T5-ARZ-341

STUDIES IN
COMPARATIVE ECONOMICS 9

Studies in Comparative Economics

1. E. H. Phelps Brown, THE ECONOMICS OF LABOR
2. Charles P. Kindleberger, FOREIGN TRADE AND THE NATIONAL ECONOMY
3. Theodore W. Schultz, TRANSFORMING TRADITIONAL AGRICULTURE
4. Jan Tinbergen, CENTRAL PLANNING
5. Abram Bergson, THE ECONOMICS OF SOVIET PLANNING
6. Joe S. Bain, INTERNATIONAL DIFFERENCES IN INDUSTRIAL STRUCTURE
7. Simon Kuznets, MODERN ECONOMIC GROWTH
8. Erik Lundberg, INSTABILITY AND ECONOMIC GROWTH

FINANCIAL STRUCTURE AND DEVELOPMENT

by Raymond W. Goldsmith

NEW HAVEN AND LONDON
YALE UNIVERSITY PRESS
1969

Library of Congress catalog card number: 69–15445
Set in Baskerville type,
and printed in the United States of America by
The Colonial Press Inc.,
Clinton, Massachusetts.
Distributed in Great Britain, Europe, Asia, and Africa by Yale University Press Ltd., London; in Canada by McGill University Press, Montreal; and in Mexico by Centro Interamericano de Libros Académicos, Mexico City.

S.F.G. in memoriam
Sapienti sat iterum

FOREWORD

Modern economics has been bred chiefly in Western Europe and the United States, and despite its aspiration toward generality it bears the stamp of institutions and issues characteristic of these areas.

But the economic world no longer revolves about London and New York. Dozens of new nations are struggling toward economic independence and industrial growth under institutional arrangements quite unlike those of the West. Economies of a novel type also extend eastward from central Europe to the Bering Strait and have been busily developing their own principles as a by-product of administrative experience. It is asserted that "Western economics" has only limited analytical value in these other countries.

The problem of the content and relevance of economics thus arises inescapably. Are the economic principles taught in the West really susceptible of general application? Or are they culture-bound and relevant mainly to industrial capitalist countries? Is it possible to create a general economics which would be as useful in Poland or India as in Canada or France? Or must we be content with several species of economics which will remain distinct in intellectual content and applicability?

"Comparative economics" has been regarded as a separate area of the economics curriculum, consisting of a botanical classification of national economies into a few loosely labeled boxes. But surely any course in economics is potentially comparative. A concern with comparative experience can profitably be infused into any of the standard branches of economic study. This series is inspired by the hope that a rethinking of particular branches of economics in world perspective, combined with a bibliography of available material from many countries, may help teachers to give their courses a broader and more comparative orientation.

In pursuing this objective, we deliberately chose autonomy over standardization. Each author was left free to determine his own approach and method of treatment. The essays thus differ considerably in length, analytical as against descriptive emphasis, geographical coverage, and other respects. How far the original intent of the series has been accomplished is for the profession to judge.

We are grateful to the authors who have struggled with possibly insoluble problems, to the Ford Foundation for its support of the enterprise, and to the staff of the Yale University Press for their helpful cooperation.

The Inter-University Committee on Comparative Economics: Abram Bergson, Arthur R. Burns, Kermit Gordon, Richard Musgrave, William Nicholls, Lloyd Reynolds (Chairman)

PREFACE

Having sinned before by excessively long prefaces, particularly in the case of *A Study of Saving*, I now prefer to err in the opposite direction and to let this book speak for itself. If I have not managed to convey the book's meaning in several hundred pages of text and to convince the reader that it deals, very imperfectly indeed, with an important problem, viz. the relation of financial structure and development to economic growth, then it is not likely that I shall be able to do so in a few additional paragraphs. I should add, however, since this is not evident from the text, that I hope to supplement this volume with another one devoted to about half a dozen country studies, as I have come more and more to feel that a highly aggregative approach such as this book represents may produce good leads, but is not likely alone to provide answers to the most interesting questions in this field.

I have been working on this volume for about six years (starting in 1962 with the unnoticed *La estructura financiera y el crecimiento economico*), though with several and sometimes long interruptions. Unfortunately I cannot claim that the result bears out the German proverb that what takes a long time comes out well ("Was lange währt, währt gut"). I only hope that the book will not be found to be all old straw threshed once more.

As a result of this long incubation period and the usual extended interval between completion of a manuscript and its appearance in book form, the statistical data end, with one minor exception (the last section of Chapter 8), with 1963, and it has not been possible to take account, again with minor exceptions, of any material published after 1966. I am not aware, however, of anything that has appeared in print in the two following years that would induce me substantially to alter or to add to the present text.

The book is not easy reading, I realize, even if the appendixes are omitted. Whoever is interested only in the substantive findings, without bothering about the conceptual structure or the underlying statistical material, may content himself with the first part of Chapter 9. For those who are looking primarily for new or substantially reworked or processed statistics, the tables of Chapters 3 through 8 and of Appendix IV may suffice. Finally, those looking for unsolved and possibly unanswerable questions may just peruse the second part of Chapter 9.

I am also aware that the scope of the book is overambitious in view of the as yet unsatisfactory status of the theory of the financial process and even more so in view of the lamentable lack of adequate primary data. As a result, I cannot expect to have escaped statistical errors and oversights, although I hope that none of them is serious enough to affect descriptions or conclusions substantially. All I can do is to take comfort in the proverb, "Nothing ventured, nothing gained," and to put my faith in those who will plow the field over again and may produce a richer harvest, in particular obtaining a higher yield per hour for their labor.

"This book should deal with the effect of sources and channels of finance on the rapidity and nature of economic growth. . . . In particular, the book should examine how and to what extent differences in financial structure have been responsible for differences in the rate and character of economic growth. This examination, naturally, should run in quantitative terms, i.e. it should relate certain measurable characteristics of financial structure to a quantitative expression of economic growth . . . The book does not follow this straight path . . . First, there is no accepted and tried kit of concepts of measuring financial structure and thus distinguishing clearly and quantitatively changes in structure over time or differences in structure between countries or regions. Second, even if we hastily fashion some new tools . . . there is great difficulty in finding data for different dates and different countries that are sufficiently comprehensive, detailed, and comparable to justify their application. Third, our measures of economic growth are still so crude, particulary if we go back more than a few decades, that differences . . . must be pronounced and persistent to be regarded as significant. Fourth, the number of "cases" from which our generalizations would have been drawn is woefully small . . . Fifth—and this will be the decisive consideration for theorists—economic growth is so complex a phenomenon, obviously determined or influenced by basic factors of a physical, technological, and mass-psychological nature, that an attempt to isolate the effects of apparently secondary forces such as the character of financial institutions and the nature of credit practices does not promise success . . . For an explanation of the differences in the speed and character of economic growth . . . financial factors will be, I am afraid, too weak and blunt a tool until our knowledge of both the economic growth and the financial structure of different countries is much further advanced than it is now."

These sentences were written fifteen years ago, exactly as they stand.[1] Unfortunately they seem to be almost as true now as they were then.

While I have gratefully received assistance on details, particularly the tables in Appendix IV, from so many government statisticians, central bank officials, and individual economists in many of the 35 countries covered by this study that it would be invidious to mention a few of them, writing this

1. Raymond W. Goldsmith, "Financial Structure and Economic Growth in Advanced Countries—An Experiment in Comparative Financial Morphology," *Capital Formation and Economic Growth* (New York, National Bureau of Economic Research, 1955), pp. 113–14, a paper presented at the 1953 meeting of the Conference on Research in Income and Wealth; the only liberty I have taken is to substitute "book" for "paper."

book has essentially been a lonely job, as it probably must be in a field like this which is only beginning to become cultivated. I want, however, to acknowledge the assistance of three of our students (as they then were) whose aid was essential in producing the tables and calculations on which much of the discussion in Chapters 4 and 5 and in Appendixes I, II, and III is based—David Chu, Steve Nelson, and Helen Stone Tice. They are, of course, guiltless of any misuse of the figures that may be found in the present text. I also owe a debt to Eli Shapiro for a careful reading of the entire text—he may remain the only mortal to suffer this ordeal—and for many criticisms and suggestions. I have not been able to adopt all of them, partly because they would have called for enough additional work to have delayed publication further and seriously. Readers nevertheless owe to Professor Shapiro that they are given the choice of reading, or not reading, the material now relegated to Appendixes I to III there rather than in the body of the book. Last, but not least, I am much in debt to my secretary, Mrs. Anne Tassi, and to the staff of the Yale University Press, particularly Mrs. Marian Ash; even a casual look will give the reader an idea of what a task the typing, retyping, stenciling, editing, and typesetting of these 500-odd pages—and there were more to begin with—must have been.

Yale University
New Haven, Conn.
November 1968

Raymond W. Goldsmith

CONTENTS

CHARTS

TABLES

APPENDIX

APPENDIX II

APPENDIX III

APPENDIX IV

APPENDIX V

SYMBOLS

FLOWS

a_1 = depreciation
a_2 = calculated retirements
a_3 = actual retirements
b = borrowing (including issuance of equity securities)
c = valuation change in financial assets (= ΔV)
d = net issues by domestic nonfinancial issuers
e = total net issues
f = issues by financial institutions
g = total gross issues
k = gross capital expenditures
l = lending
m = change in transactions cash
p = purchase of existing financial assets
q = sale of existing financial assets
r = net trade credit extension
s = saving
t = financial deficit ($k - s$)
u = financial surplus ($s - k$)
v = sales
x = net foreign issues
y = gross national product
z = retirements

STOCKS

D = debt securities (including money)
E = equity securities
F = all financial assets ($D + E$)
K = domestic tangible assets

S = net worth
V = difference between market value and original issue price of financial assets
W = national wealth ($K + X$)
X = net foreign assets

RATIOS

α = multiplier: $\alpha = (\gamma + \pi + \pi\gamma)^{-1} + 1$, where
γ = annual rate of growth of real income
π = annual rate of change in price level
β = average capital-output ratio ($\beta = W/y$)
δ = ratio of issues of nonfinancial sectors to GNP
$\bar{\delta}$ = ratio of issues of nonfinancial sectors to their sales
ϵ = ratio of all net new issues to GNP
ζ = ratio of retirements to gross issues
η = ratio of issues of nonfinancial units to their gross capital formation
θ = share of issues of equity securities in total issues of nonfinancial units
$\bar{\theta}$ = share of equity securities in market value of all financial assets at benchmark date
κ = ratio of gross capital formation to total gross national produc
$\hat{\kappa}$ = ratio of gross capital formation to sales or receipts
ι = financial intermediation ratio ($\iota = \varphi/\delta$)
λ = layering ratio (ratio of issues of financial units to other financial units to their issues to nonfinancial units)
μ = ratio of monetized to total GNP
υ = ratio of valuation changes to net issues
ξ = ratio of foreign issues to GNP
ρ = ratio of personal disposable income to GNP
σ = personal saving ratio (personal saving: personal disposable income)
τ = truncation ratio (ratio of sum of geometric series for n years to infinite series increasing at same rate)
χ = share of saving through thrift and insurance institutions in total personal saving

Symbols

ϕ = ratio of issues by financial units to GNP
$\overline{\phi}$ = adjusted ratio $\overline{\phi} = \phi(1 + \lambda)^{-1}$
ψ = average rate of change of price of price-sensitive assets
ω = ratio of inter-unit sales (other than final goods and services) to GNP
Φ = ratio of market value of assets of financial institutions to GNP

SUBSCRIPTS (IDENTIFYING TRANSACTORS OR HOLDERS AND ISSUERS)

a = all sectors
b = deposit banks
c = central banks
d = deficit units
e = business enterprises
f = all domestic financial institutions (b + c + i + t + o)
g = government
h = households
i = insurance organizations
m = money-issuing institutions
n = domestic nonfinancial sectors
o = financial institutions other than b, c, i, and t
s = surplus units
t = thrift institutions
x = foreign units
z = financial intermediaries of second degree (sometimes included in o)

FINANCIAL STRUCTURE AND DEVELOPMENT

1 THE WORLD OF FINANCE

Every economic society of which we have knowledge has possessed capital in the sense of durable physical assets that represent the product of human labor applied to natural resources. This capital may have been as modest as the simple tools—axes, adzes, scrapers, knives, and borers—of Stone Age man. Since the agrarian revolution of the sixth millennium, and still more since the urban revolution of the third, these tangible assets have gradually taken the forms with which we are now familiar—dwellings and other buildings, roads, dikes and canals, tools and machines of increasing size and complexity, wheeled vehicles, livestock, inventories of raw materials, semifinished goods and finished products, and metals in the form of ornaments, bars, or coins.

Financial instruments, i.e. evidences of claims against other economic units or of ownership in them, particularly in forms easily marketable, did not come into existence before the second millennium B.C., and at that time were known only in a few restricted areas of the Near and Middle East. They have acquired substantial importance, with a few exceptions in time and space, only in the last five hundred or, at most, one thousand years. In that process they have developed a great variety of forms. As a result, every modern economy has a superstructure of financial instruments that exists side by side with (and is connected with) the infrastructure of national wealth—the physical assets of the economy, assets which may be the gifts of nature (raw land, virgin forests, mineral deposits, water) or the work of man.

Possibly the most important and probably the oldest of these financial instruments is scriptural (nonmetallic) money in the form of bank notes and of deposits transferable by check or by a similarly easy procedure. (Full-bodied metallic money is not a financial instrument but a tangible asset—a piece of metal certified as to weight or fineness.) Other financial instruments are deposits of varying legal maturity and effective duration; loans made with or without the pledge of specific assets to governments, business enterprises, or individuals, and often repayable only after many years; claims arising out of life insurance and pension contracts, usually running over long periods; sales credit extended by one enterprise to another or to individual buyers in the form of book credit or of bills of exchange and usually repayable within a short time; and evidences of participation in the equity (i.e. the profit and loss and the net worth) of a business enterprise or a venture, of which corporate stock is the most common modern form.

Many of these financial instruments are issued or held by financial institutions (enterprises whose assets and liabilities consist primarily of financial instruments) rather than by business enterprises, governmental organizations, or households whose assets are predominantly physical, having the form of structures, equipment, durable consumer goods, inventories, and land. The most important and most common type of financial intermediaries are money-issuing institutions, such as banks of issue and the check-deposit departments of commercial banks; thrift institutions exemplified by savings banks, building and loan societies, and credit cooperatives; insurance organizations such as life or property insurance companies and pension and retirement funds; mortgage and industrial banks; sales finance companies; and investment trusts.

Countries differ with respect to their financial structure (i.e. the types of financial instruments and financial institutions in existence), with respect to the exact character and mode of operation and the relative size of the various types of existing financial instruments and institutions, with respect to the degree of concentration within the various branches of financial intermediaries, and—possibly most important from the point of view of economic analysis—with respect to the relation of the volume of financial instruments and of the funds of financial institutions to relevant economic magnitudes such as national wealth, national product, capital formation, and saving.

Countries also differ in the way in which their financial structure has changed over time, i.e. in the relative size of the various types of financial instruments and financial institutions. These differences are evident in the sequence in which the different types of financial instruments and institutions have made their appearance, in their relative rates of growth, in their penetration into the different sectors of the economy, and in the speed and character of their adaptation to changes in the country's economic structure. The differences among countries in financial development are reflected in changes in the quantitative and qualitative relations between the size and character of the financial superstructure and of financial transactions, on the one hand, and of the infrastructure of national wealth and national product, on the other.

It is the task of the comparative study of financial structure and development, first, to ascertain and describe the differences that exist in the present financial structure of individual countries and groups of countries or that have been observed in the process of their financial development and, secondly, to explore and explain the relationships between financial development and economic growth, an investigation which necessitates a theory of the basic interrelations between financial superstructure and real infrastructure.

This study can take only the first steps in each of these directions, since there does not as yet exist a theory of financial structure and development as an integral part of modern economic theory and since quantitative studies of financial structure and development of individual countries—or systematic and reasonably uniform statistical data for a large number of countries on which a comparative analysis could be based—are almost completely lacking.

After a brief description in this chapter of types of financial instruments, financial institutions, financial structure, and financial development, intended primarily for the reader not familiar with the field of finance, and after a preliminary summary of findings, Chapter 2 presents an elementary theory of financial structure and development. The second chapter has no ambitions beyond showing how financial instruments and institutions arise in the economic process and beyond indicating some of the basic economic factors which determine the size and character of the financial superstructure in relation to the real infrastructure. Chapters 3 through 7, which constitute the bulk of the study, deal individually with all the main determinants of the financial superstructure identified in Chapter 2. Thus Chapter 3 presents the data available on the volume of new issues by nonfinancial sectors—business enterprises, governments, households, and foreigners—and discusses the two main determinants of these issues, the capital formation ratio and the external financing ratio. While the analysis can for the postwar period utilize the experience of about two dozen countries, including all the main developed countries, the basis of the discussion is more restricted for earlier periods among which main attention is paid to the decade preceding World War I. Chapters 4 and 5 deal with the issues of financial institutions, first (Chapter 4) in the aggregate and then (Chapter 5) separately for the five main groups of financial institutions distinguished—central banks, deposit banks, thrift institutions, insurance organizations, and other financial intermediaries. Because of the availability of data for a larger number of countries, for a longer period of time and in more nearly comparative form, the analysis is more intensive for financial issues, and it has been found possible to present in Appendix IV an elementary econometric analysis of the main determinants of the ratio of issues of financial institutions to national product based on data for up to thirty-five countries. Chapter 6 reviews the evidence on the three factors which connect the volume of new issues of financial instruments by financial institutions and by the nonfinancial sectors with the stocks of financial instruments that are outstanding at any one time and make up the financial superstructure, viz. the new issue multiplier, the valuation adjustment which reflects changes in the prices of financial assets after their issuance, and the average capital-output ratio. As in other chapters an attempt is made to identify, and as far as possible to explain, differences among countries, particularly differences between developed and underdeveloped countries. This material is then brought together in Chapter 7, and the values of the financial interrelations ratio (which relates the volume of the superstructure of financial instruments to the infrastructure of national wealth) that can be derived from the ratio's components is compared with the observed values of the ratio. Chapter 8 is devoted to a brief discussion of a few topics that should help in understanding some aspects of financial structure and development but would have interrupted the flow of the argument of Chapters 3 through 7. While Chapters 3 through 8 are specialized in scope and predominantly statistical in character, an attempt is made in the brief final chapter (Chapter 9) to restate the findings on the basis of a set of eight charts and to explore in more general terms what contribution the findings can make to the basic problem of the relation between financial development and economic growth.

FINANCIAL INSTRUMENTS

There now exist an amazing variety of financial instruments which differ from each other in important characteristics such as the basic nature of the contract, the duration, callability, marketability, and security of the instrument, the level and character of stipulated yield, and the nature of owner and issuer. In this study, however, we need to distinguish only two basic types of instruments—claims and equity securities, here limited to corporate stock—and only three groups of issuers—business enterprises, governments, and households—mainly because it is not yet possible to find statistical information on a more detailed basis for a substantial number of countries and for a long period of time. The disregard of equities in unincorporated business enterprises is justified at the conceptual level by the common difficulty of separating business-type activities of partnerships and sole proprietorships from the household activities of the owners, and is rendered imperative at the practical level by the almost complete absence of data on assets and liabilities and hence on the equity of unincorporated business enterprises.

Among claims, there is a basic threefold distinction: claims against domestic financial institutions, claims against domestic nonfinancial sectors, and claims against foreigners. The first two groups, which in most situations are entirely predominating, are further subdivided according to groups of debtors and issuers. Thus, a distinction is made, wherever that seems essential for understanding and is statistically feasible, among claims against business enterprises, claims against governments, and claims against households. Similarly, claims against domestic financial institutions are subdivided according to the five types of such institutions that are distinguished throughout the study—central banks, deposit banks (the two being sometimes combined as the banking system), thrift institutions, insurance organizations, and other financial intermediaries.

Equities are evidences of fractional ownership in the net worth of a business enterprise. Net worth, in turn, is defined as the difference between the sum of a unit's real and financial assets and its liabilities. The legal arrangements regarding the relations between the owner of a unit's equity and the unit itself differ from place to place and from period to period. They are sometimes very complex and occasionally lead to the existence of more than one type of participation in the equity of the same economic unit, such as preferred and common stock of business corporations. Generally, however, the evidences of equity in a unit are much more homogeneous than the unit's debts and, hence, than the creditors' claims.

It has not been found possible to subdivide corporate stock into issues of financial and nonfinancial corporations, although it is known that the second category generally accounts for the bulk of all corporate stock. It is, therefore, often necessary in actual statistical work to combine claims against a given sector and equity securities (corporate stock) of the same sector, a combination that results in the three-way division of all financial instruments into those issued by domestic nonfinancial sectors, those issued by domestic financial institutions (both categories subdivided as above according to issuing subsectors), and those issued by foreigners.

Ultimate economic units—in modern economies human beings and governments—possess a net worth defined and measured in the same way as that of business enterprises, namely as the difference between the value of all assets and liabilities. However, since nobody owns these units in the sense that he may sell or otherwise dispose of his share of ownership in them, the net worth of ultimate economic units is neither an equity nor does it represent a third main type of financial instrument. The calculated net worth of ultimate economic units nevertheless is of importance for the financial process, and constitutes a significant element in a national balance sheet.

To provide an indication of the relative size of the main types of financial instruments in a modern economy, Table 1–1 shows the relevant figures for the United States in 1963 and adds comparable figures for 1900 to provide historical background. The main relationships visible in Table 1–1 indicate that in the contemporary United States:

1. Approximately three-fourths of all financial instruments are in the form of claims, while about one-fourth is corporate stock.

2. About two-fifths of all claims, or nearly three-tenths

TABLE 1–1

Financial Instruments Outstanding in the United States, 1963 and 1900

	Amount[a]		Distribution		Relation to National Wealth		New Issue Ratio[b]
	1963	1900	1963	1900	1963	1900	1901–63
	(billions of dollars)		(per cent)		(per cent)		(per cent)
	(1)	(2)	(3)	(4)	(5)	(6)	(7)
1. Money[c]	210	7.6	7.8	12.6	9.8	8.5	2.0
2. Saving deposits[d]	286	3.7	10.7	6.1	13.3	4.1	2.7
3. Insurance reserves, private	218	1.6	8.2	2.6	10.1	1.8	2.1
4. Insurance reserves, government	51	0.0	1.9	0.0	2.4	0.0	0.5
5. Finance company debentures	12	0.0	0.4	0.0	0.6	0.0	0.1
6. Claims against financial institutions (1 through 5)	777	12.9	29.0	21.3	36.2	14.4	7.4
7. Consumer credit	70	1.0	2.6	1.7	3.3	1.1	0.7
8. Security credit	16	1.3	0.6	2.2	0.7	1.4	0.2
9. Bank loans n.e.c.	79	3.9	3.0	6.5	3.7	4.3	0.7
10. Mortgages, home	182	2.6	6.8	4.3	8.5	2.9	1.7
11. Mortgages, other nonfarm	49	1.8	1.8	3.0	2.3	2.0	0.5
12. Mortgages, farm	17	2.3	0.6	3.8	0.8	2.6	0.1
13. U.S. govt. securities	310	1.2	11.6	2.0	14.4	1.3	3.0
14. State and local govt. securities	88	2.0	3.3	3.3	4.1	2.2	0.8
15. Corporate bonds[e]	101	5.2	3.8	8.6	4.7	5.8	0.9
16. Trade credit	103	5.7	3.8	9.5	4.8	6.3	0.9
17. Other claims	160	6.5	6.0	10.6	7.9	7.1	1.5

18. Claims against nonfinancial sectors (7 through 17)	1175	33.5	44.0	55.6	55.2	37.1	11.0
19. All claims (6 + 18)	1952	46.4	73.0	76.9	91.4	51.5	18.4
20. Corporate stock	720	13.9	27.0	23.1	33.5	15.5	0.9
21. All financial assets (19 + 20)	2672	60.3	100.0	100.0	124.9	67.0	19.3

[a] Market value for corporate stock; face or book value for claims.

[b] Col. 1 less col. 2 divided by aggregate gross national product 1901–63, except for col. 20 (Stock issues 1901–38 from R. W. Goldsmith, *A Study of Saving in the United States* (Princeton, Princeton University Press, 1955) *1*, 482–3; for 1939–63 from Federal Reserve Board flow-of-funds statistics).

[c] Currency and demand deposits.

[d] Including time deposits and savings and loan shares.

[e] Includes foreign bonds (1963: $7 billion).

Sources:
(*Col. 1.*) Federal Reserve Board, *Flow-of-Funds Assets and Liabilities 1945–65* (May 1966), except lines 1 and 13, which are shown on gross instead of net basis, and except line 20, which is increased by about one-fifth to account for intercorporate holdings among nonconsolidated nonfinancial corporations. (*Col. 2.*) R. W. Goldsmith, R. E. Lipsey, and M. Mendelson, *Studies in the National Balance Sheet of the United States* (Princeton, Princeton University Press, 1963) *2*, 73. Home mortgages from R. W. Goldsmith, *A Study of Saving in the United States* (Princeton, Princeton University Press, 1955) *1*, 725.

of all financial instruments, are issued by financial institutions.

3. Financial institutions are connected as holders or as issuers with approximately three-fifths of all financial instruments outstanding, and with as much as four-fifths of all claims, since financial institutions own claims against nonfinancial sectors to approximately the extent of the claims they themselves have issued.

4. Money represents less than one-tenth of all financial instruments and not much over one-tenth of all claims outstanding.

5. About two-thirds of all financial instruments are liquid in the sense that they can easily be disposed of in an open market in the customary quantities, rapidly and without sharp price changes, or can be presented to the issuer for redemption in lawful money. This includes most claims against financial institutions, approximately one-third of the claims against nonfinancial issuers and a large proportion of all corporate stock.

6. The financial superstructure, represented by claims and equity securities, has a value about one-fifth greater than than of the real infrastructure, i.e. national wealth, if claims against financial institutions are included, and a value of approximately four-fifths of national wealth if such claims are excluded as representing a duplicative layer of financial assets.

A comparison of the present financial superstructure of the United States with that of 1900 indicates half a dozen important changes, which are also found in other countries as far as their direction goes, though the exact relationships are different.

7. The ratio of the value of the financial superstructure to the real infrastructure has increased considerably from aproximately two-thirds to one and one-fourth.

8. The share of financial institutions in total financial instruments outstanding has risen from about one-fifth to three-tenths, while the share in all claims has advanced from about three-tenths to two-fifths.

9. The share of money in all financial assets has declined from about one-eighth to one-twelfth.

10. A sharp increase has occurred in the share of thrift deposits and insurance reserves in all financial assets and in all claims against financial institutions.

11. Of the claims against nonfinancial domestic sectors, consumer credit, home mortgages, and U.S. government securities have increased considerably in comparison to all financial assets and all claims. On the other hand, the shares of bank loans to business, security credit, farm mortgages, corporate bonds, and trade credit have declined considerably. These trends reflect partly shifts in importance among nonfinancial sectors (for instance, the declining share of agriculture in national wealth and product) and partly changes in the character of national wealth (such as the increasing importance of consumer durables and of homes) and in its distribution and its financing.

12. The share of corporate stock in the market value of all financial instruments was somewhat higher in 1963 than in 1900, and sharp fluctuations in the ratio have occurred in the interval.

13. During the more than sixty years since the beginning of the century the value of issues of financial instruments (net of retirements and disregarding valuation changes after issuance) has on the average been equal to almost one-fifth of the period's aggregate national product. The ratios have been about 12 per cent for the issues of nonfinancial sectors, made predominantly in the form of claims—of which about 3 per cent are accounted for by the federal government, 1 per cent by state and local governments, 3 per cent by households, and most of the remaining 5 per cent by domestic business enterprises. The ratio has averaged 7 per cent for the issues of financial institutions, of which 2 per cent represents the increase in money in circulation while about $2\frac{1}{2}$ per cent reflects household saving in the form of thrift deposits and $2\frac{1}{2}$ per cent in that of voluntary or compulsory insurance reserves.

FINANCIAL INSTITUTIONS

Financial institutions are characterized by the fact that financial instruments constitute their main assets habitually, not only occasionally, and that their activities are concentrated on, and hence their income is mainly derived from, the holding of, and transactions in financial instruments.

The nature and the relative importance of financial instruments owned and issued and of financial activities undertaken are probably the two most important principles of classification of financial institutions. As in all similar attempts, the main difficulty in devising a classification that is not too complicated and yet fits most actual situations reasonably well, and—last but not least—can be implemented statistically, is not the existence of financial institutions that differ in character, but the fact that many institutions combine several financial activities and do so in a different mixture.

Table 1–2 provides a simplified classification of about twenty major types of financial institutions based on their main sources and uses of funds. Since only seven sources and three uses are distinguished, and since the form of presentation makes it difficult to allow for a combination of more than two main sources and two main uses of funds, the allocation of the variety of financial institutions to the twenty-one fields necessarily cannot be accurate in detail, even if the classification is limited to the main types of institutions actually encountered. While the table is based primarily on financial institutions operating in Western countries in the twentieth century, the principles of classification adopted generally provide adequate room for financial institutions found in other periods and countries.

Of the twenty-one fields provided in Table 1–2, no fewer than eight are left blank, and most of the types of financial institutions distinguished are crowded into relatively few fields. The location of these fields, determined as it is by the character of assets and of liabilities, reflects the fact that there is a tendency for financial institutions to have assets and liabilities of the same type, and particularly of the

TABLE 1–2

Types of Financial Institutions

	Main Uses of Funds		
Main Sources of Funds	Short-term and Medium-Term Claims	Long-Term Claims	Corporate Stock
1. Money	Banks of issue[a] Deposit banks		
2. Short-term nonmonetary liabilities	Credit cooperatives Finance companies[b] Security dealers	Savings banks[c] Building societies	
3. Long-term marketable liabilities		Mortgage banks Development banks Investment trusts (British type)	
4. Long-term nonmarketable liabilities		Life insurance organizations[d] Retirement funds[d] Social insurance organizations[d]	
5. Marketable equities		Property insurance cos.[b] Holding companies	Open-end investment companies
6. Nonmarketable equities	Moneylenders Private bankers	Investment bankers	
7. Fiduciary		Trustee organizations[e]	

[a] Monetary metals and foreign exchange are other important uses of funds.

[b] Also use sources 2, 3, or 5 to considerable extent.

[c] Including savings departments of deposit banks.

[d] In some countries also invest substantially in corporate stock.

[e] Independent trust companies, trust departments of commercial banks, common trust funds, and public trustees.

same maturity, when only a few forms of sources and uses of funds are distinguished.

Financial intermediaries are of two major types: (1) financial institutions whose liabilities are "money" in the sense of the generally accepted medium of exchange at a given time and place, usually currency and check deposits, and (2) financial institutions whose liabilities are not money.

Depending on legal arrangements or custom, money may be issued by specialized private or governmental institutions that concentrate on this activity—i.e., the liabilities of which consist mainly of bank notes (currency) and of deposits of other financial institutions, primarily check-money-issuing banks—or by institutions for which the issuance of check money, and more rarely of bank notes, is only a part of their broader activities. The most common form of combination of issuance of money with other financial activities involves the acceptance of time or savings deposits. The issuance of money and the financial institutions issuing it, should always be separated from other financial activities and institutions, because of the specific role of money as the standard means of exchange. This separation is, however, statistically often impossible because the demand (check) deposit business is not divided in operation and in accounting from the other activities of the financial institution that issues money, a situation that is common in many countries where the deposit banks (commercial banks) provide most of the money supply but also account for a substantial proportion of all savings deposits handled by financial institutions.

The non-money-issuing financial institutions differ so much in the character of their assets, liabilities, and activities that a further subdivision is essential. The first subgroup (for which "thrift institutions" seems to be the best general and fairly neutral name) comprises financial institutions most of the liabilities of which are short- or medium-term deposits from the general public—deposits which are not being used as money—and which invest most of their assets in long-term loans and fixed-interest-bearing long-term securities. This discrepancy in the maturity of funds raised and used is possible because of the substantial stability in total deposits which, in turn, reflects a relatively slow velocity of turnover of most individual deposit accounts.

The main constituents of this group are savings banks (including the postal savings system which is of considerable importance in many countries), buildings societies (in the United States called savings and loan associations), and credit cooperatives.

The second subgroup, insurance organizations, is characterized by the fact that their financial activities are incidental to their main operating function, the provision of funds in the case of specified contingencies, which generally lie well in the future. The accumulation of large funds, which usually accompanies these operations in the case of life insurance organizations and retirement funds, is the result primarily of the adoption of the level premium principle. This accumulation does not exist in pay-as-you-go plans and for term insurance. Insurance organizations that operate on the pay-as-you-go principle, as do many social insurance schemes, do not accumulate substantial financial assets and might be excluded from the field of financial institutions. Property insurance companies represent a mixed type of financial institutions, deriving their funds partly from advance premiums (i.e., short-term but non-callable liabilities to insurers) and partly from owners' contributions and retained earnings; most of these funds are used to acquire long-term securities, both fixed-interest-bearing obligations and stocks.

The third subgroup is residual and heterogeneous, and includes both privately and governmentally owned and operated financial institutions. The main representatives of this group are finance companies, mortgage banks, development banks, investment companies, financial intermediaries of the second degree, private banks, investment bankers, security dealers and moneylenders.

Finance companies use most of their funds, obtained mainly by short- or long-term borrowing, to extend loans to consumers, primarily for the purchase of durable goods, and to acquire from merchants similar claims against consumers with a maturity of commonly not more than three years. Some finance companies, however, do a general short-term loan business, and are then distinguished from commercial banks chiefly by the fact that they do not accept check deposits.

Mortgage banks are characterized by their main source of funds (marketable long-term bonds), not by the use of their funds (long-term real estate loans), which is similar to that of some other thrift organizations. Mortgage banks are poorly represented in the United States, where they have been virtually limited to agriculture, but they have been, and sometimes still are, of great importance in continental Europe and in other parts of the world, particularly in the field of residential and farm mortgage credit.

Development banks are essentially a creation of the postwar period and are concentrated in less developed countries. Government participation in ownership, financing, and management is prevalent. Their main functions are the extension of credit, usually for the intermediate and long term, to industrial enterprises that cannot easily raise funds in the domestic or foreign capital market and the acquisition of debentures and stocks of such enterprises. Some of them are not too different from commercial banks, e.g., the Mexican *financieras*. At the other end of the spectrum, they resemble mortgage banks.

Investment companies are characterized by the predominance of marketable long-term securities among their assets. Their original representatives, the British investment trusts developed in the latter half of the nineteenth century, raised funds through the sale of common stock, preferred stock, and debentures, and used the funds to acquire both long-term fixed-interest-bearing securities and stocks. These organizations in their modern form (perfected primarily in the United States during the last three decades but now becoming common in most developed countries) concentrate on common stock both as the source and the use of funds, and thus come close to a pool of a changing group of participating investors under continuous management.

Strict adherence to the basic definition of financial intermediaries as enterprises whose assets consist mostly of financial instruments would require the inclusion of holding companies, i.e. organizations concentrating their assets in the equity securities of a relatively small number of other corporations, financial or nonfinancial, in amounts sufficient to give the holding company majority control or, if it owns only a minority interest, to assure it a substantial degree of influence in the management of the portfolio companies. Holding companies, however, have been excluded from the scope of this study. This hardly needs justification in cases where the holding company owns all or almost all the stock of the portfolio companies. Such companies are nonfinancial companies in disguise, and their true character becomes immediately evident when the accounts of the holding company are consolidated with those of its portfolio companies. A similar argument applies to a second type, personal holding companies, even if their portfolio securities do not involve majority or minority control, because such companies do not as a rule use outside funds, stock ownership being limited to members of one or a very small number of families.

The distinction between investment and holding companies becomes rather tenuous when the assets consist of substantial and influence-giving holdings of stock in a limited number of companies and of loans to them, and when these portfolio companies are otherwise independent of each other and cannot well be regarded as parts of one nonfinancial enterprise group. Such diversified, publicly owned holding companies, which are more common in financially less developed than in industrialized countries—the so-called "development banks," including some Latin American *financieras,* but also the American small business investment companies—are included in this study whenever the data are available.

Financial intermediaries of the second degree—the fourth component—are distinguished by receiving all or most of their funds from other financial institutions, most commonly saving banks or credit cooperatives, and/or making a large part of their funds available to other financial institutions or to the central government. They thus may be regarded as an additional layer within the system of financial institutions. The oldest and most important institution of this type is the French Caisse des Dépôts et Consignations, which has found followers in a few other countries, e.g. Germany, Italy, Japan, and India.

Private bankers, investment bankers, and moneylenders differ from the types of financial institutions discussed so far mainly in the source of their funds, which usually consist of these firms' own capital, contributed by partners or shareholders, or accumulated out of retained earnings, borrowed funds generally being of secondary importance only. These institutions, therefore, are to a much lesser extent engaged in the financial intermediation and debtor substitution that characterize the other types of financial institutions. With rare exceptions, their omission from this study, however, is due more to the unavailability of statistical information about their activities than to conceptual reasons. This omission is particularly regrettable because these organizations have played a large role in the early stages of the financial development of many countries.

The omission of trustee organizations, again with occasional exceptions, is justified by the fact that they differ basically from all other financial institutions in that they are not the owners of the assets they administer and do not incur liabilities of their own but hold and administer, with more or less freedom of investment decision, financial and tangible assets of the beneficiary owners, who usually are private individuals. The operations of trustees, therefore, do not constitute financial intermediation in the strict sense and no debtor substitution at all is involved. Trustees may be specialized independent institutions, either private enterprises (for instance some trust companies in the United States and Great Britain), or government organizations (e.g. the Public Trustee in the United Kingdom and in some British dominions), or they may constitute one of several departments of mixed financial institutions, e.g. the trust departments or subsidiaries of American or British commercial banks. Individuals, particularly attorneys, who often act as executors and trustees, are not to be regarded as financial institutions, even though their function with respect to an individual trust fund is very similar to that of an independent trust company or a trust department.

No classification of this type can do justice to the variety of actual experience or make allowance for the changes that occur over time in the character of the institutions included within the group of financial institutions. Description or analysis of these variations and changes are beyond the scope of this study. One example of significant differences within what is treated in the typology as one category of financial institutions may, however, be given because of its great practical importance and because of the role which it has played in financial literature. It concerns the category of commercial banks, or deposit banks as they are commonly called in the European literature. These institutions are treated as a homogeneous category in the typology of financial institutions as well as in the banking statistics of most countries. This category, however, includes, in different countries and at different times, institutions of very different character, united only by two facts. First, one type of their liabilities, and, since the turn of the century in many countries the most important one, has the form of deposits subject to check that are generally accepted as one of the means of payment; and, secondly, a considerable and generally major part of their assets consists of short-term loans to business enterprises made for the purpose of financing the latter's working capital requirements. Within these limits, however, the category includes institutions ranging from the small bank with a single office and a few employees (which uses mostly owners' rather than borrowed funds, and in which most of the deposits turn over very slowly) to branch bank systems with thousands of offices covering entire large countries—institutions in which net worth represents only a minute fraction of liabilities and in which most liabilities are due on demand and actually turn over rapidly. More important yet for financial development than variations in size, areas of operation, and sources of funds, are differences in the uses of funds. Some commercial banks, individually or in the national aggregate, invest most of their funds in government securities and in so-called money market instruments. This is usually an individual or temporary phenomenon observable on a large scale only during or immediately after wars in which the government has largely preempted the use of funds. Other banks concentrate their assets in short-term business credits. There are, however, important cases in which a substantial part of the funds of commercial banks are used in long-term financing. This may be done openly in the form of long-term mortgage loans, intermediate-term loans, and holdings of long-term corporate securities, bonds, or stocks—or less openly, by making what are in form short-term advances but become long-term credit through repeated renewals expected by both borrower and lender. This tendency may go so far that commercial banks of this type approximate diversified investment and holding companies in the character of their assets or operations.

For the purpose again of illustrating the orders of magnitude involved, Table 1–3 shows the assets of the main types of financial institutions in the United States at the end of 1963 and 1900. Since the table is intended for comparative purposes, the assets of the various groups are shown as percentages of the combined assets of all financial institutions and in relation to all financial assets and to national wealth. The figures for 1900 are included to permit a comparison with the relative importance of the various types of institutions at a considerably earlier phase of the financial development of the United States. In this case it has been possible to show figures for virtually all types of financial institutions included in the taxonomic arrangement of Table 1–3. Three characteristics of the structure of financial institutions in the United States are evident:

1. The banking system now accounts for less than two-fifths of the assets of all financial institutions. If savings

departments of commercial banks are classified as thrift institutions, which is in line with their character, the share of money-issuing institutions is less than three-tenths of the assets of all financial institutions.

2. Institutions whose main function is to provide the bulk of the population, excluding only the very poor at the one end and the very wealthy at the other, with most of their retirement and contingency funds, i.e. thrift institutions and insurance organizations, now together hold more than one-half of the assets of all financial institutions.

3. Financial institutions now own almost two-fifths of all financial assets outstanding in the United States and approximately three-fifths of all financial assets other than claims against financial institutions, and their assets are equal to almost one-half of national wealth.

Probably more interesting are the structural changes that have taken place since the turn of the century, evident from a comparison of the figures for 1963 and 1900, changes which are characteristic for virtually all developed and for many underdeveloped countries, as will appear in Chapters 4 and 5. The most important of these changes is the substantial increase in the ratio (at market values) of the assets of financial institutions compared to either all financial assets outstanding in the country or to national wealth. While the assets of financial institutions at the turn of the century were equal to not much over one-sixth of the national wealth of the United States, they are now close to one-half of national wealth. The increase in the share in total financial assets outstanding, while less spectacular, is still substantial, the share rising from not much over one-fourth to almost two-fifths of the total.

Within financial institutions there has been a marked decline in the share of the banking system from over three-fifths to less than two-fifths of the total. (If the savings departments of commercial banks are excluded, the decline is more pronounced—from slightly less than three-fifths to approximately three-tenths.) Thrift institutions, including

TABLE 1–3

Financial Institutions in the United States, 1963 and 1900

	Total Assets[a]		Distribution of Assets		Relation to National Wealth		Relation to Total Financial Assets	
	1963	1900	1963	1900	1963	1900	1963	1900
	(billions of dollars)				(per cent)			
	(1)	(2)	(3)	(4)	(5)	(6)	(7)	(8)
I. Banking system	374.8	10.0	38.1	62.9	17.4	11.2	14.7	16.6
1. Federal Reserve Banks	58.0	—	5.9	—	2.7	—	2.3	—
2. Commercial banks[b,c]	316.8	10.0	32.2	62.9	14.7	11.2	12.4	16.6
II. Thrift institutions	165.9[2]	2.9[2]	16.9	18.2	7.7	3.2	6.5	4.8
1. Mutual savings banks	49.7	2.4	5.1	15.1	2.3	2.7	2.0	4.0
2. Savings and loan associations	107.6	0.5	10.9	3.1	5.0	0.6	4.2	0.8
3. Credit unions	8.1	0.0	0.8	0.0	0.4	0.0	0.3	0.0
4. Postal savings system	0.5	—	0.1	—	0.0	—	0.0	—
III. Insurance organizations	315.1	2.2	32.0	13.8	14.7	2.5	12.4	3.7
1. Life insurance companies[d]	145.0	1.7	14.7	10.7	6.7	1.9	5.7	2.8
2. Private pension funds	53.8	—	5.5	—	2.5	—	2.1	—
3. Government funds[e]	79.3	0.0	8.1	0.0	3.7	0.0	3.1	0.0
4. Other insurance companies	37.0	0.5	3.8	3.1	1.7	0.6	1.5	0.8
IV. Miscellaneous financial institutions	127.7	0.8	13.0	5.0	6.0	0.9	5.0	1.3
1. Finance companies	36.0	.	3.7	—	1.7	—	1.4	.
2. Investment companies[f]	33.6	—	3.4	—	1.6	—	1.3	—

3. Mortgage companies	4.5	0.2	0.5	1.3	0.2	0.2	0.2	0.3
4. Land banks	3.5	—	0.4	—	0.2	—	0.1	—
5. Security dealers	9.7	0.6	1.0	3.8	0.5	0.7	0.4	1.0
6. Government lending institutions	40.4	—	4.1	—	1.9	—	1.6	—
V. All financial institutions	983.5	15.9	100.0	100.0	45.8	17.8	38.6	26.4
VI. Personal trust departments	82.2	3.0	8.4	18.9	3.8	3.3	3.3	5.0

[a] Book value except for investment companies (market value).

[b] Includes agencies of foreign banks (1963: $4 billion).

[c] Individual savings deposits in commercial banks, included in line I,2, were $0.9 billion in 1900 (R. W. Goldsmith, *A Study of Saving*, *1*, 386) and $86.6 billion in 1963 (Federal Reserve Board flow-of-funds statistics).

[d] Includes fraternal insurance companies (1963: $3.6 billion; 1900: $0.0 billion) and private insured pension funds (1963: $23.3 billion).

[e] Pension, retirement and social security funds.

[f] Includes small business finance companies (1963: $0.6 billion).

Source: Table A-33, except line VI for 1963: American Bankers' Association release (Jan. 1965) and for 1900: R. W. Goldsmith, *Financial Intermediaries in the American Economy since 1900* (Princeton, Princeton University Press, 1958), p. 74.

the savings departments of commercial banks, have just maintained their share of about one-fourth of the assets of all financial institutions. In contrast, the share of insurance organizations has increased sharply from not much over one-eighth to almost one-third of the total.

FINANCIAL STRUCTURE

Every country that has passed the primitive stage of economic development possesses some financial instruments in addition to scriptural money. Most countries also acquire at a fairly early stage of development some financial institutions, even though financial activities are often combined in mixed enterprises with nonfinancial activities, primarily with long-distance wholesale trading. The presence, nature, and relative size of financial instruments and financial institutions of the various types then characterizes a country's financial structure. Because financial structure is determined by a combination of financial instruments and financial institutions, several aspects must be taken into account and given quantitative expression wherever possible. They are: the relation of total financial assets to total tangible assets; the distribution of total financial assets and liabilities among the various types of financial instruments; their distribution among financial institutions and nonfinancial economic units, summarized in the share of financial assets held or issued by financial institutions; and the position of financial assets and liabilities in the accounts of the various economic sectors. Each of these stock relations has a corresponding flow aspect, doubling the number of relations relevant for the study of financial structure.

Measures of Financial Structure

1. The first basic aspect of financial structure, the relation between a country's financial superstructure and its real infrastructure, is reflected in the financial interrelations ratio. The ratio is obtained by dividing the total (partly

duplicated) value of all financial assets in existence at one date by the total value of tangible assets plus net foreign balance, i.e. by national wealth.

2. Equally as important as the relative size of the total financial superstructure is its composition. This is reflected, first, in the distribution of total financial instruments outstanding among their main types; and in the corresponding distribution of the financial assets of the main sectors of the economy. The same total amount of financial instruments, even if it reflects the same financial interrelations ratio, may have quite a different economic significance and may affect economic growth differently depending on its composition—for instance the share of debt and equity instruments, of short- and long-term debt instruments, of marketable instruments, and of more or less risky and price-fluctuating instruments.

3. The composition of the financial superstructure is reflected, secondly, in the distribution among economic sectors and subsectors of total financial assets and of the amount outstanding of various financial instruments. The shares of different sectors in the total amount of a given financial instrument outstanding, together with information on the number of individual holders of the instrument and on the shape of the size distribution of the instrument among holders, provides important clues to the degree of penetration of different financial instrument within the economy and to the preferences of various sectors and subsectors among financial instruments. Both of these relations are of importance in monetary analysis and in the study of economic growth.

4. The character of a country's financial structure is also considerably influenced by the relative importance of different types of financial institutions. This aspect is measured by the share of the various types of financial intermediaries in the total assets of all financial institutions, in the aggregate, or for the main types of financial instruments.

5. Because of the crucial importance of financial institutions for an understanding of financial structure and development, the share of financial institutions in the stock of financial instruments is another important characteristic of financial structure. The most general measure of this kind, comparable in this respect to the financial interrelations ratio, is the share of all financial institutions in total financial assets. This ratio is the simplest overall indicator of the degree of institutionalization of a country's financial structure. For closer analysis there is need of similar calculations separately for the main types of financial assets, i.e. for figures showing the shares of various financial assets outstanding that are held by the main groups of financial institutions.

6. A combination of the breakdown of the stock of financial assets by type of instrument and by sector yields a financial interrelations matrix, which identifies the owner and the issuer of each type of instrument. Such a matrix can be drawn up for the total of all financial instruments without distinction of type of instrument. It is, however, of much greater value if available for broad classes of instruments such as all claims or all equity securities, or for narrower types of instruments, e.g. residential mortgages.[1]

7. The preceding aspects of financial structure all are concerned with relationships among stocks existing at a given date, either relationships among stocks of financial assets and liabilities, or relationships between stocks of financial assets and stocks of tangible assets. Similar relations, of course, exist between corresponding flows during a given period, say a calendar year, a business cycle, or a longer period of one or several decades. Indeed, because flows during a period can be regarded as differences between the stocks existing at the beginning and end of the period, after elimination of valuation changes, and because stocks may be treated as cumulated flows during preceding periods, now including valuation changes, there is a close

1. For an example of financial interrelations matrices, see R. W. Goldsmith in *The Review of Income and Wealth,* Dec. 1966, 106ff.

connection between the stock and the flow aspects of financial structure and the ratios used to measure them.[2]

On the most general level the financial interrelations ratio as a measure of the relation between stocks of financial and tangible assets has a parallel among flows in the ratio of new issues of financial assets to gross national product. The relationships among stocks of different financial assets and liabilities also have their parallel among flows. Thus, important characteristics of the financial structure of a country during a given period are reflected in the distribution of total financial flows among instruments and among sectors; in the share of financial institutions in the transactions in financial instruments, in the aggregate and by type; and in the distribution of total financial transactions of the various sectors and subsectors among the different financial instruments.

8. Of particular importance for the study of financial structure is the distribution of total sources and funds of various sectors and subsectors by form and by partner. The tool here is the sources-and-uses-of-funds statement as it has been developed in many countries during the past decade as the backbone of financial transactions accounts.[3] Such a statement shows the sources of financing of the different sectors of the economy during a period of usually one year, but sometimes of only one quarter, and combines these data with information on the uses of the funds so obtained. This statement, therefore, makes possible a determination

2. For an algebraic treatment of the relationships between stocks and flows see, for instance, R. W. Goldsmith, *The Flow of Capital Funds in the Postwar Economy,* (New York, National Bureau of Economic Research, 1965), Chap. 2.

3. For an international survey of financial transactions accounts see G. S. Dorrance in *Income and Wealth,* Series IX (London, Bowes and Bowes, 1961) and in *IMF Staff Papers 13* (1966). A detailed although no longer entirely up-to-date description of the American system of financial transactions accounts is provided by the Federal Reserve Board's *Flow of Funds in the United States 1939–1953* (Washington, 1955) and by an article in the *Federal Reserve Bulletin, 45* (1959), 828ff.

of the share of internal financing (saving) and external financing (borrowing or issuance of equity securities) of different sectors, and within external financing makes it possible to distinguish the share of funds attributable to financial institutions, in the aggregate and by the main types of institutions. Flow-of-funds statements also indicate the share of direct financing (through the acquisition of loans and purchases of securities of nonfinancial enterprises and government) and of indirect financing through financial institutions. Finally, a combination of a flow-of-funds statement for all sectors permits the preparation of a financial transactions matrix—the parallel to the financial interrelations matrix—which shows the changes in the claims of each sector against every other sector (excluding valuation changes)[4] and thus provides a statistical answer—though, of course, not an analytical explanation—to the questions who finances whom, to what extent, and in what form, questions which are basic for the study of financial structure and development.

Types of Financial Structure

The indicators of specific aspects of financial structure which have been briefly discussed in the preceding section have a purpose that goes beyond the facilitation of the description of the financial structure actually existing in a given country at a given time and of changes in that structure over time. The indicators have been so conceived that in appropriate combinations they may help to identify different types of financial structure and to disclose pat-

4. It is theoretically feasible, although it has not yet actually been done on a comprehensive basis, to integrate valuation changes with flow-of-funds statistics; see G. Stuvel, *System of Social Accounts* (Oxford, Clarendon Press, 1965), Chap. 7. For a few broad sectors of the American economy and for periods of substantial length, an attempt has been made to separate changes in aggregate balance sheet values between benchmark dates into valuation changes reflecting asset price movements and net flows resulting from saving. R. W. Goldsmith and R. E. Lipsey, *Studies in the National Balance Sheet of the United States* (Princeton, Princeton University Press, 1963) *1*, Pt. 2.

terns of the financial dimension of economic development. They can do so only if it is found that the association of different numerical values of the various indicators of financial structure is not fortuitous but shows a reasonable degree of regularity, and if it appears that these typical combinations in turn are associated with indicators of the structure of national wealth and of national product in a systematic rather than random fashion. Whether this is the case is a question of fact that must be determined by investigating a sufficient number of countries over extended periods of time. Attempts in this direction will be made throughout this study. The explanation of the association of characteristics of financial structure that may thus be suggested, and an understanding of the path of financial development, however, require a theory of the financial process. Chapter 2 will attempt to develop the rudiments of such a theory. Anticipating a few of the results of this investigation, it may be helpful to outline here some of the main types of financial structures actually encountered.

In doing so it is necessary to distinguish between private enterprise (including mixed) economies and centrally planned economies in which the government owns and operates most tangible assets other than, in some instances, agricultural land. The difference in financial structure between these two types of economies does not lie primarily in the types of financial instruments and financial institutions that are in existence. Both private enterprise and centrally planned economies have similar forms of claims—paper currency, check and savings deposits, accounts receivable and payable, consumer installment credit, insurance policies, short- and long-term loans to business enterprises, and government bonds. They also have similar types of financial institutions—banks of issue, commercial banks, savings banks, life insurance companies, and industrial development banks. From this formal point of view the main differences are the absence of corporate stock among the financial instruments of centrally planned economies and the absence of investment bankers, investment companies, and trustee organizations among their financial institutions. The significant differences rather are: first, the control of financial institutions, all of them being owned and operated by the government in centrally planned economies; second, the predominance of claims against the government or government-owned enterprises among financial assets; third, the generally smaller size of the financial superstructure in centrally planned economies, which is reflected in the lower value of the financial interrelations ratio at comparable levels of economic development; and, fourth and most important, a basic difference in function—the fact that the financial system in centrally planned economies serves primarily, at least until recently though some changes are now under consideration or even in the experimental stage, as an adjunct to the authoritative direction of the real flows of labor and goods instead of acting as an independent factor in the allocation of resources.[5]

Financial structure in private enterprise and mixed economies, in the sense of the relative size of different financial instruments and financial institutions, might conceivably be unrelated to the size of the entire financial superstructure in terms of its tangible infrastructure. The share of commercial banks, for example, in all financial assets or in the aggregate assets of all financial institutions might be the same irrespective of the level of the financial interrelations ratio. Actually the character of the financial structure and the level of the financial interrelations ratio seem to be far from independent as will appear in Chapter 5. There are also theoretical reasons, as the discussion in Chapter 2 will suggest, which explain why the relative size of a country's financial structure and the character of that structure should be related to each other.

We consequently find that the different levels of the financial interrelations ratio encountered in free enterprise economies are associated with fairly distinct types of finan-

5. For an analysis of the operation of the financial system in centrally planned economies, see G. Garvy, *Money, Banking and Credit in Eastern Europe* (New York, Federal Reserve Bank, 1966).

cial structures. While any simple classification and typology does violence to the variety of experience, the common characteristics of financial structure of different countries seem to be sufficiently pronounced and regular to justify the distinction of at least three basic types of financial structure that can be distinguished in private enterprise and in mixed economies since the beginning of modern economic development.

The first type of financial structure is characterized formally by a low financial interrelations ratio (a value of from one-fifth to one-half), by the predominance of claims over equity securities, by a relatively low share of financial institutions in all financial assets outstanding, and by the preeminence of commercial banks among financial institutions. These are characteristics of an early stage of financial development in which scriptural money (bank notes and check deposits) is supplementing and gradually superseding metallic money, and in which production and distribution are conducted predominantly by enterprises of small size and family ownership. This type of financial structure (categories 5 and 7 of Table 1–4) is found in Europe (excluding peripheral areas) and in North America from perhaps the eighteenth until the middle of the nineteenth century.

A quite similar type of financial structure (categories 6 and 7) is common to most nonindustrialized countries in the first half of the twentieth century, a structure which has developed at different times depending on the individual country's history. Here, too, the financial interrelations ratio is low; claims by far exceed equity securities; and banks predominate among financial institutions. The main difference between this and the first type is the greater role of the government and of government financial institutions, reflecting the often mixed character of these economies. In some cases the existence of a sector of large corporate enterprises constitutes a second difference. Since this sector is usually foreign owned and financed, it has, however, often little effect on the country's own financial structure. An-

Table 1–4

Types of Financial Structure

Characteristics	Examples: Contemporary	Examples: Historical
1. Only commodity money; no financial institutions, but occasional credit transactions	Isolated tribal communities	Early antiquity
2. Metallic money, bills of exchange, and indigenous small-scale financial institutions (moneylenders)		India and China before ca. 1850 Japan before 1868 Classical antiquity Most of medieval Europe and large parts of Europe through 18th century
3. Central bank the only, or predominant, financial institution	U.S.S.R. and other centrally planned economies Ethiopia (until 1962)	France } early 19th Russia } century
4. Deposit banks, but no central bank and no paper money		Medieval Italian cities (from 13th century on)
5. Multiplicity of note issuing and deposit banks; beginning of other financial institutions		Scotland in first half of 19th century U.S.A. to 1913
6. Central bank; modern deposit banks; indigenous small-scale financial operators	Most of tropical Africa, Middle East, and Southeast Asia	
7. Central bank; deposit banks; beginnings of other financial institutions (particularly savings banks, mortgage banks, development banks, and insurance organizations)	Spain Latin America India Egypt	Western Europe from mid-19th century to World War I
8. Full complement of financial institutions and instruments	U.S.A., former British Dominions, Western Europe, Japan (all since late 19th or early 20th century)	

other difference is that this type of financial structure appears to be associated with a lower rate of domestic saving and capital formation—this is far from established—and a higher financial intermediation ratio than was reached in Western Europe and North America when these areas had a similar financial structure.

The third type of financial structure (category 8 of Table 1–4) is common among industrialized countries since approximately the beginning of the twentieth century. It is characterized, first, by a higher value of the financial interrelations ratio—a value in the order of unity (i.e. aggregate financial assets are equal in size to national wealth) with, however, a fairly broad range of from ¾ to 1¼ but rising occasionally to a value of 2. This type is characterized, secondly, by a higher ratio of equity securities to claims (though claims still account for over two-thirds of total financial assets), by a higher share of financial institutions in total financial assets, and by increased diversification among financial institutions, leading to a decline in the share of the banking system and a corresponding increase in the importance of thrift institutions and private and public insurance organizations.

Cases evidently exist where the main characteristics of financial structure are in a position intermediate between the three main types or where not all characteristics point to the same type of structure. This must be so because the historical transition of individual countries from one type of financial structure to another is gradual rather than abrupt and because the quantitative characteristics of the financial structures of different countries, although they do not constitute a continuous spectrum, yet are not entirely concentrated in a few narrow intervals. Nevertheless the simple classification into three main types fits most of the countries, for which the necessary calculations can now be made, without doing undue violence to the variations actually found. It is also applicable to the development in financial structure over the last century for the much smaller number of countries that have the required historical records. If the story were to be pushed back beyond the seventeenth century in Europe, and beyond comparable periods in other parts of the world, several additional types of simple financial structures would have to be added to the list. These, however, would have little relevance to the problems of financial structure and development in the world of today. This path is therefore not further pursued except for the attempt made in Table 1–4 to expand the number of types of financial structures discussed in the preceding pages sufficiently to encompass in categories 1 through 4 of the table a wider geographic and historical field and to point to examples of all those types of financial structure that seem to have existed.

The study of financial structure involves, of course, more than the classification of financial instruments and of financial institutions into rather broad and rough categories. A good deal of the actual differences in financial structure and development among countries and over time, which are the subjects in which the comparative study of finance is primarily interested, can be traced to two factors. The first of these is the existence of differences and changes over time in the character of a single type of financial instrument or a single type of financial institution that is regarded as homogeneous for purposes of typology, an assumption which is required for the preliminary exploration of the terrain and for the discovery of regularities of reasonably broad scope in space or time. The second factor is connected with the character of the relations among people participating in the network of finance, such as the relations between the officers of a financial institution and its customers, between corporate officials and the company's investment bankers, and between trustees and beneficiaries. These relations are important, although they are not easily quantifiable and vary much in character. In a study such as this it is not possible to go much, if at all, beyond the chief quantitative characteristics of financial structure and development into the details of the character of financial instruments, the operation of financial institutions, and the relations between financial and nonfinancial sectors. These matters can only be occasionally touched upon, important as they are for full understanding of financial development. This study deals on an international comparative basis with the basic elements and not with the fine structure of the financial system.

FINANCIAL DEVELOPMENT

Basic Problems

Financial development is change in financial structure. Hence, the study of financial development essentially requires information on changes in financial structure over shorter or longer periods of time. This can be provided either by information on the flows of financial transactions over continuous periods of time or by the comparison of financial structure at different points of time. For full understanding of financial development, both types of information are wanted. As a practical matter, however, because of the recency of interest in these problems and the lack of continuous data for long periods of the past, the comparative study of financial development, once it is to be pushed back beyond World War II, must rely primarily, if not exclusively, on the comparison of financial structure at benchmark dates, sometimes dates separated by several decades. In that case, the main tools of the analysis of changes in financial structure are the comparison of national balance sheets at benchmark dates and of the ratios derived from these balance sheets, such as the financial interrelations ratio, the share of financial institutions in financial assets, in the aggregate, and for important instruments, the distribution of total financial assets among instruments, and the distribution of financial institutions, i.e. the ratios which have already been discussed in the preceding section in their application to a single point of time.

Both from a conceptual and a statistical point of view these comparisons rely heavily on the fact that the change in the market value of stocks between two benchmark dates, i.e. the value of the various financial instruments outstanding and the assets of different types of financial institutions, are equal to the sum of (1) financial flows (i.e., net purchases or sales) in the interval and (2) valuation adjustments, which reflect unrealized as well as realized capital gains and losses arising from the fluctuations in the market prices of assets. This relationship makes it possible to draw inferences from the known changes in the value of assets and in asset prices between two benchmark dates on the volume of financial flows in the interval, for which direct information usually is missing. The material, however, generally permits such inferences only at the national level, and occasionally for a few broad sectors, but not for smaller subsectors which sometimes may be more important for understanding what has happened.

Here again the main question to be answered by the statistical material is: Who finances whom? This question is now interpreted in the sense of changes in the size of the financial superstructure in relation to the real infrastructure, in the distribution of financing by sources and uses, and in the terms of financing.[6]

Thus, changes in the financial interrelations ratio reflect what is probably the basic feature in financial development: the changing relation between the size of the financial superstructure and the real infrastructure. Since the financial interrelations ratio is higher the denser the net of financial interrelations in comparison to the size of national wealth or national product, one would expect the financial interrelation ratio to rise in the course of economic development and to provide a measure of the stage of financial development reached. There will be an opportunity in Chapter 9 to investigate the extent to which this hypothesis is borne out by the facts and to examine the cautions that must be observed in interpreting the levels

6. Primarily because of lack of data on an international comparative scale, this study must unfortunately remain silent on the last of these three important questions.

and movement of the financial interrelations ratio and its components.

Changes in the ratio of financial assets that involve financial institutions to the total volume of financial assets outstanding in the country reflect the institutionalization of the process of savings and investment. The higher this ratio, after allowance is made for the influence of valuation changes, the larger the share of indirect savings through financial institutions compared to that of direct saving.

Similarly, changes in the distribution of the total assets of financial institutions indicate the changing importance of the banking system in the process of saving, whether the narrow concept which includes only money-issuing institutions is used, or a broader concept is adopted that includes the entire commercial banking system and possibly even savings banks. More generally, the changes in the distribution of the total assets of financial institutions between benchmark dates reflect the development of new financial institutions and differences in the growth rates of existing types of institutions.

Types of Financial Development

There is no doubt about the existence of different types of financial structure. The comparison of national balance sheets of any recent date is sufficient to disclose great differences among countries in the level of their financial interrelations ratio, in the share of financial institutions in total financial assets, in relationships among financial instruments and their size in comparison to national wealth or national product, and in the distribution of the assets of financial institutions among banks, insurance companies, and other institutions. It is much more difficult to determine whether there have been systematic differences in the path by which countries have reached their present financial structure. In other words, do the differences in financial structure that we observe at the present time reflect nothing but differences in the position of individual countries along the same universal path of financial development, differences which in turn could be due either to differences in starting date or to differences in the speed of travel—measured in calendar time—along the path? Or is the present position the result of traveling along different paths? It is only in the second case that the problem of types of financial development arises.

One of the main tasks of this study is to determine whether different paths of financial development among countries can be distinguished. We may anticipate some of the results by stating that, apart from the different path taken since World War I or II by the countries that have a centrally planned economy in which the government owns most of the means of production, the existence of clearly different paths of financial development is doubtful. The evidence now available is more in favor of the hypothesis that there exists only one major path of financial development, a path marked by certain regularities in the course of the financial interrelations ratio, in the share of financial institutions in total financial assets, and in the position of the banking system, deviations being connected primarily with war finance and with inflation; a path on which different countries have started at different dates, in the twofold sense of different calendar dates and of different phases of their nonfinancial economic development; a path along which they have traveled at different speed, again in the sense of both calendar time and of phases of economic development; and a path from which they have deviated only to a minor extent.

In one respect, however, the differences in financial development among countries are sufficiently pronounced that one could distinguish two traces of one basic path rather than one single path. The difference between the two traces centers in the extent to which the government (central or local) participates in the ownership and the management of certain financial institutions.

In the countries following the first of these two traces virtually all financial institutions are privately owned and administered, with the exception of only, first, the central bank of issue during the latter phase of the country's financial development, and, second, of social insurance organizations. The United States is the most important country which has traveled along this trace of the path and the country which so far has adhered to it most closely, though of course not rigidly, as is evidenced, for example, by the increasing importance since the Great Depression of government lending institutions. The United States has had relatively few companions on this trace—primarily Canada and some of the countries of Western Europe such as Belgium and the Netherlands. It is almost unique in that even the central bank is owned privately, though it is under strong government influence. Whether the United Kingdom's path has been closer to this or to the other trace is arguable.

In the countries following the second trace several important types of financial institutions have been owned and managed by the government, either in their entirety or in part, and either from their inception or at a later stage of their development. Among these institutions are savings banks, mortgage banks, development banks, financial intermediaries of the second degree, trustee organizations and even some or most of the commercial banks, probably the stronghold of the private financial sector in the countries traveling along the other trace. Even in these countries, however, some types of financial institutions have almost always been outside the sphere of government ownership or management, viz. life and property insurance organizations, building societies, finance companies, investment companies, and security brokers and dealers. This trace of the path has been followed by most countries outside of Western Europe and North America. It is, therefore, predominant among the Latin American republics, and among the independent states of Africa, the Near East and Southeast Asia after they reached political sovereignty. At least one of the British dominions, Australia, should be included in this group since the turn of the century or

World War I. So should most European countries, at least since World War II, and some of them, notably France, Germany, and Italy, almost back to the beginning of their modern financial development. The second, and not entirely unrelated, characteristic of this trace of the path is the considerable foreign participation during the early stages of development of some financial institutions, particularly commercial banks and insurance companies, followed at later stages by the repatriation of foreign holdings in these institutions.[7]

One of the reasons, possibly the most important single reason, for this basic unilineality in financial development since the industrial revolution of the later eighteenth and the early nineteenth centuries is the fact that none of the non-Western countries appears to have developed an indigenous financial structure in more than rudimentary form. Certain types of financial instruments, e.g. bills of exchange, mortgages and annuities, and some financial institutions, such as banks of deposit and issue, can be found here and there in the ancient Orient, in China, and in classical antiquity.[8] Both financial instruments and institutions gained in variety and importance in the late Middle Ages. In some areas, particularly in northern Italy and the Low Countries, they sometimes have an outwardly modern look.[9] But as far as we can judge from the scanty quantitative data available, financial activities (i.e. transactions in financial instruments) remained sporadic and ancillary with the possible exception of trade credit, sea loans, and the transfer of money by check. What is more impor-

7. This feature is briefly discussed in the section "The Role of Foreign Banks" (Chapter 8).

8. For the ancient Orient see F. M. Heichelheim, *An Ancient Economic History* (Leiden, A. W. Sijthoff, 1958), *1,* 133ff., 363–65, 477–82, 505–07; for classical antiquity, see, e.g. M. Weber, *Wirtschaftsgeschichte* (München, Duncker und Humblot, 1924) p. 292.

9. For Italy see, e.g. A. Sapori, *Le Marchand Italien au Moyen Age* (Paris, Colin, 1952) who claims that the central and northern parts of the country developed a deposit banking system as early as the middle of the thirteenth century (p. XXXIV).

tant, financial instruments, institutions, and operations never seem to have acquired a volume (compared to tangible wealth or to national product) of the order of magnitude to which we are now accustomed even in financially less developed modern countries.

For the two countries that were destined to become the prototypes of modern financial structure and development—the United Kingdom and France—students seem to agree that a financial structure in the modern sense and a capital market of more than occasional nature did not develop before the second quarter of the nineteenth century, and certainly were not yet to be found in the mid-eighteenth century.[10] In the United States, the decisive formative period may be a little earlier, possibly the first quarter of the nineteenth century. Hardly any other country reached the same stage before the middle of the nineteenth century. Very few financial institutions—be they central banks, commercial banks, savings or mortgage banks, investment trusts or insurance companies—go back beyond the early nineteenth century, and those that do are of very small size until well into the nineteenth century, not only by present standards but in comparison to contemporary values of wealth and income.

The reasons for this absence of financial structure and development in the modern sense are not far to seek. They lie primarily in the as yet rudimentary separation between savers and investors, or between households and enterprises, a separation whose importance for the creation and expansion of a financial superstructure will become clear in the theoretical discussions of Chapter 2 and in the statistical evidence of Chapters 3 through 7.

10. For England see T. S. Ashton, *The Industrial Revolution, 1760–1830* (London, Oxford University Press, 1948), pp. 100–08; e.g. (p. 108): "In 1760 there was nothing that could justly be called a capital market. Lending was still largely a local and personal matter."

A BIRD'S-EYE VIEW OF THE FINDINGS

The modern epoch of financial development, the only one that justifies the use of the term financial structure and development and the measurement of the structure's size and character, thus is less than 200 and probably not more than 150 years old. During that period a financial system of the modern type, characterized by the existence of several basic forms of financial institutions (banks of issue and deposit, savings banks, mortgage banks, and insurance companies) and of financial instruments (scriptural money, bills of exchange, accounts receivable and payable, bank deposits and loans made by financial institutions, life insurance and pension contracts, mortgages, government and corporate bonds, and corporate stock) spread from Western Europe over the entire world, with the possible exception of some Communist countries. This process, though starting in different countries at different dates during the nineteenth century and in some cases, primarily limited to Africa, beginning only at the turn of this century, has shown several important regularities, again excepting Communist countries. These regularities, whose disclosure and explanation constitute the main task of this study, can preliminarily be summarized in the following dozen statements, which have purposely been expressed in essentially qualitative terms:

1. In the course of economic development a country's financial superstructure grows more rapidly than the infrastructure of national product and national wealth. Hence the financial interrelations ratio (the quotient of the aggregate market value of all financial instruments in existence in a country at a given date to the value of its tangible net national wealth) has a tendency to increase.

2. This increase in a country's financial interrelations ratio, however, is not a process that continues without limit. Both observation and theoretical considerations—the latter to be discussed in Chapter 2—indicate that once a certain

stage of development is attained, specifically when the financial interrelations ratio reaches a value between 1 and $1\frac{1}{2}$, (this occurred in Western Europe and North America early in the twentieth century) the ratio tends to level off. In the United States, for example, the financial interrelations ratio is still at about the level it reached forty years ago. Much higher values of the ratio are generally limited to short periods and reflect the effects of repressed inflations during or immediately after major wars.

3. Economically less developed countries have much lower financial interrelations ratios than those which prevail in Europe or North America. The present values of the financial interrelations ratios of less developed countries—generally between one and two-thirds—correspond to those reached and then surpassed in the United States and Western Europe during the second half of the nineteenth century.

4. The main determinant of the relative size of a country's financial superstructure is the separation of the functions of saving and investing among different economic units and groups of them. The level and movement of the financial interrelations ratio, therefore, reflect the extent to which the groups of economic units that habitually account for the bulk of capital expenditures or occasionally incur current expenditures in excess of income—business enterprises, home owners, and governments—need to resort to external financing through borrowing or through issuance of equity securities, or are able to finance their expenditures internally out of their own saving. The level of the financial interrelations ratio thus can be traced back to fundamental features in a country's economic structure, such as the concentration of production, the distribution of wealth, the incentive to invest, the propensity to save, and the extent to which business activities are legally separated from household activities by devices such as incorporation. These features are reflected in the ratio of new issues of debt and equity securities by the nonfinancial sectors of the economy to national product. The higher this ratio the

more pronounced the separation of the processes of saving and capital formation.

5. In most countries the share of financial institutions in the issuance and the ownership of financial assets has considerably increased in the process of economic development. The share has continued to advance even after the rise in the nationwide financial interrelations ratio has ceased.

6. This "institutionalization" of saving and of the ownership of financial assets has affected the main types of financial instruments differently. Institutionalization has generally made much further progress with respect to claims than to equity securities—partly because of the limitations imposed in many countries on equity ownership by financial institutions—and among claims more with respect to long-term than to short-term claims. As a result the proportion of total government securities, corporate bonds, and mortgages outstanding that are acquired or held by financial institutions is now in many countries well in excess of fifty per cent and in some of them is close to 100 per cent. Corporate stock, on the other hand—which is considerably larger compared to claims in developed than in less developed countries—is everywhere still predominantly owned directly by individual shareholders, although the proportion held by financial institutions here too is usually higher in developed countries and generally has been increasing.

7. Financial development in the modern sense has started everywhere with the banking system and has been dependent on the diffusion of scriptural money through the economy. The ratio of currency (coin and bank notes) to national wealth first increased, but later leveled off or decreased. The ratio of bank money (check deposits) has followed a similar course, but with a lag of one or several generations.

8. As economic development has progressed, the share of the banking system in the assets of all financial institutions has declined, though its share in the country's total financial assets has continued to increase for a while. Simultane-

ously the share of the newer types of financial institutions —primarily savings banks, building societies, mortgage banks, life insurance companies, government and private retirement funds, investment companies, and finance companies—has increased in relation to both the assets of all financial institutions as well as total financial assets. As a result the assets of the banking system (central and commercial banks) are now considerably below those of all other financial institutions taken together in the economically most advanced countries, while the opposite relationship is still common in less developed countries.

9. Foreign financing, as either a source of funds supplementing those domestically available or as an outlet for funds not easily utilizable within the country, has played a substantial role in some phase of the development of most countries. As a result of both economic and political trends the ratio of foreign to domestic financing, and particularly that of foreign long-term financing, has, however, failed to show a definite movement since World War I for the world as a whole, after increasing rapidly through most of the nineteenth century, an increase closely connected with the railway age.

10. Probably as important for the financial development of most countries as these flows of funds across international boundaries was the example provided by the more advanced countries. Transfer of technology and entrepreneurship have been easier to accomplish, and on the whole more successful, with respect to financial instruments and financial institutions than in many other fields. This, however, refers to the introduction of these devices rather than to their relative quantitative importance, which is primarily determined by basic economic factors.

11. The cost of financing, including interest rates and other charges, is distinctly lower in financially developed than in less developed countries, with occasional exceptions mainly reflecting the effects of inflation. There has, however, been no long-term downward trend in these costs since the mid-nineteenth century in the developed coun

tries of Europe, North America, and the British Commonwealth. Movements in the rest of the world are too diverse and irregular to permit generalization.

12. In most countries a rough parallelism can be observed between economic and financial development if periods of several decades are considered. As real income and wealth increase, in the aggregate and per head of the population, the size and complexity of the financial superstructure grow. There are even indications in the few countries for which the data are available that periods of more rapid economic growth have been accompanied, though not without exception, by an above-average rate of financial development. There is no possibility, however, of establishing with confidence the direction of the causal mechanism, i.e. of deciding whether financial factors were responsible for the acceleration of economic development or whether financial development reflected economic growth whose mainsprings must be sought elsewhere. The only financial phenomenon that has had obvious effects on the rate and character of economic development is strong inflation, and here too nonfinancial factors appear in most cases to have been responsible for initiating and maintaining the process.

This book is chiefly devoted to the documentation, illustration, expansion and explanation of these twelve theses. It tries, in briefest formulation, to answer the questions who finances whom at different stages of financial development, to what extent, through which instruments, and with what effects on economic development. It tries to do so by a comparative analysis, chiefly in quantitative terms and with reference to a system of national accounts, of the financial structure and development of between half a dozen and three dozen countries.

2 THE DETERMINANTS OF FINANCIAL STRUCTURE AND DEVELOPMENT

It is the function of a theory of finance to identify the main economic determinants of a country's financial structure, its stock of financial instruments, and its flows of financial transactions, and to describe the way in which these determinants interact to produce financial development. In the stock dimension the main statistical characteristics of financial structure are, as has been explained in Chapter 1:

1. The financial interrelations ratio, the broadest measure of the relative size of the financial superstructure, a ratio defined as the value of all financial assets divided by the value of all tangible assets (i.e. by national wealth);
2. The distribution of total financial assets (instruments) among their main components, particularly among short-term claims, long-term claims, and equity securities;
3. The ratio of financial instruments issued by financial institutions to those issued by nonfinancial units, a ratio which provides the most general indicator of the degree of institutionalization of the financial process;
4. The share of all financial intermediaries and of the principal groups of them in the total amounts outstanding of the main types of financial instruments issued by nonfinancial units, a set of ratios which furnishes a more detailed measure of financial institutionalization than (3);
5. The relative size of the main groups of financial intermediaries, particularly the central bank, the check-

issuing commercial banks, thrift institutions, and insurance organizations;

6. The degree of interrelations existing among financial institutions, which can be measured by the proportion of the combined to the consolidated total assets of financial institutions, a proportion that may be called the layering ratio;

7. The relative size of internal and external financing of the main nonfinancial sectors;

8. Within external financing the share of the different financial instruments and the share of the main domestic sectors—particularly financial institutions—and of foreign lenders in each type of debt and equity securities outstanding.

Each of the stock ratios and relationships has a parallel in the flow dimension, net acquisitions or issues taking the place of assets or liabilities, and national product being used instead of national wealth under this correspondence principle of financial analysis.

The task, then, is to identify the economic factors which determine the level of these structural characteristics—they will be defined in more detail when the relevant statistical data are studied—as well as those factors which are responsible for changes in the structure over a shorter or longer period of time, i.e. for financial development.

APPROACH

There are two ways of explaining the salient features of an economy, ways which have come to be known as the micro-economic and the macro-economic approach. These two approaches should lead to the same result, although by different paths, possibly by employing different explanatory concepts and, of course, by using different statistical data. In Appendix I an attempt has been made to explain micro-economically, i.e. on the level of the individual household, firm, or government, two important processes: first, how the volume of a unit's gross and net issues is determined and, secondly, what determines the size and the structure of a unit's financial assets. Unfortunately it has not been possible to go far in this direction because on this level very little statistical material is available that would lend itself to international comparison and to the analysis of systematic differences in financial behavior of individual economic units of different types in various countries.[1] In this situation we must turn to the macro-economic approach if we want to have any chance of providing a theoretical, i.e. a systematic, framework for the international comparison of financial structure and development that can be tested against statistical information. This requires, of course, a much higher degree of aggregation since we are in practice able to distinguish only a small number of types of financial and nonfinancial sectors and of financial instruments. The approach, however, need not to be more abstract than the micro-economic analysis, and it has the crucial advantage that some statistical information is available, even though much less than we would like and should have, on the two basic problems: the path of financial development in a number of countries over the last fifty to one hundred years and the present differences in financial structure among countries of different types and at different stages of their economic development.

We therefore need a framework which will reduce to a manageable number of determinants the most important characteristics of a country's financial structure at a point of time—the ratio of new issues of financial instruments to national product, the ratio of financial assets to national

1. The discussion at the micro-economic level—individual economic units and groups of them—has been omitted here in order to permit the majority of readers to proceed directly to the more immediately interesting analysis of financial structure and development on the macro-economic, countrywide level, the field to which the empirical material used in this study is of necessity almost entirely limited. The discussion has been relegated to Appendix I, perhaps mistakenly, so as to enable the probably few readers interested in these basic but as yet little known and controversial matters to examine what little the author may have to contribute to the discussion.

wealth, the role of direct as compared to indirect financing, the relative importance of the different types of financial institutions and financial instruments, a framework that thus will identify the determinants of the changes in structure between two points, i.e. of financial development.

To be useful in financial analysis these determinants should meet five conditions: (1) They should be measurable. (2) Each of the determinants should behave reasonably regularly although they often will exhibit long-term trends. (3) They should be economically relevant for the units to which they apply and to the country's financial process and structure, a condition for which perhaps no objective tests exists. (4) The determinants chosen should not be tied irrevocably to the individual observer's opinion of the character of certain financial relationships, i.e. the approach should be flexible enough to be useful in exploring a variety of hypotheses regarding financial behavior. (5) They should be relevant in very different types of financial structure, or they would not be usable in the comparison over extended periods and over long distances in space and wide differences in type.

The approach to the analysis of financial structure and development taken in this chapter, an approach which underlies much of the rest of this study, has been selected to meet these five criteria. It is necessarily aggregative in level and abstract in character, but it is fully adapted to statistical implementation and testing.[2] This approach may be likened to the use of the quantity theory in the analysis of money and prices. Just as in that approach, the framework of analysis that is being developed factors important observable economic magnitudes—here the volume of issues and the stock of financial instruments, there the volume of

2. Readers familiar with the financial literature of the last decade will note some similarity of the approach used here to that of J. G. Gurley and E. S. Shaw—more in "The Growth of Debt and Money in the U.S., 1800–1950; A Suggested Interpretation" in *Review of Economic Statistics, 39* (1957), 250–62, than in their *Money in a Theory of Finance* (Washington, Brookings Institution, 1960)—but only in the general character of the approach, not in the details.

monetary transactions and the stock of money—into a small number of components: here the dozen coefficients of Equation (36), for example, there either the volume of money (for several types of money) and their velocities or the volume of finished output (or its components) and the corresponding prices. These components, of course, need further analysis and they have their own determinants, a regress which, if not working ad infinitum, can certainly be followed for several steps backward. The approach used here, like the quantity theory, will have done its duty if it has identified the elements operating at one level below the surface and if it has indicated how these elements of the (so to speak) nether world cooperate to produce the observed phenomena, the explanation of which is the objective of the exercise.

It will help an understanding of the approach taken in this section if we go back to sectoral sources-and-uses-of-funds statements, distinguishing only two sectors in a closed economy, the first comprising all nonfinancial units (i.e., nonfinancial business enterprises, households, and governments), while the second includes all financial institutions.[3] These two sectors are identified in the equations that follow by the subscripts n and f respectively; where two subscripts are used the first indicates the lender (holder) and the second the borrower (issuer). We then have for any period, if k indicates capital expenditures, including inventory accumulation, s saving, l lending (i.e. the acquisition of new debt as well as of equity securities), b borrowing (i.e. the issuance of these two types of securities), and p and q the purchase and sale respectively of existing financial assets.

$$k_n + l_n + p_n = s_n + b_n + q_n \qquad (2.1)$$

$$k_f + l_f + p_f = s_f + b_f + q_f \qquad (2.2)$$

$$(k_n + k_f - s_n - s_f) + (l_n + p_n - q_n) = b_n + b_f - (l_f + p_f - q_f) \qquad (2.3)$$

Since in a closed economy total capital formation equals

3. The character of sources-and-uses-of-funds statements at the unit and sector level is discussed in Appendix I.

total saving (in an open economy net current balance is needed to insure their equality), these relationships can be summarized in a single basic equation (2.4) which shows on the left-hand side total net acquisition of securities by financial and nonfinancial units and on the right-hand side total net issues of securities of nonfinancial units, divided into their direct and indirect external financing, and the corresponding net issues of financial institutions, i.e. the increase in money, deposits, insurance reserves and other types of financial instruments issued by financial institutions

$$\underbrace{\underbrace{(l_n+p_n-q_n)}_{\text{By nonfinancial sectors}} + \underbrace{(l_f+p_f-q_f)}_{\text{By financial institutions}}}_{\text{Total net acquisition of securities}} = \underbrace{\underbrace{\underbrace{b_{nn}}_{\text{Direct}} + \underbrace{b_{fn}}_{\text{Indirect}}}_{\substack{\text{financing} \\ \text{By nonfinancial sectors}}} + \underbrace{\underbrace{b_{nf}}_{\text{Outside}} + \underbrace{b_{ff}}_{\text{Inside}}}_{\substack{\text{financing} \\ \text{By financial institutions}}}}_{\text{Total net issuance of securities}} \quad (2.4)$$

These equations can be applied either on a gross or a net basis, i.e. l and b may be gross or net of retirement of securities by their issuers; and these retirements may be introduced as separate terms in the equations if l and b are on a gross basis. Because of the scarcity of data on retirements most practical work in this field is on a net basis.

Financial structure and development, of course, have two dimensions—flows over a given period of time and stocks at a given point of time. Equations (2.1) to (2.4) refer to the flow aspect. The comparable stock relationships are set forth in Equations (2.5) to (2.8), where K and F identify tangible and financial assets, D and E stand for debt and equity issues ($B = D + E$), S is the value of earned net worth (saving), a bar above the symbol indicates valuation at market price, and the domestic nonfinancial sectors (subscript n) include nonfinancial business enterprises (subscript b) and household and governments (subscript h).

$$K_n + F_n = S_b + S_h + D_b + E_b + D_h \qquad (2.5)$$

$$K_f + F_f = S_f + D_f + E_f \qquad (2.6)$$

$$\underbrace{(K_n + K_f)}_{\text{Tangible assets}} + \underbrace{(F_n + F_f)}_{\text{Financial assets}} = S_b + S_h + S_f + D_b + D_h + D_f + E_b + E_f$$

(at national original cost)

$$= S_b + S_h + S_f + E_{nn} + E_{fn} + E_{nf} + E_{ff} + D_{nn} + D_{fn} + D_{nf} + D_{ff} \qquad (2.7)$$

$$\underbrace{(\bar{K}_n + \bar{F}_n)}_{\text{Assets of nonfinancial sectors}} + \underbrace{(\bar{K}_f + \bar{F}_f)}_{\text{Assets of financial institutions}}$$

(at market value)

$$= \underbrace{\bar{E}_{nn} + \bar{E}_{fn} + \bar{D}_{nn} + \bar{D}_{fn}}_{\text{Nonfinancial issues outstanding}} + \underbrace{\bar{E}_{nf} + \bar{E}_{ff} + \bar{D}_{nf} + \bar{D}_{ff}}_{\text{Financial issues outstanding}} + \underbrace{\bar{S}_h}_{\text{Net worth of ultimate units}} \qquad (2.8)$$

(at market value)

Some differences between the two groups of equations should be noted.[4] While in the case of flows we need not choose among alternative bases of valuation since all entries are made at actual cash flow values, the situation is more difficult in the case of stocks, i.e. for balance sheets of sectors and of the nation. The main choice here is between original cost on the one hand and market value and the nearest approximations to it on the other. If original cost is used as a basis of valuation, stocks are simply the cumulation of all previous net flows. The resulting value of stocks, however, is not realistic over longer intervals in the sense that the figures cease to be the quantities that decide or influence the holders in their actual behavior. If each asset is valued at market or nearest approximation to it, the balance sheet values cease to be summations of previous net flows, although the difference can be resolved into

4. The disappearance of the S_b and S_f terms from Equation (2.8) reflects the fact that the market value of equity securities of business enterprises includes both the original issue price, E, and the later retained profits, S, and the market value of the securities, $\bar{E}$, includes both E and S.

realized and unrealized capital gains and losses. Another difference between the flow and the stock equations is that balance sheets at market value, such as are represented by Equation (2.8), include the value of nonreproducible assets, a figure which is not the result of capital expenditures, and hence is excluded from the cumulation of capital expenditures that yields the value of tangible assets at national original cost, i.e. at the original cost at which the asset first entered the national territory. Finally it is generally not possible in balance sheets drawn up on the basis of market values to distinguish between earned surplus (cumulated saving from the flow statements), surplus resulting from realized capital gains, and contributed equity capital, i.e. the cumulation of receipts from issuance of equity securities. These three items together are reflected in the market value of equities securities, i.e. item $\bar{E}$ in Equation (2.8).[5]

For the analysis of financial structure and development greatest importance attaches, in the stock dimension, to the right-hand side of Equation (2.8) which shows the market value of financial instruments issued by nonfinancial and financial units respectively. The right-hand side also shows —and this is an important difference from the corresponding flow in Equation (2.4)—the net worth of households and governments, S_h, an item which in contrast to the net worth of nonfinancial business enterprises and of financial institutions is not a financial instrument, although it may constitute one of the bases of these units' ability to borrow, i.e., to issue financial instruments. The net worth of these ultimate units, of course, cannot be shown at market value in a strict sense similar to that of corporate stock but is entered at adjusted book value, i.e. the difference between the market value of assets and the liabilities of households and governments. Unincorporated business enterprises—partnerships and sole proprietorships—can be treated like

5. For a more adequate discussion of the problems raised by sectoral and national balance sheets see Goldsmith and Lipsey, *Studies in the National Balance Sheet, 1,* Pt. I, Chap. 2.

corporations or like ultimate units. In the first case their net worth is entered separately at adjusted book value and becomes a financial asset of the partners or proprietors. If, on the other hand, no distinction is made between the household and business activities of the partners and proprietors, then their net worth includes the difference between their business type assets and liabilities and the difference does not appear as a separate item in the national balance sheet. While the theoretical advantages of one or the other treatment may be debated, the statistical material almost forces adoption of the second alternative, i.e. inclusion of business type assets and liabilities with the household assets and liabilities of the owners and proprietors.

The formulas to be developed below have for immediate objective the factoring of the right-hand side of Equations (2.4) and (2.8), except for the net worth of ultimate units in Equation (2.8). To bring out the most important features of the annual flow of financial instruments or of the stock of financial instruments outstanding at a given balance sheet date, the formulas should distinguish three main components of total issues, i.e. the issues of the nonfinancial sectors and of financial institutions and, in the practically dominating case of an open economy, also the balance of transactions in financial instruments with the rest of the world. The formulas should be so constituted that each of the two domestic components can be subdivided to the extent that this is necessary for analysis and is feasible statistically. This means distinguishing the main nonfinancial issuing sectors—business enterprises (possibly further subdivided among main industries), households, and governments of different levels—and the main forms of financial instruments (short-term debt, long-term debt, equity securities). The formulas should be usable on a gross as well as a net basis, i.e. they should permit the separation of gross issues, retirements, and net issues, where this is appropriate and statistically feasible, and where the separation may contribute to an understanding of the financial process. Finally there should be as simple as possible a link between the formula for (annual) issues of financial instruments and that for the market value of the stock of instruments outstanding at a balance sheet date, a link requiring a specific allowance for the change in the market value of financial intruments between the dates of their issuance and the date of the balance sheet. These terms are not easy to meet, particularly if the formulas must also accord with the five basic conditions discussed earlier. No perfect solution is possible. It is hoped, however, that the formulas developed in the following sections represent a reasonable compromise between the desire for the maximum of analytic significance on the one side and the availability of data and the simplicity of the expressions on the other.

THE FLOW OF NEW ISSUES OF FINANCIAL INSTRUMENTS

The Choice of Denominators

The analysis of financial structure and development, particularly if it is conducted on an international comparative basis, is not primarily interested in the absolute value of the annual issues of financial instruments or in the market value of the stock of financial instruments outstanding at the balance sheet date expressed in the currency of the time and place. Both for international comparisons and for the analysis of one country's financial development over time the magnitudes to be explained are not so much these absolute figures, as their relations to certain macroeconomic aggregates which may be regarded as the appropriate denominator, standard of comparison, reference, or matrix. The selection of the appropriate denominator for flows of (net or gross) issues, on the one hand, and for the market value of the stock of financial instruments outstanding at one point of time, on the other, necessarily involves choice; it thus implies a judgment regarding the relative usefulness of alternative denominators, although the choice is limited by the need to select a denominator which is amenable to measurement on an international scale. One condition, however, should be met wherever possible—the macro-economic aggregate to which the flow or the stock of financial instruments is related should have the appropriate economic dimension. This means in the case of flows of financial instruments during one period that the denominator should be an economic flow relating to the same period and the same area, while for the market value of a stock of financial instruments it should be the market value of the stock of some economic assets in the same area and for the same date.

Under these conditions the macro-economic quantity best fitted to serve as the denominator of figures for the flow of financial instruments during a period seems to be the period's gross national product—the best indicator now available of the flow of final goods and services. Since one of the most important objectives of financial analysis, if not the most important one, is a clarification of the relations that exist between a country's financial superstructure and its real infrastructure, national product would seem to be the natural choice of denominator in the case of financial flows.

National product, however, has at least one competitor that must be considered, a magnitude which may be called "national sales" or "national receipts," as it has no standard name in economic theory or in national accounting practice. National aggregate sales or receipts differ from national product in that they derive, to use accounting terminology, from the combination of the accounts of all constituent units rather than from the consolidation of the current transactions of all units within a sector as is the case for national product.[6]

National sales are, as the name tries to convey, the sum of the monetary receipt from sales of goods and services of all units within the national boundaries, not excluding

6. As is well known, gross national product as usually defined is in accounting terms the sum of (1) a combination of the consolidated current income statements of the sectors being distinguished, i.e. commonly households, governments, and business enterprises, and (2) total capital formation.

sales of nondurable goods from one business enterprise to another, the "interindustry transactions" which are eliminated from national product, and not excluding transfer receipts. National sales thus are the sum of national product and interindustry sales. National sales, of course is a duplicative concept in contrast to national product, which by eliminating interindustry sales insures that only the value of the final output of durable and nondurable goods and services is included in the total. As a result, the value of national sales depends on the degree of integration within the business sector and, in comparison to national product, is the larger the lower the degree of integration.[7]

National sales thus are not invariant to differences and changes in industrial organization. They are therefore not an appropriate measure of the volume of the final output of an economy, a measure which is the objective of national product. This defect, however does not decide whether (for an individual economic unit and for certain groups of them) sales (receipts) may not be a reference magnitude preferable to the unit's contribution to national product. This is so because financial flows, particularly the issuance of financial instruments, may be more closely related to sales than to the unit's contribution to national product. Indeed, while evidence is insufficient for a categorical answer, there is good reason to believe that an individual unit's —and even a sector's—sales (i.e. for households, receipts from wage and property income and from transfers; for governments, tax and other receipts; for business enterprises, sales) may be regarded with more justification as determining the volume of financial transactions, and again particularly the volume of capital expenditures and of the issuance of financial instruments, than may the contribution of the unit or the sector to gross national product.

It is fortunately not necessary to make an exclusive choice

7. Interindustry (input-output) statistics in addition usually include some intrafirm sales in order to permit an economically more meaningful allocation of the output of multiproduct enterprises. These intrafirm transactions are disregarded in national sales as defined here.

between gross national product as the best macro-economic matrix of capital expenditures and of the issues of financial instruments and the individual unit's sales as the magnitude most likely to influence, or to determine, that unit's capital expenditures or issues of financial instruments. All that is needed is to introduce the concept of the ratio of interindustry (nonfinancial) sales in the entire economy to gross national product (y), a ratio which may be designated by ω, so that national sales are equal to $y(1 + \omega)$. This ratio, however, is meaningful only on the national level or for all nonfinancial business enterprises together.

Issues of Nonfinancial Issuers

What is wanted is an expression for the volume of issues of financial instruments by nonfinancial issuers during a given period, in practical work usually one year. It has just been argued that the sales of nonfinancial units and sectors seem to provide the most appropriate basis or denominator for this expression. Since we take into consideration only monetary sales, excluding barter transactions, and financial transactions are by definition limited to the monetized sector of the economy, we must introduce a factor which expresses the relation of monetized gross national product to total national product, including those imputations (particularly imputations for food consumed by farmers and rent on owner occupied homes) that are customarily made in national accounting. Designating sales by v (all of them by definition monetary) and calling the monetization ratio μ, we have for any one period, j, as the expression for the sales of the domestic nonfinancial sectors and hence as the denominator of issues of financial instruments by domestic nonfinancial units:

$$v_j = y_j \mu_j (1 + \omega_j) \qquad (2.9)$$

The question now arises as to the macro-economic magnitudes best fitted to explain the volume of issue of financial instruments of nonfinancial sectors, or more accurately the ratio of their issues to their sales. There is again not enough evidence for an unequivocal decision. It would seem, however, that capital expenditures, in a sense to be clarified in a moment, must be one important factor, and possibly the most important single factor, that influences or determines the volume of issues of the nonfinancial sectors, i.e. the sum of all forms of financial instruments issued by a unit. If we define the capital formation ratio ($\hat{\kappa}$) as the value of capital expenditures (k, assuming for simplicity all capital expenditures to be monetized) divided by the value of sales, and multiply $\hat{\kappa}$ by the expression for sales developed in Equation (2.9), we obtain

$$\hat{\kappa}_j = [y_j\mu_j(1 + \omega_j)]\hat{\kappa}_j \qquad (2.10)$$

Since there exist numerous reasonable possibilities of defining capital expenditures, particularly for use as a determinant of the volume of issues of financial instruments, several alternative versions of the capital formation ratio must be considered. The first uses the standard definition of gross capital formation, i.e. the expenditures on durable goods (usually of a life of one to three years or more), including major alterations and repairs, plus net increases in inventories. It is, however, sometimes preferable to deal with net capital formation, i.e. gross capital formation as just defined, less either depreciation allowances of the period as calculated by accountants or statisticians (a_1); or less calculated or actual retirements of reproducible durable assets during the period (a_2 and a_3 respectively). For individual units and for sectors capital formation also includes the net purchase or sales of existing durable goods, but these transactions cancel out for the economy as a whole. These alternatives lead to four versions of κ—which we may designate by κ_1 to κ_4, using as numerator gross monetized capital formation (k), capital expenditures net of depreciation ($k - a_1$) and capital expenditures net of retirements ($k - a_2$ or $k - a_3$), while employing in all four case the volume of sales as denominator.

For financial analysis, and particularly for the study of

the determinants of the volume of issues of financial instruments, it may, however, be preferable to define capital expenditures more broadly as the type of expenditures which are commonly financed by borrowing. This concept of capital expenditures would generally yield larger figures than the standard definition of net capital formation because it includes the unit's requirements, particularly in the case of business enterprises, for extending trade credit to customers (r) and for additional transactions cash (m) needed to handle the increasing volume of business.[8]

Use of this broader definition of capital expenditures ($k' = k + r + m$) produces four additional definitions. The first of these (κ_5) is on a gross basis and equals $(k + r + m) : v$. The three others (κ_6 to κ_8) start from capital expenditures net of depreciation and retirements respectively and thus are equal to $(k - a_1 + r + m) : v$, to $(k - a_2 + r + m) : v$ and to $(k - a_3 + r + m) : v$ respectively.

The formula, fortunately, can use any of these versions of k—or any other that may be preferred in a specific case —because, as will be seen below (footnote 9, page 68), the effect of differences in the values of k is exactly offset by differences in the ratio of issues of financial instruments to capital expenditures (η).

So much for the theory, or more correctly for that measurement of k that is likely to perform best on the basis of what we think we know about the motives of the economic units that make capital expenditures. When we try to find numerical values for κ in different countries it soon becomes evident that the value of several of the magnitudes we have used is rarely known, though there is no fundamental obstacle to their measurement. This is the case primarily for ω, but not rarely also for μ and for a_1, a_2, a_3, r, and m. We are, in fact, left with only k and y, and are forced to use a much simpler formula for the capital formation ratio in practical works on an interna-

8. See Appendix I.

tional comparative basis, and even in work on a single country if long periods of time are involved. This simplified formula is

$$\kappa = \frac{k}{y} \tag{2.11}$$

i.e. the ratio of total gross capital expenditures to total gross national product, instead of the theoretically preferable, because more informative version of Equation (2.10). The two ratios κ and $\hat{\kappa}$ are, of course, of different sizes, $\hat{\kappa}$ being usually smaller than κ. The crucial fact, however, is that both κy and $\hat{\kappa} y \mu$ $(1 + \omega)$ yield k, the volume of total gross capital formation. By using the simpler ratio κ/y we, of course, lose the contribution that ω, μ, r, and m might make to the understanding of the determinants of the capital formation ratio.

Probably the crucial, but unfortunately the empirically least explored, factor in the component of the formula which explains the volume of issues of the nonfinancial sector is the external financing ratio, η, i.e., the ratio of the value of financial instruments issued during a given period to that period's total monetized capital expenditures. Since we may want to explain the volume of gross issues or that of net issues, i.e. gross issues less retirements, and since we have several variants of the capital expenditure ratio, we are faced with the choice among numerous new issue ratios. It is important to realize, therefore, that the product of the capital expenditure ratio and the external financing ratio is the same for all variants of the capital expenditure ratio. The product is equal to the quotient of net new issues and sales in all cases where net issues are involved, while in all cases where gross issues are the quantity to be explained the product is equal to the sum of net issues and retirements divided by sales. The numerical value of $\delta = \kappa\eta$, the first component in the basic formula for the net new issue ratio of nonfinancial sectors, is therefore unaffected by the definition of capital expenditures, and the analyst may choose that version which best suits his purposes, exactly as he may choose between net and gross issues as the object of explanation, always of course limited by the availability of statistical data. If, because of limitation of data, κ is used instead of one of the versions of $\hat{\kappa}$, the result is likewise unaffected by the definition of k adopted, although all products $\hat{\delta} = \hat{\kappa}\hat{\eta}$ differ from those of $\delta = \kappa\eta$ by the scale factor $(1 + \omega)\mu$.

So far we have treated gross or net issues of all nonfinancial issuers as one undifferentiated total. This very aggregative figure, and the equally aggregative figures of the capital formation ratio and the new issue ratio of the nonfinancial sectors taken as a whole, will in many cases provide the information needed. Often, however, when finer-grained analysis is undertaken, one value for κ or for η applying to the total of all nonfinancial units will not suffice. One may, for instance, want to explain not only the total of new issues of all nonfinancial issuers but also the separate ratios for the large constituent sectors such as business enterprises, households, and governments—or equally well the ratios for subsectors within the business enterprise and government sectors, such as individual industries or central and local governments. The formula is easily capable of accommodating such a breakdown, the main limitation being the availability of statistical data. In fact, the capital formation and new issue ratios for all nonfinancial sectors together should be regarded as weighted averages of the same ratios for the constituent subsectors. Thus we may want to separate even at a very general level of analysis, the issues of business enterprises, households, and governments. We then will have the following relationships (ratios for the three subsectors being identified by the subscripts *e, h,* and *g*; the subscript identifying the period being omitted from now on):

$$\hat{\delta} = \kappa\hat{\eta} = (\hat{\kappa}_e\hat{\hat{\eta}}_e)\frac{v_e}{v} + (\hat{\kappa}_g\hat{\hat{\eta}}_g)\frac{v_g}{v} + (\hat{\kappa}_h\hat{\hat{\eta}}_h)\frac{v_h}{v} \tag{2.12}$$

If κ is used instead of $\hat{\kappa}$, we obtain in formally parallel fashion

$$\delta = \kappa\eta = (\bar{\kappa}_e\eta_e)\frac{y_e}{y} + (\bar{\kappa}_h\eta_h)\frac{y_h}{y} + (\bar{\kappa}_g\eta_g)\frac{y_g}{y} \tag{2.13}$$

where y_e, y_h, and y_g are the contributions of the three sectors to gross national product and the bar over the sectoral κ's indicates the use of the sector's contribution to national product as the denominator. These ratios, however, have no behavioral significance and little economic meaning. If sectoral sales data are, as usual, unavailable, it is preferable to use total gross national product as the denominator for all sectoral κ's so that

$$\delta = \kappa\eta = \kappa_e\eta_e + \kappa_h\eta_h + \kappa_g\eta_g \tag{2.14}$$

This difficulty does not arise in the case of the sectoral η's since the ratio of issues to capital formation is meaningful on a sectoral as well as national level.

We similarly may distinguish different kinds of financial instruments. The resulting external financing ratios, e.g. for short-term debt, long-term debt, and equity securities, all have as their denominator the capital formation of either all nonfinancial sectors together or of an individual sector or subsector. Thus the issue-type external financing ratios for either all nonfinancial units together or for subsectors of them directly sum up to the new issue ratio of the sector or of all nonfinancial sectors.

When attention is focused on types of issues rather than issuing sectors it will often be found preferable, partly because of the nature of the available data, to deal directly with the ratio of new issues to national product ($\delta = \kappa\eta$) without distinguishing the two components. Such issue ratios will be particularly appropriate for those sectors, like the central government, whose issues are not closely tied to their capital expenditures. Since these issue-type ratios all use a common denominator—national product—they are additive and sum to the aggregate new issue ratio of all nonfinancial domestic units and ultimately to the national new issue ratio (ϵ) which also includes foreign issues and the issues of financial institutions.

While the alternative of treating new issues of securities on a gross or net basis is theoretically open for all types of financial instruments, it is economically significant primarily for those with a maturity of, say, one year or more. Hence a large proportion of all financial instruments will almost always be treated on a net basis. It is only in the case of longer-term instruments, particularly mortgages, government bonds, and preferred stock, that a decision must be made whether to proceed on the net or the gross basis. Theoretically the gross basis is always preferable because it provides additional information, and because in many cases retirements are determined by factors quite different from those that govern new issues. The limiting factor is the lack of statistical data which results in net issues of debt securities being measured by differences in the amounts outstanding at the end and at the beginning of the period rather than by subtracting independently determined retirements from gross issues. Common stock, on the other hand, will almost always have to be treated on a gross basis because data on retirements are usually unavailable except in the special case of open-end investment companies, and because valuation changes preclude using the difference between the market value of outstandings at the end and at the beginning of the period, in place of new issues during the period.

We thus arrive at the following formula for the first main component of the volume of issues during a given period, i.e. the issues of nonfinancial sectors, using sales as the denominator and monetized capital expenditures as the numerator of $\hat{\kappa}$:

$$\hat{\delta} = [y\mu(1 + \omega)]\hat{\kappa}\hat{\eta} \tag{2.15}$$

where $\hat{\kappa}$ and $\hat{\eta}$ may be understood as weighted averages of the capital formation ratio and the new issue ratios for the component sectors—in practice, at least, business enterprises, households, and governments—and the new issue ratios may in turn represent the sum of ratios for different instruments, obtained in each case by dividing the sector's issues of a given type of instrument by the sector's total capital formation.

Using instead the coefficient κ, which employs total gross national product as denominator and total capital formation as the numerator, Equation (2.15) reduces to

$$\delta = \kappa\eta \qquad (2.16)$$

where $\kappa\eta$ should be understood as the weighted average of corresponding sectoral ratios. This expression holds algebraically, irrespective of its economic significance, whatever the definition of y and k.[9]

The emphasis on the nature of $\delta = \kappa\eta$ as a weighted average of sectoral values is not a formality. Since sectors differ in the value of η, i.e., the proportion in which they finance their capital expenditures by resort to borrowing or issuing stock, the distribution of capital formation among sectors, i.e., the sectoral structure of κ, is an important determinant of δ. A country in which a relatively large proportion of capital expenditures is made by the government, with the result that a relatively large proportion of tangible assets is owned by the public sector, will therefore generally show relatively high values of δ because of the usual tendency of governments to finance a larger proportion of their capital expenditures externally than do the business and household sectors. Similar effects flow from the

9. These relations may be illustrated by an example in which $y = 100$; $v = 300$; $k' = 18$; $k = 20$; $r + m = 10$; $a = 15$. Then

$$\hat{\kappa}_1 = k/v = 0.067 \qquad d = \hat{\kappa}_1\eta v = 15$$

$$\hat{\kappa}_2 = \frac{k + r + m}{v} = 0.100 \qquad = \hat{\kappa}_2\eta' v = 15$$

$$\kappa = k/y = 0.200 \qquad = \kappa\eta y = 15$$

$$\eta = d/k = 0.750$$

$$\eta' = d/k + r + m = 0.500$$

indicating that all three approaches, though differing in the definitions of capital formation ratio and external financing ratios lead—necessarily—to the same value of issues (d).

distribution of capital expenditures by type, again because (and insofar as) a systematic connection exists between types of capital expenditures and the share which is externally financed. Thus inventory investment is likely to be financed externally to a higher degree than most other types of capital expenditures, and expenditures on additions and alterations are likely to be financed to a larger extent internally than new structures or machines.

Issues of Financial Institutions

In studying the determinants of the second main component of the volume of new issues, the issues of financial institutions, it is desirable, and even necessary for a successful analysis of financial structure and development, to distinguish the issues of at least the five main types of financial institutions as they have been defined in the previous chapter: (1) the central bank; (2) the check-issuing deposit (commercial) banks; (3) thrift institutions; (4) insurance organizations, comprising both private life and other insurance companies and private and government pensions and similar funds; and (5) all other financial institutions, a rather heterogeneous group varying in content over time and among countries and including financial intermediaries of the second degree that may well be treated as a separate sixth subgroup.

From a formal point of view it is desirable to use as a denominator for the issues of the five (or six) types of financial institutions the same magnitude considered in the case of the issues of nonfinancial units, i.e. aggregate sales or receipts of the financial sectors. This quantity, however, is not likely to have a strong, economically meaningful association with the volume of issues of financial institutions. While this is again a question of judgment, it would seem that of the common macro-economic aggregates the two magnitudes most closely associated with the issues of financial institutions are gross national product and personal disposable income. If it is desired to use the same denominator for all groups of financial institutions, gross national product is preferable, particularly because it is used in the operational version of the issue ratio of non-financial sectors. There is little doubt, however, that the issues of thrift institutions and insurance organizations, as well as those of some of the institutions in the miscellaneous group, are more closely related to personal disposable income since these instruments are acquired almost entirely by households. One might therefore use personal disposable income as the denominator for these two groups, retaining gross national product as the denominator for the banking system and miscellaneous financial institutions, and then divide these two groups' ratios by the share of personal disposable income in total gross national product, a relation that fortunately is not likely to change rapidly or erratically. Hence the choice of the denominator for the issues of financial institutions will hardly make much of a difference for the efficiency of the analysis. From a practical point of view total gross national product is preferable since estimates are available for a larger number of countries and for longer periods than is the case for figures for personal disposable income. Using, then, gross national product as the denominator for all six groups of financial institutions, we have as the expression for the issues of financial institutions, f, and for the six subtotals, which are identified by the subscripts c, d, t, i, o, and z:

$$\frac{f}{y} = \phi = \phi_c + \phi_b + \phi_t + \phi_i + \phi_o + \phi_z \qquad (2.17)$$

In the case of issues of financial institutions, the choice between gross and net issues as the magnitude to be explained is of relatively little importance. Most of these issues are either of short maturity, at least legally (bank and thrift deposits), or they are of a character where retirements are essentially predetermined (insurance reserves). In this situation, and given the unavailability of data for gross issues for many types of short-term instruments, it seems preferable, at least in a first attack, to proceed on the basis of net issues. The formula can, of course, be easily adapted to the distinction between gross and net issues in those cases where this is regarded as desirable and where the data are available, by introducing the ratio ζ of retirements, z, to gross issues, g, in a way parallel to that explained for the issues of nonfinancial sectors.

The issues of financial institutions present one complication that is less important in the case of the issues in nonfinancial sectors, i.e. the issuance of financial instruments by one member of a subsector to members of the same or other subsector. The intrasector issues are particularly important within the banking system where they take the form of interbank deposits, either between the central bank and deposit banks or among deposit banks. Since these interbank deposits have their own determinants (legal and institutional factors often play a large role) and because of their great importance in monetary affairs it is necessary for analysis to separate them. This can be done easily by introducing the concept of a layering ratio (λ), i.e. the ratio of (1) the issues of financial instruments by one type of financial intermediaries to all other financial intermediaries to (2) their total issues to nonfinancial intermediaries. The volume of total issues by one type of financial intermediaries then is equal to their issues to nonfinancial intermediaries, multiplied by the layering ratio plus unity, the said ratio being defined as the ratio of total issues to issues to nonfinancial sectors. The term ϕ_c of Equation (2.17), for example, is then replaced by an adjusted ratio in which the volume of the central bank's issues to nonfinancial sectors is the numerator while national product is used as before as denominator. Thus the unadjusted ratio ϕ_c is factored into an adjusted ratio ($\bar{\phi}_c$) and the layering ratio λ_c so that $\phi_c = \bar{\phi}_c\ (1 + \lambda_c)$. Use of a similar layering ratio may also be advisable for deposit banks in countries where interbank deposits are of importance, as in the United States, and particularly for financial intermediaries of the second degree, most of whose issues are made to other financial institutions so that λ_z is high and $\overline{\phi}_z$ small compared to $\overrightarrow{\phi}_z$. For the other subsectors will generally be too small to justify complication of the formula. For all financial institutions together

$$\phi = \overline{\phi}(1 + \lambda_f) \tag{2.18}$$

where $(1 + \lambda_f)$ is, in accounting terminology, simply the ratio of the combined net issues of all financial institutions to their consolidated net issues, and where all three terms may be regarded as weighted averages of the corresponding sectoral ratios, the total unadjusted issues of each subsector providing the weights.

The splitting up of the issue ratio of financial institutions into a number of components—here six—each of which measures the relation of the subsector's issue to national product, and the accounting for intersectoral issues by the layering ratio, is of course, only a first step in the analysis. It is now necessary to explain each component, or group of components, by appropriate economic determinants. This, however, is far from easy, and the approach taken here is only one of several possible alternatives. This approach starts from the fact that the net issues of financial instruments by financial institutions, once interbank and similar deposits and issues of financial intermediaries of the second degree are eliminated, are essentially the result of two different though partly overlapping types of financial transactions. The first is the issuance of money (currency and check deposits), money which is then held by households and by other nonfinancial sectors of the economy. The second reflects the nonmonetary gross indirect financial saving of households[10] in the form of thrift deposits (with

10. The qualification "gross" is important, because it means that comparison of net financial issues with the usual figures of net indirect financial savings of households is not legitimate. The net borrowing of households from financial institutions (primarily in the form of home mortgage loans and consumer credit, but also in that of business credit if unincorporated business enterprises are included in the household sector as is generally the case) is correctly deducted from their net acquisition of claims against financial institutions in the calculations of net indirect (institutional) financial saving of house-

commercial banks, savings banks, saving and loan associations, credit unions, and similar organizations), of insurance reserves (voluntary or compulsory), of the purchase of bonds of mortgage banks and similar financial institutions, and of the purchase of equity securities of financial institutions by households. This leaves a heterogeneous third component consisting of time deposits held by enterprises, government, and foreigners, the issuance of mortgage bonds and of equity securities to others than households, undistributed earnings, and miscellaneous minor types of liabilities of financial intermediaries.

This approach, therefore, leads to the following explanatory formula for the issues of financial institutions:

$$\phi = (\phi_m + \phi_h + \phi_p)(1 + \lambda_f) \tag{2.19}$$

where ϕ_m is the ratio of net increase of money outside the nonfinancial system to gross national product, ϕ_h the ratio of nonmonetary issues to households, ϕ_p the ratio of the remaining issues to nonfinancial sectors to national product, and λ_f the overall layering ratio.

We may leave the factoring of ϕ_m to the monetary theorists and thus think of magnitudes like velocity of circulation or Marshallian *k*. The content of ϕ_p is probably too heterogeneous to justify anything but treatment as an exogeneous ratio. The third component ϕ_h may, however, usefully be factored into the personal saving rato (σ_h)—i.e. the ratio of total personal saving to personal disposable income—the share of saving through nonmonetary claims against (or equity securities of) financial intermediaries to total personal saving (χ_h), and the ratio of personal dis-

holds. These borrowings, however, must not be deducted when statistics of household saving through financial institutions are compared with figures on the net issues of financial institutions. This caveat is particularly important because the ratio of household saving through and of borrowing from financial institutions differs greatly among countries and has changed considerably over time. (Cf. R. W. Goldsmith, "Changes in the Structure of Personal Saving" in *Saving in Contemporary Economic Research,* Brussels, Caisse Générale d'Epargne, 1966, pp. 93 and 101.)

posable income to gross national product (ρ). This yields

$$\phi = [\phi_m + (\rho\chi_h\sigma_h) + \phi_p](1 + \lambda_f) \qquad (2.20)$$

Any definition of personal saving may be used—e.g. consumer durables may be included or excluded and depreciation on (or use value of) the stock of consumers' tangible assets may be allowed for or not—since use of varying definitions will simply lead to differing values for χ_h, σ_h, and ρ but will leave the value of $\rho\chi_h\sigma_h$ unchanged and the applicability of the formula unaffected.

This formula for ϕ is analytically more satisfactory than Equation (2.17). Unfortunately it cannot yet be implemented on an international comparative basis. In that field Equation (2.17) will have to serve until statistics of personal saving by form become available for more countries, particularly for underdeveloped ones, and for longer periods of time.

Foreign Issues

We are now left with the third and last, and generally the least important, component, viz., foreign issues. If, as will usually be the case, the figures for the issues by nonfinancial domestic sectors and by domestic financial institutions include issues to foreigners, it is necessary to add the balance in financial transactions with foreigners in order to obtain a correct figure for the total addition to the volume of financial instruments available within the country. This means adding the difference between the net acquisition of foreign issues (claims and equity securities) by domestic units and the net acquisition of domestic issues by foreign units, a figure which of course may be positive or negative. Some problems are posed by retained profits (both by foreign enterprises owned or controlled by domestic units but operated abroad and by foreign-owned enterprises operating within the national boundary), by the retained earnings attributable to minority shareholders of foreign nationality in domestic enterprises and to domestic minority shareholders in foreign enterprises, and by transactions in existing tangible assets, particularly in monetary metals. Whatever the decisions on these points—and they are to some extent arbitrary—when it comes to statistical implementation we usually must be satisfied with one aggregate figure taken from the balance of payments, viz. the net surplus or deficit on current account (commodity transactions, services, interest and dividends) less unilateral transfers, a figure which is regarded as measuring, with sign reversed, the net balance of international transactions in financial and existing tangible assets. It remains necessary, however, to decide whether to include transactions in monetary metals, because these are often of substantial size and the data are available. Under modern conditions it seems preferable to treat monetary metals as a form of financial instruments and thus to include them with the net foreign balance of claims and equity securities.

The question again arises as to the appropriate denominator, and as in the case of the issues of financial institutions gross national product would seem to be the least objectionable choice, although it must be admitted that the relationship between the net foreign balance in financial instruments, as defined above, and gross national product cannot be expected to be a close one, or to be constant over longer periods of time. Another of several possibilities would be to regard the net foreign balance in financial instruments as related to the volume of domestic issues or possibly only to that of the issues of nonfinancial sectors, a treatment which implies that the same factors determine both the volume of domestic issues and of the net foreign balance in financial instruments. Since no more evidence is available for this than for the alternative hypothesis, and since the latter simplifies the formula, one may as well adopt gross national product as the denominator of the net foreign balance in financial instruments. This means the introduction of a final term (ξ) into the formula, defined as the ratio of the net foreign balance in financial instruments (x) to total gross national product, or to monetized national product only (ξ').

The Aggregate New Issue Ratio (ANIR)

We thus now have the following equation for the three components of the issues of financial instruments, and hence for total issues of financial instruments ($e = d + f + x$):

$$e = y\{[\mu(1 + \omega)(\hat{k}\hat{\eta})] + [\bar{\phi}_b(1 + \lambda_b) + \phi_t + \phi_i + \phi_o + \phi_z] + \mu\xi'\} \quad (2.21)$$

Choosing the alternative expression for the financial issues ratio and also basing this ratio for the sake of consistency on monetized rather than on total gross national product (the difference in basis being indicated by an apostrophy), we obtain

$$e = y\mu[(1 + \omega)\hat{k}\hat{\eta} + (\phi'_m + \rho'\sigma_h\chi_h + \phi'_p)(1 + \lambda_f) + \xi'\} \quad (2.22)$$

If total gross national product is used as the common denominator, as is generally required by the limitations of the statistical material, the equation parallel to (2.21) becomes:

$$\epsilon = \frac{e}{y} = \hat{k}\hat{\eta} + (\phi_c + \phi_d + \phi_t + \phi_i + \phi_o + \phi_z) + \xi \quad (2.23)$$

This is probably the form best fitted for actual application, though it may be regarded as behaviorally less significant than Equation (2.22).

Another important characteristic of the financing process of nonfinancial units, the relative importance of direct financing (the issuance of financial instruments by nonfinancial units to other nonfinancial units, such as the sale of corporate bonds to households) and of indirect financing (the sale of such investments to financial institutions) can easily be incorporated into the formula. All that this requires is a splitting of the new issue ratio of the nonfinancial and foreign sectors into two components: The first is calculated as the ratio of the issues of nonfinancial domestic sectors to other nonfinancial units (d_n) to aggregate capital formation (k); the second is obtained by dividing the issues of financial instruments by nonfinancial issuers to financial institutions (d_f)—for instance loans obtained from banks or government and corporate bonds sold to insurance companies—again to aggregate capital formation. The two resulting separate ratios for direct and indirect financing of nonfinancial sectors ($\delta_n = d_n/k_n$ and $\delta_f = d_f/k_n$) are, however, considerably more difficult to calculate than the aggregate ratio δ, since they require information on the transactions in the securities issued by nonfinancial sectors between other nonfinancial sectors on the one hand and financial institutions on the other. If indirect financing by nonfinancial sectors is equated to the difference between total net new issues by nonfinancial units and the change in holdings by financial institutions of the securities of nonfinancial issuers, as usually must be done given the limitations of available statistics, then the distinction between direct and indirect financing becomes blurred—apart from the fact that this method is practicable only on a net basis—because securities of nonfinancial issuers acquired during the period by financial institutions from nonfinancial holders are regarded as part of indirect financing, even though no transaction between the nonfinancial issuers and the financial holder is involved.

This difficulty is serious only for those types of financial instruments in which change of hands after issuance is of considerable importance, in particular net sales or purchases of the financial sector to or from other sectors. This will be the case primarily for marketable securities such as government bonds and corporate stocks and bonds. Short-term instruments as well as mortgages and some other forms of long-term debt issued by the business and household sectors will only rarely be acquired or sold by financial institutions after original issuance, except from or to other financial institutions. For these instruments—and they often constitute the majority of all issues of the nonfinancial sectors—a change in the holdings of financial intermediaries is evidence of a direct supply of funds to the issuers.

If this difficulty is disregarded, the share of financial intermediaries in the total financing of domestic nonfinancial sectors, which may be called the domestic financial intermediation ratio (ι), is defined as $\iota_d = d_f/d = \delta_f/\delta$. A parallel problem exists for net foreign issues leading to the distinction of x_f, the net foreign balance of domestic financial intermediaries and x_n, the residual net foreign balance, attributable to domestic nonfinancial sectors. We then have for the national financial intermediation ratio

$$\iota = \frac{d_f + x_f}{d + x} \tag{2.24}$$

On the same conceptual basis ι can be approximated even when d_f and x_f cannot be separated from d and x by profiting from the fact that $f\ (1 + \lambda_f)^{-1}$ is equal to or very close to $d_f + x_f$. This must be the case since the counterflow to the net issues of financial intermediaries to domestic nonfinancial and foreign sectors is the net acquisition of financial instruments of the same sectors, the difference consisting only of the retained earnings of financial intermediaries, and even these only if they are not regarded as implicit issues to nonfinancial sectors, viz., the owners of financial institutions. This yields

$$\iota = \frac{f}{(1 + \lambda_f)d} = \frac{\bar{\Phi}}{\delta} \tag{2.25}$$

since $\bar{\Phi} = f[(1 + \lambda_f)y]^{-1}$ and $\delta = dy^{-1}$.

The more restrictive concept of $\hat{\iota}$, in which the numerator is limited to the financial instruments issued by nonfinancial sectors acquired by financial intermediaries directly from their issuers, is nonoperational because of absence of information on a comprehensive basis on such transactions. Fortunately, however, $\bar{\Phi}/\delta$ will usually not differ too much from $\hat{\iota}$ because, as just argued, many types of financial instruments are exclusively or predominantly acquired by financial intermediaries directly from the issuer and rarely change hands after issuance. The difference between $\bar{\Phi}/d$ and ι will therefore be greater the higher the velocity of turnover of financial instruments, or more correctly the larger the net balance in intersectoral transactions in outstanding instruments between financial intermediaries and other sectors.

The attentive reader may have noticed that the concept of financial surplus and deficit, for units, groups, or sectors, which was so stressed in Appendix I, seems to have disappeared from view in this section. In fact there is a fairly direct and simple formal connection between financial surpluses and deficits and new issues of nonfinancial units.

Introducing the shares of nonfinancial surplus and deficit units in the group's or sector's capital expenditures ($\dot{\kappa}_u$ and $\dot{\kappa}_d$) and saving ($\dot{\sigma}_u$ and $\dot{\sigma}_d$) and the ratios of new issues to the value of the financial surplus and deficit (ρ_u and ρ_d), which are explained in Appendix I, we have

$$\begin{aligned} d &= \rho_d t + \rho_u u \\ &= \rho_d(\dot{\kappa}_d k - \dot{\sigma}_d s) + \rho_u(\dot{\sigma}_u s - \dot{\kappa}_u k) \\ &= k(\rho_d \dot{\kappa}_d - \rho_u \dot{\kappa}_u) + s(\rho_u \dot{\sigma}_u - \rho_d \dot{\sigma}_d) \end{aligned} \tag{2.26}$$

From this equation it appears that for a group or a sector the volume of new issues (or, for that matter, the ratio of new issues to national product) depends on the relative size of the group's or sector's capital expenditures and saving (since the values of the two brackets are not likely to be the same), the distribution of the group's capital expenditures and saving among surplus and deficit units, and the relative size of ρ_d and ρ_u. Since ρ_d is almost certain to be larger than ρ_u, and the share of deficit units in capital formation is likely to be larger than that of surplus units (i.e., $\dot{\kappa}_d > \dot{\kappa}_u$), the multiplier of k in Equation (2.26) is bound to be positive and will be the larger the greater the excess of ρ_d over ρ_u and of $\dot{\kappa}_d$ over $\dot{\kappa}_u$. Much less can be asserted about the multiplier of s. It is quite doubtful in a given situation whether it will be positive or negative. While $\dot{\sigma}_u$ is likely to be larger than $\dot{\sigma}_d$ this difference may be more than offset by the excess of ρ_d over ρ_u.

If Equation (2.26) is applied to the entire economy (identified by subscript a) for which $k = s$, or, though not rigorously, to all nonfinancial units together, we obtain:

$$\frac{d_a}{k_a} = \delta = \rho_d(\dot{\kappa}_d - \dot{\sigma}_d) + \rho_u(\dot{\sigma}_u - \dot{\kappa}_u) \tag{2.27}$$

This equation provides the direct connection between the

new issue ratio of this section (δ) and the financial surpluses and deficits of Appendix I. Possibly its most important feature is that it indicates the dependence of the new issue ratio on the separation of surplus and deficit units. The more pronounced this separation (that is, the lower the offset ratio $\Sigma(u - d) : \Sigma(u + d)$, i.e. the ratio of the algebraic to the absolute sum of all surpluses and deficits) the higher is the ratio of new issues to capital formation, or to the absolute sum of financial surpluses and deficits. Equation (2.27) can as yet be implemented statistically only if a highly aggregative approach is used in which all units in broad sectors are combined, and the resulting sectoral net financial surpluses or deficits are treated as the individual components of Equation (2.27) and even then only where sectorized flow of funds statements are available. As a practical matter Equation (2.27) cannot yet be used for international comparisons if a fairly broad spectrum of countries is to be included, but the day on which this can be done should not be too far off.

THE STOCK OF FINANCIAL INSTRUMENTS

The stock of financial instruments at a given date, in the sense of the market value of all claims and equity securities then outstanding, can be regarded as the result of (1) the sum of net issues of financial instruments before the balance sheet date and (2) the sum of changes in value, compared to original cost, that has occurred between the date of issuance of the instruments that are still outstanding and the balance sheet date, an amount that in turn can be divided into the present holders' unrealized capital gains and losses, and capital gains and losses which have been realized in the past on the occasion of previous changes of hand of the instrument.

The New Issue Multiplier

The first component, aggregate net issues made before the balance sheet date, may, of course, be obtained by summing periodic, usually annual, figures for past net issues. This approach, however, requires information on the volume of net issues for a very long period—in principle back to the date of issue of the first financial instrument in the country still outstanding—and does not provide an insight into the basic process involved. For both these reasons, use will be made of the average rate of growth of national product in current prices and of the assumption that the new issue ratio, the determinants of which were discussed in the preceding section, has been constant in the past—or, what is equivalent, the assumption that the current value of the new issue ratios can be regarded as the average of the past values. It will be shown later that both assumptions can be considerably relaxed without seriously impairing the usefulness of the approach chosen.

If the new issue ratio ($\varepsilon = \delta + \phi + \xi$) is assumed to have been constant, the stock of financial investments at the balance sheet date at original issue prices (F'_T) is obviously proportional to the sum of national product during the period, i.e. $F'_T = \varepsilon \Sigma y$. Under the additional assumption that national product in current prices has grown at the constant annual rate of $(\gamma + \pi)$, where γ is the rate of growth of real product and π is the rate of change in the price level, the aggregate of past national products is, according to the formula for the sum of an infinite geometric series, equal to αy_t where $\alpha = (\gamma + \pi + \pi\gamma)^{-1} + 1$ and y_t is the rate of national product at the end of the period or, less accurately, during the last year of the period. Thus, if national product has been increasing at a rate of 5 per cent a year, equally divided between growth in real product and in the price level, the sum of all past values of national product will be 20.75 times the value of the current year's national product, and the sum of all past net issues of financial instruments will be $20.75 \times y_t \times \varepsilon$. Using the simple version of the formula previously developed for ε in a condensed form, we have the following expression for the value of financial instruments outstanding at the end of period *t*, as yet unadjusted for valuation changes:

$$F'_\tau = \alpha y_t \epsilon = \alpha y_t(\delta + \phi + \xi) \qquad (2.28)$$

This formula applies strictly only to a period of infinite duration in which the rate of growth and the coefficient ε are constant. For practical use it must be adapted to periods of finite length. This can be done by using an adjustment coefficient, a truncation ratio (τ), which makes the formula applicable to a period of finite length of n periods (years).[11] The value of this coefficient is $\tau = 1 - (1 + \gamma + \pi)^{-n}$. After this coefficient has been applied to Equation (2.28) to produce the formula value for a limited rather than infinite period, it is necessary to add the value (at original cost) of the stock of financial instruments at the beginning of the period covered by the formula, i.e. at $\tau - n$, in order to obtain again an expression for the original cost of financial instruments at the balance sheet date. This yields:

$$F'_\tau = \tau\alpha y_t(\delta + \phi + \xi) + F'_{\tau-n} \qquad (2.29)$$

Values of τ for periods of selected lengths and for selected rates of growth of national product are given in Table 2–1. It is evident that if the period is reasonably long—in excess of, say, 30 years—and if the annual rate of growth of national product in current prices is of the order common over the last century—approximately 5 per cent—the value of $F'_{\tau-n}$ is quite small compared to F'_t. Thus $F'_{\tau-n}$ will be less than 5 per cent of F_τ at 55 years' distance if the rate of growth of national product is 5 per cent, and at as little as 30 years' distance if the growth rate is 10 per cent a year. It therefore makes little difference whether, in cases where no reasonably reliable figure is available for $F'_{\tau-n}$, a rough estimate is used, or if it is assumed that the values of γ, π, and ε for a period from $\tau - n$ to τ may also be applied to the period preceding $\tau - n$.

Probably the most important case where the value of τ

11. Because of the limited number of letters in the Greek alphabet, τ had to be used as a symbol for the truncation ratio as well as a subscript symbol indicating a point of time. Since τ as the symbol of the truncation ratio never appears as a subscript, no confusion should arise.

TABLE 2–1

Value of τ for Selected Values of γ and π at 10, 15, 20, 30, and 50 Years

(RATIO OF SUM OF DECREASING GEOMETRIC SERIES FOR LIMITED NUMBER OF YEARS (n) TO INFINITE SERIES)

γ	π	α	τ $n = 10$	$n = 15$	$n = 20$	$n = 30$	$n = 50$
.01	.00	101.00	.09	.14	.18	.26	.39
.01	.01	50.75	.18	.26	.33	.45	.63
.03	.02	20.76	.39	.52	.62	.77	.92
.05	.025	14.11	.52	.67	.77	.89	.97
.05	.05	10.76	.62	.77	.86	.95	.99
.08	.07	7.43	.76	.89	.94	.99	1.00
.08	.12	5.77	.85	.94	.97	1.00	1.00
.08	.17	4.79	.90	.97	.99	1.00	1.00

is substantially above zero and its effect on F'_τ is not offset by $F'_{\tau-n}$ occurs after hyperinflations, which are usually of short duration, or after sharp cuts in the level of outstanding debt by monetary reform. (This could be taken into account in the formula by introducing an additional discontinuous multiplicative factor.) The volume of debt outstanding is very low at the end of the hyperinflation or after the monetary reform, particularly in relation to national product, which generally soon recovers its previous volume in real terms. In that situation some constituents of δ and ϕ, particularly net issues of short-term claims, are likely to be abnormally high, since stocks of these types of financial assets must be rapidly reconstituted, particularly holdings of money. Other components of δ and ϕ are also likely to be above their long-term level, because individuals attempt to reconstitute part of the reserves they have lost through inflation or monetary reform. Thus the aggregate value of ε will for a while be extraordinarily high but will have a tendency to decline to a more stable value. Until this happen, τ will reduce $\alpha y_t \varepsilon$ by more than $F'_{\tau-n}$.

The Valuation Adjustment

Until now we have ignored the fact that financial instruments are subject to changes in market value after they are issued. Such changes may be regarded as negligible for short-term claims and for nonmarketable long-term claims such as mortgages and insurance contracts. They are, however, sometimes substantial for marketable long-term claims, particularly for government and corporate bonds. The financial instrument for which valuation changes are often of crucial importance is, of course, corporate common stock, for which changes may come to be much larger than original cost, a relationship which never occurs in the case of claims except for some relatively unimportant hybrid forms such as convertible debentures.

Equation (2.29) must, therefore, be adjusted for valuation changes on that proportion of all financial instruments which is subject to price changes in terms of the currency unit. This can be done by assuming that throughout the period, or on the average, the proportion of total net issues of financial instruments subject to price fluctuation is θ and that the rise in the market value of such assets proceeds, at a constant, or average, annual rate of ψ per cent. Then the value of net new issues subject to price changes issued in a given year j will be $y_j\theta\varepsilon$; its value at the end of the period will be $y_j\theta\varepsilon\ [(1 + \psi) \exp\ (t - j)/2]$; and the valuation increment will be $y_j\varepsilon\{\theta[(1 + \psi\ \exp\ (t - j)/2] - 1\}$. Applying this to the issues of price sensitive instruments throughout the period which extends from $\tau - n$ to τ we obtain for the aggregate valuation adjustment (V_τ) at the end of the period

$$V_\tau = (y_t\alpha\epsilon\theta)[(1 + \psi)^{n/2} - 1] \tag{2.30}$$

where the expression in parentheses measures the stock of price-sensitive financial assets at original issue price, and the expression in brackets reflects the effect of financial asset price changes.

Combining Equations (2.29) and (2.30) we obtain the following expression for the market value (F as distinguished from F' for the original cost) of financial investments outstanding at τ, assuming a period of infinite length:

$$F_\tau = F_\tau + V_\tau = \alpha y_t\epsilon(1 + \nu) \tag{2.31}$$

where ν is the bracketed expression from Equation (2.30) multiplied by the share of price-sensitive securities in total issues, i.e. $\theta\,[(1 + \psi)^{n/2} - 1]$.

Illustrative values for ν for two periods (25 and 50 years) and for selected values of θ and ψ are shown in Table 2–2.

TABLE 2–2

Value of $\nu = \theta[(1 + \psi)^{n/2} - 1]$ for Selected Values of θ, ψ, and n

ψ	$\theta = .01$	$\theta = .02$	$\theta = .05$	$\theta = .10$
		n = 25 YEARS		
.01	.001	.003	.007	.013
.02	.003	.006	.014	.028
.05	.009	.019	.047	.093
.10	.023	.046	.115	.230
		n = 50 YEARS		
.01	.003	.006	.014	.028
.02	.006	.013	.032	.064
.05	.024	.048	.119	.239
.10	.098	.197	.492	.984

Under conditions usually encountered, where θ is in the range 0.5 to 0.10 and the average price rise for price-sensitive assets is of the order of 2 or 3 per cent a year, ν will have a value of 0.05 to 0.10 if a period of 50 years is covered by the calculation, i.e. the effect of these asset price changes will at the end of the period add 5 to 10 per cent to the value of the stock of all financial instruments at their original cost at issuance. Even if the rise of financial asset prices has averaged as much as 5 per cent a year, ν will amount to only between 0.12 and 0.24, thus constituting between approximately one-ninth and one-fifth of the market value of financial investments outstanding at the end of the 50-year period.

Matters become more complicated if the assumption that the parameters of Equation (2.31) i.e. α, ε, and ν (and hence θ and ψ), are applicable to a period as far back of the balance sheet date as we like, or at least for a period of well over half a century, is not applicable, and Equation (2.29) must be used. In that case the expression for F_T consists of two parts. The first is the market value at the balance sheet date of the issues made during the period from τ to $\tau - n$ including valuation changes on these issues during the period. The second part is the value at the balance sheet date of the financial instruments outstanding at $\tau - n$, a value which in turn is made up of two components, first the value at $\tau - n$ of investments issued before $\tau - n$, and secondly the change in value of the price-sensitive fraction of these instruments which has occurred between $\tau - n$ and τ. If this fraction is designated as $\theta_{\tau-n}$, the expression for the market value of all financial instruments outstanding at the balance sheet date becomes

$$F_\tau = \tau \alpha y_t \epsilon (1 + \nu) + F_{\tau-n}[1 + \theta_{\tau-n}(1 + \psi)^n] \qquad (2.32)$$

since the price-sensitive instruments outstanding at $\tau - n$, the market value of which is equal to $F_{\tau-n}\ \theta_{\tau-n}$, have been subject to further financial asset price movements during the entire period of n years between $\tau - n$ and τ.

THE FINANCIAL INTERRELATIONS RATIO (FIR)

The Formula

As in the case of the periodic (annual) flow of new issues of financial investments, the economic analyst's interest does not lie primarily in the absolute value of, in this case, the stock of financial instruments outstanding at a given point of time, but in an economically significant relationship of this stock to other basic macro-economic magnitudes. Here the appropriate matrix or denominator appears to be national wealth, i.e., the stock of real (tangible) assets, including the net foreign balance in the sense of the difference between the market value of the country's foreign investments, financial and tangible, such as real estate abroad directly held by domestic units, and foreigners' holdings of domestic financial and tangible assets. If the market value of national wealth at date τ is designated by W_τ, we have as the formula for the financial interrelations ratio (FIR) for a very long (theoretically infinite) period

$$\frac{F_\tau}{W_\tau} = \frac{\alpha y_t \epsilon (1 + \nu)}{W_\tau} \tag{2.33}$$

using the expression for F_τ developed in Equation (2.31) as numerator, but still assuming a period of infinite length. Since the value of national wealth at any date is equal to the value of gross national product times the average capital-output ratio (β), defined as usual as the quotient of net national wealth and gross national product, the formula for FIR finally becomes in abbreviated form and for a period of infinite length (ignoring the difference between y_τ and y_t or using an estimate such as $\frac{1}{2}(y_t + y_{t+1})$ as the year-end rate of national product):

$$\frac{F_\tau}{W_\tau} = \beta_\tau^{-1} \alpha \epsilon (1 + \nu) \tag{2.34}$$

or in more detail:

$$\frac{F_\tau}{W_\tau} = \beta_\tau^{-1}[(\gamma + \pi + \gamma\pi)^{-1} + 1][\kappa\eta + \bar{\phi}(1 + \lambda) + \xi] \{1 + \theta[(1 + \psi)^{n/2} - 1]\} \tag{2.35}$$

It is well to remember that $\kappa\eta = \delta$ should be regarded as a weighted average of sectoral δ's, and that ϕ consists of the several components indicated in Equations (2.17) or (2.20).

The last Equation (2.35) provides information, directly or by simple rearrangement or calculation, on the magnitudes which have been regarded as crucial for the analysis of financial structure or development: the relative size of the financial superstructure (FIR); the external financing ratio of the nonfinancial sectors (δ); the role of financial institutions as issuers, which may be measured by the financial intermediation ratio ($\bar{\phi}/\delta$); the importance of the main types of financial institutions (the relation among the components of ϕ); the role of international financial transactions (ξ); and the effects of the growth of real national product (γ), product price changes (π) and stock price movements (ψ). If the formula is used in a more disaggregated form it also shows the relative importance of the main nonfinancial sectors—business, government, households—as users of funds (components of $\delta = \kappa\eta$), and the role of direct and indirect financing within these sectors (relation of the ϕ's disaggregated as to sectors of destination and sectoral δ's).

Equation (2.35) is based on the assumption that the parameters, in particular the rate of growth of national product in current prices and the ratios of issues of financial instruments to national product, represent (appropriately weighted) averages for a very long period—theoretically a period of infinite length and in practice one of at least 50 or preferably 100 years. In many concrete instances, however, information is available only for shorter periods, often only for the less than 20 years of the postwar period. It is then necessary to use a different formula—Equation (2.36) in which the financial interrelations ratio for the balance sheet date consists, as in Equation (2.32) of two parts, viz. first, the ratio of the value of the issues during the period from $\tau - n$ to τ to national wealth at τ, and, secondly, the ratio of the value at τ of the instruments outstanding at $\tau - n$ again to national wealth at τ. The formula then becomes

$$\frac{E_\tau}{W_\tau} = \tau\alpha\epsilon(1 + \nu)\beta_\tau^{-1} + \frac{E_{\tau-n}}{W_\tau}[1 + \theta_{\tau-n}(1 + \psi)^n] \qquad (2.36)$$

The contribution of the two parts to the level of FIR obviously depends on the value of each of the components in the formula. In practice the length of the observation period will be the most important of these since it determines τ and also influences ν, $(1 + \psi)^n$, and E_{T-n}/W_T. The effect on $1 - \tau$ and E_{T-n}/W_T is inverse, i.e., the longer the observation period the smaller the value of $1 - \tau$ and of E_{T-n}/W_T provided the rates of growth of y and E are positive, as is generally the case. The effect on ν and $(1 + \psi)^n$ is generally direct, both being the larger the longer n, provided ψ is positive. In one special case the effects offset each other, viz., when the second part of Equation (2.36) is equal to $(1 - \tau)$ $[\alpha\varepsilon(1 + \nu)\beta_T^{-1}]$, so that FIR is simply $\alpha\varepsilon(1 + \nu)\beta_T^{-1}$. While this condition will rarely if ever be exactly met, calculations for the postwar period in Chapter 7 indicate that it is approximated in several concrete cases.

A diagram (Chart 2–1) may help in visualizing these relationships by illustrating the composition of the market value of financial instruments outstanding at the balance sheet date (E_τ). This figure is the crucial magnitude, since the financial interrelations ratio is nothing but E_τ divided by the national wealth at the balance sheet date.

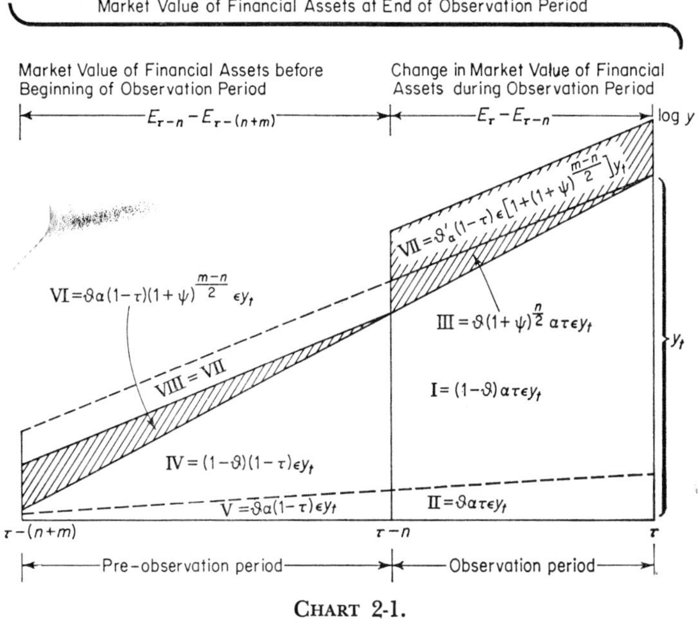

CHART 2-1.

Diagrammatic Illustration of Derivation of E_τ

Of the eight wedges of Chart 2–1, four (I, II, III, and VII) are required when the aggregate new issue ratio and the financial interrelations ratio must be calculated from the truncated formula of Equation (2.36), because data are available or can be estimated only for a relatively short observation period of n years, and when (as a result) the value of financial assets at the beginning of the period must be treated as exogenous.

The sum of wedges I and II then represents the value, at original cost, of the issues which were made during the period of observation and, of these, wedge II refers to price sensitive instruments. Wedge III measures the valuation change during the observation period, a change here assumed to be positive, of price-sensitive instruments issued during the observation period. Wedge VII accounts for the valuation change occurring during the observation period on price-sensitive instruments that had been issued before and were outstanding at the beginning of the observation period. The sum of wedges of I, II, III, and VII, then, measures the net issues of financial instruments made during the observation period plus valuation changes on new and outstanding instruments that have occurred during the observation period. This sum is thus equal to the difference between the market value of all financial instruments outstanding at the end and at the beginning of the observation period ($E_T - E_{T-n}$).

To obtain an estimate of the market value of the financial instruments outstanding at the end of the observation period (E_T) it is necessary to add the market value of financial instruments at the beginning of the period (E_{T-n}) which is represented by the sum of wedges IV, V, and VI, if one is willing to assume that the value of the constants also applies for an extended period preceding the observation period. If, however, it is known or suspected that the value of the constants was different in the earlier period from what it has been in the observation period, then the value of financial assets outstanding at the beginning of the observation period must be treated as an exogenous datum. In that case wedge VII simplifies to $E_{T-n}[1 + \bar{\theta}_{T-n}(1 + \psi)^n]$ where $\bar{\theta}_{T-n}$ is the share of the market value of price-sensitive financial instruments in the financial assets outstanding at the beginning of the period.

If the assumption that the values of the constants determined for the observation period are also applicable to a rather long pre-observation period of m years appears to be justified, or is adopted faute de mieux, only two wedges are needed. The first of these, consisting of wedges I, II, IV, and V in Chart 2–1 equal to $\alpha\varepsilon y_t$, represents the original cost of all issues outstanding at the balance sheet date; while the second, made up of wedges III, VI, and VII (or VIII), and now also simplified to $(\alpha\varepsilon y_t)\theta(1 + \psi) \exp (n + m)/2$, reflects the valuation changes of all price-sensitive issues.

It will be noticed that the first part of Equation (2.36) corresponds to the sum of wedges I, II, and III, while the second part equals wedges IV, V, VI, and VII if the period before $\tau - (n + m)$ is disregarded as being too remote to influence E_τ to any significant extent.

Relation to Interest Rates

At least one factor, however, seems to be missing from the formulas, the rate of interest. Does not the level of interest rates prevailing at any one time, or the structure of interest rates (i.e. the differentials among interest rates and equity yields on financial instruments of different type, different maturity, different issuer, and different quality) influence some of the components of the basic formulas, and thus the value of the ratio of the net issuance of financial instruments to national product or of the ratio of total financial assets outstanding to national wealth? Do not movements in interest rates affect changes in the coefficients and thus the path which the values of the aggregate new issue ratio (ANIR) and the financial interrelations issue (FIR) trace? The answer is simple. Interest and yield rates certainly do influence the level and the movements of ANIR and FIR, but they do this through their influence on most if not all of the components of the formula. Interest rates are thus secondary, though by no means unimportant, determinants of ANIR and FIR and of the value and relationships of the coefficients in the formulas. They are in the same position as other determinants of these components, such as the asset preferences of different groups of holders and issuers of financial instruments, the legal provisions affecting the issuance of securities and the operation of financial intermediaries, the policy of the monetary authorities, and the factors determining the balance of payments.

It will suffice to illustrate this indirect effect of interest rates on ANIR and FIR by a few examples. To start with the volume of the issues of nonfinancial sectors, the values of both components κ and η are influenced by interest rates, the first mainly by the level of interest rates as a whole, the second both by the level and by differentials among instruments. Other things being equal, κ (the ratio of capital formation to national product) will be low if interest rates are high in comparison to what is regarded as the normal level at the time and place. The coefficient η (the share of external in total financing) likewise probably is negatively correlated with the level of interest rates. Likewise the distribution of the issues of nonfinancial sectors among the types of financial instruments used to finance capital expenditures is strongly influenced by interest rates differentials. Indeed the empirical relationship of the distribution of total issues of nonfinancial sectors among the different types of financial instruments to interest rate differentials is much more apparent than the relationship between the aggregate level of interest rates and η, κ, or δ.

Interest rates may be expected also to influence the level of the issuance of financial instruments by financial institutions and the relationship among the different components, such as the issues by commercial banks, thrift institutions, and insurance organizations. Here again the influence of interest rate differentials on the distribution of ϕ (the ratio of financial institutions' issues to national product among its components) seems to be much more pronounced than the effect of the level of interest rates and changes in it on the value of ϕ. While it has not yet been possible empirically to establish strong and stable relationships between ϕ (or for that matter the aggregate saving ratio) and the level of interest rates, the relative share of the different financial institutions in the total issue of financial instruments by financial intermediaries, as well as the distribution of personal saving by form, are clearly influenced to a substantial degree by interest rate differentials, although more so in the short than in the long run. It is only necessary to point to the results of the extensive discussion of liquidity preference (i.e. the effect which the differential between the zero or near-zero interest rate on money and the positive rate on other financial instruments) has on general economic development and on prices as well as on financial structure and development.

The effect of interest rates is equally evident in the valuation adjustment item (ν), particularly the price movement of equity securities (ψ). The level of interest rates and the differentials between the yield on claims and on equities is one of the main, although not the sole and probably not even the strongest, determinant—compared particularly to the trend of corporate profits—of the price of equities.

While empirically a negative association exists in intercountry comparison between monetization ratio and interest rate level, one could not claim that μ depends on the level of interest rates. The causal relationship, if any, rather runs in the opposite direction, the process of monetization tending to decrease the level of interest rates as a capital market develops.

Among the factors linking ANIR and FIR, the effect of interest rates is probably quite pronounced in the case of the capital-output ratio. We may presume β to be negatively associated with the level of interest rates—in this case the yield of tangible assets rather than monetary interest rates—because low yield rates favor capital intensive techniques and industries, so that β will be the higher the lower the level of interest rates. Since β enters the formula in its reciprocal form, i.e. as the ratio of output to capital, the value of FIR should be positively associated with β^{-1} and hence with the level of interest rates, other things being equal, a condition which, of course, will rarely be met between countries or dates widely differing in the level of yield rates.

The multiplier α, finally, may be presumed to be negatively correlated with the level of interest rates, because rapid growth of gross national product in current prices is usually accompanied by a high level of interest rates, particularly if the growth is due mainly to a rise in the price level when interest rates may include a considerable element of insurance against loss of purchasing power.

The interrelations between level and structure of yield rates of different character and ANIR and thus FIR are so complex, and in many cases so indefinite, that it is impossible to claim a simple association, let alone a causal relationship, between interest rates and the values of ANIR and FIR.

The information on significant aspects of financial structure and development compressed into the formulas is thus considerable. The question, however, remains: To what extent can the formulas be statistically implemented to yield sufficiently extensive and reliable results to be of help in the analysis of a country's financial structure and development, and particularly in the international comparison of financial structure and development? To this question we shall return in the section on statistical implementation.

Algebraic Implications

Of the main components of FIR in the formula, its value is positively related to seven—the monetization ratio (μ), the nonfinancial interrelations ratio (ω), the capital formation ration (κ), the external financing ratio (η), the new issue ratio of financial institutions (ϕ), the price movement of financial assets (ψ, since θ always must be positive) and the multiplier (α); the value of FIR is negatively related to one factor—the capital-output ratio (β).[12] However, since the multiplier itself is negatively related to the rate of growth of national product in current prices, it is more significant to formulate the basic algebraic relationships of the for-

12. The two factors μ and ω have disappeared from the final formulation in Equations (2.36) and (2.37), but it should be remembered that the capital formation ratio was originally defined as $k/y\mu$ $(1 + \omega)$, so that $\kappa = \hat{\kappa}\mu$ $(1 + \omega)$.

mula by saying that the value of FIR is positively related to the new issues ratio (ε) and all of its components, since each of them enters the formula with positive sign, with the price of financial assets (ψ) and with the share of price-sensitive issues (θ), and is negatively related to the rate of growth of real income (γ) and of the general price level (π) and to the average capital-output ratio (β).

Thus one country's FIR will be higher than that of another country, or it will be higher at one time than at another, as its new issue ratio in the past has been higher (which, in turn may be due to a higher capital formation ratio, a higher external financing ratio, or a higher financial intermediation ratio or a combination of the three); as the share of price-sensitive financial assets (essentially corporate stock) in total net new issues has been higher, and the rise of financial asset prices in the past has been more pronounced; or as the monetization and industrial interrelations ratios are higher. FIR will be lower as the current capital-output ratio is higher and as the rate of growth of either real national product or of the general price level has been higher.

Of these possible relationships, the one not sufficiently appreciated in relation to its quantitative importance is the negative relation between FIR and the rate of growth of national product in current prices. It is obvious, however, that a rapid rate of growth of nominal national product—in the extreme case due to hyperinflation—will reduce the ratio of the stock of financial assets to national wealth (both at market values), other things being equal, as it devalues the relative importance of the net issues of the past, which were based on much lower levels of national product in current prices. At a rate of growth of nominal national product of 3 per cent, for example, the multiplier α will be 34 compared to a value of 21 if the rate is 5 per cent. This difference alone will, other things being equal, lead to a value of FIR more than one and one-half times as large in the first case than in the second.

This relation would be immediately evident if all financial assets had a value fixed in terms of the monetary unit, since the current value of the tangible assets that make up national wealth may be assumed to move in the same direction and to approximately the same extent as the general price level. When part of the issues of financial instruments takes the form of equity securities, the prices of which may be assumed to move over longer periods in the same direction, though not in the same proportion, as the general price level, the valuation adjustment on the stock of price-sensitive financial assets will, however, tend to counteract the depressing effect of the rise in the general price level on the ratio of the stock of claims to the market value of national wealth.

Under the usual conditions, where equities represent only a small proportion of the net issues of financial instruments —hardly ever more than one-tenth and in most cases less— and where stock prices are not likely to rise by much more than the general price level, this offset will be relatively small, though not negligible. In fact the effect of stock price movements on FIR is likely to be relatively more important in cases where the rate of increase in the general price level has been moderate, but stock prices have in the long run advanced at a rate substantially—though, of course, differing in size among countries and periods—in excess of that of the general price level.

Since not all the required parameters are known, the following example is illustrative only, though it should be reasonably close to the actual situation in the United States. It is based on an annual rate of growth of real national product (γ) of 3½ per cent, a secular rate of rise in the general price level (π) and the price of corporate stock (ψ) of 1½ per cent and 2½ per cent respectively, a share (θ) of corporate stock issues in total net new issues of financial instruments of 5 per cent, a new issue ratio (ε) of 15 per cent, and a capital-output ratio (β) of 3. In this situation the multiplier (α) is 21 and the valuation adjustment term $(1 + v)$ is about 1.25 for a period of 100 years.

The value of FIR thus would be approximately 1.30 compared to the value of 1.50, which it would have in the absence of changes in both the general price level and in corporate stock prices. Even here, therefore, price changes have in the final result reduced rather than increased FIR.

These relationships are directly relevant to the problem of the effect of inflation on ANIR and FIR and to the way in which these effects are reflected in the formulas. Inflations generally originate in deficits of the central government that are not due to capital expenditures. Such deficits, which are particularly important in wartime but are endemic in some parts of the world, increase η and raise it above unity (i.e. they may lead to a volume of new issues of nonfinancial units in excess of national gross capital formation), a situation which is never encountered under normal conditions where a substantial part of national capital formation is internally financed by the business, household, and government sectors. If the deficit is covered by sales of government securities to the banking system, not only δ but also ϕ_c and ϕ_b will increase above the customary level, thus accentuating the increase in FIR. It is the existence of a particularly heavy deadweight debt, a good part of which is held by financial institutions, that helps to explain the very high value of FIR in Great Britain since World War I. It also explains the relatively high values of FIR immediately after World War II in several other countries, including the United States.

The effects of inflation on FIR, however, are more pervasive. There are, first, two direct effects. As inflation is associated with a high rate of growth of national product in current prices, and hence a low value of α, FIR will be lower, other things equal, the more pronounced the inflationary rise in the price level. Secondly, the valuation adjustment (ν) will be larger in relation to FIR the sharper the increase in stock prices which is related to although not necessarily equal to the rise in the price level of national product. Since the influence of an increase in the valuation adjustment is usually smaller than that of the decrease in the multiplier α, the net direct result of a sharp or protracted inflation on FIR is likely to be downward. The secondary effects of inflation on FIR are, of course, numerous and complicated, but it is not likely that they will commonly exercise a sufficient upward influence on FIR to offset, or even seriously to mitigate, the direct downward effects.

Actual observations confirm these deductions, probably the best example being provided by the extremely low levels of FIR in Germany after the inflations accompanying and following World War I and II. Even today the relatively low FIR's of Germany and France, as well as those of some Latin American countries, reflect in part the inflationary price rises or the devaluations that have occurred in these countries during the last half century.

STATISTICAL IMPLEMENTATION OF THE FORMULAS FOR ANIR AND FIR

It is of little use to devise formulas of the type developed in the preceding sections unless it is possible to implement them statistically, i.e. to assign more or less accurate numerical values to the coefficients. We are therefore bound to inquire briefly into the type of statistical data that are required to implement the formulas presented here, and to consider to what extent (that is, for which countries and for which periods) these data are directly at hand or may be expected to become available in the not too distant future.

The situation is quite different for different components of the formulas or for groups of them. Thus it is usually possible to obtain information for fairly long periods, at least back to the 1930s and often back to the turn of the century, on the value of gross national product in current and constant prices and on the assets and liabilities of financial institutions, data which permit the calculation of the multiplier (α) of the formulas, as well as of the coefficient ϕ and its components. This is true for almost all developed countries in Europe, North America, and Oceania, as well as for most important countries in Latin America and in Asia, particularly for India and Japan. For Africa and the Middle East, the period for which the figures are available—commonly only since the mid-1950s—is too short to permit use of the formula for FIR. Information is more limited and usually less reliable and less comparable over time and among countries on the capital formation ratio (κ) and the net foreign issue ratio (ξ). Nevertheless, the average values of these coefficients can be calculated or approximated for most developed countries at least back to World War I and for a number of less developed countries back to the 1930s. There is hardly any evidence on which to base an estimate of the nonfinancial interrelations ratio (ω), except for about a dozen countries in the recent past. This difficulty, as well as the scarcity of information on the monetization ratio (μ), can be overcome by using as the denominator of the capital formation ratio national product rather than the sector's own sales, even though this may make the substitute ratio less significant for analysis.

Calculation of one of the components of the valuation adjustment ratio, the share of corporate stock in total issues (θ), also encounters serious difficulties, although information on the other component, the trend in stock prices (ψ) is more widely available. The estimated value of the ratio will thus often be subject to a large margin of error. Fortunately the contribution of ν to the aggregate value of FIR is in most cases relatively small, so that even a substantial error in the estimates for this ratio will not affect FIR too seriously.

Estimates of the average capital-output ratio (β), which, like the multiplier and the valuation adjustment, is required for the calculation of FIR, though not of ANIR (and even then unlike the other coefficients it is needed for only one date), are still fairly rare, even for developed countries. Moreover the range of the ratio seems to be broad enough and sufficiently erratic to preclude the application of a standard value or a value of a "similar" country in cases where no estimate of national wealth is available. It will thus be possible to calculate the value of the ratio of the stock of financial assets to national product (F_T/y_t) for many countries and dates for which FIR cannot be estimated with a reasonable degree of accuracy.

The most serious statistical problem is presented by the external financing ratio of the nonfinancial sectors (η). To calculate this ratio, and to combine it with κ to obtain δ, or to estimate it with a fair degree of confidence, it is necessary to have a sources-and-uses-of-funds statement, or information closely approximating it, for all nonfinancial sectors together or, preferably, separate statements for the main sectors. Such statements exist only for a small number of countries, almost all developed ones, and they are practically limited to the last decade. Fortunately δ may in many cases be calculated or estimated even if neither κ nor η, or if only one of the two is known. Thus δ can sometimes be estimated by the combined use of the statistics of bond and stock issues, of banking statistics on the sectoral distribution of credit outstanding, and of some other financial statistics, and η can then be found by dividing δ by κ. Unfortunately, however, very little of the basic statistical data required for this synthetic and indirect approach to an estimate of the new issue of the nonfinancial sector has been collected save for a few countries and for relatively short recent periods, in addition to the also rare cases where sources-and-uses-of-funds statements have been prepared as part of a comprehensive system of flow-of-funds statistics.

Thus a considerably more extensive application of the formulas than that which is presented in Chapters 3 through 7—more extensive in time or geographic scope—depends essentially on additional information, primarily on η and secondarily on κ, δ, θ, and β.

HOW REALISTIC IS THE BASIC FORMULA?

It is always easier to construct a formula that promises to explain a macro-economic magnitude reasonably well than it is to determine the actual values of the formula's components and coefficients, and thus to test its validity and range of application by comparing the value of the magnitude to be explained as it emerges from the formula with the values provided by statistical observation—in this case by comparing the values of the financial interrelations ratio for different countries at one or more dates (calculated, for example, from Equation (2.35) by inserting observed or experimental values for the dozen coefficients in the equations) with the values otained by dividing the market value of financial assets by that of national wealth, a value taken, if possible, from a national balance sheet or secured from other statistical sources.

Differences between calculated and observed values result from two quite different sources. The first are assumptions embodied in the formula that do not necessarily conform to reality, so that their use may—but need not—lead to systematic deviations of the calculated from the observed values. The second are imperfections in the numerical values of the coefficients inserted in the formula or imperfections in the observed value of the magnitude being measured—here FIR. Nothing can be said in general terms about errors of the second type, except that the use of as much as a dozen largely independent coefficients makes it likely that the errors in some coefficients will be offset in their effect on FIR by errors in the opposite direction in other coefficients—offset in part, but not necessarily or even probably in full.

In the formulas with which we are dealing here the two crucial simplifying assumptions, which by their very nature are not in full accord with the observed reality of financial development, are (1) the constancy of the rate of growth of national product in current prices throughout the period of observation and (2) the stability of all the other coefficients which enter into the formula. It is, therefore, necessary to consider to what extent these assumptions, unrealistic or at least overly simplistic as they obviously are, vitiate the usefulness of the formula in the sense of either producing values of FIR that significantly deviate from those observed or of falsifying the relationships among individual components of the formula or among groups of them. The problem of deviation does not arise in the case of one of the coefficients, the capital-output ratio, since it refers to one point of time, the end of the period, rather than to the entire period as all the other coefficients do.

The effects of deviations of the observed values from the assumptions of constancy must be considered separately for the rate of growth of national product in current prices ($\gamma + \pi$), on the one hand, and for the other coefficients or combinations of them, particularly the aggregate new issue ratio (ε) and the components of the valuation adjustment ratio (θ and ψ), on the other. For each of these two groups three types of deviations must be distinguished: (1) more or less regular (e.g. sinusoidal) oscillations around the constant or average value of the coefficients; (2) systematic (trendlike) deviations, exemplified by a regularly increasing or decreasing set of ratios, the average of which is equal to the coefficient used in the formula; and (3) random, and usually short-lived, deviations.

The case of regular periodic fluctuations around the average for the entire period, whether for the rate of growth of national product or for any of the other coefficients, is relatively easy to dispose of since such fluctuations are not likely to produce serious deviations of the calculated from the observed value of FIR. (The same is, of course, true of occasional, random deviations.) No significant deviation will arise if the periodic movement is regular (for instance, sinusoidal) and if the period over which the calculation extends includes a full number of cycles so that the beginning and the end of the period fall into the same cycle phase. But even if these two conditions are not met, the resulting deviation is likely to be small. This will be the case for a single coefficient.[13] It is even more likely to be true if each of the coefficients follows a sinusoidal movement of its own with varying phase length and amplitude. Only under peculiar conditions, particularly when phase lengths are equal for most or all coefficients and cyclical tops and bottoms coincide in time, or when the period being considered begins or ends at different phases of the movement of most of the coefficients, will the actual value of financial instruments outstanding, and hence the value of FIR, differ substantially from that calculated on the assumption that coefficients are constant. Even then, the deviation may be serious enough to invalidate the entire approach only in the unlikely case that the period covered is relatively short compared to the phase length of the fluctuations in the rate of growth of national product.

Turning to the effects of the deviation of the path of the annual rates of growth in national product from their average, it is necessary to distinguish the first case (in which this average is calculated as the slope of a trend fitted by the method of least squares) from the second case (in which the average is obtained, as is the rule in practice, by the short-cut method of comparing only the value of national product in the first and in the last year of the period of *n* years so that the average rate of growth is calculated as the *n*th root of the ratio of national product in the last year to that in the first year). In the first case, deviations of annual values from the average generally should lead to only small differences between the calculated and the observed value of the stock of financial instruments outstanding and of FIR. Fluctuations in the rate of growth of

13. See R. W. Goldsmith, *The National Wealth of the United States in the Postwar Period* (Princeton, Princeton University Press, 1962) pp. 18ff., for a discussion of the parallel case of fluctuations in capital expenditures and their effect on formula estimates of national wealth.

national product will have to be very large and quite irregular to create a substantial difference between the calculated and observed values of FIR.

In the second case, however, substantial differences between the observed and calculated values may occur if the path of national product deviates from a logarithmic straight line, either systematically though regularly or in a very irregular fashion. The first possibility is represented by regular acceleration or deceleration of the rate of growth in national product over the period. If the rate accelerates, then the average rate calculated on the basis of the beginning and the end point of the period will be smaller than the true average; if the rate decelerates it will be larger. Hence, the calculated value of the stock of financial instruments and of FIR will be higher, other things being equal, than the observed value if the rate of growth accelerates, and the difference will be larger the higher the degree of acceleration. Similarly, the calculated ratio will be lower than the observed ratio if the rate of growth decelerates over the period.

These differences may be quite serious if the rate of acceleration or deceleration is pronounced. For instance, if the average rate of growth for a forty-year period is 5 per cent per year, and only the value at the beginning and the end of the period are used to determine the average rate of growth, a path under which the rate of growth accelerates from 4 per cent at the beginning of the period to 6 per cent at the end will produce a total volume of financial instruments outstanding that is about one-tenth lower than that given by the formula, and hence an FIR, other things being equal, that is about one-tenth lower than its calculated value. The deviation is much more pronounced if, for instance, the rate of growth decelerates from a rate of 8 per cent at the beginning to one of 2 per cent at the end, compared to the 5 per cent average. The actual stock of financial instruments accumulated under this condition over a forty-year period will be about 50 per cent higher than the one derived from a formula in which the 5 per cent average growth rate is used. The lesson is obvious. Where annual estimates of national product are available, or at least where a long period can be broken down into subperiods of several years' duration, the average rate of growth inserted in the formula should be the average obtained by fitting a logarithmic trend to annual or period values.

The situation is theoretically similar for the coefficients that are related multiplicatively to gross national product, i.e. κ, η, ϕ, ξ, θ, and ψ. If the average value of the coefficient for the period, which is inserted into the formula, is obtained by a least-squares fit of the values for all individual years or for short subperiods, then the movement of the coefficients during the period do not matter in the sense that the formula value and the observed value of the stock of financial instruments and hence of FIR will agree. This type of average, however, is rare because of the scarcity of annual data and the consequent use of decadal averages or similar data, or of rough estimates based perhaps on information available for a few years within the period. Hence the formula value for the stock of financial instruments and for FIR may again deviate from the observed value because of systematic or irregular changes in the coefficients over the period.

These conditions apply to one coefficient taken by itself. Since the formula includes half a dozen to more than a dozen such coefficients, the number depending on the degree of disaggregation, there is a considerable chance that deviations from the averages used in the formula will offset each other more or less completely. Some offset is certain to occur since hardly ever will all coefficients have the same trend or pattern or even move in the same direction. Thus, the product of the averages of all coefficients, which then is combined with the multiplier determined by the rate of growth of national product, is certain to deviate less from more accurate appropriately weighted averages based on annual values than is the case for most or even for all individual coefficients. Hence the combined effect of deviations of the annual values of the coefficients from their averages used in the formula may not, and probably will not, lead to a substantial difference between the formula and the observed value of the stock of financial instruments and of FIR unless the deviation is very large and occurs in a coefficient having a heavy weight in the formula, such as κ, η, ϕ, and, occasionally, ψ and θ.

While these general considerations are useful, though a more rigorous treatment might better suit the mathematically proficient, it may be well to look at the situation as it presents itself in the actual experience of a number of countries over the last one or two generations. Such a test, however, is possible only for the national product multiplier α because it is the only coefficient for which annual data are available for a substantial number of countries and for extended periods of time. With these data at hand it is possible to compare the sum of the actual annual figures for national product with the formula totals based on the average rate of growth ($\gamma + \pi$) and the truncation ratio (τ), both of which can be determined, first, from the value of national product in the first and the last year of the period and, secondly, from the fitted trend line. The results of these comparisons for ten countries—all now developed—for the period 1914–63 are inconclusive if attention is centered on the differences between the three sets of multipliers for individual countries and periods, since the average deviation (disregarding sign) between the observed values of the multiplier and the values calculated on the basis of fitted or end-point rates of growth are of the same order of magnitude—about one-tenth—for the two methods of calculation and for the long and the short period. There is only one feature that merits comment as reflecting a general characteristic of the figures. This is the large difference for Italy and Japan for the period 1914–63, which reflects the unreliability of the calculated multipliers in face of one (or more) sharp inflations within the period. For the period 1949–63 the same comparison can be extended to all 35 countries included in the study, but the results are very similar. The average ratios of the fitted trend or end-point trend estimates to the observed values are 0.94 and 0.89 (compared to 0.92 and 0.88 for the ten developed countries), and the average deviations disregarding sign are 0.10 and 0.13 (compared to 0.09 and 0.13).

THE ANALYTICAL VALUE OF THE FORMULAS

The chief analytical value of the decomposition of the volume of new issues of financial instruments and of the stock of financial instruments and of the financial interrelations ratio lies in the identification and separation of a number of factors which cooperate to make the magnitudes and relations what they are at a given time and place. This decomposition is not yet an explanation, but it is a step towards this goal, admittedly only a first step but hopefully a helpful step and almost certainly a necessary one. There, of course, remain the next step or steps, viz. first the identification of the forces which determine each of the coefficients and then the discovery and explanation of the regularities in the level and movements of the coefficients. Some suggestions on these problems have been made in this chapter and others will be offered in later chapters, but they are tentative and sporadic. A systematic treatment of these problems, at a level deeper than the initial decomposition of ANIR and FIR, would entirely transcend the scope of this study. Indeed both statistical analysis and quantitative study of financial structure and development are at this moment far from able to permit such an approach at a deeper level, certainly not if the exploration of international differences is the aim.

We may again use the analogy with the quantity theory of money. The decomposition of the volume of monetary transactions into Mv (the stock of money and its transactions velocity), yk (national income and the inverse of the income velocity of money), or $q\pi$ (real national income and the price level) does not by itself explain the course of monetary developments or international differences in monetary structure, even if each of the components is subdivided according to type of money, sector, or type of output. Yet by isolating components and determinants, the quantity equations help to formulate relevant questions and pave the way for gradually finding answers to them, or at least experimenting with more promising approaches to answers. This is also the function of formulas of the type that have been developed here for the broader spectrum of all financial assets.

Such formulas are in a sense economic models, but extremely simple, or rather preliminary, ones. They can, however, be transformed into more adequate models as it becomes possible to connect each of the components with one or more behaviorally significant and measurable determinants. In the case of some determinants, and some of the most important ones, such as the rate of growth of national product, the capital-output ratio and the capital formation ratio, this connection is the task of general economic theory. For others (e.g. the new issue ratios, the financial intermediation ratio, and the valuation adjustment), the discovery of the most important determinants, the determination of the form of the relation, and the testing of the stability of the relationship—not to speak of international comparisons of these matters—remain tasks for future financial research. Suggestions will occasionally be made in later chapters on the basis of the limited material now available or developed in this study, but their tentative and fragmentary character will be obvious.

3 NONFINANCIAL ISSUES

The function of this and the following four chapters is to put some flesh on the skeleton constructed in Chapter 2 by explaining in quantitative terms the relationships between a country's financial superstructure and its real infrastructure. To this end each of the five chapters will briefly review the evidence on the numerical values of some of the coefficients that were used in Chapter 2 in building up the basic equations for, first, the ratio of net issues of financial instruments to gross national product (the aggregate new issue ratio, or ANIR) and, secondly, the ratio of the value of all financial instruments outstanding at a given date to national wealth (the financial interrelations ratio, or FIR). This chapter thus will deal with the issues of financial instruments by nonfinancial sectors—the short- and long-term obligations and equity securities of business enterprises, governments, and households—and their ratio to national product (δ) and with the two factors that have been used to explain this ratio, i.e., the ratio of net new issues to the capital formation of the nonfinancial sectors (η) and the ratio of these sectors' capital formation to national product (κ). It also deals with the ratio of foreign issues to national product (ξ), which measures another component of nonfinancial new issues. Chapters 4 and 5 consider in the same way the issues of financial instruments by financial institutions and thus will analyse, first, the coefficients ϕ and Φ, which relate the total of these issues and the assets of financial institutions to gross national product, and then the components of ϕ and Φ as well as the layering ratio within the financial sphere λ. Chapter 6 will present the evidence on those coefficients that are common to the financial instruments issued by nonfinancial and financial sectors and that link the aggregate of these issues to national wealth (i.e. the multiplier α connecting the level of national product at the balance sheet date with the sum of national product during a long period preceding it), on the capital-output ratio (β), the monetization ratio (μ), and the ratio of sales to gross national product (ω). Chapter 7, finally, will consider the way in which these three groups of components combine to produce the observed values of ANIR and FIR. This will make it possible to evaluate in quantitative terms the influence of the different components, and of groups of them, on ANIR and FIR, and to do this both from the point of view of differences among countries at different stages of financial development as well as from that of changes in individual countries during the past fifty to one hundred years.

THE RATIO OF DOMESTIC NONFINANCIAL ISSUES TO NATIONAL PRODUCT

The issues of financial instruments by nonfinancial issuers, i.e. the business, household, and government sectors as well as the rest of the world, represent one of the two main elements of a country's financial superstructure and constitute one of the main components in the basic formula. In that formula the value of the ratio of aggregate issues of nonfinancial issuers to national product (δ) is traced to four factors: the ratio of net new issues to the capital formation of the nonfinancial sectors (η), the ratio of the nonfinancial sector's capital formation to their sales (κ), the ratio of nonfinancial sectors' sales to their contribution to gross national product (ω), and the ratio of monetized to total gross national product (μ); such a breakdown is necessary for an adequate analysis of the relationships involved. Statistically, however, it is often easier to obtain directly figures for the product of the four components η, $\hat{\kappa}$, $(1 + \omega)$ and μ, i.e. for the ratio δ of the net new issues of financial instruments by nonfinancial sectors to gross national product. This requires the existence of a sectorized flow of funds statement which provides information, usually on an annual basis, on the volume of net new issues of all financial instruments by all nonfinancial sectors. Usually we are not in this fortunate position. Indeed, except for a relatively small number of developed countries and for part of the postwar period, we are forced to use more or less complete and more or less reliable approximations to the comprehensive figures of total new issues of financial instruments by all nonfinancial sectors.

One of these approximations is provided by the data on the public issues of securities (bonds and stocks) of nonfinancial sectors, which are available for a number of countries and which in some of them can be carried back to the turn of the century, although usually not in a form that is strictly comparable with more recent data. The main difficulty with this type of data, apart from some technical problems regarding their completeness and the handling of stock issues, is that they cover only part of the total issues of financial instruments by nonfinancial sectors and, what is more serious, that it cannot be assumed that the ratio between publicly offered securities and all net issues of financial instruments by nonfinancial sectors has been constant.

It is, however, often possible to supplement the data on publicly offered securities of nonfinancial issuers by fragmentary material on other types of financial instruments issued by nonfinancial sectors, such as their borrowing from financial institutions (other than in the form of publicly offered securities acquired by financial institutions), their borrowing on mortgages, trade credit among nonfinancial enterprises, and borrowing by households from other than financial institutions. In these cases annual data are usually not available, but the net volume of issues over a period must be determined as the difference between the amounts estimated to be outstanding at the beginning and the end of the period. This is possible without great error in the case of claims since valuation changes after issuance may be regarded as of minor importance or can be roughly allowed for.

The availability and reliability of data of this type is such that one must, in general, limit the analysis to developed countries if it is desired to go back to the turn of the century. For underdeveloped countries figures are scarce even for the postwar period. In the case of developed countries it has been regarded as preferable to concentrate on the comparison of two periods of approximately equal length, periods that were relatively normal in character and which in most cases remained unaffected by sharp inflations. There are the period from the turn of the century to 1913, and the years from 1949 through 1963; both World Wars and their immediate aftermath as well as the Great Depression are thus excluded.

Before World War I

We may start with the broadest picture available, the relationship of the volume of issues of financial instruments of all types by all domestic nonfinancial sectors taken together during the half-century preceding World War I. Obviously no figures exist from which such a picture could be derived directly, reliably and in detail. It is possible, however, to obtain by indirect methods an idea of the order of magnitudes involved and thus produce a picture that is not likely to be misleading in its main features. The chief sources of such estimates are the information on new issues of securities during the period 1861–1913, the value of securities outstanding on the eve of World War I, and the change during this period in the claims of financial institutions against nonfinancial sectors in the financially dominating countries, particularly the Big Four (the United States, the United Kingdom, Germany, and France). The main features of the estimates are described in the footnotes to Tables 3–1 and 3–2.

During the fifty years preceding World War I, thus going back to almost the beginning of the period in which financial instruments and financial institutions became important features in the economy of the modern world, the net issuance of financial instruments of all types—stocks, bonds, mortgages, and short-term loans—averaged somewhat less than one-tenth of gross national product for the four large developed countries.

The ratio is considerably lower—in the order of 5 per cent—for three out of four other large countries (Italy, Austria-Hungary, Russia, and Japan), which during that period could be regarded as financially semideveloped. It undoubtedly was very low for most of Latin America, Africa and Asia.

The ratio for the world as a whole seems to have been between 5 and 6 per cent as a result of the predominance during that period of the countries for which estimates are available—and other financially developed countries such as the Low Countries, Switzerland, and Scandinavia—both in the issuance of financial instruments and in national product.

Of the total for the Big Four of about 9 per cent of gross national product, approximately one-half represented public offerings of securities (government and corporate bonds and corporate stock), while one-fourth took the form of borrowing of nonfinancial sectors from financial institutions (excluding the acquisition of securities of nonfinancial issuers by financial institutions), and—the most doubtful item in the calculation—one-fourth consisted of borrowings by nonfinancial sectors from other nonfinancial sectors, primarily in the form of trade credit and private mortgages.

While the ratio of aggregate issues of financial instruments by nonfinancial sectors to gross national product is very similar among the Big Four (and Japan),[1] differences

1. In the case of Japan it is possible to check the very rough estimates of Table 3–1 against a direct calculation—(D. Ott, *Journal of Political Economy, 69,* 122–41, 1961). Ott obtained a value of 12 per cent for the ratio of "net issues of primary securities," which are con-

Table 3–1

Estimation of Ratio of Net Issuance of Financial Instruments by Nonfinancial Issuers to Gross National Product, 1861–1913

BILLIONS OF DOLLARS

	Securities (Stocks and Bonds) Owned, 1912 (1)	Increase in Assets of Financial Institutions, 1861–1913 (2)	Col. (1) Adjusted (3)	Col. (2) Adjusted (4)	GNP 1861 to 1913 (5)	New Issue Ratio (per cent of GNP) A (6)	New Issue Ratio (per cent of GNP) B (7)
1. France	22.3	9.1	12.0	11.4	300	10.5	7.8
2. Germany	21.0	20.5	10.0	25.6	335	12.3	10.6
3. Britain	29.0	10.7	12.0	13.4	410	9.7	6.2
4. U.S.A.	56.1	32.8	43.0	36.0	815	10.9	9.8
5. Total, lines 1–4	128.4	73.1	77.0	86.4	1,861	10.8	8.8
6. Austria-Hungary	5.1	5.0	4.0	6.3	200	5.1	5.2
7. Italy	3.4	3.8	3.0	4.7	150	4.8	5.1
8. Japan	3.0	1.0	2.8	1.3	45	8.9	9.1
9. Russia	6.7	3.5	5.5	4.4	280	3.6	3.5
10. Total, lines 6–10	18.2	13.3	15.3	16.7	675	4.7	4.7
11. Other Countries	11.5	20.0	10.0	25.0	1,500	2.1	2.3
12. Total, lines 1–11	158.1	106.4	102.3	128.1	4,035	6.5	5.6

Sources: Col. 1: A. Neymarck, *Bulletin de l'Institut International de Statistique*, *22*, except for line 4 which is derived from Goldsmith, Lipsey and Mendelson, *Studies in the National Balance Sheet*, *2*, 75. (Neymarck's figure for U.S.A. is much too low, but checks against fragmentary data for some other countries do not point to a similar error for them.)

Col. 2: Derived from country tables in Appendix IV, except for lines 6 and 11 which are very rough estimates.

Col. 3: Col. 1 less (*a*) estimate for bonds of mortgage banks (derived from data in Appendix IV) because they are included in col. 2; (*b*) foreign securities (from Table 3–20 for four main countries, rough estimates for others); and (*c*) unrealized capital gains on common stock holdings (estimated at one-fourth of value in 1913). The total of $102 billion is compatible with the estimate of aggregate new issues for 1871–1913 (Neymarck) of about $100 billion since the issues for 1861–70 should be about offset by the issues of financial institutions—approximately one-eighth of total—included in the estimates.

Col. 4: Col. 2, plus 25 per cent to take account of nonfinancial sectors' debt in forms other than securities, primarily trade credit and private mortgages, except for U.S.A., where figures are taken from national balance sheet (cf. col. 1). The assumed ratio of 125 per cent is higher than the observed ratio in U.S.A. because of relatively high share of interbank deposits and low volume of noninstitutional mortgages in U.S.A.

Col. 5: Based on data in Appendix V for lines 1–4, and 7–9; rough estimates for lines 6 and 11.

Col. 6: Sum of cols. 1 and 2, divided by col. 5.

Col. 7: Sum of cols. 3 and 4, divided by col. 5.

appear if the comparison is limited to domestic issues alone, as is appropriate for the determination of the values of the ratio δ in the basic formula. Then, because of the relatively larger importance of foreign issues of securities in the United Kingdom and France than in Germany, the United States, Italy, Japan, or Russia, the highest ratios for net domestic issues to gross national product appear in the United States and Germany where they are in the neighborhood of 10 per cent, while the ratios for France and the United Kingdom decline to 8 per cent and 6 per cent respectively.

For the thirteen years between the turn of the century and World War I somewhat better information is available. It is, first, again possible to derive a rough figure for the entire world. Starting from the estimate of new issues of securities (other than those of financial institutions) of nearly $30 billion[2] and adding 125 per cent of the increase in the assets of financial institutions to take account of the borrowing of nonfinancial sectors in forms other than securities, we reach a total of approximately $100 billion, equal to 6 to 7 per cent of gross national product during that period. On this basis, therefore, there would seem to have been a noticeable though not radical increase in the ratio of net new issues of financial instruments by nonfinancial sectors to gross national product between 1861 and 1900 and 1901 and 1913. This probably reflects, among other developments, the increasing importance of corporations within the business sector.

More reliable estimates can be made for the financial Big

---

ceptually identical with the net issues of nonfinancial sectors used in Table 3–1. Since the ratio is considerably lower for the years 1860–77 than for the later period and since the numerator of national income is about one-fifth lower than gross national product used in Table 3–1, Ott's figures made comparable as to period and concept with Table 3–1 would yield virtually the same value—viz. 9 per cent.

2. A. Neymarck, *Bulletin de l'Institut International de Statistique, 22* (1925). Neymarck's figures apparently are those of the *Moniteur des Intérêts Matériels* of Brussels (see e.g. issue of July 5, 1914), although they are not so identified.

Four and Japan (Table 3–2). For these countries the ratio of net issues of financial instruments by domestic nonfinancial issuers to national product averages 10 per cent. The ratio is considerably lower for France and particularly for the United Kingdom than it is for the United States and even more so than for Germany and Japan. The lower figures for France and the United Kingdom are explained primarily by the substantial proportion of foreign issues, but also reflect the relatively low level and slow growth of the assets of financial institutions, which here have been used as a basis of estimating the new issues of nonfinancial domestic sectors in forms other than publicly offered securities. The very high ratio for Germany is due primarily to the extraordinarily rapid growth of financial institutions. In this case, however, the resulting estimated figure for the borrowings of nonfinancial sectors in forms other than securities can be checked against other data, and such a comparison shows that the resulting figure of 14 per cent for the total domestic net new issue ratio of nonfinancial sectors is reasonable.

For these five countries one may even try to establish movements within the half century preceding World War I. It would then appear (Table 3–3, rows 1 and 3) that, while there was a definite upward trend in the ratio in the two countries that started the period in a relatively backward stage financially speaking—Germany and Japan—the upward movement is less pronounced in the United States and is limited to the period 1901–12, and that there is no marked trend in the two "old" countries, the United Kingdom and France. This, however, is due to the increasing share of foreign issues; if the figures included all security issues, the ratio for these two countries would also show some upward movement, though one of more modest dimensions.

Rough estimates for other developed and semideveloped countries indicate a domestic nonfinancial issue ratio of approximately 8 per cent. This is, as would be expected, somewhat below the ratios found—by more reliable meth-

TABLE 3–2

Domestic Nonfinancial Net New Issue Ratio, 1901–13, in Five Leading Countries

BILLIONS OF DOLLARS

	Net Public Issues of Securities of Nonfinancial Sectors			Increase in Assets of Financial Institutions	Gross National Product	Domestic New Issue Ratio (per cent of GNP)	
	Total	Domestic Issues	Stock Issues			A[a]	B[b]
	(1)	(2)	(3)	(4)	(5)	(6)	(7)
1. France	7.2	3.7[e]	2.2[e]	3.6	100	7.3[d]	9.0
2. Germany	6.2	5.0	1.4	12.0	140	12.1	16.3
3. Great Britain	9.5[e]	3.0[e]		4.0	140	5.0	6.4
4. Japan[c]	1.7	1.7	.5	1.1	20		14.0[f]
5. U.S.A.[d]	17.5	17.2	5.8	19.6	337		10.9[f]
6. Total	42.1	30.6		40.3	737		11.0

[a] Cols. 2 plus 4 divided by col. 5.
[b] For lines 1 through 3, col. 2, plus 1.50 × col. 4, divided by col. 5.
[c] 1902–14.
[d] 1901–12.
[e] Including issues of financial sector.
[f] All primary securities.

Sources: Cols. 1–3:
Line 1: *Annuaire Statistique, Retrospectif* (Paris, 1961), p. 232.
Line 2: K. Helfferich, cited in Neymarck, *Bulletin de l'Institut International de Statistique*, *19*(2), 232.
Line 3: A. R. Hall, *Economica* 24 (1957), 62.
Line 4: Ott, pp. 125 ff.
Line 5: Goldsmith, Lipsey, and Mendelson, *2*.
Col. 4: Tables in Appendix IV.
Col. 5: Based on table in Appendix V.

ods—for the financial Big Four and Japan but somewhat higher than the equally rough estimates for the longer period 1860–1913. It is thus likely that in those countries the ratio of net new issues of nonfinancial sectors to na-

TABLE 3–3

Trend in the Nonfinancial Domestic Net New Issue Ratio, Five Major Countries, 1861–1963
PER CENT OF GROSS NATIONAL PRODUCT

	France (1)	Germany (2)	Great Britain (3)	Japan (4)	U.S.A. (5)
1. 1861–1880	8	7	6		12
2. 1881–1900		10	8	7	11
3. 1901–1913	8	14	6	14	11
4. 1920s			8	9	13
5. 1949–1963[a]	12	10	10	35	10

[a] Includes small amounts of foreign issues.

Sources:
Lines 1–4: Same as Table 3–2, except that figures in col. 5, lines 1 and 2, are from E. S. Shaw and J. G. Gurley, *Review of Economics and Statistics 39* (1957), p. 256. Figures in line 3 cols. 1 to 3 are averages of those in Table 3–2, cols. 6 and 7.
Line 5: Table 3–4, col. 8.

tional product showed an increasing trend during the fifty years preceding World War I as it did in the Big Four and in Japan.

We are thus left with three main conclusions which are not likely to be invalidated by the more accurate statistical data that are needed for closer analysis:

1. The ratio of new issues of domestic nonfinancial sectors in the leading developed countries in the decade before World War I was in the order of one-tenth.

2. The ratio increased noticeably, but not spectacularly, in the period between the third quarter of the nineteenth century and World War I.

3. The ratio was considerably lower in financial semi-developed countries, such as Europe outside the leading countries, and was sharply lower in the rest of the world.

In the Postwar Period 1949–63

Estimates for the aggregate domestic nonfinancial issue ratio for the period of 1949–63 for one-half of the thirty-five countries, coverage of which is attempted, are shown in Table 3–4. Most of the figures can be regarded as fairly reliable as they are based on sectorized flow-of-funds data for all or for a considerable part of the period. The estimates for a few countries, however, are more precarious as they had to be derived from national balance sheets near the end of the period, sometimes in combination with flow-of-funds data for one or a few years. From these data, five conclusions may be drawn about the level and the international differences of δ during the postwar period.

1. The average of δ for all countries is slightly above 12 per cent, whether or not the two socialist countries are included. The ratio is considerably higher for the thirteen nonsocialist developed countries with 13.5 per cent than for the three less developed nonsocialist countries—obviously an insufficient sample—with 7.5 per cent. An average for a larger group of underdeveloped countries might show an even smaller value, and hence a larger difference compared to the value of δ for the developed countries.

2. One of the socialist countries included, the U.S.S.R., shows a very low value of δ, which is probably representative for this type of economy and is explained by the absence of some important types of financial instruments in their economy. The other socialist country included in Table 3–4, Yugoslavia, on the other hand, shows a very high ratio, indeed a ratio higher than those for any underdeveloped country and higher than all but two of the thirteen developed nonsocialist countries of Table 3–4. This contrast reflects institutional differences in the financial structure of these two socialist countries. In Yugoslavia a large proportion of the funds of enterprises, which are owned publicly in both countries, takes the form of borrowing from financial enterprises, including the Investment Loan Fund, but in the U.S.S.R. these funds are treated as alloca-

tions from the central budget, which are not regarded as liabilities in Table 3–4.

3. The similarity in the value of δ is most pronounced for the eleven Western developed countries which show an average of a little above 11 per cent and a range of 9 to 15 per cent. Japan and Israel, with values of 35 and 30 per cent respectively, are clearly in a class by themselves. The high values for these two countries are connected with the rapid rate of growth and the consequent heavy reliance of external financing, but cannot be completely explained in this manner.

4. Among the underdeveloped countries the value of δ is considerably higher for the two Latin American countries than for the only other country (India). From fragmentary and indirect evidence it is likely that the average for all 16 underdeveloped countries would be closer to the former than the latter value.

5. The contribution of equity securities to δ is small. Retention of earnings, it should be recalled, is not regarded as an issue of securities, and more specifically of equity securities. On the average, for the ten countries for which this information is available separately, common stock furnishes less than one-twelfth of total external financing—their share in no case exceeds one-tenth—and these issues are on the average equal to hardly 1 per cent of gross national product. While the number of cases is too small for confident conclusions, there does not seem to exist a clear relation between the relative contribution of corporate stock to δ and factors such as the level of real product per head or the rate of growth of the economy. The relative contribution of equity securities to δ is probably strongly influenced by factors specific to the country and period, both on the side of the issuing corporations and on that of individual and institutional buyers.

For the seventeen countries not included in Table 3–4, we are forced to rely on the indirect method of starting with the value ϕ of the ratio of the issues of financial institutions to national product, adjusted for intrafinancial is-

TABLE 3–4

Estimation of Domestic Nonfinancial Issues Ratio (δ) for 1949–63 in Selected Countries

	Debt Issues of Nonfinancial Domestic Sectors Outstanding		Reported Net Domestic Debt Issues			Estimated Net Issue Ratio, 1949–63		
						Debt	Stock	Total
						Per Cent of Period's GNP		
	Year (1)	Amount[a] (2)	Period (3)	Amount[a] (4)	(5)	(6)	(7)	(8)
1. Australia			1953–61	8.3	13.4	13.4	1.4	14.8
2. Belgium	1960	1,143	1958–62	345	12.0	12.0	.8	12.8
3. Canada			1949–54	15.4	12.0	12.0	.7	12.7
4. France	1960	313	1953–63	290	10.5	10.5	1.0	11.5
5. Germany	1960	359	1950–63	305	9.3	9.3	.7	10.0
6. Great Britain	1961	80	1958–61	12.1	12.6	9.0	.7	9.7
7. India	1961	242	1951–61	64.2	4.5	4.5	.2	4.7
8. Israel	1962	10				29.0		
9. Italy	1961	31				13.5		14.5
10. Japan	1961	29	1953–63	42.8	32.9	32.0	3.0	35.0
11. Mexico	1960	130	1960	19.0	12.3	10.0		
12. New Zealand			1956–62	.7[b]	8.4[b]			9.0
13. Norway	1962	66	1956–63	36.0	14.7	14.0	.8[b]	14.8
14. U.S.S.R.	1959	100	1951–59	51	3.8	4.0		4.0
15. Sweden			1956–62	27.6	8.2	8.2	.5	8.7
16. U.S.A.	1963	880	1949–63	590	9.4	9.4	.4	9.8
17. Venezuela	1962	21	1958–63	10.4[b]	7.1[b]			8.0
18. Yugoslavia	1963	5,727	1957–63	4,985	23.6	18.0		18.0

[a] Billions of national currency, except for Italy and Japan (trillions).
[b] Includes issues of corporate stock.

[illegible] R. W. Goldsmith, "The Uses of National Balance Sheets," in *Review of Income and Wealth* (June 1966), p. 128.

Line 7: M. S. Joshi, *The National Balance Sheet of India* (Bombay, 1966), p. 36.

Line 16: Federal Reserve Board, *Flow of Funds—Assets and Liabilities, 1945–65* (mimeo, May 1966).

Line 17: Banco Central, *El Fluir de Fondos de Capital*, 1964.

Cols. 4–5:

Line 1: Reserve Banks of Australia, *Flow-of-Funds, Australia, 1953–54 to 1961–62.*

Line 2: Banque Nationale de Belgique, *Bulletin d'Information et de Documentation* (Feb. 1963 and May 1966).

Line 3: W. C. Hood, *Financing of Economic Activity in Canada* (Ottawa, 1958), pp. 78 ff.

Line 4: Ministère des Finances, *Les Comptes de la Nation 1949–1959, 1963 and 1964.*

Line 5: Deutsche Bundesbank, *Monatsberichte* (July 1962 and Apr. 1966).

Line 6: J. Revell, *The Wealth of the Nation*, MS (according to the revised printed version, [Cambridge, 1967, pp. 47ff.] the figures would be somewhat higher).

Line 7: From (unpublished) flow-of-funds statistics of Reserve Bank of India. Now published in revised form in *Reserve Bank of India Bulletin*, Manl 1967.

Line 10: Bank of Japan, *Flow-of-Funds-Accounts of Japan* (1954–1963, and 1964).

Line 11: J. Lopez Gonzales, *Calculo del Ahorro Nacional*, unpublished thesis (1963).

Line 12: W. A. Poole, *Sources and Uses of Capital Funds* (Wellington, 1965).

Line 13: Statistisk Sentralbyra, *Kredittmarkedstatistikk* (1955, 1963).

Line 14: Differences between 1950 and 1959 outstanding as estimated in R. W. Goldsmith, "The National Balance Sheet of the Soviet Union," in *Essays on Econometries and Planning presented to Professor P. C. Mahalanobis*, (Calcutta, 1963), p. 98.

Line 15: Bank of International Settlements; unpublished Riksbank data.

Line 16: Same as cols. 1 and 2, line 16.

Line 17: Banco Central, *El Fluir de Fondos de Capital* (1964) and *Cuentas Nacionales* (*1963*).

Line 18: Narodna Banka, *Annual Report* (1965).

Col. 6:

Lines 1, 4, 5, 7, 10, 12–15, 18: Assumed equal to, or only slightly different from col. 5.

Line 6: Based on national balance sheets (J. Revell) for 1948 and 1961.

Line 8: Issues 1949–62 assumed equal to outstanding at end of 1962 and 1963 ratio equal to 1949–62 averages.

Line 9: Based on the assumption that four-fifths of 1961 outstanding reflect net issues of 1948–61, and that the 1949–61 ratio is also applicable to 1962–63.

Line 11: Issues 1949–60 assumed equal to 80 per cent of 1960 outstanding and 1961–63 ratio equal to 1949–60 ratio.

Line 16: Same as col. 1, line 1.

Line 17: Issues 1949–60 assumed equal to 80 per cent of 1960 outstanding and 1961–63 ratio equal to 1949–62 ratio.

Col. 7: Unless otherwise indicated same as for cols. 5 and 6.

Line 3: M. C. Urquhart and K. A. H. Buckley, eds., *Historical Statistics of Canada* (Cambridge, 1965), p. 280.

Line 6: Based on ratio (.65 for period) of issues of domestic nonfinancial quoted companies 1956–63 (*Financial Statistics*, Nov. 1964).

sues and foreign assets, as representing issues of nonfinancial sectors to financial institutions, and adding to ϕ, so adjusted (i.e. to $\bar{\phi}$), allowances for issues of nonfinancial sectors held outside the financial system—primarily government and corporate securities, mortgages, consumer credit, and trade credit. For the seventeen countries, $\bar{\phi}$ seems to have an average value of approximately 8 per cent of gross national product, resulting from values of 12 per cent for the five developed countries not included in Table 3–4 and 6 per cent for the twelve less developed countries. The contribution of government securities held by nonfinancial sectors is known to be small, as will be shown later in this chapter (in the section on issues of government securities); on the average it does not exceed one-half of 1 per cent of gross national product. The issue of corporate bonds, consumer credit, and mortgages absorbed by nonfinancial sectors is also small. The issues of corporate stock, most of which are held outside the financial system, and of trade credit, however, are far from negligible. They may, on the average, be in the order of 2 per cent of gross national product, lying somewhat above this value for developed countries and somewhat below it for less developed ones. Using these extremely rough estimates, the average values of δ for the seventeen countries would be in the order of 10 per cent, with a substantial difference of approximately 15 per cent for developed and approximately 8 per cent for less developed countries. These figures are sufficiently close, in each of the two groups, to the better established values for the eighteen countries of Table 3–4 to make the existence of a systematic and substantial difference between the two sets of countries unlikely. We would then conclude that for the postwar period the average value of δ for nonsocialist countries was in the order of 12 per cent of gross national product, being several percentage points higher than this level for developed countries, probably in the order of 15 per cent, and lower for less developed countries, probably averaging slightly less than 10 per cent. The average value of the ratio for developed countries thus would be at least one and one-half times as high as that for less developed countries as a group. This is probably as far as we can go in the present fragmentary state of our information, which is obviously much more deficient for less developed than for developed countries.

The values of δ are, of course, a combination of the corresponding ratios for the main sectors of the economy. Information on net issues by nonfinancial sectors is unfortunately even scarcer, both in geographic and time coverage, than that shown in Table 3–4 for the aggregate national new issues ratio, even if only three main sectors—business enterprises, households, and government—are distinguished. The material available for a dozen countries for a smaller or larger fraction of the entire 1949–63 period, derived almost exclusively from the different countries' flow-of-funds statistics, has been summarized in Table 3–5 in the form of the ratios of sectoral new issues of gross national product and of the share of each sector's ratio in the national aggregate ratio.

The main impression Table 3–5 gives is that of great variety in the share of the main sectors in δ, an impression reinforced by the realization that the definition and economic functions of the three sectors vary considerably among countries, e.g. in the classification of home mortgages and of the issues of unincorporated and of government business enterprises. Since this variety is considerably more pronounced than the differences in aggregate δ among countries—particularly if attention is concentrated on developed Western countries—there obviously exists a good deal of substitutability among the functions of the main sectors and of their issues.

Table 3–5 nevertheless discloses some interesting though not unexpected features. The issues of the government range all the way from 0.5 to 7 per cent of national product, and their share in total issues extends from one-eighth or less in four of the thirteen countries to one-half or more in three (Great Britain, New Zealand, and India)—or to four countries if the issues of publicly owned business en-

Table 3–5

Domestic Nonfinancial Net Issues Ratio (δ) for Main Sectors and Selected Countries in the Postwar Period

	Period	Nonfinancial Business	Households	Government	Total	Nonfinancial Business	Households	Government
		Per Cent of GNP				Share in δ		
	(1)	(2)	(3)	(4)	(5)	(6)	(7)	(8)
Australia	1953–61	4.4	4.7	5.7	14.8	.30	.32	.38
Belgium	1958–62	8.3		4.4	12.7	.65		.35
Canada	1949–54	11.1		.5	11.6	.96		.04
France	1953–63	7.0	.9	3.6	11.5	.61	.08	.31
Germany[a]	1950–63	8.8		1.2	10.0	.88		.12
Great Britain	1958–61	6.7		6.8	13.5	.50		.50
India	1951–61	.9	.7	3.1	4.7	.19	.15	.66
Japan[b]	1953–63	18.3	14.1	3.8	36.2	.51	.39[b]	.10
New Zealand	1956–62	3.8		4.6	8.4	.45		.55
Norway	1956–63	9.9		3.1	13.0	.76		.24
Sweden	1958–62	3.3	5.4		8.7	.38	.62	
U.S.A.	1949–63	4.3	3.7	1.8	9.8	.44	.38	.18
Yugoslavia	1957–63	19.1	1.3	3.0	23.4	.81	.06	.13

Note: where a single value is given for two adjacent sector columns (bracketed together in the original), it is the combined figure: Households + Nonfinancial Business for Belgium, Canada, Germany, Great Britain, New Zealand and Norway (cols. 2–3 and 6–7), and Households + Government for Sweden (cols. 3–4 and 7–8).

[a] Including unincorporated business .9 in col. 2; .09 in col. 6.
[b] Includes unincorporated business in cols. 3 and 7.

Sources: Generally same as for Table 3–4, cols. 3 and 4.

terprises in Yugoslavia are attributed to the government sector. These differences are, of course, a reflection of the varying role of the government—general government as well as public enterprises—in these countries' economy, a role related to, but not exactly measured by the government's share in national product.

The importance of households' borrowing, mainly in the form of home mortgages and of consumer sales credit, also varies greatly, although definite conclusions are hampered by the failure of several countries' flow-of-funds statistics to show separate figures for the household sector and to allocate home mortgage issues to it. Among the countries covered in Table 3–5, the relation of households' borrowing to national product and their share in δ is high—or may be presumed on the basis of other fragmentary evidence to be high—in the United States, Canada, Great Britain, Germany, Norway, Sweden, and Australia and low in France, Yugoslavia, India, and, if the issues of unincorporated business are excluded, probably also in Japan. Institutional factors (e.g. the extent of home ownership and the access of households to financial institutions), economic factors (such as the importance of consumer durables), and geographic factors (e.g. the need for expensive shelter) all would need to be taken into account in a satisfactory explanation of the differences shown in Table 3–5.

Business enterprises are in all countries the largest issuers of nonfinancial debt and equity securities. This fact is somewhat obscured in Table 3–5 because in some countries public and unincorporated private enterprises are included in the government or the household sector, and because in others all home mortgage borrowing is attributed to the nonfinancial business sector. If allowance is roughly made for these deficiencies in the basic flow-of-funds statistics, it would appear that in most of the countries covered in Table 3–5 nonfinancial, nonagricultural enterprises, whether privately or publicly owned, account for between two-fifths and four-fifths of total nonfinancial issues. The proportion is probably lowest among this dozen of countries—just over

40 per cent—in the United States on the one hand because of the heavy capital expenditures on homes and consumer durables, which are largely financed by household borrowing, and in India on the other hand as a result of heavy borrowing for general governmental purposes. The typical value seems to be in the order of three-fifths of total nonfinancial issues.

The relationship of the issues of nonfinancial, nonagricultural business enterprises to national product varies even more widely, probably from as little as 2 or 3 per cent in India to well over 20 per cent in Japan, most of the western developed countries showing ratios between 4 per cent (e.g. United States, New Zealand) and 8 per cent (Canada, France, Norway). These variations are due to differences in the rate of growth of the business sector as well as in the relationship between internal and external financing, which is reflected in the external financing ratio (η), which will be discussed in the following section.

A comparison of the nonfinancial issues ratio δ during the postwar period with the corresponding figures for earlier periods, particularly before World War I, as attempted in Table 3–6, is of great interest because it will indicate whether this basic financial ratio has undergone substan-

Table 3–6

Comparison of Nonfinancial Domestic Net Issues Ratio (δ) before World War I and after World War II

PER CENT OF GROSS NATIONAL PRODUCT

	1861–1912 (1)	1901–13 (2)	1949–63 (3)
France	7.8	7.2–9.0	11.5
Germany	10.6	12.1–16.3	10.0
Great Britain	6.2	5.0–6.4	9.7
Italy	5.1		14.5
Japan	9.1	14.0	35.0
Russia-U.S.S.R.	3.5		4.0
U.S.A.	9.8	9.3–10.9	9.8
All countries	5.6		13.0

Sources: Col. 1: Table 3–1, col. 7.
Col. 2: Table 3–2, cols. 6 and 7.
Col. 3: Table 3–4, col. 8.

tial structural changes over the past century. Scarcity of historical data unfortunately limits the comparison to half a dozen developed countries. A more serious defect is that the two bodies of data were of necessity derived by different methods, and that the figures for the period before World War I have a wider margin of error than the more recent data.

Taking the figures at their face value it would appear that for the Big Four (United States, Great Britain, France, and Germany) the average value of δ for 1949–63 of just over 10 per cent of national product is only slightly—by 1 to 2 percentage points—above the level estimated in Tables 3–1 and 3–2 for 1901–13 and for the longer period 1861–1912. The main difference is a substantial rise in the ratios for Great Britain and France, a rise which can be explained in part by the substitution of foreign issues, which were much more important before World War I, by domestic issues. In the case of Germany the 1860–1912 and 1949–63 ratios are almost identical, though that for 1901–13 is higher. All three ratios are virtually on the same level of 10 per cent for the United States. As a result of these changes the range of the ratio among the four leading countries seems to be much narrower in the postwar period—only two percentage points—than it was for in either the 1860–1912 or 1901–13 periods.

It is questionable—and even quite unlikely—that this absence of change also applies to the rest of the world. There is no doubt about a substantial rise in two countries for which data are available—Italy and Japan. It is very unlikely, to say the least, that the pre-World War I ratios could have been as high as they were in the postwar period in several developed countries (Canada, Australia) and in most underdeveloped countries, even in India. Nothing but a very rough estimate is possible, but it would seem that the postwar average of δ for the thirty-three nonsocialist countries of approximately 13 per cent represents an increase by at least 5 percentage points compared to the 1901–13 value, and that is at least twice as high as the

1860–1912 average. As a result the large difference that existed before 1914 between the Big Four (and a few other European countries) and most of the rest of the world has virtually disappeared.

Still less can be said about changes in the distribution among sectors. It is likely, however, that compared to the situation of one or more decades before World War I the share of general government is now lower and that of public enterprises and households is higher, while that of business enterprises may not have changed much.

THE DOMESTIC CAPITAL FORMATION RATIO[3]

The volume of capital expenditures and its relation to national product, the ratio κ of the basic formula, is one of the key magnitudes in the explanation of economic growth, although it may not have quite the dominating position that sometimes has been attributed to it in the discussions of the postwar period. Here, however, we need to concern ourselves with the volume of domestic capital formation and its relation to national product only because the volume of nonfinancial issues is presumably determined to a greater or smaller extent by the volume of issuers' capital expenditures. This, at least, can be assumed to be the case for business enterprises and probably for households, particularly for home mortgages debt and for government enterprises and local government. What primarily matters for the anal-

3. Readers should be reminded that of the two alternative denominators for the capital formation ratio discussed in Chapter 2 (gross national product and the volume of sales of the sectors making the capital expenditures), the first is used here because the statistical data available for its calculation are much more satisfactory. For the same reason no allowance has been made in the numerator for other uses of funds likely to give rise to issues of financial instruments such as extension of trade credit and needs for transaction cash. Thus κ is defined as k/y rather than as $(k+r+m)/v$. As a consequence there is no need for the nonfinancial interrelations ratio (ω) or for the monetization ratio (μ). This short cut is not likely to impede analysis if interest is concentrated on nationwide totals and coefficients.

ysis of the development of the financial superstructure are long-term changes in the ratio of capital formation to national product, both in the aggregate and for the main sectors. We are, therefore, interested chiefly in three questions: (1) What is the long-term trend in the aggregate gross domestic capital formation ratio κ? (2) What are the differences in the level and trend of the domestic capital formation ratio in countries at different stages of economic development or countries with differences in other economic characteristics? (3) What is the distribution of aggregate domestic capital formation among the chief sectors and the chief types of capital goods? Unfortunately, the statistical data needed are not available in comparable form for sufficiently long periods and for a sufficiently large number of countries to permit satisfactory answers to these questions, notwithstanding the great amount of work which has been done during the last few decades on the statistics of capital formation. All we can hope for is a rough idea of trends and differences in the domestic capital formation ratios of different groups of countries that may be of some help in explaining differences in the character and the development of their financial superstructure.

There is no doubt that over the past century κ, the nationwide ratio of gross domestic capital formation to national product, has shown a definite upward trend both for developed and for underdeveloped countries taken as a group.

The statistical evidence now available is limited to developed countries. For ten developed countries, including all large ones which have been in this category since the mid-nineteenth century (this therefore excludes Japan), the gross domestic capital formation ratio, as shown in Table 3-7 averaged 13 per cent (unweighted) for the period 1861–90, and 16 per cent for the following quarter-century preceding World War I. The ratio apparently stayed at that level for the interwar period 1921–39 as a whole, notwithstanding the severe effect of the Great Depression. In the postwar period, the level shifted upward, averaging 23 per

TABLE 3–7

Trend in Domestic Gross Capital Formation Ratio (Excluding Consumer Durables), 1860–1963

PER CENT OF GROSS NATIONAL PRODUCT

	Approximate Period Average				Changes			
	1861–90 (1)	1891–1914 (2)	1921–39 (3)	1948–63 (4)	1861–90 to 1891–1914 (5)	1891–1914 to 1921–39 (6)	1921–39 to 1948–63 (7)	1891–1914 to 1948–63 (8)
1. Argentina		15	13	19		− 2	+ 6	+ 4
2. Australia	17	14	17	27	−3	+ 3	+10	+13
3. Canada		22[a]	15	24		− 7	+ 9	+ 2
4. Denmark	11[b]	13	13	20	+2	0	+ 7	+ 7
5. France		14[c]	16	22		+ 2	+ 6	+ 8
6. Germany	16	23	13	25	+7	−10	+12	+ 2
7. Great Britain	9	9	9	16	0	0	+ 7	+ 7
8. Italy	11	14	18	22	+3	+ 4	+ 4	+ 8
9. Japan		11	16	33		+ 5	+17	+22
10. Norway	11[d]	14	17	30	+3	+ 3	+13	+16
11. Sweden	11	13	16	22	+2	+ 3	+ 6	+ 9
12. U.S.A.	21[e]	22	18	18	+1	− 4	0	− 4

[a] 1896–1915. [b] 1870–89. [c] 1896 and 1913. [d] 1865–89. [e] 1869–89.

Sources: Cols. 1–3: S. Kuznets, "Long-Term Trends in Capital Formation Proportions," in *Economic Development and Culture Change*, 9 (1961), except for line 1: C. Diaz Alejandro, MS; for line 5: Berthet, Carré, Dubois, and Malinvaud, MS (June 1965); and for line 9: Ohkawa and Rosovsky, *Hitotsubashi Journal of Economics*, *3* (1).

Col. 4: U.N., *Yearbook of National Accounts Statistics*, various issues (total capital formation ratio).

cent for the years 1948–63, and showed an upward movement within that period. This definite upward trend, particularly the increase in the postwar period compared to the half-century preceding World War II, is shared by all developed countries except the United States, where the postwar ratio is slightly less than that for the period before World War I. Since these figures do not include consumer durables, the upward trend would be accentuated if a broader concept of capital formation were used, in which case the downward movement for the United States would disappear.

An upward trend also was almost certainly already operative during the first half of the nineteenth century, although statistical data to document this surmise are very scarce. In the United States, gross domestic capital formation (including home-produced capital equipment but excluding consumer durables) is estimated to have increased from 15 per cent of gross national product for the period 1834–58 to 25 per cent for 1869–88.[4] For the United Kingdom, which throughout the nineteenth century had one of the lowest domestic capital formation ratios among developed countries, partly because of a very high foreign investment ratio, κ is estimated to have risen from about 6 per cent at the end of the eighteenth century—and 5 per cent at its beginning—to about 9 per cent during the second half of the nineteenth century.[5]

No comparable information exists on capital formation ratios in underdeveloped countries before World War II, but there is little doubt that the upward trend was present here too. It is even probable that the trend was at least as much if not more pronounced than in the countries which can be regarded as having been economically developed

4. R. Gallman, in *Studies in Income and Wealth, 30* (New York, National Bureau of Economic Research, 1966), 11. These figures are higher than those of Table 3–7, possibly because they are expressed in constant rather than in current prices.

5. Phyllis Deane, *The First Industrial Revolution* (Cambridge, Cambridge University Press, 1965), p. 154.

since the middle of the nineteenth century. According to estimates, κ increased in Japan from a quite low level before the Meiji era to about one-eighth in the two decades preceding World War I, when Japanese economic development started in earnest; it advanced moderately to one-sixth during the interwar period and then rose spectacularly to one-third—probably the highest rate in the world—during the postwar period. In Mexico, where the estimates are rougher than in the case of Japan, κ seems to have risen from less than one-tenth before the Revolution of 1911 and a similarly moderate level during the 1930s to about one-fifth in the 1950s and 1960s.[6] The upward trend in κ is likely to have been slower in most other underdeveloped countries. In view of the fact, however, that the average value of κ for underdeveloped countries during the postwar period is close to one-fifth, while it probably was well below one-tenth in most countries before World War I (heavily capital-importing countries like Argentina are an exception), the rate of increase of the gross domestic capital formation ratio must have been quite marked in the less developed countries.

The ratio of net domestic capital formation to national product has risen less rapidly than κ because the share of capital consumption allowances in gross capital formation has been increasing, first, because of the influence of a shortening of the average life of capital goods, which reflects the increasing share of equipment compared to structure in total capital formation, and, secondly, although less universally, because of the deceleration in the rate of increase in the volume of total gross capital formation.[7]

The significance of the upward trend in κ is that it implies an increasing ratio of the issuance of securities by non-

6. R. W. Goldsmith, *The Financial Development of Mexico* (Paris, Organization for Economic Cooperation and Development, 1966). The figures for the postwar period are based on recent upward revisions in the estimates which are not yet embodied in the official published data.

7. The decrease in the ratio of net to gross capital formation when the rate of growth of gross national capital formation decelerates is an algebraic necessity. (See E. Domar, *Economic Journal, 63* [1953], 1–32.)

financial units to national product, as well as an increasing FIR, if other factors have remained unchanged, particularly the external financing ratio (η). In that case, if κ has in developed countries been in the order of one-fifth to one-fourth during the postwar period, even excluding consumer durables, compared to a value of about one-seventh for the half-century before World War I, and probably not over one-tenth during the first half of the nineteenth century, then the ratio of the issuance of securities of nonfinancial issuers to national product (δ) would now be about one and one-half times as high as they were early in the twentieth century, and the ratios would be more than twice as high as those prevailing in the mid-nineteenth century. Actually, of course, many factors are at work to influence these ratios, and these other factors may accentuate or offset the upward pull of κ on the ratio of new nonfinancial issues to national product (δ) or on FIR. To understand these relationships, we would need to know much more about the determinants of the trend and of the international differences in κ than we now do. The general impression that κ is related, over time and between countries, to real national product per head is not enough. Indeed we know or have reason to believe that this relationship does not hold without exceptions and—which is more serious—that the form of the relationship is not the same in all countries, even those of similar economic structure and similar level of economic development, and that it has changed over time in many countries. The attempt made in Appendix II to relate the capital formation ratio of about fifty countries during the period 1956–60 to a number of these countries' economic characteristics—level and growth of national product, growth of population, price level changes, capital formation ratio, and importance of foreign trade—should be regarded as only a small and hesitant step in this direction.

THE EXTERNAL FINANCING RATIO

The ratio η of the new issues, gross or net, of financial instruments by domestic nonfinancial issuers to their capital expenditures is one of the most important relations in the analysis of financial structure and development and one of the crucial coefficients explaining the ratios of issues of financial instruments to national product (ANIR) and of the stock of such instruments outstanding to national wealth (FIR).[8] The reason is that η, and even more its components for the enterprise, households, and government sectors or subsectors of them (η_b, η_h, η_g, etc.), should provide a meaningful explanation—though necessarily only a partial one—of the volume of issues of nonfinancial sectors, particularly for the business and household sectors. It is therefore extremely regrettable that an adequate investigation of the ratio η and its determinants on an international comparative scale is not yet feasible, due primarily to the lack of the required sectoral source-and-uses-of-funds statements, except for about a dozen countries for usually short and recent periods.

Before World War I

The material now available in internationally comparable form does not permit direct estimation of the ratio of the issuance of financial instruments by nonfinancial sectors to their capital formation before the 1950s and particularly for the period before World War I, since sectorized sources-and-uses-of-funds statements are a relatively recent statistical innovation. For that period it is necessary to resort to the indirect approach of determining η by dividing the ratio of total net issues of financial instruments by non-

8. If it is necessary to distinguish the gross and net ratios, they may be identified as η' and η'', where $\eta'' = \eta'(1-\zeta)$; and ζ, it will be remembered, is the ratio of retirements to gross issues. Unless the contrary is specifically indicated, all values of η discussed in this section refer to net issue ratios.

financial sector (δ) by the national capital formation ratio (κ).[9] This has been done in Table 3–8 for five countries, including the financial Big Four.

TABLE 3–8

Indirect Estimation of Net External Financing Ratio (η) of Nonfinancial Sectors for Five Countries, 1901–13

PER CENT

	Domestic New Issue Ratio (δ) (1)	Domestic Gross Capital Formation Ratio (κ)[a] (2)	Inferred Value of η (3)
France	9	14	.64
Germany	16	20	.80
Great Britain	6	9	.67
Japan	14	14	1.00
U.S.A.	11	22	.50

[a] Excluding consumer durables.

Sources: Col. 1: Table 3–2, col. 7.
Col. 2: France and Germany: Table 3–7, col. 2.
Great Britain: C. H. Feinstein, *London and Cambridge Bulletin* No. 50 (1964), plus allowances for inventory accumulation.
Japan: Figures for 1902–11 in H. Rosovsky. *Capital Formation in Japan*, p. 9. Ohkawa and Rosovsky's estimates in 1934/36 prices in *Hitotsubachi Journal of Economics, 3* (1) (1962), 33 are considerably lower—11 per cent.
U.S.A.: *Historical Statistics of the United States Colonial Times to 1957* Washington, 1960, p. 143 for 1897 through 1911.

The results, necessarily very rough and precarious, are at least not unreasonable. They indicate a rather wide

9. This assumes that the share of the nonfinancial sectors in national capital formation is close enough to 100 per cent so that the complementary share of financial institutions can be safely neglected, given the margin of error in all capital formation estimates. This assumption is justified by whatever scattered material is available, the share of financial institutions in national capital formation usually being in the order of 1 to 2 per cent. In the United States, for example, the financial sector has since the turn of the century owned between ½ and 1½ per cent of all tangible assets (R. W. Goldsmith, R. E. Lipsey, and M. Mendelson, *Studies in the National Balance Sheet, 2,* 42 ff.) In Great Britain the ratio was 1.5 per cent in 1960 (J. Revell, *Moorgate and Wall Street,* London, Spring 1966, p. 60).

range for the value of η of between 0.50 and 1.00. This means that, on a national aggregate and a net basis (i.e. deducting retirements) between one-half and all (and on the average nearly three-fourths) of total gross capital expenditures were financed by the issuance of financial instruments in one form or another rather than out of the funds of the sectors making the capital expenditures. These ratios, of course, are a combination of comparable ratios for individual sectors, which show considerable variation. They are further influenced by the fact that some part of total issues of financial instruments, particularly by central governments and to a lesser extent by consumers, is not connected with capital expenditures but rather is used to defray current outlay. (The main example of these are military expenditures, which in the period 1901–13 were substantial but not large enough to invalidate the comparison.) The ratios, moreover, have a substantial statistical upward bias because the estimates of capital expenditures that had to be used in the calculation of η exclude expenditures on consumer durables and take incomplete account of capital expenditures by the government, which together would increase κ (and hence decrease η) by something like one-tenth to one-fifth of its measured value, i.e. such estimates would reduce the external financing ratio for the average of the five countries to between 50 and 60 per cent. Not too much importance should be attached to differences among countries in view of the indirect method of calculation and the roughness of the numerator and the denominator. The ranking of the five countries—relatively high values of the ratio for Germany and Japan and relatively low values for the United States and France—however, is not unreasonable.

During the Postwar Period 1949–63

For this period the nationwide external financing ratio (η) can be estimated indirectly, i.e. by dividing the nonfinancial issue ratio (δ) by the capital formation ratio (κ) for all eighteen countries of Table 3–9 for which the volume of nonfinancial issues is known or can be approximated. The more interesting sectoral external financing ratios, however, are limited to the smaller number of countries—about one dozen—and sometimes to the considerably shorter periods for which sectorized flow-of-funds statements are available. This material does permit some elementary international comparisons notwithstanding many shortcomings of the data and the very poor representation of underdeveloped countries.

For all eighteen countries and the entire period of 1949–63 the average value of η (net nonfinancial issues divided by gross capital formation) is close to 0.60 if the denominator excludes consumer durables, while it is slightly below 0.50 if consumer durables are included, a calculation which appears to be more appropriate since part of new issues, though generally a small one, is used to finance the acquisition of consumer durables by the household sector. This means that on this very aggregative basis about half, or three-fifths, of capital expenditures are financed externally by the incurrence of debt or by the issuance of equity securities, while the remaining one-half or two-fifths are supplied internally by gross saving which may be divided somewhat arbitrarily into earned capital consumption allowances and net saving.

While the range of η of individual countries shown in Table 3–9 is wide—from 0.27 to 0.99 (excluding the U.S.S.R.) if consumer durables are included in the denominator—there is no substantial difference between the averages for the fourteen developed and for the four underdeveloped countries. No far-reaching conclusions can be drawn from this fact in view of the insufficient representation of the latter group. However, an even rougher estimate for all sixteen underdeveloped countries covered in this study does not point to an average value of η much different from 0.60 for this group of countries. The considerable variance in η among the eighteen, or thirty-five countries must therefore be explained primarily by less obvious, and probably often by historical and institutional factors.

TABLE 3–9

Indirect Estimation of η for 1949–63 in Selected Countries

	Net Domestic Nonfinancial Issue Ratio (δ) (1)	Net Foreign Issue Ratio (1956–63) (ξ) (2)	Total Nonfinancial Issue Ratio[a] ($\delta - \xi$) (3)	Gross Capital Formation Ratio (κ) Excluding Consumer Durables (4)	Gross Capital Formation Ratio (κ) Including Consumer Durables (5)	Inferred Value of External Financing Ratio (η) (6)
Australia	14.8	−1.2	16.0	26.8	38.0	.42
Belgium	12.8	.3	12.8	17.8	26.0	.49
Canada	12.7	−3.0	15.7	24.0	30.0	.52
France	11.5	.2	11.5	22.2	38.0	.30
Germany	10.0	.9	10.0	24.6	33.0	.33
Great Britain	9.7	1.7	9.7	15.9	26.0	.37
India	4.7	−2.4	7.1	9.9	12.0	.59
Israel	30.0	−4.1	34.1	30.3	38.0	.89
Italy	14.5	−0.2	14.7	22.0	25.0	.59
Japan	35.0	−0.5	35.5	32.7	36.0	.99
Mexico	11.0	−1.8	12.8	21.0	24.0	.53
New Zealand	9.0	−0.9	9.9	25.1	35.0	.28
Norway	10.8	−2.0	12.8	29.6	36.0	.36
Sweden	8.7	−0.4	9.1	21.7	27.0	.34
U.S.A.	9.8	.2	9.8	17.6	26.6	.37
U.S.S.R.	4.0		4.0	27.0	30.0	.13
Venezuela	8.0	1.4	8.0	25.8	30.0	.27
Yugoslavia	18.0		18.0	30.0	34.0	.53

[a] See note to col. 3.

Sources: Col. 1: Table 3–4, col. 8.

Col. 2: R. W. Goldsmith, *The Determinants of Financial Structure* (Paris, OECD Development Center, 1966), Table 5, except for Mexico, for which revised figures are used (Goldsmith, *Financial Development of Mexico.*)

Col. 3: Col. 1 minus col. 2 when the figure is negative. Conceptually the numerator of the external financing ratio of the nonfinancial sectors should include only foreign issues of nonfinancial sectors, but such figures are not easily available for a substantial number of countries or long periods of time. Substitution of the more common figures for net foreign balance of all sectors, which can be obtained from the balance of payments, may be permissible where it can be assumed that the balance is dominated by capital imports of the nonfinancial sectors and capital movements in the opposite direction are relatively small. When this assumption is not justified, the use of the net foreign balance instead of the foreign issues of the nonfinancial sectors is likely to understate the total volume of issues and hence also the external financing ratio. A similar dilemma exists in the case of countries with a positive net foreign balance. If this may be assumed to represent mainly capital exports offset only to a minor extent by issues of nonfinancial sectors to foreigners, it may be best to disregard the net foreign balance in the calculation of the external financing ratio. This procedure has been followed here because it seems applicable to some of the countries with a positive net foreign balance and because the necessary data on foreign issues by nonfinancial sectors to foreigners could not easily be secured for countries where the assumption is doubtful. It seems, however, that foreign issues in these countries are small enough compared to domestic issues of nonfinancial sectors that their omission does not seriously affect any major conclusion that can be derived from the external financing ratio as here calculated.

Col. 4: U.N., *Yearbook of National Accounts Statistics*, various issues (some of the ratios refer to periods slightly shorter than 1949–63), except for U.S.S.R. and Yugoslavia for which figures are rough estimates based on data for second half of period.

Col. 5: Estimate for consumer durables based on 1955–63 relationship of gross domestic capital formation including and excluding consumer durables derived from data in U.N., *Yearbook of National Accounts Statistics, 1965*, except for U.S.A., where Department of Commerce data for 1949–63 were used and for lines 5, 7–12, 16, and 17, which are rough estimates based on partial data or on relationships in comparable countries.

Col. 6: Col. 3 divided by col. 5.

Such an explanation requires a much more intensive analysis of the situation in individual countries than is possible here, an analysis which would in any case be severely hampered by the absence of reliable figures and relevant analytical studies for many if not for most countries. Thus the relatively high values of η for Japan and Israel may be connected with an extraordinarily high rate of growth, which requires primary reliance on external financing. (There is no inconsistency in values of η very close to or even above unity since part of the proceeds of new issues is used not to defray capital expenditures—the denominator of the ratio—but to permit the increase in items like trade receivables and transactions cash which may be substantial in a rapidly expanding economy.)

Any serious analysis of η must take account of the differences in the ratio among sectors because the values of η for different sectors may be presumed to reflect sectorally varying factors, and because the share of the several sectors in total nonfinancial issues differs among countries. This is evident from Table 3–10 even though the table covers less than a dozen countries and distinguishes only three broad sectors.[10] Interpretation of the data is made difficult

10. The values of η for a given country in this table need not be identical with those in Table 3–9 because the periods covered differ, in some cases substantially. In fact, however, the difference is small—on the average for the eleven countries only 0.07 even if the sign of the difference is disregarded, and it is negligible if the value of the two averages rather than those of the components are compared.

It would have been possible for several countries to separate by rough estimates the household, business, and government sectors where the two of them are now combined in the flow-of-funds statistics, and hence in Table 3–10, by using material not included in these statistics, e.g. on government debt, on capital expenditures on dwellings and consumer durables, and on home mortgages. It might also have been possible to make the scope of the three sectors more nearly comparable by similar additional rough estimates. No attempt has been made in this direction because of limitation of resources and the uncertain promise of reliable results. The standardization of the dozen or more of national sectorized flow-of-funds statistics now being published, however, remains an important, though very laborious, task still to be done.

by differences in definition, particularly in the allocation of public enterprises and the housing sector. One significant result that emerges is, it would seem, the fact that in most countries the external financing ratio of the nonfinancial enterprise sector is not very far from 0.50, falling in most cases within the range of approximately 0.40 to 0.60. The chief exception again is Japan, where the ratio is considerably higher. The wide variations of the ratio for the government sector are partly due to differences in the treatment of public enterprises. The substantial differences in the external financing ratio of the household sector among the three countries for which the data are available—high for United States and Australia, low for France—seem to reflect genuine differences in the extent to which the purchase of homes and consumer durables is externally financed; the poor organization and high interest rates in this sector of the French capital market force households to rely much more on internal funds that in the United States and Australia, where external financing in these fields is easier and cheaper.

The external financing ratio of the postwar period of about three-fifths (excluding consumer durables) does not on the average appear to differ greatly from that estimated for the period before World War I, at least not for developed countries (the five countries for which the comparison can be made—Table 3–11—may be regarded as representative of these). This similarity is, however, the result of considerable variations in individual countries. As a result the range of the values of η for individual countries is somewhat wider in the postwar period than it was half a century earlier.

These remarks, based on the scarce aggregative and comprehensive data now available, obviously can do no more than to provide an idea of the order of magnitude involved and to raise questions rather than to answer them. Some information on the external financing ratio of nonfinancial corporations can be obtained from special studies for a few

Table 3–10

Net External Financing Ratio (η) for Main Sectors and Selected Countries, 1948–63

PER CENT OF GROSS CAPITAL EXPENDITURES

<table>
<tr><th rowspan="2"></th><th rowspan="2">Period</th><th rowspan="2">Government</th><th rowspan="2">Nonfinancial Business</th><th colspan="2">Household</th><th colspan="2">All Sectors</th></tr>
<tr><th>Excluding Consumer</th><th>Including Durables</th><th>Excluding Consumer</th><th>Including Durables</th></tr>
<tr><td>1. Australia</td><td>1953–61</td><td>.68</td><td>.54</td><td>.55</td><td>.23</td><td>.57</td><td>.40</td></tr>
<tr><td>2. Belgium</td><td>1958–62</td><td>2.30</td><td colspan="2">.51</td><td></td><td>.70</td><td>.53</td></tr>
<tr><td>3. Canada</td><td>1949–54</td><td>.12</td><td colspan="2">.53</td><td></td><td>.51</td><td>.39</td></tr>
<tr><td>4. France</td><td>1953–63</td><td>1.64</td><td>.48</td><td>.27</td><td>.09</td><td>.57</td><td>.42</td></tr>
<tr><td>5. Germany</td><td>1950–63</td><td>.39</td><td colspan="2">.42</td><td></td><td>.42</td><td>.33</td></tr>
<tr><td>6. Great Britain</td><td>1958–61</td><td>1.02</td><td colspan="2">.61</td><td></td><td>.76</td><td>.51</td></tr>
<tr><td>7. Japan</td><td>1953–63</td><td>.39</td><td colspan="2">1.24</td><td></td><td>1.02</td><td>.80</td></tr>
<tr><td>8. Norway</td><td>1956–63</td><td>.44[a]</td><td>.42[b]</td><td></td><td></td><td>.43</td><td>.36</td></tr>
<tr><td>9. Sweden</td><td>1958–62</td><td></td><td></td><td>.68[c]</td><td></td><td>.37</td><td>.27</td></tr>
<tr><td>10. U.S.A.</td><td>1949–63</td><td>.52</td><td>.41</td><td>.58</td><td>.27</td><td>.48</td><td>.35</td></tr>
<tr><td>11. Yugoslavia</td><td>1957–63</td><td>.62</td><td></td><td></td><td></td><td>.64</td><td>.59</td></tr>
</table>

[a] Including government enterprises.
[b] Housing expenditures allocated to col. 2.
[c] All housing.

Sources:

Line 1: Reserve Bank of Australia, *Flow-of-Funds, Australia, 1953–54 to 1961–62* (1965).
Line 2: Banque Nationale de Belgique, *Bulletin d'Information.*
Line 3: Hood, *Financing of Economic Activity in Canada.*
Line 4: *Les Comptes de la Nation 1949–1959* and *1963–1964.*
Line 5: Deutsche Bundesbank, *Monastberichte.*
Line 6: J. Revell, MS.
Line 7: Bank of Japan, *Flow-of-Funds Accounts in Japan 1954–1963.*
Line 8: Statistisk Sentralbyra, *Kredittmarkedstatistikk* (1955, 1963).
Line 9: Sveriges Riksbank (BIS mimeo.).
Line 10: Federal Reserve Board, *Flow-of-Funds Annual 1963–64* and *1945–62.*
Line 11: Narodna Banka, *Annual Report 1965.*

TABLE 3–11

Comparison of Inferred Value of η before World War I and after World War II for Five Countries[a]

	1901–13	1949–63	Difference
France	.64	.52	−.12
Germany	.80	.41	−.39
Great Britain	.67	.61	−.06
Japan	1.00	1.09	+.09
U.S.A.	.50	.56	+.06
Average	.72	.64	−.08

[a] Consumer durables are excluded in denominator.

Sources: *Col. 1:* Table 3–8, col. 3.
Col. 2: Table 3–9, cols. 3 and 4.

additional countries for part of the postwar period,[11] but it would not significantly add to our understanding of the causes of international differences in η even in this sector. A specialized intensive study, standardizing the basic data to provide a basis for genuine international comparisons, is needed if progress is to be made in this field.

THE ISSUES OF GOVERNMENT SECURITIES

Government securities are the only important component of the new issues of financial instruments by nonfinancial sectors, or of the stock of such instruments outstanding, for which data for most of the thirty-five countries are availa-

11. In the United Kingdom, for instance, the value of η for 2,549 nonfinancial companies, accounting for a substantial proportion of total assets of all nonfinancial businesses, was 0.53 for the period 1949–53 if tax and interest accruals are included among issues and 0.45 if they are excluded (B. Tew and R. F. Henderson, eds. *Studies in Company Finance* [Cambridge, Cambridge University Press, 1959], p. 272). In India a group of 1,000 to 1,300 joint stock companies, accounting for a high proportion of all corporations in the private sector, in 1956–63 had an external financing ratio of slightly above 0.60 (*Reserve Bank of India Bulletin* [Sept. 1961, Nov. 1965]). In Venezuela the external financing ratio for maunfacturing and commercial corporations in 1961 was 0.61 (Banco Central de Venezuela, *El Fluir de Fondos de Capital* [Caracas, 1964], p. 75). All these figures fit in reasonably well with the data in Table 3–11, Column 2.

ble, and for which it is possible to extend them back to the nineteenth century, even though complete comparability can hardly be achieved without engaging in a major undertaking of refining the statistical data now at hand. This is the reason for presenting in this section the material available on the ratio of net issues of the central government to national product.

In terms of the basic equations of Chapter 2 we are dealing in this section with a component of the ratio of domestic nonfinancial issues to gross national product, a ratio (δ_g) which has parallels in the ratios of the net issues of the household, enterprise, and foreign sectors (δ_h, δ_b and ξ). The international comparative material is not yet adequate to treat the ratios δ_h and δ_b in the same way, while ξ is discussed in the final section of this chapter. Actually the figures that had to be used in this section cover in most cases both domestic and foreign issues of governments, the former entirely predominating in developed countries. Hence this section strictly speaking deals with part of both nonfinancial domestic and foreign issues—in symbols $\delta_g + \xi_g$.

The practical necessity of using the par values of public debt outstanding and the differences in such values between benchmark dates as the means of measuring the net issues of government securities during the period does not constitute a serious drawback, because we may assume that most government securities are issued and retired at or very close to par, even though the price of outstanding long-term issues may sometimes vary considerably and decline far below par.[12]

12. Probably the classical case is that of the British consols (having no definite maturity and a coupon yield of 3 per cent to 1889, of 2¾ per cent from 1889 to 1902 and of 2½ per cent ever since) with a market value (December averages) of 94 in 1860, 99 in 1880, 97 in 1900, 72 in 1913, 53 in 1929, 54 in 1939, 78 in 1948 and as little as 45 in 1963. Notwithstanding these sharp fluctuations virtually all British government securities during the last century were issued or redeemed at or very close to par value, but of course at quite different coupon and yield rates.

Much more difficult problems arise in connection with coverage, problems which have considerable importance in view of differences in the structure of the government sector in different countries. In very centralized countries without a substantial government enterprise sector—a rather rare combination—it may be sufficient to base the calculations on the total debt (long and short, domestic and foreign) of the central government. In other, more numerous countries in which local authorities (in federations the constituent states) are substantial issuers of securities, and in which there exists a large government enterprise sector that finances itself partly by the sale of its own securities, limitation of the statistics to direct obligations of the central government would seriously misrepresent the role of the government in the financial superstructure. Even more difficult problems are presented by the issues of local governments or of business enterprises which are guaranteed by the central government as to principal or interest or both. Although some of these guaranteed securities are so close to direct government issues that the market is hardly making any distinction between them, they have been excluded here. This has been done, apart from the practical reasons that comprehensive coverage is not feasible, because in most cases guaranteed securities differ substantially from direct government securities and because it is very difficult to draw a demarcation line once one includes guaranteed securities. (How, for instance, are home mortgages or bank deposits insured by the government to be treated?)

Government securities, more narrowly or more broadly defined, fulfill four main functions in a country's financial structure:

1. They represent a type of security competing with other investments, particularly with other claims, on the basis strictly of yield and risk as evaluated by investors.

2. Sometimes government securities enjoy tax advantages which make them more attractive for broader or narrower groups of domestic or foreign investors than competing taxable investments of the same coupon, maturity, and risk. In

this case the choice made by investors may be, and generally will still be, entirely rational, and government securities enjoy an advantage which is parallel to the tariff protection of home-produced commodities.

3. Because of legislation or tradition, substantial amounts of funds must be or at least are regularly invested in government securities, even if the yield differential is greater than the risk and tax differentials and consideration of liquidity would justify. This is akin to protection by import quotas or similar administrative measures in international trade.

4. Some types of government securities, particularly those of short maturity, have developed into one of the standard liquid assets and are used widely as balancing items in the asset structure of large groups of economic units and thus acquire the quality of near-money to an even greater extent than term deposits in banks and similar financial instruments.

For a thorough analysis of the role of government securities in the financial structure one would wish to separate these four types of holdings of government securities. This, however, is not possible in practice and hardly even feasible in theory if one looks for operational definitions of the four types. We may, however, come near to such a separation by investigating the distribution of the holdings of government securities among the different sectors in the economy, because it would appear that some relation exists between the character of the holder and the nature of and the motives for holding government securities. In practice, the holding of central government securities by banks of issue, by deposit banks (with some reservations), by government insurance and trust funds, and by large nonfinancial corporations generally do not belong in the first and second of the four categories of holdings distinguished above but are predominantly of the third and fourth type. We shall, therefore, in the second half of this section devote some attention to the sectoral distribution of holdings of government securities in order to see whether significant differences in the distribution exist among countries which now are at a different stage of their financial development and to ascertain whether important trends can be observed in the distribution over the last fifty to one hundred years.

The Aggregate Debt of the Central Government

One of the main characteristics of the ratio of the net issuance of government securities to national product as well as of the ratio of the total amount of government securities outstanding at any one date to either national product or, more appropriately, to national wealth is the very great variance among countries and among periods and the dependence of these ratios, not primarily on the stage of economic or financial development, but on historical accidents, if participation in a major war may be so called; on the scope of government activities, particularly the participation of the government in the transportation, communication, heavy industry and housing sectors; and on the division of functions, primarily of capital expenditures and their financing, among the central government, the states (in federalized countries), and local authorities. This explains why the highest ratios of the net issuance of government securities to national product, or of the volume of government securities outstanding to national wealth, are always found during or at the end of long and costly wars. From this point of view it is unfortunate that none of the standard benchmark dates used throughout this study coincide with the end of World War I or World War II, although the 1948 date is near enough to the end of World War II to show the effects of that conflict clearly.

To give a few examples—the relevant data are shown in Table 3–12—the debt of the U.S. government at the end of the Civil War was equal to about two-fifths of national product and one-tenth of national wealth. The ratios were considerably higher at the end of World War II when the federal government's debt amounted to almost one-half of national wealth and slightly exceeded one year's national product. The comparable figures are much higher for Eng-

TABLE 3–12

Ratio of Central Government Debt to National Product and Wealth before and after Major Wars

	1815	1871	1913	1919	1938	1945	1963
			Ratio to gross national product				
U.S.A.	.15	.40[a]	.03	.27	.43	1.17	.52
Great Britain	2.50	.65	.27	1.15	1.45	2.35	1.01
France	.40[b]	.80[c]	.70	2.00[d]	1.15	1.80	.38[e]
Germany		.25	.38	2.00[d,f]	.19	4.00[d]	.10[e]
Japan			.56	.18	.67	1.45[h]	.04
			Ratio to national wealth[g]				
U.S.A.	.06	.10[a]	.01	.08	.10	.47	.15
Great Britain	.30	.10	.04	.40[h]	.60	.95[i]	.33
France	.05	.10	.13				.10[e]
Germany		.04	.07				.03
Japan		.00	.11	.03			.01

[a] 1865. [b] 1819. [c] 1872.
[d] Based on rough estimates of national product.
[e] 1961. [f] 1918.
[g] All ratios based on national wealth, except for 1963, are to be regarded as very rough estimates.
[h] 1920. [i] 1948.

land. Looking at the three major wars in which the United Kingdom has been involved during the last two hundred years, government debt equaled nearly two and one-half years' national product and almost one-third of the national wealth at the end of the Napoleonic wars. After a protracted decline during most of the next century to only three months' national product in 1913, that debt exceeded one year's national product at the end of World War I and rose to approximately 100 per cent of national wealth and nearly two and one half years' gross national product at the end of World War II.

Instances of high ratios of government borrowing or debt to national product or wealth as a result of inflation primarily due to and sustained by government deficits cannot be found because the rapid rise in the price level continuously wipes out—in comparison to national product or wealth—most if not virtually all or even more than the government debts being created in the inflationary process. Thus in Germany at the end of one of the most pronounced hyperinflations ever observed, the government's debt was negligible, and, even after a partial ex post facto revaluation following the end of the inflation and the introduction of a new currency, the central government's debt in 1926 equaled less than 20 per cent of national product and only 5 per cent of national wealth.

The movements in the ratio of Germany's government debt during and after World War II illustrates another characteristic of government debt—its liability to repudiation. Early in 1945 the debt of the German government at approximately 380 billion RM represented almost 400 per cent of gross national product of the last prewar year (1938), when the actual ratio had been about 20 per cent. As a result of the almost complete repudiation of this debt by the successor states, the public debt of the German Federal Republic in 1950 (consisting mostly of equalization certificates—*Ausgleichsforderungen*—arising out of the old debt) was below 15 per cent of national product. The public debt of Russia has been repudiated twice—once formally and completely after the revolution of 1917 and once informally and partially in connection with the currency reform of the 1950s. Complete or partial, temporary or permanent repudiations and reductions of public debt, for political or financial reasons, have been far from rare in other countries, both in the nineteenth and the twentieth centuries. For this reason, among others, the financial importance of public debt in a country's financial structure is better measured by the ratio of net issues of public debt to national product than by the change in the ratios of public debt outstanding to either national product or national wealth.

In the cases discussed so far we have been dealing with what could be called deadweight debt, i.e. debt no part of which has led to the creation of civilian durable assets which form part of national wealth. Much more important from an economic—though not necessarily from a financial or public finance point of view—is government debt, the proceeds of which are used to finance nonmilitary tangible assets such as roads, schools, government buildings, public housing, telephone and telegraph installations, power plants, and industrial enterprises, whether fully or partly owned by the government. Most of the debt of local authorities has been issued to finance capital expenditures of this type; in fact capital expenditures usually are in excess of the increase in local authority's debt even after allowing for depreciation on their reproducible tangible assets. Much or most of the peacetime debt of many small and a few large countries is of the same character. It is not possible to separate statistically deadweight debt from other debt, except that one may assume all increases in debt during war periods to represent deadweight debt. From the point of view of the effect on a country's financial structure this distinction, although interesting, fortunately is not essential. It makes no difference to the owner, except very indirectly, whether the proceeds of a government security which he holds were used to pay for guns or for gasworks, or to cover current deficits rather than to build schools.

The most important figures bearing on the role of the central government's debt (generally excluding government

Table 3–13

Ratio of Net Increases in Central Government Debt to Aggregate Gross National Product, 1861–1963
UNWEIGHTED COUNTRY AVERAGES (PER CENT)

	All Countries		Developed Countries		Less Developed Countries	
	No.	Aver. Ratio	No.	Aver. Ratio	No.	Aver. Ratio
1861–1880	6	1.5	6	1.5		
1881–1900	14	1.0	13	1.0	1	.4
1901–1913	21	1.2	17	1.5	4	.2
1914–1929	25	3.6	17	4.7	8	1.0
1930–1938	29	1.4	17	1.5	12	.4
1939–1948	32	6.0	18	9.5	14	.9
1949–1963	35	1.9	19	1.9	16	1.8
1881–1963[a]		2.3		3.1		.8

[a] Average of all periods, weighted by number of years in each period.
Source: Table 3–14.

enterprises) in the flow of capital funds are summarized in Table 3–13 in the form of average ratios of the net change in the central government's debt to gross national product, for all countries together and for developed and underdeveloped countries separately, for seven periods between the benchmark dates from 1860 to 1963. While variations among countries are very marked, such averages are useful in establishing the orders of magnitude and in indicating the main trends. The underlying data for individual countries are shown in Table 3–14.

TABLE 3–14

Ratio of Change in Central Government Debt to Aggregate Gross National Product for Individual Countries, 1881–1963

PER CENT

	1881 to 1900[a] (1)	1901 to 1913 (2)	1914 to 1929 (3)	1930 to 1938 (4)	1939 to 1948 (5)	1949 to 1963 (6)
Argentina		0.5	1.3	1.4	4.8	4.1
Australia		3.1	8.1	3.1	13.5	2.1
Belgium	1.8	2.7	4.3	0.6	10.5	3.3
Brazil			2.3	4.4	2.2	4.1
Canada	0.6	0.6	2.9	2.8	12.0	0.8
Denmark		0.6	0.7	−0.1	5.2	−0.2
Egypt-U.A.R.		−0.5	0.2	−0.2	1.0	2.4
France	1.5	0.6	13.2	−2.3	5.0	1.7
Germany	1.5	1.4	15.4[b,c]	1.9	21.3[c]	0.7
Great Britain	−0.2	0.0	9.2	1.6	18.0	1.4
Greece			0.6	0.2	9.8	2.2
India	1.4	0.6	1.1	0.3	2.2	3.1
Israel						15.2
Italy	1.4	0.6	4.2	4.8	10.0	−1.1
Jamaica					1.4	1.7
Japan	1.2	5.1	2.0	8.1	10.2	0.2
Mexico		1.0[d]	1.0[d]	1.0[d]	1.0[d]	0.4
Netherlands	0.5	0.0	1.7	2.5	14.7	−0.2
New Zealand	3.5	5.1	8.0	2.9	8.3	2.5
Nigeria				0	−0.1	0.6
Norway	1.3	1.1	2.1	−0.1	5.4	0.3
Pakistan						1.5
Philippines			0.2	0	1.2	1.5
Puerto Rico				−0.1	−0.4	1.2
Rhodesia					15.0[d]	9.0
Russia-U.S.S.R.		1.7	4.5[b]	1.5	1.7	1.1

South Africa			4.3	1.2	7.4	3.5
Spain		−0.5	2.5	2.0[d]	3.1	2.7
Sweden	0.4	0.7	0.9	0.9	4.9	1.3
Switzerland	0.1	0.2	1.6	0.6	3.8	−0.5
Thailand					0.8	1.2
Trinidad					0.8	1.5
United States	−0.3	−0.0	1.2	2.9	12.6	0.8
Venezuela				−0.3	0.0	0.8
Yugoslavia				−1.1		0.0
Average	1.1	1.2	3.7	1.4	6.5	2.0

[a] Averages for 1861–80: France 2.5; Germany 1.1; Great Britain −0.2; Italy 3.4; Sweden 0.9; United States 1.3; six countries 1.5.

[b] Averages, weighted by number of years, of rough estimates: Germany, 1914–18, 40 per cent; 1919–23, 7 per cent; 1924–29, 2 per cent; Russia, 1914–17, 15 per cent; 1918–29, 1 per cent.

[c] The figures for Germany refer to the periods 1914–18 and 1939–44 respectively, i.e. they represent rough estimates of the ratio of the increase in the central government's debt to the aggregate gross national product during these two periods. (The increases in central government debt during the two periods were in the order of 150 billion Marks and 380 billion Reichsmarks, respectively.) Any ratio including the hyperinflation period of 1919–23 without distinction would be meaningless. The ratio of increase in government debt for 1945 through 1948 was negligible, Germany during that period having no government of its own.

[d] Rough estimates.

Sources: Government debt:
Cols. 1, 2: Miscellaneous national sources.
Cols. 3, 4: U.N., *Public Debt, 1914–1946* (Lake Success, 1948).
Cols. 5, 6: U.N., *Statistical Yearbook* (New York), various issues.
National product: Based on Appendix V.

Of the five features which stand out in Table 3–13, the first is the sharp increase in the ratios caused by World Wars I and II, increases understated in the tables because both benchmark periods, and particularly that running from 1914 to 1929, include nonwar years; and because the averages include countries not participating in hostilities.[13]

13. There is also a conceptual problem, the treatment of the actual (U.S.S.R.) or effective (Germany) repudiation of the government debt accumulated during World War I. This difficulty has been overcome somewhat arbitrarily by deriving the ratio of net issues of government debt to national product for the entire period 1914–29—the specific war period 1914–19 is not affected—as the average of the ratios for 1914–19 and 1920–29, weighted by the number of years in each period; thus, in effect, the repudiation is ignored.

In order to remove these limitations, the relevant data have been assembled in Table 3–15 for about one dozen countries which actively participated in World War I. The absence of reliable estimates of national product for several

TABLE 3–15

Ratio of Net Issues of Central Government Debt to Gross National Product, 1914–29

PER CENT

	Ratio			Share of War Years in Total Debt Increase
	1914–19	1920–29	1914–29	
Australia	19.0	5.4	8.1	.47
Belgium	19.0[a]	3.0	4.3	.36
Canada	12.3	−1.3	2.9	1.31
France	40.0[a]	8.5	13.2	.46
Germany	40.0[a]	4.0	18.0[a]	.75[b]
Great Britain	28.6	− .8	9.2	1.06
India	.7	1.3	1.1	.20
Italy	20.9	1.0	4.2	.79
Japan	1.9	2.1	2.0	.21
New Zealand	17.0[a]	4.4	8.0	.60
Russia-U.S.S.R.	16.0[a]	1.0[a]	5.0[a]	.90[b]
South Africa	4.2	2.7	3.2	.39
U.S.A.	6.3	− .9	1.2	1.54
Average, all countries	17.4	2.3	6.1	.70
Average, excluding India and Japan	20.2	2.5	7.0	.78

[a] Round figures due to roughness of national product estimates.
[b] Disregarding formal or effective repudiation of war debt.

Sources: Government debt: U.N., *Public Debt 1914–1946.*
National product: Based on Appendix V.

important countries—France, Germany and Russia—imparts a substantial margin of error to some ratios, but it cannot seriously affect the overall picture.

It then appears that among the eleven main belligerents (omitting India and Japan whose war expenditures and debt increase were relatively small) the net issues of government securities were equal to no less than 20 per cent of gross national product of the period from 1914 through 1919. The ratio was close to 30 per cent in Great Britain and reached 40 per cent in France and Germany. These are unprecedented proportions, neither duplicated during World War II nor anticipated during the Napoleonic wars,[14] proportions which are due to the combination of high ratios of military expenditures to national product and of borrowing to military expenditures.

These ratios overstate the absorption of domestic resources by the central government's borrowing because they include issues sold abroad. Foreign borrowing was very important in World War I for most of the Allies outside of North America. Thus of the total net increase in the government's debt in the years 1914 through 1919, one-sixth represented foreign debt in the case of Great Britain and Belgium, and almost one-third in the case of France and Australia. The domestic burden was further reduced by liquidation of foreign assets, mainly in the case of Great Britain and France. The subsequent repudiation or writing down of much of the foreign war debt does not, of course, affect the absorption of resources by the borrowing government in either the earlier or the later period. The figures for the World War II period are much less affected by these considerations since foreign borrowing was relatively small, intergovernmental grants of one form or another being used instead.

In contrast, the ratio of net issues of government securities to national product during the period 1920–29 was quite low in the former belligerents, partly because of sub-

14. The ratio of net issues of government securities to national product during the war period (1794–1815) may be estimated at about 7 to 8 per cent in Great Britain, using P. Deane and B. R. Mitchell's figures—*Abstract of British Historical Statistics* (Cambridge, Cambridge University Press, 1962), p. 366—for national income, although the ratio reached 15 per cent in some years. In France the ratio was undoubtedly much lower as total government debt at the end of 1819 amounted to only 3½ billion francs. Rough estimates point to a value of between 2 and 3 per cent of the country's total national product in the period from 1790 to 1819.

stantial retirements of debt in several important countries, particularly the United States and the United Kingdom. For all twelve countries (excluding South Africa, for which no data are available before World War I) the ratio averaged 2.3 per cent for 1920–29, and thus was not much in excess of the average of 1.9 per cent registered for 1900–13. The figures for the entire period 1914–29 in Table 3–14, column 4 thus are not representative for the period as a whole, neither for participants in World War I, nor even for a few European neutrals who borrowed considerable amounts during World War I to defray military and other expenditures intended to insure their neutrality (e.g. Switzerland and Sweden).

Turning to World War II, which is fairly well represented by the standard period 1939–48, it is found that the ratio of net issues of government securities to aggregate national product was in excess of 10 per cent for most active belligerents. The ratio was as high as approximately 35 per cent for Germany, 17 per cent for the United Kingdom, 14 per cent for Australia, 13 per cent for the United States and the Netherlands, and 10 per cent for Japan but amounted to only 5 per cent for Italy and 3½ per cent for France. The lowest ratios are shown by countries which suffered a considerable dose of inflation immediately after the war, which reduces the burden of the government debt. Most of these are very high ratios, whether compared to the averages for nonwar periods or with the total issue ratios for nonfinancial sectors.

The second feature is that in periods not affected by major wars the average ratio of the net issuance of central government securities to aggregate national product has stayed between 1 and 2 per cent. These values are not negligible, although not dominant either, in comparison to the ratio of the net issues of all nonfinancial sectors to national product, a ratio which has been found on the average to be in the order of one-tenth. Variations in the ratio among countries are large. On the one hand there are several countries in which the issues of central government securities in peacetime have constituted only a small proportion of total issues by nonfinancial sectors. This is the case before World War I, for example, in the United States, the United Kingdom, Switzerland, and the Netherlands. On the other hand, the issues of the central government have been quite important in relation to gross national product and to all nonfinancial issues in several rapidly growing non-European countries before World War I, for example, Australia, New Zealand, and Japan. They have also been significant in some European countries, particularly in connection with large capital expenditures by these governments on railroads, e.g. by Germany and Russia.

Thirdly, the average ratio of the issuance of central government securities to aggregate national product has been only negligibly higher in the 1920s, the 1930s and in the period following World War II with approximately 1½ per cent than it was in the two prewar periods of 1881–1900 and 1901–13, for both of which they average close to 1¼ per cent. Of the sixteen countries for which the calculation can be made, the postwar ratio (1948–63) is above the pre-World War I ratio (1881–1913) in seven countries (Belgium, Great Britain, India, Italy, Spain, Sweden, and the United States); it is lower in six countries (Australia, Denmark, Germany, Japan, New Zealand, and Norway); and it is approximately the same in three countries (Canada, Netherlands, and Switzerland).

Fourthly, for the limited number of less developed countries for which the information is available, the average ratio was much lower than for developed countries until World War II, and it failed to show the sharp increases during both wars which are such an outstanding feature in the record of developed countries.

The relation between the government issue ratio of developed and less developed countries—and this is the fifth feature—changed sharply during the period following World War II. For these fifteen years the ratios were virtually identical at slightly below 2 per cent of national product for both groups of countries. Part of this "catching up" of the less developed countries is the result of substantial borrowing from international and U.S. lending agencies, and another part reflects a limited revival of international private lending. Most of the increase, however, was internal in origin and to a good extent resulted from borrowing from financial institutions, particularly in countries which experienced a substantial protracted inflation (e.g. Argentina, and Brazil). Among developed countries the government issue ratios were generally highest in the non-European rapidly growing countries (Israel, Rhodesia, South Africa, New Zealand).

Sectoral Distribution of Central Government Debt

The distribution of the central government's debt among the main groups of holders, shown in Table 3–16 for a recent date for the seventeen out of the thirty-five countries for which data are readily available, is characterized by the following features.

1. Most of the total debt of the central government is domestically held. The share of foreign-held debt is considerably higher in less developed countries, where much of it is in the possession of international or United States lending agencies, than it is in developed countries.

2. In all countries financial institutions (including government social security funds) are the largest groups of holders and account with very few exceptions for more than one-half of the total domestic debt of the central government. The proportion is generally higher for less developed countries, where it is often above three-fourths and sometimes exceeds 90 per cent, than in developed countries, for which it averages slightly above one-half. The difference is due to the lack in the former of a substantial market for government securities among individuals and business enterprises. In most less developed countries, debt held outside of financial institutions is negligible.

3. Particularly interesting is the share of the central government's domestic debt held by the banking system. Here

the contrast between developed and less developed countries is especially pronounced. In developed countries the central bank on the average holds about 15 per cent of the central government's total domestic debt, the highest ratio being shown for Japan, which in this respect is closer to less developed countries. In one-half of the cases of developed countries the share of the central government's domestic debt held by the central bank is below one-tenth. In less developed countries, on the other hand, the central bank on the average owns one-half of the total domestic debt of the central government and thus holds about two-thirds of the central government's debt that is in the hands of all financial institutions. This distribution reflects the small absorptive capacity of the other financial institutions. In inflationary countries it also reflects the disinclination of deposit banks, because of the artificially low yield of most of these securities, to hold more than the amount of central government debt they are forced to own.

4. In contrast the average share of deposit banks is about the same in developed as in less developed countries. There are considerable variations in the ratio of the central government's debt held by deposit banks in developed countries. The range is usually between 10 and 20 per cent, but it is considerably higher, though not above 30 per cent, in some countries and considerably lower in a few of them. Less developed countries also show considerable variation, but the share of deposit banks again usually is not in excess of 30 per cent.

5. There is a clear distinction in the share of the central government's debt held by insurance (including government social security funds) and thrift organizations. In developed countries the share averages 30 per cent. In less developed countries differences are great. In some countries the share of insurance or thrift organizations is almost zero, while in a few others, where social security funds are of substantial importance, for instance in Brazil and Spain, these organizations hold more than 20 per cent of the central government's total domestic debt.

TABLE 3–16

Distribution of Central Government Debt, ca. 1960

PER CENT

<table>
<tr><th rowspan="2"></th><th rowspan="2">Date</th><th rowspan="2">Central Govern-ment</th><th rowspan="2">Other Govern-ment Units</th><th colspan="5">Financial Institutions</th><th rowspan="2">Other Domestic</th><th rowspan="2">Foreign and International Organizations</th></tr>
<tr><th>Total</th><th>Central Bank</th><th>Commercial Banks</th><th>Insurance Organiza-tions</th><th>Others</th></tr>
<tr><td>Australia</td><td>1960</td><td>18</td><td></td><td>40</td><td>11</td><td>24</td><td>5</td><td></td><td>23</td><td>19[d]</td></tr>
<tr><td>Belgium</td><td>1960</td><td></td><td></td><td>57</td><td>10</td><td>23</td><td>10</td><td>14</td><td>32</td><td>11[d]</td></tr>
<tr><td>Brazil[a]</td><td>1960</td><td>12</td><td></td><td>85</td><td>57</td><td>5</td><td>23</td><td></td><td>3</td><td></td></tr>
<tr><td>Canada</td><td>1960</td><td>5</td><td>4</td><td>43</td><td>15</td><td>17</td><td colspan="2">11</td><td>43</td><td>5</td></tr>
<tr><td>France</td><td>1960</td><td>2</td><td>9</td><td>37</td><td>8</td><td>10</td><td colspan="2">19</td><td>42</td><td>10</td></tr>
<tr><td>Germany[a,b]</td><td>1963</td><td></td><td></td><td>60</td><td>42</td><td colspan="3">18</td><td>40</td><td></td></tr>
<tr><td>Great Britain</td><td>1964</td><td>3</td><td>1</td><td>49</td><td>9</td><td>7</td><td>17</td><td>16</td><td>35</td><td>12</td></tr>
<tr><td>India[c]</td><td>1956</td><td>4</td><td>6</td><td>52</td><td>18</td><td>25</td><td>9</td><td></td><td>36</td><td>3</td></tr>
<tr><td>Italy</td><td>1959</td><td></td><td></td><td>65</td><td>13</td><td></td><td>52</td><td></td><td>27</td><td>8</td></tr>
<tr><td>Japan</td><td>1960</td><td>5</td><td></td><td>77</td><td>43</td><td>4</td><td>0</td><td>30[e]</td><td>18</td><td></td></tr>
<tr><td>New Zealand</td><td>1957</td><td>20</td><td>1</td><td>55</td><td>7</td><td>2</td><td>5</td><td>41</td><td>15</td><td>9[d]</td></tr>
<tr><td>Pakistan</td><td>1960</td><td>4</td><td></td><td>61</td><td>42</td><td>17</td><td colspan="2">2</td><td>19</td><td>16</td></tr>
<tr><td>South Africa</td><td>1963</td><td>68[f]</td><td>0</td><td>23</td><td></td><td></td><td>4</td><td></td><td>8</td><td>1</td></tr>
<tr><td>Spain</td><td>1960</td><td>10</td><td></td><td>68</td><td>16</td><td>28</td><td>2</td><td>22</td><td>17</td><td>5[d]</td></tr>
</table>

Sweden	1960	8	1	71	26	19	13	13	19	1[d]
Thailand	1960			82	70	12			8	10[d]
U.S.A.	1960	19	7	35	9	19	7		35	4

[a] Only domestic debt.
[b] Excluding currency reform debt.
[c] Only funded domestic (rupee) debt.
[d] Assuming all foreign currency debt held abroad.
[e] Including Trust Fund Bureau (28 per cent).
[f] Public Debt Commissioners.

Source: International Monetary Fund, *International Financial Statistics*, 1965–66 Supplement, except for *Reserve Bank of India Bulletin* (Mar. 1963).

6. The share of other domestic holders, mainly individuals, is of course the complement to that of financial institutions. In some developed countries these holders absorb almost one-half of the total debt of the central government, and on the average individuals and other nonfinancial holders account for about one-third of the total domestic debt of the central government. The substantial differences among developed countries can be explained partly by the financial history of these countries and by the degree of inflation which they have experienced. The supposedly negative relation between the degree of inflation and the percentage of the central government's debt held by individuals is, however, far from very marked. In less developed countries the share of nonfinancial holders is usually very small, although in a few cases it rises to close to one-fourth of the central government's total domestic debt.

If the very long view is taken, the present distribution of the central government's debt, particularly the large proportion held by financial institutions, represents a radical structural change that has taken place over the last century. Until well after the middle of the nineteenth century, virtually the entirety of government debt was held by individuals, simply because financial institutions of the type now owning large amounts of government debt were either not yet in existence or were still very small compared to the volume of government debt outstanding. During the second half of the nineteenth century, however, the importance of banks, thrift institutions, and insurance organizations and their holdings of government securities increased, as did those of specialized institutions holding government securities for the account of either other financial institutions or for individual trust accounts (the French Caisse des Dépôts, the British National Debt Commissioners, and the Japanese Trust Fund Bureau are examples) grew rapidly, at least in now developed countries. As a result the holdings of the obligations of the central government by these institutions have constituted a substantial proportion of the total amounts outstanding ever since the turn of the century. While the proportion generally has continued to increase during the last half-century, the increase has not been very marked; and it has varied considerably from country to country reflecting institutional differences, the tempo of increase in the total government debt outstanding, particularly during wars, which tends to increase the share of individuals' holdings, even though but temporarily, and the intensity and character of inflation. In this respect probably the three most interesting countries are Great Britain, France, and the United States.

While there is no statistical evidence, we may be fairly certain that most of the British government's large debt outstanding at the end of the Napoleonic wars to the extent of £840 million in 1820—an unprecedented 270 per cent of gross national product—was held by individuals.[15] Probably the only large institutional holding was that of the Bank of England, but it amounted to only about 2 per cent of the total outstanding.

In 1880, when the total government debt had declined to £765 million, then equal to only 75 per cent of gross national product, the Bank of England still held only 2 per cent of the total, as it had done in 1820. Now, however, the deposit banks owned 6 per cent of the total, the insurance companies another 1 per cent, and the savings banks through the National Debt Commissioners 10 per cent.[16] The amount of government debt then in the hands of the discount market is not known, but it cannot have been large compared to the total outstanding. The Paymaster General held £61 million, or 8 per cent of the total, in trust for suitors in the Court of Chancery,[17] but these represented

15. It is astonishing that nobody seems to have taken the trouble of making a systematic analysis of the distribution of the British government's debt during the nineteenth century, when it was one of the main, if not the principal, financial instrument outstanding in the country, and of the economic and financial effects of such a large debt held mostly by individuals.

16. Based on data in an unpublished manuscript by D. Sheppard.

17. E. L. Hargreaves, *The National Debt* (London, E. Arnold, 1930), p. 191.

TABLE 3–17

Distribution of British Central Government Domestic Securities, 1880–1963

PER CENT, EXCEPT LINE 1

	1880	1900	1913	1929	1937	1947	1963
1. Total outstanding[a] (millions of £)	765	704	706	7,596	7,119	25,151	30,222
2. Central government (including Exchange Equalization Account)					8	5	4
3. Local authorities					1	1	1
4. Financial institutions:							
Bank of England	2	5	5	1	6	7	9
Deposit banks	5	12	11	6	11	15	7
Savings banks[b]	10	25	35	5	4	10	10
Insurance organizations[c]	1	1	4	5	12	12	17
Other financial institutions } 5. Other domestic holders	82	57	46	83	55	39	6
5. Other domestic holders							34
6. Foreign holders					3[d]	12[d]	12

[a] March 31 of the year following.
[b] Held through National Debt Commissioners.
[c] Including National Insurance Fund, held through National Debt Commissioners.
[d] Official foreign holdings only.

Sources: 1880–1929:
Line 1: B. R. Mitchell and P. L. Dean, *Abstract of British Historical Statistics* (Cambridge, 1962).
Lines 4–6: Rough estimates from various sources.
1937: Committee on the Working of the Monetary System, *Minutes of Evidence* (London, 1960), p. 111.
1948: Central Statistical Office, *Economic Trends* (London, Dec. 1961).
1963: *Bank of England Quarterly* (London, 1964).

individual and not institutional holdings. There also were undoubtedly some foreign holdings. It is probable, however, that as late as 1880 the overwhelming majority, probably close to three-fourths, of the total public debt, was owned by British individual holders.

At the eve of World War I the situation had radically changed. Of the £700-odd million outstanding—representing only 27 per cent of gross national product, or only one-tenth of the ratio of 1820—the Bank of England held 5 per cent, but deposit banks accounted for 12 per cent. The main change, however, was the increase in the holdings of the National Debt Commissioners for account of the savings banks, which totaled 35 per cent of the total public debt outstanding, and their much smaller holdings for the National Insurance Fund. The share of all financial institutions thus was close to 60 per cent, and the holdings of British individuals—as important as consols might still be for some classes of conservative investors—had been reduced to approximately two-fifths of the total amount outstanding.

If we look only at the aggregate share of financial institutions, no substantial net change occurred in the distribution of the British government's debt in the following fifty years. Early in 1964 all financial institutions together owned fully 55 per cent of a total of £30 billion debt held domestically, almost the same ratio as prevailed in 1914. Substantial changes, however, had taken place in the intervening fifty years in the distribution of the holdings among the different types of financial institutions. Insurance organizations, private and public, were the largest holders, accounting for almost 20 per cent of the domestic total. Savings banks, through the National Debt Commissioners, still held 12 per cent of the domestic total, but this was only one-third of their share in 1913. The banking system, combining the Bank of England with holdings equivalent to 9 per cent of the domestically held total and the domestic deposit banks with 7 per cent, just held its own as a haven for government securities. Another important change was the increase in foreign holdings to 12 per cent of the total, mostly in the hands of foreign central banks as a result of the role of sterling as a key currency and of international monetary institutions, reflecting the latter's assistance to sterling. There were, of course, fluctuations in the share of all financial institutions taken together within these fifty years—particularly the sharp but temporary increase in individuals' holdings after World War I—as well as in the distribution of the total among the different types of financial institutions. These changes can be followed in Table 3–17.

In France government securities have been concentrated in the hands of domestic individuals possibly to a larger extent than in any other country. From the beginning of the nineteenth century to World War I the only large institutional holder of French government securities was the Caisse des Dépôts, both for account of financial institutions such as the savings banks and the Caisse Nationale de Prévoyance and of individual and other trust funds, while the Banque de France and the deposit banks held only small amounts of government securities. The total assets of the Caisse des Dépôts, then mostly invested in government securities, increased from about one-eighth of the total government debt in 1880 to about one-fourth from 1913 to 1938. Considerable changes in the distribution of the French government's debt, however, have occurred since World War I when the Banque de France, and later the deposit banks, acquired considerable holdings of short-term government securities (Table 3–18). As a result, the Banque de France in 1963 owned 7 per cent and the deposit banks 8 per cent of government debt outstanding, while other financial institutions—mostly the Caisse des Dépôts—held another 22 per cent. Since there also were substantial holdings by local governments and general government funds, the share of domestic nonfinancial holders now has been reduced to about one-half of the total. This is still a higher proportion than prevails in most other developed countries.

The development in the United States has been strongly

influenced by the fact that U.S. government bonds from 1864–1914 constituted the backing of national bank notes and thus were particularly attractive for their issuers. As a result, the national banks by 1912 had accumulated more

TABLE 3–18

Distribution of Central Government Domestic Securities in France, 1880–1963

PER CENT, EXCEPT LINE 1

	1880	1900	1913	1929	1938	1950	1963
Total oustanding (billions of francs)	21.6[a]	30.1[a]	33.5	368[b]	424	4900	13400
Central government						3	3
Local governments						6	7
Financial institutions							
Banque de France	[c]	[c]	[c]	8[d]	9	16	7
Deposit banks	[c]	[c]	[c]		13	6	8
Other financial institutions	12[e]	18[e]	29[e]	13[e]	26	19	22
Other domestic holders[f]	88	82	71	79	52	24	49
Foreign holders				[c]	[c]	26	4

[a] Beginning of year.
[b] Excluding foreign war debt.
[c] Very small.
[d] 1927.
[e] Total assets of Caisse des Dépôts.
[f] Residual.

Sources:
1880–1938: various sources (cf. Table D-8).
1950, 1963: *International Financial Statistics*, 1965–66 Supplement.

than 60 per cent of all Treasury securities outstanding, acquired not only from former individual holders, but also from some other financial institutions, particularly mutual savings banks, which at some times had substantial holdings of Treasury securities. The large government bond issues of the Civil War period, on the other hand, had been purchased almost exclusively by domestic individuals, as was common in Europe at that time. However, as the combined result of rapid retirement of Treasury securities and purchases by national banks, individual holdings declined from about $2.5 billion at the end of the Civil War to about $1.5 billion in 1880 and to less than $500 million between the turn of the century and World War I.

In the last fifty years the ownership of Treasury securities has become thoroughly institutionalized. Individuals still absorbed most of the bonds sold to finance World War I, so that financial institutions in 1922 held less than 40 per cent of total U.S. government securities outstanding. They then rapidly increased their holdings, first as the government during the 1920s retired many of the individually held bonds and then as financial institutions absorbed the large amounts of government securities issued to cover the budget deficits of the 1930s. As a result, financial institutions in 1939 owned as much as three-fourths of the total federal debt, while the holdings of nonfinancial owners declined from $14 billion in 1922 to $12 billion in 1939. The trend was reversed during World War II when, as is usual in war periods, a substantial proportion of the newly issued securities was absorbed by individuals, so that financial institutions in 1945 held only two-thirds of the total U.S. government debt. During the following twenty years, financial institutions slowly increased both the absolute amount and their share in total government debt outstanding, but even in 1963 their proportion of 66 per cent was still below that of 1939. This, however, was partly the result of large acquisitions by nonfinancial corporations, which had not been much interested in Treasury securities before the Great Depression but in 1963 held 6 per cent of the total amount outstanding. Domestic individuals' holdings were reduced to about one-fourth of the total, still about equal to the proportion of 1939, but well below proportions prevailing during the 1920s and late 1940s.

The distribution of the aggregate holdings of Treasury securities among the different types of financial institutions, shown in Table 3–19, is the combined result of different growth rates of total assets and of changes in the proportion of total assets held by different types of financial institutions

TABLE 3–19

Distribution of Central Government Domestic Securities in the United States, 1900–1963

PER CENT, EXCEPT LINE 1

	1900	1912	1929	1939	1949	1963
Total outstanding (billions of dollars)	1.2	1.4	16.3	47.6	257.2	310.1
Financial institutions, total	54	67	46	74	63	66
Federal Reserve Banks	—	—	3	5	7	11
Deposit banks	42	65	29	34	26	22
Thrift institutions	8	1	4	9	6	4
Insurance organizations[a]	4	1	5	15	10	12
Federal government trust funds	0	0	5	9	13	16
Other financial institutions	0	0	0	2	1	1
Other domestic } Foreign	46	33	54	26[b]		
Other domestic					36[b]	30[b]
Foreign					1	4

[a] Includes all state and local government trust funds but excludes Federal insurance funds.

[b] Includes four in 1939 and six per cent in 1949 and 1963 held by nonfinancial corporations.

Sources: *1900–1949*: R. W. Goldsmith, *Financial Intermediaries*, p. 269.
1963: Economic Report of the President, 1964, and Federal Reserve Board, *Flow-of-Funds Statistics.*

in Treasury securities. Deposit banks and life insurance companies during the postwar period reduced their holdings in absolute and relative terms from the peak reached at the end of the war as other more profitable outlets for their funds were reopened; together they now hold less than one-fourth of the total U.S. government debt outstanding. On the other hand the Federal Reserve Banks and particularly private and public pension funds absorbed large amounts of Treasury securities and considerably raised their share in the total outstanding. As a result of these movements, nearly one-half of the federal securities held by all financial institutions and nearly one-third of the total amount outstanding is now in the hands of the banking system and of public and private insurance organizations.

THE FOREIGN ISSUE RATIO

In the approach followed in Chapter 2, foreign issues are regarded as a separate component of nonfinancial issues, additive to the issues of domestic nonfinancial units. Figures are therefore needed for the net issues of foreign securities, i.e. the difference between the net acquisition of foreign securities including not only bonds and stock, but also all credits not embodied in securities, such as deposits with foreign banks, reserves with foreign insurance companies, trade credit to foreign customers, and possibly even reinvested earnings in foreign subsidiaries and the sale of domestic securities of the same types to foreigners. Monetary metals may be included in, or excluded, from the figures.

The statistical material available on an international basis conforms only roughly to these concepts and is quite scarce before World War II if reliability and comparability are demanded of the data. The main differences in the value of the foreign investment ratio among countries and the main trends in the ratio over the past century are nevertheless fairly clear. The essential figures are brought together in Table 3–20.

From a large number of detailed studies of foreign lending and borrowing of individual countries it is known, even though the statistical material is often incomplete and not comparable over time and among countries, that the international flows of capital in the period between the middle of the nineteenth century and World War I led to substantial surpluses (i.e. net acquisitions of foreign securities) by a few countries in Western Europe, primarily the United Kingdom, France, Germany, the Netherlands, and Belgium, and that these surpluses were balanced by capital imports (i.e. the net sales of domestic financial instruments to foreigners) by most other countries in the world, not only by the present less developed countries but also by most of the present developed countries outside Western Europe, such as Canada, Australia, New Zealand, South

Africa, Italy, Scandinavia, and Japan, and, until the turn of the century, even the United States. Comparable statistical data, however, are available only for about the dozen countries covered in Table 3–20.

Among the major buyers of foreign securities, it was only in the United Kingdom and the Low Countries that the ratio of foreign investment to gross national product (ξ) was of the same order of magnitude as the domestic nonfinancial issue ratio (δ). Both for the thirty years ending around 1890 and for the following twenty-five years until World War I began, the net acquisition of foreign securities was equal to 4 to 5 per cent of the British gross national product, so that foreign issues made about as large a contribution to the growth of the financial superstructure of the United Kingdom as did domestic nonfinancial issues. In the two other large capital-exporting countries, France and Germany, the foreign investment ratio was considerably lower, averaging about 2½ per cent for France and 1½ per cent for Germany for the half-century before World War I. The acquisition of foreign securities in comparison to the net new issues of domestic nonfinancial issues thus was relatively much more important in France, with a ratio of almost one-half, than in Germany where foreign issues constituted only about one-fourth of the addition to the total stock of nonfinancial securities.[18] The ratios probably also were high compared to net domestic nonfinancial issues for the Netherlands and Belgium, for which not sufficient data are available, but the absolute volume of foreign issues absorbed in these countries was considerably smaller than in France, Germany, or Great Britain.

There are unfortunately only few debtor countries for which the ratio of net sales of domestic financial instruments to foreigners to gross national product or to domestic nonfinancial issues can be estimated for the period before

18. Based on K. Helfferich's figures for Germany for 1886 to 1910, cited by Neymarck, *Bulletin de l'Institut International de Statistique, 19* (1911), 232; figures for France for 1892 to 1913 are from *Annuaire Statistique, Retrospectif* (1961), p. 332.

TABLE 3–20

Trend of Foreign Investment Ratio (ξ), 1860–1963

NET FOREIGN BALANCE AS PER CENT OF GROSS NATIONAL PRODUCT

	Approximate Period Averages				Changes		
	1861–90 (1)	1891–1914 (2)	1921–39 (3)	1956–63 (4)	1861–90 to 1891–1914 (5)	1891–1914 to 1921–39 (6)	1921–39 to 1956–63 (7)
1. Australia	−6.5	−2.5	−2.0	−1.2	+4.0	+0.5	+0.8
2. Belgium, Netherlands, Switzerland	7.0[a]	5.0[a]		1.7	−2.0[a]	−3.3[a]	
3. Canada		−7.5[d]	0.5	−3.0		+8.0	−3.5
4. Denmark	−2.0[b]	−1.6	0.9	−0.3	+0.4	+2.5	−1.2
5. France	2.0	3.0		0.2	+1.0	−2.8	
6. Germany	2.0	1.1		0.9	−0.9	−0.2	
7. Great Britain	4.0	4.8	0.9	1.7	+0.8	−3.9	+0.8
8. Italy	−1.3	0.6	−1.5	−0.2	+1.9	−2.1	+1.3
9. Japan		−1.3[e]	−1.0	−0.5		+0.3	+0.5
10. Norway	0.1[b]	−4.2	−2.2	−2.0	−4.3	+2.0	+0.2
11. Sweden	−1.1	−0.8	2.6	−0.4	+0.3	+3.4	−3.0
12. U.S.A.	−0.7[c]	0.4	1.0	0.2	+1.1	+0.6	−0.8

[a] Rough estimates.
[b] 1870–89. [c] 1869–88. [d] 1896–1915. [e] 1887–1916.

Sources: Col. 1–3: Derived as unweighted averages of decadal ratios in S. Kuznets "Long-Term Trends in Capital Formation Proportions," except for lines 5 and 6, which are rough estimates based on net foreign investment in 1890 and 1914 (S. Kuznets, *Modern Economic Growth*, New Haven, 1966, p. 322); and for line 2, derived on the basis of estimate of foreign investments in 1914 ($5.5 billion according to U.N. *International Capital Movements During the Interwar Period* (Lake Success, 1949) and assumption that most of these originated after 1860).

Col. 4: Net foreign balances, excluding "errors and omissions," from International Monetary Fund, *Balance of Payments Yearbook* (Washington), various issues; national products from U.N., *Yearbook of National Accounts Statistics*.

World War I. There is no doubt, however, that the ratio was quite high—reaching or even exceeding 5 per cent of national product—for a few rapidly developing countries, such as Argentina, Canada, and Australia.[19] In most cases, however, net foreign issues equaled only a few per cent of national product, for instance, in Japan, the Scandinavian countries, Italy, and Russia. They nevertheless represented a substantial proportion of total nonfinancial domestic issues in the borrowing countries because, at least in Latin America and Asia, the ratio of domestic nonfinancial issues to national product was well below the European and American level.

The relative importance of international capital flows shrank considerably in the interwar period of the 1920s and 1930s. Thus the total value of foreign investments in 1938 was estimated at around $55 billion,[20] only about $10 billion, or one-fifth, above the 1913 level, while national products had at least doubled. So far as can be inferred from the available statistical material, the ratio of nonfinancial foreign issues to national product and to nonfinancial domestic issues was considerably smaller than before World War I. Moreover, some of the pre-World War I borrowers became net lenders. The most important of these, of course, was the United States, but the same shift can be observed in the case of Canada and Sweden.

With respect to the relative size of net foreign investment, the picture after World War II was much closer to that in the interwar period than to the situation during the heyday of international finance between the middle of the nineteenth century and World War I. The ratio of foreign lending and borrowing to national product remained low.

19. For Latin America the ratio of foreign investment may be estimated to have been as high as approximately one-fourth of fixed reproducible wealth as late as 1929 if the figures of A. Ganz for foreign investments and reproducible capital in *Income and Wealth,* Series VIII (London, 1959), are accepted.

20. C. Lewis, *Debtor and Credit Countries 1938* (Washington, Brookings Institution, 1944), pp. 48 ff.

Reflecting a high level of domestic demand for funds no important lender in the postwar period put 3 to 5 per cent of his national product into the acquisition of foreign securities as the United Kingdom, France, and probably the Netherlands and Belgium did before World War I. The highest ratio for the period 1956–63—which though short is preferable to the even less normal first decade after World War II—was in the order of 1½ per cent excepting only Switzerland where it reached 3 per cent.

Among the fifty-three countries for which information is available for the period 1956–63, the unweighted average ratio of net foreign investment to national product was 1½ per cent,[21] and it was slightly below zero even for developed countries. Since this average, including virtually all countries of importance in the international flow of capital, should be close to zero, it is probable that the available figures understate net foreign investment. Even if a liberal allowance is made for understatement, the ratio is not likely to have exceeded 1 per cent for the developed countries as a group. There appears, however, among these countries, a clear difference between European developed countries on the one hand and overseas developed countries (Canada, Australia, New Zealand, Japan, Israel, South Africa) on the other, a difference which amounts to about one- and one-half per cent of national product in favor of the European developed countries. Even for the latter, the reported ratio averages only one-fourth to one-half of 1 per cent of national product, and after adjustment for understatement probably is not in excess of 1–2 per cent of national product, so that it constitutes only one-tenth or less of domestic nonfinancial issues. The reported figures for underdeveloped countries show an average ratio of net borrowing abroad, i.e. of net sales of domestic securities of all types to foreigners, of about 2 per cent of national product. There apparently was no systematic difference in the resort to foreign borrowing between Latin American

21. R. W. Goldsmith, *The Determinants of Financial Structure*, pp. 27 ff.

countries on the one hand and the less developed countries in Asia and Africa on the other, at least not in the reported relationship between net foreign borrowing and national product.

There is no doubt that notwithstanding the lower overall average ratio, net foreign borrowing was for a minority of less developed countries substantial in relation to their gross national product and to the issuance of domestic nonfinancial securities, and that these funds financed a substantial proportion of these countries' total domestic capital formation. Figures for domestic nonfinancial issues are not available for a sufficient number of less developed countries to confirm the second statement statistically. A comparison of net capital imports, a concept close to net sales of domestic securities to foreigners (if direct investments and reinvestment of profits of foreign enterprises are included) shows an average (median) value for thirty-six less developed countries of slightly more than one-tenth of domestic capital formation, exceeding one-fifth in several important countries (Brazil, India, Nigeria, Pakistan, United Arab Republic).[22]

22. Derived from data in Goldsmith, ibid.

4 THE ISSUES OF FINANCIAL INSTITUTIONS—NATIONAL AGGREGATES

The different types of securities issued by financial institutions—such as demand and time deposits, mortgage bonds, insurance and pension obligations, as well as the shares of banks and insurance and investment companies—constitute the second main component of the flow or of the stock of financial instruments. If a few theoretically desirable though practically not essential refinements are disregarded, the statistical material on the issuance and on the stocks of financial instruments issued by financial institutions is fortunately much richer, both in time and in space, than the comparable data on the securities issued by nonfinancial sectors. For this important component of a country's financial superstructure, and at the same time for financial intermediaries as one of the most important links in the financing process, it is possible to go back to the turn of the century for a sufficient number of countries to permit an analysis on a truly comparative basis and for a period long enough to observe structural changes.

THE STATISTICAL MATERIAL

The materials on which the analysis presented in this and the following chapter rests are data on the total assets of the main types of financial institutions—ranging from half a dozen to two dozen types—in thirty-five countries for a number of benchmarks, from three to nine dates situated at irregular but internationally standardized intervals of three to twenty years between 1860 and 1963. Data are available for all the thirty-five countries for the benchmarks of 1948 (or a slightly later date for a few countries), 1960, and 1963. For two dozen countries the same information is also at hand for the benchmark dates of 1938, 1929, and 1913. The figures can be carried backwards to 1900 and 1880 for fifteen countries, all developed ones except India, while an attempt to provide the same information for the benchmark date of 1860 has been regarded as justified only for five developed countries—developed then as well as now. The countries for which the information is available for each of the benchmark dates, as well as the minor deviations of a few actual benchmark dates from the standard, can be identified in Table 4–1, while Table 4–2 shows the number of countries included at each benchmark date in the various groupings. The basic data for each country will be found in Appendix IV.[1]

These data on the total assets of the different types of financial institutions provide a basis for comparative long-time analysis, but they have two important drawbacks for detailed study, apart from a number of less serious and more technical limitations which are discussed in the introduction to Appendix IV. The first of these is the absence of a breakdown of assets and liabilities by type, the second the use of differences between assets at different benchmark dates in lieu of true flow figures for the period between these dates.

If a detailed analysis of the role of the financial institutions in each of the countries included in the study were the

1. As a result of additional information obtained after the data were originally collected and processed, the figures now shown in Appendix IV differ in a few cells—the assets of one type of institution for one benchmark year in one country—from those employed in the tabulations. The number of cases, however, is small and they are of substantive importance only in very few countries (Argentina and the Netherlands), and in these only for a few early benchmark dates. The averages for all countries or groups of them are virtually unaffected.

Table 4–1

Reference Dates for Assets of Financial Institutions

	1880[a]	1900	1913	1929	1938	1948	1960 and 1963[b]
Argentina		1901	×	×	1940	×	×
Australia		1901	1915	×	×	×	×
Belgium	×	×	×	×	1939	×	×
Brazil			×	×	×	×	×
Canada	×	×	×	×	×	×	×
Denmark	×	×	×	×	×	×	×
Egypt-U.A.R.		×	×	×	×	×	×
France	×	×	×	×	1937	×	×
Germany	×	×	×	×	×	×	×
Great Britain	×	×	×	×	×	×	×
Greece			×	×	×	×	×
India	×	×	×	×	×	×	×
Israel						1950	×
Italy	×	×	×	×	×	×	×
Jamaica						×	×
Japan	×	×	×	1930	×	×	×
Mexico		1903	1911	1930	1940	×	×
Netherlands	×	×	×	×	×	×	×
New Zealand	×	×	×	×	1937	×	×
Nigeria				×	×	×	×
Norway	×	×	×	×	×	×	×
Pakistan						×	×
Philippines			×	×	×	×	×
Puerto Rico				×	×	×	×
Rhodesia						×	×
Russia-U.S.S.R.		×	×	1928	1937	1950	×
South Africa			×	×	×	×	×
Spain	×	×	×	×	1935	×	×
Sweden	×	×	×	×	×	×	×
Switzerland	×	×	×	×	×	×	×
Thailand					×	×	×
Trinidad					×	×	×
U.S.A.	×	×	1912	×	1939	×	×
Venezuela				×	×	×	×
Yugoslavia				×	×	1952	×

[a] For France, Germany, Great Britain, Switzerland, and the U.S.A. an additional reference date is 1860.

[b] Only deviations are 1964 (instead of 1963) for Australia and 1959 (instead of 1960) for U.S.S.R.

TABLE 4–2

Number of Countries Included during Various Periods[a]

	1861–80 (1)	1881–1900 (2)	1901–13 (3)	1914–29 (4)	1930–38 (5)	1939–49 (6)	1949–63[b] (7)
I. All countries	5	15	21	25	29	31	35
II. Developed	5	14	16	17	17	17	19
1. European	4	10	11	11	11	11	11
2. Non-European	1	4	5	6	6	6	8
III. Less developed	0	1	5	8	12	14	16
1. European	0	0	1	2	3	3	3
2. American	0	0	2	3	5	6	7
3. Afro-Asian	0	1	2	3	4	5	6

[a] The figures also indicate the number of countries for which the information is available at the beginning (and in the case of col. 7 also at the end) of the period.

[b] Same numbers apply to periods 1949–60 and 1961–63, separately.

objective, it would be necessary to distinguish among the assets at least the funds made available to each of the main sectors of the economy—business enterprises, government, households and foreigners—and it would be important to separate securities of these sectors acquired in the open market from loans made directly to them, as well as to identify those assets that represent claims against or equities of other financial institutions. Similarly a distinction would have to be made between the financial institution's net worth, its short-term deposits, its time and saving deposits, and the long-term securities (such as mortgage bonds) which it has issued. An additional or alternative breakdown distinguishing the creditor sector would considerably add to the value of the analysis. Such breakdowns of the assets and liabilities of financial institutions would be particularly important in any attempt to evaluate the role of financial institutions, in the aggregate and for their main types, in the financing of the different sectors of the economy, somewhat along the lines that this can be done for the United States.[2] In the present state of the basic data it was, however, entirely out of the question to undertake this further analysis as part of this study.

The need to approximate the volume of net issues of financial institutions through the calculation of the first difference between the assets at the end and the beginning of the period is a less serious drawback. The procedure is unexceptional insofar as fixed value claims are involved on either the asset or the liability side of financial institutions, and such claims fortunately constitute the great majority of the total assets and liabilities of virtually all types of financial institutions. Indeed on the asset side, the percentage of equities, represented primarily by corporate common shares, and of tangible assets—mostly office buildings—is so small in most countries and is limited to so few types of financial institutions—primarily investment companies, and

2. See, for example, R. W. Goldsmith, *Financial Intermediaries in the American Economy Since 1900* (Princeton, Princeton University Press, 1958) Chap. 7.

in a few countries also insurance companies, pension funds, and development banks—that the error introduced by using first differences of the book value of total assets in lieu of true flow figures (i.e. the difference between acquisitions and disposal of given types of instruments) is generally very small compared to the margin of error necessarily involved in the figures that have to be used, the more so since the balance sheets of financial institutions on which the calculations are based rarely carry corporate shares and real estate at market value but more commonly enter them at a book value, which is close to actual costs of acquisition. Ignoring net worth on the right-hand side of the balance sheet of financial institutions, or more accurately treating the capital stock and surplus of financial institutions as if they were claims, is somewhat more serious, particularly for earlier benchmark dates when net worth still constituted a substantial proportion of the balance sheet total of several types of financial institutions. The difference, however, would be substantial only if the comparison were made with the market value of the shares of the banks and other financial institutions. It is much smaller if one is thinking of the adjusted book value obtained by deducting liabilities from the market value of assets. There is thus little doubt that substitution of first differences of the book value of total assets between benchmark dates for the theoretically more appropriate figures of net flows during the period cannot as a rule be seriously misleading when the figures refer to either the total of all financial institutions in a country or to those of the main types of financial institutions, particularly the banking system and other thrift institutions.

One instance in which the use of the difference in the assets of financial institutions at the beginning and the end of a period as the numerator of ϕ (issue of financial institutions divided by national product) will lead to misleading results is a period during which a country experienced a debt writedown, usually in connection with a currency reform. In such a case the change in the assets of financial institutions over a longer period may be negative although assets increased in every single subperiod. Among the data used here, the most important instances are data for Germany in the period 1914–29 and 1939–48 and for Russia in the period 1914–29. The values of ϕ shown in these three instances are therefore of very limited meaning. Their use could have been avoided if ϕ had been calculated for subperiods not affected by the writedown, e.g. for Germany for 1914–29 by calculation of separate values of ϕ for 1914–23 (or even subperiods as short as one year) and for 1923–29 and by the derivation of ϕ for the 1914–29 period as an average of the ϕs for the subperiods. Data and resources for this improvement—of minor importance in the overall picture—were, however, lacking.

THE GROWTH OF FINANCIAL INSTITUTIONS' ASSETS

Before investigating the behavior of the ratio of the net issues of financial institutions to national product (ϕ), which constitutes the subject of this chapter, it may be well to look at the rate of growth of the assets of financial institutions. It is then seen in Table 4–3 that the average annual rate of growth of the assets of financial institutions in the countries included in the tabulation for the different periods has varied between less than 5 and nearly 20 per cent if the calculation is based on book value in current prices. The range, of course, is much wider among the values for individual countries shown in Table 4–4. The averages vary between 1.5 per cent in the World War II period and almost 8 per cent in the immediately following period of 1948–63, if the influence of changes in the price level (represented by the national product deflator) are eliminated.[3] Comparison of the rates for the same period and country group in the upper and lower tier of Table 4–3 indicates how important the influence of these price movements on the rate of growth of assets of financial institu-

3. In the figures used in the text Germany is excluded for the 1914–29 period.

TABLE 4–3

Growth of Financial Institutions' Assets

UNWEIGHTED COUNTRY AVERAGES (PER CENT PER YEAR)

	Including Socialist Countries			Excluding Socialist Countries			Identical Countries	
	All (1)	Developed (2)	Less Developed (3)	All (4)	Developed (5)	Less Developed (6)	Developed (7)	Less Developed (8)
				CURRENT PRICES				
1861–1880	6.21	6.21		6.21	6.21			
1881–1900	5.24	5.31	4.36	5.24	5.31	4.35	5.31	
1901–1913	6.93	6.01	9.85	6.88	5.88	9.85	6.00	
1914–1929[a]	17.98	22.23	8.95	18.96	23.97	8.95	26.53	8.95
1930–1938	4.72	5.17	4.09	4.06	3.85	4.36	3.63	4.87
1939–1948	16.98	12.72	22.16	17.04	12.83	22.23	12.98	23.09
1949–1963	12.72	11.33	14.37	12.48	11.38	13.80	10.37	15.61
				CONSTANT PRICES				
1861–1880	6.53	6.54		6.54	6.54		6.54	
1881–1900	5.45	5.59	3.39	5.45	5.59	3.39	5.59	3.39
1901–1913	5.55	4.51	8.87	5.52	4.41	8.87	4.59	8.87
1914–1929[b]	3.73	2.01	3.89	3.66	3.56	3.88	3.00	3.89
1930–1938	4.72	4.23	5.42	4.66	4.14	5.42	3.83	4.78
1939–1948	1.47	−0.28	3.60	1.46	−0.53	3.91	−1.65	2.85
1949–1963	7.67	7.38	8.02	7.36	7.26	7.48	6.83	6.43

[a] The figures, excluding Germany, for cols. 1, 2, 4, and 5 are: 8.16, 7.26, 8.73, and 11.47.

[b] The figures, excluding Germany, for cols. 1, 2, 4, 5, and 7 are: 3.54, 2.34, 3.78, 3.10, and 3.50.

Table 4–4

Growth of Financial Institutions' Assets in Individual Countries—Current Prices

PER CENT PER YEAR

	1881–1900[a]	1901–13	1914–29	1930–38	1939–48	1949–63
Argentina		12.7	4.5	3.6	20.8	21.1
Australia		4.3	6.3	3.3	10.6	8.0
Belgium	4.2	5.7	14.8	3.4	13.1	8.2
Brazil			11.8	6.3	17.5	27.9
Canada	6.6	8.5	5.6	2.9	9.1	8.4
Denmark	5.1	5.9	5.7	3.3	8.0	7.1
Egypt-U.A.R.		14.8	4.7	−2.9	19.4	7.3
France	4.4	3.8	12.8	4.4	22.5	16.0
Germany	5.6	6.4	261.6	3.6	−5.3	14.4
Great Britain	2.5	2.7	5.7	3.6	9.2	5.4
Greece			24.6	5.8	61.1	20.4
India	4.4	7.8	6.4	7.8	16.0	7.7
Israel						31.8
Italy	3.6	8.0	12.1	4.2	36.4	16.4
Jamaica						11.5
Japan	15.0	7.2	12.1	7.9	40.0	25.0
Mexico		12.5	−0.4	11.4	23.2	15.5
Netherlands	3.3	5.8	7.3	3.6	8.8	8.9
New Zealand	4.0	5.3	6.3	5.5	8.0	6.6
Nigeria				5.4	17.3	16.7
Norway	4.2	5.7	7.9	.5	12.1	5.8
Pakistan						8.3
Philippines			9.2	5.6	13.6	10.2
Puerto Rico				−0.6	16.8	11.6
Rhodesia						11.8
Russia-U.S.S.R.		7.9	−5.6	26.2	10.9	10.4
South Africa			5.8	7.4	13.0	8.2
Spain		1.5	10.7	1.4	13.2	14.8
Sweden	4.5	5.5	5.8	4.6	6.5	8.2
Switzerland	4.7	6.8	5.3	1.1	3.8	8.0
Thailand					34.8	12.6
Trinidad					20.9	9.1
U.S.A.	6.4	6.5	8.4	2.3	9.6	6.6
Venezuela			16.2	4.3	14.5	12.3
Yugoslavia				1.1	21.3	22.9

[a] Rates for 1861–80 are 6.4 for France, 6.0 for Germany, 4.3 for Great Britain, 7.7 for Switzerland, and 6.7 for U.S.A.

tions has been.[4] Thus the average rates of growth show much more of an upward trend on the current than on the constant price basis, because the trend of prices has been upward during most of the past century. After elimination of price level changes, the average rate of growth of the assets of financial institutions for all countries included (thirty-five in the later period and on the average seventeen in the three earlier periods) has been practically the same in the postwar period at slightly less than 6 per cent a year as in the half-century before World War I, while it was twice as high—almost 13 per cent—in current prices. What may be more interesting, the average growth rates in constant prices show a definite downward trend until 1929, which was reversed during the following thirty years, the war periods of 1914–29 and 1939–48 constituting two troughs in the series. The movement of the rates in current prices, on the other hand, is irregularly upward with definite peaks in the two war periods.

There are substantial differences among groups of countries, but these differ depending on the price basis used. In current prices (Table 4–4) the average rate of growth of assets is higher for less developed countries in two of the five periods in the twentieth century, but lower from 1914 to 1938 because the inflationary price rises during World War I were more pronounced and the price declines of the Great Depression less pronounced among the developed countries. In constant prices (Table 4–5), on the other hand, the rate is higher for less developed countries in all five periods. In fact on that basis their postwar rate of asset expansion—as well as that in the period 1901–13—is higher than the rates for the developed countries back to 1860.

4. The issue ratio, of course, is the same whether based on figures in current or constant prices so long as the same deflator is used, e.g. the so-called gross national product deflator. In that case, the levels and movements of ϕ calculated from assets and national products in current prices on which the discussion is based would be unaffected by a shift to constant prices.

TABLE 4–5

Growth of Financial Institutions' Assets in Individual Countries—Constant Prices

PER CENT PER YEAR

	1881–1900	1901–13	1914–29	1930–38	1939–48	1949–63
Argentina		9.0	4.0	4.8	7.0	−3.0
Australia		1.8	3.6	4.3	6.9	2.9
Belgium	4.8	3.3	1.8	1.4	−1.4	6.5
Brazil			5.9	1.2	5.0	3.8
Canada	7.9	5.3	3.5	4.8	3.5	5.5
Denmark	5.5	5.4	2.6	3.4	−0.9	4.1
Egypt-U.A.R.		13.9	2.0	0.7	6.7	6.1
France	5.4	3.3	1.1	4.5	−8.1	8.9
Germany	5.4	5.5	−3.6	6.0	−10.2	11.6
Great Britain	3.1	2.2	1.9	3.8	2.9	2.1
Greece			4.3	1.9	−8.6	13.4
India	3.4	5.6	4.7	12.2	4.1	6.4
Israel						18.1
Italy	3.7	6.3	1.9	5.2	−6.9	12.8
Jamaica						6.9
Japan	12.9	4.4	9.3	4.9	−15.4	19.3
Mexico		15.0	−5.5	9.0	9.1	8.3
Netherlands	3.9	3.2	4.8	4.3	5.8	5.2
New Zealand	4.5	4.7	5.3	5.1	2.4	3.4
Nigeria				12.1	−6.0	14.0
Norway	4.8	4.3	5.2	0.3	3.9	1.2
Pakistan						6.8
Philippines			0.5	9.3	−1.2	8.8
Puerto Rico				1.1	11.8	7.2
Rhodesia						9.4
Russia-U.S.S.R.		6.0	−8.0	5.6	3.7	9.6
South Africa			4.2	8.4	7.7	4.7
Spain		0.8	7.2	−0.9	0.8	7.6
Sweden	4.6	4.5	3.2	2.6	0.8	4.1
Switzerland	4.5	7.4	0.6	3.5	−2.0	6.4
Thailand					3.3	9.7
Trinidad					11.5	4.9
U.S.A.	7.3	4.5	5.4	3.9	2.4	4.5
Venezuela				8.2	7.5	11.3
Yugoslavia				5.4	−0.4	16.1

LEVEL AND MOVEMENTS OF THE AGGREGATE ISSUE RATIO OF FINANCIAL INSTITUTIONS

One of the characteristics of financial structure most relevant for the analysis of the role of financial institutions in the economy is the ratio (ϕ) of the net issues of financial instruments by financial institutions to gross national product. It is therefore our first task to analyze the approximations to the aggregate financial issues ratio that can be derived for the thirty-five countries covered by this study for the periods between the standard benchmark dates, i.e. the three to ten values of ϕ, each of which refers to a period (excluding that of 1961–63) of between nine and twenty years. While annual, or even quarterly, data would be required for a study of cyclical movements in ϕ, the fact that we are necessarily dealing here with periods of substantial length has the advantage that the ratios are less affected by ephemeral developments and by minor inaccuracies in the statistics and thus are more likely to reflect changes of structural or long-term character. The aggregative financial issues ratio is then seen from Tables 4–6 and 4–7 to have three main characteristics.

The first characteristic is the marked upward trend in the ratio over the last century. This trend is possibly most clearly evident for the five countries for which it can be calculated for the full century. For these countries (United States, Great Britain, France, Germany, and Switzerland) the ratio has on the average risen from slightly above 3 per cent of gross national product for the period 1861–80 to 12.5 per cent for the fifteen years 1948–63. The picture is very similar for a group of fourteen countries, all developed ones except India, for which the statistical material has been avaialble since the late nineteenth century. The average value of ϕ for this group, which includes almost all important developed countries, rose from slightly over 4 per cent in 1881–1900 to 11 per cent in 1948–63 and to as much as 14 per cent in the much shorter period 1961–63, which may, however, turn out to be representative for the 1960s. Since the calculated figures include some valuation adjustments on the equity securities and other price-sensitive assets held by financial institutions, and since they are affected by some duplications resulting from interbank and similar balances and from the existence of financial intermediaries of the second degree, both values would be

Table 4–6

Issue Ratios of Financial Institutions (ϕ)—Unweighted Country Averages

PER CENT OF GROSS NATIONAL PRODUCT

	1881 to 1900[a]	1901 to 1913	1914 to 1929	1930 to 1938	1939 to 1948	1949 to 1960	1961 to 1963	1949 to 1963
A. INCLUDING SOCIALIST COUNTRIES								
I. All countries	4.19	5.74	5.06	4.15	9.90	9.41	12.77	10.49
II. Developed	4.48	6.62	6.24	6.00	12.68	11.29	15.97	12.82
1. European	4.30	7.04	5.71	4.81	10.46	10.09	15.26	11.60
2. Non-European	4.90	5.69	7.20	8.19	16.73	12.95	16.94	14.48
III. Less developed	0.13	2.92	2.55	1.53	6.52	7.19	8.98	7.72
1. European		0.55	4.96	1.77	7.36	12.74	16.61	14.28
2. American		5.23	2.27	2.18	7.87	8.24	7.92	8.01
3. Afro-Asian	0.13	1.78	1.23	0.55	4.40	3.18	6.40	4.10
B. EXCLUDING SOCIALIST COUNTRIES								
I. All	4.19	5.75	5.39	4.31	10.29	9.33	12.65	10.37
II. Developed	4.48	6.70	6.81	6.17	13.34	11.76	16.60	13.34
1. European	4.30	7.20	6.57	4.96	11.30	10.81	16.33	12.43
III. Less developed	0.13	2.92	2.55	1.61	6.54	6.42	7.91	6.80
1. European		0.55	4.96	2.29	7.86	9.80	12.40	10.68
C. IDENTICAL NONSOCIALIST COUNTRIES								
I. Developed[b]	4.48	6.89	6.50	7.10	6.14	11.71	16.45	13.18
II. Less developed[c]			2.55	2.07	8.16	8.41	10.85	9.00

[a] Values for 1861–80 are 3.41, 3.68, and 2.31 in lines A II, II 1 and II 2, and 3.41 and 3.68 in lines B II and II 1.

[b] Fourteen countries: Belgium, Canada, Denmark, France, Germany, Great Britain, Italy, Japan, Netherlands, New Zealand, Norway, Sweden, Switzerland and U.S.A.

[c] Eight countries: Argentina, Brazil, Egypt, Greece, India, Mexico, Philippines, and Spain.

Table 4–7

Issue Ratios of Financial Institutions (ϕ) in Individual Countries

PER CENT OF GROSS NATIONAL PRODUCT

	1881 to 1900[a]	1901 to 1913	1914 to 1929	1930 to 1938	1939 to 1948	1949 to 1963
Argentina		5.6	2.9	3.1	14.1	9.6
Australia		4.0	5.2	4.7	15.1	8.5
Belgium	3.3	5.4	6.5	3.7	9.8	10.6
Brazil			4.0	3.8	11.4	19.5
Canada	3.9	7.3	5.2	4.3	10.4	10.1
Denmark	6.5	9.9	7.4	6.7	13.7	11.8
Egypt-U.A.R.		3.2	1.7	−1.4	9.6	6.9
France	3.0	3.6	8.5	5.5	6.6	11.4
Germany	5.3	8.5	−2.9	4.2	−5.3	12.8
Great Britain	2.4	2.8	5.2	5.6	13.6	8.6
Greece			5.7	3.5	5.2	9.3
India	0.1	0.4	0.5	1.7	4.2	3.5
Israel						22.9
Italy	1.9	6.2	7.2	6.0	23.1	18.6
Jamaica						4.8
Japan	7.7	6.5	14.0	18.4	31.8	29.3
Mexico		4.9	−0.1	3.0	6.4	6.1
Netherlands	1.7	4.2	5.9	5.9	12.6	13.5
New Zealand	3.7	5.3	6.7	9.3	12.2	8.1
Nigeria				0.0	0.4	1.8
Norway	6.5	9.4	9.8	1.3	19.8	8.8
Pakistan						2.7
Philippines			1.5	1.9	3.8	5.2
Puerto Rico				−0.3	6.6	7.8
Rhodesia						14.0
Russia-U.S.S.R.		5.4	−2.9	3.3	2.1	3.3
South Africa			4.3	8.1	18.3	13.4
Spain		0.6	4.3	1.1	10.5	12.0
Sweden	5.4	7.0	6.0	7.5	9.2	10.9
Switzerland	7.1	15.1	12.2	3.4	9.9	20.4
Thailand					3.9	4.5
Trinidad					4.6	3.0
U.S.A.	4.3	5.3	7.8	4.4	12.6	9.6
Venezuela				1.3	4.1	5.4
Yugoslavia				0.7	6.4	21.5

[a] Values for 1861–80 are 2.0 for France, 2.9 for Germany, 2.8 for Great Britain, 7.0 for Switzerland, and 2.3 for U.S.A.

slightly lower if the ratios could be based, as theory demands, on the volume of new issues of financial instruments by financial institutions to nonfinancial sectors as the numerator. In that case, the increase in ϕ between 1881–1900 and 1948–63 probably would range from somewhat below 4 per cent to approximately 9 per cent of gross national product. There is thus no doubt about a definite and sustained upward trend in ϕ over the century as a whole. This trend was almost universal. Of the twenty-one countries for which the data go back far enough, all but one show an increase in ϕ between the periods 1881–1900 or 1901–13 and 1949–63, an increase which ranges from 20 per cent (Denmark) to 1,900 per cent (Spain) with a median increase approximately of 100 per cent. The one exception—Russia-U.S.S.R.—moreover, is easily explained by the radical change in the country's financial structure.

The second characteristic is the higher level—at any one date—of ϕ for developed than for less developed countries. For the recent period 1948–63 the average calculated value of ϕ was 13 per cent for developed countries compared to less than 8 per cent for the less developed countries. The lower level of ϕ for the less developed countries is to be expected in view of the secular upward trend in the ratio that has prevailed among the developed countries. In fact the present value of ϕ for the less developed countries was almost reached by developed countries as far back as 1901–13. More relevant is the substantial increase in ϕ for the less developed countries from a level of 3 per cent in 1900–13—this value must be treated with reserve because of the small number of less developed countries (five) for which the data are available for that period—to approximately 7.5 per cent for the same five countries in the period 1948–63. The relative increase in ϕ over the interval of approximately forty years is thus considerably higher for the less developed countries than for the developed countries.

Differences are smaller, but by no means negligible, within the broad groups of developed and less developed countries. Among the developed countries, the value of ϕ has been continuously lower for the European than the non-European members beginning with World War I. The difference was particularly pronounced in the 1930s and 1940s but remained substantial in the postwar period. This difference is, however, attributable in part to the very high values of ϕ for Japan. If Japan is excluded, the excess of the remaining seven developed non-European nonsocialist countries over their European counterparts disappears for the postwar period, though it remains in reduced size for earlier periods. As a result the average ratio of assets of financial institutions to national product, which reflects the cumulative process over the entire past, was in 1963 slightly higher for the non-European developed countries, while it had been substantially below the value of the ratio for the European countries at the benchmark dates of 1880, 1900, and 1913. Among less developed countries the differences are much larger, even if the high values for the European less developed countries, which for the postwar period are as high as those for European developed countries, are ignored because of the small number (three) and heterogeneous character of the countries in this group. Thus the ratio has been consistently higher for the American than for the Afro-Asian countries, in fact until 1960 generally at least twice as high. Whether the sharp reduction of the difference in 1961–63 will endure remains to be seen. From the 1940s until 1960 the values of ϕ for the American less developed countries have actually been closer to those of the European developed than to those of the Afro-Asian countries.

The third characteristic is provided by significant temporal variations within the general upward trend of the ratio. These variations appear more clearly in the figures for individual countries than in the averages for all of them or even in those for all developed and all less developed countries. Thus the accelerated increase in ϕ during World War I is not visible in the averages, because only part of the countries included participated in hostilities, and because the period 1914–29 is so long that developments during the 1920s partly offset those during World War I. On the other hand the sharp reduction in ϕ during the 1930s, which reflects the deflation on the Great Depression, is evident in the decline of the average for all countries from 5.1 per cent in 1914–29 to 4.2 per cent for the period 1930–38. The averages similarly show in full clarity the accelerated increase in ϕ during World War II and its aftermath in the increase in ϕ from 4.2 per cent in 1930–38 to 9.4 per cent for the period 1949–60. It is possible that a division of this period would show that ϕ did not rise further, or even declined, during the middle and later 1950s. Another quite remarkable increase in ϕ is shown during the short final period 1961–63—it apparently has continued for the following two or three years[5]—when ϕ reached its all-time high of almot 13 per cent of national product.

The discussion of the differences in ϕ among broader or narrower groups of countries has so far been based on unweighted arithmetic averages for all countries included for a given period. This is at once the simplest procedure and probably the one best adapted to a comparative study where every observation—for one country and for one period—may be regarded as of equal importance. It may be argued, however, that, as countries differ considerably in their economic importance, the average for groups of countries and for all of them should take account of these differences and that the analysis therefore should be based on weighted averages of the ratios for individual countries. This approach immediately raises the difficult conceptual problem of deciding on the nature of the weights appropriate for such an international comparison, and the no less difficult practical problem of actually determining the weights for as many countries as are involved here and for as extended a period. In view of these difficulties, the only weighting system that has actually been used is based on the various countries' gross national product, the original figures being reduced to a uniform standard by neither the ex-

5. See "Recent Developments" (Chapter 8).

change rates prevailing during the different period or, more ambitiously, though even more precariously, by constant purchasing power equivalent rates, here U.S. dollars of 1960 purchasing power. Though averages have actually been calculated on both bases, use is made of only those expressed in constant purchasing power equivalents as reflecting better—or less inadequately—the relative size of the different countries' national product.

While an unweighted average attributes equal significance to the ratio for countries with small and with large national products, the weighted averages are, of course, dominated by the ratios of the large countries, the degree of dominance depending on the size distribution of national products among all countries included in an average. It so happens that national product is highly concentrated among the thirty-five countries as well as in the universe of countries. In particular, the United States alone has accounted for between one-fourth and two-fifths of the total national product (in 1960 dollars) of all countries included, and for between one-third and three-fifths of that of all developed nonsocialist countries, and, of course, has completely dominated the average for non-European developed countries. The six largest countries, ranked on the basis of their 1963 national product (United States, U.S.S.R., Germany, Great Britain, France, and Japan), have since the turn of the century had a weight of almost three-fourths of the total for the thirty-five countries and a weight of five-sixths of that for the nineteen developed countries. While concentration is not quite as pronounced among the less developed countries, in 1948 and 1963 the largest two of the sixteen countries included (India and Brazil) accounted for about one-half, and the largest six countries (India, Brazil, Spain, Mexico, Argentina, and Pakistan) for approximately four-fifths of the group's aggregate national product.

The weighted averages, therefore, primarily reflect the situation in these few large countries. For that reason the figures are shown only for aggregate ϕ in Table 4–8 and are not discussed in detail. It must be recognized, however, that

TABLE 4–8

Issue Ratios of Financial Institutions (ϕ)—
Weighted Country Averages[a]
PERCENT OF GROSS NATIONAL PRODUCT

	1881 to 1900[b]	1901 to 1913	1914 to 1929	1930 to 1938	1939 to 1948	1949 to 1963
A. INCLUDING SOCIALIST COUNTRIES						
I. All countries	3.30	4.95	4.29	4.74	9.50	10.22
II. Developed	3.86	5.45	4.65	5.19	9.81	10.45
1. European	3.43	5.44	2.37	4.75	5.45	8.81
2. Non-European	4.66	5.48	8.00	5.61	14.90	11.96
III. Less developed	0.13	1.25	1.93	1.98	7.18	8.93
1. European		0.55	4.51	1.43	8.45	14.14
2. American		5.20	2.93	3.34	10.90	13.39
3. Afro-Asian	0.13	0.66	0.65	1.36	4.37	3.68
B. EXCLUDING SOCIALIST COUNTRIES						
I. All countries	3.30	4.88	5.33	4.91	10.64	11.42
II. Developed	3.86	5.46	5.93	5.41	11.22	12.06
1. European	3.43	5.45	4.06	5.16	6.80	12.23
III. Less developed	0.13	1.25	1.93	2.03	7.22	8.37
1. European		0.55	4.51	1.61	9.12	11.38
C. IDENTICAL NONSOCIALIST COUNTRIES						
I. Developed	3.86	5.48	5.94	5.41	11.11	12.10
II. Less developed			1.93	2.09	7.53	9.22

[a] Weighted by gross national product in dollars of 1960 purchasing power.

[b] Values for 1861–80 are 2.5 in lines A I, A II, B I, and B II; 2.6 in lines A II 1 and B II 1; and 2.3 in line A II 2

there are substantial differences between the weighted and the unweighted averages, and not only in details but in a few important points. These differences will be the more marked the more pronounced the systematic correlation between ϕ and the size of the various countries' national product.

For all countries taken together, the weighted average value of ϕ is lower for all periods except 1930–38 than the unweighted average, as Table 4–8 shows, but the difference has a declining trend. Thus, in the first three periods the unweighted average of ϕ is above the weighted average by 0.8 to 0.9 per cent of gross national product, or by one-sixth to more than one-third of the absolute value of the weighted average. On the other hand, since 1939 the difference has amounted to only 0.3 to 0.4 per cent of national product or 3 per cent of the absolute value of the weighted average. As a result, the increase in ϕ is considerably larger on the weighted basis (8.2 per cent of national product or 210 per cent of the 1881–1900 value) than it is for the unweighted basis (6.7 per cent of national product or 150 per cent of the starting value).

The differences are more pronounced, but do not have the same character, if we look separately at developed and less developed countries. For developed countries the unweighted average is higher than the weighted average in all periods, the difference on the average amounting to between 1 and 1.5 per cent of gross national product. Furthermore, in contrast to what has been observed for all countries taken together, the difference does not show a tendency to shrink relatively in terms of percentages of gross national product. It even increases. This relationship reflects primarily the very heavy weight of the United States and the fact that the level of ϕ in the United States is somewhat lower than the average of the other developed countries. Among less developed countries the weighted average is below the unweighted one before 1929 but above it since, indicating for the later period, when coverage is less inadequate, a positive correlation of the level of ϕ with the size of the country measured by its gross national product expressed in dollars.

The effect of these differences between unweighted and weighted averages on the gap in ϕ between underdeveloped and developed countries is erratic. The result, however, is that unweighted figures show a widening of the gap while the gap narrows, although irregularly, if weighted averages are used.

To discuss the movements of the net issue ratio of financial institutions individually for each of the countries included in the analysis would require more space than is available and would call for studies of the financial history of each country much more intensive than are possible within the framework of a broad comparative analysis. All that can be done here is to point to a few special features of the level or movements of ϕ for some of the countries, features that seem to have interest for financial analysis (the ratios for individual countries and periods will be found in Table 4–7):

1. Japan has shown the highest values of ϕ not only in the postwar period but also for the entire span from 1880 to 1963 and for most of the subperiods. This feature, explained to some extent by level and movement of the components of ϕ, may be ascribed to a combination of an extremely high personal saving ratio and a very high indirect external financing ratio of business.

2. Among European developed countries, Switzerland ranks first in level of ϕ for the entire period 1881–1963 and for most subperiods. However, while the value of ϕ for Switzerland was almost twice as high as the average for all developed countries from 1881 to 1929, it was hardly in excess of the average in the following thirty-five years, though the difference had again reached a high value at the end of the period (1961–63). There is no easy explanation of this early and sustained extraordinarily large role of financial institutions. The inflow of foreign funds is too small to explain more than a minor part of the difference and, of course, does not contribute at all to the explanation for the period before World War I, when it is particularly needed.

3. Notwithstanding the early development and the variety of its financial institutions, Great Britain has since the late nineteenth century had a lower financial institutions' issue ratio than most other developed countries. For the entire period from 1881 to 1963, the British average value of ϕ of 5.7 per cent compares with values of 6.3 per cent for France, of over 6.5 per cent for Germany, and of 7.0 per cent for the United States.

4. The smaller developed countries seem to have had higher financial institutions' issue ratios than the larger countries in this group. Thus the average value of ϕ for the period 1881–1963 is 6.7 per cent for the Netherlands, 7.0 per cent for New Zealand, 7.4 per cent for Sweden, 8.5 per

cent for Norway, 9.7 per cent for Denmark, and 11.5 per cent for Switzerland.

5. Among the less developed countries, Argentina, Brazil, Spain, and Yugoslavia show the highest financial institutions' issue ratios, particularly since 1939 (12 per cent for Argentina and Spain, 16 per cent for Yugoslavia, and 17 per cent for Brazil). These ratios obviously reflect, at least in part, the rapid inflation which finds its first expression in a sharp expansion of the assets of the banking system. The values for these less developed countries are well above those shown for developed countries other than Japan and Israel.

6. For several of the other less developed countries the value of ϕ for the last quarter century is at a level common among developed countries in the period between 1880 and World War I. Thus the value of ϕ for the period 1949–63 is 8 per cent for Egypt-United Arab Republic, Greece, and Puerto Rico, 6 per cent for Mexico, and 5 per cent for the Philippines and Jamaica. It is still considerably below that level for most countries in Southeast Asia and Africa south of the Sahara. Thus the value is approximately 4 per cent for Thailand, 3 per cent for India, Pakistan, and Trinidad, and 2 per cent for Nigeria.

VARIABILITY AND CONGRUENCE OF ϕ

The justification for using averages for groups of countries in international comparison depends to a considerable extent on the size of the variations among the values, in this case ϕ and its components, for the individual countries. The larger the variation among the individual country ratios, the less typical is any average for groups of countries. One measure of variability that is often used is the coefficient of variation, i.e., the standard deviation (the average of squared deviations from the arithmetic average) divided by the average. A coefficient of variation of 0.50, for example, indicates that the standard deviation is one-half as large as the average, and hence that under the usual assumptions about the normality of the distribution about two-thirds of the country values will lie between 75 and 125 per cent of the average and about 87 per cent will be found between 50 and 150 per cent of the average. In order to obtain an idea of the variability and hence of the representative nature of ϕ and its components the coefficients of variation are shown in Table 4–9 for each of the seven periods and for all nonsocialist countries, as well as for developed and underdeveloped countries separately. From this table, four conclusions can be derived that are relevant in this connection.

TABLE 4–9

Coefficient of Variation of Issue Ratios of Financial Institutions (ϕ)

	1881 to 1900[a]	1901 to 1913	1914 to 1929	1930 to 1938	1939 to 1948	1949 to 1963
A. INCLUDING SOCIALIST COUNTRIES						
I. All countries	0.51	0.55	0.78	0.89	0.71	0.60
II. Developed	0.42	0.44	0.66	0.61	0.63	0.47
1. European	0.46	0.48	0.78	0.36	0.71	0.41
2. Non-European	0.33	0.20	0.45	0.60	0.43	0.50
III. Less developed		0.73	0.74	1.01	0.54	0.71
1. European			0.14	0.68	0.31	0.36
2. American			0.77	0.68	0.46	0.63
3. Afro-Asian			0.44	2.46	0.67	0.41
B. EXCLUDING SOCIALIST COUNTRIES						
I. All	0.51	0.57	0.69	0.87	0.69	0.59
II. Developed	0.42	0.45	0.52	0.60	0.58	0.43
1. European	0.46	0.49	0.57	0.35	0.64	0.33
III. Less developed		0.73	0.74	0.99	0.56	0.64
1. European			0.14	0.51	0.34	0.12
C. IDENTICAL NONSOCIALIST COUNTRIES						
I. Developed	0.42	0.44	0.52	0.63	0.63	0.43
II. Less developed			0.74	0.77	0.46	0.52

[a] The coefficient for the period 1861–80 is 0.54 in lines A I, A II, A II 1, B I, B II, and B II 1.

First, the variability of ϕ, measured by the coefficient of variation for all nonsocialist countries, has not shown a definite trend over the period covered by the study. Thus there is no clear or pronounced tendency for the values of ϕ for all the countries to converge more definitely towards a typical value.

Secondly, the coefficients are in all periods substantially lower for developed than for less developed countries. For the average of the five periods running from 1900 to 1963, a mean of 0.50 for the developed countries compares with one of 0.73 for the less developed countries. This indicates that the eighteen developed countries are more homogeneous with respect to ϕ than the fifteen less developed countries. This difference, however, cannot be used as a basis for arguing that all developed countries are more similar with respect to ϕ than are all less developed countries, because a few developed and many less developed countries are not included in the calculations, and because there are many factors that may be presumed to influence ϕ that are not allowed for in the comparison, for instance the fact that the proportional range of real income per head is larger for less developed than for developed countries.

Thirdly, interesting deviations from this pattern can be observed within some groups of countries. Thus the decline of the coefficient is considerably smaller for the ten or eleven European developed countries, i.e., these countries' financial institutions issue ratios have been relatively similar since the middle of the nineteenth century. The series, however, shows upward movements in the two World War periods, probably reflecting the substantial differences then existing between countries actively participating in hostilities and in other countries (cf. the figures for individual countries in Table 4–7).[6] The particularly low value of the coefficient of variation for the 1930s may reflect common effects of the Great Depression. While the coefficient for the non-European developed countries also has a downward trend, the decline is more pronounced than for the European countries, and the coefficient fails to show the in-

6. The average values of ϕ for European developed countries for the two periods 1914–29 and 1939–48 would be higher—probably about 8 and 13 per cent respectively, excluding in both cases the U.S.S.R., if meaningful period ratios could be calculated for Germany.

creases during the two war periods. During the 1930s the ratio rises moderately as a result of the very differing response to the Great Depression in, on the one hand, Japan, South Africa, and New Zealand, where the ratio increased, and, on the other, in the United States, Canada, and Australia where it declined like in most European developed countries.

Fourthly, the dispersion of the values of ϕ among less developed countries has shown a noticeable decline only for the Afro-Asian group, but the number of countries in this, as in other subgroups of less developed countries, is too small for reliable results. Whether the higher level of the coefficient for American than for Afro-Asian less developed countries is significant could be decided only if both groups were increased considerably beyond their present membership of seven and six countries respectively.

The main conclusion to be drawn from a study of the level and movements of the coefficient of variation of ϕ, then, is one of slow convergence, more within than between country groups, features which may be interpreted economically as a tendency of the role of financial institutions within the economy, as measured by the ratio of changes in their assets to aggregate national product, to become slightly and slowly more similar.

THE ELASTICITY OF DEMAND FOR THE ISSUES OF FINANCIAL INSTITUTIONS

Since ϕ has shown an increasing trend over the last century, it is obvious that for all countries taken together the income elasticity of the issues of financial institutions must be above unity. Hence according to the usual classification of demand theory the issues of financial institutions are, from the point of view of the holder, a "luxury" rather than a "necessity." It is, nevertheless, worthwhile to ascertain somewhat more closely the values of the income elasticity for the issues of financial institutions for different periods and for different groups of countries. The average values for the usual groupings of countries are shown in Table 4–10 while the figures for individual countries and periods will be found in Table 4–11. Elasticity is in all

Table 4–10

Income Elasticity of Net Issues of Financial Institutions

RATIO OF AVERAGE RATES OF GROWTH OF ASSETS OF FINANCIAL INSTITUTIONS TO AVERAGE RATES OF GROWTH OF GNP

	1881 to 1900[a]	1901 to 1913	1914 to 1929	1930 to 1938	1939 to 1948	1949 to 1963
A. INCLUDING SOCIALIST COUNTRIES						
I. All countries	2.11	2.17	1.11	1.48	1.24	1.26
II. Developed	2.04	1.40	1.02	2.18	1.37	1.18
1. European	2.04	1.54	0.87	2.86	1.55	1.20
2. Non-European	2.05	1.10	1.29	0.93	1.02	1.14
III. Less developed	3.04	4.65	1.32	0.40	1.10	1.35
1. European		0.74	1.48	0.32	0.94	1.36
2. American		7.40	0.85	2.03	1.28	1.06
3. Afro-Asian	3.04	3.86	1.68	−1.60	0.97	1.70
B. EXCLUDING SOCIALIST COUNTRIES						
I. All countries	2.11	2.20	1.22	2.27	1.25	1.24
II. Developed	2.04	1.38	1.16	3.39	1.37	1.15
1. European	2.04	1.53	1.09	4.87	1.58	1.16
III. Less developed	3.04	4.65	1.32	0.48	1.11	1.34
1. European		0.74	1.48	1.06	0.94	1.29
C. IDENTICAL NONSOCIALIST COUNTRIES						
I. Developed	2.04	1.42	1.15	3.45	1.37	1.17
II. Less developed			1.32	0.41	1.05	1.22
D. COEFFICIENT OF VARIATION[b]						
I. All countries	0.53	2.40	0.79	5.54	1.06	0.31
II. Developed	0.54	2.72	0.80	4.68	1.29	0.26
1. European	0.58	3.37	0.82	4.09	1.39	0.28
2. Non-European	0.44	2.99	0.86	7.39	0.30	0.23
III. Less developed	2.52	1.50	0.77	4.35	0.24	0.33

[a] Values for 1861–80 are 2.89 in lines A I, A II, B I, and B II; 3.16 in lines A II 1 and B II 1; and 1.82 in line A II 2.

[b] Excluding socialist countries.

cases calculated as the ratio of average annual rate of growth of the assets of financial institutions to the rate of growth of gross national product, both in current prices, for the standard nine- to twenty-year periods. In the discussion, the period 1930–38 is usually omitted; during this period the elasticity coefficient was often negative as a

Table 4–11

Income Elasticity of Issues of Financial Institutions in Individual Countries

RATIO OF ANNUAL RATE OF CHANGE OF FINANCIAL ASSETS TO ANNUAL RATE OF CHANGE OF GNP

	1881 to 1900[a]	1901 to 1913	1914 to 1929	1930 to 1938	1939 to 1948	1949 to 1963
Argentina		1.41	1.22	3.22	1.13	0.77
Australia		0.84	1.10	3.80	1.31	0.83
Belgium	1.53	1.26	0.89	−2.14	0.77	1.63
Brazil			1.41	1.30	1.03	0.93
Canada	2.27	1.11	1.05	−1.47	0.79	1.19
Denmark	1.78	1.45	1.01	1.27	0.80	1.00
Egypt-U.A.R.		5.44	1.02	0.45	1.33	1.25
France	4.16	1.21	0.93	−16.27	0.73	1.31
Germany	1.71	1.69	0.95	1.53	8.13	1.06
Great Britain	0.97	1.39	1.38	2.43	1.22	0.86
Greece			1.04	1.06	0.86	1.44
India	3.04	2.27	2.00	−2.26	1.03	1.62
Israel						1.34
Italy	4.18	1.89	0.99	62.42	0.78	1.77
Jamaica						1.05
Japan	3.03	1.24	1.80	0.92	0.68	1.68
Mexico		13.39	−0.08	2.02	1.17	1.18
Netherlands	1.82	1.66	1.35	−1.54	0.89	1.03
New Zealand	1.12	1.20	1.08	1.95	1.06	0.79
Nigeria				−1.70	0.61	2.61
Norway	1.43	1.39	1.45	0.16	1.17	0.68
Pakistan						1.87
Philippines			2.03	−2.89	0.85	1.45
Puerto Rico				0.76	1.41	1.22
Rhodesia						1.16
Russia-U.S.S.R.		1.66	−1.34	−17.24	1.29	1.60
South Africa			1.35	2.12	1.50	1.00
Spain		0.74	1.92		1.02	1.14
Sweden	1.58	1.19	1.01	1.61	0.83	1.04
Switzerland	1.26	2.12	0.89	−0.78	0.49	1.20
Thailand					1.03	1.38
Trinidad					1.73	0.87
U.S.A.	1.81	1.09	1.36	−1.75	0.78	1.15
Venezuela				4.38	1.20	1.39
Yugoslavia				−0.42	0.94	1.51

[a] The values for 1861–80 are 4.82 for France, 2.17 for Germany, 2.54 for Great Britain, 3.10 for Switzerland, and 1.82 for U.S.A.

result of a positive (negative) rate of growth of assets and a negative (positive) rate of gross national product.

It is then seen that for all the remaining six periods the average income elasticity of demand for the total issues of financial institutions in all countries taken together is above unity, although the excess becomes very small for the period 1939–48 if we omit the extraordinarily high value for Germany that results from the sharp cutting down of outstanding issues in connection with the currency reform of 1948. These values again reflect the fact that the assets of financial institutions have throughout the periods grown at a rate somewhat more rapid than national product. More important is the observation that elasticity is considerably higher before World War I, when its value is between 2.1 and 2.9 for the three periods, than it is during the later three periods, for which it is very close to 1.25, reflecting the fact that the rate of growth of the assets of financial institutions was much more in excess of that of national product before World War I than in the following half-century. It is during this early period that most of the developed countries, which then dominated the averages, experienced the most rapid expansion of their financial superstructure.

The average elasticity is in all periods higher for less developed than for developed countries, though in the case of 1939–48 this is true only if Germany is excluded. This relationship is not astonishing since one might expect that the less developed countries, starting from a very low level of the share of assets of financial institutions in national product, would increase this proportion more rapidly than the developed countries, which by the turn of the century already had passed the initial period of financial growth. In fact, however, the value of the elasticity for the average of less developed countries in the postwar period is still much lower than it was for developed countries before World War I. It would therefore appear that the phase of rapid expansion of the financial superstructure compared to national product has not yet been reached in the less developed countries, or at least that the acceleration in the growth of share of the assets of financial institutions compared in national product is not yet as pronounced as it was in the developed countries in Europe and North America in the fifty years before World War I.

If attention is focused on narrower, and particularly on more homogeneous, groups of countries, a few additional trends and relations emerge. Thus the tendency for the coefficient of elasticity to decline becomes much more pronounced for the developed countries as a group and even more so for the two subgroups of European and of identical developed countries. There is, however, this difference that the value of the coefficient is considerably lower in the postwar period than for 1901–13 in the case of European developed countries, while the difference is insignificant for non-European or for identical developed countries, in both cases because of the high level of the coefficient for Japan in the postwar period.

The movements of the coefficient are rather erratic for the less developed countries, due to their nonhomogeneity as a group and the small number of countries in each subgroup. For the eight identical less developed countries for which the information is available back to World War I, no trend in the coefficient is discernible, the excess of the rate of growth of the assets of financial institutions over that of national product being only slightly lower in the postwar period than in 1914–29 after having disappeared for the 1930s. These countries did not at any time—except for the very short final period of 1961-63—have values of the coefficient as high as those shown for developed countries before World War I.

THE RELATION OF THE ASSETS OF FINANCIAL INSTITUTIONS TO NATIONAL PRODUCT

While national wealth rather than national product is the dimensionally appropriate denominator for the assets of financial institutions,[7] and the assets of financial institutions are the sum of the issues during the preceding periods and hence dependent on them, a separate brief look at the ratio of the assets of financial institutions to national product—which may be designated by Φ—seems useful. The necessary data are given for the usual group of countries and benchmark dates in Table 4–12 and for individual countries in Table 4–13.

The upward trend in the financial institutions' new issue ratio, which has been observed above in the section on the level and movement of ϕ, is necessarily also evident in the ratio of financial institutions' assets to national product. The trend, however, is less pronounced and the movements are smoother because the assets of financial institutions are the accumulation of their issues over long periods. Thus the average ratio of financial institutions' assets to gross national product for all countries increased only from 83 per cent in 1900 to 115 per cent in 1963, while ϕ rose from 4.2 per cent in the period 1881–1900 to 10.5 per cent in 1949–63.

The fluctuations in ϕ have been large enough to be reflected twice in a decrease of the ratio of financial institutions' assets to gross national product, first between 1913 and 1929, when the reduction is insignificant, and again between 1938 and 1948 when the decline in Φ from 110 to 95 per cent is a result not of a reduction in ϕ—the value of ϕ actually was considerably higher in the 1939–48 period than before—but of the very sharp rise in gross national product in current prices in most countries during the second half of the period, a development which produced the downward effect of inflation on both Φ and the financial interrelations ratio (FIR), which has already been mentioned several times, an effect we might call (in remembrance of Solon's debtors' relief operation) a quasi-seisachtheia.

The same effect is partly responsible for the persistence

7. For some data on the ratio of financial assets to national wealth, see Table 7–8.

TABLE 4–12

Assets/GNP Ratios of Financial Institutions (Φ)—Unweighted Country Averages

PER CENT

	1880[a]	1900	1913	1929	1938	1948	1963
A. INCLUDING SOCIALIST COUNTRIES							
I. All countries		83.9	96.2	94.2	109.8	95.4	114.5
II. Developed	72.9	102.5	122.8	131.1	159.5	132.5	155.9
1. European	81.5	106.2	137.7	131.9	158.7	133.9	152.6
2. Non-European	51.4	94.4	95.7	129.6	161.0	130.5	160.4
III. Less developed		24.2	39.6	41.9	49.5	51.3	65.4
1. European			45.8	64.7	75.2	62.7	108.5
2. American		35.1	54.5	44.8	48.3	59.2	56.3
3. Afro-Asian		7.0	20.5	21.1	35.4	36.6	54.5
B. EXCLUDING SOCIALIST COUNTRIES							
I. All countries		85.1	96.6	98.2	113.9	98.3	116.0
II. Developed	72.9	105.5	125.2	137.8	168.0	138.3	162.1
1. European	81.5	111.0	142.8	142.7	172.3	144.5	163.5
III. Less developed		24.2	39.6	40.7	47.2	50.3	60.6
1. European			45.8	69.4	73.6	60.2	94.0
C. IDENTICAL COUNTRIES[b]							
I. Developed	72.9	105.2	131.0	143.5	173.8	138.9	164.1
II. Less developed			39.5	46.3	60.2	63.6	71.8
D. COEFFICIENT OF VARIATION[b]							
I. All countries	55.8	52.9	61.7	67.3	63.6	61.7	51.4
II. Developed	47.9	29.6	41.4	40.7	29.8	37.8	22.6
III. Less developed		63.0	51.8	58.5	51.4	54.7	40.2

[a] The values for 1860 (five countries) are 39.9 in lines A II, B II, and C I; 43.0 in lines A II 1 and B II 1; and 27.8 in line A II 2.

[b] Excluding socialist countries.

Table 4–13

Assets/GNP Ratios of Financial Institutions (Φ) in Individual Countries

PER CENT

	1880[a]	1900	1913	1929	1938	1948	1963
Argentina		44	66	74	97	113	52
Australia		108	98	106	131	165	129
Belgium	71	94	109	85	140	102	161
Brazil			36	59	67	70	55
Canada	43	87	96	101	155	124	149
Denmark	95	147	184	186	198	166	166
Egypt-U.A.R.		10	42	43	60	90	111
France	50	96	104	90	130	63	104
Germany	73	114	158	89	99	107	124
Great Britain	95	93	103	131	158	184	162
Greece			57	65	66	37	83
India	2	4	7	11	30	35	53
Israel						61	138
Italy	36	61	97	95	137	67	174
Jamaica						46	50
Japan	13	82	97	223	212	61	217
Mexico		26	62	20	33	41	56
Netherlands	46	62	83	110	187	169	176
New Zealand	100	109	121	130	160	167	130
Nigeria				6	12	5	20
Norway	107	136	166	241	187	219	148
Pakistan						22	37
Philippines			12	25	48	39	60
Puerto Rico				46	41	62	82
Rhodesia						136	169
Russia-U.S.S.R.		58	86	25	23	27	44
South Africa			71	89	124	184	185
Spain		37	35	74	81	83	105
Sweden	89	123	136	138	161	142	148
Switzerland	153	184	287	261	325	225	272
Thailand					27	29	47
Trinidad					19	40	33
U.S.A.	49	86	91	129	185	147	167
Venezuela				25	33	41	66
Yugoslavia				55	79	68	138

[a] The 1860 ratios are 19 for France, 40 for Germany, 57 for Great Britain, 56 for Switzerland, and 28 for U.S.A.

of a fairly large difference in the values of Φ between developed and less developed countries, notwithstanding a diminishing spread in the values of ϕ. On the eve of World War I, the value of Φ for developed countries of 123 per cent was three times as high as that for less developed countries. The gap was still wide in 1963—156 per cent for developed against 65 per cent for less developed countries. This is, of course, partly the result of the fact that in the developed countries the most pronounced increases in Φ occurred before 1913. The ratio in 1880 was as low as 73 per cent, which is not much above the 1963 level of Φ for less developed countries.

Within developed countries the early advantage of the European countries diminished after World War I and both groups have virtually shown the same value of the ratio for the four benchmark dates from 1929 to 1963. The ratios for the subgroups of less developed countries also show a tendency to converge, particularly if the few European less developed countries are omitted. This is due both to the absence of any increase in Φ for American less developed countries after 1913, reflecting the quasi-seisachtheia effect of inflation in some of these countries (Argentina, Brazil, and Mexico) and partly to the continued increase in the ratio in the Afro-Asian countries, particularly during the 1930s and since World War II.

The tendency towards convergence is evident also in the decline of the coefficient of variation for less developed countries and, although in a considerably less regular and marked manner, of that for developed countries. That the coefficient fails to show a similar downward movement for all countries taken together reflects the persistence of the large gap in the averages of the two groups and points to the existence of two separate populations.

The movements of Φ for individual countries are too varied to permit easy summarization, and a country-by-country explanation would, as is true for ϕ, require case studies of their financial history. All that can be done here is to point to some features of the level or movements of the ratio of individual countries which seem to have some broader interest, even though it is not possible to identify in each case the factors that are likely to have been responsible. The order in which these features are taken up is no indication of their importance.

1. The opposite effect on Φ of repressed and of open inflation is particularly evident in the period from 1939 through 1948, which is dominated by World War II and its financing. Compared to an average decline in Φ for thirty-odd countries by one-seventh, the ratio fell on the average by one-third for the nine countries in which prices rose by more than 300 per cent (in ascending order of price rise: the Philippines, Spain, Thailand, Nigeria, Yugoslavia, France, Italy, Japan, and Greece). In the four countries where the price level multiplied twentyfold or more the decline in Φ averaged as much as 55 per cent. On the other hand, Φ increased or declined only slightly in the countries in which wartime inflation was small or was kept fairly well repressed. In ten countries in which prices at most doubled (Australia, Canada, Great Britain, India, Mexico, New Zealand, Norway, South Africa, Sweden, and Venezuela) the ratio on the average increased by about one-eighth. The exception to this behavior is Switzerland, which showed a decline in Φ by about 30 per cent even though the price level rose by only approximately 80 per cent.

2. The highest values of Φ are usually found in the small developed countries, although the difference between them and the other developed countries has been declining. Thus, for the six smallest developed countries (Belgium, Denmark, Netherlands, New Zealand, Norway, and Switzerland) Φ averaged 160 in 1913 and 175 in 1963, while the average value of Φ was less than 110 per cent in 1913 and about 155 per cent in 1963 for the six largest developed countries (France, Germany, Great Britain, Italy, Japan, and the United States). The reasons for this differential or its movement are not evident. (They may have something to do with the greater openness of the small countries.)

3. Some now developed countries seem to have built up a full-fledged financial system, measured by the value of Φ, early in their development, others only later. Thus, a ratio of 100 per cent or more was shown as early as 1880 for Denmark, Germany, New Zealand, Norway, Switzerland, and possibly Australia. In most of the other developed countries

it took until World War I—for instance in Belgium, France and the United Kingdom—or even until the 1920s to reach this ratio, for instance in Canada, Japan, the Netherlands, and the United States.

4. While most of the changes in the ratio were gradual unless influenced by sharp inflations, a few cases of explosive movements are visible in Table 4–12. Examples are the rise in Φ for Japan from 13 to 82 in the last two decades of the nineteenth century and the second sharp increase from less than 100 to well over 200 between 1913 and 1929, the quadrupling of the rate for Egypt between 1900 and 1913, the tripling of the Indian rate in the 1930s, and the tripling of the rate for Switzerland between 1860 and 1880. Obviously most of these explosive movements occurred early in a country's financial development when the starting value of Φ was low. Some of the other large developed countries probably would show a similar movement if figures were available for the thirty to fifty years preceding 1860.

AN ELEMENTARY ECONOMETRIC ANALYSIS OF ϕ AND Φ[8]

In earlier sections suggestions have occasionally been made about possible or probable determinants of some of the observed features of the net issue ratio of financial institutions (ϕ) or of the ratio of the assets of financial institutions to national product (Φ), and we shall continue to make similar suggestions in the following chapters. To proceed in this direction more systematically and thoroughly would call for an intensive econometric analysis of the data. This would require experimentation with a large number of economic factors which might have influenced the level, the movements, the differentials, and the interrelations of ϕ and Φ, and would necessitate trying out many alternative formulations of the relationships between ϕ and Φ and the independent determining variables. All this, however, is a

8. For details see Appendix III.

task which goes well beyond the author's competence and the resources that were available for this study.

A limited and preliminary attempt in this direction is nevertheless possible and was regarded as worthwhile, and its results are presented and briefly discussed in Appendix III. These are essentially simple and multiple linear correlations between ϕ and Φ for individual countries and for each benchmark date or period as alternative dependent variables (developed and less developed countries usually are treated separately) and a few characteristics of the level and the movements of real gross national product per head and of the price level as independent variables and determinants of ϕ and Φ. The main results of this experiment are summarized in the following paragraphs.

1. In most periods two of the independent variables covered by the experiment (the rate of growth of real gross national product per head and the rate of change in the price level) explain at least one-third of the observed differences among countries, but they very rarely explain more than two-thirds of the differences. These two factors thus are undoubtedly among the most important determinants of the ratio of new issues of financial institutions to national product, although several other factors not identified are of substantial, and sometimes even of greater, importance in explaining these differences.

2. In general, though not always, the rates of change of real national product per head and of the price level explain a slightly larger proportion of intercountry differences in ϕ for developed and less developed countries than for all countries taken together. This suggests that as far as the financial new issue ratio is concerned, developed and underdeveloped countries behave as if they belonged to separate populations rather than to one universe.

3. The proportion of intercountry differences explained by the rate of change of real product per head and of the price level does not vary substantially among the six periods, except that it is particularly low for the World War II years 1939–48.

4. There existed substantial, though far from complete, continuity in the ranking of countries with respect to the value of their financial new issues ratio, suggesting that the relative values of the ratio are not erratic but reflect enduring characteristics in the financial and economic structure of the various countries. This continuity was considerably more pronounced among developed than among less developed countries. It was also generally more marked—anticipating subjects to be discussed in Chapter 5—for thrift and insurance organizations than for central and commercial banks whose issues are apparently more subject to irregular influence such as repressed or open inflation and deflation.

5. In the case of the ratio of the assets of financial institutions to national wealth (Φ), the level of real national product per head emerged as generally the most important single determinant. Its explanatory value, however, showed considerable variations over the period and was usually considerably lower for developed than for less developed countries. For the latter, however, it explained between four-fifths and five-sixths of intercountry differences in Φ for 1929, 1938 and 1948, though only one-seventh in 1963.

5 THE STRUCTURE OF THE NET ISSUE RATIO OF FINANCIAL INSTITUTIONS

As it is known that the share of the main components of ϕ—the ratios of the issues of central banks, deposit banks, thrift institutions, insurance organizations, and miscellaneous financial intermediaries—differs among countries, and that the various components of ϕ have followed different paths over the last one hundred years, it would be desirable to treat each of the five components in the same way and in as much detail as this has been attempted for the aggregate net issue ratio of financial institutions (ϕ) in the preceding chapter. Since the basic data for the assets of all financial institutions, and hence for ϕ, have been built up from similar data on the assets of each individual type of financial intermediaries in each country, data which were then grouped into five or six broad categories of institutions, there is no fundamental obstacle to such an approach. For the reasons set forth at the end of the preceding chapter, the treatment of the five components of ϕ in this chapter must, however, be much briefer and, what is more serious, the discussion must stop even earlier in an attempt to explain the observed behavior of the components and identify the main determining factors. These limitations will be the more keenly felt since two of the five components —the new issue ratios of central banks and of deposit banks —are closely connected with the core of monetary theory and policy, and since an adequate comparative study—adequate as to the number and character of countries included and as to the length of the period covered—is still lacking.[1] Even narrow comparative quantitative studies are rare, although the situation has been improving in recent years. It should be clear, therefore, that this chapter cannot claim to close the gap. At best it may provide some leads for a later, more intensive analysis, an analysis that would have an opportunity of using a larger and more refined body of data and of applying more powerful statistical methods to them.

THE ISSUES OF CENTRAL BANKS

The central banks' issue ratio (ϕ_c), shown in Table 5–1, is the only one of the components of ϕ for which the average for less developed countries is higher now, and has been higher during most periods since the turn of the century, than it is for the more developed countries. This relationship reflects the fact that the central banks' issue ratio is the result of three chief components—first, and usually most important, the ratio of the net issuance of bank notes, which in most countries now constitute the bulk of currency in circulation; secondly, the deposits which commercial banks in many countries keep with their central bank by law or custom, and which vary greatly in relative importance; and, thirdly, government and sometimes private deposits.

It is not yet possible to follow the distribution of the issues of central banks among these categories for a number of countries and a period long enough for confident generalizations. There is little doubt, however, that throughout the past century the issuance of bank notes has in most countries and during most periods accounted for the bulk of ϕ_c. It is only since World War I, and even more since the 1930s, that bankers' and governments' deposits have come to account for a substantial part of ϕ_c, particularly in less developed countries.

1. As far as the postwar period goes, this gap will be filled by a study by Professor H. C. Wallich, to be published in this series

During the postwar period, the central banks' issue ratio in the thirty-five countries, as shown in Table 5–2 ranged from less than 0.4 per cent of national product in a few

TABLE 5–1

Net Issue Ratios of Central Banks and Their Share in Issues and Assets of All Financial Institutions
UNWEIGHTED COUNTRY AVERAGES (PER CENT)

	Relation to GNP		Relation to Change in GNP	Share in Total of All Financial Institutions	
	Issues[a]	Assets[b]	Change in Issues[c]	Issues[a]	Assets[b]
			ALL NONSOCIALIST COUNTRIES		
1881–1900	.24	8.3	8.5	5.2	11.9
1901–1913	.39	8.4	9.1	6.2	13.6
1914–1929	.70	10.0	13.2	16.2	12.0
1930–1938	.92	16.1	−31.5	26.1	12.2
1939–1948	2.88	21.2	25.4	28.8	17.7
1949–1963	1.35	15.7	13.0	13.9	17.4
			DEVELOPED NONSOCIALIST COUNTRIES		
1861–1880	.15	8.1	9.9	6.6	13.7
1881–1900	.25	7.9	9.1	5.6	12.7
1901–1913	.36	7.8	9.0	5.2	8.7
1914–1929	.68	10.3	12.2	7.5	6.5
1930–1938	1.16	18.6	−54.8	25.5	8.6
1939–1948	3.34	24.9	30.1	20.8	11.3
1949–1963	1.11	16.6	12.4	7.3	10.6
			LESS DEVELOPED NONSOCIALIST COUNTRIES		
1881–1900		9.5			
1901–1913	.48	9.5	9.3	9.1	28.2
1914–1929	.72	9.4	15.0	3.7	21.7
1930–1938	.56	12.9	5.9	26.9	17.4
1939–1948	2.29	16.7	19.6	38.5	25.5
1949–1963	1.63	14.7	13.7	21.9	25.5

[a] Change in assets during period as per cent of cumulated GNP of period.
[b] Assets at end of period as per cent of GNP of last year of period.
[c] Ratio of first differences in issues and in GNP of successive periods.

developed countries (in ascending order Norway, United States, Denmark, New Zealand, and Great Britain) to 4.9 per cent in Yugoslavia, 5.6 per cent in Israel, and 8.7 per cent in Brazil, all countries having expanded rapidly to the

Table 5–2

Net Issue Ratios of Central Banks (ϕ_c) in Individual Countries

PER CENT OF PERIOD'S GROSS NATIONAL PRODUCT

	1880 to 1900[a]	1901 to 1913	1914 to 1929	1930 to 1938	1939 to 1948	1949 to 1963
Argentina		1.86	.87	−.08	2.29	2.51
Australia			.58	.29	4.81	.60
Belgium	.45	.60	1.25	1.65	2.93	1.30
Brazil			.81	2.28	3.85	8.70
Canada				.97	1.54	.31
Denmark	.10	.45	.25	.58	3.85	.20
Egypt-U.A.R.		.59	1.25	−.73	6.15	1.04
France	.30	.35	2.45	.93	1.79	1.55
Germany	.20	.25	.66	.52	.75	.92
Great Britain	.06	.02	.53	.38	1.27	.40
Greece			1.53	1.44	3.62	2.77
India				1.03	2.19	.66
Israel						5.62
Italy	.20	.51	1.02	−.27	6.23	1.80
Jamaica						.79
Japan	1.41	.88	.79	.93	8.07	1.30
Mexico			.19	1.88	1.78	.93
Netherlands	.09	.28	.61	1.41	2.63	.65
New Zealand				2.31	2.90	.35
Nigeria				.06	.16	.67
Norway	.31	.56	.56	.76	.93	−.14
Pakistan						.88
Philippines			.24	.58	1.68	.97
Puerto Rico						
Rhodesia						2.07
Russia-U.S.S.R.		.73	.29	3.04	1.69	2.44
South Africa			.70	1.38	2.65	.60
Spain		−.03	.91	−.25	2.73	1.71
Sweden	.42	.56	.40	1.40	1.43	.70
Switzerland		.96	.69	3.57	1.73	1.63
Thailand					2.41	1.89
Trinidad					.95	.13
U.S.A.			.43	1.76	1.83	.13
Venezuela					2.07	.74
Yugoslavia				−.24	6.67	4.86

[a] The figures for 1861–80 are .45 for France, .20 for Germany, and .09 for Great Britain.

accompaniment of pronounced and sustained price rises. The mean for all thirty-five countries was 1.5 per cent, the result of averages of 1.2 per cent for nineteen developed and of 1.8 per cent for sixteen less developed countries. While the difference between developed European and non-European countries was small—the higher value for the latter is due to the inclusion of Israel—the seven American less developed countries with an average of 2.0 per cent were far ahead of the six Afro-Asian less developed countries whose average of 1.0 per cent was even below that for all developed countries. The European less developed countries showed the highest average for any group—3.1 per cent—but this position is of limited significance since the group includes only three countries (Greece, Spain, and Yugoslavia).

The long-term trend of the central banks' issue ratio has been sharply upward (Table 5–3), probably reflecting—except in the Afro-Asian and some of the American less developed countries—the substitution of bank notes for coin within currency in circulation and the introduction of reserve requirements for deposit banks, more than an increase in the monetization ratio of the economy or in the liquidity preference for bank notes over other claims. During the second half of the nineteenth century, when the information is essentially limited to European developed countries, the increase in central banks' assets averaged as little as 0.2 per cent of national product. It is not astonishing that during that period central banks could not in general exercise a far-reaching influence on the economy, nor did they usually wish to do so. In the European developed countries the ratio doubled in the dozen years before World War I. The further increase shown for the period 1914–29 fails to bring out the full effect of World War I because ϕ_c was in most countries considerably higher between 1914 and 1920 than during the 1920s. The increase continued during the 1930s, but differences among countries were very great, as some countries gave free rein to the deflationary forces of the Great Depression, while others in an antideflationary effort considerably expanded the volume of lending of their central banks. This diversity is reflected in the increase of the coefficient of variation for all nonsocialist countries from 0.77 in the period 1914–29 to

TABLE 5–3

Net Issue Ratios of Central Banks (ϕ_c) in Different Groups of Countries
Unweighted Country Averages
PER CENT OF PERIOD'S GROSS NATIONAL PRODUCT

	1881 to 1900[a]	1901 to 1913	1914 to 1929	1930 to 1938	1939 to 1948	1949 to 1963
A. INCLUDING SOCIALIST COUNTRIES						
I. All Countries	.24	.41	.68	.95	2.96	1.48
II. Developed	.25	.38	.66	1.27	3.26	1.18
1. European	.21	.48	.79	1.27	3.05	1.04
2. Non-European		.18	.42	1.27	3.63	1.37
III. Less developed		.48	.72	.49	2.61	1.83
1. European		−.03	1.22	.32	4.34	3.11
2. American		.93	.62	.82	1.82	1.97
3. Afro-Asian		.29	.50	.22	2.52	1.02
B. EXCLUDING SOCIALIST COUNTRIES						
I. All countries	.24	.39	.70	.92	2.88	1.35
II. Developed	.25	.36	.68	1.16	3.36	1.11
1. European	.21	.45	.84	1.09	3.19	.91
III. Less developed		.48	.72	.56	2.29	1.83
1. European		−.03	1.22	.60	3.17	2.94
C. IDENTICAL COUNTRIES[b]						
I. Developed	.25	.39	.69	1.21	3.30	.79
II. Less developed			.72	.77	3.03	2.41
D. COEFFICIENT OF VARIATION[b]						
I. All countries	1.48	1.16	.77	1.03	.75	1.24
II. Developed	1.41	.86	.81	.76	.73	1.12
III. Less developed		1.50	.70	1.65	.68	1.25

[a] The figures for 1861–80 are: .15 in lines A I, A II, B I, and B II; and .18 in lines A II 1 and B II 1.

[b] Nonsocialist countries.

1.02 in 1930–38. World War II, of course, led to an unprecedented expansion of central banks' issues, carrying ϕ_c to a high of 3.0 per cent of national product for the period 1939–48. The movement was quite general as shown, first, by the fact that ϕ_c increased in all but three of the twenty-eight countries and, secondly, by the decline in the coefficient of variation from 1.02 to 0.75, the lowest value for any of the nine periods.

The expansion of central banks' assets relative to national product during the postwar period naturally was considerably slower than it had been during the 1940s, reflecting the existence in many countries of excess liquidity at the end of World War II, but in most of them ϕ_c remained well above prewar levels. For all countries included it averages 1.35 per cent, i.e., almost twice the average for the twenty-five years before World War II and more than three times the level in the period 1901–13. Whether the acceleration observed in the early 1960s will continue—the average for the years 1961–63 was as high as 1.65 per cent compared to a value of 1.37 for 1949–60—remains to be seen.

In interpreting the level and movements of ϕ_c it is necessary to keep in mind not only the position of the central bank in the monetary system—indicated, for example, by the relation of central bank money to deposit bank money—but also differences in the relative share of what are for most central banks the three main types of their issues, viz. currency, bankers' deposits, and government deposits.

The share of bankers' deposits in central banks' assets and issues differs considerably among countries reflecting their financial history and monetary organization. In 1963, for example, bankers' deposits—representing mainly reserves required by law—averaged 14 per cent of central banks' total assets for the thirty-two countries, omitting Puerto Rico which has no central bank and the two socialist countries. The ratio was considerably higher for developed than for less developed countries and among developed countries higher for non-European than for European countries. While the ratio was below 10 per cent for one-half of the thirty-two countries, it exceeded 20 per cent in seven countries (Australia, Canada, Germany, Israel, New Zealand, Switzerland, and the United States), all developed countries and most of them strongly influenced in their monetary structure by the United States' example of using reserve requirements for monetary control.

Government deposits constitute a substantial part of the issues of central banks in only a few countries. In 1963 they exceeded one-tenth of total liabilities in Denmark, Israel, Jamaica, the Netherlands, Norway, the Philippines, Rhodesia, South Africa, Thailand, and Venezuela—the list does not include any of the large developed countries—and their share averaged 8 per cent for all thirty-two countries, being slightly higher in less developed than in developed countries (10 as against 7 per cent).

Since high shares of bankers' and of government deposits do not generally coincide and the share of capital funds and miscellaneous liabilities is generally small, bank notes constitute the majority of issues of central banks in almost all countries. Thus in 1963 the share of bank notes in central banks' total assets was above 50 per cent in twenty-six of the thirty-two countries, exceeded 75 per cent in ten of them, and averaged 67 per cent for all thirty-two countries as well as for developed and less developed countries separately. The average ratio was, however, higher (77 per cent) for European than for non-European developed countries (52 per cent). It is thus the factors which determine the ratio of money to national product and the share of bank notes in total money supply that must be relied upon in first instance to explain level and movements of ϕ_c and differences among them, although the relative importance of bankers' and government deposits, which largely reflect differences in institutional arrangements, exercise an important additional influence.

Not enough is known on a sufficiently wide international basis, and particularly for a sufficiently long period, to venture more than a few remarks on these factors. Looking at the whole period and all thirty-five countries, there can, of course, be little doubt that the share of central bank note issues in the total money supply has increased compared to coin, particularly to gold in circulation, but has declined in relation to monetary (check) deposits. For the most important developed countries and for the world as well, the share of bank notes in the total of notes and monetary deposits decreased between 1885 and 1913 from approximately two-fifths to one-fourth, but remained at that level until the early 1960s.[2] Thus for the last half century the increase in ϕ_c would seem to be attributable primarily to a rise in the ratio of money to national product, i.e. to a decline in the income velocity of money and, secondarily, to the rise in bankers' and government deposits with central banks, rather than to an increase in the share of bank notes in total monetary circulation, which had been an important factor in the preceding half-century.

Turning to the determinants of intercountry differences in ϕ_c, the differences among or within groups of countries in the ratio of bank notes in circulation (which can statistically be divided into differences in the ratio of money issues to national product and in the share of bank notes in total money issues) are known to be very great, but they do not seem to be amenable to simple explanations, as the recourse to differences in "payment and hoarding habits" does not provide a satisfactory answer. That the issuance of bank notes represents, on the average, a higher proportion of national product in less developed than in developed countries (for the period 1949–63 the ratios were 0.9 and 0.6 per cent of national product respectively, or slightly more than one-half of ϕ_c in both cases) may be expected in view of the fact that bank notes represent on the average a considerably higher proportion of total money in circulation in less developed countries—in 1963 nearly one-half against approximately one-third in developed countries. But the variations in ϕ_c within these two groups of countries are large, and often enduring, and do not seem to yield to easy explanations.

2. See R. Triffin, *The Evolution of the International Monetary System: Historical Reappraisal and Future Perspectives* (Princeton, Princeton University, 1964), Tables 2 and 6.

THE ISSUES OF DEPOSIT BANKS

Total Issues

The ratio of the net issues of financial instruments by deposit (commercial) banks to aggregate national product (ϕ_b) is the largest single component of ϕ, reflecting the fact that commercial banks have in most periods and countries issued larger amounts of financial instruments than any other single group of financial institutions, and often have accounted for the majority of issues of all financial institutions. These issues are the sum of three components which are of very different character from the point of view of economic and financial analysis.

The first component are the check (demand) deposits which form part, and often represent the bulk, of total money supply, and are held mostly by domestic business enterprises, households, and governments. The second component consists of time and savings deposits of households, which are very similar to household deposits with specialized thrift institutions, such as savings banks and building societies. The third component is a heterogeneous remainder, the two most important components of which are the deposits of other banks and the issues of deposit banks' own stock, primarily to domestic individuals. This third component also includes time deposits held by domestic business and government and by foreigners, as well as miscellaneous minor items. It is not yet possible to separate these three components for all countries over the long period covered here—even in the United States the official separation of demand and time deposits in banking statistics goes back only to 1914. It is not even possible to identify that part of the issues of commercial banks which forms part of the money supply on such a broad international basis except for the postwar period. Hence the discussion must be based on the undivided value of ϕ_b, which is derived as the ratio of the change in the total assets of deposit banks to aggregate national product. The statement occasionally made about the contribution of one or the other of the three components can be based on evidence from only a few countries insofar as the period preceding 1948 is involved.

The outstanding features of the level and movement of ϕ_b may be summarized as follows, on the basis mostly of the figures shown in Table 5–4 to 5–6:

1. The average value of ϕ_b for all countries has moved irregularly, rising slightly from less than 2 per cent of

TABLE 5–4

Net Issue Ratios of Deposit (Commercial) Banks (ϕ_b) and Their Share in the Total for All Financial Institutions

UNWEIGHTED COUNTRY AVERAGES (PER CENT)

	Relation to GNP		Relation to Change in GNP	Share in Total of All Financial Institutions	
	Issues[a]	Assets[b]	Change in Issues[c]	Issues[a]	Assets[b]
			ALL NONSOCIALIST COUNTRIES		
1881–1900	1.78	30.8	.55	40.5	44.0
1901–1913	2.58	37.1	.83	45.5	48.9
1914–1929	2.29	43.6	.46	56.3	49.9
1930–1938	.33	42.9	−.11	11.0	38.5
1939–1948	3.50	38.9	.33	33.8	37.1
1949–1963	3.45	38.3	.40	35.0	35.5
			DEVELOPED NONSOCIALIST COUNTRIES		
1861–1880	1.66	32.9	.79	42.8	45.9
1881–1900	1.90	45.7	.59	38.3	42.2
1901–1913	2.95	54.6	.73	42.4	43.2
1914–1929	2.76	56.4	.56	35.5	40.2
1930–1938	.26	52.7	−.27	15.7	29.7
1939–1948	4.34	46.6	.42	30.8	34.8
1949–1963	3.95	48.7	.49	26.9	28.8
			LESS DEVELOPED NONSOCIALIST COUNTRIES		
1901–1913	1.48	21.7	1.16	54.8	59.2
1914–1929	1.35	23.3	.26	97.9	64.1
1930–1938	.42	21.9	.14	49.9	49.3
1939–1948	2.46	20.2	.22	37.5	39.8
1949–1963	2.86	25.7	.30	44.7	43.5

[a] Change in assets during period as per cent of cumulated GNP of period.

[b] Assets at end of period as per cent of GNP of last year of period.

[c] Ratio of first differences in issues and in GNP of successive periods.

gross national product in the period 1861–80 to 2.6 per cent in the years preceding World War I. After a sharp decline during the Great Depression, the value of ϕ_b has apparently settled at the higher level of about 3.5 per cent of gross national product for both periods 1938–48 and 1948–63. As a result, the ratio of the assets of deposit banks to national product has risen from 0.17 in 1860 to 0.43 in 1913 but then has declined to 0.36 in 1963. The ratio thus was not higher in 1963 than in 1900.

TABLE 5–5

Net Issue Ratios of Deposit Banks (ϕ_b) in Different Groups of Countries
UNWEIGHTED COUNTRY AVERAGES
PER CENT OF PERIOD'S GROSS NATIONAL PRODUCT

	1881 to 1900[b]	1901 to 1913[b]	1914 to 1929	1930 to 1938	1939 to 1948	1949 to 1963
A. INCLUDING SOCIALIST COUNTRIES						
I. All countries	1.78	2.56	2.13	.28	3.27	3.26
II. Developed	1.90	2.90	2.50	.25	4.09	3.74
1. European	1.70	2.97	2.36	−.74	3.25	3.43
2. Non-European	2.41	2.74	2.76	2.06	5.62	4.16
III. Less developed	.09	1.48	1.35	.32	2.28	2.68
1. European		.34	2.75	.02	1.70	3.10
2. American		3.29	1.21	.57	3.32	3.21
3. Afro-Asian	.09	.24	.56	.24	1.37	1.86
B. EXCLUDING SOCIALIST COUNTRIES						
I. All countries	1.78	2.58	2.29	.33	3.50	3.45
II. Developed	1.90	2.95	2.76	.26	4.34	3.95
1. European	1.70	30.6	2.75	−.81	3.58	3.78
III. Less developed	.09	1.48	1.35	.42	2.46	2.86
1. European		.34	2.75	.43	2.61	4.66
C. IDENTICAL COUNTRIES[a]						
I. Developed	1.90	3.06	2.96	.06	4.30	4.20
II. Less developed			1.35	.54	2.88	3.44
D. COEFFICIENT OF VARIATION[a]						
I. All countries	.83	.77	.73	5.71	.69	.77
II. Developed	.76	.65	.60	9.04	.57	.81
III. Less developed		1.18	.92	1.47	.75	.57

[a] Nonsocialist countries.
[b] Figures for 1861–80 are 1.66 in lines A II and B II, 1.74 in lines A II 1 and B II 1, and 1.32 in line A II 2.

2. Except during the Great Depression, ϕ_b has always been higher in developed than in less developed countries,

Table 5–6

Net Issue Ratios of Deposit Banks (ϕ_b) in Individual Countries
PER CENT OF PERIOD'S GROSS NATIONAL PRODUCT

	1881 to 1900[a]	1900 to 1913	1914 to 1929	1930 to 1938	1939 to 1948	1949 to 1963
Argentina		1.80	1.27	1.83	6.69	4.12
Australia		1.43	1.85	1.75	3.56	1.76
Belgium	1.19	2.54	3.40	−1.82	3.15	2.84
Brazil			2.84	0.34	4.07	6.32
Canada	1.85	4.53	2.83	−0.21	4.76	3.06
Denmark	1.52	2.93	1.96	0.89	3.31	4.84
Egypt-U.A.R.		0.18	0.48	−0.29	2.33	3.02
France	0.45	1.42	2.57	−0.54	2.21	3.37
Germany	1.10	2.58	0.17	−0.79	−0.48	2.17
Great Britain	1.06	0.97	1.83	1.08	5.39	1.73
Greece			3.28	0.57	0.61	3.39
India	0.09	0.31	0.25	0.20	1.66	1.01
Israel						6.50
Italy	0.24	2.19	3.00	−1.12	7.34	5.99
Jamaica						2.36
Japan	4.36	2.66	5.87	7.71	11.31	13.65
Mexico		4.77	−0.49	0.35	1.38	1.02
Netherlands	0.43	1.23	2.62	−1.43	3.77	2.39
New Zealand	0.67	1.58	1.67	1.57	3.05	1.07
Nigeria				0.03	0.23	1.07
Norway	2.92	3.80	3.02	−2.59	4.71	1.97
Pakistan						1.22
Philippines			0.95	1.01	1.72	2.74
Puerto Rico				−0.56	4.17	4.31
Rhodesia						2.68
Russia-U.S.S.R.		2.05	−1.63			
South Africa			0.80	1.55	5.73	2.01
Spain		0.34	2.21	2.94	4.62	5.92
Sweden	3.02	3.92	1.99	0.89	2.71	3.12
Switzerland	5.07	8.98	6.98	−2.71	3.69	10.03
Thailand					0.90	2.19
Trinidad					2.91	2.19
U.S.A.	2.77	3.50	3.53	−0.01	5.29	2.54
Venezuela				0.89	0.68	2.13
Yugoslavia				−0.79	−0.11	

[a] Ratios for 1861–80 are 0.46 for France, 0.81 for Germany, 1.61 for Great Britain, 4.59 for Switzerland, and 1.32 for U.S.A.

but the difference has been shrinking. Thus, in the period 1901–13, ϕ_b in developed countries (almost 3 per cent) was twice as high as in less developed countries. In the postwar period, on the other hand, ϕ_b has an average value for less developed countries of 2.9 per cent, which is equal to the ratio reached in developed countries half a century earlier, so that the value of ϕ_b for developed countries was now only 1 per cent ahead of that for the less developed countries. The difference is, however, more marked in the ratio of the assets of deposit banks to gross national product, because this ratio is influenced by the values of ϕ_b over a long period of the past. Thus the 1963 ratio of almost 50 per cent for developed countries was still about twice as high as that then prevailing for less developed countries. This represents, nevertheless, a substantial change from the situation around the turn of the century, when the ratio had been aproximately four times as high in developed than in less developed countries.

3. The share of deposit banks in the total issues and in the assets of all financial institutions has been considerably lower since the Great Depression than it had been before. There are, however, no substantial differences within the period 1881–1929, during which the ratio varied only between 44 and 49 per cent, and again since World War II, when the share has remained close to one-third.

4. The share of deposit banks in the assets of all financial institutions has at all periods been higher in less developed than in developed countries, although the figure was lower after the Great Depression than before in both groups of countries. The value of the share for less developed countries of a little over 40 per cent observed during the period 1949–63 is close to that prevailing in developed countries in the period 1881–1929.

5. Among developed countries, the value of ϕ_b has been considerably higher for non-European than for European countries since World War I. The difference is particularly marked for the period from 1929–48, when the ratio for European developed countries is as low as 1.4 per cent of gross national product, compared to 3.9 per cent for non-European developed countries. The difference reflects, first, the fact that the total assets of deposit banks in the European developed countries declined during the 1930s under

the impact of the Great Depression, while they continued to increase, although at a somewhat slower pace than before, in non-European countries that followed more energetic antideflationary policies. It reflects, secondly, the considerably higher values of ϕ_b in non-European developed countries during World War II and its aftermath. For the postwar period as a whole, the value of ϕ_b for the non-European developed countries was 0.7 per cent of gross national product, or about one-fifth, above that of the European countries, but the difference was reduced to only one-twentieth for the period 1961–63. As a result, the ratio of the assets of deposit banks to national product in 1963 was somewhat higher at 54 per cent for the non-European countries than for the European countries, for which it averaged 43 per cent. The difference, however, was largely due, as is also true for part of the differences in the value of ϕ_b, to the high value for Japan, the average for the other non-European countries only slightly exceeding that for the European countries.

6. Considerable differences also exist among less developed countries. Possibly the most interesting feature is the relatively high level of ϕ_b for the American less developed countries. For these countries, ϕ_b has been slightly above 3 per cent of gross national product both for the period 1900–13 and since 1938, and thus has been at or a little above the level of all developed countries. The high values of ϕ_b for the American less developed countries are due in part to the continuous inflation which has affected some of them. The values of ϕ_b for the Afro-Asian less developed countries are considerably lower if longer periods are considered, but the gap may be closing since the ratio for this group of countries was as high as 3.3 per cent of gross national product for the period 1961–63, a ratio equal to that observed for the American less developed countries and almost as high as that of the European developed countries. The ratio of the assets of deposit banks to national product at the end of the period (1963), however, was about the same—at a little less than one-fourth of gross national prod-

uct—for both the American and the Afro-Asian less developed countries, because the higher values of ϕ_b for the American countries were in the long run offset by the effective devaluation of the older issues of deposit banks which occurred in the process of inflation.

7. The difference in the values of ϕ_b and of the share of deposit banks in the assets of all financial institutions persists if we turn to individual countries. Thus, in 1963 the share of deposit banks was below one-fifth in four of the thirty-three countries. Three of these were developed countries (Germany, South Africa, and New Zealand) and the low value for the only underdeveloped country (Mexico) is explained by the existence of a group of special financial institutions (*financieras*) that are quite similar to commercial banks in many of their operations although they do not issue check deposits. At the other end of the scale, all five of the countries having a share of deposit banks of more than 50 per cent are in the less developed group (Jamaica, Nigeria, Philippines, Puerto Rico, and Trinidad). So are six of the nine countries showing a share of deposit banks in the assets of all financial institutions of between 35 and 50 per cent. The only developed countries in that group are Sweden, Switzerland, and Japan.

Components of ϕ_b

On an international scale, the distribution of the issues of deposit banks among the three main sources—monetary deposits, time and saving deposits, and miscellaneous sources—and hence, by inference, the composition of ϕ_b, does not seem to have changed radically since the turn of the century. While the evidence for the period before 1948 is too scanty for confident conclusions, it would seem that the proportion of both monetary and nonmonetary deposits has slightly increased while that of net worth (issues of the bank's own stock and retained earnings) and of miscellaneous liabilities has decreased substantially, as is the case in the United States.

The share of time and saving deposits in the total assets

of deposit banks was in the order of one-third in 1913 and in 1929, when data are available for about one-half of the thirty-five countries, and it was at the same level in 1963 both for these selected countries and for all thirty-three nonsocialist countries, as shown in Table 5–7. There is, however,

TABLE 5–7

Relation of Time and Savings Deposits to Assets of Deposit Banks
UNWEIGHTED COUNTRY AVERAGES (PER CENT)

	1913 (1)	1929 (2)	1948 (3)	1963 (4)
All nonsocialist countries	33	35	25	36
Developed countries	32	39	25	36
European	26	31	27	38
Non-European	38	41	23	34
Less developed countries	39[a]	24[b]	24	36
European			21	51
American			28	38
Afro-Asian			22	30
Number of countries	14	18	32	33

[a] Two countries only (Brazil and Greece).
[b] Five countries only (Argentina, Brazil, Greece, Mexico, and Spain).
Source: Derived from data in Table 5–8.

some evidence that the share of time and saving deposits had been increasing during the thirty to fifty years before World War I and that it had been declining substantially between 1938 and 1948. For the postwar period, for which the statistical material is available for all nonsocialist countries, a substantial rise from 25 per cent in 1948 to 36 per cent in 1963 is evidenced. The increase, however, apparently did not do more than restore the ratio to the level that had been reached before the Great Depression. From these movements one may infer that the share of the issues of time and saving deposits in ϕ_b increased before 1913, showed little change between the beginning of World War I and World War II, declined sharply from 1939 to 1948, and increased sharply from 1949 through 1963. In the postwar period, the ratio of the net issuance of time and saving deposits to aggregate national product, which we may designate as ϕ_{bt}, was 1.3 per cent of gross national product or nearly two-fifths of aggregate ϕ_b for all non-socialist countries together.

The postwar period is the only one for which information is available for a sufficient number of countries to investigate possible systematic differences between developed and less developed countries or among subgroups of countries. It then appears that the share of time and saving deposits in the total assets of deposit banks increased both for developed and less developed countries and to about the same extent, i.e. by one-half of the 1948 value of the ratio. Among the developed countries the increase was similar for the European and the non-European groups. So was the somewhat smaller increase for the American and the Afro-Asian less developed countries. The extraordinary increase for the European underdeveloped countries shown in Table 5–7 loses in significance because the group includes only two countries (Greece and Spain). The ratio of the net issues of time and saving deposits to gross national product was slightly higher for developed countries (fully 1.4 per cent) than for less developed countries, for which it averaged a little less than 1.1 per cent, the difference reflecting the higher level of ϕ_b for the developed countries.[3]

Since the issues of time and saving deposits by commercial banks are very similar in character to the issues of thrift institutions a comparison between these two types of issues is called for but unfortunately must be limited to the postwar period. During these fifteen years the average ratio of issues of time and saving deposits by deposit banks for the thirty-three non-socialist countries of 1.3 per cent is not much lower than the ratio of 1.6 per cent for the similar is-

3. A study by J. D. Khazzoom, *The Currency Ratio in Developing Countries* (New York, Praeger, 1966), which covers a larger group of less developed countries—thirty-one countries, including ten of the fifteen nonsocialist countries included here—seems to indicate a somewhat more rapid rise for less developed countries, viz. from 20 to 38 per cent of total money supply (currency plus demand, time and saving deposits) between 1951 and 1961 for all thirty-one countries and from 24 to 51 per cent for the ten countries. The two set of figures are, however, not entirely comparable.

sues of specialized thrift institutions. The relation, however, is quite different for developed and for underdeveloped countries. While ϕ_{bt} was not much over half the size of ϕ_t for developed countries (1.4 against 2.4 per cent), it was more than twice as large as ϕ_t for underdeveloped countries (1.1 against 0.5 per cent). As a result, the difference between developed and underdeveloped countries in the level of the sum of $\phi_{bt} + \phi_t$ for the postwar period is considerably smaller than it is for ϕ_t alone but is considerably larger than the difference is for ϕ_{bt}. This would point to substitutability between ϕ_{bt} and ϕ_t, the relation between the two being determined by institutional differences in the various countries' financial structure as well, and possibly as much, as by basic economic factors, such as the level of real income per head or the personal saving ratio. This question, however, can be decided only on the basis of a comparison of the movements of ϕ_{bt} and ϕ_t for individual countries.

Such a comparison for the period since World War I indicates that differences in the level of ϕ_{bt} compared to ϕ_b are an enduring characteristic of a country's financial structure. With a few exceptions, the same countries show a relatively high or relatively low ratio of time and saving deposits to the aggregate assets of deposit banks at all benchmark dates. Thus the share of time and savings deposits is relatively high in the Scandinavian countries, Australia, Canada, South Africa, Japan, and India and is relatively low in France, Belgium, the Netherlands, and Brazil. Pronounced long-term trends in the ratio are rare since the turn of the century. The most important example of such a trend is provided by the United States, where the share of time and saving deposits in the total assets of commercial banks has increased from about one-tenth at the turn of the century to two-fifths in 1963, most of the increase having been concentrated in the decade before World War I and in the post-World War II period.

One obvious explanation of the differences in the level of the share of time and saving deposits in the aggregate assets of deposit banks is the existence and the importance

TABLE 5-8

Relation of Time and Savings Deposits to Total Assets of Deposit Banks in Individual Countries

PER CENT

	1913 (1)	1929 (2)	1937 (3)	1948 (4)	1963 (5)
Argentina		51		34	34
Australia	57	65		21	27
Belgium	18	17	15	20[a]	29
Brazil	19	20		25	4
Canada	40	41	48	47	41
Denmark	38	49		42	48
Egypt-U.A.R.				21[b]	25
France	5	6		2	13
Germany				19[c]	34
Great Britain					31
Greece	58	24		3[d]	49
India			45[e]	28	47
Israel				19[f]	36
Italy				18	26
Jamaica				44[d]	57
Japan	35	46	50	33[d]	41
Mexico		8		18	20
Netherlands	19	23	16	10	35
New Zealand	38	46	37	20	14
Nigeria				20[d]	17
Norway	55	52	73	55	62
Pakistan				16	37
Philippines				22	41
Puerto Rico				17	26
Rhodesia				5	35
South Africa	36	46	28	12	40
Spain		21		38[b]	52
Sweden		53		59	64
Switzerland	20[e]	24	18	21[g]	38[g]
Thailand				22	38
Trinidad				41	56
U.S.A.	21	29	25	26	40
Venezuela				12	33

[a] 1950. [b] 1952. [c] 1951. [d] 1953. [e] Rough estimates. [f] 1955.
[g] Including bank obligations of 38 in 1948 and 45 in 1963.

Sources: Cols. 1–3: League of Nations, *Les Banques Commerciales*, 1913, 1929–34, 1937, except for Japan (*Historical Statistics of Japan*) and for the U.S.A. (Goldsmith, *A Study of Savings*, *1*).

Cols. 4–5: International Financial Statistics, 1964–65 Supplement, except for Puerto Rico, Rhodesia, and Trinidad (national banking statistics).

of specialized thrift institutions whose issues are near substitutes for time and saving deposits in commercial banks. Countries in which these thrift institutions are long established and well developed usually show relatively low ratios of time and saving deposits in commercial banks to the total assets of these institutions. Another explanation is inflation, countries and periods of sharp rises in the price level usually showing low or declining ratios of time and saving deposits to total assets of commercial banks and low or declining shares of the issues of time and saving deposits in commercial banks to aggregate ϕ_b, partly because of the existence of the transactions demand for check deposits, which has no counterpart in the field of time and savings deposits.

THE ISSUES OF THRIFT INSTITUTIONS

Although thrift institutions are known by various names in different countries—titles like savings banks, building societies, popular banks, and credit cooperatives are the most common ones—they are more homogeneous in the character of their issues, though not in that of their assets, than any other group of financial institutions, the great majority of their issues having the form of interest bearing deposits of households, deposits which show a relatively low velocity of turnover. Most of these institutions also have in common the feature that they are not operated for profit and are administered either by central or local governments or by groups of independent trustees. In a few countries privately owned thrift institutions operated for profit are, however, of substantial though generally secondary importance in this field, for instance in Australia (private savings banks) and in the United States (stock saving and loan associations). In many countries very similar financial instruments are also issued by deposit banks and these have already been discussed in the preceding section. Indeed, for the average of all countries covered by this investigation, the volume of time and saving deposits issued by deposit banks is of a size comparable, though somewhat smaller, than the issues of specialized thrift institutions.

The issues of thrift institutions are characterized by three features evidenced in Tables 5–9 to 5–11. The first is a

TABLE 5–9

Net Issue Ratios of Thrift Institutions and Their Share in Issues and Assets of All Financial Institutions

UNWEIGHTED COUNTRY AVERAGES (PER CENT)

	Relation to GNP		Relation to Change in GNP	Share in Total of All Financial Institutions	
	Issues[a]	Assets[b]	Change in Issues[c]	Issues[a]	Assets[b]
	(1)	(2)	(3)	(4)	(5)
		ALL NONSOCIALIST COUNTRIES			
1881–1900[d]	.86	15.7	33.4	22.3	15.9
1901–1913	.94	16.1	23.4	17.1	13.8
1914–1929	.93	17.3	20.0	16.5	14.0
1930–1938	.93	19.8	81.4	12.5	16.1
1939–1948	1.52	15.3	16.9	13.6	13.2
1949–1963	1.60	18.7	19.7	13.8	13.7
		DEVELOPED NONSOCIALIST COUNTRIES			
1861–1880	.54	16.3	24.2	16.8	16.1
1881–1900	.92	20.8	35.6	22.2	19.6
1901–1913	1.25	23.7	30.6	20.0	19.2
1914–1929	1.32	27.8	29.7	20.3	19.6
1930–1938	1.40	32.5	130.0	17.4	20.3
1939–1948	2.49	25.3	28.4	20.4	18.1
1949–1963	2.54	30.5	31.9	19.5	19.3
		LESS DEVELOPED NONSOCIALIST COUNTRIES			
1901–1913	.05	.9	1.9	8.5	4.0
1914–1929	.16	1.8	3.8	9.1	5.9
1930–1938	.24	4.2	3.6	5.4	10.9
1939–1948	.33	3.4	2.7	5.2	7.2
1949–1963	.48	4.5	5.2	7.0	7.0

[a] Change in assets during period as per cent of cumulated GNP of period.

[b] Assets at end of period as per cent of GNP of last year of period.

[c] Ratio of first differences in issues and in GNP of successive periods.

[d] Includes one less developed country (India).

substantial increase in ϕ_t, the ratio of the issues of thrift institutions to aggregate national product, from a plateau of a little less than 1 per cent (which extends from the late nineteenth century until World War II—contrary to some other types of financial institutions no decline is visible in the 1930s) to fully 1.5 per cent in the war and postwar periods.

TABLE 5–10

Net Issue Ratios of Thrift Institutions (ϕ_t) in Different Groups of Countries
UNWEIGHTED COUNTRY AVERAGES
PER CENT OF GROSS NATIONAL PRODUCT

	1881 to 1900[a]	1901 to 1913	1914 to 1929	1930 to 1938	1939 to 1948	1949 to 1963
A. INCLUDING SOCIALIST COUNTRIES						
I. All countries	.87	.98	.88	.89	1.43	1.53
II. Developed	.92	1.20	1.22	1.33	2.35	2.44
1. European	1.05	1.20	1.00	1.10	1.62	2.20
2. Non-European	.73	1.18	1.64	1.77	3.69	2.77
III. Less developed	.03	.05	.16	.25	.31	.45
1. European		.12	.25	.50	.35	.91
2. American			.12	.18	.38	.41
3. Afro-Asian		.06	.13	.14	.19	.28
B. EXCLUDING SOCIALIST COUNTRIES						
I. All countries	.87	.95	.93	.93	1.52	1.60
II. Developed	.98	1.25	1.32	1.40	2.49	2.54
1. European	1.04	1.28	1.14	1.18	1.76	2.35
III. Less developed	.08	.05	.15	.24	.33	.48
1. European		.12	.25	.58	.55	1.36
C. IDENTICAL COUNTRIES[b]						
I. Developed	.93	1.28	1.34	1.41	2.23	2.69
II. Less developed			.16	.32	.39	.64
D. COEFFICIENT OF VARIATION[b]						
I. All countries	.61	.92	1.19	1.37	1.34	1.11
II. Developed	.54	.65	.89	1.05	.93	.75
III. Less developed		1.08	.86	.96	1.09	1.09

[a] Figures for 1861–80 are: .54 in lines A I, A II, A II 1, B I, B II and B II 1; and .55 in line A II 2.
[b] Nonsocialist countries.

The second and more important characteristic is the sharp difference in the level of ϕ_t between developed and less developed countries. For developed countries, the value of ϕ_t since World War II has been in the neighborhood of 2.5 per cent of gross' national product, which is about

Table 5-11

Net Issue Ratios of Thrift Institutions (ϕ_t) in Individual Countries

PER CENT OF PERIOD'S GROSS NATIONAL PRODUCT

	1880 to 1900[a]	1901 to 1913	1914 to 1929	1930 to 1938	1939 to 1948	1949 to 1963
Argentina			0.08	0.03	0.04	0.16
Australia		1.53	1.49	0.62	3.99	2.11
Belgium	1.08	1.10	0.44	0.99	1.31	2.04
Brazil			0.26	0.62	1.03	0.76
Canada	0.30	0.13	0.06	0.07	0.37	0.43
Denmark	1.76	1.18	1.67	0.74	2.35	1.33
Egypt-U.A.R.		0.03	0.04	0.31	0.40	0.20
France	0.63	0.30	0.92	1.02	0.82	2.38
Germany	1.55	2.94	−0.93	2.22	−2.77	4.91
Great Britain	0.53	0.53	0.93	2.51	3.08	1.53
Greece			0.07	0.59	−0.00	0.55
India	0.03	0.08	0.18	0.28	0.01	0.76
Israel						0.47
Italy	0.72	1.54	1.70	1.75	4.56	4.35
Jamaica						0.66
Japan	1.00	1.76	4.16	6.11	7.97	8.74
Mexico				0.12	0.31	0.32
Netherlands	0.38	0.65	1.02	1.06	2.22	2.27
New Zealand	0.94	1.88	2.25	1.66	4.16	2.27
Nigeria				0.00	0.04	0.01
Norway	1.88	2.73	3.35	−0.76	2.75	1.70
Pakistan						0.06
Philippines			0.19			0.22
Puerto Rico				0.11	0.15	0.83
Rhodesia						3.51
Russia-U.S.S.R.		0.45	0.39	0.25	0.17	0.62
South Africa			0.87	1.98	4.54	2.57
Spain		0.12	0.44	0.58	1.11	2.17
Sweden	1.21	1.33	1.71	1.57	2.64	2.68
Switzerland	0.31	0.56	0.58	0.74	0.67	0.94
Thailand					0.52	0.43
Trinidad					0.54	0.09
U.S.A.	0.72	0.62	0.98	0.17	1.13	2.03
Venezuela				0.05	0.02	0.05
Yugoslavia				0.34	−0.06	

[a] Figures for 1861–80 are: 0.06 for France, 0.97 for Germany, 0.43 for Great Britain, 0.77 for Switzerland, and 0.55 for U.S.A.

twice the level for the periods running from 1901 through 1938. For less developed countries, the value of ϕ_t was only about 0.5 per cent, even in the postwar period, a level which had been reached by the developed countries as far back as the third quarter of the nineteenth century. However, ϕ_t has been increasing at a more rapid rate for the less developed than for the developed countries. Thus the 1949–63 ratio for the less developed countries is four times as high as that for the 1914–29 period and almost ten times as high as that of the 1901–13 period, while among developed countries the ratio only approximately doubled within this span.

In this comparison one must keep in mind that, as has been pointed out in the preceding section, the ratio of the issues of time and saving deposits by deposit banks to the issues of specialized thrift institutions is higher for less developed than for developed countries. As a result, the difference in the level of the ratio of all time and saving deposits to national product is a little less unfavorable to the less developed countries than ϕ_t alone would indicate. For the postwar period, the only one for which sufficient data for time and saving deposits in deposit banks are available, the issues of time and saving deposits by deposit banks were on the average more than twice as high as the similar issues by specialized thrift institutions for less developed countries, while the same ratio averaged less than one-half in the case of developed countries. However, even if the issues of time and saving deposits by deposit banks and by specialized thrift institutions are combined, the postwar level of the ratio for developed countries with approximately 3½ per cent of gross national product would still be more than twice as high as the comparable ratio for less developed countries, which is in the order of 1½ per cent.[4]

4. Among the fifteen nonsocialist less developed countries, the increase in time and saving deposits with deposit banks exceeded the similar increase in savings deposits of specialized thrift institutions in twelve cases (in nine of them to the extent that the issues of time and saving deposits in deposit banks were at least twice as large as

This relationship reflects the relatively late start and the often still limited scale of operation of savings banks and credit cooperatives and the absence of building societies in most less developed countries, as well as the fact that deposit banks in less developed countries function as the universal nonspecialized credit institution.

For developed countries it is possible to carry the comparison between the issues of saving-type deposits of deposit banks and of thrift institutions back to the late nineteenth century. It then appears that the issue of time and saving deposits by deposit banks was of the same order of magnitude as that by thrift institutions in the two periods between 1880 and 1913, viz. 1 per cent of gross national product or a little more, so that the ratio of issuance of saving-type deposits by both groups of institutions averaged between 2–2.5 per cent. In the 1914–29 period, however, the ratio of issuance of saving-type deposits by deposit banks to gross national product declined both absolutely to a little less than 1 per cent and relatively to about two-thirds of that by specialized thrift institutions. The ratio of all saving type deposit issues to gross national product at 2.25 per cent, however, did not show a marked change. During the 1930s the issue ratio of thrift institutions, which remained at its previous level, was probably considerably in excess of that of saving-type deposits by deposit banks—the ratio of all issues by deposit banks declined to almost zero—although the evidence is not sufficient for a more confident statement. There is little doubt that the issue ratio of saving type deposits by thrift institutions during the period 1939–48, reaching a new plateau at 2.5 per cent of gross national product was again in excess of that for deposit banks, since the share of saving deposit in total issues by deposit

those of specialized thrift institutions), while among the eighteen nonsocialist developed countries the increase in the deposits of specialized thrift institutions was in excess of the increase of time and saving deposits with deposit banks in thirteen cases (in nine of them to the extent of more than twice the increase in time and saving deposits with deposit banks).

banks declined sharply. The combined ratio of saving type deposit issues to national product nevertheless reached a high of 3–3.5 per cent but probably remained well below the 4 per cent level of the postwar period.

The third characteristic is that the share of the issues of saving deposits by specialized thrift institutions and the share of the assets of these institutions in the total issues and assets of all financial institutions have been remarkably stable in developed countries over the last century, viz. in the order of one-sixth to one-fifth for all seven periods of nine to twenty years. In the case of less developed countries the movement is rather irregular, reflecting in part the small number of countries covered by the averages.

The majority of the issues and assets of thrift institutions is accounted for by savings banks, whether private or governmental, and a small part is contributed by credit unions. In a number of countries, however, there exists another specialized thrift institution, the building society (in the United States more recently known as saving and loan association), which is similar to a savings bank in that the issues are held predominantly by households and have a fairly low velocity of turnover, but which differs from a savings bank in that most assets consist of home mortgages. Building societies have operated in only about one-third of the thirty-five countries covered, and, as appears from Table 5–12, they have been of substantial importance in the financial structure only in about half a dozen of them. Building societies are at the present time the largest single type of thrift institutions in five countries (Great Britain, Puerto Rico, Rhodesia, South Africa, and the United States). In these countries they account for between two-fifths and four-fifths of the total assets of all specialized thrift institutions and for about one-tenth or more of the assets of all financial institutions. They are of some, though lesser, importance also in Australia, Germany, New Zealand, Sweden, and Trinidad. This regional distribution is explained in part by the fact that building societies originated and first achieved importance in Great Britain and from there

TABLE 5–12

Share of Building Societies in Assets of All Thrift Institutions and of All Financial Institutions

PER CENT

	Australia	Germany	Great Britain	New Zealand	Puerto Rico	South Africa[a]	Sweden	Trinidad	U.S.A.
A. SHARE IN ASSETS OF ALL THRIFT INSTITUTIONS									
1880			34	39					34
1913	8		14	13		42			14
1938	5	1	33	11		64	3	51	33
1948	7	4	20	7	11	62	3	32	20
1963	13	9	44	14	79	83	6	32	44
B. SHARE IN ASSETS OF ALL FINANCIAL INSTITUTIONS									
1880			4.6	5.5					4.6
1913	1.4		2.4	3.4		5.9			2.4
1938	1.5	0.5	8.3	3.0		13.4	0.7	24.7	8.3
1948	1.3	0.3	4.7	2.0	0.3	14.6	0.8	5.4	4.7
1963	3.4	3.4	9.0	3.9	7.2	17.1	1.6	2.2	9.0

[a] Figures for Rhodesia for 1963 are 67 in Section A and 15.3 in Section B.

Source: Country tables in Appendix IV.

spread to the British Dominions, except Canada, and to the United States. The substantial importance of these institutions in Puerto Rico and in Trinidad—the only two underdeveloped countries out of the group of ten—are obviously attributable to the example of the mother countries. Similarly the rapid development of building societies in postwar Germany was modeled after the precedent in Great Britain and the United States.

THE ISSUES OF INSURANCE ORGANIZATIONS

The ratio of the issues of insurance organizations to gross national product (ϕ_i), taking as before the change in the assets of insurance organizations to represent their net issues, is the component of ϕ which has shown the most rapid growth, both in absolute value and in its share in aggregate ϕ (Table 5–13). This is due, first, to the marked rise in the ratio of issues of life insurance companies to national product, particularly until the 1930s and, secondly, to the development of two new types of insurance organizations—public social security funds and private retirement funds—which have grown very rapidly since the 1930s, particularly after World War II. The third component of ϕ_i, the issues of property insurance companies, has been of secondary importance since World War I.

The main characteristics of the net issues of insurance organizations other than property insurance companies are, first, that they represent almost exclusively the contractual or compulsory saving of households and, secondly, that these issues have a low velocity of turnover compared not only to demand deposits, but also to thrift deposits and most types of securities held by individuals. The four main immediate determinants of ϕ_i (as also those of ϕ_{bt}) are therefore the ratio of personal to total national saving, the personal saving-income ratio, the ratio of indirect to total personal saving, and—the most directly relevant factor—the share of insurance in total indirect personal saving. While the data are not sufficient for separation of these four components on an international basis, there is no doubt that the increase in ϕ_i is due mostly to the rise in the third and fourth components. In the United States, where the com-

TABLE 5–13

Net Issue Ratios and Share in Issues and Assets of All Financial Institutions of Insurance Organizations
UNWEIGHTED COUNTRY AVERAGES (PER CENT)

	Relation to GNP		Relation to Change in GNP	Share in Total of All Financial Institutions	
	Issues[a]	Assets[b]	Change in Issues[c]	Issues[a]	Assets[b]
			ALL NONSOCIALIST COUNTRIES		
1881–1900[d]	.46	8.5	17.9	12.5	8.8
1901–1913	.66	11.1	17.3	11.8	10.5
1914–1929	.77	13.2	17.0	13.2	11.4
1930–1938	1.41	21.4	65.6	29.0	14.8
1939–1948	1.46	17.1	17.3	13.6	13.2
1949–1963	2.03	23.6	27.0	19.5	17.5
			DEVELOPED NONSOCIALIST COUNTRIES		
1861–1880	.32	5.5	16.4	10.8	7.1
1881–1900	.50	11.1	19.2	13.0	10.8
1901–1913	.86	16.0	22.0	14.4	14.3
1914–1929	1.18	21.0	24.4	19.5	16.1
1930–1938	2.24	36.3	98.4	46.6	21.7
1939–1948	2.08	27.2	26.6	17.9	17.5
1949–1963	3.00	37.4	42.1	25.3	22.8
			LESS DEVELOPED NONSOCIALIST COUNTRIES		
1901–1913	.07	1.3	3.0	4.2	3.8
1914–1929	.10	1.8	2.3	.6	4.6
1930–1938	.21	3.2	13.0	13.3	6.4
1939–1948	.70	5.0	5.8	8.2	8.0
1949–1963	.85	7.1	9.0	12.5	11.2

[a] Change in assets during period as per cent of cumulated GNP of period.
[b] Assets at end of period as per cent of GNP of last year of period.
[c] Ratio of first differences in issues and in GNP of successive periods.
[d] Includes one less developed country (India).

ponents can be disentangled, ϕ_i has increased from 1.0 per cent in 1901–13 to 3.3 per cent in 1949–63 in the absence of a definite upward trend in the personal saving-income ratio or in the share of personal in total national saving; thus, mainly as a result of an increase in the share of indirect saving in total personal net saving, ϕ_i has increased from less than 40 per cent in 1909–14 to 70 per cent in 1950–64 while the share of insurance in total indirect personal saving has risen from 25 to nearly 45 per cent.[5]

For all nonsocialist countries together, ϕ_i has shown an uninterrupted increase over all the seven periods, rising from 0.3 per cent of gross national product in the period 1861–80 to 2.0 per cent in the postwar period, a process which can be followed in Table 5–14. The rise was very slow, though continuous, until 1929. The ratio then almost doubled between 1914–29 and 1930–38, reflecting a continued absolute increase in the net issues of insurance organizations in the face of a decline in national product. The ratio advanced again substantially between 1939–48 and 1949–63, this time exclusively as a result of a very sharp increase in the issues of social security organizations and private pension funds.

The increase in ϕ_i, however, is also substantial if it is compared with the movements of aggregate ϕ, which in itself showed a marked upward trend. While ϕ_i accounted from 1861 to 1900 for only about one-tenth of the aggregate value of ϕ, the proportion has risen to about one-fifth in the postwar period. The ratio of almost one-third shown for the period 1930–38 is, of course, abnormal and reflects the continued high and even increasing level of issues by insurance organizations in the face of a stagnating or even declining volume of issues of all financial institutions taken together.

Even for the postwar period, the value of ϕ_i of nonsocialist developed countries with 3.0 per cent of national product was more than three times as high as the ratio of 0.9 for underdeveloped countries. The gap, however, has narrowed considerably since the period before the Great Depression, when the ratio for less developed countries of 0.1 per cent was almost insignificant compared to the ratio

5. Goldsmith, "Changes in the Structure of Personal Saving," Table I.

of 1.1 per cent for developed countries. Putting it another way, ϕ_i for less developed countries increased 8½ times in not much over thirty years between 1913–29 and 1949–63, while the ratio only tripled during the same time in the

TABLE 5–14

Net Issues Ratios of Insurance Institutions (ϕ_i) in Different Groups of Countries
UNWEIGHTED COUNTRY AVERAGES
PER CENT OF GROSS NATIONAL PRODUCT

	1881 to 1900[b]	1901 to 1913	1914 to 1929	1930 to 1938	1939 to 1948	1949 to 1963
A. INCLUDING SOCIALIST COUNTRIES						
I. All countries	.46	.64	.73	1.32	1.37	1.92
II. Developed	.49	.81	1.03	2.11	1.96	2.85
1. European	.40	.76	.77	1.95	1.53	2.40
2. Non-European	.78	.92	1.50	2.40	2.75	3.46
III. Less developed	.01	.07	.10	.19	.65	.82
1. European		.06	.13	.02	.49	.50
2. American		.12	.10	.39	1.10	1.14
3. Afro-Asian	.01	.00	.07	.08	.21	.60
B. EXCLUDING SOCIALIST COUNTRIES						
I. All countries	.46	.66	.76	1.41	1.46	2.03
II. Developed	.49	.86	1.10	2.24	2.08	3.00
1. European	.40	.83	.86	2.14	1.68	2.64
III. Less developed	.01	.07	.10	.21	.70	.85
1. European		.06	.13	.02	.72	.58
C. IDENTICAL COUNTRIES[a]						
I. Developed	.49	.86	1.05	2.23	1.89	2.83
II. Less developed			.10	.22	.92	1.12
D. COEFFICIENT OF VARIATION[a]						
I. All countries	.74	.70	1.00	.88	.94	.78
II. Developed	.67	.43	.67	.43	.69	.48
III. Less developed		.54	.70	1.18	1.09	.80

[a] Nonsocialist countries.
[b] Figures for 1861–80 are: 0.32 in lines A II, A II 1, B II and B II 1; and 0.34 in line C I.

case of developed countries. Nevertheless the level of ϕ_i for less developed countries during the postwar period was only where that of developed countries had been fifty years earlier.

Considerable differences in ϕ_i also exist within developed and within less developed countries (Table 5–15). Thus

Table 5–15

Net Issue Ratios of Insurance Organizations (ϕ_i) in Individual Countries

PER CENT OF PERIOD'S GROSS NATIONAL PRODUCT

	1881 to 1900[a]	1901 to 1913	1914 to 1929	1930 to 1938	1939 to 1948	1949 to 1963
Argentina		0.14	0.13	0.85	2.50	1.62
Australia		0.81	1.19	1.83	2.28	2.43
Belgium	0.21	0.57	0.39	0.97	0.97	2.22
Brazil			0.13	0.41	1.97	2.35
Canada	0.77	1.29	2.27	2.56	3.29	4.20
Denmark	0.19	0.57	0.75	1.91	2.58	1.82
Egypt-U.A.R.		0.07	0.08	0.00	0.50	1.78
France	0.56	0.54	0.28	0.99	0.25	0.48
Germany	0.65	1.03	−0.90	1.40	−1.28	1.71
Great Britain	0.49	0.83	1.44	1.59	2.66	3.43
Greece			0.02	0.01	0.04	0.09
India	0.01	0.02	0.04	0.16	0.34	0.75
Israel						4.41
Italy	0.10	0.30	0.69	1.61	1.04	1.30
Jamaica						0.73
Japan	0.14	0.27	1.22	2.39	0.73	1.86
Mexico		0.09	0.03	0.14	0.54	0.64
Netherlands	0.29	0.71	1.06	4.87	3.31	5.34
New Zealand	1.43	1.23	1.16	2.60	1.66	2.89
Nigeria				0.00	0.01	0.05
Norway	0.63	1.29	1.51	1.73	2.75	2.78
Pakistan						0.26
Philippines			0.09	0.14	0.11	0.67
Puerto Rico				0.17	1.01	1.67
Rhodesia						3.05
Russia-U.S.S.R.		0.09	−0.08	0.06	0.03	0.04
South Africa			1.67	2.75	4.58	5.59
Spain		0.06	0.24	0.03	1.39	1.07
Sweden	0.56	0.90	1.37	2.92	1.81	3.04
Switzerland	0.33	1.56	2.02	3.41	2.73	5.25
Thailand					0.08	0.10
Trinidad					0.24	0.61
U.S.A.	0.60	1.01	1.52	2.29	3.97	3.26
Venezuela				0.37	0.36	0.37
Yugoslavia				0.03	0.03	0.34

[a] The figures for 1861–80 are 0.28 for France, 0.21 for Germany, 0.32 for Great Britain, 0.45 for New Zealand, and 0.34 for U.S.A.

during the postwar period the ratio of ϕ_i for developed countries has ranged from slightly over 5 per cent of gross national product in the case of South Africa, Switzerland, and the Netherlands to 1.3 for Italy and to a low of 0.5 for France, although seven of the eighteen countries showed a value for ϕ_i of between 2.0 and 4.0 per cent. The value of ϕ_i apparently was influenced not so much by the level of real income per head as by three other factors, the existence of a social security system accumulating funds (rather than operating on a pay-as-you-go basis), the level of ϕ_t, and the degree of inflation in the not too distant past. These factors however, are not sufficient to explain fully some of the extreme values, particularly the extraordinarily low value of ϕ_i in France. The ranking of developed countries with respect to ϕ_i has been fairly stable, indicating that we are dealing here with an enduring characteristic of the countries' financial structures. The main exceptions have been the downward movement in the ranking order between 1901–13 and 1949–63 of Germany and Norway and the upward movements of Japan, Netherlands, and Great Britain. Among the fifteen countries the average change in rank within this half-century, however, has been only three positions, and the rank correlation coefficient for the two periods is 0.63.

Differences in ϕ_i are more pronounced among less developed countries and here mainly reflect the existence and degree of accumulation by the social security system. Compared to an average of 0.9 per cent of national product for all nonsocialist underdeveloped countries, the value of ϕ_i is below 0.1 per cent in a few countries without a social security system such as Greece, Thailand, and Nigeria, but ranges from 1.6 to 2.4 per cent of national product in countries with a system accumulating a considerable part of its income as for instance Argentina, Brazil, Egypt, and Puerto Rico.

Until the 1930s, the issues and assets of social security funds and of employee pension funds, whether governmental or private, played only a minor role within the insurance sector, and their importance was still smaller within the total of all financial institutions. The only important exception among the thirty-five countries is Germany, where as far back as 1913 social security funds accounted for about one-fourth of the assets of all insurance organizations and for nearly 3 per cent of the assets of all financial institutions. Other examples at that date are the United Kingdom, where the assets of the social security fund represented nearly 1 per cent of the total for all financial institutions, New Zealand (approximately 2 per cent) and Norway (about 4 per cent). Social security and government employee retirement funds began to acquire substantial importance in a larger number of countries during the 1920s and 1930s. After World War II personal private retirement funds were added to them and in a few countries came to exceed government social security and pension funds in size—in 1963 this was the case in Denmark, Israel, the Netherlands, and Spain.

As a result at the end of 1963 approximately one-half of the total assets of all insurance organizations, and presumably a similar though probably somewhat smaller share of the net issues of all insurance organizations in the postwar period, was accounted for by life insurance. Most of these were private companies, but government life insurance organizations were predominant or important in a number of countries (e.g. Denmark, France, India, Italy, New Zealand, and U.S.S.R.) although in the total of the thirty-five countries they accounted for only a relatively small part of the assets or issues of all life insurance organizations. Approximately one-tenth of the assets of all insurance organizations were in the hands of property insurance (fire, marine, accident, etc.) companies, practically all of which were privately owned and administered. Private retirement funds held somewhat more than one-tenth of the total assets of all insurance organizations and, because of their rapid growth throughout the postwar period, accounted for a somewhat larger proportion of total issues. Government employee pension funds, which occupy a position between private retirement funds and social security organizations, held somewhat less than 10 per cent of the total, while the remaining assets (a full fifth of the total) was accounted for by social security organizations. Thus about two-thirds of the total funds and issues of all insurance organizations now belong to the private sector of the economy, the remaining one-third being under government control and administration.

The distribution of the assets and issues of insurance organizations among the main component groups does not appear to be very different as between developed and less developed countries. There was however a tendency for government employee and social security funds to account for a larger proportion of the total—close to two-fifths—among less developed countries than among developed countries, where their combined share was on the order of one-fourth. On the other hand, the share of private retirement funds was larger in developed than in underdeveloped countries. Property insurance companies were of considerably larger importance in developed than in less developed countries, although even among the former group they did not account for much over one-tenth of the total assets of all insurance organizations. Life insurance organizations accounted in both groups for nearly one-half of the total assets, but the fraction of this share represented by government life insurance organizations was considerably larger among less developed than among developed countries.

THE ISSUES OF MISCELLANEOUS FINANCIAL INTERMEDIARIES

The Group as a Whole

The share of the issues of miscellaneous financial intermediaries in ϕ has been in the neighborhood of one-fifth both for the three periods extending from 1860 through 1913 and again during the 1930s and in the post-World War II period, and this applies to all countries as well as to developed countries alone, as is evident from Tables 5–16 to 5–18. The share of ϕ_o was considerably lower in the two

TABLE 5–16

Net Issue Ratios of Miscellaneous Financial Organizations and Their Share in Issues and Assets of All Financial Institutions
UNWEIGHTED COUNTRY AVERAGES (PER CENT)

	Relation to GNP		Relation to Change in GNP	Share in Total of All Financial Institutions	
	Issues[a]	Assets[b]	Change in Issues[c]	Issues[a]	Assets[b]
			ALL NONSOCIALIST COUNTRIES		
1881–1900	0.83	15.7	34.3	19.5	16.9
1901–1913	1.16	17.7	30.4	19.3	17.8
1914–1929	0.70	14.9	14.6	7.8	15.3
1930–1938	0.72	17.6	156.0	21.5	12.4
1939–1948	0.92	10.1	8.8	10.3	12.9
1949–1963	1.94	19.7	23.5	17.8	15.9
			DEVELOPED NONSOCIALIST COUNTRIES		
1861–1880	0.74	13.1	37.7	23.0	21.8
1881–1900	0.89	20.2	36.8	20.9	18.1
1901–1913	1.27	23.5	32.9	18.0	18.9
1914–1929	0.94	22.1	19.7	17.3	17.5
1930–1938	1.11	27.9	249.0	26.2	15.5
1939–1948	1.07	14.3	108.3	10.0	17.0
1949–1963	2.74	28.9	34.5	21.1	18.4
			LESS DEVELOPED NONSOCIALIST COUNTRIES		
1901–1913	0.83	6.1	23.1	23.4	14.5
1914–1929	0.22	4.3	4.6	11.3	11.3
1930–1938	0.17	5.0	7.1	14.6	8.0
1939–1948	0.75	5.0	6.3	10.6	7.9
1949–1963	0.98	8.6	10.3	13.9	12.8

[a] Change in assets during period as per cent of cumulated GNP of period.
[b] Assets at end of period as per cent of GNP of last year of period.
[c] Ratio of first differences in issues and in GNP of successive periods.

periods affected by World Wars I and II, i.e. 1914–29 and 1939–48. It might thus seem that in the long run ϕ_o has increased more or less in step with ϕ. This apparent stability, however, hides considerable changes in the makeup of this heterogeneous group. Before World War I its most important component were mortgage banks. Beginning with the

1930s, however, the category of miscellaneous financial intermediaries came to be dominated in most countries, particularly in less developed ones, by government credit institutions, mainly institutions extending long-term credit to

TABLE 5–17

Net Issue Ratios of Miscellaneous Financial Institutions (ϕ_o) in Different Groups of Countries

UNWEIGHTED COUNTRY AVERAGES

PER CENT OF PERIOD'S GROSS NATIONAL PRODUCT

	1881 to 1900[a]	1901 to 1913	1914 to 1929	1930 to 1938	1939 to 1948	1949 to 1963
A. INCLUDING SOCIALIST COUNTRIES						
I. All countries	.83	1.21	.60	.72	.87	2.30
II. Developed	.90	1.33	.82	1.04	1.02	2.61
1. European	.99	1.62	.79	1.23	1.01	2.53
2. Non-European	.67	.67	.88	.68	1.04	2.73
III. Less developed		.83	.22	.27	.68	1.93
1. European		.07	.61	.91	.49	6.66
2. American		.90	.23	.21	1.25	1.28
3. Afro-Asian		1.14	−.04	−.13	.11	.34
B. EXCLUDING SOCIALIST COUNTRIES						
I. All countries	.84	1.16	.70	.73	.92	1.94
II. Developed	.90	1.27	.94	1.11	1.07	2.74
1. European	.99	1.58	.97	1.36	1.09	2.76
III. Less developed		.83	.23	.17	.75	.98
1. European		.07	.61	.66	.80	1.84
C. IDENTICAL COUNTRIES[b]						
I. Developed	.89	1.35	1.05	1.22	1.13	2.67
II. Less developed			.22	.24	.94	1.39
D. COEFFICIENT OF VARIATION[b]						
I. All countries	.87	.99	1.36	1.58	1.18	.73
II. Developed	.81	.92	1.14	1.20	1.18	.46
III. Less developed		1.21	1.33	2.25	1.09	.96

[a] Figure for 1861–80 is .74 in lines A II and B II; .90 in lines A II 1 and B II 1; and .10 in line A II 2.

[b] Nonsocialist countries.

industry and agriculture. In a few developed countries a substantial proportion of ϕ_o is now accounted for by two types of financial institutions which expanded most rapidly in the postwar period, consumer credit institutions (sales finance companies or hire-purchase organizations and personal credit organizations) and investment companies, but

TABLE 5–18

Net Issue Ratios of Miscellaneous Financial Intermediaries (ϕ_o) of Individual Countries

PER CENT OF PERIOD'S GROSS NATIONAL PRODUCT

	1881 to 1900[a]	1901 to 1913	1914 to 1929	1930 to 1938	1939 to 1948	1949 to 1963
Argentina		1.80	0.54	0.43	2.36	1.14
Australia		0.25	0.11	0.24	0.47	1.58
Belgium	0.36	0.56	1.00	1.86	1.47	2.24
Brazil				0.14	0.52	1.34
Canada	0.95	1.38	0.01	0.88	0.41	2.12
Denmark	2.95	4.76	2.79	2.54	1.56	3.58
Egypt-U.A.R.		2.29	−0.12	−0.71	0.19	0.86
France	1.06	1.02	2.29	3.07	1.57	3.58
Germany	1.79	1.72	−1.90	0.80	−1.56	3.05
Great Britain	0.22	0.42	0.49	0.06	1.25	1.47
Greece			0.77	0.86	0.92	2.55
India			0.01	0.04	0.04	0.28
Israel						5.90
Italy	0.00	1.64	0.82	4.03	3.91	5.18
Jamaica						0.23
Japan	0.77	0.90	1.92	1.23	3.70	3.76
Mexico			0.15	0.52	2.42	3.19
Netherlands	0.54	1.29	0.57	−0.04	0.67	2.89
New Zealand	0.70	0.63	1.64	1.16	0.46	1.51
Nigeria						0.05
Norway	0.73	0.96	1.31	2.13	0.30	2.52
Pakistan						0.24
Philippines				0.14	0.34	0.59
Puerto Rico					1.28	0.94
Rhodesia						2.72
Russia-U.S.S.R.		2.09	−1.05	0.09	0.23	0.24
South Africa			0.28	0.43	0.83	2.60
Spain		0.07	0.46	0.46	0.68	1.14
Sweden	0.17	0.32	0.50	0.73	0.61	1.34
Switzerland	1.43	3.07	1.90	−1.57	1.09	2.58
Thailand						0.01
Trinidad					−0.03	0.02
U.S.A.	0.25	0.21	1.33	0.17	0.36	1.61
Venezuela					0.98	2.09
Yugoslavia				1.40	−0.14	16.28

[a] Figures for 1861–80 are 0.72 for France, 1.32 for Germany, 0.33 for Great Britain, 1.23 for New Zealand, and 0.10 for U.S.A.

because of their absence in less developed areas their average share in the total for all thirty-five countries is still small. This is also true for another, though much older, component, the so-called financial intermediaries of the second degree, which have been of considerable importance in a few developed countries.

Mortgage Banks

The most homogeneous component of miscellaneous financial intermediaries and, from some points of view the most interesting, are mortgage banks. These institutions are characterized on the asset side by the concentration on long-term agricultural, urban real estate, or local authority loans, and on the liability side by reliance on the issuance of long-term bonds bought by individual investors. They first developed into important parts of the financial structure in France and Germany early in the nineteenth century and from there spread to many neighboring countries—Denmark, Sweden, Netherlands, Norway, Switzerland, Italy, Spain, and Russia among those covered in this study. They were also around the end of the nineteenth century successfully transplanted to at least three countries outside of Europe—Argentina, Egypt, and Japan. They never became important in English-speaking countries where their functions were performed to a substantial extent by other financial institutions, either deposit banks or some of the specialized thrift institutions, particularly building societies.

Mortgage banks reached their greatest importance within the financial structure in the period between 1880 and World War I. In 1913 they accounted on the average for fully one-tenth of the assets of all financial institutions. Interestingly enough the relative importance of mortgage banks among the total assets of financial institutions was greatest in the few underdeveloped countries in which they operated, particularly in Argentina and Egypt—they had been introduced into these countries from abroad and most of their issues were absorbed by foreign investors—than they were in the developed countries of Europe (Table 5–19).

TABLE 5–19

Mortgage Banks' Share in Assets of All Financial Institutions[a]

PER CENT

	1880	1913	1938	1948	1963
Argentina		19	20	7	7
Denmark	29	43	39	24	25
Egypt-U.A.R.		70	19	2	2
France	15	12	4	2	7
Germany	27	23	9	3	10
Israel				4	8
Japan	9	12	10	5	4
Netherlands	9	22	8	3	3
Norway	15	10	11	4	5
Russia		23			
South Africa		5	5	3	4
Spain		4	7	2	2
Sweden	25	8	8	7	8
Switzerland	15		8	7	6

[a] Only countries in which share of mortgage banks was at least 5 per cent at one of the five dates.

Source: Country tables in Appendix IV.

Since mortgage banks and their issues are particularly susceptible to the effects of inflation, the share of mortgage banks in the assets of all financial institutions was sharply reduced from World War I on. In 1929 they accounted, on the average, for 4.5 per cent of the assets of all financial institutions compared to a share of 10.5 per cent in 1913. By the end of World War II, mortgage banks had become relatively insignificant in the international picture, accounting on the average for only 2 per cent of the assets of all financial institutions in the thirty-three nonsocialist countries, and in no country did they represent more than 7 per cent of the assets of all financial institutions. During the postwar period, mortgage banks experienced a considerable recovery in France and Germany, but on the whole they did not manage to do much better than to expand in step with all other financial institutions.

Consumer Credit Institutions

Of the other types of miscellaneous financial intermediaries, one, the investment company or trust, originated in Great Britain around the middle of the nineteenth century; the second, consumer credit institutions, is an American innovation which developed beginning with the 1920s. Notwithstanding a considerable growth in relation to all financial institutions, particularly in the United States, and their spread during the postwar period to about a dozen of the thirty-five countries the average share of the assets of specialized consumer credit institutions in the total of all financial institutions at the end of 1963 was only in the neighborhood of 1 per cent, while their share in the assets of all miscellaneous financial institutions was not in excess of 5 per cent.

In 1963 there were only nine countries—out of the thirty-five—in which the share of specialized consumer credit institutions in the assets of all financial institutions exceeded 1 per cent; there were seven countries in which investment companies accounted for more than 1 per cent of the total, and four in which both types exceeded this limit. Among these, Australia, in which consumer credit institutions and investment companies together held more than 9 per cent of the assets of all financial institutions, was followed by the United Kingdom, the United States, and Canada with shares of 7 to 8 per cent each. Consumer credit institutions are as yet of substantial importance in the financial structure in only very few less developed countries. Their share was highest in Puerto Rico with about 4 per cent of the total, obviously influenced by the example of the United States; in Jamaica their share was about 3 per cent and in Nigeria 2 per cent.[6] Investment companies are

6. Figures for the share of specialized consumer credit institutions in the assets of all financial institutions cannot be used as a measure of the relative importance of consumer credit because in many countries other financial institutions, or even nonfinancial business enterprises, extend as much or more consumer credit than do specialized con-

as yet without substantial importance in any less developed country.

Development Banks

In most underdeveloped countries the largest component of the miscellaneous group are government credit institutions, particularly those of the development bank type, which provide long-term credit to industry and agriculture and are mostly financed by their countries' treasuries or, in the postwar period, by international lending organizations.[7] The country in which organizations of these types have been most important—and in this case including private institutions issuing both short- and long-term obligations—is Mexico. There the issues of government development banks, mostly organized in the 1930s, have accounted for about one-fourth of the issues of all financial institutions from 1941 to 1948 and for about 30 per cent in the 1949–63 period. The largest of the government development banks alone (Nacional Financiera) has been responsible for one-seventh of all issues of financial institutions during the postwar period. Private institutions of this type (*financieras*) which, however, also do a considerable amount of short-term lending and borrowing, have added another 7

sumer credit institutions. Even in the United States, specialized consumer finance institutions accounted for less than two-fifths of all consumer credit extended by financial institutions and not much more than one-fifth of total consumer credit outstanding in 1948 as well as in 1963.

7. As an obvious innovation in the field of finance, and virtually the only one widely used in less developed countries, development banks have given rise to a literature generally distinguished more by number and repetitiveness than by quality, and characterized by lack of comparative quantitative treatment. Among the descriptive publications, mention may be made of the recent comprehensive *Les Banques de développement dans le monde* (1963, 1965). The most detailed and statistically based study of development banks sponsored by the Organization for Economic Cooperation and Development has not yet been published in full; a first volume was issued in 1967: J. D. Nyhart and E. F. Janssens, *Repertoire des banques de développement situées dans les pays en voie de développement.*

per cent in 1941–48 and another 16 per cent from 1949 to 1963. In the postwar period, public and private development banks, in the widest sense of the term, have thus accounted for nearly one-half the issues of all financial institutions. Other countries in which development banks have been responsible for a substantial proportion of the issues of all financial institutions during the postwar period are Argentina, Brazil, Egypt, Greece, India, Nigeria, Pakistan, the Philippines, Puerto Rico, Spain, Venezuela, and Yugoslavia—all less developed countries. In these countries the share of development banks in the issues of all financial institutions has been much lower, generally in the order of 5 to 10 per cent, except in Greece and Yugoslavia. Because of the absence of development banking institutions in developed countries, the average share of these banks in the issues of financial institutions of all thirty-three nonsocialist countries is only in the order of 5 per cent and would be considerably lower if the average took account of the relative economic size of the countries concerned.

Financial Intermediaries of the Second Degree

The category of miscellaneous financial intermediaries finally includes the so-called financial intermediaries of the second degree—public institutions that receive all or most of their funds from other financial institutions (usually also public ones) and predominantly savings banks. The prototype of these financial intermediaries of the second degree is the French Caisse des Dépôts et Consignations, which was founded early in the nineteenth century.[8] Similar organizations of substantial importance are found in a few other continental countries, for instance, Germany, Italy, and Greece, as well as in Japan. In these countries, the secondary financial intermediaries account for a considerable part of the total assets of all financial institutions. The Caisse des Dépôts, for instance, held on the average approximately one-fifth of the assets of all French financial

8. See R. Priouret, *La Caisse des Dépôts* (Paris, Presses Universitaires, 1966).

institutions, its share ranging from 14 to 23 per cent at the different benchmark dates. In recent years, as its investments have become more diversified (formerly they were limited to French government securities), the Caisse has developed into one of the most important factors in the French financial structure. This tendency to outgrow their initial function of acting as a conduit between certain types of thrift institutions and a few standardized outlets for their funds, primarily government securities, and to develop into more diversified and independent financial institutions can also be observed in some other countries (e.g. in Germany in the central organizations of the German savings banks—the *Girozentralen*—and credit cooperatives, as early as the interwar period). The share of the Italian counterpart of the Caisse des Dépôts, the Cassa Depositi e Prestiti, was approximately one-fifth of the assets of all financial institutions until World War I, but since the 1920s has declined to about one-tenth. In Germany, the central organizations of the savings banks and credit unions have accounted since World War I for nearly one-tenth of the assets of all German financial institutions. The Trust Fund Bureau has since World War I held approximately one-tenth of the assets of all Japanese financial institutions.

Since these secondary financial intermediaries are of importance in only a few countries, their average share in the total assets of financial institutions in all countries is rather low. Since the turn of the century it has been in the order of 2 per cent for all countries taken together, although it has amounted to approximately 3 per cent for all developed countries where most of the secondary financial intermediaries operate. Their importance within the miscellaneous group has, however, declined considerably for all countries from about one-sixth to one-twelfth of total assets and for developed countries alone from fully one-third until World War II to one-fourth or less more recently.

Documents were lacking for a detailed examination of the balance sheets of intermediaries of the second degree in order to determine the extent of their liabilities to other financial institutions. Table 5–20, however, shows the relation of the total assets of those institutions of this type, most of whose funds could be assumed to represent interfinancial transactions, to the assets of all financial institu-

TABLE 5–20

Share of Financial Intermediaries of the Second Degree in Total Assets of All Financial Institutions in Selected Countries[a]

PER CENT

	1880	1900	1913	1929	1938	1948	1963
France	17	15	12	8	11[b]	8	9
Germany			2	9	10	9[c]	11
Greece				2	4	0	3
India				7	4	1	5
Italy		16	20	11	21	10	10
Japan		3	7	10	12	8	7

[a] The following institutions have been regarded as financial intermediaries of the second degree:
France: Caisse des Dépôts (own funds)
Germany: Central organizations of savings banks and credit unions
Greece: Consignment and Loan Fund
India: Central cooperative and land mortgage banks
Italy: Cassa Depositi e Prestiti
Japan: Trust Fund Bureau
[b] 1937. [c] 1950 (1947:19).

tions in the country. The ratios of Table 5–20 thus are higher than the term $\phi_z (1 + \lambda_z)$ that is required in the basic equation. On the other hand there undoubtedly exist a number of financial institutions in various countries which perform similar functions with respect to part of their assets and transactions, but which have not been identified, or which have been omitted because it appeared that their interfinancial transactions were relatively small.

Because of the heterogeneous character of the miscellaneous group it is hardly worthwhile to discuss the determinants of the group's share in the issues of all financial institutions or the relation of its issues to national product beyond the indications that have already been given for some of the larger and more homogeneous subgroups.

THE COMPOSITION OF THE AGGREGATE FINANCIAL INSTITUTIONS' ISSUE RATIO

Now that we have reviewed the level and course of the five main components of ϕ and have tried to provide some explanation for them, it is necessary to compare some of the important characteristics of these component ratios. To this end this section briefly discusses three of the characteristics of the components of ϕ: their level and trend, by means of a discussion of the share of the five component ratios in the aggregate value of ϕ; their variability and convergence, by a look at their coefficients of variation; and their reaction to changes in national product, by the calculations of their income elasticities. It hardly needs emphasis that the discussion is in each case limited to elementary features since an adequate treatment would have required intensive studies for which the data are often lacking and would have called for a substantial amount of econometric analysis. Time and resources for such special studies were unfortunately lacking.

As in the case of the aggregate net issue ratio, the discussion of the level and movements of the component of ϕ may usefully be introduced by a presentation in Table 5–21 of the average rates of growth of assets of the five groups of financial institutions in current prices as well as in constant (1960) prices.[9]

Asset growth rates were highest for insurance organizations both in developed and less developed countries with an average rank for the seven or six periods among the

9. Since the denominator of the net issue ratios—national product—is the same for all five groups, the relations among the five component ratios for any one period and country grouping will be related to the differences among components shown in Table 5–21, but the relations of one country grouping or one period to another will be different for growth rates than for issue ratios since the growth rates of national product are far from perfectly correlated with the rate of growth of assets of each group of financial institutions.

Table 5–21

Growth of Assets of Main Types of Financial Institutions

PER CENT PER YEAR, UNWEIGHTED AVERAGE OF NONSOCIALIST COUNTRIES

	Developed Countries					Less Developed Countries				
	Central Banks	Deposit Banks	Thrift Institutions	Insurance Organizations	Miscellaneous	Central Banks	Deposit Banks	Thrift Institutions	Insurance Organizations	Miscellaneous
	(1)	(2)	(3)	(4)	(5)	(6)	(7)	(8)	(9)	(10)
				CURRENT PRICES						
1861–1880	1.80	7.05	5.92	7.47	7.05					
1881–1900	1.21	5.00	5.32	6.14	5.37		3.92	6.20	5.64	
1901–1913	2.44	6.47	5.55	7.86	5.61	4.79	8.97	5.93	7.38	8.61
1914–1929	23.20	23.85	23.67	24.86	23.28	8.20	10.03	5.02	9.07	2.34
1930–1938	5.64	.21	4.53	8.20	4.43	4.54	1.90	7.18	6.84	3.34
1939–1948	20.33	13.88	12.29	9.19	9.24	23.68	19.47	14.59	25.05	14.23
1949–1963	5.17	9.99	11.31	13.79	15.72	10.87	14.90	11.65	16.52	12.82
				CONSTANT PRICES						
1861–1880	2.12	7.38	6.25	7.80	7.38					
1881–1900	1.47	5.29	5.77	6.59	5.62		2.95	5.22	4.66	
1901–1913	1.49	4.99	4.08	6.35	4.14	3.75	8.02	5.15	6.51	7.50
1914–1929	3.18	2.77	2.86	4.21	2.69	3.89	4.98	3.26	4.15	1.49
1930–1938	5.86	.49	4.82	8.50	4.71	4.02	2.98	7.61	7.36	3.37
1939–1948	5.80	.33	.92	−3.27	−3.75	5.41	1.96	1.80	6.09	1.13
1949–1963	1.96	5.93	7.24	9.56	11.43	4.86	8.57	5.89	10.16	7.21

five groups of 1.8. Central banks ranked lowest for developed countries (3.6) and next to lowest for less developed countries (3.8). Deposit banks similarly had relatively higher asset growth rates in less developed than in developed countries with average ranks of 2.5 and 3.4 respectively. Thrift institutions occupied approximately the same position in both groups of countries (average rank 3.0), while the heterogeneous miscellaneous group was in a slightly lower position in less developed countries (average rank 3.8) than in developed countries (3.6).

Possibly more interesting are differences in position among periods with respect to rate of growth of assets. Thus central banks ranked well ahead of their seven- or six-period average during both World Wars in developed as well as in less developed countries, a reflection of the inflation which originated in the issuance of central bank money and which affected many countries during these two periods. Miscellaneous financial organizations, on the contrary, ranked lower in these two periods than in any other. Deposit banks slipped considerably during the Great Depression in both groups of countries, actually falling to the lowest position among all five groups.

If we look at the entire century ending in 1963 and at the average for all countries, the important features in the relative composition of ϕ evident from Table 5–22 are the increasing importance of the issues by central banks and insurance organizations, the declining share of the issues of deposit banks, and the absence of a definite trend in the issues of thrift institutions and miscellaneous financial intermediaries. The movements, of course, do not generally proceed without interruption. Deviations from the trend are particularly obvious, first, in the 1930s as a result of the Great Depression, which is characterized by an abnormally low level of ϕ_b, a feature which in turn reflects the concentration of the deflation of this period on deposit banks among financial institutions; and, secondly, during World War II, when the share of ϕ_c was abnormally high, reflecting the general prevalence of inflation more or less successfully repressed, due to war financing by money creation.

There is also clearly evident a break around World War I in the case of central and deposit banks. The share of ϕ_c

TABLE 5–22

Share of Main Types of Financial Institutions in ϕ
UNWEIGHTED COUNTRY AVERAGES (PER CENT)

	Central Banks (ϕ_c)	Deposit Banks (ϕ_b)	Thrift Institution (ϕ_t)	Insurance Organization (ϕ_i)	Miscellaneous Institution (ϕ_o)
	ALL NONSOCIALIST COUNTRIES				
1881–1900	5.2	40.5	22.3	12.5	19.5
1901–1913	6.2	45.5	17.1	11.9	19.3
1914–1929	6.2	56.3	16.5	13.2	7.8
1930–1938	26.1	11.0	12.5	29.0	21.5
1939–1948	28.7	33.8	13.6	13.6	10.3
1949–1963	13.9	35.0	13.8	19.5	17.8
	DEVELOPED NONSOCIALIST COUNTRIES				
1861–1880	6.6	42.8	16.8	10.8	23.0
1881–1900	5.6	38.3	22.2	13.0	20.9
1901–1913	5.2	42.4	20.0	14.4	18.0
1914–1929	7.5	35.5	20.3	19.5	17.3
1930–1938	25.5	−15.7	17.4	46.6	26.2
1939–1948	20.8	30.8	20.4	17.9	10.0
1949–1963	7.3	26.9	19.5	25.3	21.1
	LESS DEVELOPED NONSOCIALIST COUNTRIES				
1881–1900	—	71.0	22.5	6.4	—
1901–1913	9.1	54.8	8.5	4.2	23.4
1914–1929	3.7	97.9	9.1	0.6	−11.3
1930–1938	26.9	49.9	5.4	3.3	14.6
1939–1948	38.5	37.5	5.2	8.2	10.6
1949–1963	21.9	44.7	7.0	12.5	13.9

has been considerably higher since World War I than before, while that of ϕ_b has been substantially lower. The increase in the share of ϕ_c reflects at least three developments: (1) the creation of central banks in several important countries where none existed before, particularly in the United States; (2) the inclusion of an increasing number of less developed countries, which as a rule have a higher share of ϕ_c than developed countries; and (3) a rise in the importance of ϕ_c in a number of both developed and less developed countries. The break in the share of ϕ_b, which begins in the 1930s rather than at the time of World War I, and which has reduced the share of deposit banks in ϕ by almost ten percentage points, is fairly widespread.[10] It reflects an important change in financial structure, in particular a decrease of the share of the issues of money in the total issues of all financial instruments by financial institutions.

If we compare the period 1901–13 (the first period for which data are available for a sufficient number of both developed and less developed countries) with the postwar period 1949–63, the main changes in the distribution of ϕ among its five components are a doubling of the share of ϕ_c from only 6 per cent of total ϕ to 13 per cent, a decrease in the share of ϕ_b from the dominating 45 per cent to 33 per cent, and a sharp increase in the share of ϕ_i from 12 to 20 per cent, while the shares of ϕ_t and ϕ_o decline slightly to approximately 14 and 18 per cent respectively. While these changes are significant, the relative stability in the structure in the flow of issues of financial institutions seems more impressive in view of the rapid and far-reaching changes in the world economy that have occurred during these fifty years. This is particularly so if we divide ϕ_b between the issuance of money and of thrift deposits, and if we eliminate financial intermediaries of the second degree from ϕ_o. Then the share of the issues of monetary institutions (i.e. the issues of central banks and of demand liabilities of deposit banks) declines only a few percentage points from about 40 per cent in 1901–13 to fully 35 per cent in the postwar period, while that of thrift and insurance organizations increases from about 45 to 50 per cent and that of miscellaneous financial institutions falls from about 15 to 10 per cent, a decline in the relative importance of the issues of mortgage banks not being fully

10. The value of ϕ_b in 1963 was below that of 1929 in 23 of the 30 countries (14 of the 17 developed countries and 9 of the 13 underdeveloped).

compensated by an increase in the issues of newer forms of miscellaneous financial institutions, such as development banks and investment companies.

The share of ϕ_c is considerably higher in less developed than in developed countries in all periods, while the share of ϕ_t and ϕ_i is much lower, and the difference in ϕ_o is small and irregular. Thus in the postwar period ϕ_c and ϕ_b together accounted for almost two-thirds of the aggregate value of ϕ in the case of less developed countries, as against a share of slightly below two-fifths in developed countries, while the opposite relationship obtained for the shares of ϕ_t and ϕ_i, which amounted to one one-fifth in less developed countries but fully two-fifths in developed countries. The difference is even more marked if the issues of time and saving deposits by commercial banks are combined with the issues of thrift and insurance institutions and the issues of financial intermediaries of the second degree are eliminated from ϕ_o. If this is done, the share of issues of money (currency and demand deposits in central and deposit banks) is as high as about 60 per cent for the average of less developed countries against a share of 30 per cent for developed countries, while thrift and insurance issues account for only about 30 per cent of the aggregate value of ϕ in underdeveloped countries compared to more than 55 per cent in developed countries. This divergence reflects a basic difference in the financial structure between developed and less developed countries, the much larger importance of money, and the correspondingly smaller importance of thrift deposits and insurance reserves, in less developed countries. In this respect, less developed countries at the present time again are closer to developed countries fifty to one hundred years ago than they are to the present situation of developed countries. In the period 1861–80, for instance, the share of issues of money among developed countries—at that time only five countries including the Big Four are covered by the statistics—was about two-fifths of the aggregate value of ϕ, while the issues of thrift deposits and insurance reserve accounted for only one-third of the total, a relationship not too different from the one observed in less developed countries in the postwar period. The details of the differences in the development of the share of each of the component ratios can be followed in Table 5–22.

It may, finally, be worthwhile to look in Table 5–23 at

TABLE 5–23

Distribution of Assets of Financial Institutions
Unweighted Nonsocialist Country Averages
PER CENT

	Central Banks	Deposit Banks	Thrift Institutions	Insurance Organizations	Miscellaneous Institutions
			ALL COUNTRIES		
1900	13.6	44.0	15.9	8.8	17.8
1913	12.0	48.9	13.8	10.5	15.3
1929	12.2	49.9	14.0	11.4	12.4
1938	17.7	38.5	16.1	14.8	12.9
1948	26.5	37.1	13.2	13.2	10.1
1963	17.4	35.5	13.7	17.5	15.9
			DEVELOPED COUNTRIES		
1860	13.7	38.7	17.0	8.9	21.7
1880	12.7	45.9	16.1	7.1	18.1
1900	8.7	42.2	19.6	10.8	18.8
1913	6.5	43.2	19.2	14.3	17.5
1929	8.6	40.2	19.6	16.1	15.5
1938	11.3	29.7	20.3	21.7	17.0
1948	18.2	34.8	18.1	17.5	11.5
1963	10.6	28.8	19.3	22.8	18.4
			LESS DEVELOPED COUNTRIES		
1900	28.2	49.6	4.8	2.9	14.5
1913	21.7	59.2	4.0	3.8	11.3
1929	17.4	64.1	5.9	4.6	8.0
1938	25.5	49.3	10.9	6.4	7.9
1948	36.4	39.8	7.2	8.0	8.5
1963	25.5	43.5	7.0	11.2	12.8

the share of the five groups in the total assets of all financial institutions, rather than at their share in ϕ, i.e. at the distribution of Φ among the five components (Φ_c, etc.). These shares may, of course, be regarded as weighted averages of the shares in ϕ for the past, and are thus likely to show slower and less abrupt movements. They also have the advantage of reaching back beyond the first period for which the ϕ ratios could be calculated. Differences between the two distributions shown in Tables 5–22 and 5–23 are therefore relatively most pronounced for the early dates and for the period of the Great Depression, which affected the distribution of assets among the five groups much less than the distribution of flows which are nothing but first differences in assets. Otherwise the main features of the two distributions are quite similar.

VARIATION AND CONGRUENCE OF COMPONENT RATIOS

The components of ϕ vary not only in their level and their movements over the past century, but also in the extent to which the values for the individual countries are scattered around the averages for broader or narrower groups of countries, i.e. in the level of their coefficients of variation and in the degree to which the scatter has narrowed, a tendency which is reflected in a decline in the coefficient of variation and indicates an increasing similarity among individual countries in their ratios of the issues of different groups of financial institutions to national product.

It is seen from Table 5–24 that the unweighted average of the coefficients of variation for the seven periods for all thirty-three nonsocialist countries is highest for ϕ_b (1.50) and lowest for ϕ_i (slightly less than 0.80), the three other ratios ϕ_c, ϕ_t, and ϕ_o occupying an intermediate position at values of slightly above unity. These relations are, however, strongly influenced by the figures for 1930–38, a period during which the coefficient of variation of ϕ_b was extraordinarily high. If we exclude this rather abnormal decade, the value of the coefficient of variation declines for all components and the range is considerably reduced, now stretching from about 0.75 for ϕ_i to 1.00 for ϕ_o, and the value of ϕ_b (0.80) now becomes the second lowest instead of the highest of the five.

The lower level of the coefficient of variation for developed compared to less developed countries found for total ϕ also is applicable to all components of ϕ for the average of the five periods 1901–63 for which the comparison can be made, with the exception of ϕ_d, but this anomaly disappears if the period 1930–38 is excluded. The relationship also holds for most subperiods. Indeed, of the forty-five

TABLE 5–24

Coefficient of Variation of Financial Institutions' New Issue Ratios
$\left(\frac{\text{STANDARD DEVIATION}}{\text{MEAN}}\right)$

	Total (ϕ)	Central Banks (ϕ_c)	Deposit Banks (ϕ_b)	Thrift Institutions (ϕ_t)	Insurance Organizations (ϕ_i)	Miscellaneous Institutions (ϕ_o)
		ALL NONSOCIALIST COUNTRIES				
1881–1900	0.51	1.48	0.83	0.61	0.74	0.87
1901–1913	0.57	1.16	0.77	0.92	0.70	0.99
1914–1929	0.69	0.77	0.73	1.19	1.00	1.36
1930–1938	0.87	1.03	5.71	1.37	0.88	1.58
1939–1948	0.69	0.75	0.69	1.34	0.94	1.18
1949–1963	0.59	1.24	0.78	1.11	0.78	0.73
Average	0.65	1.07	1.59	1.09	0.84	1.12
		DEVELOPED COUNTRIES				
1861–1880	0.54	1.15	0.94	0.54	0.25	0.65
1881–1900	0.42	1.41	0.76	0.54	0.67	0.80
1901–1913	0.45	0.86	0.65	0.65	0.43	0.92
1914–1929	0.52	0.81	0.60	0.89	0.67	1.14
1930–1938	0.60	0.76	9.04	1.05	0.43	1.20
1939–1948	0.58	0.73	0.57	0.93	0.69	1.18
1949–1963	0.43	1.12	0.81	0.75	0.48	0.46
Average	0.51	0.98	1.91	0.76	0.52	0.92
		LESS DEVELOPED COUNTRIES				
1901–1913	0.73	1.50	1.18	1.08	0.54	1.21
1914–1929	0.74	0.70	0.92	0.86	0.70	1.33
1930–1938	0.99	1.65	1.47	0.96	1.18	2.25
1939–1948	0.56	0.68	0.75	1.09	1.09	1.09
1949–1963	0.64	1.25	0.57	1.09	0.80	0.96
Average	0.73	1.27	0.98	1.02	0.86	1.37

cases, the coefficient of variation is higher for less developed countries in all but ten instances.

There thus seems to be a considerable amount of substitutability among the components of ϕ, i.e. among the different types of issues of financial instruments by financial institutions. This already is indicated by the fact that the coefficient of variation for total ϕ is lower than that for any of its five components. It is confirmed by the values of the coefficient of variation for combinations of ϕ_c, ϕ_b, and ϕ_t, all of which are for most periods lower than the coefficients of individual components. One would expect such a relationship in view of the fact that similar functions are performed in different countries by institutions belonging to different categories of financial intermediaries, the function of issuing money in particular being performed by central banks and by deposit banks, while the function of issuing saving deposits is discharged to a varying extent by both deposit banks and thrift institutions.

The trends in the coefficients of variation for the five components and combinations of them, finally, also show considerable differences. Interestingly enough, none of the series for all countries shown in the upper tier of Table 5–24 exhibits a definite downward trend, which would indicate increasing similarity among countries. The series coming nearest to this pattern is the coefficient of variation for the net issue ratio of deposit banks, but even here the difference between the values for the most recent period and those before World War I is small. On the contrary, two of the series, those for the issues of thrift institutions and miscellaneous financial institutions, show if anything a slight tendency to rise.

The picture changes if developed and less developed countries are separated. There then appears among developed countries a slight tendency for the coefficients to decline, but the extent of the movements remains small and erratic. For less developed countries, on the other hand, the values of the coefficient for the postwar period are in all cases except thrift institutions below those for the initial period 1901–13 as well as those for the two following periods running from 1914 through 1938, and the reduction is substantial for central and deposit banks and for miscellaneous financial institutions. In this group of countries, the issue ratios for most types of financial institutions seem to have become considerably more similar since the 1940s than they were before.

THE INCOME ELASTICITY OF THE ISSUES OF DIFFERENT TYPES OF FINANCIAL INSTITUTIONS

The differences among the main types of financial institutions in the income elasticity evident in Table 5–25 are

TABLE 5–25

Income Elasticity of Issues of Financial Institutions in All Nonsocialist Countries
UNWEIGHTED COUNTRY AVERAGES

	All	Central Banks	Deposit Banks	Thrift Institutions	Insurance Organizations	Miscellaneous
ABSOLUTE VALUES (RATIO OF AVERAGE RATES OF GROWTH OF ASSETS AND GNP)						
1861–1880	2.89	1.11	3.47	2.50	3.40	3.42
1881–1900	2.11	0.56	1.93	2.73	2.83	2.01
1901–1913	2.20	0.72	2.31	1.52	2.03	1.57
1914–1929	1.22	0.88	1.22	1.12	1.47	0.89
1930–1938	2.27	−1.57	−0.64	2.46	5.48	7.14
1939–1948	1.25	1.00	1.09	1.27	1.52	1.03
1949–1963	1.24	0.74	1.23	1.19	1.57	1.45
PERCENTAGE OF VALUE FOR ALL FINANCIAL INSTITUTIONS						
1861–1880	100	38	120	87	118	118
1881–1900	100	27	92	129	134	95
1901–1913	100	33	105	69	92	72
1914–1929	100	72	100	92	121	73
1930–1938	100	−69	−28	108	242	314
1939–1948	100	80	87	102	122	82
1949–1963	100	60	99	96	127	117
COEFFICIENT OF VARIATION						
1861–1880	0.60	1.16	0.72	0.59	0.64	0.66
1881–1900	0.53	1.13	0.57	0.89	0.63	0.80
1901–1913	2.40	1.32	1.16	16.10	0.88	0.83
1914–1929	0.79	0.80	0.59	0.89	0.54	0.92
1930–1938	5.54	−4.07	−12.40	6.19	5.60	5.53
1939–1948	1.06	1.70	0.61	1.75	1.87	2.20
1949–1963	0.31	0.72	0.45	0.56	0.41	0.55

substantial, but they have shown a tendency to decline. Thus in the three periods before World War I the coefficient of income elasticity for the issues of each of the five types of financial institutions differed on the average by fully one-fourth from the coefficient for the issues of all financial institutions taken together, while the difference declined to about one-sixth in 1939–48 and 1949–63.

The issues of central banks showed the lowest elasticity in all but one of the seven periods—the 1930s—i.e. they reacted less to a given change in national product than any of the other four types of financial institutions. (Since the coefficients are based on averages for periods of nine to twenty years' duration, this says very little about behavior in the short or intermediate run.) Indeed for the average of six of the seven periods the elasticity of the issues of central banks was slightly below unity, indicating that an average annual increase in national product by 1 per cent was accompanied by an increase of the issues of central banks by 0.85 per cent. In the seventh period—the 1930s—the issues of central banks increased in the face of declining national product—a result of antideflationary monetary policies.

All other elasticities are above unity—with the exception of that for the issues of deposit banks in the 1930s, which is negative and again reflects that period's antideflationary expansion in some countries, and of that for miscellaneous financial institutions for 1914–29. Elasticity was on the average highest for insurance organizations; the average values for the other three groups are similar if the 1930s are disregarded. Elasticities were considerably smaller for all groups beginning with the 1940s than they had been before the Great Depression, reflecting the fact that the rate of growth of issues of all types of financial institutions was farther ahead of the expansion of national product in the earlier than in the later periods.

Comparing the elasticities for developed and less developed countries, period by period and type by type of institution, it appears from Table 5–26 that the elasticity is higher for less developed countries in eighteen out of twenty-eight cases. If the often abnormal values for the 1930–38 period are excluded, the difference is more pronounced, the less developed countries showing a higher elasticity in sixteen of twenty-three cases. This is only another way of expressing the fact that for most periods and types of institutions the volume of issues increased more in comparison with the rise in national product in less developed than in developed countries. This is to be ex-

TABLE 5-26

Income Elasticity of Issue of Financial Institutions in Developed and Less Developed Countries
RATIO OF AVERAGE ANNUAL RATES OF GROWTH OF ASSETS OF FINANCIAL INSTITUTIONS AND OF NATIONAL PRODUCT
UNWEIGHTED COUNTRY AVERAGES

	All Fin. Institutions	Central Banks	Deposit Banks	Thrift Institutions	Insurance Organizations	Miscell. Fin. Institutions
			DEVELOPED COUNTRIES			
1861–1880	2.89	1.11	3.47	2.50	3.40	3.42
1881–1900	2.04	0.60	1.87	2.62	2.75	2.15
1900–1913	1.38	0.58	1.53	1.29	1.87	1.35
1914–1929	1.16	0.82	1.05	1.17	1.41	1.11
1930–1938	3.39	−2.84	−1.25	3.28	6.90	11.33
1939–1948	1.37	0.93	1.14	1.66	1.74	1.37
1949–1963	1.15	0.56	1.01	1.20	1.40	1.64
			LESS DEVELOPED COUNTRIES			
1901–1913	4.65	1.14	4.63	2.18	2.52	2.22
1914–1929	1.32	1.01	1.56	1.01	1.59	0.46
1930–1938	0.48	0.47	0.33	1.15	3.20	0.44
1939–1948	1.11	1.08	1.02	0.78	1.25	0.61
1949–1963	1.34	0.96	1.49	1.17	1.77	1.21

pected, since for identical calendar year periods the less developed countries find themselves at an earlier stage of their financial development than do the developed countries. If we compare the period 1949–63 for less developed countries with the 1901–13 period for developed countries to give some recognition to this lag, the difference disappears, indicating a similar response to the expansion of the issues of the main types of financial institution to the same relative increase in national product. If the comparison is made with the values of elasticities for the developed countries in the period 1914–29, thus implying a lag of approximately thirty-five years instead of one of nearly fifty years, all values are higher (except one which is equal) for less developed countries by about one-fifth on the average.

THE LAYERING RATIO

For financial analysis two of the most important classifications of the flows and of the assets and liabilities of financial institutions are, on the one hand, the division between those assets that represent supply of funds to other sectors and those that take place within the financial institutions sector and, on the other hand, the distinction between fund flows and liabilities (and equity securities) that are provided by other sectors and, again, those that occur within the financial institutions sector. Since financial institutions abroad are regarded as a part of the nonfinancial foreign sector, the proportion of interfinancial flows—and of interfinancial assets and liabilities—to the totals of flow or of assets and liabilities of financial institutions will be the same whether or not the economy is closed, provided consistent methods of accounting and valuation are used.

Four main types of interfinancial flows and assets and liabilities need to be ditinguished. The first are the claims and liabilities within the deposit banking system, which are particularly important in cases where no central bank exists —such as in the United States before 1914—and which tend to lose in importance as the concentration process within the system of deposit banks progresses. Reserves kept by deposit banks with the central bank, either voluntarily or more commonly in accordance with law or regulation, constitute the second and often the quantitatively and qualitatively most important part of interfinancial assets and liabilities. It is the central bank's control over these deposits which constitutes the chief instrument of monetary policy in most developed and in many underdeveloped countries. The third component consists of the checking and other deposits held by nonbank financial institutions with deposit banks, just as such deposits are kept for transactions purposes and for temporarily idle funds by nonfinancial business enterprises and by other sectors. This type of interfinancial assets is generally of relatively small importance, particularly in developed countries where other and usually higher yielding instruments for the investment of short-term liquid funds exist. The fourth type of interfinancial assets is of a different character, being limited to a few countries but having substantial importance in these. This type is represented by special institutions, which have been called financial intermediaries of the second degree because most or all of their assets and liabilities consist of claims against, or of obligations to, other financial institutions.[11]

This important phenomenon of layering within the financial institutions sector can be taken into account in the basic formula in at least two ways. The simpler of these, followed in Chapter 2, is to ignore the differences among the four types of interfinancial flow or assets and to express the sum of all four types as a per cent (λ) of the total flow-of-funds or of total assets of all financial institutions. Then ϕ $(1 - \lambda)$ is the ratio of the net flow of funds from financial institutions to other sectors to gross national product. Alternatively, if we start from the funds that financial institutions make available to nonfinancial sectors, $\bar{\phi}$ $(1 + \bar{\lambda})$ is equal to the ratio of the total supply of funds from financial institutions to all sectors to gross national product.[12]

We may, on the other hand, wish to distinguish between the four types, or at least between three of them, omitting the deposits of nonbank financial institutions with deposit banks, because they are relatively small and no comprehen-

11. See "Financial Intermediaries of the Second Degree," above. In some cases funds of the type are administered not by a separate organization, but by treasury officials or by a special committee, for instance the National Debt Commissioners in the United Kingdom. These funds have not been regarded as a type of financial institution and are not included in the layering ratio, even though the difference to some financial institutions of the second degree is small.

12. The relation can also be expressed in terms of the ratio of interfinancial assets to total assets instead of that used above of interfinancial net to total net flows. The formulas are identical in structure, although of course the numerical values of Φ and Λ will differ from those of ϕ and λ.

sive information exists on an international basis. In that case the formula becomes more complicated. We introduce an additional subsector of financial institutions, consisting of financial intermediaries of the second degree and identified by subscript z (the subscript o′ now identifying the o-z sector) and distinguish λ_c as the ratio of changes (net flows) in reserves held by deposit banks with their central bank to total net flows; we also distinguish λ_b as the ratio of changes in deposits among deposit banks to their total net flows and λ_z as the ratio of changes in the assets of financial intermediaries of the second degree received from other financial institutions to changes in these organizations' total assets (these ratios can be derived either from the sources or uses side of a flow-of-funds statement or from either the assets and liabilities side of a balance sheet). The detailed formula then becomes, instead of Equation (2.18) of Chapter 2:

$$\phi = \phi_c + \phi_b(1 - \lambda_c - \lambda_b) + \phi_t + \phi_i + \phi_o + \phi_z(1 - \lambda_z)$$

What are the possibilities of obtaining numerical values for these λ coefficients for a sufficient number of countries at benchmark dates to justify statements about trends and differences in the layering ratio among countries of different types? What are the results insofar as such figures can be obtained?

Trying to answer these questions, we find ourselves in the same position in which we are so often in comparative financial analysis. The raw material for the answer exists, although it is widely dispersed. Nobody, however, has taken the trouble of collecting the material systematically and of putting it into a form where comparison would be relatively easy. We must, therefore, again be satisfied with presenting scattered evidence. This should, however, suffice for settling the order of magnitudes involved, and the answers should not be in danger of seriously misleading us on important points.

The situation is least unsatifactory from the statistical point of view for the first and second of the four types of interfinancial assets or flows distinguished above—the deposits kept by deposit banks (1) with their central bank and (2) with other domestic deposit banks. Table 5–27 shows the ratio of the deposits held by deposit banks with their central banks to the total combined assets of the banking system for the postwar period for all the thiry-one countries to which the calculation is applicable, i.e. excluding the two Communist countries and the two countries without a central bank in 1963 (Puerto Rico and Trinidad).

A second table (Table 5–28) permits us to follow the trend in the ratio of interbank deposits of both types to the total assets of the banking system since the turn of the century for the few countries for which data of this character are easily available.[13]

From these two tables and from some collateral statistics not shown here, one can draw the following tentative conclusions about differences in the ratio of interbank deposits and borrowings to the assets of the banking system among countries during the postwar period and about the long-run trend of this ratio in developed countries:

1. At the present time interbank deposits, both with the central bank and with other domestic commercial banks, account on the average for only 6 per cent of the total assets of the banking system. For general financial analysis, these interbank deposits are therefore of secondary importance, and it does not matter much whether the analysis is based on the combined or the consolidated balance sheet of the banking system, or on a combined or a consolidated flow-of-funds statement.

2. The interbank layering ratio ($\lambda_c + \lambda_b$) now is somewhat lower in developed than in less developed countries. In the former countries, the average value of the ratio in 1963 was in the neighborhood of 5 per cent compared with an average of approximately 7 per cent for underdeveloped

13. Because in some countries deposit banks keep reserves with their central bank in excess of their borrowing from the central bank, while the opposite relation prevails in other countries, Table 5–27 is based on the larger of the two items as best reflecting the degree of interfinancial flows of assets within the banking system.

TABLE 5–27

Ratio of Deposit Banks' Reserves with (or Borrowing from) Their Central Banks in the Postwar Period to Total Assets of Banking System[a]

PER CENT[b]

	1948[c]	1963	Change 1948–63	Marginal Rate[d]
Argentina	28.8	27.4	−1.4	27.2
Australia	11.5	7.5	−4.0	−14.8
Belgium	2.5	2.2	−0.3	1.9
Brazil	4.3	10.0	5.7	10.1
Canada	5.5	3.4	−2.1	1.9
Denmark	7.8	4.2	−3.6	1.2
Egypt-U.A.R.	9.8	5.6	−4.2	4.0
France	12.7	13.4	0.7	13.5
Germany	9.5	5.8	−3.7	3.6
Great Britain	3.6	1.9	−1.7	−2.5
Greece	5.7	3.4	−2.3	2.2
India	2.2	1.4	−0.8	0.6
Israel	4.4	11.6	7.2	11.7
Italy	1.3	3.5	2.2	4.7
Jamaica	[e]	2.8		
Japan	10.5	6.2	−4.3	5.2
Mexico	10.3	7.9	−2.4	7.4
Netherlands	0.8	1.1	0.3	0.1
New Zealand	19.5	12.0	−7.5	1.0
Nigeria	[e]	5.9		
Norway	4.5	2.3	−2.2	−0.2
Pakistan	3.4	4.0	0.6	4.3
Philippines	6.6	3.4	−3.2	2.1
Rhodesia	[e]	3.2		
South Africa	15.7	5.0	−10.7	−4.1
Spain	11.8	7.3	−4.5	6.0
Sweden	2.4	0.5	−1.9	−0.6
Switzerland	3.8	5.8	2.0	6.8
Thailand	5.4	3.1	−2.3	0.3
U.S.A.	10.7	5.0	−5.7	−2.3
Venezuela	6.4	7.2	0.8	7.4

[a] Central banks and deposit banks.

[b] Numerator is the larger of reserves or borrowings; denominator is total assets of central and deposit banks.

[c] Starting year slightly later (1949–55) for lines 3, 7, 9, 10, 11, 13, 14, 15, 17, 22, and 24 because of unavailability of earlier data.

[d] Change in reserves or borrowing divided by change in total assets.

[e] Central banks organized in 1956 (Rhodesia), 1959 (Nigeria), and 1961 (Jamaica).

Sources of bank data: International Financial Statistics, 1965/66 Supplement.

countries. There are, however, substantial differences within both of these groups. Among developed countries, interbank balances are much less important in European countries, where they average only 4 per cent, than in the developed countries outside of Europe, where the average is close to 7 per cent. Among the less developed countries the inter-

TABLE 5–28

Changing Importance of Interbank Deposits

PER CENT OF TOTAL ASSETS OF CENTRAL AND DEPOSIT BANKS

	1880	1900	1913	1929	1938	1948	1960
United States							
Total		13.1	12.3	8.5	19.4	18.0	9.8
With central bank				3.5	12.1	10.2	5.8
With other banks[a]		13.1	12.3	5.0	7.3	2.8	4.0
Canada							
Total	2.2	0.9	0.3	0.2	5.4	5.9	4.3
With central bank					5.3	5.1	4.0
With other banks[a]	2.2	0.9	0.3	0.2	0.1	0.8	0.3
Great Britain							
Interbank deposits	2.2	4.0	3.5	6.1	4.0	0.8	1.4
South Africa							
With central bank				5.7	15.7	16.3	6.0

[a] Only other domestic deposit banks.

Sources:
U.S.A.: *Historical Statistics* (1960) and *Continuation* (1965).
Canada: Urquhart and Buckley, *Historical Statistics of Canada.*
South Africa: *Union Statistics for Fifty Years* (Praetoria, 1960).
Great Britain: D. K. Sheppard, (MS) for interbank deposits; Table A–10 for total bank assets.

bank layering ratio is much higher in Latin America—the average for the three countries included in Table 5–27 is over 13 per cent—than in the other less developed countries, which show an average ratio only slightly in excess of 4 per cent. Thus, as in some other financial ratios, the non-American less developed countries are much closer to developed countries as a group, particularly to European developed countries. These conclusions must be treated with great caution since they are based on less than thirty countries, and the number of countries included is quite small in some of the subgroups. However, somewhat more comprehensive tabulations show essentially the same results.[14] These differences in the average values of the interbank layering ratio are mainly institutional in origin. They depend to a good extent on the existence and the level of reserve requirements laid down in the laws of different countries and on the degree of concentration existing among a country's deposit banks.

3. The interbank layering ratio showed a definite decline between 1948 and 1963. For all countries together, it fell from approximately 8 to 6 per cent. The decline was of about equal size—two percentage points—for developed and less developed countries, but it was considerably larger in the non-European developed countries and considerably smaller in the Latin American countries. Such a downward tendency in the postwar period is to be expected, since in many countries the banking system was still extremely liquid in 1948 as a result of the methods of financing employed during World War II, and the commercial banks in consequence held substantial amounts of excess reserves.[15]

4. The long term trend in the interbank layering ratio is affected by two tendencies which work in opposite directions. The creation of central banks in a number of countries that did not have them before World War I and the introduction or increase of reserve requirements in other countries resulted in a rise in the value of λ_c on an inter-

14. See Goldsmith, *Determinants of Financial Structure,* Table 5; in that table, it should be noted, the denominators of the ratio are the assets of only commercial banks, not as in Table 5–28 the combined assets of commercial and central banks.

15. The discussion in the text is based on the ratio of interbank assets to the total assets of the banking system. Table 5–27, however, also shows in col 4 a corresponding flow magnitude, viz. the ratio of the change in interbank assets to the change in the total assets of the banking system. Because of the generally downward tendency of the ratio between 1948 and 1963 (col. 3) and the abnormally high level of the 1948 value in many developed countries, the ratios in col. 4 are very low or even negative (average 3.5 for all countries, 1.5 for developed and 6.5 for underdeveloped countries), and cannot be regarded as typical of the current level of the flow ratio. The 1963 stock ratios (col. 2) probably provide a better basis for this purpose.

national scale. On the other hand, the process of concentration within the commercial banking system, which has now resulted in the dominating position of a very small number of nationwide branch banking systems in virtually all countries outside the United States, will usually be accompanied by a decline in λ_b. This process, however, had been of greater influence in the half century before World War II than it was in the postwar period. Some of these tendencies are visible in Table 5–28, unfortunately limited to less than half a dozen countries for which comparable statistics are available back to the turn of the century.[16] In these countries—all developed ones—the increase in λ_c has more than compensated for the decline in λ_b. It is impossible to tell at the moment whether the same development would be observed for a more representative group of countries. The tendency towards an increase in the aggregate interfinancial layering ratio is, however, to be expected for less developed countries because of the creation and expansion of central banks which has occurred in most of them over the last fifty years. In view of the present low average value of even the combined λ_c and λ_b ratios, it is, however, unlikely that changes in them could have seriously affected the level and movements of ϕ since the turn of the century.

The financial intermediaries of the second degree that give rise to λ_z have already been discussed. It was shown there[17] that the average value of λ_z for all countries together, or for broad groups of them, has been very small—perhaps in the order of 0.02.

16. Table 5–28, in contrast to Table 5–27, also provides information on balances among deposit banks.

17. See p. 260.

6 THE COMMON ELEMENTS

The three preceding chapters have reviewed the material on the net issuance of securities by nonfinancial sectors (Chapter 3) and by financial institutions (Chapters 4 and 5) and have investigated the relation of these issues to national product and to other relevant economic variables. They have tried, in particular, to ascertain whether differences can be found in the value of the two overall ratios (δ and ϕ) and in their components among countries that are now at different stages of their financial development and whether definite trends can be observed in these ratios over the last fifty to one hundred years.

A similar review of the values of those determinants of the total issues of financial instruments outstanding at any one point of time that apply to both the issues of nonfinancial sectors and of financial institutions (i.e. a review of the coefficients that relate the volume of issues of new financial instruments during a period to the stock of such instruments outstanding at a given date) is therefore in order. Since the issues of financial instruments have so far been expressed as a ratio of total gross national product, this means that now, where we shift from the flow to the stock dimension, we must first ascertain what determines the relationship between the old denominator and the new denominator—total national wealth. We also want to see how the use of total gross national product as denominator instead of the theoretically preferable concepts of monetized national product or sales (a substitution required by the statistical situation) affects some of the coefficients actually used.

The four coefficients necessary to effect the shift in dimension from the aggregate new issue ratio (ANIR) to the financial interrelations ratio (FIR) as well as to substitute total national product (y) for monetized product (μy) or sales $[\mu y(1 + w)]$ are, as has been explained in Chapter 2, the gross national product multiplier (α), the monetization ratio (μ), the capital-output ratio (β), and the valuation adjustment term (ν). These relationships are recapitulated in the equations below in which F_n, F_x and F_f stand for the market values of domestic nonfinancial, foreign (net) and financial institutions' instruments outstanding, and d, x, and f for the corresponding flows of net new issues, and W for the market value of national wealth (domestic physical assets plus net foreign balance).[1]

$$\text{ANIR} = \frac{d + x + f}{y} = \delta + \xi + \phi \qquad (6.1)$$

$$= [\mu\bar{\kappa}\eta(1 + \omega)] + \xi + \phi \qquad (6.2)$$

$$= \kappa\eta + \xi + \phi \qquad (6.3)$$

$$\text{FIR} = \frac{F_n + F_x + F_f}{W} \qquad (6.4)$$

$$= [\alpha\beta^{-1}(1 + \nu)](\kappa\eta + \xi + \phi) \qquad (6.5)$$

This chapter, then, deals with the expression in square brackets of Equation (6.5), as well as with μ and ω of equation (6.2), whereas Chapters 3 to 5 were devoted primarily to the four coefficients in the second parenthesis of Equation (6.5).

THE NEW ISSUE MULTIPLIER

NIM, the net new issue multiplier,[2] i.e. the ratio of a

1. For derivation of the formulas, see Chapter 2.

2. To call α the "net new issue multiplier" is justified only in the context of the basic formula, i.e. on the assumption that the ratio of net new issues (e) to gross national product is constant throughout the period to which α applies, or that e and its components are appropriately weighted averages of new issue ratios for shorter, and ultimately annual, periods.

period's aggregate gross national product to the gross national product during the last year of the period (or—more correctly but statistically less conveniently and hardly differently—to the rate of gross national product at the end of the last year, i.e. at the balance sheet date) is a combination of the rate of growth of real national product (γ) and the rate of change in the general price level (π), i.e. the GNP deflator. If the period is of infinite length—or, practically speaking, extends over half a century or more—and if γ and π are constant or represent appropriately measured averages, NIM can be expressed by the simple formula explained in Chapter 2, viz. $\alpha = [(\gamma + \pi + \pi\gamma)^{-1} + 1]$. If these two assumptions are not met, the formula becomes more complicated. The value of α, however, can always be determined as the quotient of the sum of past gross national product and of current national product. Provided estimates of gross national product are available on an annual basis, or in the form of averages for longer periods, this approach is applicable, irregular as the course of the national product over the period may have been. Whether α can be factored into its components γ and π depends on whether estimates exist for gross national product both in current and constant prices or whether π can be estimated on the basis of a combination of price indices that may be entirely independent of the GNP calculations.

It is well beyond the scope of comparative financial analysis to explain the values of γ and π for different countries and different periods, except to the extent that these values are determined by financial factors. We must, however, at least review the values of α and its components γ and π, first, in order to see whether there exist systematic differences in α, γ, and π among countries with different types of economic and financial structure; and secondly, to determine whether the values of α, γ, and π have shown definite trends over the past century. Such a review is required in order to evaluate the effects of differences in α on differences in FIR, ANIR, and other important financial ratios.

Since the magnitude of α is for practical purposes determined by the values of national product in the thirty to fifty years preceding the benchmark date—unless the sum of γ and π is very small, say below .02, in which case a longer period is needed—we shall usually look at the average value of γ and π for periods of this length that precede the most important benchmark dates in the study, i.e. 1880 (rarely possible), 1913, 1938, and 1963. The values of α are shown in Table 6–1 for the thirty-five countries used throughout this study as far as the necessary data are available or can be roughly estimated. Because of unavailability of annual data for many countries and periods, the values of α are calculated in a considerable proportion of cases only from the values of the initial and final year of the period, i.e. $(\gamma + \pi)$ is determined as the *n*th root (*n* being the number of years in the period) of the ratio of gross national product in current prices at the beginning and end of the period; π is similarly derived from the value of the GNP deflator index in the two years; and γ is obtained from the values of gross national product in constant prices. These values of α are therefore not exactly equal to the quotient of the sum of the period's GNP and that of its last year, or to α determined by fitting a logarithmic trend to annual or period data.

Any review of the new issue multiplier α must distinguish sharply between the period from the late nineteenth century to World War I and the half-century following it.

During the first period the value of NIM was generally much higher than during the second one. In most countries and subperiods, γ lay between 0.02 and 0.04; population growth accounted for between 0.01 and 0.02 of this, while the annual rate of increase in real income per head rarely exceeded 0.02 and, more commonly, was in the neighborhood of 0.01. The value of π was even smaller for the period as a whole, as the decline in the price level prevailing during the 1870s to 1890s offset much or even all of the increase that occurred during the rest of the period, particularly during the fifteen years preceding 1913.

For the period from 1880 through 1913, which is long

TABLE 6–1

Net New Issue Multiplier (α)[a]

	1881 to 1913	1914 to 1929	1914 to 1963	1930 to 1963	1949 to 1963
Argentina		(28.1)	(9.3)	(7.1)	4.6
Australia	45.2	18.3	16.2	11.1	12.9
Belgium	(29.9)	(7.0)	(11.7)	(17.5)	21.2
Brazil		(12.9)	(7.4)	(6.3)	4.5
Canada	27.8	(19.9)	19.9	12.9	16.1
Denmark	31.2	27.5	19.5	15.4	14.5
Egypt-U.A.R		(22.7)	(21.9)	(21.6)	16.1
France	(54.3)	(8.2)	(7.9)	(7.8)	10.4
Germany	26.5	(38.6)	(27.1)	(23.8)	10.1
Great Britain	47.7	42.8	24.1	16.6	16.6
Greece		(5.2)	(5.0)	(4.9)	8.8
India	(45.3)	(32.2)	(22.9)	(20.2)	23.4
Israel					5.2
Italy	47.3	9.2	7.1	5.3	12.4
Jamaica					11.2
Japan	15.5	13.0	5.8	4.1	8.4
Mexico		(15.4)	(10.7)	7.9	8.6
Netherlands	(41.4)	21.7	20.3	12.7	13.4
New Zealand	(26.8)	(18.2)	(16.5)	(15.8)	15.4
Nigeria				(11.3)	21.4
Norway	(30.3)	36.7	20.2	13.1	15.0
Pakistan					17.9
Philippines		(23.0)	(17.0)	(15.1)	15.5
Puerto Rico				(13.7)	12.6
Rhodesia					10.1
Russia-U.S.S.R.		(42.2)	(11.5)	(8.7)	15.9
South Africa		(24.3)	(17.2)	(15.2)	13.4
Spain		(18.9)	(12.2)	(10.5)	11.5
Sweden	27.3	29.9	19.5	12.5	14.1
Switzerland	(29.4)	(17.8)	(20.4)	(22.0)	16.3
Thailand					13.7
Trinidad					10.8
U.S.A.	(24.3)	17.1	19.9	13.9	19.1
Venezuela				(14.1)	12.7
Yugoslavia				(8.7)	8.3

[a] Data in brackets are determined from estimates of national product in initial and terminal years of period only; other figures are derived by fitting a logarithmic trend to annual values.

enough to produce a significant figure, NIM, based on the average rate of growth of aggregate gross national product in current prices, is shown in Table 6–1 to have averaged 33 for the eight of the thirty-five countries covered in this study for which the necessary annual national product estimates are available. (The multiplier is only little higher on the average for eight additional countries, for which it is based on estimates of national product in only the initial and terminal year of the period.) The values of NIM ranged from 16 for Japan, then probably the most rapidly growing country, to over 45 for Great Britain, Italy, and Australia. The number of then (and now) less developed countries for which national product estimates are available—even on a less than annual basis—is too small to permit a determination of average or range. Since most of these countries were then growing rather slowly—this certainly was the case for the two largest countries in this group, India and China—and since their price level was in many cases tied to that of the world market, NIM should typically have been fairly high.

The situation has changed radically since World War I, in at least four respects. First, a number of European countries experienced one or usually two sharp price inflations or currency reforms connected with the two world wars, events which resulted in values of π well above those observed in the century before 1914, whether the period 1913–63 is regarded as the appropriate basis for calculation or a somewhat shorter span is preferred. Secondly, secular inflation at substantial average annual rates made its appearance for much of the period in a number of less developed countries, particularly in Latin America. Thirdly, the average rise in prices in developed countries remained considerably higher after World War II than before 1939. Thus, for the period 1948–63, the annual rise in the general price level averaged 4.0 per cent for seventeen developed countries (3.3 per cent if we exclude Japan and Israel). Finally, the typical values of γ have been considerably higher for the period following World War II than before

World War I both in developed and in less developed countries, though in many cases not for the period since 1914 taken as a whole, an increase reflecting an acceleration in the rate of growth of both population and of real product per head.

As a result of these tendencies, the values of NIM for the last thirty to fifty years—and it is these figures that enter the formula explaining the current (1963) values of FIR and of the ratio of financial institutions' assets to gross national product—are considerably lower than they were before 1914, and for that matter before 1929 or 1938, with the exception, in the latter two cases, of the European countries that experienced a pronounced inflation during or after World War I. Thus for the ten countries of the total of thirty-five for which annual data are available, the average value of NIM for the period 1914–63 was 17.[3] For the period 1948 to 1963, which is too short for a valid determination of NIM, but for which figures are available for all thirty-five countries, the average (mean or median) values of α are 13 for all, 14 for developed, and 12 for less developed countries.[4]

3. The average is practically the same for the twenty-five countries for which NIM can be calculated on the basis of the value of gross national product in 1913 and in 1963 alone. Among these countries an average of 17 for the much better represented sixteen developed countries compares with one of 13 for the nine less developed countries. For a slightly larger group of eighteen developed countries and fourteen less developed countries, the typical (median) value of α for the half-century ending with 1963 (determined from initial and terminal year values) is 15 for the thirty-four countries, 16 for the developed, and 11 for the less developed countries (Goldsmith, *Determinants of Financial Structure,* Table 7).

4. For a considerably larger group of thirty-six less developed countries the typical (median) value of α, based again on the actual experience of the 1948–63 period, is 14, resulting from γ of 0.046 and π of 0.030 (ibid., p. 34), so that the difference between developed and less developed countries disappears. (It reappears, and is even enlarged, if unweighted arithmetic averages of the values for the sixteen and thirty-six countries are used instead of medians which reduce the influence of extreme values.)

THE CAPITAL-OUTPUT RATIO

The capital-output ratio, in the form of the ratio of the current net value of total wealth (i.e. depreciated reproducible plus nonreproducible assets within the country with or without addition of the net foreign balance) to gross national product, is for the purposes of financial analysis, and in particular in connection with the basic formula developed in Chapter 2, one of several factors that must be treated as exogenous. The ratio reflects, first, technological input-output relationships, and secondly the level of yield rates prevailing in the country. Since technology differs considerably among sectors (compare the much higher capital-output ratios in agriculture and housing with the lower ratios in manufacturing and trade and particularly in services), since the relative importance of the several sectors varies from country to country and with changes over time, and since the level and structure of yield rates differ among countries and show not only secular trends but probably also long-term swings, it is to be expected that capital-output ratios will show both intercountry differences and movements over time. These differences and movements influence FIR although not ANIR, since the function of β^{-1}, i.e. the inverse of the capital-output ratio, in the basic formula is to reduce the denominator of the ratio to the same dimension as the numerator (the volume of financial assets outstanding at the point of time) by shifting the ANIR (the flow ratio of aggregate net issues of financial instruments to GNP gross national product) to its equivalent denominator in the stock dimension, national wealth, thus yielding FIR.

In view of this function of the capital-output ratio, it is not necessary to analyze its determinants, and we may limit ourselves to a brief review of the existing estimates of capital-output ratios for the present and the past in order to see whether systematic differences exist among countries that are related to their stage of financial development and to ascertain whether long-term movements can be observed in the figures. This modest program, however, is severely handicapped by the scarcity and lack of comparability of the existing figures over both time and space. Incredible as it may seem in view of the crucial importance which the capital-output ratio has played in much of the theories and the models of economic growth that have been developed during the postwar period, there does not exist a thorough critical review of the statistical data on an international comparative or even on a national historical scale.

In this situation the best that can be done without intensive study is to bring together figures for a few countries covering several benchmark dates since the turn of the century derived by one estimator, presumably by the same method and hence reasonably comparable over time. Unfortunately such time series are available for only half a dozen countries, all developed ones. These are shown in Table 6–2. On the other hand, there exist collections of estimates for about one dozen countries for the years 1888 and 1914 which were made or selected by one author, estimates that therefore may be presumed to be more nearly comparable in time and method than any collection of one-shot estimates that could be brought together. These two sets are reproduced in Table 6–3, together with estimates for the same as well as for a few other countries for a date close to 1960. The latter estimates, while not strictly comparable, have at least been derived in most cases by the same approach, as far as reproducible assets are concerned, viz. the perpetual inventory method, which involves the cumulation of past capital expenditures properly adjusted for depreciation and price changes.

With all due caution suggested by the roughness of the figures, particularly the incomplete comparability of most of the older figures with the more recent estimates,[5] five con-

5. While most of the more recent estimates of reproducible tangible wealth are derived by the perpetual inventory method and thus are comparable in their basic approach, the estimates that necessarily must be used for the period before World War II are in many countries

clusions can be drawn with a reasonable degree of confidence from these two bodies of data:

1. The aggregate average capital-output ratio, the relationship which is used in the basic equation for FIR, has shown a definite downward trend since the late nineteenth century, after probably having increased during most of the preceding one hundred years. There are two obvious reasons for this decline: first, the decreasing importance of agriculture with its high capital-output ratio and the consequent fall in the share of land in the capital-output ratio and, secondly, the disappearance of most of the large net foreign investments held by Western European countries, investments which before World War II accounted for as much as one-third of the total capital-output ratio in Great Britain and for one-tenth or more in France, Germany, and the Low Countries.

2. The downward movement of the aggregate capital-output ratio reached its lowest point in most countries around the end of World War II. Since then the ratio has generally moved upward, but it has advanced in only a few of them sufficiently to offset the previous decline entirely.

3. The ratio of reproducible tangible assets to gross national product has shown an only irregular and on balance generally small decline since World War I, the average remaining slightly above 3. The data are not reliable, comparable, or detailed enough to attempt an explanation of this relative stability in the ratio and of the differences in level that are still found among countries.

4. There is no definite difference in the level of the aggregate capital-output ratio as between developed and less developed countries. This tentative finding may well have to be revised when capital-output ratios become available

very heterogeneous in method and of varying quality. Of the older estimates used in Table 6-2, those for the United States, Canada, Germany, Norway, Australia, South Africa, and Argentina are not subject to this reservation for the period beginning with 1928—and in some cases with 1913 and 1900—since they are obtained by the perpetual inventory method.

TABLE 6–2

Time Series of Average Capital-Output Ratios for Selected Countries, 1900–55

	Argentina[a,b] (1)	Australia[c] (2)	Belgium[a,b] (3)	Canada[a,b] (4)	Germany[a] (5)	Great Britain[c] (6)	Norway[a,b] (7)	South Africa[c] (8)	United States[c] (9)
TOTAL WEALTH									
1900		6.4	7.6			4.1			4.7
1913		5.6	6.4		5.4	4.2			4.4
1928		5.2	4.7			3.4			4.1
1938			5.5			3.3			4.2
1948		3.9	4.0			2.4			3.5
1955		4.0			4.0				3.4
REPRODUCIBLE WEALTH									
1900	4.1	4.4			3.7	2.2	4.1		3.2
1913	5.1	4.1			3.7	2.1	3.9	4.7	2.9
1928	4.2	3.9		3.0	3.9	2.2	3.7	2.7	3.0
1938	3.2			2.5	3.2	2.2	3.6	2.7	3.2
1948	3.1	3.0		1.9	3.4	2.1	2.9	2.2	2.8
1955	3.2	3.3		2.1	2.3		3.4	2.3	2.8

[a] Constant price estimates.
[b] Inventories excluded.
[c] Current price estimates for wealth and income.

Sources of wealth data used in calculating capital-output ratios (when necessary ratios have been shifted to GNP as denominator):

Col. 1: A. Ganz, *Income and Wealth,* Series VIII, p. 246. Ratios are based on series in 1950 prices and before 1955 on five-year averages.

Col. 2: J. M. Garland and R. W. Goldsmith, ibid., p. 312.

Col. 3: Th. v. d. Weide, ibid., p. 30.

Col. 4: Urquhart and Buckley, *Historical Statistics of Canada*, pp. 132, 139. Ratios based on figures in 1949 dollars.

Col. 5: F. Grünig, *Income and Wealth,* Series VIII, pp. 154, 156.

Col. 6: J. Revell, "Changes in the Social Distribution of Property in Great Britain During the 20th Century," in *Review of Income and Wealth* (1967); figures for 1913 refer to 1910.

Col. 7: O. Aukrust and J. Bjerke, *Income and Wealth,* Series VIII, p. 116.

Col. 8: D. G. Franzsen and J. J. D. Willers, ibid., p. 312.

Col. 9: Goldsmith, Lipsey and Mendelson, *Studies in the National Balance Sheet, 2.*

for a larger number of less developed countries and increase in quality and detail. The outward similarity is apparently the result of higher ratios of land to national product and lower ratios of reproducible tangible assets in the less developed countries.

5. Condensing all the available evidence, it appears that the overall capital-output ratio has declined from an average of nearly 7 late in the nineteenth century to not much over 5 at the eve of World War I and then to its present level of about 4. Thus β^{-1}, which is the factor entering the basic equation, has risen from about 0.15 before the turn of the century to 0.25 at the present time. As a consequence, FIR would now be about two-thirds higher than it was late in the nineteenth century, and about one-fourth higher than it was before World War I, if all other components of

TABLE 6–3

Capital-Output Ratios, 1888, 1914, and ca. 1960

	Including Land			Excluding Land		
	1888 (1)	1914 (2)	ca. 1960 (3)	1888 (4)	1914 (5)	ca. 1960 (6)
Argentina	5.1	4.8		4.0	3.4	3.2
Australia	7.9	4.1	4.0	5.0	3.9	3.3
Belgium	5.0	3.8	4.5	3.2	3.0	3.2
Canada	6.3	4.1		4.5	2.9	2.1
Denmark	5.9	3.6		2.8		
France	7.1	6.4	3.9	4.9	4.8	3.1
Germany	5.8	5.9	3.6	4.1	4.7	2.9
Great Britain	7.0	5.6	3.2	5.8	5.1	
India			3.6			2.3
Israel			3.2			2.6
Italy	6.6	4.4	3.1	4.0	2.7	2.3
Japan		5.2	2.8		2.8	2.0
Mexico			3.8			2.9
Netherlands	8.0	4.0	4.8	6.3		4.0
Norway	4.1	2.9	5.3	2.4		4.5
Russia-U.S.S.R.	5.0	5.8	2.7	3.5		2.0
South Africa						2.3
Spain	7.1	5.7		4.3	3.5	
Switzerland	7.0	4.4		3.9		
Sweden	4.4	4.4	6.0	2.8	3.3	5.4
U.S.A.	4.5	5.5	4.3	3.7	3.7	3.6
Yugoslavia						4.0

Sources: Cols. 1, 4: M. G. Mulhall's estimates of national wealth (*Dictionary of Statistics*, 1899, p. 589) divided by his estimates for national income (*Dictionary of Statistics*, 1892, p. 320), the ratio then being reduced by one-sixth to shift to GNP basis. While Mulhall changed many of his national wealth estimates between the 1892 and the 1899 editions but continued to attribute them to 1888, he did not make any changes in his estimates of national income. The figures in col. 4 were obtained by reducing Mulhall's estimates of total national wealth in the 1899 edition in proportion to the share of land as given in the 1892 edition.

Cols. 2, 5: Estimates of various authors as selected by J. C. Stamp, *Journal of the Royal Statistical Society, 82* (July 1919), divided by the GNP estimates of 1913 used throughout this study. While the figures are listed by Stamp in his summary table (p. 491) under the heading of "at the outbreak of war in 1914," most of them actually refer to a slightly earlier date (1912 or 1913).

Cols. 3, 6:

Lines 1, 2, 4, 17: From Table 6–2 (for 1955).

Lines 3, 6–13, 15, 16: Derived from wealth data in Goldsmith, "The Uses of National Balance Sheets," p. 128.

Line 21: Based on national wealth estimates for 1964 by J. W. Kendrick in *The Morgan Guaranty Survey* (New York, Aug. 1966).

Line 22: Based on national wealth estimates by I. Vinski.

Figures for numerator (gross national product) taken throughout from U.N., *Yearbook of National Account Statistics*, various issues.

FIR had remained unchanged. Similarly FIR would now be somewhat lower, possibly by something like one-tenth, than it was at the end of World War II.[6]

6. In an unpublished analysis of the capital-output ratios of seventeen countries, mainly developed ones, undertaken in 1958 in connection with the International Economic Association meeting in Corfu and based on wealth estimates for the early 1950s, I made an attempt to correlate several versions of the aggregate capital-output ratio with a number of independent variables that could be presumed to exercise an influence on the level of the capital-output ratio, such as the level and the rate of growth of real gross national product per head, the degree of industrialization, and the growth rate of the population. These calculations did not succeed in identifying factors having a close connection with the capital-output ratio. The results were generally better for capital-output ratios in which the numerator was limited to reproducible tangible wealth. Even here the simple correlation coefficient (r) with real product per head amounted to only 0.26, that with the growth of real income per head to 0.34, and that with the degree of industrialization measured by the share of industry

THE VALUATION ADJUSTMENT TERM

One of the most interesting components of FIR and ANIR, and in some cases a very important one, is the valuation adjustment term that measures the effect of changes in financial asset prices, primarily the prices of corporate common stock, on the total value of all financial assets outstanding. It is therefore unfortunate that we do not have sufficient information for an internationally comparative analysis over a reasonably long period. This is due partly to conceptual and theoretical difficulties but mainly reflects the lack of data for all but a few of the thirty-five countries, almost all of them developed countries, on the volume of new issues of corporate common stock, the main focus of valuation gains, and of data on stock prices back to the turn of the century.

We recall from Chapter 2 that the relative contribution of the valuation adjustment term (ν) to the level of FIR or ANIR depends essentially on two factors. The first is the ratio of issues of corporate common stock to the total net issuance of financial instruments (θ), and the second is the index of common stock prices (ψ). These two factors are joined in the approximate formula $\nu = \theta \quad (1 + \psi)^{n/2}$, where n is the period (number of years) covered by the calculation and θ is a fraction of the value of all issues of financial instruments during the observation period. Thus if, for example, $\theta = 0.05$, $\psi = 0.03$, and $n = 100$, the value of ν is 0.17, indicating that the market value of all financial instruments at the balance sheet date exceeds their original issue price by about one-sixth.

in the labor force also to 0.34. Real product per head, its growth and the share of dwellings and government structures in reproducible tangible wealth together yielded an R^2 i.e. a measure of the share of these three independent variables in the total variance among the capital-output ratios, of 0.42 for the capital-output ratio, including land, and one of 0.46 for the ratio excluding land. The attempt thus proved inconclusive, except that it indicated that the intercountry differences in capital-output ratios probably cannot be explained as the result of a few simple independent variables.

The Share of Price-Sensitive Issues

An adequate analysis of θ requires information on both the volume of issues of corporate common stock and of the net volume of issues of all financial instruments for extensive periods of time. If it is already difficult to obtain data on the volume of stock issues for long periods and for a sufficiently large number of countries, it is virtually impossible to do the same for the issuance of all financial instruments as this requires a comprehensive flow-of-funds system. We therefore, again, must be satisfied with approximations.

The most important of these approximations is the use of national balance sheets at benchmark dates. Since the valuation changes in claims are small enough to be ignored —and since most national balance sheets are drawn up on the basis of the face value of claims rather than on that of their market values—the ratio of the market value of corporate common stock to the value of all financial assets provides, in general, an upper boundary to the ratio of the issuance of common stock to net issues of all financial instruments in the past. From fragmentary data, particularly for the United States, it is known that the share of valuation gains in the total market value of corporate common stock outstanding has hardly ever been below one-half during the twentieth century, meaning that the cumulated net sales of corporate common stocks have generally been below one-half of the market value of corporate stock shown for a benchmark date in the national balance sheet.[7]

7. On the basis of the data for common stock issues and the value of corporate stock in the national balance sheet, it may be estimated that in the United States the share of valuation gains in the market value of corporate common stock outstanding was in the order of one-half for the benchmark dates of 1900, 1938, and 1948. It was higher after periods of either rapid rise in stock prices (such as in 1929 when the ratio was of the order of three-fourths), after a long period of relatively low stock issues, or after periods combining both characteristics, such as the benchmark date of 1963, when the share of valuation gains in the total market value of corporate common stock then outstanding was in the order of five-sixths.

Applying this approximation to the ratios of the market value of corporate stock to that of all financial assets shown in the national balance sheets of a dozen countries for a date in the neighborhood of 1960,[8] it appears that the average value of θ is not likely to have been much in excess of 0.05 if we take the period from the turn of the century to the 1960s as a whole. There were, however, considerable variations among countries and over time. The value of θ, for example, was probably considerably higher in the period 1901–13 than in the postwar period. The ratios of the market value of corporate stock to that of all financial assets range from only a few per cent to almost one-fourth, but it is certain that the range of θ is considerably smaller because of a positive association between the level of the ratio and that part of it that is attributable to stock price movements. In other words, countries now showing a high ratio of the market value of corporate stock to all financial assets are likely to be those in which valuation gains represent a relatively high proportion of the total market value of corporate stock, with the result that the ratios of the net flow of funds into corporate common stock to the flow into all financial instruments, which is the relationship which θ measures, would show substantially smaller international differences.

The number of countries for which these data are available is too small and some of the figures are too uncertain to permit us to make confident statements about statistical relations between the value of θ and the stage of a country's financial development. It is, however, likely that developed countries do on the average have a slightly higher value of θ than have underdeveloped countries, although the association is apparently irregular, some underdeveloped countries (for instance Mexico) showing a relatively high ratio of corporate stock to total financial assets, and some developed countries showing relatively low ratios.

Turning to the trend of θ during the last fifty to one

8. See R. W. Goldsmith, "The Uses of National Balance Sheets," *Review of Income and Wealth,* no. 4 (1967), p. 128.

hundred years there is little doubt that the value of θ was considerably higher in the heyday of security capitalism—in most developed countries, the period between, say, 1880 and the Great Depression—than it has been during the last thirty years. In the United States, the only country for which the course of θ can be traced statistically since the turn of the century, it has declined from an average of fully 0.10 in the period 1900 to 1929 to only 0.02 since World War II.[9]

Since flow of funds statistics have become available during the last decade for an increasing number of countries, we are somewhat better and more directly informed about the level of θ in the postwar period. These data point to rather low values of θ, at least in developed countries, the only ones for which sufficient data are available. Thus for the ten developed countries covered in Table 3–4, the average ratio of stock issues to national product is about 1 per cent, and the average share of stocks in total new issues is less than 4 per cent, ranging from about 2 per cent in the United States and Sweden to 5–6 per cent in Australia, France, and Japan. These values are substantially below the similar figures for the period 1900–30 where comparable data are available.

9. A second approximation to the value of θ is the ratio of the issues of common corporate stock of domestic nonfinancial corporations to the sum of public issues of bonds by nonfinancial sectors and the increase in the assets of financial institutions. The numerator is too low because the statistics of public offerings of corporate stock do not include stock sold without assistance of the investment banking machinery, which in some countries and in some periods may account for substantial proportions of the reported public offerings of corporate stock. The denominator, on the other hand, is considerably too low because it does not include trade credit and private (noninstitutional) mortgages as well as consumer borrowing from noninstitutional sources. This effect is only partly offset by the inclusion in the change of assets of financial institutions of the usually small part of publicly offered securities that is acquired by these institutions. In view of these limitations and the scarcity of statistics of appropriate scope, this approach can yield only rough estimates of the orders of magnitude. It has therefore not been pursued here.

Changes in the Price of Equity Securities

The second component of the valuation adjustment term is the change in stock prices. In this case fairly adequate data are available for the developed countries and the postwar period, and possibly back to 1929, but the material is again insufficient for an adequate analysis for the earlier part of the period and for less developed countries.

The postwar period is characterized by the extraordinary rise in stock market prices in developed countries, a rise which averaged 9 per cent a year for the fifteen years ending in 1963 and which exceeded the increase in the general price level by no less than 5 per cent a year.[10] Such a difference has never been observed before for a similar length of time and is not likely to endure.[11] It certainly cannot be

TABLE 6–4

Relation of Changes in Stock Prices and in General Price Level, 1929–63

AVERAGE ANNUAL PERCENTAGE RATE OF CHANGE

	Stock Prices	GNP Deflator	Difference
Italy	13.1	13.2	−0.1
Japan	12.7	18.8	−6.1
France	8.1	12.9	−4.8
Mexico	5.7	6.8	−1.1
South Africa	4.3	2.6	+1.7
Australia	4.2	3.7	+0.5
Sweden	3.6	3.9	−0.3
Great Britain	3.5	3.2	+0.3
India	3.4	3.2	+0.2
U.S.A.	2.9	2.0	+0.9
Denmark	2.9	4.2	−1.3
Norway	2.9	4.0	−1.1
Canada	2.6	2.2	+0.4
Spain	1.1	8.0	−6.9

Sources: Stock prices: U.N., and League of Nations, *Statistical Yearbook,* various issues.
GNP deflator: U.N., *Yearbook of National Accounts Statistics* and *Statistical Yearbook.*

10. Cf. Goldsmith, *Determinants of Financial Structure,* Table 5.

11. Indeed in the two years 1964 and 1965 stock prices have declined in most countries except the United States and Canada (where the

regarded as typical of the long-range values of ψ or $\psi - \pi$. These extraordinary values of ψ may be explained by the abnormally low level of stock prices after World War II in countries such as Germany, Japan, France and Italy greatly affected by the war or by inflation. But the excess of ψ over the general price level is above 5 per cent also in the United States, Canada, and Switzerland, which were not so affected. In contrast, in the six less developed countries for which stock price indices are available during the postwar period, stock prices just managed to rise as much as the general price level, i.e. by 3 per cent, only about one-third of the rate observed for developed countries. Some of the less developed countries included in the study do not have a substantial market for corporate stock (e.g. Jamaica, Nigeria, Thailand, Trinidad, and, of course, Yugoslavia). For the remaining less developed countries there are no data on stock price movements during all or most of the postwar period, but it is very unlikely that the rate of increase in stock prices in these countries would be sufficiently in excess of the rise in the general price level, if such a difference existed at all, to result in a positive difference between the rise in stock price and the general price level for the group of less developed countries as a whole.

Information is available for fourteen countries for the period from 1929 to 1963, which should be sufficiently long a span to determine a meaningful value for the average rate of growth of common stock prices (ψ), although the period starts in most countries with an extraordinarily high level of stock prices and thus yields a considerably lower average value for ψ than would be obtained if one had started the period in the early 1920s or in 1913. Unfortunately the stock price indices do not reach that far back in a sufficient number of countries.

There is an obvious relationship evident in Table 6–3,

---

decline was delayed until 1966). Using fourth-quarter averages the decline has averaged 4 per cent for fourteen countries (7 per cent for ten countries in Europe) compared to an increase of 26 per cent in the United States.

which confronts the average rate of increase of common stock prices (ψ) and the general price level as reflected in the gross national product deflator (π), between the rate of increase of stock prices and in the general price level. The correspondence, however, is far from perfect. In eight of the fourteen countries, the rise in the stock price indices was lower than that in the national product deflator, and substantially so—the difference exceeding one-tenth of the growth rate of the general price level—in six of them. Stock prices advanced more than the general price level in six countries, substantially so—again using the test of one-tenth of the rise in the general price level—in five of them, viz. South Africa, Australia, India, the United States, and Canada, interestingly enough all developed non-European countries with one exception. Unfortunately not too much trust can be put in this comparison because many if not most of the indices of stock prices do not accurately reflect the fate of a fixed portfolio of common stocks adequately adjusted for splits, stock dividends, and similar events. There is reason to assume that the available indices of stock prices have some downward bias on these points. However, even if tentative allowances are made for this, it is not likely that the average of stock price indices for all countries advanced as much as the general price level in the period from 1929 to 1963; and it would appear that in general the more pronounced the rise in the general price level the more pronounced the lag of stock prices. This differential, however, might well disappear if data were available for a sufficient number of countries for the entire half-century between 1913 and 1963, a period which may be regarded as providing a more adequate comparison, because less distorted by the out-of-line level of stock prices at one of the end points.[12] No generalization, and no comparison

12. Thus, in the United States, the average annual rate of increase in stock prices for the period from 1900 through 1963 was 4.0 per cent, which compares with an average rate of increase in the general price level of only 2.2 per cent. In France, one of the inflationary countries, on the other hand, the rate of increase in stock prices is shown by

among countries, is possible for such long periods as 1900 to 1963. The material, however, is sufficient for one conclusion that is important in this connection.

The rise in stock prices was on the average considerably lower for the period 1900–63 or, for that matter, for most periods of a generation or more between 1880 and the end of World War II, with the exception of the late 1920s, than it has been during the postwar period, just as the rise in the general price level was usually considerably higher in the postwar period than in the preceding fifty to one hundred years. It is thus likely that, with the exception of a few cases of sharp and protracted inflation, the value of ν has usually fallen within the range of 0.05 and 0.15. The order of magnitude of ν therefore is such that systematic differences in ν that may exist among countries at different phases of development, or differences in the long-term trend of ν in individual countries, are not large enough to result in either substantial differences in FIR among countries or in substantial trend movements upwards or downwards in a country's FIR.

THE MONETIZATION RATIO

This and the following section provide information on the order of magnitude of two coefficients of the full formula, Equation (2.2) of Chapter 2—the monetization ratio (μ) and the industrial interrelations ratio (ω)—which it has been possible to omit from the operational versions of the formula in Chapters 3 through 5, because of their unavailability for a sufficient number of countries and of periods of time, as a result of a redefinition of another coefficient,

---

the available figures to be slightly below the advance in the general price level—8.8 per cent against 9.6 per cent. Although not too much significance should be attached to small differences between statistical series spanning such long periods in which they necessarily undergo numerous variations in method and content, it is unlikely that French stock prices advanced as much as, let alone more than, the general price level since the turn of the century.

the capital formation ratio κ. As in the case of the other coefficients an attempt is made, which here can be only at the most elementary level, to indicate systematic differences that may exist between developed and less developed countries and trends that may be observed over the last century.

The proportion of the total of goods and services of an economy that is monetized, in the sense of being paid for in money by the purchaser, is one of the most important characteristics of the level and course of economic development. It therefore should be a major concern of quantity-minded economic historians. In view of the importance of this ratio, the statistical information now available is woefully inadequate, both for the present situation in less developed countries and for the values of the ratio during earlier stages of development of the now advanced countries. Enough is known about this ratio, however, to feel confident that for the period with which we are dealing in this study, i.e. the last one hundred years for now developed countries and the last fifty years for the rest of the world, the change in the monetization ratio is not great enough to explain a substantial proportion of either present differences between developed and less developed countries in the level of FIR or of the ratio of financial issues or assets to national product, or to account for much of the trend of the ratio in either developed or less developed countries.[13]

In the United States, which is one of the few countries for which the necessary estimates are available, the ratio of nonmonetized total gross national product is now in the order of 8 per cent if nonmonetized income is limited in the main to the three standard items of agricultural production consumed by farmers, imputed rent on owner-occupied homes, and imputations for financial services. One may, however, well take a broader view in which nonmonetized income includes the use value of the stock of government structures and of consumer durables, two items that are

13. One of the few publications dealing in some detail and at least in quantitative terms with this problem is S. Ghosh, *Monetization of an Economy* (Calcutta, World Press, 1964).

excluded from gross national product in the estimates of most countries, a view which leads to a substantially lower value of μ. The monetization ratio for the United States at the present time then is 0.93 if the narrower concept of nonmonetized income is used, and about 0.85 if the broader definition is adopted.[14] In Japan, to cite another developed country, though one in which development is more recent and less complete than in the United States, the value of μ for 1962–64 is put at 0.88, using the narrower, and at nearly 0.85, using the broader definition of nonmonetized income figures, which indicate almost as high a degree of monetization as in the United States.[15]

A ratio of approximately this magnitude is probably also applicable at the present time, as well as for the last generation, for most developed countries. In the United States, for instance, the share of nonmonetized income may be estimated at nearly 10 per cent in 1929, using the narrow definition, and about 15 per cent, applying the broader definition, so that μ would be 0.90 and 0.85 respectively. The relatively small size of the difference between these values separated by more than thirty years is the result of partly offsetting changes in, on the one hand, the self-consumption of farmers, which tends to decline as the share of agriculture in national income is reduced and agriculture is progressively commercialized, and, on the other hand, the increasing use value of government structures and consumer durables, which reflects the rising share of government in the economy and the spread of expensive consumer durables such as the automobile and electric household appliances. It is likely that similar tendencies have prevailed in other developed countries so that μ has since World War I been

14. U.S. Department of Commerce, *The National Income and Product Accounts of the United States, 1929–1965,* Washington, 1966, pp. 152–53. If an even broader view is taken of nonmonetized income, and the use value of government and consumer durables as well as the value of housewives' unpaid services are included, the value of μ would be reduced to something like 0.65 for 1963. (J. Kendrick, *Statistisk Tidskrift,* 3rd. series, *4,* 1966, 360 ff.)

15. Communication from Japanese Economic Planning Agency.

within a range of 0.85 to 0.95 for the narrow definition, and 0.80 to 0.90 for the broader definition of nonmonetized income.

The monetization ratio is almost certain to have increased between the middle of the nineteenth century and World War I. In the absence of statistics, it is not possible, or at least is very difficult, to indicate the order of magnitude of the rise in μ, and thus to give an idea of its contribution to the movements of FIR or the ratio of financial assets to national product.[16] The material available on the present situation in less developed countries, which will be briefly reviewed in the following paragraphs, makes it unlikely that the rise in μ can have been very sharp in these countries, or that it can explain a substantial part in the increase in the financial interrelations ratio or the ratio of financial assets to national product which occurred throughout the world in the half century preceding World War I. The opposing tendencies in the main components of nonmonetary income were at work also during this earlier period, increasing μ as a result of a decline in the share of self-consumption in agriculture and in the hand trades, but decreasing μ as the importance of financial services, government structures, and consumer durables rose, and hence as nonmonetized use value gained in importance.

Cases can undoubtedly be found in which μ is even now below one-half. Thus, it has been estimated that in 1950–51 in the Bantu areas of South Africa only approximately one-fifth of the national product was monetized if remittances of residents from earnings outside these areas are excluded, and that μ was not in excess of 0.30 even if these earnings

16. One formerly important component of nonmonetized income, the value added by household manufacturing is estimated to have declined in the United States from $137 million in 1839 and $218 million in 1859 to $89 million in 1889, and thus to have fallen precipitously from nearly 8 per cent of gross national product in 1839 to 5 per cent in 1859 and to less than 1 per cent in 1889. (See R. Gallman in *Studies in Income and Wealth, 30* [1966], 26 and 35.)

are included.[17] No independent country, however, is known for which μ is at the present time below one-half or even close to that value. In Tanzania (Tanganyika), for example, μ has been estimated for 1960 on the basis of national accounting data at approximately three-fifths, the result of monetization ratios as low as one-fourth in livestock and one-half in agricultural production, but of slightly above two-thirds in construction and close to unity in manufacturing and mining.[18] Where foreign enclaves, particularly plantation agriculture, are more important, μ seems to be in the order of two-thirds to three-fourths, as for example in Kenya, Uganda, and the former Belgian Congo,[19] or in the Ivory Coast[20] and Togo.[21]

India is of particular importance as being the largest of the less developed countries, and as having been in close contact with and economically to a substantial extent under the control of a European economy for over two centuries. Here it has been estimated that nonmonetized consumption declined from 35 per cent of consumer expenditures in 1953–54 to 32 per cent in 1958–59.[22] Since the monetization ratio is likely to be higher for capital formation and government activities, μ should be somewhat higher than 0.70 and possibly as high as 0.75 for the entire economy. This figure obviously does not leave a wide margin until the level of now developed countries is reached.

Estimates of monetization ratios in planned economy countries are rare. In Yugoslavia the ratio has been esti-

17. H. J. J. Reynders, in *African Studies in Income and Wealth* (London, Bowes and Bowes, 1965), p. 244.

18. *Statistical Abstract, 1961* (Dar es Salaam), pp. 25–26.

19. P. Ady, *African Studies in Income and Wealth,* p. 62.

20. Direction de la Statistique, *Comptabilité économique* (Abidjan), 1961.

21. Banque Centrale des États de l'Afrique de l'Ouest, *Comptes économiques, Togo, 1956–1957–1958,* 1961.

22. India, Ministry of Finance, Economic Division, Taxation Research Unit, *Incidence of Indirect Taxation,* 1958–59, as cited in *Economic Development and Cultural Change,* 1963, p. 49.

mated at 0.73 in 1953 and 0.91 in 1963,[23] an unusually rapid rise due partly to institutional changes and partly to industrialization. In this case, there is no significant difference in μ compared to free enterprise economies of similar level of development. Fragmentary information about the situation in the U.S.S.R. and the planned economy countries in Eastern Europe point to the same conclusion.

THE INDUSTRIAL INTERRELATIONS RATIO

A knowledge of the numerical value of ω—the ratio of all sales of goods and services by nonfinancial units to their sales of final goods and services only, i.e. roughly speaking to their share in consumer expenditures, in government exhaustive (nontransfer) expenditures, and in gross capital formation—is required only if the net new non-financial issue ratio uses nonfinancial sectors' sales as the denominator. This was the approach taken in Chapter 2 in defining the ratio κ, and this formulation was adopted because nonfinancial sectors' sales seemed to be the most relevant of the various magnitudes that could be considered as the matrix of these sectors' gross capital expenditures. If, however, the statistically easier and theoretically not unreasonable approach is taken in which the capital expenditures of nonfinancial sectors are related to gross national product, an aproach which yields the ratio $\kappa = k/y$, then separate estimation of ω is not required, since it is subsumed in δ, the latter coefficient being the product of the three separate ratios η, κ, and ω distinguished in Chapter 2.[24]

23. D. Dimitrijevic, *The Financial Structure in a Changing Economy*, mimeographed report (National Bank of Yugoslavia, Belgrade), Dec. 1965, p. 5. The figures in the text probably do not include nonmonetized income on government structures and equipment and on consumer durables and hence must be compared with the narrower definition of nonmonetized income.

24. In symbols: $\delta = \eta\,\kappa\,\omega = (e/k) \times (k/v) \times (v/y) = e/y$, where e, k and v are the nonfinancial sectors' net new issues, capital formation, and sales respectively, and y is gross national product. (Because of the usually negligible size of the capital expenditures of financial institu-

There is probably less direct statistical information on ω than on any of the other components of FIR. The determination of ω presupposes the existence of an input-output table, or of information very close to it. Such tables have as yet been constructed for only about two dozen countries, but, what is a serious defect for the analysis of FIR, with the exception of the United States they are generally available only for one or very few years during the postwar period.

The data are, however, sufficient to provide an indication of the present relative importance of interindustry transactions in countries at different levels of economic development. Comparison of about a dozen input-output tables has confirmed the common sense feeling that the ratio of interindustry transactions to national product rises with the level of real national product per head, but the rise is rather slow.[25] As measured by the standard input-output tables, this ratio typically increases from less than 0.40 when real income per head is $100, to fully 0.50 when it reaches $500, to 0.58 at an income level of $1,000, and to 0.67 when real income per head is as high as $3,000.[26]

This ratio of intermediate output to gross national products is unfortunately not identical with ω as defined in Chapter 2, because intermediate output as used in the ratio does not include the total value of intermediate sales in trade, but only that part of such sales that represents value added by trade, i.e., the trade margin. The value of ω required for the equations is therefore higher than the ratio cited in the preceding paragraph, and the difference will be the larger the more numerous the number of enterprises

---

tions, the capital formation of the nonfinancial sectors is regarded as identical with the national total.)

25. H. B. Chenery, "The Use of Interindustry Analysis in Development Programming," in T. Barna, ed., *Structural Interdependence and Economic Development* (New York, St. Martin's Press, 1963), pp. 12 ff.

26. These values are derived from Chenery's regression equation $x = 0.1038 + 0.0869 \log y$, where y is real income per head in dollars and x is the ratio of intermediate demand to total production.

through which a commodity moves on its way to the ultimate user. There is little doubt, however, that the positive association with the level of real income per head also holds for ω, although the rate of an increase in the ratio to that of real income per head may be somewhat different.

There are no data available, even for the United States, permitting us to follow the trend of ω in the past,[27] and it is doubtful whether the association between ω and the level of real income per head deduced from contemporary data for countries at different income levels is applicable to the trend of ω in a single country.

The virtual absence of data on ω forces us in actual application to omit it from the formula, and to revert to versions of κ that use national product rather than sales as denominator. This severely limits the possibilities of breaking down the national capital formation ratio into sectoral components, in which both numerator and denominator may be presumed to have direct relevance for the sector's behavior. It does not prevent us, of course, from implementing the formula statistically at either the national or the sectoral level.

27. Although input-output tables exist in the United States for selected years back to 1919, they are not sufficiently comparable to permit an empirical determination of the trend of ω.

7 THE NEW ISSUE RATIO AND THE FINANCIAL INTERRELATIONS RATIO

The time now has come to put together the pieces presented individually in the four preceding chapters, even if each piece is less complete, less reliable, and less polished than one would desire, and even if it meets these tests to a lesser extent than would be possible with substantial additional effort within the limitations of the relevant basic data.

The formula which explains the relationship between the size of a country's financial superstructure and its real infrastructure, as it is reflected in the financial interrelations ratio, consists, it may be recalled, of three main elements. The first is the ratio of new issues by nonfinancial domestic and by foreign issuers to gross national product ($\delta + \xi$); the second is the ratio of the issues of domestic financial institutions to national product (ϕ). The third element is made up of three "operators," the first of which (ν) reflects valuation changes in financial instruments that occur after their issuance; the second (α) shifts the numerator of the ratio from the flow to the stock dimension by the use of the new issue multiplier; and the third (β) effects the comparable shift for the denominator by substituting national wealth for national product by means of division by the capital-output ratio.

The first two of the following four sections will deal with the first two components of the basic formula, which together make up the new issue ratio. They will concentrate on the crucial problem of the relationship between the new issue ratio of nonfinancial and of financial issuers which is an indicator of the degree of financial intermediation and of changes in it. The third section will investigate the transition from the new issue ratio to the financial interrelations ratio with particular attention to the question of whether, in historical or cross-country comparison, the level of the new issue ratio and the combined effect of the three operators tend to reinforce each other, so that a high and rising (or low and declining) new issue ratio and a high and rising (or low and declining) financial interrelations ratio go together, the question of whether the two tend to offset each other, or whether, finally, they seem to be unrelated. At this point a comparison of the financial interrelations ratio for a number of countries calculated according to the formulas with the observed values of the same ratio will become necessary and will require an explanation of such discrepancies between calculated and observed values as may be disclosed. This is the subject of this chapter's fourth section.

The first three sections are essentially summaries of materials discussed in some detail in Chapters 3 through 6, although some of the material is put to new uses and additional material is introduced on some points. Because of the scarcity of relevant data, the discussion in this chapter unfortunately must be limited to the postwar period and to about one-half of the thirty-five countries covered in Chapters 4 and 5 and the varying number of countries used in Chapters 3 and 6. What is possibly more serious is that there are only very few less developed countries that can be included in this overview, so few indeed that we cannot claim them to be typical for this group of countries, although they may finally turn out to be so.

THE NEW ISSUE RATIO

The first three columns of Table 7–1 show the average values for the postwar period of the ratio of issues by nonfinancial sectors, of foreign issues and, of issues of financial institutions to gross national product for each of the

TABLE 7–1

Aggregate New Issue and Financial Intermediation Ratios, 1949–63

PER CENT OF GROSS NATIONAL PRODUCT

	Domestic Nonfinancial Issues δ (1)	Net Foreign Issues ξ[a] (2)	Issues of Domestic Financial Institutions ϕ (3)	Aggregate New Issue Ratio ϵ (4)	Ratio[b] A ϕ/δ (5)	Ratio[b] B $\phi/(\delta+\xi)$ (6)
Australia	.15	−.01	.09	.23	.60	.64
Belgium	.13	.00	.11	.24	.85	.85
Canada	.13	−.03	.10	.20	.77	1.00
France	.12	.00	.11	.21	.92	.92
Germany	.10	.01	.13	.24	1.30	1.18
Great Britain	.10	.02	.09	.21	.90	.75
India	.05	−.02	.04	.07	.80	1.33
Israel	.30	−.04	.23	.49	.77	.88
Italy	.14	−.00	.19	.33	1.36	1.36
Japan	.35	−.01	.29	.63	.83	.85
Mexico	.11	−.02	.06	.15	.55	.67
New Zealand	.09	−.02	.08	.15	.89	1.14
Norway	.15	−.02	.09	.22	.60	.69
Sweden	.09	−.03	.11	.17	1.22	1.83
U.S.A.	.10	.00	.10	.20	1.00	1.00
U.S.S.R.	.04		.03	.07	.75	.75
Venezuela	.08	.01	.05	.14	.63	.56
Yugoslavia	.18	−.00	.22	.40	1.22	1.22

[a] 1956–63.
[b] This ratio is higher than the financial intermediation ratio (cf. text).

Sources: Col. 1: Table 3–4.
Col. 2: Same as Table 3–20, col. 4.
Col. 3: Table 4–7.

eighteen countries for which estimates of the nonfinancial issues ratio, which turns out to be the limiting factor in the measurement of the aggregate new issue ratio (ε), could be derived in Chapter 3. Of these, the values for the foreign issues ratio are undoubtedly the weakest component, both conceptually[1] and statistically—they could be obtained on a comparable basis only for the period 1956–63—but the consequently substantial margin of error in the estimates of the foreign issues ratio cannot seriously affect the aggregrate

1. See "The Stock of Financial Instruments" (Chapter 2).

new issue ratio except in one or two countries, particularly in Israel, because of the relatively small size of the foreign issue ratio compared to the ratio of domestic issues of financial and nonfinancial issuers to national product.

For the eighteen countries, the new issue ratio averages 0.24 of gross national product, whether or not the two socialist countries are included. This is a result of an average value of 0.13 for the new issue ratio for nonfinancial issuers, 0.12 for the new issue ratio of financial institutions, and of −0.01 for the net foreign issue ratio. The ratio is much higher for the thirteen developed nonsocialist countries (0.28) than for the three less developed nonsocialist countries, for which it averages 0.13. While the number of less developed countries is much too small as a basis for confident conclusions, it is likely, judging on the basis of other fragmentary data, that the level of the new issue ratio of approximately one-eighth of gross national product is reasonably representative for a larger number of less developed countries. Among the thirteen nonsocialist developed countries, the ratio keeps within the relatively narrow range of 0.15 to 0.24 in ten cases. The exceptions are Italy, Israel, and particularly Japan, with ratios ranging from about one-third to almost two-thirds of national product.

In view of the rather narrow range of the ratio for most developed countries—and fragmentary information indicates that the new issue ratio for most other developed countries during the postwar period is of the same order of magnitude—it is not profitable to search for simple explanations of the differences. What needs explanation are the three exceptional ratios, and an attempt has been made in Chapter 3 to explain the high level of the ratio of nonfinancial issues to national product, basic in this connection, by the high values of both the capital formation ratio, which is in turn affected by the rapid rate of growth of the three countries, and of the external financial ratio. Similarly the low new issue ratios of less developed countries reflect low values of both the capital formation and the external financing ratios.

It may be well to bring together at this point the information on the new issue ratio and its components for periods before World War II that has already been presented piecemeal in Chapters 3 and 4. The limiting factor, as always in the study of the new issue ratio, is the availability of data on the ratio of issues of nonfinancial sectors to national product. Table 7–2 is therefore unfortunately limited to five developed countries and to the period 1901–13.

TABLE 7–2

New Issue Ratio before World War I (1901–13) in Five Large Countries
PER CENT OF GROSS NATIONAL PRODUCT

	Issues of Nonfinancial Sectors δ (1)	Net Foreign Issues[a] ξ (2)	Issues of Financial Institutions ϕ (3)	New Issue Ratio ϵ (4)	Ratio A ϕ/δ (5)	Ratio B $\phi/(\delta+\xi)$ (6)
France	9.0	3.0	3.6	15.6	.40	.30
Germany	16.3	1.1	8.5	25.9	.52	.49
Great Britain	6.4	4.8	2.8	14.0	.44	.25
Japan	14.0	−1.3	6.5	19.2	.46	.51
U.S.A.	10.9	0.4	5.3	16.6	.49	.47
Average, 1901–13	11.3	1.6	5.3	18.3	.47	.41
Average, 1949–63	15.2	0.5	14.3	30.0	.99	.98

[a] 1891–1914.

Sources: *Col. 1:* Table 3–2, col. 7.
Col. 2: Table 3–20, col. 2.
Col. 3: Table 4–2, cols. 3 and 9.
Line 7: Table 3–4, col. 8.

Three main conclusions can be drawn from the figures assembled in Table 7–2, notwithstanding their roughness:

1. The level of the new issue ratio before World War I is considerably lower than after World War II. This is true not only for the average of the five countries, for which the ratio increases from 0.18 to 0.30, but also for four out of the

five countries, the ratio being virtually identical in both periods in the fifth country, Germany. There is every reason to believe that a substantial increase in the aggregate new issue ratio between the first decade of this century and the post-World War II period would also be found to exist for other developed countries, and probably for less developed countries too.

2. The three countries with the lowest aggregate new issue ratio in the post-World War II period—France, Great Britain, and the United States—occupy the same position in 1901–13. Similarly, the two countries with the highest ratio in the recent period—Germany and Japan—also hold the first two places before World War I, although their position has been reversed, and the lead of Japan in the post-World War II period is much greater than that of any country before World War I. Indeed, if Japan is excluded, the average aggregate new issue ratio for the other four countries rises only from 0.18 to 0.22, and the range of the ratio is narrower after World War II (0.20 to 0.24) than it was before World War I (0.16 to 0.26).

3. Finally, and most importantly, the increase in the aggregate new issue ratio is due primarily to an advance in ϕ, the issue ratio of financial institutions. While the new issue ratio of nonfinancial sectors increased on the average only from 11.3 to 15.2 per cent and the net foreign issue ratio actually declined from 1.6 to 0.5 per cent of national product, the value of the new issue ratio of financial institutions almost tripled, rising from 5.3 to 14.3 per cent. Moreover, the direction of the movement was the same in all five countries. As a result, the ϕ/δ ratio, to which we turn in the following section, on the average more than doubled, advancing from slightly below one-half before World War I to almost unity in the post-World War II period. The increase of the ratio was fairly similar in all five countries—the ϕ/δ ratio in 1949–63 is between 1.8 and 2.5 times as high as that of 1901–13—suggesting that we are here facing a trend towards increasing institutionaliza-

tion of the financial process, which is common to all developed countries; this probably also applies to less developed countries.

THE FINANCIAL INTERMEDIATION RATIO

One of the most important characteristics of a country's financial structure and development is the extent to which the issues of domestic nonfinancial and of foreign issues are absorbed or held by domestic financial institutions rather than by domestic nonfinancial sectors or by foreigners, particularly by domestic households. It is this relation which reflects the degree of institutionalization in the country's financial structure and the relative importance of direct and indirect financing.

Statistically, the financial intermediation ratio is determined in the flow dimension as the ratio of the net acquisition during a given period by domestic financial institutions of instruments issued by domestic nonfinancial sectors and by the rest of the world to total issues of such instruments. In the stock dimension, the ratio is found by dividing the market value of debt and equity securities of domestic nonfinancial and foreign issuers held by domestic financial institutions at a given date by the total value of such instruments outstanding. The net acquisitions, or the holdings, of financial institutions include debt and equity securities of nonfinancial domestic sectors and of foreign issuers issued during the period as well as similar instruments previously issued. The financial intermediation ratio, as calculated here, therefore will differ from the proportion of the period's new issues of domestic nonfinancial sectors and of foreigners which is absorbed by domestic financial institutions to the extent that financial institutions have a net purchase or sales balance in previously issued instruments of this type. The calculation of the financial intermediation ratio presupposes the existence of a sectorized flow-of-funds statement or national balance sheet, and therefore is as yet feasible only for about one dozen countries and is limited to the postwar period.

The ratio, $\phi/(\delta + \xi)$, or in the stock dimension the ratio between the holdings of financial institutions and total outstandings of financial instruments, is, as already indicated, only an approximation to the financial intermediation ratio. It will be in excess of the financial intermediation ratio to the extent that the new issue ratio of financial institutions (or of the assets of financial institutions) to national product includes the counterpart of issues of financial institutions (or of their liabilities and net worth) that do not represent issues of domestic nonfinancial or foreign issuers. These "extraneous" assets of financial institutions include claims against, or equity securities of, other domestic financial institutions, tangible domestic assets, and monetary metals. The data now at hand are not sufficient to adjust the $\phi/(\delta + \xi)$ ratios country by country. It would appear, however, that on the average such an adjustment would reduce the values of $\phi/(\delta + \xi)$, as the ratios are shown, for instance, in Table 7–1, by between one-sixth and one-fourth. This would yield an average financial intermediation ratio for the period 1949–63 of between 75 and 85 per cent for the eighteen countries listed in the table. The fact that for countries such as Italy and Sweden the $\phi/(\delta + \xi)$ ratio remains in excess of unity, even after this adjustment, or very close to unity, which is very unlikely for long periods of time, points to the possibility of an underestimation of the nonfinancial domestic or the foreign issue ratios in some countries or, what is less likely, to an overestimation of the financial institutions' new issue ratio.

For a number of countries it is fortunately possible to derive a financial intermediation ratio that has the advantage of being not only more reliable but that can also be calculated separately for a few important types of financial instruments. The relevant data that can be extracted, sometimes not without difficulty, from the flow-of-funds statistics available for substantial parts of the postwar period for seven countries are summarized in Table 7–3. During that

TABLE 7–3

Share of Financial Institutions in Net Issues of Nonfinancial Sectors, Selected Countries, 1950s and 1960s

PER CENT

	Australia 1954–62	Belgium 1958–62	France 1953–63	India 1952–61	Japan 1954–63	Norway 1956–63	U.S.A. 1949–63
All nonfinancial issues							
Total	39	73[b]	56	62	60	49	67
Debt	39	86[b]	58	64	64	53	66
Government issues							
Total	45	70[c]		65	77[c]	34[c]	55
Central	32				73[c]	42[c]	47
Local	83				95	24[c]	60
Corporate issues							
Bonds	31	52[d]		42	89	72	100
Stock	36	4	31	22	33	3	120
Mortgages							
Home				66			92
Other							93
Consumer debt	65[a]			66[e]			80

[a] Installment credit only.
[b] Domestic issues only.
[c] Including issues of government enterprises.
[d] Including other medium and long term issues: 98.
[e] All home mortgages.

Sources: Table 3–4, cols. 3 and 4.

period financial institutions absorbed on the average about three-fifths of all new issues of nonfinancial sectors and of foreigners.[2] The ratio is a few percentage points higher for debt issues alone but averages less than one-third for corporate stock. Although the range of the ratio is substantial—for all issues together from two-fifths in Australia to four-fifths in Belgium—the average of three-fifths can probably be regarded as representative for developed countries as a group. The ratio for the only less developed country for which these data are available, India, happens to be close to the average for the six developed countries, but this cannot be taken as an indication that the average is also applicable to a larger group of less developed countries, although there is fragmentary evidence to suggest that this may be so. If the average value of the ratio of approximately three-fifths is representative, at least for developed countries during the postwar period, this would indicate that the rough estimates of the financial intermediation ratio that can be derived from the adjusted $\phi/(\delta + \xi)$ ratio are somewhat too high but that they are of the right order of magnitude.

There are, of course, some differences in the financial intermediation ratio for the few types of financial instruments for which the ratio can be separately calculated, but these differences are not sufficiently clear-cut in view of the small number of countries for which they are available to draw conclusions that could be applied to all countries or

2. These more reliable figures are in all cases below the rough estimates of Table 7–1, which were obtained by dividing ϕ by $\delta + \xi$. For the seven countries covered in Table 7–3, the average value of the financial intermediation ratio is 0.58 compared to the unadjusted $\phi/(\delta + \xi)$ ratio of Table 7–1 of 0.90. Part of the difference, of course, is due to the failure of ϕ to be adjusted downward for interfinancial issues (including monetary metals), and part to statistical shortcomings of the estimates of ϕ, δ, and ξ. The fact that Table 7–3 covers in general only the latter half of the period on which Table 7–1 is based may also contribute to the difference, although it is not evident why discrepancies on this point should tend in all seven countries in the same direction.

even to all developed countries. The data presented in Table 7–3 however, suggest that for developed countries as a group the differences in the financial intermediation ratio may be fairly small for the main types of financial instruments such as government securities, corporate bonds, mortgages, and consumer credit, but that the ratio is substantially lower for corporate stock than for debt instruments.

Information on the ratio of issues of nonfinancial sectors held by financial institutions derived from national balance sheets generally confirms the conclusions that could be drawn from flow-of-funds statistics. On the most aggregative level, the average ratio of claims against financial institutions to all nonfinancial issues outstanding, shown in Table 7–4 for the dozen countries for which national balance

TABLE 7–4

Relation of Claims against Financial Institutions to Value of All Financial Assets and of Nonfinancial Issues

PER CENT

		Relation to			
		All Financial Assets	Nonfinancial Issues		Ratio of Financial Assets to National Wealth
	Year		All	Debt Issues[a]	
Belgium	1960	37	59	71	.70
France	1960	34	49	80	.64
Germany	1962	40	67	86	.73
Great Britain	1961	27	37	52	1.64
India	1959	25	33	40	.35
Israel	1962	44	78	84	1.14
Italy	1961	28	39	65	1.05
Japan	1961	47	89	109	1.40
Mexico	1960	27	37	51	.45
Norway	1962	38	61	66	.68
U.S.A.	1958	28	39	58	1.16
U.S.S.R.	1959	37	58	58	.35

[a] Figures are somewhat too high because numerator includes equity securities and tangible assets held by financial institutions.

Source: Derived from estimates in Goldsmith, in *The Review of Income and Wealth* (1967), p. 128.

sheets are available around 1960, is nearly 55 per cent. More relevant is the ratio of claims against financial institutions to only total debt issues outstanding, because financial institutions keep only a small proportion of their funds in corporate stocks and hold only a relatively small share of all stock outstanding. This ratio cannot be exactly calculated from the figures available because of the lack of figures on the holdings of corporate stock and tangible assets by financial institutions, all the calculations having been based on these institutions' balance sheet totals. (These incomparabilities explain, though possibly not completely, the Japanese ratio of slightly above unity in column 4 of Table 7–4, a ratio which of course is impossible if numerator and denominator are exactly comparable.) The average value of the share of financial institutions in all debt issues of nonfinancial sectors calculated without adjustment is close to 0.70. This figure is somewhat too high and a ratio between 0.60 and 0.65 is likely to reflect the situation more correctly.

The range of the ratios is fairly wide, stretching from less than one-half in India and Mexico to about four-fifths —if rough allowance is made for the adjustment just discussed—in Japan, Israel, and possibly Germany. While only two less developed countries are included, the fact that their ratios are lower than those for the developed countries in Table 7–4 is not unreasonable.

Turning to the share of financial institutions in the amounts outstanding of different types of issues of nonfinancial sectors, it is found from Table 7–5, (which unfortunately covers only half a dozen countries, and which, because of the scarcity and summary nature of the most sectorized national balance sheets, usually distinguishes less than half a dozen types of financial instruments), that the differences in the shares of the several instruments are sufficiently large and erratic to prevent generally applicable conclusions. These shares obviously are strongly influenced not only by the relative size of financial institutions, as measured for instance by the ratio of their total assets to

TABLE 7–5

Share of Financial Institutions in Nonfinancial Issues Outstanding in 1961–63 in Selected Countries

PER CENT

	Belgium (1963) (1)	Great Britain (1961) (2)	Japan (1963) (3)	Norway (1963) (4)	U.S.A. (1963) (5)	Venezuela (1962) (6)
All nonfinancial issues	60[a]	31	55	56	45	22
All nonfinancial debt issues	74[a]	35	56	59	63	
Selected types of issues						
Government, total	62	38	81[b]	44[b]	59[c]	25
Government, central	60	38		47[b]	59[c]	
Government, local	73	40		36[b]	58	
Corporate bonds		70	92	57	97[d]	
Corporate stock	3	22	33	5	12	25[e]
Home mortgages		78			89	12[f]
Consumer debt		77			76	

[a] Apparently does not include trade debt.
[b] Includes issues of government enterprises and corporations.
[c] U.S. government securities held by U.S. agencies netted.
[d] Includes foreign bonds.
[e] All issues of business, including agriculture.
[f] All urban real estate mortgages.

Sources: *Col. 1:* Banque Nationale de Belgique, *Bulletin d'Information* (1966), p. 620.
Col. 2: J. Revell, *The Wealth of the Nation* (1967), pp. 54–55.
Col. 3: Bank of Japan, *Flow-of-Funds Accounts in Japan, 1954–1963* (1964), p. 26.
Col. 4: Statistisk Sentralbyra, *Kredittmarkedstatistikk* (1963), pp. 26 ff.
Col. 5: Federal Reserve Board, *Flow-of-Funds Assets and Liabilities 1945–65*, mimeo. (May 1966).
Col. 6: Banco Central de Venezuela, *El Fluir de Fondos de Capital* (1964), p. 31.

the aggregate volume outstanding of nonfinancial issues or of debt issues only, but also by factors peculiar to each country. These factors may be operating either on the supply side, e.g. the relative size of the different types of financial institutions and instruments; or on the demand side, where they are exemplified by the asset preferences of the different types of financial institutions and by laws and regulations governing the investments of financial intermediaries. There are, however, two tendencies that are applicable to all six countries, and probably also are at work in other countries. The first, already noticed from national balance sheets and flow-of-funds statements of wider country coverage, is the much lower share of financial institutions in equity than in debt issues. The second is the particularly high share of financial institutions in the total amount of corporate bonds outstanding.

THE THREE OPERATORS

Since the character of the three operators—the valuation adjustment ratio, $(1 + \nu)$, the new issue multiplier (α) and the capital-output ratio (β)—their current level, their probable movements over time, and their intracountry differences have already been discussed in the first three sections of Chapter 6, as far as that is possible on the basis of the fragmentary material now available, it only remains to consider their interactions and their product, which, together with the aggregate new issue ratio (ε), determines the value of the unadjusted financial interrelations ratio. The necessary data are shown in Table 7–6 for the sixteen countries for which they are available for the postwar period. While the estimates of the new issue multiplier and of the capital-output ratio are based on respectable though far from uniform or entirely satisfactory data, the figures entered in column 1 for the valuation adjustment are nothing but the roughest of estimates, intended to indicate the order of magnitude. For that reason they are shown only in multiples of 0.05. For most countries we

TABLE 7–6

The Three Operators and Their Product, Selected Countries, 1949–63

	Valuation Adjustment 1949–1963 ν (1)	New Issue Multiplier 1949–1963 α (2)	Capital-output Ratio, 1963 β (3)	Product $(1+\nu)\alpha\beta^{-1}$ (4)
Australia	.10	12.9	4.0	3.55
Belgium	.05	21.2	4.5	5.04
Canada	.10	16.1	3.0	5.90
France	.10	10.4	3.9	2.93
Germany	.10	10.1	3.6	3.09
Great Britain	.10	16.6	3.2	5.71
India	.05	23.4	3.6	6.83
Israel	.10	5.2	3.2	1.79
Italy	.20	12.4	3.1	4.80
Japan	.05	8.4	2.8	3.15
Mexico	.10	8.6	3.8	2.49
Norway	.05	15.0	5.3	2.97
U.S.A.	.20	19.1	4.3	5.33
U.S.S.R.		15.9	2.7	5.89
Venezuela	.10	12.7	4.5	3.10
Yugoslavia		8.3	5.0	1.66

Sources: *Col. 1:* Rough estimates.
Col. 2: Table 6–1.
Col. 3: Table 6–3 for lines 1, 2, 4–14; rough estimates for lines 3, 15, and 16.

do not have the information on the share of corporate stock in total new issues and on stock prices that would enable us to make a more accurate calculation, and such a calculation is further complicated by the irregularity of the movements of the ratio of corporate stock in total issues and of stock prices. Finally the shortness of the period—fifteen years—makes calculation by formula, which may be permissible for periods of thirty to fifty years, hazardous.

The range of the product of the three operators is wide, extending from 1.7 to 6.8 compared to an average of 4.0 for the sixteen countries. No substantial differences in the averages for developed, less developed, and socialist countries appear, but there are too few countries in the last two groups to permit us to draw conclusions. Thus, the values of the two socialist countries are at or near the two extremes of the range as are the values for two of the three less developed countries. It is only the eleven developed countries (excluding Israel) which show more concentration, the ratios ranging only from 2.9 to 5.9, while the average of 4.4 is not much higher than that for all sixteen countries.

More important than the value of the product of the three operators are, on the one hand, the interactions among them and, on the other, the relation of the product of the three operators to the aggregate new issue ratio, since these together determine the unadjusted value of the financial interrelations ratio.

In view of the generally small absolute value and the large margin of error in the valuation adjustment term, we may concentrate on the interactions between the new issue multiplier (α) and the output-capital ratio (β^{-1}). There apparently exists only a slight negative correlation between these two magnitudes even if the two socialist countries are omitted.[3] There thus appears no marked tendency for a country with a high new issue multiplier that reflects a rapid rate of growth of national product in current prices to have a high capital-output ratio or a low value of its reciprocal. The most that can be said is that the effects of the new issue multiplier and the output-capital ratio do not seem to offset each other to a substantial extent.[4]

3. Within the observed range of the new issue multiplier (from 8 to 23) the value of β^{-1}, calculated from the regression equation for fourteen nonsocialist countries, declines, however, by about one-fifth from 0.30 to 0.24, yielding a calculated value of the three operators of between 2.6 and 5.8, assuming $\nu = 0.10$ in all cases.

4. This finding is compatible with the results of an investigation by H. Leibenstein ("Incremental Capital-Output Ratios and Growth Rates in the Short Run," in *Review of Economics and Statistics, 48,* [Feb. 1966]), which covers a larger group of countries, but uses the marginal rather than the aggregate capital-output ratio and constant rather than current prices and refers to annual values. Leibenstein found a positive relationship between the rate of growth of national product and the capital-output ratio.

New Issue Ratio and FIR

The picture is also far from conclusive for the relationship between the product of the three operators and the aggregate new issue ratio. For all sixteen countries together, there appears to exist a negative correlation associating relative low values of the product of the three operators with high values of the issue ratio. As a result, the calculated unadjusted values of the financial interrelations ratio, i.e. the product $\varepsilon\alpha\beta^{-1}(1 + \nu)$, show a narrower range (from 0.42 for U.S.S.R. to 1.98 for Japan) than the aggregate new issue ratio (0.07 to 0.63) and the product of the ranges of the new issue ratio and of the three operators (0.12 to 4.30), but not than the product of the three operators alone (1.66 to 6.83). This, however, is due to a marked negative correlation among the few less developed and socialist countries. For the eleven developed countries alone, no correlation, positive or negative, appears to exist. For most of them the aggregate new issue ratio lies in the range of 0.20 to 0.25, irrespective of the value of the product of the three operators.

We therefore come to the conclusion that for this period and for the relatively small number of countries for which data are available, no marked systematic association appears to exist between the aggregate new issue ratio and the product of the three operators or among the three operators. There is, it is true, some evidence of a slight negative correlation between the product and the ratio and between the two main components of the product, the multiplier and the aggregate new issue ratio (ANIR), but these relationships would have to be corroborated by data for a larger number of countries and other periods before being accepted as significant influences on the value of the financial interrelations ratio (FIR).

Here again, a look back at the situation before World War I is instructive, even if the data are available for only five developed countries—including however all leading ones—and even if they are more subject to the hazards of estimation than the figures for the postwar period. Fortunately, the differences between the two periods are so

Table 7–7

The Three Operators, 1881–1913 and 1949–63 in Five Large Countries

	France	Germany	Great Britain	Japan	U.S.A.	Average
I. 1881–1913						
1. Valuation adjustment (ν)	.05	.10	.10	.05	.15	.09
2. Multiplier (α)	54.3	26.5	47.7	15.5	24.3	33.7
3. Capital-output ratio, 1913 (β)	6.4	5.4	4.2	5.2	4.4	5.1
4. Product $[(1+\nu)\alpha\beta^{-1}]$	8.9	5.4	12.5	3.1	6.4	7.2
II. 1949–63						
1. Valuation adjustment (ν)	.10	.10	.10	.05	.20	.11
2. Multiplier (α)	10.4	10.1	16.6	8.4	19.1	12.9
3. Capital-output ratio, 1963 (β)	3.9	3.6	3.2	2.8	4.3	3.6
4. Product $[(1+\nu)\alpha\beta^{-1}]$	3.0	3.1	5.7	3.2	5.3	4.0
III. Ratio of Product 1949–63 to 1881–1913	.34	.57	.46	1.03	.83	.65

Sources: *Line I 1:* Rough estimates.
Line I 2: Table 6–1.
Line I 3: Tables 6–2 and 6–3.
Lines II 1, 3: Table 7–6.

marked that it is unlikely that the substitution of more accurate figures for those in Table 7–7 would invalidate the main conclusions.

The outstanding difference is the much higher value of the product of the three operators in the pre-World War I period. With an average of 4.1 in the post-World War II years, this product was 35 per cent below its level in the pre-World War I period. Moreover, the sharp decline over this interval of half a century is shared by four of the five countries, although the relationship of the post- and pre-World War II ratios varies considerably, from one-third in France to over four-fifths in the United States and slightly above unity in Japan. The range of the value of the product of the three operators narrowed considerably, from a range of 1 to more than 4 in the period before World War I to a range of from 1 to less than 2 in the postwar period.

The decline is due almost exclusively to the sharp fall in the multiplier from an average of 34 to 13, a decline which reflects an equally sharp increase in the rate of growth of national product in current prices, which, in turn, is due to an advance in both the rate of growth of real income and to an acceleration in the rise in the price level. While all five countries show a decline in the multiplier, the extent differs considerably ranging from only one-fifth in the United States to almost two-thirds in Germany and to over four-fifths in France. This increase in the multiplier has been offset, but only in part, by a decline in the capital-output ratio from an average of 5 to approximately 3.5, a movement shared to an about equal extent by all five countries except the United States.

This sharp reduction in the product of the three operators has one very important effect on the financial interrelations ratio. With the same aggregate new issue ratio the average financial interrelations ratio for these five countries would have been less than two-thirds as high in 1963 as in 1913; or, alternatively, a financial interrelations ratio of 1963 as high as that of 1913 would have required an aggregate new issue ratio of over one and a half times the level of the pre-

World War I period. Since, as we have just seen, the aggregate new issue ratio for the period 1949–63 was about two-thirds above that of 1901–13, we would expect for 1963 an average value of the financial interrelations ratio for these five leading countries only slightly higher than that of 1913.

CALCULATED AND OBSERVED VALUES OF FIR, 1963

Before discussing the values of the financial interrelations ratio for 1963 that can be derived by use of the formula from the data on the individual components reviewed in the preceding section and in the first section of this chapter, and before comparing the results with the observed values of the ratio, it is necessary to adjust the product of the aggregate net issue ratio and the three operators for the fact that the data cover only the fifteen-year period from 1949 through 1963 rather than the considerably longer period required for an unqualified application of the formula, disregarding for the moment the difficulties introduced by the deviations of the actual movements of the several components from their period averages. As already explained in Chapter 2, the adjustment requires a reduction of the product of the aggregate new issue ratio and the three operators, first, by a truncation ratio τ, which depends on the multiplier and the length of the period, here fifteen years, and, secondly, by the addition of the observed or estimated ratio of the value of financial assets at the beginning of the period (i.e. the end of 1948, adjusted for the rise in value during the period 1949–63 of price-sensitive assets outstanding at the end of 1948) to the national wealth at the benchmark date (i.e. the end of 1963).

While the value of τ can be easily calculated for the sixteen countries for which the other necessary data are available, the second adjustment factor must be estimated in a very rough manner since for most countries there are no observed values for financial assets at the end of 1948. The ratio of financial assets in 1948 to the national wealth of 1963, must therefore usually be based on fragmentary data, particularly data on the assets of financial institutions, government bonds outstanding, and the value of corporate stock because the last two items are generally held predominantly outside financial institutions. Fortunately the value of the second adjustment is relatively small in a number of countries in which national product has grown rapidly during the postwar period. If, for instance, gross national product has increased at an average annual rate of 8 per cent, which has not been uncommon in this period, if price sensitive assets constituted one-tenth of all financial assets at the end of 1948 and the rise in stock prices has averaged 3 per cent per year, and if the financial interrelations ratio for 1963 is in the order of unity, then the adjustment calculated in accordance with the procedures explained in Chapter 2 would amount to only 0.37, so that even a substantial error in estimating the value of financial assets at the end of 1948 would not seriously affect the estimates of the financial interrelations ratio for 1963. Column 5 of Table 7–8 shows estimates of the financial interrelations ratio for 1963, based on the aggregate new issue ratio for the period 1949–63, the truncation ratio τ, and a rough estimate of the ratio of financial assets in 1948 (adjusted for valuation changes) to national wealth in 1963. These estimates may then be compared to the observed values for fourteen countries for a date in the neighborhood of 1960 shown in column 6.

In evaluating the differences between the calculated and observed values of the financial interrelations ratio for 1963, two points should be kept in mind. First, the observed values are subject to a not negligible margin of error since they are derived from often rather rough estimates of the value of financial assets and of national wealth in 1963. The error in the latter figure, however, should not affect the comparison since the same figures are used in the calculation of the capital-output ratio for 1963 which is a factor in the estimated value of the financial interrelations ratio in column 5. Secondly, the calculated values of the financial interrelations ratio are not adjusted for irregularities in the

Table 7–8

Calculated and Observed Values of Financial Interrelation Ratio, 1963

	Aggregate New Issue Ratio ϵ	Product of Three Operators $(1+\nu)\alpha\beta^{-1}$ 1949–1963	Truncation Ratio τ	$\frac{\text{Financial Assets 1948}^{a}}{\text{Wealth 1963}}$	Financial Interrelations Ratio	
					Calculated 1963	Observed
	(1)	(2)	(3)	(4)	(5)	(6)
Australia	.23	3.55	.65	.25	.78	
Belgium	.24	5.04	.47	.30	.87	
Canada	.20	5.90	.56	.50	1.16	
France	.21	2.92	.73	.25	.70	.64 (1960)
Germany	.24	3.08	.74	.15	.70	.76 (1960)
Great Britain	.21	5.71	.55	1.05	1.71	1.72 (1961)
India	.07	6.83	.43	.15	.35	.35 (1960)
Israel	.49	1.79	.94	.05	.88	.88 (1962)
Italy	.33	4.80	.67	.30	1.37	1.06 (1961)
Japan	.63	3.15	.81	.15	1.75	1.70 (1963)
Mexico	.15	2.49	.80	.20	.50	.50 (1963)
Norway	.22	2.98	.59	.30	.69	.68 (1962)
U.S.A.	.20	5.33	.50	.70	1.23	1.27 (1963)
U.S.S.R.	.07	5.90	.57	.12	.36	.35 (1959)
Venezuela	.14	3.11	.65	.10	.39	.40 (1959)
Yugoslavia	.40	1.66	.81	.05	.59	.40 (1960)

[a] Adjusted for change in value of price-sensitive assets.

Sources: *Col. 1:* Table 7–1, col. 4.
Col. 2: Table 7–6, col. 4.
Col. 3: Calculated on basis of rate of growth of national product $[\tau = 1 - (1 + \rho)^{-15}]$.
Col. 4: Rough estimates.
Col. 5: Product of cols. 1, 2, and 3, plus col. 4.
Col. 6: Goldsmith in *The Review of Income and Wealth* (1966), p. 128, except for Japan, Mexico, and U.S.A.

rates of growth of national product during the period 1949–63 that affect the multiplier and the truncation ratio, or for variations in the aggregate new issue ratio during the period. It is not possible to say without detailed examination in which direction these adjustments would tend for individual countries or for an average of groups of them. In general, however, adjustments of the type should not be too large in relation to the calculated value of the financial interrelations ratio.

The comparison of the financial interrelations ratio for 1963 so calculated, with the observed value of the ratio for a date in the neighborhood of 1960 made in Table 7–8, yields a reasonably satisfactory picture provided we take all the fourteen countries together. In that case, the average value of the calculated financial interrelations ratio for 1963 of 0.86 compares with an average of the observed values of 0.81, a difference of approximately 6 per cent. This difference would, moreover, be reduced by a few percentage points by virtue of the fact that the calculated values refer to 1963 while the observed values refer on the average to a date two years earlier, and it is likely that in the early 1960s the value of financial assets increased in most countries more rapidly than that of national wealth, thus increasing FIR. The difference between the calculated and observed values of the financial interrelations ratio is lower for the ten developed countries with 6 per cent than for the four less developed countries with 10 per cent, but this is due entirely to the large difference in one of the four cases (Yugoslavia).

The situation is not unexpectedly less satisfactory for individual countries. Among the fourteen countries the calculated ratio is within 10 per cent of the observed ratio (without allowance for the probably higher value of the observed ratio in 1963 than those shown in Table 7–8 for a slightly earlier date) in all but three countries (Belgium, Italy, and Yugoslavia) for which the calculated and observed values of the ratio differ by more than could be explained by the slight difference in dates or by minor inaccuracies.

The difference in fact is negligible—less than 5 per cent—in nine countries (Great Britain, India, Israel, Japan, Mexico, Norway, the United States, and Venezuela), but this close correspondence is likely to be fortuitous in some cases.

In view of the considerable margin of error in the observed values of the numerator—total financial assets—used in the calculation of the observed value of the financial interrelations ratio, it is not possible to assume that the entire difference between the two values is attributable to an error in the calculated value. (It has already been pointed out that the undoubtedly substantial errors in the observed values of national wealth do not affect the comparison because national wealth appears with the same values in one of the components of the formula, the capital-output ratio.) It is nevertheless likely that a substantial part, if not most, of the difference between the observed and calculated values is due either to errors of measurement in one or more of the dozen of components or to serious deviations of the movements of the components over the period from their fifteen-year average. Considering the relative weight of the various components on the calculated value of FIR and the reliability of the estimates of each of them it is likely that the most serious errors, measured by the effect on the calculated value of FIR, have occurred in the aggregate new issue ratio ε, particularly in that of the nonfinancial sector δ. Countries in which no sectorized flow-of-funds statistics are available for all or most of the period are particularly liable to serious errors in the estimation of the aggregate new issue ratio. This may help to explain the size of the difference in Belgium, Italy, and Yugoslavia.

Resolution, or even substantial reduction, of the differences between the calculated and observed values of FIR would require much more intensive work on individual countries and much closer first-hand familiarity with their financial statistics than is possible within the framework of a comparative study undertaken by an individual. Fortunately the differences, severe as they are in a few cases, are not such as to affect substantially the ranking of the various countries with respect to their FIR—with the exception of Yugoslavia—or to invalidate any of the economically relevant major conclusions that may be drawn from the split-up of the observed values of FIR on the basis of the formula. For, obviously, to the extent that the calculated values of FIR are reasonably close to the observed values there exists at least a presumption that the values of the components from which the calculated value of FIR has been built up are also valid. Offsetting errors certainly have been at work, but it is not likely that they could have been of a character to produce a reasonable degree of similarity between calculated and observed values of FIR for a dozen countries unless there existed also a similar likeness between the values of the components used in building up the calculated values of FIR and the true values of these components.

Here once more a look backward is useful, even if the estimates are again more hazardous than those for a more recent date. The derivation of the estimated value of FIR in 1913 in six developed countries is shown in Table 7–9. The average value of FIR for these six countries is 0.81, and the range extends from 0.40 in Japan to a high of 1.30 for the United Kingdom. These values may be compared with an average of 1.20 for the observed value of FIR in 1963 for the same six countries. Observed values, unfortunately, can be obtained in 1913 for only two countries, Great Britain and the United States. In both cases the difference between observed and calculated values is substantial but tends in different directions. Unless the calculated value of FIR in 1913 for the other four countries is much more different from the observed value than is the case in 1963, it is likely that over this half-century a considerable increase has occurred in FIR for developed countries. It may also be surmised that a similar movement took place in underdeveloped countries.

The comparison of Table 7–10 also indicates that the relationship between FIR in 1963 and in 1913 is quite different for individual countries. The ratio actually seems to be slightly lower in 1963 than it was in 1913 for France and Germany, while it is substantially higher in 1963 in Great Britain, Italy, and the United States, and it is radically higher (1.70 as against 0.40) in Japan. These relationships are not unreasonable. In France and Germany the financial interrelations ratio in the 1960s was still held down by the reduction in the volume of financial assets outstanding resulting from inflation or currency reform in the late 1940s or early 1950s. The spectacular increase in Japan's FIR, already alluded to several times in this study, mirrors the rapid growth of the economy, a high external financing ratio and a high financial intermediation ratio. The increase in the value of FIR from 1913 to 1963 in Great Britain and the United States reflects the intermediate position of these countries, and in the case of Great Britain also a sharp increase in government debt. There remains to explain the fairly rapid increase in FIR in Italy, notwithstanding an inflation in the postwar period similar to the one experienced in France. It is possible that we have here a case of rapid catching-up of a formerly financially less developed country.

Because of the absence of figures for the value of all financial assets outstanding before the postwar period, except for the United States and Great Britain, it is not possible to compare the calculated value of FIR in 1913—or for that matter similar values for the benchmark years of 1880, 1900, 1929, and 1938—with the observed values of the ratio.[5] It is, however, feasible to calculate the ratio of the assets of financial institutions to national wealth for ten countries and the results of this attempt are shown in Table 7–11. These ratios provide some indication of the trend and of the intercountry differences of the financial interrelations ratio, because it is known that at the present

5. If the figures of Table 7–9 are used, the observed value of the ratio is 16 per cent above the calculated value for the United States, but 20 per cent below it for Great Britain. If, instead, Revell's estimate for national wealth is used, the difference almost disappears.

Table 7–9

ANIR and FIR, 1881–1913, in Six Large Countries

	France	Germany	Great Britain	Italy	Japan	U.S.A.
1. Nonfin. dom. issue ratio (δ)[a]	.08	.11	.06	.05	.09	.10
2. Financial inst. issue ratio (ϕ)	.03	.07	.02	.04	.07	.05
3. Foreign issue ratio (ξ)[b]	.03	.01	.05	.01	−.01	.00
4. ANIR ($\delta + \phi + \xi$)	.14	.19	.13	.10	.15	.15
5. Valuation adjustment (ν)	.05	.10	.10	.05	.05	.15
6. Multiplier (α)	54.3	26.5	47.7	47.3	15.5	24.3
7. Capital-output ratio, 1913 (β)	6.4	5.4	4.2	4.4	5.2	4.4
8. Product $[(1 + \nu)\alpha\beta^{-1}]$	8.9	5.4	12.5	11.3	3.1	6.4
9. ANIR × line 8	1.26	1.03	1.63	1.13	.47	.96
10. Truncation ratio (τ)	.47	.71	.58	.54	.81	.67
11. Line 9 × line 10	.59	.73	.95	.61	.38	.64
12. Fin. assets, 1880: natl. wealth, 1913	.20	.15	.35	.20	.02	.07
13. FIR, 1913, calculated values[c]	.79	.88	1.30	.81	.40	.71
14. FIR, 1913, observed values			1.04			.80

[a] 1860–1912. [b] 1891–1914.

[c] Sum of lines 11 and 12. Adjustment to line 12 for change in value of price-sensitive assets outstanding in 1880 has been omitted because of small size and lack of data.

Sources:

Line 1: Table 3–6.

Line 2: Table 4–7.

Line 3: Table 3–20.

Line 5: Rough estimates of order of magnitude only.

Line 6: Table 6–1.

Line 7: Table 7–7 and 6–3 (for Italy).

Line 10: Calculated from same data as line 6 on basis of formula $1 - (1 + \gamma + \pi + \pi\gamma)^{-34}$, where γ and π are average rates of increase of real gross national product and of price level for period 1881–1913.

Line 12: Rough estimate, except for U.S.A.

Line 14, Great Britain: Financial assets (including net foreign investment) from Revell, Table 3–10; for national wealth, Stamp's estimate (14.5 billion) which is used in other tables, e.g. in calculating the capital-output ratio, slightly reduced to eliminate increases in 1911–13. Revell's own estimate of FIR for 1910 is much higher because he does not include net foreign assets in denominator, and estimate of value of domestic tangible assets apparently is far below Stamp's. Using Revell's estimate for tangible domestic assets and including his figures for net foreign balance in the denominator, the ratio is 1.35.

Line 14, U.S.A.: Goldsmith, Lipsey and Mendelson, *Studies in the National Balance Sheet, 2,* 75 (financial assets exclude equity in unincorporated business). Figures refer to 1912.

TABLE 7–10

Rise in FIR, 1913 to 1963, in Six Large Countries

	1913 (1)	1963 (2)	Change 1913–1963 (per cent) (3)
France	.79[a]	.65[b]	−18
Germany	.88[a]	.75[b]	−15
Great Britain	1.04	1.70[c]	+63
Italy	.81[a]	1.05[c]	+29
Japan	.40[a]	1.70	+275
U.S.A.	.80	1.27	+59
Average	.81	1.19	+47

[a] Calculated Values. [b] 1960. [c] 1961.

Sources: Col. 1: Table 7–9, lines 13 and 14.
Col. 2: Table 7–8, col. 6.

time the assets of financial institutions usually represent between three-tenths and two-fifths of all financial assets in

TABLE 7–11

Relation of Financial Institutions' Assets to National Wealth in Ten Developed Countries, 1880 to 1960

	1880[a]	1913	1929	Ca. 1960
Australia		.24	.21	.33[b]
Belgium	.07	.29	.10	.32
Canada	.05	.25	.19	.50[b]
France	.06	.16	.19	.23
Germany	.09	.27	.20	.29
Great Britain	.11	.19	.30	.44
Italy	.07	.22	.33	.44
Japan	.01	.19	.28[b]	.53
Russia-U.S.S.R.	.03	.16		.14
U.S.A.	.12	.17	.32	.46
Average	.07	.21	.24	.37

[a] Figures should be slightly increased except for U.S.A., because denominator refers to 1888 instead of 1880.

[b] Based on very rough estimates of national wealth.

Sources: Assets of financial institutions Appendix IV.
National Wealth
1880: Mulhall, *Dictionary of Statistics*, 1899, p. 589 (figures refer to 1888); for U.S. estimates for 1880, Goldsmith in *Income and Wealth*, Series II (1952) pp. 306, 310.
1913: Stamp, p. 491.
1929: Dresdner Bank, *Economic Forces of the World* (Berlin, 1930).
1960: Goldsmith, "The Uses of National Balance Sheets," p. 128

developed countries, and it is also known that this ratio has been increasing over the past fifty to one-hundred years. In the United States, for instance, financial institutions in 1880 held about one-eighth of all financial assets outstanding, while their share was in the order of one-fourth in 1900, 1912, and 1929 and has been at the level of one-third or more since the 1930s.[6] While it is hazardous to apply a multiplier derived from such relationships in estimating the financial interrelations ratio for individual countries, the danger is less serious for groups of reasonably homogeneous countries such as those in Western Europe and North America.

Table 7–11 shows that the ratio of the assets of financial institutions to national wealth increased sharply for virtually every one of the ten countries from 1880 to 1913 and from 1929 to the early 1960s while the direction of the movement between 1913 and 1929 was indecisive. The average of the ratio for the ten countries (nine in 1880 and 1929) rose from approximately 0.08 in 1880 to 0.21 in 1913, was hardly higher with 0.24 in 1929, and then sharply increased to 0.37 (0.42 excluding U.S.S.R.) in 1960. If we assume, using trends of the ratio in the United States and Great Britain, that the ratio of all financial assets outside financial institutions to those held by financial institutions was cut in half between 1880 and 1913 and again decreased by one-third between 1913 and 1960 and that it now stands in the neighborhood of two-fifths, we obtain a rough estimate for the average value of FIR of developed countries of the order of 0.65 in 1880 and 0.85 in 1913, compared to somewhat above unity now. These figures are entirely compatible with those derived for 1913 in Table 7–9 by a less cavalier method for four large European countries and the United States. We may, therefore, hopefully put some faith in the indicated increase of the financial interrelations ratios of developed countries by more than 50 per cent between 1880 and the present time. Not enough is

6. Goldsmith, Lipsey, and Mendelson, *Studies in the National Balance Sheet, 2.*

known to venture a similar estimate for the trend of the financial interrelations ratio in less developed countries. It is, however, likely that the increase in the ratio between 1880 or 1913 and the present time was even more pronounced for less developed than for developed countries. In other words, in 1880 or in 1913, the financial interrelations ratio of less developed countries, particularly those in Latin America and Southeast Asia, was even farther below the level of the ratio of developed countries than it is now.

These considerations, speculative as some of them are, at the very least seem to justify a presumption that the approach toward a quantitative analysis of the relationships between a country's financial superstructure and its real infrastructure, developed in Chapter 2, is operational and that it leads to results which are in reasonably good agreement with the observed differences among countries and the trends observed over the past century in individual countries. This may be regarded as not much of an achievement in absolute terms, but it possibly represents about as much as can be expected from a first attempt made in the present sad state of the basic data.

8 ADDITIONAL ASPECTS OF FINANCIAL STRUCTURE AND DEVELOPMENT

There are, of course, many important aspects of financial structure and development that have found no place in Chapters 6 and 7, where the main determinants of the new issue ratio and the financial interrelations ratio were discussed. Only a few of these aspects can be briefly studied in this chapter. Their selection from among a much larger number of problems that need and deserve study has been determined mainly by the availability of data and the lack of time and also, let it be admitted, by limitations of the author's interests and competence. As a result, this chapter deals only with three supplementary aspects of financial structure and development: first, the varieties of financial institutions existing at various points of time in the countries included in this study; secondly, the penetration of financial intermediaries in the various countries' economic systems; and, thirdly, the role of foreign banks in financial development. Addition of a short and fragmentary fourth section on developments since 1963, the closing date for the statistics used in Chapters 3–7, may be regarded as an apology for delays in publication.

THE VARIETIES OF FINANCIAL INSTITUTIONS

Notwithstanding the limitations of the characterization of financial development by the number of the different types of financial institutions in operation,[1] two tendencies

1. There is some degree of arbitrariness in deciding what is regarded as a separate type of financial institution at a given place and date,

that stand out clearly in Table 8–1 seem to be significant: (1) the increase in the number of types of financial institutions operating in each country and (2) the larger number of institutions in operation in developed than in less developed countries.[2] Thus, in the five developed countries that are covered in the tables since 1860 (United States, Great Britain, France, Germany, and Switzerland), the average number of types of financial institutions in operation rose from less than ten in 1860 to a little over thirteen in 1913 and to nearly twenty-one in 1963. The increase is much slower in the average for all countries for which information is available at any one benchmark date—from less than ten in 1860 to almost fifteen in 1963—because in the additional countries for which the data go back to the turn of the century (Argentina, Egypt, India, Mexico, and Spain), the increase in the average number of types of financial institutions in operation is even larger than it is for the developed countries, rising from six in 1913 to over sixteen

---

an arbitrariness that results in part from the way in which the basic statistical data are arranged. Thus, in some countries all deposit banks are shown as a single group of financial institutions (this rule has been adopted throughout in Table 8–1), while in some others two or even three groups of such banks are distinguished, for instance, nationwide and local banks or domestic and foreign banks. Similarly life insurance and property insurance companies are combined in some countries, but separated in others. The social insurance organizations are sometimes shown as one type of institution, while in other instances up to half a dozen funds are shown separately. Finally, and possibly most importantly, government credit institutions are in some country tables shown in one line or combined in a few groups, while in others each of the individual institutions is counted separately, this treatment increasing the number of types substantially in Japan and Spain and to a lesser extent in Norway, Mexico and Venezuela. The figures in Table 8–1 are, therefore, best regarded as a count of the separate types of institutions distinguished in the country tables of Appendix IV.

2. Since the figures in Table 8–1 correspond to the number of separate types of institutions for which asset data are shown or marked "unknown" in the country tables of Appendix IV, some types of institutions having very small assets are omitted for one or more benchmark dates.

TABLE 8–1

Varieties of Financial Institutions

NUMBER OF TYPES OF FINANCIAL INSTITUTIONS IN OPERATION

	1860	1880	1900	1910	1929	1938	1948	1963
Argentina			5	7	7	8	10	10
Australia			7	7	9	11	13	15
Belgium		10	11	12	15	18	18	20
Brazil				6	7	8	11	12
Canada		11	11	11	13	16	17	17
Denmark		7	9	9	12	12	12	16
Egypt-U.A.R.			5	5	5	6	8	10
France	9	9	11	11	13	14	19	20
Germany	12	12	15	18	20	21	22	23
Great Britain	13	14	16	17	23	23	23	23
Greece				4	7	7	8	8
India		5	5	8	10	14	17	18
Israel							12	14
Italy		11	12	14	14	15	17	17
Jamaica							8	11
Japan		5	10	10	13	15	19	33
Mexico			4	4	9	16	20	20
Netherlands		10	11	11	16	17	18	18
New Zealand		8	8	11	11	12	14	14
Nigeria					4	4	5	7
Norway		6	10	12	12	12	16	16
Pakistan							6	12
Philippines				6	6	8	9	12
Puerto Rico					5	5	9	14
Rhodesia							7	10
Russia-U.S.S.R.			6	6	4	4	4	4
South Africa				8	10	10	13	16
Spain			6	6	10	11	12	14
Sweden		8	12	15	18	18	20	22
Switzerland	7	7	7	11	15	15	18	17
Thailand						5	6	7
Trinidad					7	7	8	8
U.S.A.	7	9	10	12	19	19	19	20
Venezuela				3	3	3	6	14
Yugoslavia					9	9	2	8

in 1963. If the calculation is limited to the fifteen countries for which information is available back to 1880, the average rises much more sharply from nine to twelve in 1913, sixteen in 1939 and twenty in 1963. The average for all developed countries in 1963 of nearly nineteen is substantially but not radically in excess of the value of slightly less than twelve for all less developed countries, excluding

U.S.S.R. and Yugoslavia. Obviously it is not the existence or the complete absence of certain types of financial institutions which explains either the rise in the ratio of the assets of financial institutions to national product or wealth over the past century, or the present difference in these ratios among countries, particularly the wide gap between developed and less developed countries. These differences are due mainly to the larger relative size—i.e. the higher ratio of their assets to national product or wealth—of most types of financial institutions in developed compared to less developed countries, and in the rise of these ratios over the past fifty to one hundred years in both developed and less developed countries.

THE PENETRATION OF THE FINANCIAL SYSTEM

The ratios of all financial assets, or of the assets of financial institutions, to either national or personal wealth and income, which have been used throughout this study to measure the relative importance of the financial superstructure and its components, do not provide a direct indication of the degree of penetration of the financial system, because these ratios can be high while only a small proportion of households actually own financial assets and use financial institutions. Worse still, the ratios can rise without a corresponding (and theoretically even without any) increase in the proportion of households owning financial assets or using financial institutions. The process of penetration of the financial system, which is important for economic as well as for sociological and political analysis, can be adequately studied only on the basis of information (in praxis necessarily on a sample basis) obtained from households at one or more dates, information which indicates the proportion of households of different characteristics that own various types of financial assets. Unfortunately household sample surveys of this type have been undertaken only in a very few countries, and even in these only during the postwar period or for a single recent year. It is therefore impossible to base an international or intertemporal comparison of the penetration of the financial system on this type of material.[3] We are then forced to fall back on aggregative data on the number of depositors, policyholders, and stockholders or similar material. The advantage of this type of data is that they are available for a fairly large number of countries and in some cases for extended periods of time. The aggregative data, however, have two main drawbacks. First, they are with few exceptions available only for very few types of financial assets. Secondly, and this is an even more serious flaw, the information refers only to the number of accounts or policies or shareholdings, which is not identical with the number of households owning an account or holding life insurance policies or owning corporate shares, since one household may and not rarely does own more than one saving account, more than one life insurance policy, and shares in more than one corporation, and since the degree of duplication cannot be assumed to have been stable over time or to be the same for different countries.

Savings Bank Deposits

A serious study of the penetration of thrift deposits in the economy requires information on the number of accounts, or even better on the number of individual depositors, in all types of thrift institutions, including savings departments of commercial banks. Comprehensive data of this type for an extended period exist in only very few countries. If we want to cover a reasonable proportion of the thirty-five countries on which this study is based, and if we also want to follow developments over a substantial period of time, we must limit ourselves to the number of accounts in savings banks and in postal savings institutions;

3. For a partial review of data of this type, see E. Lisle and M. Massonaud, *Bibliographie d'études étrangères sur l'épargne* (Paris, Centre de Recherche Économique sur l'Épargne, 1962).

even then we will succeed in including only one-half of the thirty-five countries and only very few of the less developed countries.

The figures available without undertaking a special study going back to primary sources are brought together in Table 8–2. The main drawback of the figures is that the propor-

TABLE 8–2
Trend in Penetration of Savings Banking
NUMBER OF ACCOUNTS[a] AS PER CENT OF POPULATION

	1850 (1)	1871/75 (2)	1910 (3)	1963 (4)
Australia			36	100
Belgium		2.5	39	94
Denmark	2.5[b]	17.4	50	96
France	1.6	5.6	36	59
Germany	1.6	8.4	33	56
Great Britain	4.0	9.7	30	61
India			0.5	26
Italy	0.3	2.5	22	
Japan			37	198
Netherlands		2.8	32	81
New Zealand			44	112
Norway	b	12.6	42	92
Russia-U.S.S.R.		0.1	5	24
Spain			3	43
Sweden	b	13.1	39	160
Switzerland	2.0	23.3	53	
U.S.A.	1.1	4.0	10	12

[a] Includes accounts with Postal Saving organizations.
[b] Figure refers to Denmark, Norway, and Sweden together.

Sources: *Col. 1:* Mulhall, *Dictionary of Statistics* (1892), p. 86.
Col. 2: *Statistique Internationale des Caisses d'Épargne* (Bureau Statistique du Royaume d'Italie, 1876), pp. 83 ff.
Col. 3: M. Seidel and J. Pfitzner *Das Sparkassenwesen* (Wien, 1916), except for India.
Col. 4: National sources, usually official statistical year books.

tion of total thrift accounts which is held in savings banks and postal savings organizations differs considerably among countries and has changed in the same country. The number of accounts in savings banks and postal savings organizations alone, therefore, can give only a rough indication of the level and of the movement of all thrift accounts, particularly in countries where other thrift organizations are of substantial importance, such as savings and loan associations in the United States, Great Britain, and South Africa, or where a considerable or even a predominant part of savings accounts is kept with commercial banks. Notwithstanding these reservations, a few conclusions of some interest can be derived from Table 8–2.

First, the penetration of thrift accounts has increased spectacularly during the last century. In European develloped countries only 1 to 2 per cent of the population had savings bank accounts in 1850, while the ratio of savings accounts to population is now in the order of 100 per cent. The rate of increase is even larger for all types of thrift accounts taken together because in 1850 there were no or only a few accounts in savings and loan associations, credit unions, and commercial bank savings departments.

Secondly, the penetration of savings accounts in the economy has been particularly rapid during the half-century preceding World War I. As a result, the ratio of savings accounts to population in 1910 was in the order of 40 per cent with a range of 30 to 50 per cent for most developed European countries. Since then the further penetration has proceeded more slowly, even if it has done so in most countries somewhat more rapidly than Table 8–2 indicates, since the newer forms of thrift institutions, particularly the savings and loan associations and credit unions, as well as the savings departments of commercial banks, have grown more rapidly than savings banks and postal savings organizations.

Thirdly, the degree of penetration of thrift accounts in the United States is low compared to European developed countries. This is spectacularly so if the figures for the United States are limited to mutual savings banks and the postal savings organizations but is true even if all other thrift accounts are included, in which case the ratio of thrift accounts to population is in the neighborhood of 75 per cent.

Fourthly, although the number of less developed countries included in Table 8–2 is too low to permit any generalization, it is suggested—and is corroborated by collateral fragmentary information—that the penetration ratio of savings as well as of all thrift accounts in these countries is very low. This is illustrated by the figures for India, which may be regarded as representative of the least developed countries. The present ratio of less than 3 per cent is diminutive compared to that observed in developed countries, but it is well to remember that the present Indian figure is approximately at the same level as the ratios observed in now developed countries about one century ago.

Fifthly, a scatter diagram shows a rough correlation between the proportion of population having a savings account and the level of real gross national product in 1963, but the diagram also discloses enough substantial deviations, even if allowance is made roughly for the varying proportion of thrift accounts held by savings banks and postal saving organizations, to indicate a considerable influence of other factors on the penetration ratio.

It might be thought that the course of the penetration ratio of savings banks would be identical with, or parallel to, the movements of the ratio of assets of thrift institutions to gross national product, i.e. parallel to the ratio ϕ_8 of Chapter 5. Table 8–3 shows that this is not the case for the fourteen countries for which the data are available.

The main reasons for the more rapid rise of the penetration ratio compared to the asset/GNP ratio is the slower increase of the average holding per account (or the average face value per policy) compared to national product per head or to average personal income. This difference is, in turn, partly due to an increase in the duplication ratio, i.e. the number of accounts or policies per spending unit, and to that extent should be eliminated from the series being compared. The remaining difference reflects changes in the ratio of the average holding of savings deposits, or of life insurance policies, in comparison to the average spending unit's income. Since average holdings are especially liable to lag behind average income during sharp inflations, it is not astonishing that the lag is more pronounced in periods and in countries subject to rapid or protracted price rises, leading in such cases even to a decline in the assets/GNP ratio in the face of a rise in the penetration ratio. This discrepancy may be observed in the figures for Germany

TABLE 8–3

Penetration Ratio and Asset/GNP Ratio of Savings Banks, 1871–75, 1910, and 1963

PER CENT

	Penetration Ratio			Assets of Savings Banks[a]: GNP		
	1871–75 (1)	1910 (2)	1963 (3)	1880 (4)	1913 (5)	1963 (6)
Belgium	3	39	94	7	20	28
Denmark	17	50	96	30	35	20
France	6	36	59	3	12	11
Germany	8	33	56	15	36	22
Great Britain	10	30	61	7	10	12
India		0.2	2.6	0.3	1.1	1.9
Italy	3	22		6	23	31
Netherlands	3	32	81	3	11	16
Norway	13	42	92	36	50	28
Russia-U.S.S.R.	0.1	5	24		8	7
Spain		3	43		3	18
Sweden	13	39	160	12	26	32
Switzerland	23	53		24	(15)	9
U.S.A.	4	10	12	10	11	8
Average lines 1–4, 8, 9, 12, 14	10	37	81	14	25	21
Average, all countries (partly estimated)	8	28	65	13	19	17

[a] Including postal savings.

Sources: *Cols. 1–3:* Table 8–2.
Cols. 4–6: Country tables in Appendix IV.

and France between 1913 and 1963 in Tables 8–3 and 8–6. There is, however, another factor at work which almost necessarily leads to a less rapid rise in the asset/GNP ratio than in the penetration ratio even in the absence of inflation. This is the fact that as the number of depositors, or policyholders, increases, the new depositors or policyholders are likely to come, on the average, from groups of the population that rank lower on the income and wealth scale than the old depositors and policyholders. An illustration of this process of "dilution" is provided in Table 8–4, which

TABLE 8–4

Relations between Penetration Ratio and Asset/GNP Ratio, Illustrated by Case of Life Insurance Policies in United States, 1880, 1913, and 1963

Symbol	Definition	1880	1913	1963
N	Number of ordinary policies (millions)	.69	8.5	101.4
P	Population (millions)	51.2	98.2	190.8
A	Assets of life insurance companies (billions of dollars)	.42	4.5	141.4
a	Assets per policy[a] (thousands of dollars)	.61	.53	1.39
Y	Gross national product (billions of dollars)	9.3	37.3	590.5
y	National product per head (thousands of dollars)	.18	.38	3.10
b	a/y	3.40	1.40	.46
δ	Number of policies per spending unit (duplication ratio)	1.2	1.8	2.5
π	Penetration ratio N/P (per cent)	1.4	8.7	53.0
π'	Penetration ratio $N/P\delta$ (per cent)	1.2	4.8	21.2
α	Asset ratio A/Y (per cent)	4.5	12.1	24.0
F	Face amount of ordinary policies (billions of dollars)	1.55	18.7	418.9
R	Reserves against ordinary policies (billions of dollars)	(.35)	(3.5)	69.1
ρ	Reserve ratio R/y	.23	.19	.17
f	Face amount per policy (thousands of dollars)	2.3	2.2	4.1
β	π/α	.31	.72	2.21
β'	$\pi/\alpha\delta$	.26	.40	.89

[a] Too high because numerator also includes assets attributable to other than ordinary policies.

Sources: Historical Statistics of the U.S.; Statistical Abstract; Life Insurance Fact Book, various issues; rough estimates for δ.

shows the relevant figures for ordinary life insurance policies in the United States for the three benchmark dates 1880, 1913, and 1963. It is unfortunately impossible to repeat this calculation for all countries and dates covered in Tables 8–3 and 8–6 for both life insurance policies and savings banks deposits.

Life Insurance Policies

The measurement of the penetration of life insurance policies and the interpretation of the data is even more difficult than it is for thrift deposits, both on the conceptual and the statistical level. The main difficulty resides in the fact that the different types of life insurance policies provide quite different kinds of protection and that the degree to which the possession of life insurance policies has been supplemented by other forms of protection, particularly by social security and by private pension funds, varies considerably among countries and has changed over time in most countries in the direction of a decrease in the share of the protection provided by life insurance policies alone. At the statistical level we must contend with the practically complete absence of internationally comparative information on the number and types of life insurance policies. In this situation, all that it has been found possible to do is to show in Table 8–5 the differences now existing in the degree of penetration (by calculating for eighteen of the thirty-five countries the ratio of the number of policies to population, separating ordinary and industrial policies because of the much smaller amount of protection provided by the latter) and to follow, in Table 8–6, the trend since 1880 in the ratio of the number of policies to population for ordinary life insurance policies for the nine countries for which the data could be ascertained.

Table 8–5, shows, as may be expected, first, a rough positive association between the penetration ratio for ordinary life insurance policies to real gross national product per head and, secondly, considerable irregularities.

Among developed countries, and these are the only ones for which a sufficient number of cases is available to establish even rough relationships, the marginal income elasticity of penetration, as it might be called, seems to be high. For four European developed countries with an average national income per head in 1963 of about $1,700 (1960 purchasing power), the penetration ratio for ordinary policies is very close to 0.20, while for four other developed countries having a national product per head in the $2,000 to

TABLE 8–5

Penetration of Life Insurance, 1963

NUMBER OF POLICIES AS PER CENT OF POPULATION

	Ordinary	Industrial and Group	Total
Australia	34	32	66
Belgium	15	30	45
Canada	43	11	54
Egypt-U.A.R.			15
Germany	19	62	81
Great Britain	13	230[a]	243
India	2		2
Israel			10
Italy	5	4	9
Japan			57
Netherlands	61	159	220
New Zealand	56	15	71
Pakistan			0.2
Spain	2		
Sweden	27	26	53
Switzerland	47	9	56
U.S.A.[b]	57	76	133
U.S.S.R.	5		5

[a] Includes collecting societies.
[b] Includes fraternal insurance.

Sources: Annual statistical abstracts of various countries except lines 4, 13, 14 and 18, which are based on data in *Die Versicherungsmärkte der Welt.* (Schweizerische Rückversicherungs-Gesellschaft, Zürich, 1964)

$2,300 range the ratio averages 0.45 and in all cases exceeds 0.30. The United States, finally, with real income per head of $3,000, has a penetration ratio of 0.60, thus occupying the top position on both scales. Any serious interpretation of these figures would have to take account of the degree of protection provided by private pension funds and by social security, but no internationally comparative data of this type are available.

The trend of the penetration ratio of life insurance poli-

TABLE 8–6

Trend in Penetration of Life Insurance[a]

NUMBER OF ORDINARY POLICIES AS PER CENT OF POPULATION

	1880	1900	1913	1929	1948	1963
Canada	1.1		12[d]			43
France	0.6			4[e]		
Germany	1.3	3	4	5	10[f]	19
Great Britain	2.6			10[e]		13
India					1[f]	2
Italy		1			7[f]	5
Sweden	0.3	4	15	35	58	53
Switzerland	1.9[c]	4	8	22	44	47
U.S.A.[b]	1.4	10	17	33	48	57

[a] Ordinary life insurance only except for Sweden (ordinary insurance in 1963: 27 per cent).

[b] Includes fraternal life insurance.

[c] 1886. [d] 1907. [e] 1923. [f] 1950.

Sources:

Lines 1–4, 1880: Mulhall, *The New Dictionary of Statistics* (London, 1892).

Line 1, 1907: A. D. Webb, *Dictionary of Statistics* (London, 1911).

Lines 2, 4, 1923: W. S. Woytinsky, *Die Welt in Zahlen, 5* (Berlin, 1927).

Line 3, 1900, 1913: A. Manes, ed., *Versicherungslexikon* (Berlin, 1924).

1929, 1950: Handwörterbuch der Sozialwissenschaften, 6, (Stuttgart, 1956).

1963: Statistisches Jahrbuch (Berlin, 1964).

Line 4, 1963: Annual Abstract of Statistics (London, 1964).

Lines 5, 6, 1950, 1963: Die Versicherungsmärkte der Welt (1964).

Line 7: Historisk Statistik för Sverige (Stockholm, 1960) and *Statistisk Årsbok* (Stockholm), 1964.

Line 8: Statistisches Handbuch der Schweiz (1965).

Line 9: Statistical Abstract of the U.S., various issues.

cies can be made out dimly from the data shown in Table 8–6. The trend differs from that observed for savings bank accounts in that the increase in the penetration ratio slows down less during the interwar period. Ordinary life insurance policies seem to have come into general use, measured by the level of the penetration ratio, one or two generations later than savings bank accounts. This may be connected with the fact that ordinary life insurance policies involve on the average a larger accumulation than do savings accounts and are therefore used primarily by people in higher income brackets. In this respect, industrial insurance policies are more similar to thrift accounts, and it is therefore interesting that the penetration ratio for industrial policies in the one country for which a long series is available (the United States) also shows its sharpest increase before World War I, rising from less than 1 per cent in 1880 to 30 per cent in 1913, a level which is only a good half below the present one. There remains the question why people in the middle and upper income brackets, who are the main users of ordinary life insurance policies, turned to them only at a relatively late state of financial development. One possible explanation is that this move is connected with a general shift of individuals towards indirect saving through financial institutions and the accompanying decline in the importance of direct saving through government and corporate securities, mortgages, and equity in owner-operated businesses. It will need an intensive investigation to do more than to present this conjecture which is not incom-

TABLE 8–7

Penetration Ratio and Asset/GNP Share of Life Insurance Companies, 1880–1963

PER CENT

	Penetration Ratio			Assets of Companies / Gross National Product		
	1880	1913	1963	1880	1913	1963
Canada	1.1	12	43	3.4	13	31
France	0.6			5.5	14	4
Germany	1.3	4	19	2.4	10	6
Great Britain	2.6		20	12.8[a]	12[a]	31[a]
India			2	0.1	0.3	5
Italy		1	5		2	6
Sweden	0.3	15	53	2.4	10	20
Switzerland	1.9[b]	8	47		11	19
U.S.A.	1.4	17	57	4.8	12	25
Average lines 1, 3, 7, 9	1.0	12	43	3.3	11	21
Average (all)[c]	1.3	10	31	4.5	9	16

[a] Includes non-life insurance companies.
[b] 1886.
[c] Partly estimated.

patible with what is known about financial development in now developed countries.

Here again, the trend in the penetration ratio differs considerably from the ratio of the assets of life insurance companies to national product, as is evident from Table 8–7, the penetration ratio increasing more rapidly than the asset/GNP ratio throughout the period as observed for savings bank deposits.

Stock Ownership

Like many characteristics of financial structure, the penetration of share ownership, measured by the proportion of the total population that is estimated to own one or more issues of corporate stock, is definitely different as between developed and less developed countries, but there does not seem to exist a clear relationship within the two groups between the degree of penetration and the level of real national product per head, the degree of industrialization, or concentration of income or any simple indicator of the level of economic development. The limited amount of information on this subject now available is summarized in Table 8–8, the ratio generally being rounded to the nearest full per cent in view of the roughness of virtually all the estimates of the number of shareholders.

In the early 1960s, the proportion of shareholders lay between 2 and 10 per cent of the population in most developed countries. The United States showed the highest proportion, exceeding 10 per cent, as well as the highest level of gross national product. Among the other developed countries, however, no clear relationship existed between income level and the degree of penetration. Thus the percentage of stockholders was relatively low—around 3 per cent of the population—in three developed countries with relatively high real income per head: Canada, Sweden, and South Africa (here, of course, using only the white population as denominator). On the other hand, the highest ownership ratios among developed countries, next to the United

States, were shown by the Netherlands, Great Britain, France, and Japan, which do not belong to countries with the highest real income per head group, the difference being particularly striking in the case of Japan. It is there-

TABLE 8–8

Penetration of Stockownership

NUMBER OF STOCKHOLDERS AS PER CENT OF TOTAL POPULATION

	Recent Estimates		Earlier Estimates	
	Year	Ratio	Year	Ratio
Argentina	[a]	1		
Belgium	[a]	6		
Canada	1959	3		
France	1957	5		
Great Britain	[a]	7	ca. 1950	4
India	[a]	0.1		
Italy	[a]	2–4		
Japan	1963	5	1946	.5
Netherlands	1961	7		
Rhodesia	[a]	1[b]		
South Africa	1963	4[b]		
Sweden	1957	2.5	1951	1.5
U.S.A.	1965	10	1948	4
			1937	7
			1900	2
Venezuela	[a]	1		

[a] No date given; presumably early 1960s.
[b] White population.
[c] Stockholders in public corporations.

Sources: Based on data on number of shareholders in New York Stock Exchange, *Individual Shareownership Around the World*, New York. (Dec. 1963), except for United States. For various U.S. estimates cf. E. B. Cox, *Trends in the Distribution of Stock Ownership* (Philadelphia, 1963).

fore obvious that other factors, particularly historical and sociological peculiarities as well as inflation consciousness, have played a larger role in determining the present value of the penetration ratio than the level of gross national product per head or another similarly simple figure. It seems, however, that a tendency towards convergence has been at work since the end of World War II among developed countries. This is indicated by the narrower spread among the penetration ratios observed around 1960 than among those before or immediately after World War II for the relatively few developed countries for which estimates are available.

Information on less developed countries is so rare that no generalizations can be based on the few figures available. There seems to be no doubt, however, that the penetration ratio for these countries is much lower than for developed countries, apparently not exceeding 1 per cent of the population in many (if any) cases and as low as 0.1 per cent in as important a less developed country as India. The much lower level of the penetration ratio in less developed countries is due to at least two factors. The first is the much smaller importance of business corporations in the country's economic and financial structure, the second is the fact that in less developed countries most corporations are still closely held by a small number of shareholders, who usually belong to one or a few families or to otherwise connected groups of investors. Corporations with more than, say, 10,000 shareholders or, alternatively, with one shareholder for every 10,000 population, are quite numerous in developed countries but extremely rare in less developed countries. Thus the most widely held Indian corporation (Tata Iron and Steel Corporation) has only 70,000 shareholders, well under two per 10,000 of India's population. Such a ratio would correspond in the United States to about 30,000 shareholders, and the number of corporations with more than that number of shareholders is well in excess of one hundred. (The average number of shareholders in all the 1500 odd companies listed on the New York Stock Exchange in 1965 exceeded 20,000.)

The United States is the only country for which the long-term trend in the number of shareholders and their proportion to the population can be established, even though many of the figures are subject to a substantial margin of error and an entirely comparable series of figures is not available. Interpreting the existing estimates as best as possible, it appears that the number of shareholders was in the neighborhood of 2 per cent of the population in 1900 and that the penetration ratio increased only slowly until World War I. The ratio seems to have been in the order of 5 per cent in 1929. In 1937, the year for which the most detailed and reliable estimates have been made,[4] it was around 7 per cent. From World War II on, a different series must be used which shows for 1948 a considerably lower ratio of approximately 4 per cent.[5] While some decline in the ratio between 1937 and 1948 is not unlikely, it would seem that the break indicated by the figures now available is exaggerated. It is certain, however, that the penetration ratio increased rapidly in the post-war period rising from about 4 per cent in 1948 to fully 10 per cent in the mid-1960s.[6] There thus is no doubt either that a spectacular increase in the proportion of the population owning corporate stock has taken place over the last half-century. While the penetration ratio is considerably, but not radically, lower for a number of European developed countries, it is likely that in their case too the ratio has been increasing substantially, although the extent of the rise, its speed, and its timing may have differed considerably from that observed in the United States. The rise of the Japanese ratio within less than a decade from about 0.5 to 5 per cent of the population is relatively more rapid than that observed in the United States in more than half a century.

THE ROLE OF FOREIGN BANKS[7]

There is no doubt that the transmission of financial technology, as well as the more far-reaching establishment of new types of financial institutions by foreigners, has played

4. *The Distribution of Ownership of the 200 Largest Corporations,* Temporary National Economic Commission Monograph No. 29 (Washington, 1938).

5. The estimates for the period beginning with the late 1950s are based on sample surveys conducted for the New York Stock Exchange.

6. New York Stock Exchange, *Shareownership U.S.A.* (New York, 1965).

7. This section is based mainly on the following sources, apart from

a large part in the financial development of most countries, indeed all of them except Great Britain, France, the United States, possibly Germany, and a few other European countries. There is equally little doubt that of all these interconnections, the establishment by foreigners of commercial banks, and to a lesser extent of central banks, has been the most important single influence. It therefore seems appro-

---

the standard literature on foreign investments and the statistical abstracts of some of the countries involved:

Baster, A. S. J. *The Imperial Banks* (London, P. S. King and Sons, 1929).

Baster, A. S. J. *The International Banks* (London, P. S. King and Sons, 1935).

Beckhart, B. H., ed. *Banking Systems* (New York, Columbia University Press, 1954).

Cameron, R., ed. *Banking in the Early Stages of Industrialization* (New York, Oxford University Press, 1967).

Crick, W. F., ed. *Commonwealth Banking Systems* (Oxford, Clarendon Press, 1965).

Ducruet, J. *Les Capitaux Européens au Proche-Orient* (Paris, Presses Universitaires, 1964).

Gindin, I. P. *Russkie kommertcheskie banki* (Moskva, Gosfinizdat, 1948).

Joslin, D. *A Century of Banking in Latin America* (New York, Oxford University Press, 1963).

Jucker-Fleetwood, E. E. *Money and Finance in Africa* (New York, Praeger, 1964).

Lewis, C. *America's Stake in International Investments* (Washington, Brookings Institution, 1938).

Ol, P. V. *Innostrannie kapitali v Rossii* (Petrograd, Gosudarstvenaia Tipografia, 1922).

Phelps, C. W. *The Foreign Expansion of American Banks* (New York, Ronald Press, 1927).

Riesser, J. *Die deutschen Grossbanken,* 4th ed. (Jena, G. Fischer, 1912).

Ronin, S. L. *Innostrannie kapitali i russkie banki* (Moskva, Isdatelstvo Kom. Universiteta J. M. Sverdlova, 1926).

Sayers, R., ed. *Banking in the British Commonwealth* (Oxford, Clarendon Press, 1952).

Strasser, K. *Die deutschen Banken im Ausland* (München, E. Reinhardt, 1925)

Willis, H. P. and Beckhart, B. H., eds. *Foreign Banking Systems* (New York, H. Holt, 1929).

priate to summarize briefly this development, even though the subject has never been treated adequately on an international basis and though the material is scarce, even for the development of foreign banks in individual creditor or debtor countries. Notwithstanding these limitations, the main features of the process are reasonably clear:

1. The process of establishing commercial banks abroad started in Great Britain in the first half of the nineteenth century, and Great Britain has kept its preeminent role in this field until the present time. A rough indication of British predominance in this field is given by the fact that, of the approximately 2,600 branches of foreign banks operating in 1913, well over 80 per cent belonged to British organized and owned institutions.[8] While the preponderance of British banks probably was not as extreme in terms of loans and deposits, it was still very marked.

2. After a halting and partly unsuccessful beginning in the 1830s and 1840s, the overseas expansion of British banks started seriously in the 1850s and proceeded intensively until World War I and more slowly through the 1920s. The main banks operating within the British Empire and in other foreign countries are estimated to have increased the number of their branches from about 450 in 1880 to 1,500 in 1913 and to 2,300 in the late 1920s.[9]

3. France and Germany followed on a large scale from the 1880s on and ceased expanding on a substantial scale by the beginning of World War I. The United States and Canada, on the other hand, started commercial bank operations abroad only during World War I and have continued to expand them substantially until the present time. The Netherlands, Belgium, Italy, Japan, and even Spain participated in this movement on a smaller scale.

4. The colonies and dependencies of each of the European countries, as well as later those of the United States and Japan, were regarded, and often legally treated, as preserves

8. Lewis, p. 191.

9. Baster, *The Imperial Banks,* p. 261; *The International Banks,* p. 245.

of the mother country. This was particularly important for Great Britain, since it gave the country a practical monopoly in a large part of the world outside of Europe insofar as the operation of foreign banks went. It was only in Latin America and to a lesser extent in the less developed European countries, the Near East, and China that the developed countries competed with each other in the field of foreign banking. Even here the British were usually in first position except in the less developed European countries, particularly in Russia, where French interests occupied this spot.

5. Until World War I, foreign banks held a dominating, or at least a very strong position, in virtually all countries in which they operated at all. Thus even by 1913, when the share of foreign banks had already declined from its peak, they accounted for approximately one-third of total banking resources in Latin America and for well over one-half in South Africa, Egypt, Turkey, China, and a few other countries.[10]

6. The influence of foreign banks was much more short-lived in European countries. The outstanding example is Italy. German banks originally controlled the two largest Italian commercial banks organized after the crisis of the early 1890s—the Banca Commerciale and the Credito Italiano—but control of both institutions had already been acquired by Italian interests before World War I.

7. Developments during the interwar period are characterized, first, by the entrance of the United States and Canada on a substantial scale, primarily in Latin America and the West Indies where they became predominant and by the declining influence of Germany, which lost many of its outposts as a result of World War I.

10. In Argentina, the share of foreign banks in the deposits of all commercial banks declined from almost two-fifths in 1901 to not much over one-fifth in 1913; it remained at this level through the 1920s and 1930s and in 1966 still amounted to 18 per cent. (*La Economía Bancaria Argentina 1901 a 1935* (Buenos Aires, 1937) and *Boletín Estadistico* of Banco Central.)

8. The interwar period is characterized, secondly, by a decline in the relative importance of foreign banks in virtually all areas in which they operated. In Russia, activities of foreign banks were completely eliminated as the result of the revolution. In Turkey, foreign banks, which had been the dominating factor before World War I through the Banque Ottomane, by 1939 held only one-eighth of total bank deposits. In Brazil, the share of foreign banks, which had been as high as two-fifths in 1913, was reduced to about one-tenth by 1948.

9. Developments after World War II tended in the same direction. The main features are the further decline in the share of foreign banks in total banking resources of most of the countries in which they operated and the relative increase in the importance of American banks.

10. While comprehensive statistics for the postwar period are lacking, the data available virtually all show a decline in the relative share of foreign banks. Thus the share of the foreign (exchange) banks in India declined from 22 per cent in 1938 to 12 per cent in 1960. The decline in the same period in Australia was from over 30 to less than 25 per cent, in Puerto Rico from over 55 to 40 per cent, to cite two examples more or less at random. It apparently was only in some South American countries, e.g. Argentina, that the decline was absent or insignificant.

11. The growing importance of American banks operating abroad is indicated by the increase in the number of their branches, which had been slightly in excess of 100 from the 1920s to the mid-1950s, to somewhat over 200 in 1965, and still more by the increase in their total assets from about $2 billion in 1955 to $9 billion in 1965, an increase which must have been well in excess both of the increase in the assets of all foreign banks as well as of the banks in the territories in which American branches and subsidiaries are operating. The foreign expansion of American banks, however, differs considerably from that of British and other banks in that a substantial part is taking place in the developed rather than in less developed countries. Thus in 1965

more than one-half of the total assets of the overseas branches of Federal Reserve member banks were held by European branches, predominantly those in London.

12. During the postwar period, tropical Africa developed into a new field of activity for foreign branches and subsidiaries, primarily for British and French banks. In terms of quantity, however, this expansion was far from offsetting the relative decline in the importance of foreign banking in the rest of the world.

13. While foreign banks were of great and sometimes decisive importance for the financial development of some of the countries in which they operated, they have absorbed only a relatively small part of the financial resources of the mother countries, partly because their operations were financed chiefly by funds raised in the countries in which the foreign banks operated, except for a relatively brief initial period. As a matter of fact, cases in which foreign banks raised larger amounts of funds in the areas in which they operated than they used in these areas, and thus provided a net source of funds to the mother country, are probably as numerous and important, if not more so, than the cases in which they acted as a net source of funds for the foreign countries.

14. At the present time, foreign banks are without substantial importance in Europe (except for the American banks), in the Near East, and in the Far East except in Hong Kong. They are still of substantial, though reduced, significance in Latin America, and even there they usually account for only a relatively small proportion—less than one-fifth—of the total banking resources of the countries in which they operate. Banks, the majority of whose shares are owned in Great Britain and which have their head office in London, still are of substantial importance in South Africa and less so in Australia and New Zealand, but they have become more and more nationalized in their operations and management. It is only in tropical Africa that foreign banks still dominate the picture. However, the fact that foreign banks account for most of the resources of commer-

cial banks (in Nigeria, for instance, for about two-thirds of the total at the present time) has considerably less importance than a similar ratio would have had in the nineteenth century, since the central banks, which now are always owned and controlled by the home government, as well as in some cases state-owned development banks, are relatively much larger in comparison to commercial banks than was the case before World War I.[11]

15. The significance of the organization and operation of usually entirely foreign-owned, mainly foreign-managed, and partly foreign-staffed commercial banks (all three criteria became attentuated as time went on) in the financial development of most countries outside of Western Europe and North America has possibly been even greater than indicated by the figures that measure the share of foreign banks in the assets of all commercial banks or of all financial institutions. The reason is twofold. First, commercial banks have in virtually all countries outside of Western Europe and North America constituted the earliest form—with the exception in some countries of banks of issue—and the most important form of financial intermediaries; they entirely predominated among financial institutions in less developed countries in Latin America and in the Far East until at least World War I and often until World War II and still do so in Africa and the Near East. Foreign banks have in most countries played a decisive role in introducing deposit and investment banking and in nursing it over its first difficult stages of adaptation to an environment differing very much from that of the Western European homeland. Secondly, commercial banks have in many of these countries exercised a far-reaching influence on commercial and industrial development, in particular on foreign trade, and thus have indirectly extended the influence of foreign share-

11. To use Argentina again as an example, the share of foreign commercial banks—and there were only a few, relatively small foreign financial institutions of other types—in the assets of all financial intermediaries declined from about 30 per cent in 1900 to 15 per cent in 1913 and 1929; by 1963 it had been reduced to about 7 per cent.

holders and managers far beyond the immediate sphere of the activities of foreign banks. What is remarkable is that this influence has not been due, except to a limited extent in the earliest stages, to the importation of substantial amounts of funds from the homelands but to the transfer of financial technology requiring virtually no capital and effected only in part through the importation of skilled foreign labor, from bank managers to accountants and clerks. One gains the impression from the rapid organization and spread of expatriate commercial banks all over the world, particularly between about 1870 and World War I, that the transfer of technology and labor has been much easier in this field, than it has been in agriculture, in commerce and in industry. Certainly the requirement for foreign funds has been much lower than in any of these fields. The reasons for the greater ease of transfer of financial technology in the field of banking, though much less so in that of other financial institutions and instruments, remain to be investigated in detail and on a geographic scale befitting the importance of the process of the financial and economic development of most of the world in the last one hundred years. The fact that banking is considered a white-collar occupation and is hence acceptable to the educated classes in many less developed countries, groups which shy away from manual work, may well have been a contributing factor, but is not a sufficient explanation.

RECENT DEVELOPMENTS

Since 1963 is the last year for which the statistical information required for the study was available for the thirty-five countries (the basic tables were frozen in mid-1966 in order to stop the never-ending process of corrections and additions), it is tempting to see whether the tendencies observed during the postwar period, and particularly between the benchmark dates of 1960 and 1963, have continued in the following three or four years.

Such a look at recent developments is unfortunately limited to one aspect of the study, if it is to cover all or most of the thirty-five countries, viz. the assets of financial intermediaries, their issues, and the relationship of the latter to national product. Table 8–9 therefore summarizes devel-

TABLE 8–9

Recent Development of Issues by Financial Institutions
PER CENT OF GROSS NATIONAL PRODUCT

	Unweighted Average of Ratios		Change 1961–63 to 1964–66	
	1961–63	1964–66	Points	Per Cent
CENTRAL BANKS				
All countries (32)	1.53	1.32	−.21	−13.7
Developed countries (17)	1.22	.81	−.41	−33.6
Less developed countries (15)	1.89	1.90	+.01	+0.5
DEPOSIT BANKS				
All Countries (32)	4.68	4.16	−.52	−11.1
Developed countries (17)	4.72	4.50	−.22	−4.7
Less developed countries (15)	4.64	3.79	−.85	−18.3
SAVINGS DEPOSITS				
All countries (31)	2.91	2.71	−.20	−6.9
Developed countries (16)	3.79	3.48	−.31	−8.2
Less developed countries (15)	1.96	1.88	−.08	−4.1
LIFE INSURANCE COMPANIES				
All countries (15)	1.35	1.31	−.04	−3.0
Developed countries (14)	1.42	1.36	−.06	−4.2
Less developed countries (1)[a]	.48	.60	+.12	+25.0
MAIN FINANCIAL INSTITUTIONS[b]				
All countries (20)	8.47	8.38	−.09	−1.1
Developed countries (14)	9.19	8.87	−.32	−3.5
Less developed countries (6)	6.78	7.21	+.43	+6.3

[a] Very small in most less developed countries.

[b] Includes, in addition to central and deposit banks, building associations (in three countries), cooperative banks (3), life insurance companies (16), postal checking systems (5), savings banks (19), and selected specialized institutions, e.g. mortgage or development banks (10).

opments during the three years 1964–66 and compares them with the equally long period of 1961–63. The table is limited to the banking system (the central bank and deposit banks) and to thrift institutions and life insurance companies in most cases where they are important. Comparable data on these institutions are provided in the International

Monetary Fund's *International Financial Statistics,* while the collection of similar data for all other types of financial intermediaries which are included through 1963 in the basic tables would have required recourse to statistical publications and unpublished material of the individual countries. Even then it would have had to remain incomplete because of serious delays in publication of some of the figures in a substantial number of countries. The banking system, however, together with thrift institutions and life insurance companies, should be sufficient to give an idea of the trend of assets of all financial institutions during the years 1964–66.

The main result of this look at recent developments is that, notwithstanding substantial deviations in a few countries, the movement of the assets of financial intermediaries during the years 1964–66 has continued at the level of 1961–63 and thus has remained well above the level of the 1950s. This means that financial intermediaries have in most countries continued to expand at an historically rapid rate and have continued to grow about as rapidly as gross national product.

Table 8–9 permits a comparison of the development, during the 1960s for thirty-two countries,[12] by showing the ϕ ratios (change in assets divided by aggregate gross national product) for central and deposit banks, for time and savings deposits, for life insurance companies, and for these four types of institutions together.[13]

There is virtually no difference at all between the two

12. Three countries (Puerto Rico, Rhodesia, and U.S.S.R.) are excluded because they are not covered by *International Financial Statistics.*

13. The data on which Table 8–9 is based are not identical with, though very similar to, those used in Chapter 4. While the differences are substantial in a few cases, the averages are little affected by them. Thus the 1961–63 average for central banks of 1.53 in Table 8–9 compares well with 1.64 for the same thirty-two countries in the tables used in Chapter 4, and the difference is of the same relative size, though in the opposite direction (4.68 as against 4.41) for deposit banks.

triennial periods of 1961–63 and 1964–66 in the broadest measure—the ratio of the increase in the combined assets of the main types of financial institutions (central and deposit banks and, in most countries where they are of substantial importance, thrift institutions and life insurance companies) to gross national product. This ratio averaged nearly 8½ per cent in the twenty countries for which data are available,[14] both for 1961–63 and for 1964–66. Since the similar ratio in Chapter 4 had shown an increase by about one-fourth between 1949–60 and 1961–63, the failure of the ratio to increase further in 1964–66 may indicate a change in trend. It will take data for developments during a few more years, as well as a breakdown of the twelve-year period 1949–60, before the hypothesis that the upward trend in ϕ, which has been observed during most of the 1940s and 1950s but has come to a halt during the 1960's, can be confirmed or rejected.

Similarly, it will take data for a longer period and for a larger number of countries to decide whether the narrowing of the gap between developed and less developed countries from nearly 2½ percentage points in 1961–63 to not much over 1½ points in 1964–66, which resulted from a fractional decline in the ratio for the developed countries and a slight increase for the less developed ones, is enduring and significant.

Differences between the two periods were smallest for savings deposits and life insurance company assets, which usually show less short-term movement than the corresponding ratios for banks. The picture for the banking system is mixed, the ratio falling considerably for developed countries' central banks (mostly due to a sharp reduction in the case of Israel as inflation was throttled) and for deposit banks in less developed countries, largely reflecting slowing

14. The ratio is well below the ratio of 12.8 per cent of Table 4–6, mainly because the institutions for which *International Financial Statistics* reports assets on the average account for only about three-fourths of the assets of all financial institutions, omissions being particularly pronounced in the insurance sector.

down of inflationary bank credit expansion in Brazil and Yugoslavia.

The similarity between the 1964–66 and 1961–63 periods is also evidenced in the even distribution of countries in which the assets of financial institutions increased more or less rapidly than national product. Of the 130 ϕ ratios summarized in Table 8–9, sixty-eight increased and sixty-two decreased. The only instances in which the number of increases or decreases differed by more than two cases are the ratios for deposit banks. Here increases outnumbered decreases in the ratio of two to one for less-developed countries, while the opposite relationship prevailed among developed countries.

For the period 1961–63, the rate of growth of assets of the selected institutions included in the tabulations is in virtually all countries very close to that of all financial institutions that underlie the discussion in Chapter 4. There is no reason to assume that the parallelism would be less pronounced in the 1964–66 period. The conclusion derived from the incomplete data used in this section, viz. that the new issue ratios in 1964–66 were on the same level as in 1961–63 therefore probably also applies to all financial institutions. This fact, together with less comprehensive information for a smaller number of countries, provides a basis for the suggestion that on an international scale financial development in 1964–66 showed no substantial differences from the characteristics of the preceding three-year-period. The relationships discussed in more detail in Chapters 4 and 5 for 1961–63 may therefore be regarded as still valid in the late 1960s.

9 FINANCIAL DEVELOPMENT AND ECONOMIC GROWTH

This concluding chapter has two main functions. The first is to present a summary, primarily in the form of charts, of the evidence which has been set forth at length, although in scattered form, throughout Chapters 3 through 7 in support of the preliminary conclusions formulated in the final section of Chapter 1. The second is an attempt to relate the process of financial development, which is the main subject of this study, to modern economic growth.

GRAPHIC SUMMARY OF EVIDENCE[1]

The main features of the character of the financial superstructure and of the relationships of that superstructure to the real infrastructure were summarized without providing factual evidence in the sections on financial structure and development in Chapter 1. An attempt was made in Chapter 2 to formulate these relationships in terms of a simple model, while Chapters 3 through 8 produced as much statistical evidence on the character of financial structure and development in a number of countries as is possible, considering the as yet very deficient information and the even more unsatisfactory state of detailed analyses of financial development in individual countries. It is the purpose of this section to bring together the main findings of these

1. This section repeats in somewhat different form the findings of Chapters 3 through 7, in order to make them accessible to readers who may have skipped these chapters. This section cannot be well understood, however, unless Chapters 1 and 2 are read.

predominantly statistical chapters in the form of seven charts in order to summarize the evidence for readers who have not plowed through Chapters 3 to 8 and in order to provide a basis for very brief comments on some of the basic problems of financial structure and development on an international comparative scale.

Since we have used the financial interrelations ratio (FIR) —the value of all financial instruments outstanding divided by the value of national wealth—as the main single characteristic of the level of a country's financial development, and since the two main problems towards which this study has been oriented are the present differences in financial structure among countries and the trends in financial development over the past century, we shall start with two charts summarizing the evidence on these two points, fragmentary as it is. Thus, Chart 9–1 relates the current value of the financial interrelations ratio for eighteen countries to the level of economic development reflected in real national product per head, while Chart 9–2 shows the trend of the financial interrelations ratio over the past century for the four developed countries for which such figures can be obtained.

Chart 9–1 permits us to draw both positive and negative conclusions on the relationships between the financial interrelation ratio and the stage of economic development as far as it is reflected in gross national product per head at purchasing power equivalents, always keeping in mind the supplementary data presented in Chapters 3 through 7. The first conclusion, which is positive, is that at the present time developed countries do indeed have a higher FIR than less developed countries. This is true not only if we look at developed and less developed countries as two groups, but also to the extent that FIR is higher for each of the twelve developed nonsocialist countries than it is for any of the six less developed countries that are included in Chart 9–1. While we cannot yet calculate the value of FIR for a substantial number of other countries, enough is known about the size of their financial superstructure to make it fairly

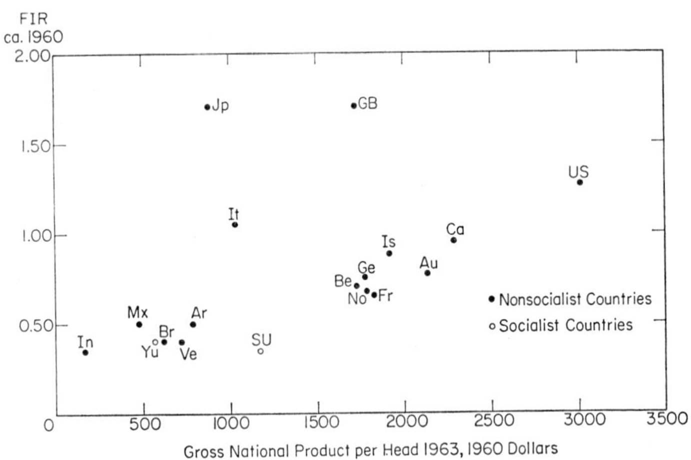

CHART 9-1.

FIR and Level of Real National Product per Head

Source: FIR, Table 7-8.

Country Abbreviations for Charts 9-1 and 9-5

Argentina	Ar	Israel	Is	Rhodesia	Rh
Australia	Au	Italy	It	South Africa	SA
Belgium	Be	Jamaica	Jm	Spain	Sp
Brazil	Br	Japan	Jp	Sweden	Sv
Canada	Ca	Mexico	Mx	Switzerland	Sw
Denmark	Dk	Netherlands	Ne	Thailand	Th
Egypt-U.A.R.	Eg	New Zealand	NZ	Trinidad	Tr
France	Fr	Nigeria	Ng	U.S.S.R.	SU
Germany	Ge	Norway	No	United States	US
Great Britain	GB	Pakistan	Pk	Venezuela	Ve
Greece	Gr	Philippines	PI	Yugoslavia	Yu
India	In	Puerto Rico	PR		

certain that these statements would hold, and would probably even be reinforced, if we had the information on a larger number of less developed countries. It is evident, however, from Chart 9–1 that the association, though certainly present, is only a loose and irregular one. Three countries (Japan, Great Britain, and Italy) have a much higher FIR than the level of their real product per head would lead one to expect and one (the Soviet Union) has not unpectedly a much lower one. The coefficient of determination (R^2) is 0.19, indicating that statistically real gross national product per head (1948 and 1963 average) accounts for only approximately one-fifth of the intercountry variations in FIR from the basic relationship.[2]

These facts, and similar relations of FIR with a few other presumably relevant independent variables, lead to the main negative conclusion, namely that real national product per head alone, or any other similarly simple indicator of the level of economic development, is unable to account for the observed values of FIR except within a rather wide range.[3] This conclusion is entirely in accord with the results

2. The regression equation, which is not significant at the 5 per cent level, is $\text{FIR} = \underset{(0.18)}{0.48} + \underset{(0.15)}{0.28}y$, where y is the 1948 and 1960 average of real gross national product per head in thousands of dollars of 1960 purchasing power. The equation is obviously unsatisfactory since an FIR of over 0.50 would be attributed to even an extremely poor country

3. Experimentation with a few simple other indicators (rate of change of real gross national product per head or price level in the period 1949–63) and separation of developed and less developed countries indicates that the correlations are statistically insignificant for all twelve developed countries included in Chart 9–1, but acquire some significance for either all the five less developed countries (of which four are in Latin America) or for the eight developed nonsocialist countries if Great Britain and Japan are excluded. Real income per head (average of 1948 and 1960) accounts, for instance, for about two-fifths of the variations in FIR for the five less developed nonsocialist countries and for nearly one-half for the eight developed nonsocialist countries. None of these, or similar, regressions can be regarded as very satisfactory. The first equation is $\text{FIR} = 0.341 + 0.183y$ ($R^2 = 0.39$); the second is $\text{FIR} = 0.419 + 0.264y$ ($R^2 = 0.48$), where y is real income per head, 1948 and 1960 average, in thousands of dollars of 1960 purchasing power. These equations indicate an FIR of 0.43 at an income level of $500 for less developed nonsocialist countries and one of 0.95 at an income level of $2,000 for the selected developed countries. If both regressions could be applied at an income level of $1,000, they would indicate a value of FIR of 0.52 on the basis of the regression for less developed and one of 0.68 on the basis of the selected developed countries.

of the theoretical approach taken in Chapter 2. It was there shown that FIR is essentially the result of three factors, the new issue ratio of nonfinancial sectors, the financial intermediation ratio, and the multiplier, the latter in turn depending on the rate of growth of real national product and the movements of the general price level. Since the multiplier does not seem to be systematically related to the level of national product per head, a close relationship of FIR to that level would depend on the relationships existing between (1) national product per head and the new issue ratio of nonfinancial sectors and (2) national product per head and the financial intermediation ratio. There is no doubt that both these ratios show some positive association with the level of real national product per head in the sense that they are generally higher for countries which have a high level of national product per head. The relationships, however, again are not very close ones, either when the two coefficients are taken alone and still less so when they are combined multiplicatively as is the case in the explanatory formula for FIR. What is more serious, the multiplier exercises a great influence on the value of FIR; and at least one of its components, the rate of change in the price level, is erratic even in the long run in the sense that it reflects the vicissitudes of individual countries, primarily sporadic wartime open or repressed inflations or secular open inflations. FIR at any given time therefore is strongly influenced by the path by which the country has reached its present position, particularly the path of the price level, but also the paths of the rate of growth of real product, of the new issues ratio of nonfinancial sectors, and of the financial intermediation ratio. FIR thus is a profoundly historical ratio. This does not mean that it cannot be explained in terms of a number of economically relevant factors, but only that the values and combination of the factors which together determine FIR vary sufficiently among countries, even among countries of similar economic level and structure, to produce in the end only a loose association—but a positive and undeniable association nevertheless—between

FIR and real gross national product per head or a similar simple measure of the level of economic development.

The positive though irregular association between the level of real national product per head and FIR, as well as the strong influence of historical accidents on the course of FIR, are corroborated in Chart 9–2, which shows the move-

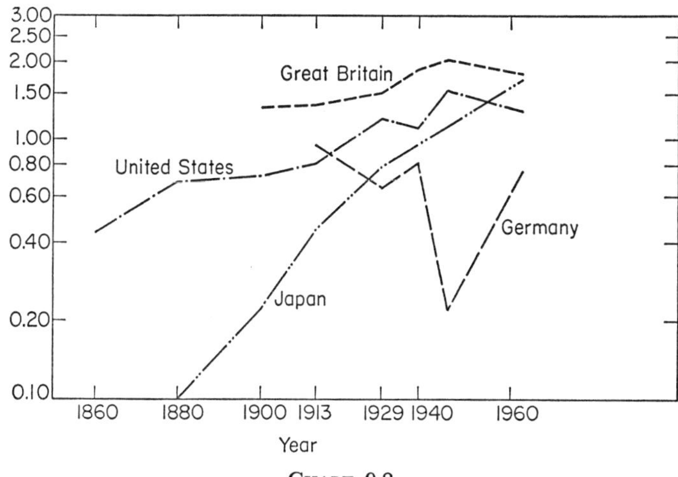

CHART 9-2.

The Trend of the Financial Interrelations Ratio in Four Countries, 1860–1963

Sources: Around 1963, Table 7-9; other years, rough estimates.

ments of FIR over the past century for four developed countries, the only ones for which the data are available—and some of these are very rough estimates—for at least half of the period. These four countries fortunately include the two financially leading nations (the United States and the United Kingdom), Japan (as an example of the only important country which, during the last century, has moved from a backward to a practically fully developed economy), and Germany (a country whose FIR was probably more affected by the vicissitudes of its political and economic history than any other non-Communist country).

If data were available for all four countries for the whole century they would in all cases show a substantial increase in FIR. As it is, the increase is evident in Chart 9–2 for the two countries for which the figures cover all or most of the century (the United States and Japan) and for the United Kingdom since the turn of the century. The trend of the German ratio, available only from 1913 on, is irregularly downward, but there is no doubt that the 1960 figure is well above that of 1860, even if one prefers not to risk an estimate of the latter's numerical value. Here again, however, the influence of the historical path of economic development is clearly evident. In the United States, which of all major countries has been least affected during the century by war and inflation, FIR approximately tripled between 1860 and the early 1960s, but almost all of the increase occurred before 1930. The movement in the United Kingdom is similar, but the level of FIR is well above that of the United States at the same calendar date. Japan's FIR, virtually zero at the time the country was opened to international intercourse, is now almost twenty times as high as it was in 1885, but even here the rate of increase in the value of FIR has slackened, if some irregular movements between benchmark dates are disregarded, particularly the temporary decline in FIR after World War II. The movements of the German ratio reflect the effects of hyperinflation following World War I and of the large-scale cutting down of debt following the repressed inflation of World War II.

What is probably the most important conclusion that can be drawn from Chart 9–2 is that even in the long run there is no close correlation between the rate of growth of real national product and of FIR, although again some positive association between the two magnitudes cannot be denied. Thus, of the four countries for which the figures are shown in Chart 9–2 for the last half-century, the two with the highest rate of growth of national product—the United States and particularly Japan—also show a more pronounced increase in FIR than do the other two countries. The association would probably be clearer if we had figures for the United Kingdom and Germany for the first half of the period. In that case the ranking of the four countries in accordance with the increase in FIR might coincide with the ranking of their rates of growth in real national product per head.[4]

Chart 9–2 also illustrates another important conclusion—viz. that the effects of temporary inflation, even at a very rapid rate, and of debt cut-down are short-lived. This is brought out most clearly in the movements of the curve for Germany, but it is also evident in the decline of FIR in the United States and the United Kingdom from the peak reached near the end of World War II.

The level of the financial interrelations ratio and its movements are of less importance for financial analysis than are the level and trends in the main elements, particularly in the two chief components of the aggregate new issue ratio, the ratios of the issues of nonfinancial sectors and of financial institutions to national product (δ and ϕ in terms of the symbols used in earlier chapters), and the financial intermediation ratio (δ/ϕ). Chart 9–3 therefore shows the relationship between the new issue ratio of domestic nonfinancial sectors and the rate of growth of real national product per head, both for the period 1949–63. This relationship has been illustrated rather than the relation of the issue ratio to the level of real national product per head since these two magnitudes do not seem to be closely connected. Even in the case of the rate of growth of real national product per head, the relationship to the value of the new issue ratio of nonfinancial sectors is not a close one. There is undoubtedly a tendency for the ratio to be positively associated with the rate of growth of real income per head during the postwar period, but the scatter is wide, and the country with the highest growth rate among the

4. The secular rates of growth of real national per head, from about 1860 to the early 1960s are 1.35 per cent per year for Great Britain, 1.50 for Germany, 1.60 for the United States, and 2.40 for Japan. (S. Kuznets, *Modern Economic Growth* [New Haven, Yale University Press, 1966], pp. 64–65.)

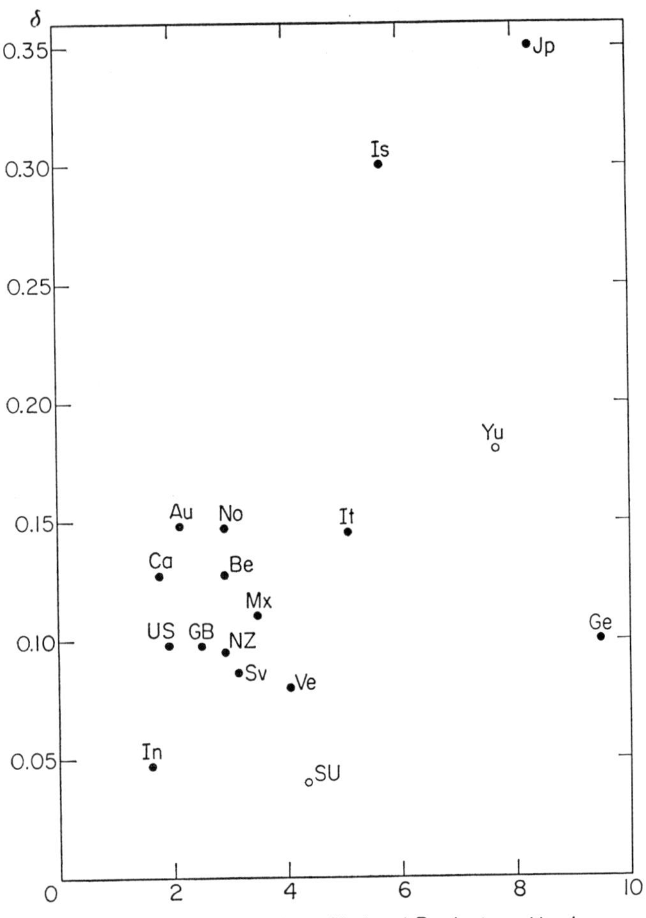

CHART 9-3.

Relation of New Issue Ratio of Nonfinancial Sectors (δ) to Rate of Growth of Real GNP per Head in the Postwar Period

Source: δ, Table 3-4.

seventeen countries included (Germany) shows a rather low value of the new issue ratio for nonfinancial sectors, a ratio reflecting the low value of these sectors' external financing ratio.

If we now turn to the movements of the new issue ratio for nonfinancial sectors, we find in Chart 9–4 no trend over the past one hundred years for the three Western countries for which we have at least approximate data. In the United States, the United Kingdom, and Germany the new issue ratio of nonfinancial sectors (including the foreign sector) has been at approximately the same level before World War I as well as during the 1920s and during the postwar period, i.e. in the neighborhood of one-tenth and one-eighth. There are, of course, some fluctuations in the ratio, some of which may be spurious since all estimates are rather rough ones, but none of them is very marked and none constitutes a definite trend. The picture is entirely different for Japan. Here also no marked trend is visible in the new issue ratio of nonfinancial sectors for the late nineteenth century, the period before World War I, and the 1920s, and the level of the ratio is very similar to that observed in Western countries. During the postwar period, however, Japan shows a ratio of approximately one-third, which is of an altogether different order of magnitude, whether compared to Japan's earlier experience or to the contemporary experience of other countries with the exception of Israel. In this case, a connection apparently exists between the rate of growth of real income per head and the level of the new issue ratio of nonfinancial sectors, but the fact that other countries have had similar rates of growth without similarly high rates of the new issue ratio of nonfinancial sectors (e.g. Germany in the postwar period) shows that such an association is not a necessary one, although its presence or absence can be explained in accordance with the basic formula by the level of the capital formation ratio, the external financing ratio, and the capital-output ratio.

The stability of the ratio of funds made available to domestic and foreign nonfinancial users to national product

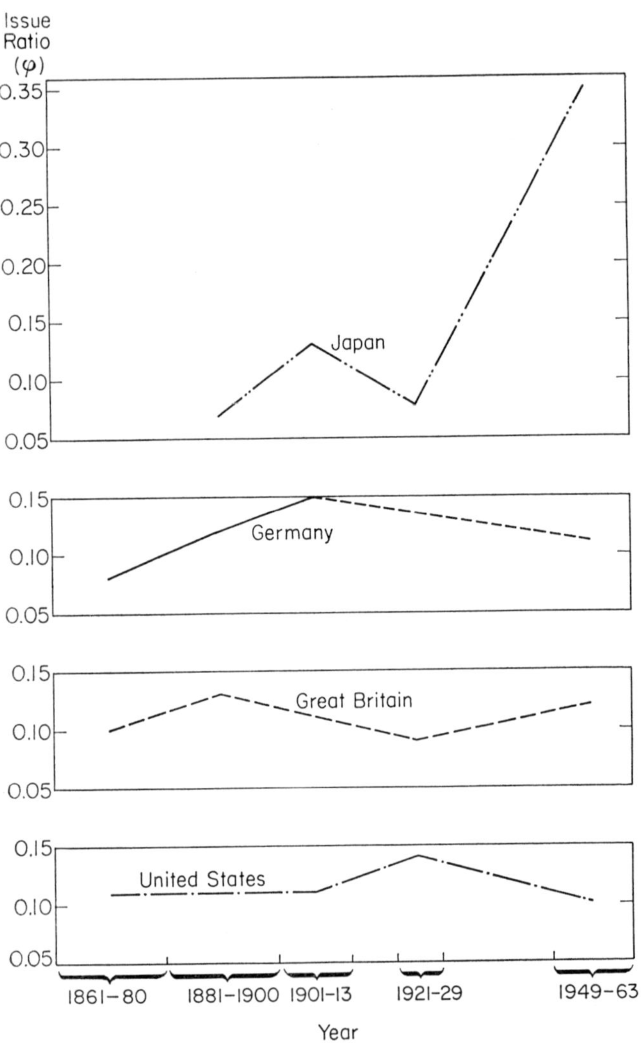

CHART 9-4.

The Trend of the Nonfinancial New Issue Ratio (δ) in Four Countries, 1860–1963

Sources: Tables 3-3 and 3-20.

and the additional similarity in the level of the ratio among the four developed Western countries as well for Japan (except for the period after World War II) seem rather remarkable. Both features are, of course, in part the result of similarities in the capital formation ratio and the external financing ratio, but because the new issue ratio of nonfinancial sectors is the result of these two distinct and not always similar factors, part of the absence of a trend and part of the similarity of the level of the ratio among countries is due to offsetting differences in the movement or in the level of the two components. The data are unfortunately too poor, particularly for the period before World War II, to permit an exploration of this subject in a manner befitting its importance, an exploration for which one would have to proceed from the highly aggregative figures used here to separate calculations for at least the main nonfinancial sectors.

The failure of the new issue ratios of nonfinancial sectors to show a clear association with the level of real income per head or with its rate of growth, or for that matter with other similarly simple measures of economic structure and development, either among a cross section of countries for the postwar period or in the trend for the few countries for which we can follow the movements, suggests that if more than a loose relationship exists (except, of course, the algebraic necessity for the net new issue ratio of nonfinancial sectors to be the product of the capital formation ratio and the external financing ratio), it is of a more complicated and as yet insufficiently understood nature.

Chart 9–5, a scatter diagram comparing the ratio of issues by financial institutions with the level of real national product per head (average of 1948 and 1963 values expressed in dollars of 1960 purchasing power) seems, at first sight, to lack any clear systematic feature. On closer inspection, however, two relationships appear. The first is fairly definite association between the ratio of issues of financial institutions (ϕ) and the level of real income per head for less developed countries, for which the ratio rises rapidly with the level of the income. Thus Spain, Greece, Argentina, and Puerto Rico all combine a value of ϕ in the order of 0.10 with an average real income of between \$500 and \$850. On the other hand, Nigeria, Pakistan, India, Thai-

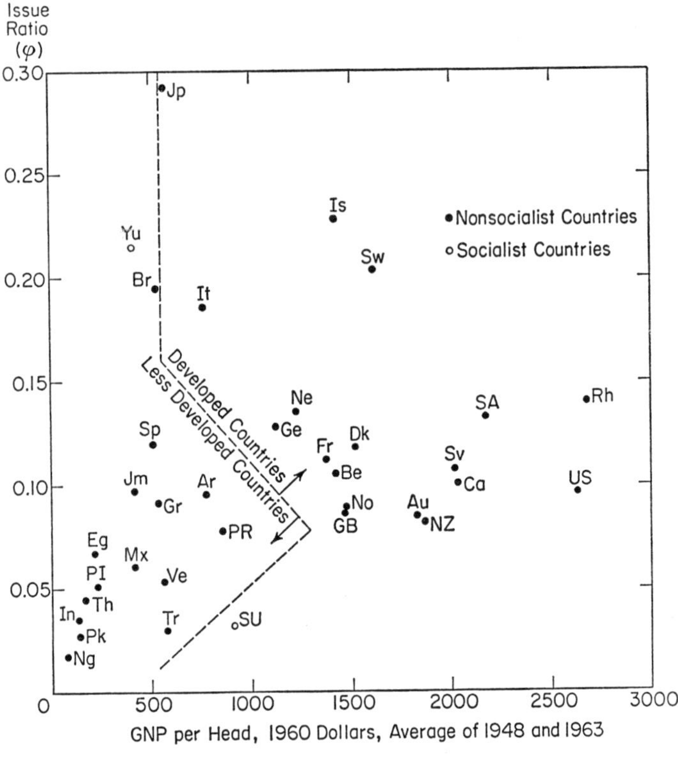

CHART 9-5.

Relation of New Issue Ratio of Financial Institutions (ϕ), 1949–63, to Level of Real GNP per Head, 1963 and 1948 Average

Source: φ, Table 4-7.

land, and the Philippines, with average incomes of less than \$200 all have a ratio of financial institutions' issues to national product of less than 0.03, while the ratio is in the order of 0.05 for Mexico and Jamaica, both of which have incomes of about $400. Even here, however, a few countries have considerably high values of ϕ (e.g. Brazil as a result of rapid inflation) or lower values (Venezuela and Trinidad) than would be expected on the basis of their income level. These irregularities among less developed countries nevertheless compare favorably with the picture presented by developed countries. Here the value of the new issue ratio of financial institutions seems to be quite unrelated to the level of income; twelve of the sixteen developed countries have a value of ϕ close to 0.10, although their average income per head ranges from about $1,000 to more than $2,500. Moreover, among the four countries for which value of ϕ is well above this level, three have the lowest income in the group (Japan, Italy, and Israel) while the fourth (Switzerland) falls in the middle range of incomes. These relationships point to the fact that among developed countries the level of national product is not an important factor in determining the level of financial institutions' issue ratio—barring rapid inflation—but that this ratio depends rather on the rate of growth of national product, on the new issue ratio of nonfinancial sectors and even more on the financial intermediation ratio. However, even if these factors are taken into account, they leave unexplained a considerable part of the differences existing among developed countries in the level of ϕ during the postwar period, a situation which is discussed in the final section of Chapter 4 and in Appendix III.

The existence of a definite though rather weak association between the financial institutions' issue ratio and the level of real national product per head, visually evident in Chart 9–3 is confirmed by the calculation of simple correlation coefficients, the results of which are summarized in Table 9–1. Hardly any correlation is evident if developed and less developed countries are merged, though the correlation is slightly higher if ϕ is regressed on the logarithm of real gross national product per head than on its original value, particularly if the two planned economy countries are omitted. When developed countries are separated from less developed countries the coefficients increase substantially, although they do so considerably more for developed than for less developed countries. For developed countries, gross national product per head alone explains nearly two-fifths of the intercountry variations in ϕ if the semilogarithmic form of the relationship is used, and both the constant term of the equation and the slope of the regression line are significant at the one per cent level. What may be astonishing is that the association is negative rather than positive, i.e. the higher a developed country's real national product per head, the lower its financial institutions' issue ratio in the 1949–63 period. This is the result of the extraordinarily high new issue ratios of Japan and Israel (both countries

TABLE 9–1

Correlations between Financial Institutions' New Issue Ratio 1949–63 (ϕ)[a] and Real Gross National Product per Head (y)[b]

	R^2	F
ALL 35 COUNTRIES		
1. $\phi_1 = 8.34^{**} + 0.00213y$	0.06	2.14
$\quad (1.86) \quad (0.00146)$		
2. $\phi_2 = -6.84 + 2.63^{*} \log_e y$	0.15	5.30
$\quad (7.50) \quad (1.12)$		
33 COUNTRIES EXCLUDING SOVIET UNION AND YUGOSLAVIA		
1. $\phi_3 = 7.76^{**} + 0.00252y$	0.10	3.25
$\quad (1.82) \quad (0.00140)$		
2. $\phi_4 = -9.17 + 2.96^{**} \log_e y$	0.20	7.92
$\quad (7.04) \quad (1.05)$		
18 DEVELOPED COUNTRIES EXCLUDING SOVIET UNION		
1. $\phi_5 = 22.00^{**} - 0.00523^{*}y$	0.26	5.68
$\quad (3.76) \quad (0.00219)$		
2. $\phi_6 = 80.94^{**} - 9.20^{**} \log_e y$	0.39	10.26
$\quad (21.08) \quad (2.87)$		
15 LESS DEVELOPED COUNTRIES EXCLUDING YUGOSLAVIA		
1. $\phi_7 = 2.94 + 0.00937y$	0.25	4.23
$\quad (2.15) \quad (0.00456)$		
2. $\phi_8 = -13.47 + 3.48^{*} \log_e y$	0.30	5.64
$\quad (8.60) \quad (1.09)$		

[a] Change in assets of financial institutions between 1948 and 1963 as per cent of aggregate gross national product from 1949 through 1963.
[b] Average of 1948 and 1963 net income per head in thousands of U.S. dollars of 1960 purchasing power.
* Significant at 5 per cent level. ** Significant at 1 per cent level.

with a relatively low real income per head) as well as of the relatively low issue ratio of the United States and Canada. Among less developed countries, the association is, as expected, positive, but it is much less well established statistically (high ratio of standard error to coefficient), and the slope of the regression is considerably flatter, at least in the semilogarithmic form which yields more satisfactory results for both groups of countries.

The relationships expressed in the equations of Table 9–1 can, of course, be regarded only as descriptions of the specific situation existing in the postwar period. They cannot be used as indications of a causal relationship running from the level of real income per head to the level of the issue ratio of financial institutions, a relationship that would also be valid for other periods or for considerably different groupings of countries. Indeed, the similar but more systematic correlations reviewed in Appendix III make it abundantly clear that the relations between the level of real income per head and ϕ have varied considerably over time and that the level of real income per head alone generally explains only a modest fraction of intercountry variations in ϕ.

The picture is clearer when we turn to the trend in the ratio of financial institutions' issues to national product. We then see in Chart 9–6 a definite upward movement in ϕ in both the group of developed countries, for which figures go back to the mid-nineteenth century, and the group of less developed countries, for which the trend can be followed only since the beginning of this century. For developed countries, we observe two periods of sharp increases in the ratio. The first extends from the middle of the nineteenth century to World War I; during this period the value of ϕ doubled from approximately 3.5 to 7 per cent. The second period, dominated by World War II, again leads to a doubling of the level and, what is more important, the maintenance of this level during the postwar period. For less developed countries, no continuous trend appears. There is only one sharp step upward, again during the

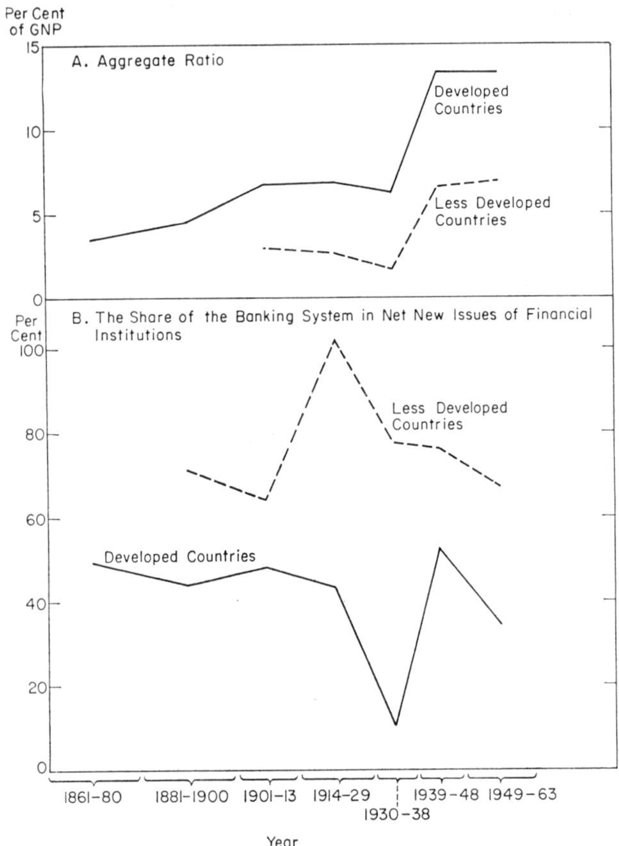

CHART 9-6.

The Financial Institutions' New Issue Ratio (ϕ) in Nonsocialist Developed and Less Developed Countries, 1860–1963

Source: Table 5-22.

1940s, from the level of only 2–3 per cent (which prevailed from the turn of the century to the late 1930s) to a level of 8–9 per cent (in the 1940s and 1950s).

The upward trend in ϕ is accompanied in the case of developed countries by an irregular downward movement in the share of the banking system in the total issues of all financial institutions, a trend which results in a reduction from a level of about one-half between 1860 and World War II to one of less than two-fifths in the period after World War II. In the case of less developed countries, a drop from the 1940s to the postwar period is also evident, although it is less pronounced than for developed countries, but the movement during the first half of the century is

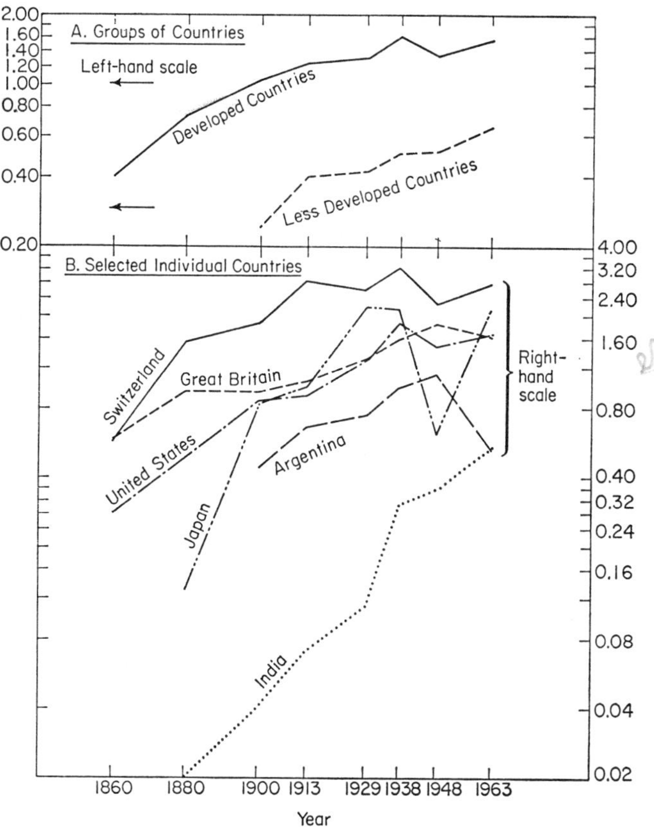

CHART 9-7.

The Ratio of Financial Institutions' Assets to GNP (Φ), 1860–1963

Sources: Tables 4-12 and 4-13.

irregular. The upward trend in ϕ and the downward movement in the share of the banking system's issues, illustrated in Chart 9–6 on the basis of the experience of about two dozen countries, are found in virtually all countries in both groups.

We conclude with a simple chart showing a well-defined movement—the ratio of the assets of financial institutions to national product. This ratio, illustrated in the upper half of Chart 9–7, shows an almost continuous upward movement since the middle of the nineteenth century for both developed and less developed countries. In the case of developed countries, the speed of the upward movement has been declining from the beginning, while no similar tendency is as yet visible for the less developed countries. This is not astonishing since the absolute value of the ratio of financial institutions' assets to national product in less developed countries in 1963 is still below the ratio observed in developed countries in 1880. The lower part of Chart 9–7 illustrates the trend for six of the most important developed and less developed countries and shows that there is a fairly common tendency of movement among them. The two apparent exceptions, the decline in the ratio for Japan between 1938 and 1948 and that for Argentina between 1948 and 1963, reflect rapid inflation and thus confirm the deductions from the basic formula.

FINANCIAL DEVELOPMENT AND MODERN ECONOMIC GROWTH

One of the most important problems in the field of finance, if not the single most important one, almost everyone would agree, is the effect that financial structure and development have on economic growth. Does it make a measurable difference in the speed and character of economic growth how large a country's financial superstructure is compared to its national wealth and product; how rapidly and regularly the financial superstructure expands in nominal and real terms; how much of a country's investment is financed externally through the issuance of financial instruments rather than internally out of investors' own saving or through involuntary transfer like taxation; what types of financial instruments exist; what are their relative importance and penetration throughout the economy; what are the character, the methods of operation, the degree of specialization and concentration, and the geographic distribution of financial institutions; and whether financial institutions are owned or operated privately, cooperatively, or by the government?

These questions and many others directed toward the nature of the financial superstructure and of changes in it are easy to pose, but most questioners are unaware how difficult and precarious the answers are, both methodologically and factually. Some of the reasons should have become evident in the course of the preceding eight chapters. Others will become clear in the next few pages.

To assess the role of financial development and structure in economic growth we may turn, depending on our philosophical predilections, to economic theory or to economic history. We shall unfortunately find that in the present state of the theory of economic growth and with the present lack of sufficiently intensive historical studies of financial development we cannot get definite answers from either discipline. The reader who is looking for simple, unambiguous, and enduring solutions may as well, therefore, stop here.

Some Theoretical Considerations

Turning first to economic theory, it is not difficult to make a case for the hypothesis that the separation of the functions of saving and investment, which is made possible by the introduction of financial instruments (though commodity money may already permit the few first halting steps in this direction), as well as the enlargement of the range of financial assets, which follows from the creation of financial institutions, increase the efficiency of investment and raise the ratio of capital formation to national product; and that financial activities through these two channels increase the rate of growth, assuming industrial and financial technology, consumers' tastes, and attitudes toward risk to remain unchanged.

This conclusion is based on two main assumptions. The first assumption, hardly in need of verification, is that the members of an economic community differ in their ability to combine factors of production and to utilize assets acquired by saving or inheritance, in their attitude toward uncertainty, and in the value they put on future compared to present utilities. The second, equally self-evident, assumption is the existence of economies of scale within a producing unit and of externalities within the economy, i.e., the fact that not all, and probably not many, production functions are homogeneous of degree zero.

Once these assumptions are accepted, it is evidently possible to increase output, without changes in resources, technology, tastes, and attitudes toward risk, by a division of work in which some units—those with less entrepreneurial ability and with a higher degree of risk aversion—save more than they invest, while others invest more than they save, the excess saving being transferred to investors through financial instruments.

The theoretical justification for the existence of a financial superstructure and for the presumption that it facilitates and accelerates economic growth is thus similar to the textbook argument regarding the advantages of indirect exchange over barter, an advantage realized by the introduction and increasing use of money, initially commodity money and then paper money, as the first and most important financial instrument in theory and probably also in history. Indirect exchange vastly enlarges the circle of potential buyers and sellers and of potential transactions, eliminating the need for every buyer and seller to find a partner for the same object at the same place and at the same time, given the very limited possibilities of long-distance barter trade and of intertemporal barter.

In a parallel manner the creation of the whole gamut of financial instruments frees households and other economic units from the indissoluble tie between their own saving (nonconsumed income) and their investment (expenditures on durable assets). In the absence of financial instruments each unit's saving is necessarily equal to its investment. Once financial instruments exist, a unit's investment may be larger or smaller than its saving. This is where the importance of nonmonetary financial instruments lies, as saving not invested within the unit will now yield income and will thus provide an incentive to saving in excess of the sterile accumulation of money.

These facts, however, are not sufficient to prove that the introduction of financial instruments will accelerate economic growth. That hypothesis requires at least two additional prerequisites. The first is the unequal distribution of entrepreneurial opportunities and abilities among the population, whether along the normal curve or following any other differentiating distribution function. If all individuals were equally able investors, i.e. if they obtained the same rate of return from the capital expenditures they made, the separation of the function of saving and investment and the transfer of savings from one unit to another for investment by the latter would not increase national product or accelerate economic growth. Once such inequalities exist, the process of separating saving and investment will, or at least can, have positive effects on economic growth, and can continue until the (discounted) rate of (expected) net return of all investing units has been equalized.

The unequal distribution of the opportunity and ability to invest is strongly reinforced as an accelerator of growth by the indivisibility of many investments, often those promising high returns. It is theoretically possible, and evident in practice, that the volume of saving required for many production processes, if they are to operate at the minimum cost level, is far in excess of the saving of any one economic unit except possibly the central government. Such large investments become possible only through forcible appropriation of part of the income of many units by means of taxation (including the forced saving of inflation) or by tribute and similar noneconomic means, or voluntarily through the use of financial instruments which transfer saving from a large number of savers to a small number of investors. Indeed, the indivisibility of investments of potentially high return might accelerate economic growth through the introduction of financial instruments even in the absence of the unequal distribution of opportunities and abilities among economic units. Here again the positive effect of the use of financial instruments on economic growth may be expected to continue until the expected return from such "large" investments, after due allowance for the cost of financial intermediation, is reduced to the level of return on "small" investments that are within the reach of individual economic units.

These arguments are relevant chiefly to what have been called primary financial instruments, i.e. debt issues and equity securities of nonfinancial economic units such as business enterprises, households, and governments. Another set of considerations argues that an additional impetus to economic growth is given by the operation of financial institutions—economic units whose assets conceptually consist exclusively, and in practice are made up predominantly, of primary financial instruments and money and which issue secondary financial instruments (e.g. deposits, insurance contracts, and their own equity securities) that are held for the most part by nonfinancial units and to a lesser extent by other financial institutions.

The argument here is that in many situations indirect financing through financial institutions is more efficient than direct financing through the issuance of primary securities. Since conceptually financial institutions neither save nor invest, and actually do so to only a small extent, the growth-inducing effect of financial institutions can come only from one of two sources. The first is the increase of the aggregate volume of investment and saving beyond what it would have been in the absence of financial institutions when savers and investors would have been limited to direct financing. The second is the increase in the marginal rate of return on investment that results from a more efficient allocation of saving among potential investments, the reallocation reflecting the operation of financial institutions.

As the introduction of primary securities cuts the umbilical cord between a unit's saving and its investment and enables capital expenditures anywhere in the economy to be financed by saving everywhere else, at least theoretically, so the introduction of financial institutions and of the secondary securities issued by them as well as of the financial assets acquired by them severs the direct connection between an individual saver and an individual investor or an individual item of capital expenditure.

The interposition of financial institutions in the process of saving and investment does not, it is true, necessarily increase the total volume of saving and investment. It will do so only to the extent that secondary issues of securities are not simply substitutes for primary issues. There are, however, good theoretical reasons and some empirical evidence to support the hypothesis that part of secondary issues—the proportion varying from case to case—elicits saving and permits capital expenditures that would not have come into existence if economic units had been limited in their choice of uses and sources of funds to primary securities.

In addition, the interposition of financial institutions may change the allocation of funds among alternative sources and particularly among alternative uses even within a given total. This possibility rests on the fact that financial institutions may finance other types of capital expenditures, differing in form, durability, industry, location, or any other characteristic, from the distribution that would have obtained if primary securities had been the only way of financing capital expenditures in excess of own saving and the only outlet for saving in excess of own investments. The effect of financial institutions on economic growth must therefore be investigated from the point of view of both the total volume and the allocation of saving and investment.

The existence and importance of secondary securities issued by financial institutions in addition to primary securities issued by business enterprises, governments, and households depends on the preference that some lenders have under certain conditions for secondary over primary securities and on the preferences, again in certain situations, of some borrowers for financial institutions rather than nonfinancial units as sources of funds. These choices between primary and secondary securities, i.e. between direct and indirect financing, can be understood only if it is kept in mind that any financial asset represents a bundle of utilities and costs and that the evaluation of the several utilities and costs attached to the various types of primary and secondary securities by potential lenders and borrowers determines the extent to which these various instruments are used.

Among the most important factors that affect the choice of lenders and borrowers are the expected yield of the instrument—average level, variability, certainty, and responsiveness to changes in taxes and in the purchasing power of money; the cost and ease of acquisition and sale for the lender and of incurrence and redemption for the borrower; and the accumulation motives of savers. On almost all these points financial institutions have an advantage as borrowers or lenders in comparison with all nonfinancial units with the possible exception of the central government.[5]

Claims against financial institutions are generally easier to liquidate (i.e. to turn into cash without or with only insignificant delay, formality, and cost) that are primary debt securities. They have the additional great advantage of being completely divisible, whereas primary securities are usually issued in fixed amounts and often in amounts that make them very inconvenient for purchase and sale when lenders have small resources and when numerous individual purchase and sale transactions are involved. Some types of claims against financial institutions, particularly insurance

5. Cf. R. W. Goldsmith, *Financial Intermediaries* (New York: National Bureau of Economic Research, 1958, mimeo.), Appendix H.

organizations, have advantages, e.g. insurance protection, which cannot or are not easily provided by primary securities. Most financial institutions are better known and, rightly or wrongly, regarded as better risks than otherwise comparable primary securities, possibly again excluding the central government, given all the advantages financial institutions have as debtors.

What is the relevance of these characteristics of secondary compared to primary securities for economic growth?

It is obvious that from the point of view of the lender primary securities are not perfect substitutes for secondary securities nor is the issuance of primary securities to nonfinancial lenders a perfect substitute for their sale to financial institutions. The question remains, however, whether in actuality the volume of issues of primary securities, and hence the volume of capital expenditures in excess of the investor's own saving, is the same whether or not financial institutions operate. It is very difficult to visualize a situation in which the aggregate volume of primary securities issued would not be smaller if there were no financial institutions in operation. This is more evident from the point of view of nonfinancial lenders. It is almost certain that there exists a fringe of lenders, particularly households, who would save less if there were no secondary securities among the financial assets to choose from. To some extent this is a matter of yield, so that the volume of saving might be the same while the reservation price (the marginal interest rate demanded by lenders) would be higher, with the result that the aggregate volume of saving and investment would remain unaffected, though only if the demand for funds were extremely elastic in that neighborhood. There is little doubt, however, that there is a fraction of current income of households, size admittedly unknown but certainly little sensitive to interest rates, that can be attracted to secondary securities but not into primary securities, apart even from the volume of voluntary or involuntary saving that takes the form of increasing money stocks. These assets constitute additions to aggregate saving and hence permit additional capital expenditures.[6]

Irrespective of whether or not the existence and development of a financial superstructure increases the aggregate volume of saving and investment and thus accelerates the rate of economic growth beyond what it otherwise would have been, there is no doubt that it results in a different allocation of capital expenditures among and within sectors, types of tangible assets, and regions. From a practical point of view this influence on the distribution of capital expenditures may be of more significance for economic development than the possible effect of the operations of the financial superstructure on aggregate saving and investment.

Such a reallocation is, as has already been indicated, the necessary concomitant of the operation of a financial superstructure, both at the level of direct financing through primary securities and at that of indirect financing through financial institutions. To evaluate the possible or probable influence of the financial superstructure it is necessary to consider the directions which this reallocation of capital expenditures is likely to take and to speculate upon what difference the reallocation is likely to make in relative yields and in rates of economic development.[7]

Theoretical considerations, then, lead to the conclusion that the existence of a financial superstructure, particularly one that is not limited to the issuance of fiduciary money, will have a tendency toward equilization of the marginal yield of investment on different types of capital expendi-

6. Those offended by this implied primacy of saving may reformulate the statement to say that the preference for secondary securities by some units reduces the amount of forced saving for a given increase in the price level.

7. It should be recalled that the discussion always proceeds on the assumption of reallocation of a given aggregate of capital expenditures, without consideration of either the effect of the financial superstructure on the total volume of capital expenditures or the possible uses of methods other than external financing, such as the investors' own saving, taxation, and other involuntary sources of finance, including inflation.

tures. In doing so it will tend to increase the share of capital expenditures made by business enterprises and governments on large projects and to reduce the share of relatively small projects by households. This will, of course, increase the share of the types of structures and equipment and of industries in which large projects are of above-average importance and will reduce the share of other types and of other industries. There will be similar effects on the regional distribution of capital expenditures, although these will generally be less pronounced since the relative importance of projects favored by the existence of a financial superstructure is likely to differ less among regions than among industries and among types of tangible assets. At least one exception to this statement must be noted: capital expenditures abroad. There is little doubt that the existence of a financial superstructure, and here particularly the operation of financial institutions, tends to increase the relative importance of foreign investment in both lending and borrowing countries.

It is difficult to make more specific deductions about the reallocation of capital expenditures since these will be strongly influenced by the country's economic structure and by the size and character of the financial superstructure and often will be affected also by the regulations under which financial institutions operate. This is true with respect to the positive or negative influence of the financial superstructure on the share of the government, housing, agriculture, large and small business enterprises, consumer durables, and foreign borrowers in capital expenditures.

The influence is probably particularly marked in the case of the government, and here especially in connection with financing the government's deficit spending, primarily for military expenditures and secondarily for current deficits. Such financing has little parallel in other sectors of a modern economy, although it is of great importance in the form of household borrowing for consumption purposes in earlier stages of economic development. There are two opposing tendencies at work here. On the one hand, the existence of a developed financial superstructure, and particularly of financial institutions, greatly facilitates borrowing by the government. On the other, this very facility makes it less necessary to have recourse to taxation and other involuntary levies that do not use the financial mechanism to cover deficits. The net result will usually be an increase in the share of aggregate saving that is absorbed by the government.

These influences of the financial superstructure on the real infrastructure vary greatly from country to country and change substantially over time. It is only by intensive case studies that such influences can be traced in a specific situation and only by an accumulation of such case studies that their prevalence and their role in economic development on the direction of causation between the financial superstructure and the real infrastructure can be made plausible.

The theoretical discussion of the effects of the financial superstructure on economic development may then be condensed, with some but not a decisive loss of accuracy, into one statement: The financial superstructure, in the form of both primary and secondary securities, accelerates economic growth and improves economic performance to the extent that it facilitates the migration of funds to the best user,[8] i.e. to the place in the economic system where the funds will yield the highest social return.

The real difficulties with this formulation arises in the definition of "highest social return" in its relation to externalities, both economies of scale and uncompensated losses and benefits; monopoly and oligopoly; imperfections of information and foresight; and the shape of the social welfare function. These difficulties, however, are common to all welfare economics and indeed to all economic theory. It is a matter of opinion, but of opinion reinforced by theoretical considerations and empirical observation, that the

8. I am adapting the phrase from a well-known principle ("Wanderung des Bodens zum besten Wirt") enunciated long ago by Aereboe for agricultural land. I have been unable to trace the phrase in a rapid check, but a passage in *Agrarpolitik* (Paul Parey, Berlin, 1928), p. 506, contains the sense if not the words.

actual operation of the financial superstructure has, in most countries and in most periods, aided this migration and thus has accelerated economic growth. There have certainly, however, been exceptions—probably the greatest and most common being the financing of military expenditures. What is more serious for economists, we have not yet succeeded in developing reliable methods to measure the extent and the results of this facilitating function of finance, to determine the optimal size of the financial superstructure in relation to the real infrastructure of the economy, and to distinguish effectively the contribution of different forms of financial structure to economic growth.

Some Historical Evidence

Generalizations about the influence of financial development on economic growth cannot well be expected from those economic historians, probably the majority of the profession, who continue to regard their task as "ideographic," in Rickert's terminology.[9] But even if one is prepared to essay such generalizations one is faced with the absence of sufficiently intensive analysis of the problem even for individual countries and for limited periods and the often contradictory conclusions of the specialized literature that exists for some countries and periods. It is therefore not astonishing that few economic historians have been willing to commit themselves to generalizations on this difficult problem. To make matters worse, economic historians have devoted most of their attention in this field to the early part of the modern period, say before 1870, in Western and Central Europe, i.e. to the period when financial institutions were relatively small even in now developed countries and during which they were entirely dominated by commercial banks, and they have but rarely dealt intensively with what is probably the crucial period in financial development in Western countries, from the 1870s to World War I, let

9. H. Rickert, *Die Grenzen der naturwissenschaftlichen Begriffsbildung* (Tübingen, 1902).

alone with developments during the last half-century and with nonbanking financial institutions.

Though it is often difficult to be certain to exactly what countries and periods a specific generalizing statement on the relationship between financial development and economic growth refers, it seems fairly clear that some of the economists and historians who have concerned themselves with the problems are inclined to attribute an important and implicitly causal role to financial institutions, primarily commercial banks, while others are doubtful about such influence or deny it.[10] Virtually all authors, however, agree that the situation has differed greatly as between countries and periods and that no far-reaching generalizations are possible.

The students inclined to ascribe a positive, growth-inducing role to financial institutions—at least in some specific situations—such as Cameron,[11] Cameron and Patrick,[12] Gerschenkron,[13] and many German authors led by Schumpeter, seem to have been primarily influenced by developments in Central European countries during the second half of the nineteenth century and in Japan. The more negative attitude of other authors, particularly Gurley,[14] appears to be the result of concentration of attention on non-European countries and on more recent periods.[15]

10. Cameron and Patrick conclude that "Most economists regard financial institutions as a passive factor," an attitude that they feel "disposes of a complex matter far too summarily." (*Banking in the Early Stages of Industrialization* [New York, 1967], p. 8.)

11. Chapter IX.

12. Chapter I.

13. A. Gerschenkron, *Economic Backwardness* (Cambridge, 1962), e.g. pp. 12ff., 45.

14. J. C. Gurley, *American Economic Review* (1967), pp. 950ff.

15. Tilly, however, concludes that "financial factors explain neither the overall economic movements nor the specific developments of individual economic sectors. Differences in the process of industrialization cannot be explained by differences in monetary or banking institutions." (*Banking in the Early Stages of Industrialization,* p. 477.) Borchardt expresses himself even more categorically in a similar vein: "The extension of the net of credit is obviously not a conditio sine qua non of

The conclusions are in many cases expressed with hesitation and in no case are they based on an intensive quantitative study of the role of financial institutions and instruments in the process of economic growth. Indeed, it is not unfair to characterize virtually all of the statements on the causal relationship, if any, between financial development and economic growth as impressionistic. This is not astonishing since it is extremely hard to isolate the role of any one single factor in the process of economic growth, particularly of a factor like a country's financial structure, which is extremely difficult to quantify in its manifold ramifications throughout the economy. To add to the difficulties, the theoretical framework on which empirical investigations and case studies could appropriately be based has been put together only during the past decade and even now is far from fully developed.[16]

---

economic development." (*Jahrbücher für Nationalökonomie und Statistik, 173* [1961], 415.)

A statement on Sweden is particularly interesting because it differentiates between primary and secondary financing: "For the first 30 or 40 years industrial take off went on very nicely with a financial structure almost altogether lacking commercial bank credits and bonds. . . . So during the Swedish take off financial institutional form did not matter very much." (T. Gårdlund, cited in W. Stolper, *Planning Without Facts* [Cambridge, 1966], p. 233.)

Conclusions may be easier to reach regarding the more sporadic and less extensive developments in the financial sphere before the industrial revolution. Thus it is claimed that "the Medici Bank contributed little to economic growth, and its funds instead of being invested productively were mainly used to finance either conspicuous consumption of royal courts or military campaigns." (R. de Roover, *The Rise and Decline of the Medici Bank 1397–1494* [New York, 1966], p. 374.)

16. A recently published study (I. Adelman and C. T. Morris, *Society, Politics and Economic Development* [Baltimore, Johns Hopkins Press, 1967]) provides some additional information on the connection between some aspects of financial structure and development on the one hand and the level and movement of gross national product per head and about three dozen political, social, and economic factors on the other. The investigation covers over 70 countries, but excludes the developed countries in Europe and North America, though including South Africa, Israel, and Japan, which by financial criteria belong to

It may be worthwhile nevertheless to look briefly at the case that has often been regarded as the classical example of the influence of differences in financial structures in two countries on their rate of economic growth—the United Kingdom and Germany in the half-century before World War I. During that period, and particularly during the second half of it, German economic expansion was felt to

---

the developed group. The two financial factors considered, labeled "Level of Effectiveness of Financial Institutions, 1961" and "Degree of Improvement in Financial Institutions since 1950," are essentially based on the ratio of the level and of the increase in money and bank deposits to gross national product and on the gross domestic saving ratio.

It is difficult to summarize the results of the numerous factor analyses that constitute the core of the study. Possibly the best way is to look at the value of the factor loadings for the two financial factors, particularly in comparison to those for other economic, social, and political factors included in the analysis. It then appears that the factor loadings for both financial factors are usually in the upper half of the comparable values for all three dozen factors. The level of financial development usually is in the top quartile, but that for the change never is. Factor loadings are generally higher, both in absolute value and in rank, for the countries with high incomes (mostly Latin American countries, but also Greece, Israel, and Japan) and intermediate incomes (mostly Middle Eastern and Asian countries) than they are for the low income (mostly African) countries, but the difference is more pronounced for the "level" than for the "improvement" factor. For low income countries financial factors, just as most other economic factors, do not help to explain differences in the rate of growth in the postwar period. In contrast, these as well as other economic factors contribute substantially to an explanation of such differences for intermediate and still more so for high income less developed countries.

We may thus conclude that in the postwar period and among generally less developed countries the level of financial development—at least as evaluated by the two authors—has been associated fairly closely, compared to other economic and noneconomic factors, with differences in the level and the rate of growth of real national product per head and that the intensity of the association has been more pronounced for the countries with relatively higher incomes. This association, of course, does not say anything about the existence or direction of causation nor does it justify extending the conclusions to developed countries or to periods before World War II.

be more rapid than British, and Germany was regarded as making inroads on Britain's position as the leading industrial producer and exporter. These developments were often attributed, both by popular and professional opinion, to differences in the financial structure of the two countries, particularly to differences in the operation of their banking systems, although the process was hardly ever documented in detail.[17]

Throughout this period the German commercial banks combined the short-term loan and demand deposit business, to which the British banks essentially limited themselves, with credits that in effect were medium-term and with participation in the security issues of their clients, both as intermediating investment bankers and as temporary holders of the new securities—a development that has been called "the German path to industrialization." [18] This readier access to bank credit of more than short duration and to the securities market and the concomitant ease of supplementing internal with external sources of financing enabled German industry, so the argument ran, to expand more rapidly than its British competitors.[19] The closer relationship between banks

17. A statement by two leading German economists—Adolf Wagner and Franz Oppenheimer—may be regarded as fairly representative of the more moderate professional opinion. Wagner and Oppenheimer asserted that "the clumsiness and backwardness of British banking and of the organization of the London stock exchange" were "one of the more important causes . . . why Great Britain had to lose out to the more powerful German competition." (C. W. von Wieser, *Der Finanzielle Aufbau der Englischen Industrie* [Jena, 1919], Foreword, p. vi.) It might be kept in mind that Wagner and Oppenheimer wrote this sentence in 1916 in the middle of World War I.

18. K. Borchardt, in *Jahrbücher für Nationalökonomie und Statistik, 173* (1961), 416.

19. While less specific, obiter dicta about the decisive causative influence of the German financial system, essentially the large mixed banks, on the growth of German industry and trade are common in the literature. Cf. e.g. W. O. Henderson, *The Industrial Revolution in Europe 1815–1914* (Liverpool, 1954), p. 62, and P. B. Whale, *Joint Stock Banking in Germany* (London, 1930), p. 328.

and industry also had the advantage, it was claimed, of fostering the concentration movement among producers, thus reducing cost and increasing market power.

As a result of more recent statistical studies of the economic development of the United Kingdom and Germany, the thema probandum unfortunately has almost disappeared. If economic development is measured by the growth in real national product per head, then the rate of growth of the two countries was not much different, about 1.55 per cent per year per head for Germany against 1.35 per cent for the United Kingdom, for the half-century from 1850 to 1913, the longest period for which estimates are available for both countries and also the span that is most relevant for the comparison as it covers the entire period during which German commercial banks operated and German industry reached international importance.[20]

During the second half of the period from 1880 to 1913 the rate of growth was considerably higher in Germany, with 1.65 per cent per year, than in the United Kingdom, with less than 1.10 per cent, it is true. In the preceding 30 years, however, the position was reversed, the British rate of 1.65 per cent being slightly ahead of the German rate of 1.55 per cent.

Since modern economic development started earlier in the United Kingdom than in Germany, it may be more appropriate to compare Germany in the period from 1880 to 1913 with the United Kingdom from 1860 to 1880. In that case the British rate of growth of real national income per head of 1.65 a year was virtually identical with the German rate. On that basis there is no clear evidence of a more rapid economic development of Germany in the two generations before World War I. There remains a marked advantage in favor of Germany if the comparison is limited to manufac-

20. The German growth rates have been derived from data in W. G. Hoffmann, *Das Wachstum der Deutschen Wirtschaft* (Berlin, 1965), pp. 827–28, while the British figures were obtained from recently published calculations of Phyllis Deane, *The Review of Income and Wealth* (1968), pp. 106–07.

turing production or to the exports of manufactured goods.

The rate of growth of national income per head is, of course, the combined result of many economic and non-economic influences. The fact that no marked difference can be detected in the rate between the United Kingdom and Germany does not yet disprove the thesis that the financial system did no more for economic growth in Germany than it did for the United Kingdom in a comparable phase of development, offsetting other factors—not immediately visible, it is true—that would otherwise have held the German rate of growth below the British one. Verification or refutation of this possibility would require much more detailed analysis than has yet been undertaken by any contemporary or modern student of the period. It is however interesting that the relatively most intensive investigation of the problem—characteristically now more than fifty years old—concluded "it is not possible to ascertain how the effectiveness of British industry has been affected by the defects of the country's financial organization. Indeed it is not possible to prove beyond doubt for industry as a whole that such an influence has actually been at work, but this can be done only in isolated cases," the electric industry being claimed as one example.[21]

A Scotch verdict thus seems to be the only conclusion that the insufficient data and analysis now available permit. One cannot well claim that a superiority in the German financial structure was responsible for, or even contributed to, a more rapid growth of the German economy as a whole compared to the British economy in the half-century before World War I, since there was no significant difference in the rate of growth of the two economies. It is however pos-

21. Wieser, *Der finanzielle Aufbau,* p. 439. Kindleberger reaches a similar conclusion for this period: "By and large it is very hard to make an argument that the supply of credit . . . was responsible for slowing down the British and French rates of growth." (*Economic Growth in France and Britain 1851–1950* [Cambridge, 1964], p. 68.) So does the most recent investigation, though it deals only very briefly with the problem. (A. L. Levine, *Industrial Retardation in Britain 1880–1914* [London, 1967], pp. 120/21.)

sible and is even likely that the better performance of Germany in certain fields, particularly the growth of certain industries and the expansion of manufacturing exports, was influenced by differences in the financial structure of the two countries. Even here the more rapid growth rates may primarily reflect the fact that during this period Germany was in an earlier phase of its economic development, particularly an earlier phase of industrialization, rather than provide evidence of the specific influence of differences in financial structure.

By Way of Apology

The result thus is the same whether we turn to economic theory or to economic history, possibly because there is after all some communication between the two fields. Both assure us that the existence and development of a superstructure of financial instruments and financial institutions is a necessary, though not a sufficient, condition of economic growth, and both point out that the relationships between financial development and economic growth are very complicated and not easily amenable to generalization. Both however fail to answer the question in which we are primarily interested: Does finance make a difference, i.e. are there historically observed or theoretically inferred differences in the speed and pattern of economic development that are the result primarily, even if not exclusively, of differences in financial structure and development? [22]

Even in the case of the most spectacular of the influences on the financial superstructure—inflation (in the sense of a substantial and protracted rise in the general price level)—theoreticians and historians are far from agreeing whether

22. It does not help much, for example, to be told in a fairly typical statement, summarizing a pamphlet specifically dealing with this problem, that "growth will take place if a financial system is so constituted that it meets in a noninflationary fashion the legitimate need for funds on the part of business firms, agriculture, individuals and government." (B. H. Beckhart, *The Criteria of a Well-Functioning Financial System* [Brisbane, University of Queensland Press, 1961], p. 5.)

it accelerates or delays the rate of economic growth or leaves it unchanged or whether it substantially and permanently affects economic structure.[23] If this is the situation for a relatively clear-cut phenomenon like large-scale inflation, how small the chances are for discovering relationships, and particularly cause and effect relations, valid over a broad range of situations between less pronounced differences in financial superstructure and economic growth.

The two preceding sections could easily have been expanded and supplemented by additional cautionary statements and additional footnote references to directly or, more often, only indirectly relevant literature. I doubt, however —a subjective judgment, it is true—that such an expansion would have left readers or author more satisfied (or less dissatisfied) or would have brought us considerably closer to answers to the questions with which we started. The reason is, it would seem, that at this moment neither economic theory nor economic history is in a position to provide these answers. Whether this is due to insufficient attention to these questions by economic theoreticians and historians and a failure to discover the right approach or whether it reflects the conceptual impossibility of ever determining causal relations between as complicated phenomena as economic growth and financial development need not be decided here. The question certainly cannot be settled before the theory of finance is developed much further in the direction of analyzing the process of financial development and its relation to economic growth in operational testable terms and before we possess a substantial number of intensive case studies, for different representative countries and periods, that use the framework of such a financial theory. We are still, it seems, many years from that crucial point.

23. See, for example, H. G. Johnson's conclusion (and note the qualification "probably") that "whether inflation promotes growth depends on how the proceeds of this inflation tax are spent: if they are spent on investment growth will probably be promoted, whereas if they are spent on consumption growth will probably be retarded." (*Indian Economic Review, 6,* 65.)

APPENDIXES

I. SOME ASPECTS OF FINANCIAL STRUCTURE AND DEVELOPMENT OF INDIVIDUAL ECONOMIC UNITS AND OF GROUPS OF UNITS*

INDIVIDUAL ECONOMIC UNITS

The basis of the financial activity of any economic unit, and hence an important determinant of its role in the country's financial structure and development, is the unit's financial surplus or deficit, i.e. the difference between the unit's saving and its capital expenditures, preliminarily defined as expenditures on fixed assets and inventories.

During any one period some units have a financial surplus, some have a financial deficit, and some have neither because their saving and their capital expenditures both are zero, or because their saving is fortuitously exactly equal to their capital expenditures. Similarly there exist at any one point of time units for which the value of the financial instruments they own exceeds the value of the financial instruments they have issued, i.e. their liabilities and the proceeds from their equity securities outstanding. This difference is the result of the fact that, if valuation changes are absent or are ignored, the aggregate past financial surpluses of these units are in excess of their financial deficits. Other units show in their balance sheets issues outstanding in excess of financial instruments held because their past aggregate financial deficits exceed their financial surpluses.

* The symbols in this Appendix are independent of those used in Chapters 1 through 9.

For some units, finally, financial assets held are equal, or very nearly so, to the issues of their own financial instruments. This is likely only for financial intermediaries which do not own any nonfinancial assets. In a closed economy the sum of any one period's financial surpluses of some units is, of course, equal to the sum of financial deficits of the other units; and the value of financial assets held at a balance sheet date by all units is equal to the value, disregarding valuation changes of total liabilities and equities.

The amount of financial surpluses and deficits are determined by four flows, which are indicated in Table A–1. These are: income, which in turn is the difference of two

TABLE A–1

Main Elements of Uses and Sources of Funds

USES		SOURCES	
Cost of sales[a]	c	Sales proceeds	v
Other current expenditures	e	Final output	x
Distributions to owners	d	Other	$v-x$
Capital expenditures	$k+j$	Other income	w
Fixed	k	Income $(v+w-c-e)$	y
Increase in inventories	j	Saving $(y-d)$[a]	s
Financial deficit $(k+j-s)$	d	Financial surplus $[s-(k+j)]$	u
Retirement of own issues	z	Borrowing	b
		Trade credit	t
From financial institutions	z_f	Other short debt	g
From others	z_o	From financial institutions	g_f
		From others	g_o
		Long debt	h
		From financial institutions	h_f
Lending	l	From others	h_o
Transactions cash	m	Equity securities	e
Trade credit	r	From financial institutions	e_f
Acquisition of other financial assets[b]	p	From others	e_o
		Sale of financial assets held[c]	q
From financial institutions	p_f	To financial institutions	q_f
From others	p_o	To others	q_o

[a] Before or after capital consumption allowances.

[b] Includes money other than transactions cash.

[c] Includes repayments received on account of claims or equity securities held.

flows—receipts from sales and other income on the one hand, cost of sales and other current expenditures on the other; distributions to owners, i.e. in the case of corporations dividend payments; saving, the difference between income and distributions; and investment, i.e. expenditures on fixed assets and on inventories.

The analysis of the determinants of these flows is not part of a theory of finance. In financial analysis, these flows, and particularly the amounts of financial surpluses and deficits as their combined result, may be regarded as exogenously given. It is, however, necessary for an understanding of the financial process to study the empirical characteristics of the financial surpluses and deficits of individual economic units of different types at a given place and time and to be aware of the nature of the determinants of financial surpluses and deficits and of the way in which they influence the financial process, and through it the economic process. What matters is not the behavior of any one specific economic unit, but the pattern of behavior among groups of individual units (i.e. the typical value of financial surpluses and deficits in relation to basic economic characteristics of the unit such as its income, its assets, its saving, and its capital expenditures) and the scatter of individual values around these group averages.

In the comparative study of financial structure and development, the subject of analysis is, or should be, the typical relation to significant financial and real variables of financial surpluses and deficits of units in the main sectors of the economy in different countries and at different times. Unfortunately this is a field in which empirical data and hence statistical analyses are as yet almost entirely lacking. This state of affairs is probably attributable to, on the one hand, the virtual absence of systematically collected and analyzed data on sources and uses of funds of individual units—business enterprises or households—in all but a very few countries and, on the other hand, to the recency of the realization of the crucial importance of financial surpluses and deficits for financial analysis. It is therefore at this moment impossible to study statistically the relation between financial surpluses and deficits of individual economic units and other economic variables on an international comparative basis—or for that matter even on a national scale. All that can be hazarded are a few generalizations based on common fragmentary information.

Using the symbols of Table A–1, the basic financial equation for any economic unit having a financial deficit for the period can be written in the form of Equation (A.1); the unit's gross issuance of the main types of securities (g, h, and e) during the period appear on the left-hand side of the equation, while the right-hand side lists the determinants of the volume of gross issues. Equation (A.2) is based on the simplifying assumption that the change in net trade credit granted ($r - t$) and in transactions cash required (m) are linearly related to changes in the unit's volume of sales by means of coefficients α and β, and that nondiscretionary retirements (z') of own issues bear a constant proportion (γ) to the amount of such issues outstanding at the beginning of the period (B).

$$g + h + e = (k + J - s) + (r - t) + m + z + (p - q) \quad \text{(A.1)}$$

$$g + h + e = d + (\alpha + \beta)\,\Delta v + \gamma B + (z'') + (p - q) \quad \text{(A.2)}$$

where $z'' = (z - z')$ indicates discretionary retirements.

The corresponding basic equations for surplus units are:

$$(s - k - j) + g + h + e = (t - r) + m + z + (p - q) \quad \text{(A.3)}$$

$$g + h + e = (\alpha + \beta)\,\Delta v + \gamma B + (z'') + (p - q) - u \quad \text{(A.4)}$$

If a financial surplus is treated as a negative financial deficit (i.e. if it is designated by $-d$), both types of situations can be subsumed under one equation, which explains gross issues in terms of their main determinants:

$$g + h + e = d + (\alpha + \beta)\,\Delta v + \gamma B + (z'') + (p - q) \quad \text{(A.5)}$$

For net issues the corresponding equation is

$$(g + h + e) - [\gamma B + (z'')] = d + (\alpha + \beta)\,\Delta v + (p - q) \quad \text{(A.6)}$$

This approach raises several problems. First, how stable

are the coefficients α, β, and γ, and what determines them? Secondly, how erratic are discretionary retirements (z'') and the net acquisition or disposal of financial assets other than transactions cash and own securities, i.e. $(p - q)$? Thirdly, what determines the relative size of g, h, and e, and of the different types of instruments which each of the three terms includes?

To pose the questions in this way means that the size of the unit's financial surplus or deficit for the period is regarded as exogeneously determined, and that the other terms in the equation are supposed to adapt themselves to the size of the financial deficit or surplus. This assumption is needed unless the discussion is to cover the wide and controversial field of the determinants of financial surpluses and deficits, and hence of saving and capital expenditures, but it is not quite realistic. The volume of capital expenditures and, though possibly to a lesser extent, that of saving are influenced by the availability and cost of funds for expansion and by the outlets for and yield of funds and these are not independent of capital expenditures.

Even if the relationship between a unit's gross or net issues and its financial surplus and deficit were stable, the volume of issues would fluctuate in line with changes in d and u. In that case, the volume of gross issues $(i = g + h + e + t - r)$ would be a constant multiple (μ) of the unit's financial surplus or deficit. Similarly net issues $(n = i - z)$ would constitute a constant multiple of surplus or deficit $[n = \mu\ (1 - \zeta)]$, where ζ is the ratio of retirements to gross issues, since retirements would constitute a constant fraction of surplus or deficit and hence of gross issues. We would then have, if the subscripts u and d are used to identify surplus and deficit units:

$$i_d = \mu_d d; \qquad i_u = \mu_u u \tag{A.7}$$

$$n_d = \nu_d d; \qquad n_u = \nu_u u \tag{A.8}$$

The relationships expressed in Equations A.7 and A.8 are important when we proceed from the level of a single accounting period to that of a sequence of such periods extending from a to z. Under the assumptions made so far, the volume of gross and net issues would simply be the algebraic sum of the financial surpluses and deficits of the n subperiods. Thus, concentrating attention from now on on net issues:

$$\sum_a^z n_d = \nu_d \sum_a^z d; \qquad \sum_a^z n_u = \nu_u \sum_a^z u \tag{A.9}$$

This simple relationship would not be disturbed by the alteration of subperiods showing financial deficits with those showing surpluses if $\nu_d = \nu_n$. That, however, is extremely unlikely. Hence the cumulated volume of a unit's net issues will depend on the relation of the aggregate deficits of some subperiods (indicated by indices a to m) to the aggregate surpluses of other subperiods (indices n to z), i.e.

$$\sum_a^z n = \nu_d \sum_a^m d + \nu_u \sum_n^z u \tag{A.10}$$

The ratio of the period's gross or net issues to the absolute sum of financial surpluses or deficits or to their algebraic sum (where deficits offset surpluses) will therefore be a weighted average of the subperiods' ν's (or μ's), the values of the surpluses and deficits providing the weights. The greater the weighted difference between ν_d and ν_u or between μ_d and μ_u, the greater the effect of the alternation of financial surpluses and deficits on the volume of gross or net issues.

The alternation of a unit's financial surpluses and deficits has, of course, also a more direct, and generally a much more pronounced, effect on the volume of net issues if ν_u is negative, i.e. if a financial surplus is accompanied by an excess of retirements over gross new issues. In that case, Equation (A.10) changes to

$$\sum_a^z n = \nu_d \sum_a^m d - \nu_u \sum_n^z u \tag{A.11}$$

The sum of a period's net issues thus is influenced by the period's rotation ratio (ρ), which may be defined as the ratio of the arithmetic to the absolute sum of the subperiods' surpluses and deficits,

$$\rho = \frac{\sum_{a}^{m} u - \sum_{n}^{z} d}{\sum_{a}^{m} u + \sum_{n}^{z} d} \tag{A.12}$$

This ratio fluctuates between zero (when the sum of surpluses in some subperiods is exactly equal to that of deficits in the others) and plus or minus unity (when all subperiods show either surpluses or deficits).

We do not have sufficient evidence to say whether v_u is likely to be negative rather than positive. The probability that an excess of saving over capital expenditures will lead to a net retirement of debt rather than to a net addition to it, however, must be regarded as high for at least two reasons. First, most economic units are likely to prefer a lower to a higher level of debt, other things being equal, a reflection of the still widely prevalent horror debendi. (Periods of rapid inflation may constitute exceptions.) Secondly, and more importantly, the cost of borrowing is generally higher than the yield on financial assets held, particularly for households except at some periods for the yield on corporate stock if capital gains are included. Indeed, if all issues could be repaid without penalty by the issuers, one would feel reasonably certain that v_u would in most cases be negative. It is difficult to envisage a nonfinancial unit that has a financial surplus one period after another and still increases its debt continuously. One would rather assume that such a unit would reduce its net indebtedness by a large proportion of its financial surplus, so that v_u would be negative and close to unity, and would incur little or no new net indebtedness, once its old debt had been paid off, when v_u would be zero. The fact that considerable amounts of debt are not repayable at issuers' choice or only at a penalty, however, leads to a lag between the occurrence of surpluses and of net reductions in debt. But this is primarily a short-run phenomenon. For an individual unit, whether household, firm, or government, the long-run (average) value of v_u is therefore likely to be negative. Since the rotation ratio probably is substantially below unity for most units—we unfortunately have hardly any direct information on its value for individual firms or households—this means that the alternation of a unit's financial surpluses and deficits, as measured by its rotation ratio, is one of the determinants of the unit's net issues.

The rotation ratio cannot influence the volume of gross issues directly since μ cannot be negative. The alternation of subperiods of financial surplus and of deficit will, however, influence the value of μ, as this value is likely to be higher if the same total financial surplus or deficit of a period is the result of alternating surpluses or deficits of subperiods. This is particularly so for units which have a net financial surplus over the period as a whole, but experience financial deficits for protracted subperiods—the typical financial life cycle of a household. Notwithstanding a net financial surplus over the like cycle, many, if not most, households will show gross as well as net borrowing at least in the subperiods during which they acquire a home and major consumer durables.

There are two main reasons why gross issues exceed net issues for most units over all except very short periods. The first has just been discussed. The second, much more obvious and much more important, is the limited life of most issues. It is only corporate stocks and very rare obligations which have a life exceeding the usual time horizon of a unit, which may be set at fifty years and certainly does not exceed a hundred years. Most issues are retired after a shorter or longer life—and it is the actual not the originally stipulated life which matters here. If we deal with annual periods and assume that the life of a given instrument is λ years ($\lambda > 1$) and suppose that issues are distributed regularly over the year and have been of equal amount (a) for at least λ years, then retirements in a given year will be equal to a and net issues will be zero. If the volume of issues has been fluctuating, relations become more complicated. However, if the additional assumption is made of a regular increase in the volume of gross issues at an annual rate of growth $\gamma/100$, the relationship between gross and net issues is rather simple.[1] In that case retirements resulting from earlier issues falling due are equal to $a(1 + \gamma)^{-\gamma}$, that is, the higher the rate of growth of gross issues in the past and the longer the average life of past gross issues, the more net issues will exceed gross issues. For instruments with an effective life of thirty years—probably as long as will be found in practice except for common stock—and a growth rate of 3 per cent per year, retirements will be equal to about two-fifths of gross issues, i.e. gross issues will be one and two-thirds times as large as net issues. For issues of shorter effective life, the difference between net and gross issues is much larger. For five-year issues, for instance, the ratio of retirements to gross and net issues is much higher, viz. about seven-eighths and eight times, respectively, again assuming an annual growth rate of issues of 3 per cent. Higher growth rates, will, of course, reduce the relative importance of retirements. Thus if gross issues have in the past been growing at 6 per cent, the ratio of retirements to gross issues will be approximately three-fourths for five-year and not much over one-sixth for thirty-year (effective lives) issues. If the original issues are not repayable in their entirety at maturity or call, as assumed hitherto, but are retired in equal installments over their life, the formula relating retirements (z) and gross and net issues becomes more complicated, viz.: $z = a[1 - (1 + \gamma)^{-\lambda}](\gamma\lambda)^{-1}$. Retirements under this assumption will always be larger than in the previously discussed case of lump sum retirement at maturity or call. Thus, if again $\gamma = 3$ per cent and $\lambda =$ thirty years, retirements will equal about two-thirds of gross issues (as against two-fifths), and for five-year lives the ratio will be about 93 per cent (as against 86 per cent).

We do not have the evidence to answer the questions just

1. The situation is similar to the well-known relationship between gross and net capital expenditures (cf. e.g. Domar, *Economic Journal* 1953, pp. 1ff).

raised except by speculation, because hardly any systematic investigation has as yet been undertaken of the determinants of gross and net issues at the micro-economic (firm, household, or governmental unit) level. The material is therefore entirely inadequate for an international comparison at that level or even for a judgment about possible changes in these relationships in one country in the course of its development. In other words, we are not yet in a position to assign numerical values to the coefficients in Equations (A.5) and (A.6), or to the rotation ratio. We cannot even assert that the equations could be fitted to the data for groups of households, firms, and governmental units in one or more countries for a shorter or longer period in a way that would meet the tests of statistical significance and analytical usefulness.

To provide at least some empirical background to the discussion in the preceding pages, Table A–2 shows the rotation ratios for a group of 565 large American nonfinancial corporations in the twelve-year period 1952–63, the only information of this type that could be obtained. While these ratios obviously cannot be regarded as applicable to other countries, or to other groups of economic units or to earlier periods in the financial history of the United States, they serve at least as one piece of evidence for the conjecture that not only broad sectors, such as all nonfinancial business enterprises, but also more narrowly defined groups are made up of units with very different absolute and relative (e.g. in relation to sales and assets) financial surpluses and deficits, which often change direction from year to year, units which consequently show low values of ρ and thus are not very homogeneous with respect to surplus or deficit status, all facts which make the prevailing absence of data on the financial surpluses and deficits of individual units and of small and presumably more homogeneous groups of units a serious drawback to effective financial analysis.

Only few of the firms have a financial surplus or deficit in each of the twelve years of the period. The proportion

Table A–2

Frequency Distribution of Rotation Ratios for 565 American Nonfinancial Corporations, 1952–63

	All Industries	Capital Goods	Consumer Goods	Miscellaneous Manufacturing	Transportation and Communication	Trade
Number of companies	565	205	143	160	16	41
Mean rotation ratio	−.21	−.20	−.15	−.16	−.63	−.57
Standard deviation	.47	.43	.42	.54	.43	.40
Percentage of companies with rotation ratios of:						
−1.0 to −0.7	15	10	10	13	63	51
−0.7 to −0.5	13	15	10	14	19	10
−0.5 to −0.3	16	20	15	13	6	20
−0.3 to −0.1	19	19	24	21	0	7
−0.1 to +0.1	14	16	13	14	0	7
+0.1 to +0.3	8	7	10	9	6	2
+0.3 to +0.5	6	5	10	4	0	0
+0.5 to +0.7	4	4	4	4	6	0
+0.7 to +1.0	5	4	4	8	0	2

Source of basic data: Compustat tape of Standard and Poor's Corp.

of firms in which financial surpluses or deficits predominate to the extent of 70 per cent or more—i.e. in which the algebraic sum of financial surpluses and deficits is in excess of 0.7 times the absolute sum of surpluses and deficits—is only one in five. On the other hand almost one-half of all the 565 firms have a rotation ratio lying between +0.3 and −0.3, indicating a considerable alternation of years with financial surplus and years with financial deficit.

It is not astonishing that the number of firms with a negative rotation ratio exceeds that having a positive ratio —the mean rotation ratio for all 565 firms is −0.21—since it is known from aggregative sectoral flow-of-funds statements that nonfinancial corporations usually have a net financial deficit. More relevant is the lack of concentration of the ratios evidenced by the coefficient of variation (mean value of the rotation ratio divided by its standard deviation) which is as high as 2.2.

There are, of course, some differences in the average value of the rotation ratio and in its distribution among industries. Thus transportation, communication and trade show much higher negative average rotation ratios than manufacturing industries, indicating that they are more regularly in deficit status. One would expect such high negative ratios from firms which must finance most of their capital expenditures externally. It is not too astonishing either that the average rotation ratio for capital goods industries is slightly higher than that for consumer goods or miscellaneous manufacturing industries. More interesting is the fact that the absolute value of the standard deviation and of the coefficient of variation do not exhibit large differences among the broad industry groups although they do so among narrower industrial groups not shown in Table A–2.

In view of the scarcity of actual data and the complete absence of data on an international scale, a few conjectures, necessarily of a rather vague character, about some of the features of the basic equations may be permissible. The first of these is the distinction between, on the one hand, predetermined retirements, transactions cash, and trade credit and, on the other hand, voluntary retirements and changes in holding of other financial assets, including non-transactions cash.

There is reason to assume that the relation of even capital expenditures, trade credit, transactions cash, and statutory retirements to financial surpluses or deficits varies greatly as between groups of units and that for units of the same type it differs among countries. This relationship can be ascertained from statistical material, and one may hope that the ratios will prove to have a reasonably narrow range and to be reasonably stable, although they are, of course, subject to long-term trends. Sufficient basic data are available for a number of countries to test these conjectures, but they have never been organized and explored from this point of view.

The situation is quite different for nontransactions cash, for the net acquisition or disposal of other financial assets, and for discretionary retirements. These items undoubtedly have some relation to the unit's volume of economic activities and must, other things being equal, be reflected in the volume of net and gross issues. But it is very difficult even to speculate about the form of the relationship and about differences existing between units of different types and between different periods and countries. It stands to reason, however, that these items will be much more important for surplus than for deficit units. In particular they are likely to be decisive for households in surplus status. These households, however, generally will not have large net or even gross new issues of their own and thus are of interest primarily as sources of funds of issues of other sectors.

A little more can be said about the third problem, the distribution of total gross or net issues by type, primarily between debt issues and equity issues and among debt issues of different stipulated and effective maturity. To begin with, the choice is for many units considerably limited by law or custom. Households and government units are by their very nature precluded from issuing equity securities and unincorporated business enterprises generally find themselves in a similar position. For these units choice is limited to different types of debt issues and this choice is further restricted by the prevailing practices of lending and borrowing, e.g. the great difficulty for most units—viz. household and small business enterprises—to borrow on medium- or long-term except on real estate and securities.

Within these legal and institutional limitations, it is, however, possible—and this is the second point—to bring into play the general principle of minimization of cost of borrowing. This principle is certainly in many, if not most, cases followed loosely rather than applied in rigorous calculation, and it is usually modified by the restricted choices open to or at least known to many issuers, restrictions reflected, for example, in the oligopolistic nature of some credit markets and the existence of credit rationing. The principle nevertheless would seem to retain in most cases a certain degree of validity and considerable influence on the actual distribution of issues. This does not, of course, mean that the issuer selects, let alone secures, that distribution of his total volume of issues that minimizes cost, i.e. total discounted interest cost and connected expenses over the life of the issue or for a given period. It refers rather to a minimization that takes account of the issuer's requirements regarding maturity, callability, and other factors of the ancillary conditions of the issue, e.g. the pledges required or the restrictive covenants involved.

Attenuated as the application of the principle of minimization of cost to issuers—and the corresponding principle of maximization of return to the lender—may be in practice, it remains, it would seem, of sufficient influence on the distribution of issues by type to justify, and possibly even to call for, the introduction of interest (yield) rates in some shape into the basic equations, probably in the form of rate differentials rather than in the form of the absolute level of the rates.

Appendix I

GROUPS OF ECONOMIC UNITS (SECTORS)

Turning from individual units to smaller or larger groups of units, it may be assumed that gross or net borrowing are related in the same way to financial surpluses and deficits as they are for individual units so long as all units in the group are in surplus or in deficit status for the period considered. We could therefore repeat Equations (A.1) through (A.10) with the only difference that the variables now would be aggregates for the group—k, for instance, would then be the sum of fixed capital expenditures of all units in the group, while the coefficients become weighted averages of the coefficients for individual units.

When the group contains both surplus and deficit units, the relationships change. This is likely to be the case for all except very small and homogeneous groups and would certainly be true for groups as numerous and diverse as the broad sectors distinguished in the national accounts—households, nonfinancial business enterprises, financial intermediaries, and government—or even for subsectors such as individual industries or households of differing income and wealth levels, age and occupation of head, residence, etc. Then the degree to which the financial surpluses of some units in the group are offset by the financial deficits of other units during the same period becomes very important for financial analysis, and turns out to be a crucial factor in the determination of the volume of the group's total borrowing and issuance of securities.

In this case, the one commonly encountered in practical statistical analysis, it is necessary to separate the surplus and the deficit units within the group so that the basic equation for gross issues of the group or sector becomes

$$\sum i = \mu_u \sum u + \mu_d \sum d \qquad \text{(A.13)}$$

where the left-hand term includes all units in the group, while the first and second term on the right side of the equation refer to the aggregate of surplus and deficit units in the group. It is still assumed, as in the previous section, that there exists a definite, though stochastic, relationship between any unit's surplus or deficit and the volume of its gross issues, a relation which is expressed in the ratios μ_u and μ_d respectively and which depends, in addition to gross capital expenditures, on the unit's retirements of its own issues (or its requirements for transactions cash and net trade credit) and on its other net acquisitions or sales of financial assets. For net issues the corresponding equation is, if ζ is the ratio of retirements to gross issues,

$$\begin{aligned} \sum n &= \mu_u(1 - \zeta_u) \sum u + \mu_d(1 - \zeta_d) \sum d \\ &= \nu_u \sum u + \nu_d \sum d \end{aligned} \qquad \text{(A.14)}$$

In both equations the group or sectoral ratios μ, ζ, and ν are regarded, to repeat, as weighted averages of the same ratios for individual units. The analytical value of Equations (A.13) and (A.14) therefore depends on the representative character and the stability of these coefficients. The broader the range and the less regular the distribution of the individual values of μ, ζ, and ν among surplus and deficit units within the group and the more pronounced and erratic the movement of these values over time, the less the value of the equations.

In this situation the ratio of gross or net issues of a group or sector to its aggregate surplus or deficit will depend on the relative size of aggregate financial surpluses and deficits within the sector and on the difference between the average values of ν for the surplus and deficit sectors, since

$$\frac{\sum n}{\sum |u + d|} = \nu_u \left(\frac{\sum u}{\sum |u + d|} \right) + \nu_d \left(\frac{\sum d}{\sum |u + d|} \right) \qquad \text{(A.15)}$$

This expression is transformed into $\Sigma n/[\Sigma(u + \mathrm{d})]$, where the denominator is the algebraic sum (deficits having a minus sign) rather than the absolute sum of the units' financial surpluses and deficits, by means of multiplication with the offset ratio (ω), which may be regarded as a measure of homogeneity with respect to surplus or deficit status within the group and which is defined as

$$\omega = \frac{\sum (u - d)}{\sum |u + d|} \tag{A.16}$$

so that

$$\frac{\sum n}{\sum (u + d)} = \nu = \omega(\nu_u \sigma_u + \nu_d \sigma_d) \tag{A.17}$$

where σ_u and σ_d are the shares of aggregate surpluses and deficits in the absolute sum of the group's surpluses and deficits.

Here, as in the case of the rotation ratio, empirical evidence is practically nonexistent. The only available piece of evidence refers to the same group of 565 American large nonfinancial corporations for the period 1952–63. While the data are insufficient for any generalization regarding the offset ratio and the relationship of gross to net issues within a group of economic units, they permit a few interesting though preliminary conclusions.

The first of these is that in the United States during the postwar period the offset ratio shows a clear relationship to the business cycle. Thus while the ratios are generally negative, indicating for the 565 corporations taken together an excess of financial deficit over surpluses, the ratio is positive in two of the three recession years of the period (1954 and 1958); in the third (1961), although negative, the ratio is below that of the adjacent years. The same pattern is evidenced for the three major industry groups shown in Table A–3 as well as for most of the sixteen industry groups for which the data have been tabulated but are not shown. This means that in recession years there is no or only small prevalence of companies with deficits over those with financial surpluses and that the ratio of gross to net issues is higher than it is in years of expansion.

Secondly, an irregular trend toward reduction of the value of the offset ratio can be noticed. Thus for the first half of the twelve-year period the ratio averages −0.48, compared to a value of −0.35 for the second half of the period.

Thirdly, the value of the offset ratio depends to some extent on the size of the company. The ratio is higher, i.e. the prevalence of financial deficits, and hence the depend-

TABLE A–3

Offset Ratio and *U/D* Ratio of 565 Nonfinancial Corporations, 1952–63

	Offset Ratio				*U/D* Ratio			
	All Corporations	Consumer Goods	Capital Goods	Other	All Corporations	Consumer Goods	Capital Goods	Other
1952	−.65	−.27	−.80	−.67	.21	.58	.11	.20
1953	−.53	−.36	−.55	−.57	.31	.47	.30	.28
1954	.08	.02	.68	−.26	1.16	1.03	5.17	.59
1955	−.30	−.40	.16	−.51	.54	.43	1.38	.32
1956	−.81	−.84	−.75	−.84	.10	.09	.15	.09
1957	−.64	.17	−.71	−.79	.22	1.42	.11	.12
1958	.02	.49	.08	−.18	1.05	2.96	1.18	.69
1959	−.33	−.03	−.24	−.46	.50	.95	.61	.37
1960	−.46	−.13	−.68	−.44	.37	.77	.19	.38
1961	−.33	−.03	−.23	−.42	.50	.73	.63	.41
1962	−.38	.21	.13	−.68	.45	1.53	1.29	.19
1963	−.27	−.12	.16	−.47	.58	.78	1.36	.36
Average	−.41	−.12	−.23	−.52	.50	.98	1.04	.33
Median	−.36	−.08	−.24	−.49	.47	78	.62	.34

ence on external financing, are more pronounced for larger than for smaller companies (all 565 corporations are fairly sizable compared to the universe of corporations operating in the United States). Thus the average offset ratio for companies with assets of less than $1 million in 1963 was in the neighborhood of −0.25, compared to a ratio of around −0.35 for corporations with assets between $2 million and $100 million and to a ratio of −0.52 for the giant corporations with assets of more than $1 billion.

Fourthly, as may be expected, there is a definite relationship between the value of the offset ratio and the rate of growth of the corporation measured by the ratio of its assets at the end of 1963 to that at the end of 1952. While the relatively few companies whose assets were smaller at the end than at the beginning of the period have a positive offset ratio (+0.31), and those which expanded relatively slowly—not more than doubling their assets in the twelve-year period—had a small negative ratio (ranging between −0.04 and −0.22), the rapidly growing companies, with assets at the end of 1963 at least two and a half times as large as those of 1952, had on the average an offset ratio of nearly −0.70.

More directly relevant to an appraisal of the effect on the volume of issues of the existence of surplus and deficit units within a group for which only the algebraic aggregate net surplus or deficit is known—in practice the usual situation—is the ratio of surpluses to deficits. (The same rotation ratio $(\Sigma u - \Sigma d)/(\Sigma u + \Sigma d)$ may, of course, reflect any number of $\Sigma u/\Sigma d$ ratios.) If we assume that surplus units have no net issues and that deficit units' net new issues are equal to their deficits, then the ratio of the group's net issues to aggregate net surplus or deficit is $\nu' = d/(u - d) = [(u/d) - 1]^{-1}$. The u/d ratio thus indicates the extent to which, under the simplifying assumptions made here, the net new issues of a group exceed its aggregate net financial surplus or deficit; and the formula shows that the relation is direct, i.e. the more the u/d ratio deviates from unity, the more do the group's net issues exceed its aggregate net financial surplus or deficit. Thus, if the *u/d* ratio is one-third, issues are one and one-half times aggregate net financial deficit (disregarding sign), while when the *u/d* ratio rises to two-thirds, issues are three times the net deficit.

The *U/D* ratios shown in columns (5) to (8) of Table A–3 show, as expected, considerable similarities in their year-to-year movements and in the interindustry differences to the offset ratios of columns (1) to (4). Thus the *U/D* ratio is lowest late in the upswing (1952–53, 1956–57, 1960) when the offset ratio is highest, and it is highest in recession years (1954, 1958) when the offset ratio is positive. Similarly the *U/D* ratio is highest for capital goods industries and lowest for "other" industries (particularly public utilities), indicating a higher ratio of issues to aggregate sectoral financial deficit in the former than in the latter group.

Table A–3 indicates a mean *U/D* ratio for all 565 corporations of just over two-fifths. Thus if the two assumptions made above (that surplus units have no net issues and that deficit units' net new issues are equal to their deficits) applied to this group of economic units, net issues would be one and two-thirds times as large as the group's aggregate net deficit.

Since we do not have information on the issues of these 565 corporations, it is not possible to ascertain how far this calculated ratio is from the observed ratio of issues to combined financial surplus or deficit. However, if we assume that the 565 corporations are representative of all nonfinancial corporations, such a comparison can be made. It then appears from the Federal Reserve Board's flow-of-funds statistics that net issues of all nonfinancial corporations aggregated about $125 billion for the years 1952–63 and that this was equal to 4.1 times their aggregate financial deficit. The substantial discrepancy may be due to one or more of the following factors: The *U/D* ratio is higher for the other and generally much smaller corporations than for the 565 corporations; the volume of net issues of corporations having a financial deficit is on the average larger than their deficit, partly because net issues are used to finance expenditures other than on plant, equipment, and inventories (net trade credit extended by all nonfinancial corporations, for example, increased by nearly $20 billion or 0.7 times aggregate financial deficit); and corporations having a financial surplus in one or more years of the period nevertheless made new issues during these years. Probably all three factors, and some others too, were at work indicating that if financial surpluses and deficits are to be used as an explanation of the volume of net nonfinancial issues, offsetting of the surpluses of some units against the deficits of others must first be avoided; and, secondly, a broad concept of "capital expenditures," including at least net trade credit extended, should be used.

It is possible at the present time to determine the value of ν and (though more rarely) μ for the main sectors of the economy from the national income and product account and from flow-of-fund statistics. Values for ν and μ can also be ascertained for smaller groups, particularly in the business sector. There is, however, hardly any information available that would permit us to analyze the way in which the individual units in a group, or the subsectors of one of the large sectors in common use in national accounts, interact to produce the observed sectoral values. In this situation any international comparison is necessarily limited to the ratios of gross or net issues to the aggregate net financial surpluses and deficits of large sectors. Some of this aggregative material is reviewed briefly in the following subsection; an exhaustive exploration and utilization is a large task that remains to be done.

AN INTERNATIONAL COMPARISON OF SECTORAL FINANCIAL SURPLUSES AND DEFICITS, 1950–59 [2]

In order to make an analytically useful international comparison of the sectoral financial surpluses and deficits

2. Apologies are in order for the inclusion of this section, a longer version of which was prepared considerably earlier than the bulk of

and to avoid being misled by irrelevant differences, data are needed for a large number of countries of different types of financial structure and in different stages of financial development, for periods long enough to be unaffected by short-term movements and to show trends, for identically defined sectors, and for statistics implying the same degree of grossness.

Actually we are very far from this ideal situation. The best that can be done is to compare the financial surpluses and deficits for a relatively small number of countries (twenty-four) for a period of ten years after World War II. Even this limited material is of considerable interest, not only, or even primarily, for what it shows, but rather for the indications it provides of what could be done with more adequate data, which are now beginning to become available for an increasing number of countries.

The only body of data that is readily available and covers a substantial number of countries is found in the *World Economic Survey, 1960* of the United Nations and is derived from the national income and product accounts of individual countries. The figures are obtained by deducting capital expenditures from saving of the two main domestic sectors (business, which in principle includes housing and government enterprises, and government proper) and by adding the financial saving of households, as well as the net foreign balance (exports less imports of commodities and services), which is treated like the saving or investment surplus of a domestic sector. The advantage of this set of data is its availability for a dozen each of developed and underdeveloped countries. The disadvantages, from the point of view of financial analysis, are that the figures are given only in one aggregate for the decade 1950–59, that capital expenditures on housing are allocated to the business sector while home mortgages are treated as an offset to the saving of the

the study. Updating and revision to conform to other parts of the study would, however, be extremely difficult, given the absence of a body of readily available material more recent, more comprehensive, or more detailed than the one used here.

household sector, thus increasing sectoral financial surpluses and deficits above the level obtained from a more consistent treatment (both expenditures and borrowing allocated either to the business or preferably the household sector), and that expenditures on consumer durables are treated as current outlay rather than as investment, thus further increasing sectoral surpluses and deficits by the amount of net investment (expenditures less depreciation) in consumer durables.

Aggregate Financial Surpluses and Deficits

This body of data, summarized in Table A–4, shows for the twenty-four countries for which the information is available, an average ratio for the years 1950–59 of the absolute sum of sectoral financial surpluses and deficits to gross domestic product (henceforth simply designated as the "ratio") of 15 per cent, but a range of 5 to 28 per cent. The average for the fourteen developed countries (including South Africa and Rhodesia)[3] of 18 per cent is substantially above that of 11 per cent for the ten less developed countries. There thus exists a fairly pronounced, though not radical, difference in the ratio between developed and less developed countries. Some less developed countries, however, have a ratio not only higher than some developed countries, but also above the average for all fourteen developed countries.

The questions in which we are interested here is whether

3. South Africa and Rhodesia are examples of "dual economies," having both a European and a native sector. Practically all financial assets and liabilities as well as the bulk of tangible wealth and national product are accounted for by the European sector, although it includes only the minority of the population. This sector shows all the characteristics of developed countries. The average level of income of the entire population, on which the United Nations classification is based, is misleading for purposes of financial analysis. A similar argument could have been made, although with less justification, for the (formerly Belgian) Congo; a shift of this country, would not, however, noticeably affect the averages. For this reason South Africa and Rhodesia are classified as developed in the rest of the study, and the national product per head used in comparison is that of the white population only.

Table A–4

Ratio of Sectoral Surpluses and Deficits, Investment Ratio, and Rates of Growth, 1950–59, Twenty-four Selected Countries

PER CENT

	Ratio of Sectoral Surpluses and Deficits	Investment Ratio	Rate of Growth		Level of Income per Head in 1958 Dollars
			Total	Per Head	
	(1)	(2)	(3)	(4)	(5)
Germany	28.0	21.3	7.5	6.6	938
Australia	26.8	25.8	4.3	2.0	1214
Rhodesia	26.0	29.0	7.0	4.0	(1800)[b]
Norway	25.2	28.4	3.4	2.5	1035
Japan	23.6	22.3	9.1	7.7	285
Costa Rica[a]	19.0	20.0	6.0	1.9	365
Denmark	18.6	17.7	2.7	2.0	975
South Africa	18.0	23.0	5.0	2.3	(1450)[b]
Venezuela	17.0	27.0	8.0	3.5	971
Belgium	16.2	15.7	2.7	2.1	1031
Honduras[a]	16.0	15.0	4.0	2.0	193
Canada	15.0	23.1	3.9	1.3	1767
Netherlands	14.2	22.2	4.6	3.3	767
Sweden	12.0	20.2	3.3	2.7	1313
Congo[a]	12.0	26.0	5.0	2.6	87
Morocco[a]	12.0	16.0	2.0	−1.2	159
France	11.2	16.9	4.2	3.4	1113
U.S.A.	11.0	16.7	3.3	1.6	2361
Brazil	8.0	16.0	6.0	2.9	250
Ecuador[a]	8.0	14.0	5.0	1.7	179
United Kingdom	6.4	14.6	2.5	2.1	1085
India	6.0	8.0	3.0	1.1	67
Ceylon[a]	6.0	11.0	3.0	0.2	123
Philippines	5.0	9.0	6.0	2.5	194
Average (unweighted)	15.1	19.1	4.7	2.5	822
Median	14.6	19.0	4.0	2.1	958

[a] Not included among the thirty five countries used throughout Chapters 2 to 8.

[b] Rough estimate.

Sources: *Col. 1:* *World Economic Survey* (1960), pp. 25, 33, 52, 58, 61, 68, and 72.

Col. 2, 3: Op. cit., pp. 16, 58.

Col. 4: Column 3 less rate of population growth, derived from *U.N. Statistical Abstract* (New York).

Col. 5: Gross domestic product per head from U.N. *Yearbook of National Accounts Statistics* (1965), pp. 493 ff.; figures for South Africa and Rhodesia refer to white population only.

the average aggregate ratio of sectoral financial surpluses and deficits to national product is related to one of the factors that may be regarded as crucial in economic development, such as the rate of growth of national product, the investment ratio, or the level of national product per head.

A comparison of the ratio of sectoral surpluses and deficits and the rate of growth of national product during the 1950s for developed and underdeveloped countries suggests that in both groups of countries a positive relation does exist between the ratio and the rate of growth. The wide scatter of points in both cases, however, indicates that the relationship is not a very close one.

For instance, among developed countries, France, Canada, and Australia have very similar growth rates of about 4 per cent per year, but their *S/D* ratio differs widely—11, 15, and 28 per cent. On the other hand, Japan with a ratio of 24 per cent has a growth rate which is more than two and one-half times as high as that of Norway, whose ratio of 25 per cent is at least on the Japanese level.

The connection is, if anything, less pronounced among less developed countries, although it is not entirely absent here either. Among these countries too there are great differences in the rate of growth for countries having the same ratio and great differences in the ratio among countries having the same rate of growth. Thus Costa Rica, Brazil, and the Philippines have the same rate of growth of 6 per cent, but this is accompanied by ratios of 19, 8, and 5 per cent. Venezuela and Honduras show almost the same ratio (16 per cent), but the growth rate of Venezuela of 8 per cent is twice as high as that of Honduras.

The differences between developed and less developed countries are particularly marked in the relation between the ratio and the level of real income per head. If the ratio is compared with real national product per head for all twenty-four countries, it is hardly possible to detect a systematic relationship. There is a slight positive relation—the higher income per head, the higher the ratio—but the scatter is extremely wide. When the two groups are separated, however, it appears that the relationship is negative among developed countries, meaning that the ratio is lower the higher income per head, though the scatter remains very wide. Less developed countries, on the other hand, show a positive relation between the ratio and the rate of growth.

These observations are quantified by a correlation analysis, some results of which are summarized in Table A–5.

Table A–5

Correlations between Ratio of Sectoral Surpluses and Deficits to Gross National Product and Four Economic Indicators

	Rate of Growth, 1950–59		Investment Ratio 1950–59	Income Level 1960
	Aggregate	Per Head		
All countries (24)	.42	.55	.76	.14
Developed countries, including South Africa and Rhodesia (14)	.62	.49	.75	−.45
Less developed countries, excluding South Africa and Rhodesia (10)	.35	.38	.73	.56
Developed countries, excluding South Africa and Rhodesia (12)	.57	.48	.71	−.38
Less developed countries, including South Africa and Rhodesia (12)	.47	.60	.83	.34
Developed countries, excluding Japan (11)	.57	.43	.71	.28
European developed countries, plus Australia (9)	.56	.37	.73	−.03

The correlation between the ratio of financial surpluses and deficits and the rate of growth per head is statistically significant, although it is not very high, explaining less than one-third of the difference in growth rates per head among all 24 countries. The correlation is more pronounced for developed countries, both for aggregate and per head growth rates.

These relationships between the ratio and the growth rate

are affected by the fairly close relationship that exists between the ratio and the investment ratio on the one hand and the investment ratio and the rate of growth of real income per head on the other, relationships which make it difficult to decide how much of the connection between the ratio and the growth rate can be ascribed to the effect of differences in the ratio alone. The partial and multiple correlation coefficients shown in Table A–6, however, point to the existence of a residual effect of the ratio even after differences among countries in the investment ratio are taken into account.

Sectoral Financial Surpluses and Deficits

The second aspect of the figures on which interest centers is the distribution of financial surpluses and deficits among sectors rather than their absolute sum. One of the outstanding features of Table A–7, which provides the relevant data for both developed and less developed countries is the great variety of the distribution of surpluses and deficits among the four sectors.

For all twenty-four countries, the household sector shows a saving surplus on the average, i.e. an excess of saving over capital expenditures of nearly 5 per cent of gross domestic product, the rest of the world adding about 1 per cent in the form of capital imports and the government contributing about 0.3 per cent for a total of about 6 per cent of gross domestic product. The surpluses of these three sectors are offset entirely by the saving deficit, i.e. the excess of capital expenditures over saving, of the business sector.

Before analyzing these figures, it should be recalled that capital expenditures on housing are allocated to the business sector, even when made by households, and that capital expenditures on saving through consumer durables, are entirely neglected. If, as is more consistent and appears to be more realistic, capital expenditures on housing are shifted to the household sector, the saving surplus of that sector as well as the saving deficit on the business sector probably would be reduced by 1 to 2 per cent in most countries. A

Table A–6

Partial and Multiple Correlations among Sectoral Surplus and Deficit Ratio, Investment Ratio, Income Level, and Rates of Growth

I. Partial Correlations

First Variable	Second Variable	Constant	24 Countries	12 Developed Countries	12 Less Developed Countries
Sectoral surplus and deficit ratio	Aggregate growth rate	Investment ratio	.19	.51	−.07
	Per head growth rate	Investment ratio	.41	.53	−.03
	Aggregate growth rate	Income level	.49	.47	.38
	Per head growth rate	Income level	.57	.33	.53
	Investment ratio	Aggregate growth rate	.71	.67	.68
	Investment ratio	Per head growth rate	.71	.73	.71

II. Multiple Correlations

Independent Variable	First Dependent Variable	Second Dependent Variable	24 Countries	12 Developed Countries	12 Less Developed Countries
Aggregate growth rate	Sectoral surplus and deficit ratio	Investment ratio	.44	.58	.60
		Income level	.56	.67	.71
	Investment ratio	Income level	.56	.60	.74
Per head growth rate	Sectoral surplus and deficit ratio	Investment ratio	.55	.54	.73
		Income level	.58	.73	.65
	Investment ratio	Income level	.43	.69	.74

TABLE A–7

Sectoral Surpluses of Saving or Investment (–)

PER CENT OF GROSS DOMESTIC PRODUCT

	Households	Enterprises	Government	Rest of World	All Sectors[a]
All countries	4.8	−6.3	0.3	1.0	12.5
Developed countries	6.1	−7.6	1.3	−0.1	15.3
Less developed countries	3.5	−4.9	−0.7	2.1	11.2

[a] Arithmetic average of absolute sum of sectoral surpluses and deficits.

Source: Same as for Table A–4.

further reduction would occur if account were taken of net investment in consumer durables. After these adjustments, both the saving surplus of households and the saving deficits of enterprises would be reduced by at least two points. In that case the average of total sectoral surpluses and deficits would be in the order of 4 per cent of gross domestic product rather than the 6 per cent now indicated by the figures.

The averages used so far, however, are of limited significance for analysis because of the wide variation among countries. Any conclusions must, therefore, take account of the distribution of ratios of financial surpluses and deficits to national product among the twenty-four countries. Table A–8 provides frequency distributions of the ratios, which allows us to separate averages that reflect a typical situation from those that lack such character.

It then appears that two features of the averages can be regarded as typical, since they occur in virtually all countries. These are, first, the fact that the household sector has a saving surplus and the business sector (which in principle includes government enterprises) has a saving deficit. This would remain true in most countries even if housing expenditures were shifted from the business to the household sector. In most countries the saving surplus of households and the saving deficit of enterprises are of similar size and

Table A–8

Frequency Distribution of Sectoral Surpluses and Deficits among Twenty-four Selected Countries

Relation to Average	Aggregate Sectoral Total			Household Saving Surplus			Enterprise Saving Deficit		
	All Countries (24)	Developed (12)	Less Developed[a] (12)	All Countries (24)	Developed (12)	Less Developed[a] (12)	All Countries (24)	Developed (12)	Less Developed[a] (12)
Negative	0	0	0	1	0	1	1	0	1
0 to 40%	2	1	1	1	1	0	3	1	2
40 to 80%	7	3	4	6	3	2	5	5	2
80 to 120%	6	4	2	7	4	6	6	1	2
120 to 160%	7	3	4	5	2	0	5	3	1
160 to 200%	1	1	0	2	2	2	2	2	3
200 to 240%	1	0	1	2	0	1	2	0	1
Over 240%	0	0	0	0	0	0	0	0	0
Average[b]	15.0	17.3	12.8	4.8	6.1	3.5	−6.3	−7.7	−4.9

	Government Saving Surplus			Capital Imports		
	All Countries	Developed	Less Developed[a]	All Countries	Developed	Less Developed[a]
	(24)	(12)	(12)	(24)	(12)	(12)
Less than −160%	9	0	1	1	5	0
−160 to − 80%	0	1	2	4	0	0
− 80 to − 40%	0	1	1	2	0	1
− 40 to 0%	0	0	0	1	0	0
0 to 40%	1	2	1	3	0	1
40 to 80%	0	2	1	0	0	4
80 to 160%	0	3	1	4	0	3
Over 160%	14	3	5	9	7	3
Average[b]	0.2	1.4	−0.7	1.1	−0.1	2.1

[a] Including South Africa and Rhodesia.
[b] Per cent of gross national product; arithmetic average of values for 12 or 24 countries.

together determine the level of the ratio, i.e. the proportion of gross domestic product represented by the absolute sum of all sectoral financial surpluses and deficits.

Considerable differences, however, exist between developed and less developed countries. First, sectoral surpluses and deficits are higher in relation to gross domestic product in developed than in underdeveloped countries, both for households and enterprises. Secondly, the saving surplus of the government is much larger in relation to national product in developed than in less developed countries, but even in the former it amounts to only one-fifth of household saving. This proportion would be raised to between one-third and one-half it capital expenditures on housing were shifted to the household sector and account taken of net saving through consumer durables. Thirdly, for less developed countries capital imports supply two-fifths of all sectoral surpluses, while among developed countries, capital exports represent only an insignificant proportion of all uses of funds. This is possible because (apart from the fact that the table covers only twelve countries in each group) five of the developed countries were, on balance, capital importers during the 1950s and because the absolute values of product and of sectoral surpluses and deficits is much larger in the developed than in the less developed countries.

The main problem, then, is the relation of the structure of sectoral financial surpluses and deficits to the rate of growth. It is difficult to draw conclusions from the available material, because in most countres the household sector accounts for the bulk of all sectoral surpluses and the enterprise sector accounts for most deficits. This leaves only the share of the surplus or deficit of government proper and of the rest of the world to vary widely in its relations to the absolute sum of sectoral surpluses and deficits.

Among developed countries there appears to exist some association between the share of saving supplied to the rest of the world and the rate of growth. The countries with a relatively high share of capital exports to product (Germany, Japan, the Netherlands, and Belgium) are generally also countries with relatively high growth rates (Belgium is an exception). On the other hand, high rates of capital imports to domestic product (Australia, Canada, and Norway) do not seem to have been associated with high, but only with average, growth rates. The developed countries with low growth rates do not show an evident association with the direction or size of the foreign balance, though this balance is small in all cases (except for Belgium) in relation to domestic product.[4]

The association between the share of saving supplied by the rest of the world in domestic product and the rate of growth appears to be more pronounced among less developed countries. The relation, of course, is in the opposite direction from that observed for the developed countries, i.e. the higher net capital imports, the higher the rate of growth. (On the average, the rate of growth changes by 1 per cent with an equal change in the ratio of capital imports to national product, the rate of growth without capital imports being about 3 per cent.) The scatter again, however, is wide. Venezuela with net capital imports of 3 per cent of domestic product has almost as high a rate of growth as Rhodesia, whose capital imports were equal to 9 per cent of gross domestic product. Of the three countries with a rate of growth of 6 per cent, Costa Rica had capital imports equivalent to 4 per cent of domestic product, while the ratios for the Philippines and Brazil were as low as 2 and 1 per cent respectively. Similarly, the rates of growth of the four countries with capital imports of 1 per cent of gross domestic product range from 3 per cent in India to 6 per cent for Brazil.

Finally there appears to exist a slight positive relationship between the relative size of the government's saving surplus and the rate of growth in both developed and underdeveloped countries, but the scatter is wide in both groups. There are, however, serious doubts about the sta-

4. The relationship might be improved if the accumulation of gold and foreign currencies were separated from other capital imports which supposedly are used productively.

tistical and economical significance of the relation. If one can draw any inference on the relation in developed compared to underdeveloped countries, it is that differences in the ratio of the government's saving surplus to national product seem to have greater influence on the rate of growth for underdeveloped than for developed countries. In other words, accumulation of financial assets by the government needs to be much greater in relation to gross domestic product in developed than underdeveloped countries to be associated with the same change in the rate of growth.

II. DETERMINANTS OF THE CAPITAL FORMATION RATIO, 1956-60

While this is not a primary preoccupation of this study, it is tempting to look at the determinants of the capital formation ratio (κ), mainly to see whether some of these determinants are financial in nature or are the result of factors that also influence other components of the basic equation. Unfortunately, the material for an international comparative analysis of κ is as yet quite inadequate.[1] Apart from the level and the rate of growth of real national product per head, no economic variable (or for that matter no noneconomic variable that has been considered) has been found to be closely associated statistically with differences in κ among countries, or to be of a nature that would be more likely to influence the volume of capital formation than to be influenced by it. International cross-section analyses of κ, which the material now available limits to be postwar period, thus still leave a considerable portion of intercountry differences in κ unexplained. This suggests that factors not easily measurable on an international basis, such as government policies and the attitudes of savers and investors, have considerable influence on the level of κ and are responsible for a substantial proportion of the differences in κ among countries observed during the postwar period.

Possibly the most remarkable feature of a comparison of the average rate of κ (gross domestic capital expenditures, excluding consumer durables, expressed as per cent of gross

1. This analysis was undertaken in a very early phase of this study and it was not feasible to bring it up to date. Similar data for the period before 1956 are too scarce for an analysis of this type.

national product) for different types of countries during the period 1956–60, which are presented in the upper panel of Table B–1 on the basis of the data published in the United Nations' *Yearbook of National Accounts Statistics* is the smallness of the difference between developed countries on the one hand (23 per cent) and less developed countries on the other (19 per cent). Indeed the difference between the average of κ for Latin American (20 per cent) and for Asian and African less developed countries (16 per cent) is as large as that existing between developed and underdeveloped countries, each taken as a group. No substantial difference appears in the share of inventory accumulation in gross domestic capital formation between developed and less developed countries, although again the ratio for Latin American countries is higher than that for Afro-Asian less developed countries.

The difference between developed and less developed countries almost disappears for the net domestic capital formation ratio, because the importance of depreciation is smaller in less developed than in developed countries, although this may be a transitory phenomenon. Again the difference between Latin American and Afro-Asian less developed countries is greater than that between all less developed and all developed countries.

The relationships are not much different if averages weighted by the size of aggregate gross national product are used as is done in the lower panel of Table B–1. As a matter of fact, the difference between developed and less developed countries, or between Latin Amerian and Afro-Asian less developed countries, is even smaller when weighted averages are used, indicating that some large developed countries—large in terms of aggregate national product—have a relatively low κ (this is actually the case for the United States), and that some large Latin American countries also have a κ that is relatively low compared to the other countries in their group. (An example is provided by Argentina.)

The significant differences between developed and less de-

TABLE B–1

International Differences in Capital Formation Ratios, 1956–60

PER CENT OF GROSS NATIONAL PRODUCT

	All	Developed	Less Developed	European Developed	American	Afro-Asian
					Less Developed	
	UNWEIGHTED AVERAGES					
Gross domestic capital formation	20.7	23.3	19.1	21.7	20.4	16.2
Same plus net exports	17.1	22.2	14.2	22.6	14.4	12.2
Depreciation	7.3	9.0	6.2	9.1	7.5	5.0
Gross fixed capital formation	19.0	22.0	17.3	20.8	19.9	14.4
Change in stocks	1.5	1.6	1.5	1.4	1.7	1.1
Net fixed capital formation	12.1	13.1	11.5	11.7	12.2	9.3
Net domestic capital formation	13.7	14.3	13.4	12.4	13.8	11.1
Public gross capital formation	5.5	5.8	5.3	4.5	4.6	5.5
Private gross capital formation	12.9	16.1	10.5	16.3	13.8	8.2
Saving, total	10.5	13.4	8.6	13.9	7.7	7.3
Public saving	3.6	4.0	3.2	4.2	4.0	2.9
Private saving	7.5	9.4	5.7	9.7	4.5	5.7
	WEIGHTED AVERAGES[a]					
Gross domestic capital formation	20.0	20.3	18.8	21.0	19.1	17.1
Same plus net exports	19.9	20.8	15.5	22.1	16.1	13.3
Depreciation	8.5	9.2	5.2	8.6	7.6	2.8
Gross fixed capital formation	18.5	19.1	16.0	19.6	17.2	14.2
Change in stocks	1.4	1.3	1.8	1.6	2.0	1.4
Net fixed capital formation	10.1	9.9	11.5	11.0	9.9	12.1
Net domestic capital formation	11.5	11.1	13.7	12.4	11.8	14.3
Public gross capital formation	4.2	4.1	5.1	4.1	5.3	5.0
Private capital formation	14.2	15.0	9.6	15.6	10.5	8.8
Saving, total	11.4	11.5	10.9	13.2	9.0	11.5
Public saving	2.8	2.8	3.0	3.5	4.4	1.7
Private saving	8.6	8.7	8.0	9.8	5.1	10.6

[a] Weights are aggregate GNP in 1960 at purchasing power parities of currencies.

Sources of basic capital formation and national product data: U.N. *Yearbook of National Account Statistics* (1961). Number of countries varies among lines because of unavailability of some breakdowns for some countries. Gross domestic capital formation and Depreciation are based on data for fifty-five countries.

veloped countries appear in two different relations. The first is the distribution of total gross domestic capital formation between the government and private sectors. In less developed countries the government accounts for fully one-third of total domestic gross capital formation, while the comparable ratio is only slightly in excess of one-fourth for all developed countries and is not much in excess of one-fourth for the European developed countries. But this difference hides sharp differences among the group of less developed countries. In Latin American less developed countries the share of the public sector in gross domestic capital formation is at the level of the developed countries, while in Asian and African countries (the number covered by Table B–1 is relatively small but includes the most important one—India) the government is responsible for about two-fifths of total gross domestic capital formation.

The second significant difference is evident in the method of financing gross domestic capital formation, and this difference is particularly important for financial analysis. In less developed countries, about 30 per cent of total gross national capital formation is provided by earned depreciation allowances, such as they are reported in the various countries' national accounts, while nearly one-half is financed by net domestic saving, thus leaving approximately one-fourth of gross domestic capital formation and two-fifths of net domestic capital formation to be covered by capital imports. The shares of capital imports and of total domestic sources are similar in Latin American and in Afro-Asian less developed countries, but in Latin American countries depreciation is considerably higher in comparison to net domestic saving as a source of financing capital formation that is the case in the Afro-Asian countries.

In marked contrast, earned capital consumption allowances finance about two-fifths of total gross domestic capital expenditures in developed countries, and net domestic saving provides most of the remaining three-fifths, so that capital imports or exports remain relatively small in comparison to gross domestic capital formation. The European developed countries differ in these respects even more from less developed countries, depreciation allowances providing more than two-fifths and domestic net saving more than three-fifths of gross domestic capital formation, leaving the equivalent of approximately 5 per cent of gross domestic capital formation available for capital exports. The non-European developed countries (United States, Canada, Australia, New Zealand, South Africa, and Japan) here are more similar to less developed countries than are the European developed countries.

The larger importance of government in less developed countries has already been noted in the case of capital formation, but it also applies to net saving. In less developed countries nearly one-third of total net saving is accounted for by the government compared to a share of not much over one-fifth in developed countries. There are again substantial differences within the groups of less developed countries, as well as among individual countries. Thus, in Latin America, the government sector accounts for nearly one-half of net national saving against a share of only one-third in the Afro-Asian less developed countries, a ratio which is hardly above that prevailing in developed countries, both inside and outside Europe. In the methods of financing their capital expenditures the Afro-Asian countries thus are more similar to developed countries at this very high level of aggregation than are the Latin American countries, while the opposite relation prevails in the case of capital formation.

Significant differences may also exist in the distribution of gross domestic capital formation and its financing by smaller sectors, in the share of structures compared to equipment, and in the share of different types of structure and equipment. The statistics available unfortunately are not sufficiently detailed or reliable to confirm or to refute hypotheses which one might want to formulate on the basis of our knowledge of economic structure, of climatic conditions (which should, for example, influence the share of residential construction in total gross domestic capital formation), and of other economic and noneconomic factors in the different groups of countries.

To push the analysis of the determinants of κ one step farther, the relation of the main ratios, such as the share of gross and net domestic capital formation in national product, to a number of independent variables that were thought on the basis of theoretical considerations to be related to the different variants of κ was studied by calculating average values of κ for different ranges of the dependent variables (Tables B–2 and B–3) as well as by the standard method of simple correlation (Table B–4). The determinants of κ include the level of aggregate or per head national product in 1960 either at foreign exchange rates or at purchasing power equivalents, the rate of growth of aggregate and of real national product per head during the decade 1950–60, the rate of price rise from 1950 to 1960, the ratio of international capital movements to gross national product for the 1956–60 period, the foreign trade ratio in 1960, the share of agriculture or the government in gross national product in 1960, and the density of population in 1960 and the rate of population growth in the 1950's. The results were not decisive or encouraging. A number of the relationships were found to be significant by the usual statistical tests—i.e., it was very unlikely that the observed correlation resulted from a chance combination of κ with independent variables—but each of the independent variables included in the experiment explained only a relatively small proportion of the observed differences in κ among countries. This was true whether all the fifty-odd countries are regarded as one group, or whether five groupings of countries are considered (developed, European developed, less developed, Latin American less developed, and Afro-Asian less developed). It was therefore not felt that multiple correlation analysis, measuring the joint relationship of several of the same variables with κ, would yield sufficiently better results to justify the effort.[2]

2. The simple correlations obtained by B. M. Russett and associates in their *World Handbook of Political and Social Indicators* (New

Since the character of the association between the share of domestic capital formation and the several independent variables is easier to observe in Tables B–2 and B–3, although Table B–4 must be consulted to obtain an idea of the closeness of the association (the value of R^2) and its statistical significance, the following brief comments will be based primarily on the first pair of tables.

Looking first at the fifty-odd countries together, it is difficult to find clear associations between the values of κ, on a gross or net basis, and any of the independent variables. There is a tendency toward positive association of the capital formation ratio with the level of real national product per head in 1960 as well as with the rate of growth of real national product in the 1950s. Thus the most rapidly growing group of countries[3]—on the basis of real national product per head—had an average κ of 25 per cent, compared to a ratio of 8 per cent for the most slowly growing group of countries. Similarly the group of countries with the highest

---

Haven, Yale University Press, 1964), which became available after completion of Tables B–2 to B–4, are equally inconclusive, even though their calculations covered a slightly larger number of countries and a somewhat longer period of time, for many countries 1950–59. They found a coefficient of determination (R^2) of 0.33 for the relation of κ to the rate of growth of real national product per head, the only independent variable identical with those used here, compared with the value of 0.19 in Table B–4. Their correlations of κ with social and political indicators showed even lower coefficients, e.g. 0.33 for inhabitants per hospital bed (inverse), 0.29 for share of agriculture in national product (inverse), 0.26 for share of general government in total employment, and 0.25 for life expectancy. All of these coefficients reflect a moderate degree of association between various indicators or reflections of the level of real income per head and κ, a relation which is measured directly in several ways in Table B–4, yielding even lower coefficients for all countries taken together.

3. The boundaries of the values of the independent variables in Tables B–2 and B–3 were so selected that each of the four groups distinguished included approximately the same number of countries, so that each group is very similar to a quartile of a frequency distribution. This is true only for the entire group of countries included in the calculations, not for developed and less developed countries taken separately.

Table B–2

Gross Domestic Capital Formation Ratio, 1956–60, for Selected Groupings of Countries

UNWEIGHTED AVERAGES (PER CENT OF GROSS NATIONAL PRODUCT)

Classifier	Class Boundaries	All Countries	All Developed	All Less Developed	European Developed	American Less Developed	Afro-Asian Less Developed
I. Real GNP per head (1960 purchasing power)	Over $1,500	23.8	22.3	29.3	21.6	29.8	
	$700–1,500	21.6	22.7	20.0	21.8	20.0	
	$300–700	20.6	32.3[a]	19.8		19.8	16.2
	Below $300	16.9	30.4[a]	16.0		15.6	16.2
	All	20.7	23.3	19.1	21.7	20.4	16.2
II. Annual rate of growth of real GNP per head, 1950–60	Over 4.75%	24.8	26.2	23.3	24.0	24.0	
	2.50–4.75	20.1	21.9	18.7	21.9	9.6[a]	22.4
	1.50–2.50	17.5	20.2	15.4	21.1	16.4	13.8[b]
	Below 1.50	17.9	25.8[a]	16.3		17.3	12.5[a]
	All	20.4	23.2	18.4	22.8	18.7	17.9
III. Annual rate of growth of aggregate real GNP, 1950–60	Over 5.75%	22.9	26.5	20.8	23.4[b]	20.8	20.9[b]
	4.25–5.75	18.9	23.6	17.1	23.6	17.1	17.3[b]
	3.00–4.25	19.4	22.8	13.6	23.6	10.0[a]	15.4[b]
	Below 3.00	19.8	17.0[b]	22.6	17.0	22.6[b]	
	All	20.4	23.2	18.4	22.3	18.7	17.9
IV. Annual rate of growth of population, 1950–60	Over 2.75%	19.4	28.6[b]	18.2		20.6	14.6
	2.00–2.75	21.4	24.8	19.2		18.1	20.4
	1.00–2.00	22.9	25.0	21.4	25.0	21.1	16.8
	Below 1.00	20.0	20.0	19.8	20.0	22.4[a]	
	All	20.8	23.3	19.4	21.7	20.4	16.6

V. Annual rate of price rise, 1950–60	Over 5.00%	18.8	27.4	17.1		17.1	15.7[b]
	2.75–5.00	23.9	23.9	23.8	21.4	22.4[a]	19.6
	1.25–2.75	21.4	21.6	21.3	22.6	22.8	19.3
	Below 1.25	18.4	22.2	17.1	21.0	22.6	12.5
	All	20.7	23.3	19.1	21.7	20.6	16.2
VI. Share of foreign trade in GNP, 1960	Over 30%	22.5	22.9	22.2	21.7	27.3	17.3
	20–30	21.0	22.4	19.8	22.2	21.5	16.1[a]
	15–20	19.9	25.7	16.1	22.0	13.1	18.3[b]
	Below 15	18.7	22.9	16.6	21.0	18.2	14.9
	All	20.8	23.3	19.1	21.7	21.1	16.7
VII. Share of agriculture in GNP, 1960	Over 34%	15.0		15.0		15.7	14.5
	23–34	20.7	14.2[a]	21.2	14.2[a]	22.9	17.3
	11–23	24.0	26.0	22.0	22.2	21.8	23.1
	Below 11	22.7	22.3	24.4[b]	22.5	27.4[a]	
	All	20.6	23.1	19.3	21.7	20.6	16.2
VIII. Net domestic investment rate, 1956–60	Over 16%	27.4	28.3	26.7	26.8	28.3	20.7[b]
	12–16	21.6	23.4	20.2	23.0	19.9	20.4
	9–12	17.5	19.6[b]	16.6	19.6	18.5	11.3[a]
	Below 9	15.2	17.8	13.3	17.9	16.3	11.0
	All	21.3	23.3	19.3	21.7	21.8	16.2

[a] One country only. [b] Two countries only.

Sources of Classifiers for Tables B–2 and B–3:

I: P. N. Rosenstein-Rodan, *Review of Economics and Statistics*, vol. 43 (May 1961).

II, III, VI, VII, VIII: Based on data in U.N., *Yearbook of National Accounts Statistics* (1961).

IV: Derived from data in U.N., *Demographic Yearbook* (1961).

V: Based on wholesale price indices as given in U.N., *Statistical Yearbook* (1960) or International Monetary Fund, *International Financial Statistics.*

Table B–3

Net Domestic Capital Formation Ratio, 1956–60, for Selected Groupings of Countries

UNWEIGHTED AVERAGES (PER CENT OF GROSS DOMESTIC PRODUCT)

Classifier	Class Boundaries	All Countries	All Developed	All Less Developed	European Developed	American Less Developed	Afro-Asian Less Developed
I. Real GNP, per head (1960 purchasing power)	Over $1,500	15.1	12.8	23.9[a]	12.0	23.9[a]	
	$700–1,500	12.9	14.2	11.0	13.3	11.0	
	$300–700	15.5	22.7[a]	14.8		13.5	10.4
	Below 300	11.3	23.0[a]	10.3		7.6	11.2
	All	13.7	14.3	13.4	12.4	13.8	11.1
II. Annual rate of growth of real GNP per head, 1950–60	Over 4.75%	16.9	17.1	16.6	14.7	16.8	
	2.50–4.75	13.6	13.3	13.9	13.3		14.9
	1.50–2.50	10.6	10.8	10.4	11.8	10.1[b]	10.8[b]
	Below 1.50	7.6	13.9	6.4		5.8	8.5[a]
	All	12.8	14.0	11.8	13.3	11.1	12.4
III. Annual rate of growth of aggregate real GNP, 1950–60	Over 5.75%	16.8	17.6	16.3	14.5[b]	17.4	14.9[b]
	4.25–5.75	11.7	14.3	10.6	14.3	10.9	9.6[b]
	3.00–4.25	11.6	13.0	9.2	14.4	2.1[a]	12.8[b]
	Below 3.00	7.7	8.8	6.6[b]	8.8[b]	6.6[b]	
	All	12.8	14.0	11.8	13.3	11.1	12.4
IV. Annual rate of growth of population, 1950–60	Over 2.75%	14.2	20.9	13.0		15.7	8.3
	2.00–2.75	13.0	15.9	10.9		6.7[b]	13.5
	1.00–2.00	15.3	15.4	15.2	15.5	13.6	13.0
	Below 1.00	12.2	10.9	15.0	10.9	15.1[a]	
	All	13.8	14.3	13.5	12.4	13.8	11.3

V. Annual rate of price rise, 1950–60	Over 5.00%	11.3	19.4[b]	9.2		7.4	10.2[b]
	2.75–5.00	16.7	15.4	19.6	12.9	15.1	17.3[a]
	1.25–2.75	14.7	12.8	16.0	14.0	16.6	14.9
	Below 1.25	11.6	10.7	12.0	9.7	19.1	7.9
	All	13.7	14.3	13.4	12.4	13.8	11.1
VI. Share of foreign trade in GNP, 1960	Over 30%	15.3	13.5	16.6	11.9	20.9	11.0
	20–30	12.9	13.9	11.7	13.4	11.9	
	15–20	12.8	16.4	10.4	12.5[a]	7.0	12.6[b]
	Below 15	12.1	13.9	10.9	12.4[b]	11.0[b]	10.8
	All	13.6	14.3	13.1	12.4	14.1	11.3
VII. Share of agriculture in GNP, 1960	Over 34%	10.5		10.5		10.7	10.4
	23–34	14.7	8.8	15.3	8.8	16.5	10.6
	11–23	15.6	17.3	13.9	13.1	13.2	17.3[a]
	Below 11	13.1	12.2	17.6	12.5	17.5[a]	
	All	13.5	13.8	13.4	12.3	13.8	11.1

[a] One country only. [b] Two countries only.

Table B–4

Relation of Gross and Net Domestic Capital Formation Ratio to Selected Independent Variables, 1956–60[a]

VALUE OF R^2

Independent Variables	All Countries	Developed	Less Developed	European Developed	American	Afro-Asian
					Less Developed	
GROSS						
Real GNP per head						
Exchange rates	.11*	.19	.22*	·	.31*	·
Purchasing power equivalent,[b] 1960	.12*	.19	.27**	·	.43*	·
Growth of real GNP, 1950–60						
Aggregate	·	.24	.09	.20	.02	·
Per head	.19*	.13	.15	·	.27	.16
Price rise, 1950–60	.07	·	.08	·	·	.25
Population density, 1960	.06	.23	·	.17	.23	·
Foreign trade ratio, 1960	·	·	.13	·	.61*	·
Capital movement ratio, 1956–60	·	.09	.02	·	·	·
Government share in GNP, 1960	.05	·	·	.55*	.17	·
NET						
Real GNP per head						
Exchange rates	·	.29*	.19*	·	.35	·
Purchasing power equivalent,[b] 1960	.03	.29*	.34**	·	.59**	·
Growth of real GNP, 1950–60						
Aggregate	.32**	.32	.31*	.31	.60*	·
Per head	.44**	.21	.51**	·	.61*	·
Price rise, 1950–60	.10	.18	.22*	·	.35	.43
Population density, 1960	.02	.18	·	·	.15	·
Foreign trade ratio, 1960	·	·	.11	·	.53*	·
International capital movement ratio, 1950–60	·	.14	·	·	·	·
Government share in GNP, 1950–60	·	·	·	.15	·	·

[a] Dots indicate degree of correlation zero or very low (less than .01).
[b] Estimates of P. Rosenstein-Rodan (*Review of Economics and Statistics*, 1961).
* Significant at 5 per cent level. ** Significant at 1 per cent level.

per head income in 1960 showed an average gross domestic capital formation ratio in 1956–60 of 24 per cent, compared to a ratio of 17 per cent for the group with the lowest per head income—a rather small difference, given the very wide range of incomes per head. A positive, though weak, association can also be observed for the foreign trade ratio; the countries in which foreign trade (in 1960) accounted for a large proportion of gross national product had a slightly higher average κ than countries in which foreign trade was less important.

The independent variable possibly of most interest for financial analysis, the rate of increase in the general price level in the 1950s, showed a reasonably clear relation to the domestic capital formation ratio, a relation which might be described as concave in form because the average value of the ratio was higher for the two groups of countries having experienced a moderate rise in prices (between 1½ and 2¾ per year) than for the two groups with the mildest or sharpest price rises. The differences were relatively more pronounced for the net than for the gross capital formation ratio. In the first (net) case the difference was between 16 per cent for the two middle groups, compared with 11 per cent for the two extreme groups; in the second (gross) case the spread was only between 23 and 18 per cent. These relationships may suggest that for this period a moderate rise in the price level was more conducive to, or to be more cautious, was more compatible with, a high rate of capital formation than were deflation or price stability or a pronounced inflation (i.e. a rise in the price level at a rate of more than 5 per cent per year).

When attention is turned to the more homogeneous groups of developed and less developed countries, or to the subgroups of European developed and Latin American and Afro-Asian less developed countries, some of the relationships observed for the entire set of countries are attenuated, or vanish for one or the other group of countries, while others—and these are more numerous—become more pronounced, and a few new relations appear. The details can be observed in Tables B–2 and B–3 by comparing the entries in columns (2) to (6).

The relatively small part of the differences in capital formation ratios among countries that can be explained by a group of independent variables, which are suggested by a priori consideration, may be due to several factors or combinations of them. First, the set of the independent variables used here, and by other investigators, may miss the variables that determine the ratios and that might be found if the search were conducted on a larger scale, i.e. for more countries, for longer periods of time, and by experimenting with a much larger number of independent potentially explanatory variables and with alternative forms of the relation. Secondly, some of the variables used may have a greater influence than the simple methods used here disclose, an influence that would become evident if more powerful methods of analysis were brought into play. Thirdly, the number of determinants may be so large and their interrelations may be so irregular that a satisfactory statistical explanation is beyond reach. Whatever the ultimate answer may be, it would seem that for the time being financial analysis must treat the capital formation ratio as an essentially exogenous figure, subject only to the few and rather loose relations that are shown in Tables B–2, B–3, and B–4, which have been summarized in the preceding paragraphs.

III. AN ELEMENTARY ECONOMETRIC ANALYSIS OF ϕ AND Φ

The purpose of this appendix, as explained in the final section of Chapter 4, is to report on the results of an attempt to relate the values of the various countries' ratio of nonfinancial issues to national product (ϕ) and the values of the stock of nonfinancial issues to national wealth (Φ) to the level or the movement of a few characteristics of these countries' gross national product per head and to their price level as independent variables. The choice of these independent variables has been guided, within the restriction of the availability of data—and this is a severe limitation because up to thirty-five countries are involved for periods of up to a century—partly by preliminary experimentation, and partly by the feeling that within the necessarily limited scope of the analysis general characteristics of an economy that are likely to influence a phenomenon as broad as the issues and assets of financial institutions, characteristics such as the level and the movement of real gross national product per head, are more useful than more specialized independent variables. Following that principle, it is true, one should also have tested the influence of the level and the change in interest rates, but there were not sufficient data available on an international comparative basis for a sufficiently long period.

THE NET ISSUE RATIO OF FINANCIAL INSTITUTIONS (ϕ)

As a first step in this exploration of the possible determinants, a number of economic factors likely to have ex-

TABLE C–1

Correlation (R) between Ratio of Change in Assets of Financial Institutions to Period's GNP (ϕ) and Selected Independent Variables

	1881 to 1900	1901 to 1913	1914 to 1929	1930 to 1938	1939 to 1948	1949 to 1963
ALL NONSOCIALIST COUNTRIES						
GNP per head						
At exchange rate		.17	.23	.33	.26	.26
At purchasing power parity		.37	.40*	.40*	.32	.35
Rate of growth in period						
GNP, aggregate		.55**	.41*	.35	−.04	.47*
GNP per head		.62**	.58**	.43*	.04	.45*
GNP deflator		−.18	−.46	.43*	.25	.29
Population		.10	−.07	−.25	−.30	.06
DEVELOPED COUNTRIES						
GNP per head						
At exchange rate	−.35	−.25	−.12	−.35	−.19	−.54
At purchasing power parity	−.37	−.04	−.09	−.29	−.15	−.47*
Rate of growth in period						
GNP, aggregate	.44	.50*	.43	.48*	.08	.68**
GNP per head	.50	.56*	.55*	.43	.06	.60**
GNP deflator	.57*	−.44	−.70**	.57*	.60*	.32
Population	.10	−.04	−.02	.42	.16	.21
LESS DEVELOPED COUNTRIES						
GNP per head						
At exchange rate		.55	.26	.16	.38	.12
At purchasing power parity		.53	.76*	.48	.67**	.46
Rate of growth in period						
GNP, aggregate		.89*	.59	.25	.14	.11
GNP per head		.74	.20	.28	.28	.10
GNP deflator		−.11	.62	.68*	−.23	.75**
Population		.74	.58	.01	−.35	.02

* Significant at 5 per cent level. ** Significant at 1 per cent level.

erted influence on ϕ and Φ, for which sufficient data were available, were examined by means of simple correlation. The results are shown in Tables C–1 and C–2 in the form of the coefficients of correlation (R) or of determination

TABLE C–2

Correlation of ϕ with Level and Rate of Growth of National Product per Head and with Rate of Change in Price Level

VALUE AND SIGNIFICANCE OF R^2

	Real National Product per Head		Price Level Change	*a* and *b*	*a* and *c*	*b* and *c*	*a*, *b*, and *c*
	Level (*a*)	Growth (*b*)	(*c*)				
ALL NONSOCIALIST COUNTRIES							
1901–1913	.13	.38**	.03	.43**	.18	.38*	.43*
1914–1929	.16*	.34**	.21	.37**	.34*	.40**	.44**
1930–1938	.16*	.18*	.18*	.29*	.30	.39**	.45**
1939–1948	.10	.00	.06	.11	.28*	.11	.31*
1949–1963	.12	.21*	.08	.34**	.24*	.33**	.51**
DEVELOPED COUNTRIES							
1881–1900	.13	.25	.32*	.68**	.32	.71**	.76**
1901–1913	.00	.31*	.19	.32	.21	.37	.39
1914–1929	.01	.30*	.49**	.36	.58**	.54**	.66**
1930–1938	.08	.18	.32*	.26	.36	.50*	.53*
1939–1948	.02	.00	.36*	.08	.45*	.57**	.58*
1949–1963	.22*	.36**	.11	.37	.28	.39*	.40
LESS DEVELOPED COUNTRIES							
1901–1913	.28	.55	.01	.68	.41	.68	.70
1914–1929	.57*	.04	.39	.68*	.78*	.47	.92*
1930–1938	.23	.08	.47*	.28	.48	.62*	.62
1939–1948	.45**	.08	.05	.45*	.45*	.08	.47
1949–1963	.22	.01	.56**	.23	.60**	.70**	.70**

* Significant at 5 per cent level. ** Significant at 1 per cent level.

(R^2), the latter indicating the proportion of the total variation of the dependent variables, i.e. ϕ and Φ, from their mean which is explained by differences in the independent variable. The coefficients R or R^2 are shown for each benchmark period or date separately for underdeveloped and developed countries as well as for all countries together, the varying number of countries included already having been shown in Table 4–2. Values of the coefficients, which are significant at the level of 5 per cent or 1 per cent (i.e. the probability of their being the result of chance are only 1 in 20 or 1 in 100) are distinguished by one or two asterisks respectively; the calculations make allowances for the number of observations.

Table C–1, setting forth the values of R for ϕ in different periods and for different groups of countries as the dependent variable, shows the following main results.

High values of the correlation coefficients are rare, say values of R of at least 0.60, which imply that the independent variable statistically explains about three-eighths of the total variance in the dependent variable. Of the ninety-six values in Table C–1 only eleven are above this limit, nine of which are also significant at the 5 per cent level. High values of R include:

1. For all countries, the rate of growth of real gross national product per head for the period 1901–13.
2. For developed countries
   The rate of growth of real gross national product, in the aggregate and per head for 1949–63.
   The rate of change in the price levels for 1914–29 and 1939–48.
3. For less developed countries
   The level of gross national product per head 1914–29.
   The rate of growth of real gross national product, in the aggregate and per head, in the 1901–13 period.
   The rate of change in the price level, 1914–29, 1930–38, and 1949–63.
   The rate of population growth for 1901–13.

On the basis of this criterion the results are more satisfactory, i.e. the values of R^2 are higher, for the less developed than for the developed countries or for all countries taken together. Among the six independent variables, the results are best—or rather least unsatisfactory—for the rate of growth of real national income per head and for the rate of change of price level. The results are a little more satisfactory for the periods 1901–13 and 1914–29 than for 1930–39 and, particularly, than for 1881–1900 and 1939–48.

The results are in general the same if the evaluation is based on the average value of the correlation coefficient (disregarding sign) for the several independent variables for the different groups of countries and the different periods. In that case the relation is most pronounced among the six independent variables in the case of the rate of change in the national product deflator and is least satisfactory for the rate of growth in population. Among groups of countries, the average values of R are highest for less developed countries and lowest for developed countries; the coefficients for all countries together occupies an intermediate position. Finally, among the seven periods, the average of R is generally lowest for the period 1939–48, upset by developments of World War II, while the systematic differences among the other periods are not very pronounced, although a slight tendency can be detected for the values of R to be somewhat higher for the period 1901–13 and 1914–29 than for 1930–38 and 1949–63 and also higher than the values for the earliest period 1881–1900, for which the number of countries included is smallest and limited to developed countries. It therefore looks as if, for the restricted range of independent variables to which experimentation has been limited, their relationship to ϕ was somewhat more pronounced in the earlier part of the twentieth century than since the 1930s.

The examination of the correlations of ϕ with five independent variables for up to nine periods and for three groups of countries, based on the coefficents of correlation in Table C–1, thus indicates that one of the variables (gross national product per head translated at current foreign exchange rates) generally performs more poorly than the alternative variable of gross national product per head using purchasing power parities, and that a second variable, population, only rarely has a significant influence on ϕ. These two variables, therefore, were eliminated from the multiple correlations which thus were limited to the three remaining variables—real gross national product per head based on purchasing power parities, the rate of growth during the period of real gross national product per head, and the rate of change of the general price level measured by the gross national product deflator. The coefficients of determination for the four possible combinations of these three variables are shown in Table C–2, which for ease of comparison adds the values of R^2 for each of the three variables taken alone. Table C–3 lists the sixteen multiple regression equations together with the standard errors of each of the terms, which, in combination with the number of observations indicated in Table 4–2, permits a judgment about their statistical significance.

Starting with the coefficient of determination of ϕ—which indicates the proportion of the variation in ϕ explained by variations in the independent variables—we find that none of the three independent variables alone is able to explain as much as two-fifths of the total variation in the dependent variable, except in a few cases.

Since the three independent variables whose effect on ϕ is being investigated are not too strongly intercorrelated (the correlation is considerably higher among the level and the rate of growth of real national product per head than between either of these two and the rate of change in the price level), but since each of them explains a small part of the variance of ϕ, we may expect that combinations of two or three variables will increase the proportion of the total variance that is being explained. This is borne out by the coefficients of multiple correlation shown in Table C–2, columns 4 through 7, both in the increase in the number of cases having a value of R^2 in excess of a given level and in the increase in the proportion of coefficients significant at the 5 per cent or the 1 per cent level. Thus, of the total 64 coefficients of multiple correlation—16 for each of the four combinations of two or three variables—38 are significant at the level of 5 per cent or better, of which 19 are highly significant, and all of these have a value of more than 0.30.

The proportion of significant coefficients is substantially higher for all countries taken together—16 out of 20—than it is if developed and less developed countries are analyzed separately, in which case only every second coefficient meets the test of significance (13 out of 24 for developed and 9 out of 20 coefficients for less developed countries). There is little difference in the proportion of coefficients that are significant in relation to the variables being combined, at least at the 5 per cent level. The largest proportion appears when the rate of growth of real national product per head and the rate of change in the price level (or all three variables) are combined (11 of 16 coefficients); the lowest proportion (8 of 16) appears when the level of real income per head and the rate of change in the price level are combined. In the more stringent test of significance at the 1 per cent level, however, the combination of rate of growth of real income per head and price level change ranks first with 7 of the 16 coefficients meeting the test. The combination of all three variables is not far behind (6 of 16 coefficients), but the two other combinations—the level of real national product per head combined with either its rate of growth or the rate of change in the price level—show only 2 or 4 coefficients out of 16 significant at the 1 per cent level. This confirms the importance of the rate of change in real income per head and in the price level as explanatory variables for ϕ since they are involved in both the highest scoring combinations. It also confirms the relatively small importance of the level of real national income per head.

Differences in the proportion of coefficients of significance among periods are rather small. The period 1914–29 appears as the one most amenable to explanation by a combination of three simple variables, R^2 being significant at the five per cent level in ten of the twelve cases, and significant at the 1 per cent level in one-half of the total number. However, the period 1949–63 is almost at the same

TABLE C-3

Regression Equations for ϕ Correlated with Level (a) and Rate of Growth (b) of Real National Product and with Rate of Change of Price Level (c)

	$\phi =$								R^2	F
	ALL NONSOCIALIST COUNTRIES									
1901–1913	.0113	+0.0000751 (0.0000668)	a	+	2.152 (0.817)	b	−	0.026 (0.521)	.43*	4.01
1914–1929	.0225	+0.0000389 (0.0000310)	a	+	1.521 (0.814)	b	−	0.0197 (0.0125)	.44**	5.25
1930–1938	.0291	+0.0000485 (0.0000305)	a	+	0.703* (0.276)	b	+	0.616* (0.233)	.45**	6.36
1939–1948	.0140	+0.0000769 (0.0000290)	a*	+	0.480 (0.528)	b	+	0.224* (0.085)	.31*	3.67
1949–1963	−.0163	+0.0000293 (0.0000090)	a**	+	1.664** (0.414)	b	+	0.476** (0.152)	.51**	10.10
	DEVELOPED COUNTRIES									
1881–1900	.0233	−0.00137 (0.00095)	a	+	2.215** (0.541)	b	+	1.114 (0.613)	.76**	9.69
1901–1913	.0668	−0.0000536 (0.0000946)	a	+	1.578 (0.890)	b	−	0.839 (0.790)	.39	2.30
1914–1929	.0956	−0.0000741 (0.0000370)	a	+	1.159 (0.712)	b	−	0.344** (0.011)	.66**	7.61
1930–1938	.0820	−0.0000485 (0.0000340)	a	+	0.715* (0.337)	b	+	1.330* (0.508)	.53*	4.53
1939–1948	.0501	+0.0000181 (0.0000581)	a	+	1.217 (0.659)	b	+	0.410** (0.111)	.58*	5.39

(Each c coefficient above is followed by the variable c.)

1949–1963	.1011	− 0.0000147 *a* (0.0000275)	+ 1.255 *b* (0.744)	+ 0.419 *c* (0.554)	.40	3.09
			UNDERDEVELOPED COUNTRIES			
1901–1913	−.0144	+0.000109 *a* (0.000373)	+ 2.933 *b* (2.955)	+ 0.285 *c* (1.024)	.70	.79
1914–1929	−.0260	+0.000189 *a*** (0.000040)	+ 1.568* *b* (0.579)	+ 0.164 *c* (0.047)	.92*	15.57
1930–1938	.0192	+0.0000079 *a* (0.0000754)	+ 0.319 *b* (0.195)	+ 0.333* *c* (0.132)	.62	3.88
1939–1948	−.3210	+0.000180 *a** (0.000070)	− 0.399 *b* (0.670)	− 0.042 *c* (0.0733)	.47	2.66
1949–1963	.0045	−0.0000168 *a* (0.0000348)	+ 1.247 *b* (0.633)	+ 0.562** *c* (0.135)	.70**	8.61

a = Gross national product per head at end of period in purchasing power dollars.
b = Rate of growth of real gross national product per head during period.
c = Rate of change of price level (gross national product deflator).
* Significant at 5 per cent level. ** Significant at 1 per cent level.

level, with 9 significant coefficients of which again 6 are significant at the 1 per cent level. The 1930–38 and 1939–48 periods with 7 significant coefficients—although in each case only two of them at the 1 per cent level—are not too far behind. The only period in which the proportion of significant coefficients remains much smaller (2 out of 12) is 1901–13, but this is due partly to the smaller number of countries included, which raises the value of R^2 required for a given level of significance. The earliest period, 1881–1900, also shows itself as very amenable to this simple explanation, three of the four possible combinations resulting in a coefficient which is significant at the 1 per cent level. Indeed, the values of R^2 for this period, which includes fourteen developed countries (ten of them in Europe), are the highest for all periods in the case of three of the four combinations of variables.

The conclusion, thus, is not expectedly that a combination of the three variables—level and rate of growth of real national product per head in purchasing power terms and the rate of change of the general price level—provides the most satisfactory explanation within this very simple framework, the only one tested. However, the advantage of this three-variable combination over the combination of the rate of change in real national product per head and in the price level alone is rather small, 11 of the 16 coefficients being significant at a level of 5 per cent or better in both cases—9 of them being identical as to period and country grouping—and the value of the 16 coefficients averaging 0.55 against 0.45. Thus, the combined effect of the three variables considered here explains, on the average, five-ninths of the variations in ϕ, and the coefficients are not likely to be the result of chance to the extent of more than 1 in 20 in eleven of the sixteen cases. Indeed the likelihood of the coefficients in the three-variable combination being the result of change is less than 1 in 20 if all countries are taken together in every one of the six periods and, for developed countries, in four out of six periods (all except 1901–13 and 1949–63), though it cannot be ruled out for less developed countries in three of the five periods. Among the five periods for which separate coefficients can be calculated, the coefficients are significant for all countries together as well as for developed and less developed countries separately in one period (1914–29); they are significant in all countries and in developed countries in the periods 1930–38 and 1939–48 and in all countries and in underdeveloped countries for the period 1948–63.

Of the sixteen regression equations using the three variables shown in Table C–3, one-half have a coefficient of multiple correlation that is significant or highly significant and which on the average explains fully one-half of the variations in ϕ. The coefficient is significant or highly significant for four of the six equations for all countries, and for three of the five for developed countries, but for only one of the five equations for less developed countries, though the values of R^2 are on the average somewhat higher for underdeveloped countries than for developed or all countries.

Turning to the individual coefficients, the level of real product per head is found to be significant in four of the sixteen equations, the rate of growth in real product per head in six, and the rate of change in the price level in seven equations. There is only one equation (all countries for the 1949–63 period) in which all three coefficients are significant; there are two more (all countries for 1939–48 and underdeveloped countries for 1914–29) in which two of the three meet this test. On the other hand, four of the sixteen equations do not have a single significant coefficient.

The influence of each of the three coefficients, as well as of the constant term, on the calculated value of ϕ can be assessed only if the appropriate values for the independent variables (shown in Table C–4) are inserted in the equations. This may be illustrated in the case of the equation that yields the statistically most satisfactory result—the equation for all countries during the 1949–63 period. In that case the average real product per head in 1963 is $1,365 at purchasing power equivalents, the average rate of growth of real product per head in the 1949–63 period is 3.42 per

Table C–4

Unweighted Country Averages of Independent Variables (*a*, *b*, and *c*)

	All Nonsocialist Countries			Developed Countries			Less Developed Countries		
	Real GNP per Head			Real GNP per Head			Real GNP per Head		
	Level[a] $	Rate of Growth Per Cent per Year	Price Level Change Per Cent per Year	Level[a] $	Rate of Growth Per Cent per Year	Price Level Change Per Cent per Year	Level[a] $	Rate of Growth Per Cent per Year	Price Level Change Per Cent per Year
	(1)	(2)	(3)	(4)	(5)	(6)	(7)	(8)	(9)
1860–1880	142	1.55	−.30	142	1.55	−.30			
1881–1900	155	2.08	−.26	155	2.08	−.26			
1901–1913	202	1.46	1.30	241	1.58	1.42	85	1.08	.94
1914–1929	390	1.27	15.88[b]	504	1.48	21.37[b]	160	.85	4.90
1930–1938	315	.29	−.53	448	.71	−.27	121	−.31	−.92
1939–1948	627	.91	16.14	929	.64	14.31	256	1.25	18.41
1949–1960	1204	3.53	4.76	1816	3.79	3.94	468	3.23	5.76
1961–1963	1365	3.00	5.26	2061	3.43	3.35	529	2.49	7.55
1949–1963	1365	3.42	4.82	2061	3.71	3.79	529	3.07	6.06

[a] End of period.
[b] The figures, excluding Germany, are 4.61 in col. 3 and 4.46 in col. 6.

cent a year, and the average rise in the price level 4.82 per cent. We therefore have, since the observed value for ϕ is 10.37 per cent:

$$\begin{aligned} 0.1037 &= -0.0163 + 0.0000293 \times 1{,}365 + 1.664 \\ &\quad \times 0.0342 + 0.476 \times 0.0482 \\ &= -0.0163 + 0.0400 + 0.0570 + 0.0230 \end{aligned}$$

In this case the rate of growth of real product per head accounts for 55 per cent of the observed value of ϕ, the level of real income per head for 39 per cent, and the rate of change in the price level for 22 per cent, while the constant term reduces the sum of these three components by 16 per cent. The contribution of the constant term and of each of the three independent variables to the observed averaged value of ϕ for the group of countries involved differs, of course, from period to period. So does, in particular, the relative contribution of the constant term and of the sum of the three independent variables. The shares of these four factors, calculated as in the example above are shown in Table C–5. It is thus seen, for example, that for the period 1949–63 the contribution of the four components ($\phi = 100$) is as follows:

		Real Income per Head		
	Constant Term	Level	Growth Rate	Rise in Price Level
All countries	−15	38	55	22
Developed countries	76	−23	35	12
Less developed countries	7	−13	56	50

It is interesting to observe that the contribution of the level of real income is larger for all countries taken together than it is for developed or less developed countries taken separately and that it is positive, whereas it is negative in each of the two other groups. This confirms the impression gained from scatter diagrams that developed and less developed countries constitute two separate populations with different averages for ϕ and a (the level of real income per head) both higher in developed than in under-

TABLE C–5

Structure of Regression Equations for New Issue Ratio of Financial Institutions (ϕ)

	PER CENT OF VALUE OF DEPENDENT VARIABLE				
			Rate of Growth of		
	Constant Term	Level of Real Income per Head	Real Income per Head	Price Level	Value of ϕ
	ALL NONSOCIALIST COUNTRIES				
1901–1913	20	26	54	−0	.0575
1914–1929	41	28	35	−6	.0539
1930–1938	67	35	5	−7	.0431
1939–1948	14	47	4	35	.1029
1949–1963	−15	38	55	22	.1037
	DEVELOPED COUNTRIES				
1881–1900	51	−47	102	−6	.0453
1901–1913	100	−19	37	−18	.0670
1914–1929	140	−54	25	−11	.0687
1930–1938	133	−35	8	−6	.0617
1939–1948	37	13	6	44	.1333
1949–1963	76	−23	35	12	.1334
	LESS DEVELOPED COUNTRIES				
1900–1913	−49	32	108	9	.0292
1914–1929	−102	118	52	32	.0265
1930–1938	119	6	−6	−19	.0161
1939–1948	49	70	−7	−12	.0654
1949–1963	7	−13	56	50	.0680

developed countries, within each of which the association between ϕ and a is weak and negative, the result being a positive and fairly strong association if all countries are treated as one population.[1] It is also evident that the rate of growth of real income per head has in all three groups a stronger influence on ϕ than either of the two other independent variables. The large contribution of the constant term for the developed countries is indicative of the higher

1. The null hypothesis (i.e. developed and less developed countries constitute one population) is rejected for the three periods 1914–29, 1930–38, and 1939–48 at the 1 or the 5 per cent level (1930–38), but cannot be rejected at the 5 per cent level for the periods 1901–13 and 1949–63.

degree of uniformity among them than among underdeveloped countries or all countries taken together.

THE RATIO OF FINANCIAL INSTITUTIONS' ASSETS TO NATIONAL PRODUCT (Φ)

Tables C–6 to C–8 provide the same information on the correlation coefficients and regression equations for the ratio of the assets of financial institutions to gross national product (Φ) that was given in Tables C–1 to C–3 for the corresponding flow ratio of net issues (ϕ), i.e. change in assets between benchmark dates. In view of the considerable similarity in many characteristics of the two sets of correlations—a similarity which is not astonishing since the Φ's may be regarded as averages of the φ's of preceding periods —it will suffice to note some of the differences.

The most important difference is the predominant influence on Φ of the level of real gross national product per head in dollars of purchasing power equivalents among the determinants considered in the correlations. This is indicated, first, in Table C–6 by the considerably higher levels of the value of the correlation coefficients and the higher proportion of the coefficients that are significant at the 1 or 5 per cent levels. Thus of the seventeen coefficients for each independent variable those for the level of real income per head are significant or highly significant in nine cases if the original data are reduced on the basis of purchasing power parities, and in six cases if exchange rates are used, compared to three cases for the rate of change in the price level, two for the rate of growth of population, and one for the rate of growth of aggregate real gross national product. Indeed the level of real gross national product per head (purchasing power equivalents) is significant or highly significant for all five dates from 1913 to 1963 in the case of all countries, and in three of the five dates (1929, 1938, and 1948) for less developed countries alone, though in the case of developed countries it meets this test in only one of the seven dates (1948), the date for which the coeffi-

TABLE C–6

Correlation (R) between Ratio of Assets of Financial Institutions to GNP (Φ) and Selected Independent Variables

	1880	1900	1913	1929	1938	1948	1963
ALL NONSOCIALIST COUNTRIES							
GNP per head							
At exchange rate			.25	.20	.63**	.74**	.71**
At purchasing power parity			.51*	.42*	.68**	.77**	.72**
Rate of growth in preceding period							
GNP, aggregate			.35	.12	−.04	.09	.08
GNP per head			.55*	.29	.13	.21	.21
GNP deflator			−.29	−.07	.19	−.47**	−.24
Population			−.07	−.15	−.64**	−.39*	−.19
DEVELOPED COUNTRIES							
GNP per head							
At exchange rate	−.48	.05	−.17	−.34	−.13	.50*	−.04
At purchasing power parity	−.37	.03	.08	−.26	−.07	.48*	−.15
Rate of growth in preceding period							
GNP, aggregate	.41	.37	.34	.07	−.02	.51*	−.03
GNP per head	.66	.54	.50*	.11	−.00	.48*	.01
GNP deflator	−.58	.07	−.71**	−.24	−.06	−.74**	−.37
Population	−.35	−.09	−.17	−.04	−.11	.35	−.06

LESS DEVELOPED COUNTRIES

GNP per head					
At exchange rate	.58	.69*	.57*	.42	.28
At purchasing power parity	.68	.92**	.79**	.66**	.37
Rate of growth in preceding period					
GNP, aggregate	.80	.45	−.48	.15	.26
GNP per head	.77	−.02	−.47	.27	.44
GNP deflator	−.23	.52	.55	−.30	−.05
Population	.62	.54	−.34	−.29	−.34

* Significant at 5 per cent level ** Significant at 1 per cen level.

TABLE C-7

Correlation of Φ with Level and Rate of Growth of National Product per Head and with Rate of Change in Price Level

VALUE AND SIGNIFICANCE OF R^2

	Real National Product per Head		Price Level Change	*a* and *b*	*a* and *c*	*b* and *c*	*a*, *b*, and *c*
	Level (*a*)	Growth (*b*)	(*c*)				
			ALL NONSOCIALIST COUNTRIES				
1913	.26*	.30*	.08	.45**	.37*	.31*	.48*
1929	.17*	.08	.00	.19	.18	.08	.19
1938	.46**	.02	.04	.46**	.46**	.06	.47**
1948	.59**	.04	.23**	.59**	.62**	.23*	.65**
1963	.51**	.04	.06	.58**	.53**	.09	.59**
			DEVELOPED COUNTRIES				
1880	.13	.43	.34	.62	.36	.44	.65
1900	.00	.29	.00	.34	.02	.32	.34
1913	.01	.25*	.50**	.25	.50*	.56**	.56*
1929	.07	.01	.06	.10	.18	.06	.18
1938	.00	.00	.00	.01	.01	.00	.01
1948	.23*	.23*	.55**	.27	.55**	.56**	.56*
1963	.02	.00	.14	.03	.18	.15	.19
			LESS DEVELOPED COUNTRIES				
1929	.84**	.00	.03	.94**	.92**	.08	.94**
1938	.63**	.22	.30	.94**	.64**	.45	.95**
1948	.44**	.07	.90**	.45	.46*	.10	.52
1963	.14	.19	.00	.32	.24	.32	.35

* Significant at 5 per cent level. ** Significant at 1 per cent level.

cient for all other independent variables except population are also significant. (In the case of ϕ, it will be recalled, none of the independent variables is equally dominant, the rate of growth of real national product shows a significant value of R^2 in more cases than its level does, and the rate of change in the price level is significant in as many cases as the level of real national product in purchasing power terms.)

Because of the predominance of the effect of the level of real national product per head among the independent variables, the multiple correlation coefficients using all three variables are not as much in excess of the coefficients obtained on the basis of one variable only than is the case for ϕ. The difference is nevertheless substantial. Thus the average value of the sixteen multiple (three-variable) coefficients of determination (R^2) is 0.48, compared to an average of only 0.28 for real income per head alone; but the difference is much less pronounced if only significant coefficients are taken into account, in which case the values of the averages are 0.57 and 0.50 respectively.

For the three variable combinations the average value of R^2 is slightly lower for Φ than for ϕ (0.48 against 0.55) if all sixteen coefficients are averaged, but slightly higher (0.65 against 0.57) if the comparison is limited to the eight or eleven statistically significant coefficients. The three variables together thus explain both ratios ϕ and Φ about equally well, but their specific contribution to this explanation differs.

In particular, the relatively high explanatory value of the level of real product per head in the case of Φ, and the difference of this situation from that observed in the case of ϕ, would seem attributable to a good extent to the fact that the value of assets of financial institutions at a given date is the result of a cumulative process extending over long periods. Hence factors like the rate of change in aggregate or per head real product or in the price level over a period of about one decade preceding the balance sheet date may be presumed to have less influence on the value of Φ than the same changes in these variables have on ϕ for which they are contemporary. For the same reason the predominating influence of a variable like the level of real product per head, which is also the result of development over a long period, is easier to explain here than it would be for a flow magnitude like ϕ.

According to this reasoning, the difference between the coefficients for Φ and ϕ should be least pronounced—given a similar and high share of claims in total financial assets at the beginning of the period—in periods, or for countries, that experience a rapid and protracted inflation (say an average rate of at least 10 per cent per year for at least a decade) because such an inflation rapidly eliminates the ef-

TABLE C–8

Regression Equations for Φ on Level (*a*) and Rate of Growth (*b*) of Real National Product per Head and on Rate of Change in Price Level (*c*)

	Φ =							R^2	F
	ALL NONSOCIALIST COUNTRIES								
1913	.281	+	.00263 *a**	+	25.986 *b*	−	9.217 *c*	.48*	4.997*
			(.00115)		(14.088)		(8.994)		
1929	.523	+	.00105 *a*	+	10.863 *b*		.017 *c*	.19	1.573
			(.00065)		(17.071)		(.263)		
1938	.467	+	.00239 *a***	−	.105 *b*	+	2.514 *c*	.47**	6.744
			(.00057)		(5.121)		(4.321)		
1948	.628	+	.00098 *a***	−	5.047 *b*	−	1.036 *c*	.65**	15.678
			(.00018)		(3.233)		(.519)		
1963	.345	+	.00047 *a***	+	6.925 *b*	−	1.360 *c*	.59**	13.648
			(.00008)		(3.714)		(1.360)		
	DEVELOPED COUNTRIES								
1880	−1.889	+	.00122 *a*	+	61.032 *b*	−	14.329 *c*	.65	.607
			(.00158)		(67.470)		(71.236)		
1900	.603	−	.00148 *a*	+	32.556 *b*	+	.866 *c*	.34	1.553
			(.00271)		(15.483)		(17.544)		
1913	1.593	−	.00040 *a*	+	15.036 *b*	−	31.563 *c**	.56*	4.642
			(.00137)		(12.884)		(11.430)		
1929	1.992	−	.00118 *a*	+	2.653 *b*	−	.271 *c*	.18	.857
			(.00090)		(17.361)		(.263)		

Year	Constant		a		b		c	R^2	F
1938	1.804	−	.00029 *a*	−	.039 *b*	−	2.496 *c*	.01	.038
			(.00106)		(6.654)		(10.037)		
1948	1.816	−	.00011 *a*	+	2.060 *b*	−	2.051 *c**	.56*	5.105
			(.0038)		(4.356)		(.724)		
1963	2.230	−	.00016 *a*	−	.519 *b*	−	6.707 *c*	.19	1.089
			(.00020)		(5.478)		(4.081)		
					LESS DEVELOPED COUNTRIES				
1913	− .167	+	.00567 *a***	+	15.903 *b*	+	1.081 *c*	.97**	18.147
			(.00094)		(7.217)		(1.089)		
1929	− .144	+	.00330 *a***	+	7.725 *b*	+	.278 *c*	.94*	21.613
			(.00043)		(6.270)		(.510)		
1938	.072	+	.00346 *a***	−	6.916 *b***	−	.331 *c*	.95*	45.016
			(.00041)		(1.052)		(.715)		
1948	.339	+	.00144 *a**	−	5.168 *b*	−	.622 *c*	.52	3.186
			(.00052)		(4.953)		(.542)		
1963	.363	+	.00019 *a*	−	4.829 *b*	−	.106 *c*	.35	1.094
			(.00031)		(5.687)		(1.216)		

* Significant at 5 per cent level. ** Significant at 1 per cent level.

fect of previously accumulated claims on Φ. To test the hypothesis, it is necessary to compare the values of R^2 of both Φ and ϕ regressed on the movements of the general price level. A preliminary check comparing the difference between the values of Φ and ϕ for the three groups of countries and the five or six periods—a total of sixteen cases—with the unweighted average rate of price change shows evidence of the postulated relationship for less developed countries (the difference between Φ and ϕ being considerably higher for the period 1901–13 and 1948–63 than for 1914–29 and 1939–48, when it is negligible) but fails to do so for developed countries—except for a disappearance of the difference in the inflationary period 1939–48—and for all countries together. If the relationship exists, more specific and detailed tests are obviously needed to disclose it.

As in the case of ϕ, the average value of R^2 is highest for less developed countries, whether or not the comparison is limited to statistically significant coefficients. The situation, however, differs in that the values of R^2 are generally lowest for developed countries—i.e. they are below less developed countries, both alone and for the two groups together —in the case of Φ, while for ϕ the values for all countries together are slightly lower than those for either component groups. With respect to the level of the coefficients for different periods or dates, Φ differs from ϕ in that the values of R^2 show for all countries together a mild tendency to rise, which is absent in ϕ; and exhibit for less developed countries a definitely lower value of R^2 for 1948 and 1963 than for 1929 and 1938, a relation not in evidence in the values of ϕ. Here, as in the comparison for the three groupings of countries, the similarities are more pronounced than the differences, and it is not easy to find simple explanations for the divergencies.[2]

2. The hypothesis that developed and less developed countries form one rather than two statistically distinct populations is rejected for 1929, 1938, and 1948 at the 5 per cent level and for 1963 at the 1 per cent level, but cannot be rejected at that level for 1913, a result very similar to that noted for ϕ.

Table C-9

Structure of Regression Equations for Ratio of Assets of Financial Institutions to National Product

PER CENT OF VALUE OF DEPENDENT VARIABLE

	Constant Term	Level of Real Income per Head	Rate of Growth of Real Income per Head	Rate of Growth of Price Level[a]	Value of Φ
		ALL NONSOCIALIST COUNTRIES			
1913	26	50	35	−11	1.07
1929	49	38	13	0	1.07
1938	39	62	0	−1	1.21
1948	61	60	−5	−16	1.03
1963	30	55	20	−5	1.16
		DEVELOPED COUNTRIES			
1880	−224	206	113	5	.84
1900	57	−22	65	0	1.05
1913	124	−7	18	−35	1.29
1929	145	−43	3	−4	1.38
1938	107	−7	0	0	1.68
1948	127	−7	1	−21	1.43
1963	137	−20	−1	−16	1.62
		LESS DEVELOPED COUNTRIES			
1929	−31	114	14	1	.46
1938	14	81	4	1	.52
1948	64	70	−12	−22	.53
1963	60	17	24	−1	.61

[a] During preceding period.

Table C–9 provides information on the contribution of each of the three variables to the observed value of Φ for a given date and group of countries. In interpreting these data it is necessary to keep in mind the differing degree of statistical significance of the coefficients on which Table C–9 is based, differences that can be seen in Table C–8.

As for ϕ, the equations for the different dates are more regular for all countries taken together than for either of the two constituent groups. For the former the level of real income per head has the largest weight, while the influence of the change in the price level is small, but generally negative, i.e. it slightly reduces the value of Φ as would be expected since the price level has been generally rising since the turn of the century. For developed countries, on the other hand, the constant term is dominant except for the two earliest dates. The equations for less developed countries again are mainly influenced by the level of real income per head except in 1963.

It would have been possible to repeat these experiments in order to explain the level and movements of ϕ and of Φ (the results of which were summarized in the preceding few pages) for each of the five components of financial issues as well as for combinations of them, such as the issues of all banking institutions. The data on the dependent variables—the five sets of ϕ and Φ ratios—have been assembled and are discussed without the use of econometric tools in Chapter 5, while in the case of the independent variables the experiment could have started with the tools that have been used in this Appendix in the analysis of ϕ and Φ for the aggregate of all financial institutions. Similarly the cross-sectional study based on the data for a larger or smaller number of individual countries for a given benchmark date or period could have been supplemented as a first step by a time series analysis for the substantial number of countries—approximately twenty—for which data reaching back to the turn of the century or to World War I are available, thus providing for each country at least half a dozen observations; and as a second step by a systematic comparison of the result of the regression equations for individual countries.

The temptation to make an effort in this direction was great since there is little doubt that we would understand the movements of aggregate ϕ and Φ data better, and possibly much better, if we could connect them with differences in structure evidenced in differing and changing shares of the five types of issues and assets in aggregate issues and in aggregate assets of all financial institutions. (This, incidentally, might be achieved by introducing a characteristic of structure, such as the share of the banking system in the total issues or assets of all financial institutions, as an additional independent variable into the multiple regression equations of the aggregate ϕ and Φ ratios instead of calculating separate regressions for each of the five components.) The temptation, however, has been resisted—at least on this occasion—partly, and perforce, by the unavailability of funds and time for the extensive additional computations and interpretations of the results that would have been required; and partly, though reluctantly, by a realization of the limitations of the author's energy and competence and the reader's absorptive capacity.

THE STABILITY OF RANKS

An exception may be made for one very simple exploration of the data, the calculation of rank correlation coefficients. The purpose of this calculation is to ascertain the extent to which countries that have relatively high or low new issue ratios in one period—compared to other countries—continue to do so in the following period. The rank correlation coefficients between two adjacent periods thus provide some indication of continuity or randomness in the relative position of individual countries over time. These coefficients are shown in Table C–10 for all nonsocialist countries as well as for developed and less developed countries separately.

The general impression conveyed by Table C–10 is one of a substantial but far from perfect continuity in the ranking of individual countries over the past eighty years, perfect continuity being expressed in a series of coefficients of +1.00. In view of the difficulties of interpreting the value of rank correlation coefficients in absolute terms, attention may be concentrated on differences in the coefficients as between groups of countries, periods and types of financial instruments. It is then seen that ranking is hardly more regular among less developed than among developed countries.

Among forms of financial instruments there is a marked difference between the high values of the coefficients for thrift institutions and particularly for insurance organizations—of the dozen coefficients for all countries taken together, all are positive and all but one are in excess of 0.50, and their average is 0.65 for thrift institutions and 0.80 for insurance organizations—and the much lower values for

TABLE C–10

Period-to-Period Rank Correlation Coefficients of the New Issue Ratios of Financial Institutions and its Components, 1901–63[a]

	ϕ	ϕ_c	ϕ_d	ϕ_s	ϕ_i	ϕ_o
ALL COUNTRIES						
1901–13 and 1881–1900	.81	.69	.86	.83	.79	.87
1914–29 and 1901–13	.43	.53	.38	.65	.72	.24
1930–38 and 1914–29	.47	−.25	−.34	.40	.81	.50
1939–48 and 1930–38	.54	−.02	.11	.57	.71	.34
1949–63 and 1939–48	.59	.25	.41	.65	.87	.59
1961–63 and 1949–60	.78	.75	.69	.78	.91	.79
DEVELOPED COUNTRIES						
1901–13 and 1881–1900	.77	.65	.83	.79	.74	.84
1914–29 and 1901–13	.26	.55	.49	.53	.60	.19
1930–38 and 1914–29	−.02	−.14	−.44	.07	.58	.37
1939–48 and 1930–38	.36	−.18	.19	.43	.57	.37
1949–63 and 1939–48	.14	−.09	.15	.42	.87	.47
1961–63 and 1949–60	.69	.72	.79	.57	.87	.72
LESS DEVELOPED COUNTRIES						
1914–29 and 1900–13	0	.15	−.20	.82	0	−.05
1930–38 and 1914–29	.31	−.41	.29	.24	.41	.83
1939–48 and 1930–38	.23	−.08	0	.39	.59	.46
1949–63 and 1939–48	.85	.81	.68	.18	.83	.86
1961–63 and 1949–60	.66	.68	.61	.81	.89	.64

[a] The subscripts identify central banks (*c*), deposit banks (*d*), thrift institutions (*s*), insurance organizations (*i*), and miscellaneous financial intermediaries (*o*).

central and deposit banks. Irregularity or discontinuity are most pronounced in the case of the issues of central banks, i.e. primarily of money. Here two of the six coefficients for all countries taken together (as well as those for developed and less developed countries) are negative, viz. those for the two periods extending from 1930 through 1948, indicating a more pronounced increase in ϕ_c for countries in which the value of ϕ_c in the preceding period is relatively low, a situation that will lead towards equalization of the ratios. (The same tendency is reflected in relatively low or declining coefficients of variation of ϕ_c in these periods.) In the case of deposit banks the coefficient is high only for the period 1901–13, indicating a considerable stability in ranking during the relatively undisturbed period of 1881–1913; but it is low for the two war periods 1914–29 and 1939–48, which were characterized in many countries by violent and uncoordinated movements in the ratios. The negative coefficient for the Great Depression (1930–38) suggests, as does the comparable coefficient for central banks, that deflation was less pronounced in financially less developed countries.

Differences in the values of the coefficients among periods are substantial, a few examples already having been mentioned. The outstanding feature of this comparison, however, is the much greater stability of the aggregate ratio for all financial instruments (ϕ) compared to the movements of most of the components. For the aggregate of all countries the ratio stays between 0.43 and 0.81, averaging 0.60 for all six periods. The value is high for the first and the last period, which is not astonishing in the latter case because of the short duration of the period, and shows a regular rise from the low of 0.43 for 1914–29 to 0.78 for 1961–63.

This regularity, however, disappears as do most of the other movements, if developed and less developed countries are separated. In that case the movements become considerably more erratic, partly because they sometimes run in different directions in the two groups of countries. This is probably another reflection of the fact that we are dealing with two distinct groups of countries, almost "noncompeting groups" of economic theory, within each of which changes in ranking are rather frequent without exhibiting a systematic pattern except in the short final period and, what is more important, for less developed countries also between 1949–63 and 1939–48. The rank correlations for that period for less developed countries are generally the highest found in the table, averaging 0.70 and thus indicating close continuity in ranking with respect to the financial institutions' issue ratios.

The existence of two distinct groups of countries is confirmed in Table C–11, in which the ranking of the various

TABLE C–11

Rank Correlation Coefficients of the New Issue Ratios of Financial Institutions in the 1901–13 and 1949–63 Periods[a]

	ϕ	ϕ_c	ϕ_d	ϕ_s	ϕ_i	ϕ_o
All nonsocialist countries	.51	.41	.21	.74	.76	.33
Developed countries	.45	.52	.46	.58	.63	.68
Less developed countries	.30	.36	.10	.82	.20	−.10

[a] Subscripts identified in note to Table C–10.

countries is compared over an interval of half a century, using the periods 1948–63 and 1901–13. The rank correlation coefficient for the aggregate issue ratio (ϕ) for all countries is higher than that for either developed or less developed countries. This is also true for one of the five components, that for the issues of insurance organizations. For the other four components the coefficient for all countries is always lower than that for at least one of the two groups. It is interesting that for all countries taken together the rank correlation coefficients for ϕ_s and ϕ_i are much higher than for the three other coefficients, while this is true in the case of the less developed countries only for ϕ_s, though for the developed countries ϕ_o joins the group of high coefficients. This relationship may perhaps be interpreted to mean that the effects of the development of a relatively large insurance organization sector, and particularly of a large thrift institutions sector, are more enduring than is the case for central and commercial banks, which are more subject to changes in monetary policy. It may appear strange that the coefficient for central banks is higher than that for deposit banks in all three groups of countries. This may possibly be due to the spread of check money during the twentieth century, which has made countries more equal in this respect, a tendency which would naturally be reflected in a low rank correlation coefficient.

IV. THE ASSETS OF FINANCIAL INSTITUTIONS IN THIRTY-FIVE COUNTRIES, 1860–1963

INTRODUCTION TO THE TABLES

This appendix contains thirty-five tables, each of which presents figures on the total assets of all important types of financial institutions in one country for a set of nine benchmark dates running from 1860 to 1963 whenever figures are available for those dates. These countries now account for about 70 per cent of the population of the world outside China. While similar tables could be compiled for a few more countries, it is doubtful that it would be possible to do so in a substantial number of cases if the figures are to reach back to at least World War I. To increase substantially the number of less developed countries would be difficult even if one attempted to trace the figures only to the 1920s or 1930s, provided that all important types of financial institutions are to be included.

In the tables estimated figures are identified by parentheses, dots indicate absence of figures or estimates, dashes the non-existence, or negligible size, of a given type of institution at the benchmark date.

Scope of Assets

An attempt has been made to base all tables on the total assets at the end of the calendar year (or in a few cases the fiscal year) of each of the different types of financial institutions included. Guarantees, endorsements, and intrabank, safekeeping, custodial, and agency accounts have been omitted wherever possible. In some instances it was necessary to use data on one or a few main asset or liability items (particularly deposits in the case of savings banks, bonds issued for mortgage banks, and reserves for insurance organizations) in place of unavailable data for total assets. In other similar cases, total assets were estimated on the basis of the data for selected assets and liabilities, provided the relation between these and total assets could be approximated from the information available for neighboring years or for other benchmark dates.

The figures for total assets include claims and liabilities among different groups of financial institutions, as well as intergroup holdings of corporate stock and intragroup claims and holdings. The total for all types of financial institutions therefore contains duplications and overstates the amount of funds made available by the entire financial system to other domestic sectors or to foreign countries, or of the funds absorbed from these sectors. A systematic elimination of these claims and holdings within the financial system is impossible with the material now available. The most important duplicative items are the deposits of commercial banks with their central bank (data on these deposits for the postwar period may be found in the International Monetary Fund's *International Financial Statistics*) and the deposits of one type of financial institution redeposited with another (e.g. the deposits of French savings banks redeposited with the Caisse des Dépôts).[1]

The overwhelming majority of total assets of financial institutions, of course, consists of claims and, to a much smaller extent, of corporate stock. Tangible assets included are limited to the relatively small real estate holdings of financial institutions (including both their own buildings and other owned real estate) and monetary metals held by the central bank and occasionally by other financial institutions. For some purposes of analysis, particularly the comparison of the financial assets of financial institutions with

1. Cf. discussion in Chapter 5, section 5, 4 (Financial Intermediaries of the Second Degree).

those held by other sectors, it would have been desirable to eliminate, or at least to identify, the nonfinancial assets included in the total. This again was not feasible on a comprehensive basis with the material now available, at least not without a very large amount of additional investigation. Holdings of monetary metals, however, can be ascertained fairly easily from international publications specializing in this subject, for instance for the postwar period from *International Financial Statistics,* and for the benchmark dates 1913, 1929, and 1938 from the *Statistical Yearbook of the League of Nations.*

Total assets also include in principle foreign assets held by the central bank, which have been of importance only in the post-World War II period, as well as the foreign assets—including balances held by central and commercial banks with foreign banks for current operating purposes—of other domestic financial institutions. An attempt has been made to exclude foreign assets of financial institutions—almost exclusively commercial banks and insurance companies—which operate abroad as well as within the domestic territory. Outstanding examples are the British, French, and Dutch banking institutions with headquarters in London, Paris, or Amsterdam that operate abroad through a network of local branches or subsidiaries. The elimination of the foreign assets of these institutions, however, depended on the availability of statistics. These assets are therefore as a rule included in those countries where they play a relatively small role, such as is the case in the United States. For the postwar period the foreign assets of the commercial and central banks again can be ascertained from *International Financial Statistics,* but it would be very difficult, if not impossible, to carry through the distinction for the period before World War II for a large number of countries.

Total assets, as reported in the balance sheet, have been used as the basic magnitude because they are the most comprehensive figure characterizing the size of financial intermediaries of different types that can at the present time be obtained for a large number of countries and for a long period of time. For analytic purposes it would often be desirable to eliminate all items that appear identically on the asset and liability side of the same institution as well as creditor-debtor and holder-issuer relations among financial institutions. This, however, cannot be done on a systematic basis for many countries and over a long period of time, or would require an amount of work quite unjustified by the results. For other purposes, an even more restricted concept such as funds made available to domestic nonfinancial sectors might be preferable. Again, however, the necessary adjustments cannot be made for a sufficient number of countries and a sufficient number of types of institutions. A step in the desired direction, however, has been taken by eliminating from the balance sheet items such as guarantees, endorsements, and trustee and custodian accounts, insofar as they could be identified.

Valuation

The figures reflect book values in almost all cases, investment companies being the only institution for which they generally are based on market values. The differences from market values may sometimes be quite significant, particularly for institutions that hold a substantial proportion of their assets in stocks or in real estate, which is the case in several countries for insurance companies and for private retiremment funds.

In order not to obscure significant movements and differences in level (as well as in order to avoid a spurious impression of accuracy) the figures are generally shown only to the extent of three or four digits.

Omissions

The main difficulties encountered, and the main work involved, resulted from the need of including all types of financial institutions of importance, rather than limiting the list, as is often done in tabulations of this kind, to the central bank, the commercial banks, and a few miscellaneous and often arbitrarily selected financial institutions. The omission of some important less developed countries (e.g. Indonesia) is due mainly to the impossibility of finding sufficient statistical information on financial institutions outside of the banking system. Even so, one type of financial institution had to be left out in almost all cases, viz. private (unincorporated) bankers and money lenders. These units are of particular importance in Europe before World War I and in less developed countries until at least World War II. There are simply no figures, or even usable estimates, for this group of financial institutions save in a very few developed countries. Institutions administering funds as trustees, such as trust companies in the United States or the public trustees in a number of British countries, have been omitted from the tables.

Estimates

In many cases, particularly for the period before World War II, it has been necessary to use estimates, sometimes of a rather speculative character, instead of firm figures from official statistics or other reliable sources if the tables were to be completed at all. These estimates—printed within parentheses—are usually the rougher the further we go back in time. They were required in several countries for as basic an item as the assets of commercial banks, and there is hardly any country in which they have not had to be resorted to occasionally. Rough as the resulting figures are, the preparation of these estimates has often been laborious, and it has not been possible to describe their derivation in detail in the table notes, although indications of the type of material used is usually given. Some of these estimates undoubtedly could have been replaced by firmer figures if time and resources had been unlimited. They were retained primarily in cases where it either was fairly certain that no better figures existed, or where a more intensive search for existing estimates or a more elaborate estimating procedure seemed unjustified in view of the small size of the item or the probably small error in the estimate.

Appendix IV

Benchmark Dates

The standard benchmark dates for which the figures are shown for all countries when data are available are 1860, 1880, 1900, 1929, 1938, 1948, 1960, and 1963. The reasons for the selection of some of these dates are obvious; the choice of 1913, 1929, and 1938, for instance, reflects the situation before World War I, the Great Depression, and World War II respectively; 1948 is the first year of postwar normality in a substantial number of countries; and 1963 is the last year for which data were available for all countries at the time most of the statistical work was completed. Figures are included for 1960 notwithstanding the short distance from 1963 because some of the more detailed cross-section analyses of Chapters 4 and 5 that use data for a larger number of countries are based on figures for that year. The selection of the three benchmark dates before 1913 is more arbitrary, except that 1880—and, for a few countries, 1860—may be regarded as the earliest date when a fairly developed financial system existed in Europe and North America. In the case of less developed countries, the tables generally start with 1929 or 1938, and in some cases even with 1948, the main exceptions being Argentina, Egypt, India, Mexico, and Spain, for which it was found possible and interesting, though difficult and somewhat hazardous, to extend the figures to the turn of the century. The relatively few deviations (of seldom more than one or two years) from these standard benchmark dates, which are summarized in Table 4–1, are due to developments specific to individual countries, to the absence or the more difficult derivation of data for one or two of the standard benchmark dates, or finally to the fact that some country tables were prepared earlier when a slightly different set of benchmark dates was used.

Selection of Countries

The selection of countries for which tables are presented, or were attempted, was influenced by the relative importance of the country, the availability of data (particularly the existence of publications providing long series), the willingness of a national expert to review the draft tables, and the necessity of limiting the time-consuming work of assembling the data. As a result, all developed non-Communist countries in Europe, North America, Asia (Japan), Australasia, and Africa (South Africa, Rhodesia) are included with the exception of only four of the smallest European countries (Austria, Finland, Ireland, and Luxembourg). For the developed countries, the tables are in most cases carried back to at least 1900 (with the exception of South Africa and, of course, Rhodesia) and generally to 1880. American less developed countries are represented by four of the largest (Argentina, Brazil, Mexico, and Venezuela) and by three smaller countries (Jamaica, Puerto Rico, and Trinidad), which are worth particular attention because of their rapid economic growth since World War II, and because they present interesting features for comparison. The only Asian country for which information of this type is available back to the turn of the century is India. The inclusion of only the Philippines and Thailand is fortuitous, although data going back before World War II are available for but a very few other Asian countries. The situation is similar in Africa, where only one country could be found for which even rough and partial figures extend well beyond World War II—Egypt. Data are shown for only two centrally planned economies, the U.S.S.R. (for which the figures reach back to the turn of the century, though applying to a country of entirely different financial structure) and Yugoslavia.

All the figures refer to the boundaries of the country at the various benchmark dates. Hence for some countries, the most important of which are Germany, India, and Russia, the figures do not, at all benchmark dates, refer to the same or even an almost identical territory. This should be taken into account in making comparisons over time. For the two main purposes to which the figures are put—the relation to national income or national wealth and the comparison of one type of financial institution with another —these changes in territorial coverage are not only unavoidable but appropriate.

Scope and Classification of Financial Institutions

In view of the substantial institutional differences, it has, of course, not been possible to give data in all countries for exactly the same types of financial institutions. It has, however, been possible to show in almost all cases figures for the central bank, the commercial (deposit) banks, savings banks, and other important types of thrift institutions, such as savings and loan associations and credit cooperatives, mortgage banks (where they exist or are of importance), government credit institutions, life insurance companies, private retirement funds, and governmental pension funds.

The number of types of financial institutions for which separate data are given varies greatly, depending on the existence first of the different types in the given country and secondly of the detail provided in the financial statistics. Thus, generally only between half a dozen and a dozen different types of financial institutions can or need to be distinguished in less developed countries. In developed countries, on the other hand, the number of separate types of financial institutions that are important enough to merit separate presentation and for which data can be procured is usually well in excess of one dozen and generally in the neighborhood of two dozen.

In choosing the name for each type of financial institution, an attempt has been made to use those English terms which, according to American terminology, most nearly reflect the character of the institution. In some cases, however, particularly for government institutions, the actual foreign name has been retained. It must not be thought, of course, that institutions which are listed under the same English name are exactly or even closely similar in all countries in which they exist.

The different types of financial institutions have been

arranged in broadly the same sequence in all countries. Thus, the tables always start with the central bank, followed by the commercial (deposit) banks, the different types of thrift institutions, other private short- or long-term credit institutions, governmental credit institutions, and private insurance organizations, and end with government pension and insurance funds.

A special problem exists in those countries which do not have a central bank but use currency issued either by a governmental agency or by the central bank of another country, usually the "mother" country. (The latter situation is practically limited to colonial territories or dependencies such as Puerto Rico.) In these cases an attempt has been made to provide information on the volume of such currency circulating in the country since it may be regarded as the equivalent of the assets of the money-issuing authority in other countries.

Another special problem is presented by central government pension and social security funds. These funds operate in some countries on a pay-as-you-go basis, so that no substantial amount of assets is accumulated. In other countries, funds are accumulated and invested either exclusively or predominately in claims against the central government, usually in nonmarketable form. The amount of the funds accumulated is generally less than an actuarially calculated reserve would be. In this situation it is impossible to treat the funds in all countries on a comparable basis, or even to put them on a basis where the amounts entered for the assets correspond to their position in the country's capital market. As a compromise, assets have been shown wherever they are accumulated and either exact information on their size was available or a rough estimate could be made. It is believed that this has been done in virtually all cases in which funds of this type hold a substantial amount of assets. No attempt has been made to indicate the amount of unfunded liabilities (only very few countries provide any information on them), neither in cases where liabilities are partially funded nor where they are entirely unfunded. Since the assets of the central governments' insurance funds are always shown separately, they can easily be eliminated from the total assets of financial institutions shown in the tables by those users who regard these funds as an internal bookkeeping item of the government without economic significance.

Totals A *and* B

All tables show two totals. The first, identified by *A*, is simply the sum of the figures for all types of financial institutions for which figures are shown for a given benchmark date. The second total, labeled *B*, includes, where necessary, rough estimates for the aggregate of those types of financial institutions which are known to have existed for the given benchmark date but for which no documented figures were available or for which estimates could not be made with a reasonable degree of confidence. The *B* totals thus are more nearly comparable over time, but they are necessarily subject to a larger margin of error than the *A* totals. The difference between the two totals, fortunately, is usually significant only for the earliest benchmark dates.

Sources

An attempt has been made to base the tables as far as possible on primary, or near-primary, sources, i.e. in practice chiefly on the annual volumes of the different countries' statistical abstracts or, when they are available, on official publications giving these data for reasonably long periods, such as *Historical Statistics* in the United States and the relatively few comparable volumes existing, for example, for Japan, South Africa, and Sweden.

Since financial data are in most countries a stepchild of the official statisticians, these sources hardly ever provide all the necessary data, even for recent decades. For the earlier periods, financial data in the standard official publications are often limited to information on the main (but as a rule not total) assets and liabilities of the central bank, the commercial banks (even this information is unavailable not only for less developed but also for some developed countries), and the savings banks. These sources, therefore, needed to be supplemented by data in international statistical publications and in a host of government and nongovernmental publications for individual countries.

Financial statistics again are relatively neglected in the usual international statistical sources. The chief exceptions are the annual supplements to the International Monetary Fund's *International Financial Statistics.* These, however, furnish data only for the 1960, 1963, and (generally) 1948 benchmarks and are usually limited to information on central and commercial banks, though data for savings banks and life insurance companies are given in a number of cases. Moreover, since *International Financial Statistics* often modifies the original figures to meet its own definitions, it is sometimes necessary to use the original data for these dates and institutions in order to preserve continuity over time—albeit at the expense of international comparability. Some other international publications, for example *Die Wirtschaft des Auslandes* (1928 and 1929 volumes) and *Die Versicherungsmärkte der Welt* (1964), were very useful in filling gaps, the first for the benchmarks of 1900, 1913, and 1929, the second for life insurance companies in 1948 and 1960. Among the unofficial sources, I should like to single out the statistics of financial institutions in Great Britain prepared by Mr. D. K. Sheppard (as yet unpublished), without which the tables for this important country would have been much the worse, and *Historical Statistics of Canada* by Urquhart and Buckley.

Since these tables cover thirty-five countries at very different statistical levels for a period of up to one hundred years, it was obviously out of the question to undertake a comprehensive systematic examination of all official and unofficial publications—serials and monographs—that might contain relevant information. I have, unfortunately but unavoidably, had to rely to a good extent on memory about sources to consult, and on the accumulation of notes collected over many years, alas not too systematically.

To guard against gross errors and omissions, drafts of the

tables at various stages of their completion were sent to or discussed on the spot with the appropriate official organizations in a large proportion of the thirty-five countries. Most of the officials so approached have been kind enough to respond, in some cases going to considerable trouble in their attempts to help. I do not name these organizations and individuals, aside from occasionally identifying them as the source of otherwise unavailable figures; distinctions would be invidious, and I do not want to implicate them even indirectly in the errors which must remain in a pioneering enterprise of this type. But I must express sincere thanks to them not only on my own behalf but also in the name of the readers of this book and the (probably rarer) users of this Appendix.

TABLE D–1

Assets of Financial Institutions in Argentina

BILLIONS OF PESOS

	1901	1913	1929	1940	1948	1960	1963
1. Banco Central	—	—	—	2.29	8.6[d]	150.4	226.8
2. Banco de la Nacion[a]	.24	.81	2.09	2.03	23.5[d] (items 2–3)	221.7 (items 2–3)	382.2 (items 2–3)
3. Deposit banks	(.45)	(1.35)	3.00	(3.00)			
4. Postal savings[b]	—	.00	.10	.14	.8	9.0	12.9
5. Credit cooperatives	—	—	—	—	—	2.2	7.4
6. Mortgage banks	.30	.63	1.95	2.20	3.5	42.7	53.0
7. Banco Industrial	—	—	—	—	5.2	43.5	55.2
8. Life insurance companies	(.01)	(.08)	(.25)	.40	1.1	10.0 (items 8–9)	22.8 (items 8–9)
9. Other insurance companies	—	—	—	—	—		
10. Social security funds	—	—	—	.83	7.0	82.4	116.0
Total A	1.00	2.87	7.39	10.89	49.7	561.9	876.3
Total B[c]	1.12	3.27	7.77	11.00	50.0	570.0[e]	950.0[e]

( ) Estimated figures.

[a] Based on capital, reserves, cash, loans, and deposits for 1901 through 1950.

[b] Deposits through 1940.

[c] Including rough allowances for institutions for which no specific information is available for some dates; also including government paper currency held by public (1901, 12; 1913, .40; 1929, .38).

[d] After deduction of central bank credits to commercial banks (19.0) and of commercial bank deposits with central bank, both of which were of unusual size from the mid-1940s to the monetary reform of 1957 as a result of the so-called "nationalization" of bank deposits.

[e] Includes rough allowances for saving and loan associations (5.0 in 1963) and for finance companies.

Sources:

Lines 1–3, 1900–29: Based on data in P. J. Baiocco, *La Economia Bancaria Argentina 1901–1939* (Buenos Aires, 1937). *1940:* Banco Central, *Estadisticas Monetarias y Bancarias, Años 1940–1960* (1962). *1948–63: International Financial Statistics*, 1965–66 Supplement.

Line 4, 1913–63: Caja Nacional de Ahorro Postal, *Memoria* (1960, 1963).

Line 5, 1960–63: Based on balance sheets of cooperatives.

Line 6, 1900, 1913: Annual reports of Banco Hipotecario Nacional. *1929: Censo Bancario* . . . (1925). *1940–63:* Same as for lines 1–3.

Line 7, 1948–63: Annual reports of Banco Industrial.

Line 8, 1900–29: Estimated on basis of insurance in force and premium receipts (*Annuario Estadistico*). *1940: Annuario Geografico Argentino* (1941), p. 536. *1948: Die Versicherungsmärkte der Welt. 1960, 1963:* Superintendencia de Seguros, *Memoria* (1960, 1963), estimated on basis of premium receipts.

Line 10, 1940: Revista del Instituto Nacional de Prevision Social. 1948: Rough estimate obtained by extrapolation. *1960, 1963:* Estimates of Consejo Nacional de Desarollo.

Table D–2

Assets of Financial Institutions in Australia[a]

MILLIONS OF POUNDS

	1901	1915	1929	1938	1948	1960	1964
1. Commonwealth Bank[b]	—	—	55	73	711	1,070	1,255
2. Deposit banks	122	180	355	465	938	1,971	2,538
3. Savings banks[c]	31	92	225	260	767	1,596	2,359
4. Short-term money dealers	—	—	—	—	—	80	178
5. Commonwealth Development Bank	—	—	—	—	12	50	72
6. Development finance companies	—	—	—	—	—	11	33
7. Building societies	(4)	5	13	17	40	242	365
8. Pastoral finance companies	(15)	(25)	(35)	40	(70)	188	238
9. Installment credit companies	—	—	—	(10)	25	578	867
10. Investment companies	—	—	—	—	(5)	97	153
11. Friendly societies[d]	(3)	7	14	17	22	49	72
12. Life insurance companies[e]	(25)	49	136	221	383	1,016	1,497
13. Other insurance companies	(5)	(10)	(23)	(30)	(60)	240	345
14. Government superannuation funds	—	—	(5)	(15)	(70)	291	462
15. Private superannuation funds	—	—	—	(10)	(60)	273	422
Total	205	368	861	1,158	3,163	7,752	10,856

( ) Estimated figures.

[a] June 30.

[b] Since 1960, Reserve Bank of Australia.

[c] Deposits only through 1929.

[d] Includes health societies beginning in 1960.

[e] Australian assets only.

Sources:

1901: Rough estimates (usually based on 1906 or 1909 data), except for lines 2 and 3.

1915–48: Official Yearbook of Australia, various issues, except for line 1 (from annual reports of Commonwealth Bank) and lines 8, 13, and 15 for 1915 and 1929, lines 9, 14, and 15 for 1938, and lines 8, 10, and 13–15 for 1948, which are estimates.

1960: Reserve Bank of Australia, *Flow-of-Funds, Australia, 1953–54 to 1961–62* (1965).

1964: Research Department of Reserve Bank of Australia.

Table D–3

Assets of Financial Institutions in Belgium

BILLIONS OF FRANCS

	1880	1900	1913	1929	1939	1948	1960	1963
1. National Bank	.48	.81	1.31	15.1	29.5	97.5	150.9	192.2
2. Rediscount Institute	—	—	—	—	.6	2.6	2.4	2.6
3. Government Security Stabilization Fund	—	—	—	—	1.0	4.5	9.8	11.8
4. Postal checking system	—	—	.01	2.0	4.3	28.4	45.6	48.7
5. Deposit banks	.81	1.68	3.80	39.2	21.0	70.0	162.5	256.8
6. Investment banks[a]					5.2	5.3	8.0	10.4
7. Government Savings Bank	.15	.90	1.76	6.3	14.0	34.8	96.7	121.9
8. Communal savings banks	.01	.01	.01	.0	.1	.1	.2	.3
9. Private savings banks[b]	.02	.03	.05	.	1.3	10.8	49.2	72.2
10. Credit unions	.02	.05	.09	.4	—	—	—	—
11. S.N. Credit à l'Industrie	—	—	—	1.4	1.2	6.5	43.8	55.8
12. Credit Communal	.29	.55	1.02	9.6	18.0	26.4	54.6	76.3
13. Other government credit institutions[c]	—	—	—	—	.6	11.6	21.2	30.4
14. National Housing Co.	—	—	—	.8	1.2	2.4	20.1	24.2
15. Investment funds	—	—	—	—	—	—	4.9	5.6
16. Consumer credit companies	—	—	—	.	.	.	(6.7)	8.4
17. Life insurance companies	.	.	.	.	3.7	12.1	52.2	(67.0)
18. Other insurance companies	.	.	.	.	.	1.5	7.5	11.2
19. Savings bank life insurance[d]	.00	.04	.25	1.7	6.4	12.2	28.7	32.8
20. Workmen's accident insurance	—	—	—	—	—	.	14.3	18.5
21. Social security funds[e]	—	.	.	.	.	.	55.6	68.6
Total A	1.78	4.07	8.30	76.5	108.1	326.7	834.9	1,115.7
Total B[f]	1.80	4.25	8.75	80.0	112.0	340.0		

( ) Estimated figures.

[a] Resulted from split-up of formerly mixed banks.

[b] Includes Caisses Raiffeisen and Boerenbond and mortgage and capitalization companies.

[c] Caisse Nationale de Crédit Professionel and affiliates; Institut National de Crédit Agricole; Office Central du Crédit Hypothécaire; Société Nationale de la Petite Propriété Terrienne.

[d] Includes endowment insurance funds and very small amounts of accident insurance funds.

[e] Excluding interorganization accounts; including Miners' Pension Fund.

[f] Including rough allowance for institutions for which no specific information is available for some dates.

Sources: Unless otherwise indicated *Annuaire Statistique de Belgique*, various issues, and *Bulletin Mensuel* of National Bank, supplemented by information from Research Division of National Bank.

Line 5, 1880–1929: B. S. Chlepner, *Le Marché financier Belge depuis cent ans* (Bruxelles, 1930), pp. 94, 131. *1948–63: International Financial Statistics*, 1964–65 Supplement.

Line 17, 1939: Schweiz. Rückversicherungsgesellschaft, *Versicherungsmärkte der Welt* (1964), p. 15. *1948–63: International Financial Statistics*, 1964–65 Supplement.

Table D–4

Assets of Financial Institutions in Brazil

BILLIONS OF CRUZEIROS

	1913	1929	1938	1948	1960	1963
1. Monetary authorities	.9[a]	3.4[a]	(10.0)	45.0	533	2,326
2. Deposit banks	(1.2)	(10.0)	(11.0)	48.0	438	1,704
3. Banco do Brasil[b]	.	.	(10.0)	(40.0)	400	2,392
4. Federal savings banks	.2	.	2.0	8.8	53	150
5. State savings banks	.	.	(.8)	3.4	27	61
6. Bank for Cooperative Credit	—	—	—	—	2	3
7. National Development Bank	—	—	—	.	81	260
8. Other development banks	—	—	—	.	17	84
9. Capitalization companies	—	.	.4	1.9	6	9
10. Life insurance companies	.	.	.6	2.4	} 26	} 68
11. Other insurance companies	.	.	.5	2.2		
12. Social security organizations	—	—	.7	15.1	220	568
Total A	2.3	13.4	26.0	126.8	} 1,403	} 5,233
Total B[c]	2.5	15.0	26.0	130.0		

( ) Estimated figures.
[a] Government bank notes in circulation.
[b] Included partly in line 1 and partly in line 2.
[c] Including rough estimates for institutions for which no specific information is available for some dates.

Sources:
Line 1, 1913–29: Annuario Estatistico, 1949. *1938–63: International Financial Statistics*, 1965–66 Supplement (1938 estimated on basis of 1937 figures).
Line 2, 1913, 1929: Estimated on basis of data for main balance sheet items (*Annuario Estatistico*). *1938–63:* Same as for line 1.
Line 3, 1960, 1963: Banco do Brasil, *Relatorio* (figures exclude interbranch accounts).
Lines 4–12, 1913: Institut International de l'Épargne, *L'Épargne dans le monde* (1935). *1938, 1948: Annuario Estatistico* (1939, 1949). *1960, 1963:* Superintendencia de Moeda, *Relatorio* (1964).

TABLE D–5

Assets of Financial Institutions in Canada

BILLIONS OF DOLLARS

	1880	1900	1913	1929	1938	1948	1960	1963
Bank of Canada	—	—	—	—	.41	2.06	3.04	3.45
Chartered banks	.19	.50	1.55	3.52	3.43	8.52	16.92	22.09
Government saving institutions	.01	.05	.06	.05	.06	.13	.20	.21
Quebec savings banks	.01	.02	.04	.08	.09	.19	.31	.37
Credit unions	•	•	•	.01	.02	.25	1.31	1.89
Mortgage loan companies	•	•	•	•	•	.27	.95	1.54
Trust companies	•	•	(.05)	.22	.23	.37	1.27	2.32
Installment and other finance companies	—	—	—	•	•	.23	2.32	3.19
Industrial development banks	—	—	—	—	—	.03	.11	.21
Loan companies	(.01)	(.15)	(.45)	.21	.19	.24	.75	(1.00)
Small loan companies and moneylenders	•	•	•	•	.01	.04	.55	(.75)
Investment companies	—	—	—	•	•	•	(1.50)	1.73
Life insurance companies	(.02)	.11	.34	1.77	2.82	5.14	10.71	13.14
Fraternal benefit societies	•	•	•	.07	.09	.11	.22	.21
Fire and casualty insurance companies	•	(.04)	(.08)	.17	.09	.35	1.32	1.53
Trusteed pension plans	—	—	—	—	•	(.20)	3.62	5.18
Government Annuity Fund	—	—	—	.02	.11	.43	1.20	(1.28)
Total A	.24	.87	2.57	6.12	7.55	18.56	46.30	60.09
Total B[a]	.25	.90	2.65	6.20	8.00	18.70		

( ) Estimated figures.

[a] Including allowance for institutions for which specific information is missing for some dates.

Sources:

1880–1948: Urquhart and Buckley, *Historical Statistics of Canada.*

1960, 1963: *Canada Year Book* (1965) and Bank of Canada, *Statistical Summary* (1964).

Table D–6

Assets of Financial Institutions in Denmark

BILLIONS OF KRONER

	1880	1900	1913	1929	1938	1948	1960	1963
1. National Bank	.12	.14	.25	.47	.80	5.71	5.65	6.71
2. Postal transfer system[a]	—	—	—	.03	.08	.36	.72	1.00
3. Commercial banks	.16	.48	1.20	2.91	3.37	7.31	18.34	30.86
4. Savings banks[b]	.25	(.60)	.87	2.22	2.59	5.25	8.70	11.04
5. Cooperative savings bank[a]	—	—	—	—	—	—	.10	.13
6. Mortgage credit associations[b,c]	(.23)	(.85)	(2.00)	4.39	5.82	7.73	15.60	22.40
7. Credit Association Local. Auth.	—	.00	.02	.11	.13	.21	.74	1.30
8. Cooperative Society[a]	.03	.05	.07	.21	.26	.60	1.07	1.34
9. Manufacturers' Finance Corp.	—	—	—	—	—	—	.05	.15
10. Ship Credit Fund	—	—	—	—	—	—	—	.24
11. Real property loan funds	—	—	—	—	—	—	.10	1.75
12. Life insurance companies	.	.03	.13	.46	1.00	2.45	4.64	5.73
13. Govt life insurance organizations	—	—	.	.	.	.70	(1.45)	(1.70)
14. Other insurance companies	.	.	.	.	.	1.25	3.10	(3.70)
15. Pension funds	—	—	—	.	.31	.67	1.86	2.48
16. Social insurance organization	—	—	—	.	.	.17	(.60)	.75[e]
Total A	.79	2.15	4.54	10.80	14.36	32.41	62.72	91.28
Total B[d]	.80	2.17	4.60	11.20	15.00			

( ) Estimated figures.

[a] Deposits.

[b] As of Mar. 31 of following year.

[c] Assets 1880–1913 estimated on basis of debt.

[d] Including rough allowance for institutions for which no information is available for some dates.

[e] Sickness benefit associations and unemployment insurance funds.

Sources: *Statistisk Årbog*, various issues; E. Hoffmeyer, *Strukturaendringer pa penge-og kapitalmarkedet* (København, 1960) for lines 2, 3, 6, 7, 11, and 15, and information from Det Statistiske Departement (lines 1, 2, and 6, for 1880, 1900, and 1913).

TABLE D–7

Assets of Financial Institutions in Egypt–U.A.R.

MILLIONS OF POUNDS

	1900	1913	1929	1938	1948	1960	1963
1. Central Bank[a]	3.3	14.5	70.9	53.0	413	516	603
2. Commercial banks	·	(5.0)	·	·	156[e]	426	707
3. P.O. Savings Bank[b]	.1	.7	2.3	9.8	33	48	(70)
4. Mortgage Bank[c]	7.0	50.5	45.0	21.6	11	29	30
5. Agricultural Credit Bank	—	—	—	6.0	28	66	154
6. Industrial Bank	—	—	—	—	—	12	12
7. Insurance companies	·	·	·	·	(25)	68	(85)
8. Provident funds	—	—	—	—	·	14	(18)
9. Insurance and pension funds	—	—	—	—	(5)	71	(180)
10. Social insurance organizations	—	—	—	—	—	14	(75)
Total A	10.4	70.7	118.2	90.4	671	} 1,264	} 1,934
Total B[d]	12.0	72.0	150.0	115.0	675		

( ) Estimated figures.

[a] National Bank of Egypt through 1948, Central Bank of Egypt thereafter, including banking and note issue departments.

[b] Deposits until 1929.

[c] Through 1948 capital, reserves, and bonds, hence somewhat below total assets.

[d] Including rough allowance for institutions for which no specific information is available for some dates.

[e] Main assets of clearing banks.

Sources:

Line 1, 1900, 1913: *Annuaire Statistique* (1914). *1929–48:* Weekly reports of Central Bank. *1960, 1963:* National Bank of Egypt, *Economic Bulletin.*

Line 2, 1913: Based on share capital (*Annuaire Statistique*, 1914). *1960–63:* Same as for line 1.

Lines 3, 4, 1900–48: *Annuaire Statistique* (1960–61). *1960–63:* National Bank of Egypt, *Economic Bulletin.*

Lines 5, 6, 1938–63: National Bank of Egypt, *Economic Bulletin.*

Lines 7, 8, 1960: *Egyptian Insurance Yearbook*, 1961.

Lines 9, 10, 1960: Ministry of Economy, *Indicators of Economic Development in U.A.R.*

TABLE D–8

Assets of Financial Institutions in France

BILLIONS OF (OLD) FRANCS

	1860	1880	1900	1913	1929	1937	1948	1960	1963
1. Banque de France	1.30	3.39	5.14	6.98	90.2	113.7	1,176	4,268	6,179
2. Commercial banks[a]	(.40)	2.50	5.09	12.52	(96.0)	(81.0)	1,152	6,777	10,534
2a. Large deposit banks[b]	.31	1.48	3.28	7.07	38.0	36.4	709	(4,000)	5,807
3. Postal checking	—	—	—	—	3.9	5.2	250	1,446	1,715
4. Savings banks, private	.38	.66	3.26	4.01	20.3	36.3	206	1,741	2,637
5. Savings bank, national	—	—	1.01	1.82	16.7	25.1	192	1,205	1,668
6. Banque Commerce Exterieur	—	—	—	—	—	—	13	368	701
7. Crédit Populaire	—	—	—	—	—	(1.5)	40	320	542
8. Crédit Agricole	—	—	—	—	—	—	114	1,879	3,376
9. Caisse des Dépôts									
Own funds	.62	2.17	4.40	5.62	27.5	52.7	372	2,493	3,741
Administered funds	.27	.40	1.93	3.95	20.2	57.1	256	1,407	2,019
10. Crédit National	—	—	—	—	34.0	38.2	381	572	888
11. Crédit Foncier	.37	1.95	4.12	5.80	11.5	23.1	73	1,999	2,781
12. Sous-Comptoir Entrepreneurs	.01	.06	.23	.66	.7	.7	4	924	1,070
13. Caisses Crédit Coopératif	—	—	—	—	—	—	3	103	230
14. C.C.M.C.M.T.[c]	—	—	—	—	—	—	—	482	798
15. Installment finance companies	—	—	—	—	—	—	3	179	411
16. Life insurance companies	·	(1.00)	(3.20)	(4.50)	(7.0)	(18.0)	102	711	1,158
17. Caisse National Prévoyance	.06	.41	1.00	2.16	8.0	19.0	57	161	240
18. Other insurance companies	·	·	·	·	·	5.1	30	132	196
19. Social insurance organizations	—	—	—	—	—	—	—	79	152
Total A	3.41	12.54	29.38	48.02	336.0	476.7	4,424	27,246	41,036
Total B[d]	3.70	12.75	30.00	49.00	338.0				

( ) Estimated figures.

[a] Excludes assets outside of metropolitan France (1960: 1,142; 1963: 990).

[b] Crédit Lyonnais, Société Générale, Comptoir National d'Escompte, and, from 1937 on, Banque Nationale pour le Commerce et l'Industrie (1860: Comptoir; Crédit Industriel; Crédit Mobilier).

[c] Caisse de Consolidation et de Mobilisation du Crédit à Moyen Terme.

[d] Including rough estimates for institutions for which no specific information is available for some dates.

Sources: Unless otherwise indicated below, the data are taken for 1880–1948 from *Statistiques et Études Financières* (Ministère des Finances), Supplements nos. 123, 144, 175, or *Annuaire statistique de la France—retrospectif* (1961) or *Conseil National du Crédit*, various issues.

Line 1, 1860: Research Department, Caisse des Dépôts.

Line 2, 1900, 1913: Crédit Lyonnais, Library.

Line 2a, 1860–1913: J. Bouvier et al., *Le Mouvement du profit en France au 19e siècle*, Appendix 2. *1963:* Annual reports of four banks.

Line 6, 1963: Annual report of Banque Française Commerce Exterieur.

Line 7, 1937: Chambre Syndicale des Banques Populaires.

Line 9, 1860, 1929: Caisse des Dépôts.

Line 10, 1929–63: Annual reports of Crédit National.

Lines 11, 12, 1860–1963: Annual reports of Crédit Foncier and Sous-Comptoir respectively.

Line 13, 1948–63: Conseil National du Crédit, Service d'Information.

Line 15, 1948–63: *Rapport de la Commission de Contrôle des Banques* (Ministère des Finances), various issues.

Lines 16, 18, 1900: Based on estimates of paid-in capital (.07) in *Congrès International des Valeurs Mobilières* (1901). *1948–63:* *Rapport sur la Situation des Sociétés d'Assurance* (Ministère des Finances), various issues.

Line 17, 1860–1963: Caisse des Dépôts.

Line 19, 1960, 1963: UNEDIC, *Bulletin de Liaison* (Dec. 1961 and Dec. 1964). Figures cover only mutual unemployment insurance organizations (part of funds of private pension funds included in lines 9 and 17; no information on others; funds of government social insurance organizations are small).

Table D–9

Assets of Financial Institutions in Germany

BILLIONS OF MARKS

	1860	1880	1900	1913	1929	1938	1947[d]	1950	1960	1963
1. Central bank[a]	.95	1.57	2.57	4.03	7.05	10.73	38.60	17.03	38.85	46.26
2. Large (nationwide) banks	.39	(1.35)	6.96	8.39	13.77	9.01	17.94	7.59	28.49	36.93
3. Regional (local) banks				13.65	8.60	7.34	16.10	4.71	26.39	36.62
4. Private bankers	(1.50)	(2.50)	(3.50)	4.00	3.27	1.26	1.85	1.81	6.49	7.75
5. Specialized commercial banks	.	.	.	.98	2.89	7.30	10.40	.40	2.06	2.92
6. Postal saving check system	—	—	—	.	.64	1.08	5.46	1.11	6.06	8.63
7. Savings banks, local	.51	2.78	9.45	20.80	12.78	22.47	58.57	8.02	56.15	82.08
8. Savings banks, central	—	—	—	1.76	6.41	9.67	31.58	4.26	29.02	44.52
9. Credit unions, local	.01	.59	1.68	5.73	4.32	5.99	16.67	2.64	14.15	21.80[e]
10. Credit unions, central	—	—	.	.47	.85	1.50	16.70	1.25	5.05	7.85
11. Private mortgage banks	.04	1.85	7.50	13.55	5.82	6.24	8.01	1.06	16.64	22.58
12. Public mortgage banks	.68	1.76	4.05	(7.20)	2.94	3.63		1.29	15.65	22.51
13. Specialized credit institutions[b]	.	.	.	.	2.16	3.67	5.63	4.75	27.90	43.02
14. Installment credit institutions	—	—	—	—	—	.	.	.26	3.01	4.49
15. Building societies, private	—	—	—	—	.18	.38	.69	.30	6.14	9.36
16. Building societies, public	—	—	—	—		.13		.28	4.24	6.74
17. Investment companies	—	—	—	—	—	—	—	—	3.15	2.92
18. Life insurance companies	.07	.44	2.42	5.64	2.28	7.07	.	2.67	14.40	22.26
19. Pension funds, private	—	—	—	—			.	1.30	4.51	6.71
20. Property insurance companies	.	(.35)	(.83)	2.05	.77	1.54	.	.88	5.48	7.52
21. Social insurance organizations										
Invalidity (workers)	—	—	.87	2.11	1.58	3.11	.	.66	9.53	14.12
Employees	—	—	—	.14	1.31	3.88	.	.33	4.75	8.00
Miners	—	—	.	.19	.19	.36	.	.06	.67	(.90)
Total A	4.15	13.19	39.83	90.69	77.81	106.36	228.20	62.66	328.80	466.49
Total B[c]	4.25	13.50	40.50	91.00		107.00	260.00			

( ) Estimated figures.

[a] Includes until 1929 other banks of issue.

[b] Includes Kreditanstalt für Wiederaufbau.

[c] Including rough allowance for institutions for which no specific information is available for some years.

[d] Mar. 31, 1948. [e] Agricultural 8.85; nonagricultural 12.95.

Sources:

Line 1, 1860–1938: W. Hoffmann et al., *Das Wachstum der Deutschen Wirtschaft* (Berlin, 1965), pp. 733 ff. *1948:* Statistical annex to *Report of the Military Governor U.S. Zone* (also for 1948 data for other lines). *1950–63: Monatsberichte* of Deutsche Bundesbank and *Statistisches Jahrbuch*, various issues (also for 1950–63 data for other lines).

Lines 2, 3, 1860–1900: Der Deutsche Oekonomist. 1913, 1929: Reichsbank, *Untersuchung des Bankwesens* (1933), Part II.

Line 4, 1913–1931: Monatsberichte, Deutsche Bundesbank (Nov. 1961). *1929–38:* Reichsbank, *Untersuchung des Bankwesens* (partly estimated).

Line 5, 1913: Untersuchung des Bankwesens. 1929–38: Statistisches Jahrbuch.

Line 6, 1929–38: Länderrat, *Statistisches Handbuch von Deutschland 1928–44* (1949).

Lines 7, 8, 1860–1913: Hoffmann. *1929, 1938: Statistisches Jahrbuch*, various issues; *Untersuchung des Bankwesens.*

Lines 9, 10, 1860–1913: Hoffmann. *1929, 1938: Jahrbuch des Deutschen Genossenschaftsverbandes.*

Lines 11–13, 1860–1913: Hoffmann. *1929, 1938: Statistisches Jahrbuch.*

Line 14, 1950–63: Deutsche Bundesbank.

Lines 15, 16, 1929: Statistisches Handbuch. 1938: Statistisches Jahrbuch.

Lines 17–20, 1860–1913: Hoffmann (line 20 is the difference between Hoffmann's figures for all organizations and for life insurance organizations). *1929–38: Statistisches Jahrbuch.*

Line 21, 1900–38: Statistisches Jahrbuch. 1950: Bundesministerium für Arbeit, *Arbeits- und Sozialstat. Mitteilungen.*

TABLE D–10

Assets of Financial Institutions in Great Britain[a]

MILLIONS OF POUNDS

	1860	1880	1900	1913	1929	1938	1948	1960	1963
1. Bank of England	(55)	75	93	100	495	665	1,863	2,998	3,097
2. Deposit banks	(150)	432	879	1,146	2,424	2,860	7,303	9,230	(10,300)
3. Private banks[b]	(120)	(200)	62	53	68	61	113	151	(160)
4. Foreign and colonial banks	.	.	.	.	.	.	1,000	(2,000)	3,145
5. P.O. savings banks	—	35	134	187	285	509	1,948	1,710	1,791
6. Trustee savings banks	42	47	57	71	130	250	820	1,347	1,730
7. Birmingham Municipal Bank	—	—	—	—	12	30	84	87	(90)
8. Railway savings banks	—	—	.	.	16	30	44	45	(45)
9. Building Societies	(10)	54	60	65	313	759	1,038	3,166	4,359
10. CWS and SCWS banks	—	—	1	6	44	114	247	183	(175)
11. Accepting houses	.	.	.	.	165	.	(200)	556	1,038
12. Discount houses	.	35	37	67	140	153	(800)	1,198	1,285
13. Hire-purchase finance companies	—	—	—	—	(10)[c]	(40)[c]	(60)[c]	(550)	796
14. Investment companies and trusts		.	(100)	.	(350)	(400)	(400)	2,190	3,218
15. Life insurance companies[d]	} 80	155	311	530	1,252	1,824	2,904	7,156	9,200
16. Other private insurance companies									
17. Collecting societies	.	.	5	11	48	85	166	318	350
18. Industrial and provident societies	.	11	34	78	222	361	(650)	1,048	1,179
19. Friendly societies	.	.	33	54	104	152	206	251	260
20. Private superannuation funds[d]	—	—	—	—	} (35)	} (80)	} 500	(1,900)	2,872
21. Superannuation funds, local authorities[d]	—	—	—	—				562	727
22. Other public superannuation funds	—	—	—	—				710	925
23. National insurance funds[e]	—	—	—	21	154	194	1,027	1,745	(1,800)
24. Special finance corporations	—	—	—	—	.	.	(60)	(165)	(235)
Total A	457	1,044	1,806	2,389	6,267	8,567	} 21,433	} 39,266	} 48,777
Total B[f]	500	1,150	1,900	2,700	6,600	9,000			

( ) Estimated figures; estimates for 1963 mostly on basis of 1962 figures.

[a] Figures include Eire through 1913.

[b] Banks included in statistics of *Economist*, plus Yorkshire Penny Bank.

[c] Based on figures for eight companies, which in 1962 accounted for about 60 per cent of total.

[d] Since holdings are carried at book value and there are substantial holdings of common stock, market value of assets is considerably higher.

[e] Held by National Debt Commissioners in government securities (Mar. 31 of following year).

[f] Including rough allowance for institutions for which no specific information available for some dates.

Sources: Figures from 1880 through 1960, except where indicated below, are taken with kind permission of the author from two mimeographed memoranda of D. K. Sheppard of University of Birmingham *Financial Statistics—U.K. Banks 1880–1962* and *Financial Statistics—U.K. and G.B. Financial Intermediaries* (Aug. 1965).

Line 1, 1880–1929: Bank of England returns. *1948–63: International Financial Statistics*, 1965–66 Supplement.

Line 2, 1860, 1880: Based on figures for notes, deposits, and capital in 1844 and 1884 in W. F. Crick and J. E. Wadsworth, *A Hundred Years of Joint Stock Banking* (London, 1936).

Line 4, 1963: Financial Statistics (May 1965). Figures refer to "current and deposit accounts" and acceptances; total assets are slightly higher.

Lines 5, 6, 10, 1860: Mitchell and Deane, *Abstract of British Historical Statistics* (lines 5 and 6 only). *1963: Financial Statistics* (May 1965).

Lines 11, 12, 1900: W. T. C. King, *History of the London Discount Market* (London, 1936). *1913–38:* T. Balogh, *Studies in Financial Organization* (Cambridge, 1947). *1960–63: Financial Statistics* (May 1965), "current and deposit accounts" plus "acceptances"; *International Financial Statistics*, 1965–66 Supplement.

Lines 14, 1900, 1929: Based on data in H. Linhardt, *Die Britischen Investment-Trusts* (Berlin, 1935). *1960, 1963: Financial Statistics* (May 1965).

Line 15, 1963: Annual Abstract of Statistics.

Line 18, 1880–1963: Annual Abstract of Statistics, various issues.

Lines 20–22, 1929–48. J. Revell, *The Wealth of the Nation* (Cambridge, 1967), p. 94. For 1929 and 1938 based on Revell's estimates for 1927 and 1937.

Line 23, 1960: Annual Abstract of Statistics. Figures refer to Mar. 31 of following year and cover National Insurance Fund, including Reserve and Industrial Injuries Fund.

TABLE D–11

Assets of Financial Institutions in Greece

BILLIONS OF DRACHMAS

	1913	1929	1938	1948	1960	1963
1. Bank of Greece	—	9.13	18.65	4,690	28,320	35,200
2. Commercial banks	.88[b]	20.23	23.97	806	20,450	38,200
3. P.O. Savings Bank	.00	.39	4.26	0	2,450	6,050
4. National Mortgage Bank	.	2.28	2.63	222	3,050	3,550
5. Agricultural Bank	—	1.47[d]	5.49	954	13,150	18,710
6. Economic Development Organization	—	—	—	—	3,460	3,980
7. Consignment and Loan Fund	—	.78	2.09	26	2,220	3,030
8. Insurance companies	.	.	.	.	690[e]	(1,000)[e]
Total A	.88	34.28	57.09	6,698	73,790 (Total A and B)	109,720 (Total A and B)
Total B[a]	1.02[c]	34.40	57.25	6,750		

( ) Estimated figures.

[a] Including rough allowance for which no specific information is available for some dates.

[b] One of commercial banks (National Bank of Greece) was also bank of issue and a mortgage bank.

[c] Includes government paper money (.13).

[d] 1930.

[e] Greek companies only.

Sources:

Lines 1–3, 1913–38: Statistical Yearbook of Greece (1938) and League of Nations (e.g. *Money and Banking 1942–44*). *1948: Monthly Statistical Bulletin. 1960, 1963:* Bank of Greece, *Monthly Statistical Bulletin.*

Line 4, 1929–48: Annual Report of National Mortgage Bank (1949). *1960:* D. Psilos, *Capital Market in Greece* (Athens, 1964), p. 210.

Lines 5–7, 1929, 1938: Statistical Yearbook of Greece, 1938.

Line 6, 1960, 1963 International Financial Statistics, 1964–65 Supplement.

Line 7, 1948–63: From National Bank of Greece

Line 8, 1960: Psilos, p. 205.

Table D–12

Assets of Financial Institutions in India

BILLIONS OF RUPEES

	British India[a] 1880 (1)	1900 (2)	1913 (3)	1929 (4)	1938 (5)	1946 (6)	Indian Union 1948 (7)	1960 (8)	1963 (9)
1. Reserve Bank of India	—	—	—	—	2.25	18.14	15.74	23.50	28.96
2. State Bank of India[b]	.15	.21	.50	.91	.93	2.94	3.06	6.20	6.71
3. Other commercial banks[c]	.04	.20	.59	1.46	1.88	10.80	9.95	19.96	26.48
4. State cooperative banks[d]	—	—	—	.08	.12	.25	.24	1.82	2.96
5. Central cooperative banks	—	—	·	.29	.29	.45	.42	2.59	4.22
6. Agricultural cooperative banks[e]	—	—	·	.32	.32	.33	.35	2.44	4.17
7. Nonagricultural cooperative societies	—	—	·	.14	.26	.53	.61	1.51	2.06
8. Central land mortgage banks	—	—	—	—	.04	.05	.05	.39	.89
9. Primary land mortgage banks	—	—	—	—		.04	.04	.22	.59
10. P.O. savings banks	.03	.10	.23	.37	.82	1.42	.27	2.85	3.66
11. Investment finance companies	—	—	—	·	(.10)	(.15)	(.18)	(2.10)	·
12. Industrial Finance Company of India	—	—	—	—	—	—	(.10)	.46	.89
13. State financial corporations	—	—	—	—	—	—	·	.29	.57
14. Life insurance companies	·	·	.07	.26	.62	1.52	1.93	6.22	8.79
15. Other insurance companies	·	·						.76	(.90)
16. P.O. life and endowment funds[f]	—	—	—	.01	.01	.01	.01	.17	.20
17. Employees provident funds	—	—	—	—	—	—	—	2.05	3.64
18. Central government provident funds	—	—	—	—	—	—	.80	2.89	4.21
Total A	.22	.51	1.39	3.84	7.64	36.63	33.75	76.42	99.90
Total B[g]	.25	.55	1.50	3.90					103.00

( ) Estimated figures.

[a] Some figures include Burma for all or some of cols. 1–6.

[b] For cols. 1–3 the three Presidency Banks; for cols. 4–6 Imperial Bank of India.

[c] Capital, reserves, and deposits for cols. 1–5.

[d] For lines 4–9, June 30 until 1948; working capital (slightly below total assets).

[e] Until 1929, includes lines 8 and 9.

[f] Mar. 31 of following year.

[g] Including rough allowance for institutions for which no specific information is available for some dates.

Sources:

1880–1948: Reserve Bank of India, *Banking and Monetary Statistics of India* (1954).

1960, 1963: Reserve Bank of India, *Statistical Bulletin*, and information from Research Department; *Statistical Abstract of the Indian Union.*

TABLE D–13

Assets of Financial Institutions in Israel

MILLIONS OF POUNDS

	1950	1960	1963
1. Bank of Israel	—	1,086	2,405
2. Commercial banks	181	1,350	2,967
3. Credit cooperatives	34	139	234
4. Mortgage banks	13	227	820
5. Industrial investment banks	33 (lines 5–9)	685 (lines 5–9)	694
6. Agricultural credit funds			364
7. Specialized credit institutions			380
8. Household finance companies			44
9. Investment companies			269
10. Life insurance companies	6	88 (lines 10–11)	239[a] (lines 10–11)
11. Other insurance companies	1		
12. Provident funds	22	501	1,089
13. Social security system[b]	—	181	587
Total A	290 (Total A, B)	4,257 (Total A, B)	10,092 (Total A, B)
Total B			

[a] Includes foreign companies (33).
[b] Mar. 31 of following year.

Sources:

Lines 1, 4, 12, 1950–63: Annual Reports of Bank of Israel.

Lines 2, 3, 1950–60: M. Heth, *Banking Institutions in Israel. 1966: International Financial Statistics.*

Lines 5–9, 1950: R. Floersheim, *Financial Intermediaries in Israel: 1950–1954* (Jerusalem, 1962). *1960, 1963: Annual Reports* of Bank of Israel.

Lines 10, 11, 1950: Floersheim. *1960, 1963: Annual Reports* of Bank of Israel.

Line 13, 1960, 1963: Reports of Social Security System (in Hebrew).

Table D–14

Assets of Financial Institutions in Italy

BILLIONS OF LIRE

	1880	1900	1913	1929	1938	1948	1960	1963
Banks of issue[a]	(1.50)	2.00	3.31	21.6	18.4	1,319	3,652	5,595
Postal checking	—	—	—	—	—	.	155	333
Banks, large[b]	(.80)[i] (large and private local combined)	(1.50) (large and private local combined)	2.00	20.0	22.0	583	3,178	5,092
Banks, private local			3.00	33.0	13.2	433	3,079	4,734
Banks, government[c]	—	—	2.00	8.0	12.6	563	3,481	5,626
Banks, cooperative	(.30)	.70	1.00	5.0	7.5	217	1,495	2,373
Savings banks, ordinary[d]	.69	1.47	3.70	20.5	21.1	399	3,121	5,024
Savings banks, P.O.	.05	.70	2.10	11.8	29.2	342	2,462	3,913
Central institutions[e]	—	—	—	—	—	.	454	591
Special industrial institutions	—	—	—	—	9.9	100	2,648	5,356
Special real estate institutions	(.40)	1.07	.	3.7[k]	6.7	17	802	1,793
Special agricultural institutions	.03	.01	.	1.6	4.8	126	492	658
Cassa Depositi e Prestiti[f]	.	(1.50)	4.91	16.3	47.5	515	3,098	4,767
Istituto Nazionale Assicurazione	—	—	.02	2.4[j]	6.4	29	(280)	455
Other insurance companies	.	.	.60[j]	3.1[j]	7.9	140	(744)	1,116
Istituto Nazionale Previdenza	—	.01	.18	5.6	12.6	59	597	1,079
Other social insurance organizations[g]	.	.	.31	2.4	5.5	21	461	674
Total A	3.77	8.96	23.13	155.0 (Total A and B combined)	225.3 (Total A and B combined)	4,863	30,199 (Total A and B combined)	49,179 (Total A and B combined)
Total B[h]	4.50	9.30	25.00			5,000		

( ) Estimated figures.

[a] From 1929 on Banca d'Italia; Banco di Napoli and Banco di Sicilia included through 1913.

[b] Nationwide commercial banks, controlled by the government since 1930s (Banca Commerciale Italiana; Credito Italiano; Banco di Roma).

[c] Banco Nazionale del Lavoro: Banco di Napoli; Banco di Sicilia (these two are included in line 1 through 1913—assets 1913 about .80 billion lire); Monte dei Paschi di Siena; Istituto Bancario San Paolo di Torino.

[d] Until 1900 saving deposits only. From 1913 on includes monti di pietà.

[e] Central Organizations (Istituti di Categoria) of popular and savings banks.

[f] Includes P.O. savings bank deposits redeposited with CDP.

[g] Mostly pension funds for government employees.

[h] Includes rough allowance for institutions for which no specific information is available for some years. Includes government bank notes (1880: .94; 1900: .46; 1913: .66; 1929: .08).

[i] Mulhall's figure for capital, reserves, and deposits for 1881 (*Dictionary of Statistics*, 1892, p. 80) is 26 million £ (.65 billion lire) for 113 joint stock banks.

[j] Life insurance reserves only.

[k] Loans outstanding.

Sources: Annuario Statistico (for 1880 through 1948). *Bolletino* of Banco d'Italia (for 1960 and 1963). *Sommario di Statistiche Storiche Italiane* (for P.O. savings banks through 1948).

TABLE D–15

Assets of Financial Institutions in Jamaica

MILLIONS OF POUNDS

	1948	1960	1963
Bank of Jamaica	—	—	21.49
Currency Board[a]	2.61	9.57	·
Commercial banks	15.15	54.83	71.25
Government savings bank	2.44	5.20	6.53
Building societies	2.24	7.27	9.83
People's cooperative banks[b]	1.00	2.01	3.45
Credit unions	·	(1.00)	1.95
Development Finance Corp.	—	—	1.43
Hire-purchase organizations[b]	·	11.48	3.92
Life insurance companies[c]	(3.50)	(13.50)	19.56
Provident funds[a]	·	(.75)	(1.00)
Sugar workers' pension funds[a]	·	1.46	.61
Total A	26.94	107.07	141.02
Total B[d]	27.50		

( ) Estimated figures.

[a] Mar. 31 of following year. [b] Loans outstanding.

[c] Liabilities to Jamaican residents (Jamaican assets 1960: 10.57; 1963: 14.56); figures for 1938 to 1960 linked to 1963 value on basis of face value of policies and of premium receipts.

[d] Including rough estimates for institutions for which no specific information is available for some years.

Sources: Monetary Statistics; Bank of Jamaica, *Digest of Statistics; Auditor General's Report* (for sugar workers' pension funds).

TABLE D–16

Assets[a] of Financial Institutions in Japan

BILLIONS OF YEN

	1880 (1)	1900 (2)	1913 (3)	1930 (4)	1938 (5)	1948 (6)	1960 (7)	1963 (8)
1. Bank of Japan	—	.31	.67	2.18	3.48	405	1,436	2,396
2. Commercial banks, city	} .10	} 1.06	} 2.15	4.12	9.41	384	7,939	14,416
3. Commercial banks, local				9.19	14.70	199	3,454	6,361
4. Trust banks	—	—	—	—	—	4	405	754
5. Savings banks[b]	—	.11	.36	2.45	4.46	—	—	—
6. Postal savings	.00	.02	.21	2.50	4.74	81	1,123	1,795
7. Trust Fund Bureau	—	.06	.30	3.22	6.55	123	1,947	3,324
8. Long term credit banks	.01	.18	.55	4.19	5.83	74	1,150	2,061
9. Central Bank for Commercial Cooperatives	—	—	—	—	.02	2	193	361
10. Mutual loan and savings banks	—	—	—	.11	.26	16	1,147	2,517
11. National Federal Credit Association	—	—	—	—	—	—	94	199
12. Credit associations	—	·	.04	.23	.44	11	1,075	2,439
13. Credit cooperative associations	—	—	—	—	—	—	212	528
14. Labor credit associations	—	—	—	—	—	—	49	94
15. Central Cooperative Bank of Agriculture	—	·	—	.12	.32	44	298	608
16. Prefectural credit federations	—	·	.03	.21	.60	51	539	1,039
17. Agricultural cooperative associations	—	—	—	—	—	86	905	1,752
18. Federal fishery credit cooperatives	—	—	—	—	—	—	26	53
19. Fishery cooperative associations	—	—	—	—	—	—	49	126
20. Security finance corporations	—	—	—	—	—	—	80	96
21. Peoples Finance Corp.	—	—	—	—	.08	4	129	190
22. Reconversion Finance Corp.	—	—	—	—	—	112	—	—

23. Housing Loan Corp.	—	—	—	—	—	—	206	317
24. Japan Development Bank	—	—	—	—	—	—	642	830
25. Export-Import Bank	—	—	—	—	—	—	130	314
26. Agricultural Finance Corp.	—	—	—	—	—	—	205	309
27. Small Business Finance Co.	—	—	—	—	—	—	152	247
28. Medical Loan Corp.	—	—	—	—	—	—	1	26
29. Hokkaido Development Finance Corp.	—	—	—	—	—	—	52	91
30. Local Public Enterprise Finance Co.	—	—	—	—	—	—	36	96
31. Investment companies	—	—	—	—	—	·	691	1,361
32. Small Business Credit Institute	—	—	—	—	—	—	15	23
33. Life insurance companies	·	.02	.11	1.56	3.61	19	753	1,475
34. P.O. life insurance	—	—	—	.48	1.59	11	702	1,072
35. Non-life insurance companies	·	·	·	.41	.60	12	216	347
Total A	.11	1.76	4.42	30.97	56.69	1,638	26,051	47,617
Total B[c]		1.80	4.45					

[a] Main assets or liabilities only for lines 9–35.
[b] Converted into or absorbed by commercial banks beginning 1943.
[c] Including rough allowance for categories for which no specific information is available for certain dates.

Sources:
1880–1913: Bank of Japan, Statistics Department, except for lines 2–3 col. 1 and line 33 cols. 1–3, which are taken from H. Patrick (MS).
1930–60: Economic Statistics of Japan (1961, Statistics Department Bank of Japan).
1963: Japan Statistical Yearbook (1964).

TABLE D–17

Assets of Financial Institutions in Mexico

BILLIONS OF PESOS

	1903	1911	1930	1940	1948	1960	1963
1. Banco de Mexico	—	—	.11[b]	1.08	3.83	13.20	18.37
2. Commercial banks	.32	.84	.55	.73	2.92	13.35	18.84
3. Savings banks	—	—	—	.04	.38	2.90	4.38
4. Private finance companies	—	—	·	.07	.82	9.06	16.90
5. Capitalization companies	—	—	·	.06	.33	.63	.68
6. Mortgage banks	·[c]	·[c]	0	.08	.19	.47	1.96
7. Building societies	—	—	—	—	.01	.12	.12
8. Credit unions	—	—	—	.02	.17	.40	1.05
9. Investment companies	—	—	—	—	·	.17	·
10. Trustee companies	—	—	—	.00	.03	.19	.22
11. Nacional Financiera	—	—	—	.02	1.30	8.92	16.75
12. B.N. Credito Agricola	—	—	·	·	.14	1.54	2.20
13. B.N. Credito Ejidal	—	—	—	·	.61	2.23	(2.50)
14. B.N. Commercio Exterior	—	—	—	.04	.10	.85	.74
15. B.N. Hipotecario Urbano	—	—	—	.04	.31	2.44	3.61
16. Other government credit institutions	—	—	.03	·	.12	3.56	5.25
17. Life insurance companies	(.02)	(.03)	(.05)	.12	.58	1.52	1.93
18. Other insurance companies						1.92	2.20
19. Social security system	—	—	—	—	(.20)	2.06	4.52
20. Gov't employees pension system	—	—	—	—	·	(1.60)	(2.40)
Total A	.34	.87	.74	2.30	12.04	67.13	104.70
Total B[a]			.80	2.35	12.20		105.00

( ) Estimated figures.

[a] Including estimates for categories for which no specific information is available for some dates.

[b] Main assets. [c] Included with commercial banks.

Sources:

Lines 1–16, 19, 20, 1903, 1911: D. Cosio Villegas, *Historia Moderna de Mexico El Porfiriato La Vida Economica* (Mexico, 1966), pp. 835, 862. *1930:* O. E. Moore, *Evolucion de las Instituciones Financieras en Mexico* (Mexico, 1963). *1940–63:* Banco de Mexico, *Informe Annual*, various issues, and information from Departamento de Estudios Economicos.

Lines 17, 18, 1903–30: Linked to 1940 figures on basis of premiums received and insurance in force (*Annuario Estadistico* 1942, p. 1261). *1940–63:* Same as for lines 1–16 and 19, 20.

TABLE D–18

Assets of Financial Institutions in the Netherlands

BILLIONS OF GUILDERS

	1880	1900	1913	1929	1938	1948	1960	1963
Netherlands Bank	.24	.27	.34	.93	1.87	4.66	7.12	7.83
Postal check system	—	—	—	.15	.33	1.39	2.02	2.80
Transfer institutions[a]	—	—	—	.03	.03	.06	.33	.41
Deposit banks	(.10)	(.22)	(.82)	3.00	2.08	5.45	11.86	15.58
P.O. savings banks	—	.09	.20	.44	.85	1.67	2.99	3.98
Private savings banks	.04	.08	.14	.42	.65	1.15	3.23	4.61
Agricultural credit organizations	·	.00	.05	.56	.61	1.90	5.22	7.76
Mortgage banks[b]	(.04)	(.09)	.55	1.04	.87	.61	1.57	2.53
Bank for Local Authorities	—	—	—	—	.05	.12	6.80	9.04
Investment companies[c]	—	—	—	—	(.02)	(.04)	1.87	2.95
Reconstruction Bank	—	—	—	—	—	.38	.53	.54
Sales finance companies	—	—	—	·	·	(.02)	.33	.57
Other consumer credit institutions	—	—	—	·	·	.01	.07	.11
Building associations	·	·	·	·	·	.04	.18	.28
Miscellaneous credit institutions[d]	·	·	·	.09	.05	.09	.28	.45
Life insurance companies	(.02)	.11	(.30)	.81	1.45	3.14	9.47	12.49
Property insurance companies	·	·	(.01)	(.05)	(.11)	(.21)	1.32	1.76
Pension funds[e]	·	·	·	(.50)	1.53	2.00	10.85	15.70
Social security foundations[e]	—	—	—	(.40)	.61	1.24	3.09	3.76
Total A	.44	.86	2.41	8.42	11.11	} 24.18	} 69.13	} 93.15
Total B[f]	.45	.90	2.50	8.45	11.15			

( ) Estimated figures.
[a] Giro transfer system of municipality of Amsterdam and, for 1960 and 1963, security credit institutions.
[b] Investments; from 1948 on, only mortgages.
[c] Figures refer to ten companies listed on Amsterdam Stock Exchange.
[d] Includes burial associations, tontine banks, and, for 1963, municipal social credit banks and credit stamp associations.
[e] Investments.
[f] Includes rough estimates for institutions for which no specific figures are available for some years.

Sources:
1880–1948: Jaarcijfers voor Nederland and *Annual Report of Netherlands Bank.*
1960, 1963: Maandstatistiek van het finanziewesen.

TABLE D–19

Assets of Financial Institutions in New Zealand

MILLIONS OF POUNDS

	1880	1900	1913	1929	1937	1948	1960	1963
1. Reserve Bank	—	—	—	—	29.8	137.8	217.7	192.2
2. Trading banks	14.2	18.4	30.7	65.5	85.8	199.4	363.1	368.1
3. Trustee savings banks	0.3	0.9	1.8	9.2	13.3	32.2	71.4	105.0
4. P.O. savings banks	1.1	5.9	17.1	49.4	63.1	151.2	299.4	356.2
5. National savings accounts	—	—	—	—	—	40.2	57.6	48.8
6. Building societies	1.1[b]	1.1	2.9	7.8	10.2	16.1	57.3	82.0
7. Friendly societies	0.3[b]	0.8	1.6	3.9	5.1	6.6	10.0	11.5
8. Installment credit finance companies	—	—	—	—	—	—	11.1	13.1
9. State Advances Corp.	—	4.4	9.3	43.5	58.5	75.0	230.0	300.5
10. Life insurance companies	·	7.9	13.5	25.2	49.1	92.2	275.2	362.0
11. Non-life insurance companies	·	·	·	·	·	(16.5)	34.6	(46.8)
12. Government life insurance office	0.6	3.2	5.1	8.2	10.9	16.3	47.5	64.3
13. Government Superannuation Fund	—	—	1.3	5.4	5.5	5.6	35.3	45.0
14. National Provident Fund	—	—	0.0	2.6	5.1	10.2	45.5	77.0
Total A	17.6	42.6	83.3	220.7	336.4	799.3	1,755.7	2,072.5
Total B[a]	20.0	43.5	85.0	225.0	345.0	800.0		

( ) Estimated figures.

[a] Including rough estimates for institutions for which no specific information is available for some dates.

[b] 1884.

Sources: New Zealand Official Year-Book, various issues; W. A. Poole, *Sources and Uses of Capital Funds* (New Zealand Institute of Economic Research, 1965) for lines 8 and 11. Figures refer either to end of calendar year or to March 31 of the year following.

TABLE D–20

Assets of Financial Institutions in Nigeria
MILLIONS OF POUNDS

	1929	1938	1948	1960	1963
Central Bank	—	—	—	82.4	99.2
Notes in Circulation	·	.3[e]	8.2[e]	60.8	69.3
Deposit banks	(3.5)[f]	(5.0)[f]	16.7	117.9	162.6
P.O. Savings Bank[a]	.0	.2	2.2	3.4	3.0
Hire-purchase companies[b]	—	—	·	(2.6)	5.2
Investment Company of Nigeria	—	—	—	1.0	·
Insurance companies	·	·	·	1.7[g]	(2.0)
National Provident Fund	—	—	—	(4.0)	·
Total A[c]	3.5	5.5	27.1	213.0	272.0
Total B[d]	3.5	5.6	27.5	213.0	278.0

( ) Estimated figures.
[a] Deposits.
[b] Credits outstanding for a sample of companies.
[c] Excluding notes in circulation from 1960 on.
[d] Including rough allowance for institutions for which no specific information is available for some dates.
[e] Mar. 31 of following year.
[f] Estimated on basis of deposits.
[g] 1961.

Sources:
1929, 1938: G. K. Helleiner, *Peasant Agriculture, Government and Economic Growth in Nigeria* (Homewood, 1966), pp. 543–45.
1948–63: Central Bank, *Economic and Financial Review; Statistical Digest.*

Table D–21

Assets of Financial Institutions in Norway

BILLIONS OF KRONOR

	1880	1900	1913	1929	1938	1948	1960	1963
Bank of Norway	.07	.10	.17	.48	.71	8.82	7.93	8.26
Postal checking system	—	—	—	—	—	.12	1.10	1.68
Postal savings system	—	—	—	—	—	.04	.73	1.06
Deposit banks	.15	.43	.91	2.59	1.81	5.81	9.73	11.88
Savings banks	.16	.34	.68	2.54	2.30	4.68	8.51	10.21
Mortgage credit associations	—	—	.01	.10	.33	.70	1.96	2.58
Mortgage Bank	.07	.14	.21	.53	.55	.38	.51	.53
Housing Bank	—	—	—	—	—	.13	4.06	4.74
Other government banks	—	—	.04	.36	.75	.68	2.53	3.78
Life insurance companies	·	·	.10	.51	.89	2.02	5.18	6.76
Private pension funds	—	} .00	} .01	} .05	} .12	} .52	1.82	2.26
Communal pension funds	—						.53	.74
Accident insurance companies	·	.03	.06	.21	.25	.58	1.45	1.88
Other private insurance companies	—	—	—	—	—	.09	.34	.39
Government pension funds	—	.03	.06	.11	.22	.24	.42	.45
Social security funds[a]	·	.01	.02	.21	.13	.57	2.58	2.29[c]
Total A	.45	1.08	} 2.27	} 7.69	} 8.06	} 25.30	} 49.38	} 59.49
Total B[b]	.48	1.10						

[a] Excluding interfund assets.

[b] Includes rough allowance for institutions for which no specific information is available for some dates.

[c] Break in series.

Sources:

1880–1948: Statistisk Sentralbyrå *Statistisk Oversikter* (1948 and 1958); *Statistisk Årbog*, various issues; and H. Skanland, *Norges Kredittmarked etter 1900* (Oslo, 1966).

1960, 1963: Statistisk Sentralbyrå, *Kredittmarkedstatistikk* (1961, 1964).

TABLE D-22

Assets of Financial Institutions in Pakistan

BILLIONS OF RUPEES

	1948	1960	1963
1. State Bank	2.97	5.81	6.44
2. Deposit banks[a]	1.06	3.63	5.88
3. P.O. Savings Bank[b]	.30	.50	.54
4. Cooperative societies	.35	.78	(.80)
5. Industrial Credit and Investment Corp.	—	—	.29
6. Industrial Development Bank	—	—	.17[f]
7. Agricultural Development Bank[c]	—	.04	.23
8. Home Building and Finance Corp.	—	.08	.19
9. Refugee Rehabilitation Finance Corp.	—	.04	—
10. Life insurance companies[d] / 11. Other insurance companies[d]	(.10)	(.34)	.49
12. Provident societies, life funds	(.05)	(.04)	(.04)
13. Government employees provident funds	.02	.42	(.65)
Total A / Total B[e]	4.85	11.68	15.72

( ) Estimated figures.

[a] Scheduled banks (assets of unscheduled banks at all three dates .02), National Bank included. Figures for Agricultural Development Bank (line 7) deducted.

[b] Deposits.

[c] Before 1961 Agricultural Development Finance Corporation and Agricultural Bank. Figures refer to loans and advances.

[d] Includes foreign companies (1963: .20 in line 10, and .06 in line 11).

[e] Including rough allowance for institutions for which no specific information is available for some dates.

[f] June 30.

Sources:

Lines 1, 2: *International Financial Statistics*, 1965/66 Supplement.

Lines 3–9: State Bank, *Banking Statistics of Pakistan*, 1963–64.

Lines 4, 12, 13: S. R. Lewis and M. I. Khan, in *Pakistan Development Review* (Spring 1964).

Lines 10, 11: *Pakistan Insurance Yearbook* (1964) for 1963 and Lewis and Khan for 1948 and 1960.

TABLE D–23

Assets of Financial Institutions in the Philippines

BILLIONS OF PESOS

	1913	1929	1938	1948	1960	1963
1. Central Bank	.03[a]	.08[a]	.17[a]	.91	1.95	2.38
2. Commercial banks	.06	.26	.39	1.17	2.34	5.38
3. Postal Savings Bank	.00	.01	(.02)	.03	.06	.07
4. Savings banks	—	—	—	.01	.07	.10
5. Rural banks	—	—	—	—	.08	.19
6. Credit cooperatives	—	—	—	—	(.01)	.02
7. Building and loan associations	.00	.03	.02	.00	.01	.01
8. Development Bank of Philippines	—	—	—	.17	.47	.99
9. Private development banks	—	—	—	—	—	.10
10. Agricultural Credit Administration	—	—	—	—	.08	.08
11. Insurance companies, life } 12. Insurance companies, other	(.01)	(.03)	(.06)	(.10)	.32	(.60)
12. Insurance companies, other					.20	
13. Government Service Insurance System	—	—	.00	.00	1.24	1.35
14. Social security system	—	—	—	—	.11	.30
Total A and B	.10	.41	.66	2.39	6.94	11.57

( ) Estimated figures.
[a] Government paper money.

Sources:

Lines 1–10, 1913: Census of the Philippine Islands, 1918, 4. 1929, 1938: Yearbook of Philippine Statistics (1940). *1948–63:* Central Bank of the Philippines, *Statistical Bulletin.*

Lines 11, 12, 1913–38: Annual Report of the Insurance Commissioner.

Lines 13, 14, 1938–63: Financial Report of Government Service Insurance System and social security system (mimeo).

TABLE D–24

Assets of Financial Institutions in Puerto Rico[a]
MILLIONS OF DOLLARS

	1929	1938	1948	1960	1963
1. Commercial banks					
Local	39	25	150	414	712
Foreign	43	47	121	317	493
2. Postal savings	0	2	8	3	2
3. Savings and loan associations	—	—	1	90	149
4. Credit unions	—	—	0	(20)	37
5. Government Development Bank	—	—	55	86	143
6. Bank for Cooperatives	—	—	—	4	4
7. Puerto Rican Housing Bank	—	—	—	—	4
8. P.R. Prod. Credit Association[b]	—	—	6	13	21
9. National Farm Loan Association[b]	—	—	—	2	3
10. Consumer finance companies	—	—	—	(50)	(80)
11. Investment companies	—	—	—	(2)	(10)
12. Life insurance companies	·	·	(25)	(110)	156
13. Government pension and insurance funds	·	·	·	162	265
Total A	82	74	366	1,273	2,079
Total B[c]	90	85	400		

( ) Estimated figures.
[a] June 30 of following year.
[b] Excludes loans in Puerto Rico by U.S. government agricultural credit organizations.
[c] Including rough estimates for institutions for which no specific information is available for some dates.

Sources:

Line 1, 1929, 1938: H. J. Rivero, *Introduccion a la Moneda y la Banca* (San Juan, 1965), p. 203. *1948–63: Annuario Estadistico*, various issues.

Line 2, 1929–48: B. de Venuti, *Banking Growth in Puerto Rico* (1955), p. 99. *1960, 1963:* Information from Post Office Department.

Line 3, 1948: Based on de Venuti, p. 98 *1960: Statistical Abstract of the U.S.* (1962), average of values for Dec. 31. *1963: Report on Finances and Economy* (Puerto Rico Department of the Treasury, 1964).

Line 4, 1963: Information from Puerto Rico Department of the Treasury.

Lines 5–7, 1948–63: Report on Finances and Economy, various issues.

Lines 8, 9, 1960, 1963: Statistical Abstract of the U.S., various issues.

Lines 10, 11, 1960, 1963: Rough trade estimates (line 10, 1960, Development Bank, *Instruments of the Capital Market in Puerto Rico*, 1962, p. 9).

Line 12, 1963: Report on Finances and Economy (1964); 1960 and 1948 estimates based on premium receipts; figures refer to Puerto Rican assets of companies operating in Puerto Rico.

Line 13, 1960, 1963: Net assets of six funds (government employees, teachers, Water Resources Authority, university, judiciary, state death and disability) plus Government Employees' Association (30 in 1960, 47 in 1963).

Table D–25

Assets of Financial Institutions in Rhodesia[a]

MILLIONS OF POUNDS

	1948 (1)	1960 (2)	1963 (3)
1. Bank of Rhodesia	—	43.8	57.7
2. Commercial banks	(45.0)	90.2	110.6
3. Post Office Savings Bank[b]	(11.0)	33.0	31.7
4. Building societies	—	71.0	65.3
5. Life insurance companies	(12.0)	51.7	78.6
6. Other insurance companies	(1.0)	7.6	9.2
7. Hire-purchase finance companies	—	6.3	7.9
8. Accepting houses	—	13.2	13.9
9. Discount houses	—	8.8	16.0
10. Land Bank	(2.0)	16.3	20.7
11. Industrial Development Boards	—	11.5	12.2
Total A / Total B[c]	78.0[d]	353.4	423.8

( ) Estimated figures.

[a] Where possible, only (former) Southern and Northern Rhodesia, excluding Nyasaland.

[b] Includes Post Office Saving Certificates (1953: 1.0; 1956; 4.2; 1960: 7.9; 1963: 6.1).

[c] Including rough allowance for institutions for which no specific information is available for some dates.

[d] Including estimate (7.0) for currency in circulation.

Sources:

Lines 1–11: Quarterly Bulletin of Statistics, and *Quarterly Bulletin of Financial Statistics*, various issues.

TABLE D-26

Assets of Financial Institutions in Russia–U.S.S.R.
BILLIONS OF (OLD) RUBLES

	Russia		U.S.S.R.				
	1900	1913	1928	1937	1950	1959	1963
Central bank[a]	1.4	3.0	4.1	57.3	205	480	(620)
Deposit banks	(1.4)	6.2	—	—	—	—	—
Savings banks	.7	1.7	.2	4.5	19	101	140
Mortgage banks	(2.5)	4.3	—	—	—	—	—
Other credit institutions	·	3.4	3.7[c]	·	·	50[d]	·
Insurance companies	(.1)	.3	·	·	·	10	·
Total, A	6.1	} 18.9	} 8.0	61.8	224	} 641	(760)
Total B[b]	7.0			65.0	250[e]		850

( ) Estimated figures.

[a] State (Imperial) bank to 1913, Gosbank since 1928.

[b] Including rough allowance for institutions for which no specific data available for some dates.

[c] Estimated at close to 90 per cent of Gosbank on basis of situation in 1926 (G. Menz, *Das Sowietische Bankensystem*, 1963, p. 25). An alternative estimate—S. G. Strumilin's total of 8.5 billion (*Vestnik Finansov*, 1928, reprinted in *Izbrannie Proizvedenia*, *1*, 472) less lines 1 and 3—yields a figure of 4.2 billion.

[d] Liabilities of Investment Bank (E. Ames, *Soviet Economic Processes*, 1965, p. 167).

[e] Total assets of the U.S.S.R. banking system were estimated by Ames —apparently on a consolidated basis—at 64 billion rubles in 1940, 193 billion in 1950, and 438 billion in 1959.

Sources: Col. 1:
Line 1: Reichsbank, *Vergleichende Notenbankstatistik* (1925), p. 32.
Line 2: S. Ronin, *Innostrannie Banki* (1926), p. 113.
Line 3: P. A. Khromov, *Economic Development of Russia in the 19th and 20th Century*, p. 284.
Line 4: Congrès des Valeurs Mobilières (1900); data for 1898 from *Moniteur des Intérêts Matériels*.
Cols. 2–6: Goldsmith, "The National Balance Sheet of the Soviet Union," p. 98.
Col. 7: *Narodnoie Khoziaistvo SSSR v 1963g.* (Line 1 linked to 1959 on basis total short-term bank credit outstanding.)

TABLE D–27

Assets of Financial Institutions in South Africa

MILLIONS OF POUNDS

	1913	1929	1938	1948	1960	1963
1. S.A. Reserve Bank	—	20	52	190	236	327
2. Commercial banks[a,b]	44	67	103	401	626	859
3. Postal savings banks[c]	7	7	20	83	75	71
4. Union savings certificates	—	5	7	32	30	42
5. Private savings banks	·	3	3	(5)	22	30
6. Building societies[c]	5	22	53	197	612	748
7. Popular banks	—	—	—	2	8	12
8. Acceptance houses	—	—	—	—	38	96
9. Discount houses	—	—	—	—	37	97
10. Installment finance corps.	·	·	2	(15)	66	146
11. Land and Agricultural Bank	4	12	20	46	147	161
12. Industrial Development Corp.[d]	—	—	—	4	75	85
13. National Finance Corp.	—	—	—	—	66	72
14. Insurance companies[b]	15	45	75	178	535	682
15. Pension funds, government[c]	·	28	62	(120)	460	590
16. Pension funds, private	—	—	—	·	256	375
Total A	75	} 209	} 397	1,273	} 3,289	} 4,393
Total B[e]	85			1,350		

( ) Estimated figures.

[a] Assets in South Africa.

[b] Figures for 1913 and 1929 estimated on basis of main assets.

[c] March 31 of following year.

[d] June 30.

[e] Including rough allowance for institutions for which no specific information is available for some dates.

Sources:

1913, 1929: Union Statistics for 50 Years (1960), except for lines 5, 13, 15, and 17 in 1929, which are estimates of G. de Kock in *Ons Eerste Halfeeu.*

1938: De Kock.

1948–1963: Statistical Yearbook (1964); for lines 7, 12, 13, 14, and 16, Research Department of South African Reserve Bank; for line 15, W. F. Crick, ed., *Commonwealth Banking Systems* (Oxford, 1965), p. 334.

Table D–28

Assets of Financial Institutions in Spain

BILLIONS OF PESETAS

	1900	1913	1929	1935	1948	1960	1963
1. Bank of Spain	2.85	2.80	6.75	6.30	32.2	134.1	183.6
2. Deposit banks	(.60)	1.00	10.62	11.15	55.0	296.3	480.0
3. P.O. savings	—	—	.25	·	.8	5.4	10.9
4. Other savings banks	.18	.35	2.00	3.00	13.0	87.1	156.9
5. Banco Hipotecario	.10	.20	1.50	1.70	3.1	14.7	19.6
6. B.C.[a] Local	—	—	.58	1.10	4.0	11.9	14.8
7. B.C. a la Construccion	—	—	—	.10	1.7	21.3	34.3
8. B.C. Industrial	—	—	.10	.10	.5	6.4	9.7
9. B.C. Agricola	—	—	·	·	.2	4.8	12.2
10. B.C. Maritimo	—	—	—	—	—	.5	.6
11. Rural credit unions	—	—	—	—	—	1.0	1.8
12. Insurance companies	·	·	·	·	6.0	24.0	34.0
13. Mutual insurance associations	·	·	·	·	·	25.0	35.7
14. National Security Institute	—	—	—	—	·	15.6	22.0
Total A	3.73	4.35	21.80	23.45	116.5	} 648.1	} 1,016.1
Total B[b]	3.80	4.50	23.00	25.00	125.0		

( ) Estimated figures.
[a] Banco de Credito.
[b] Includes rough estimates for institutions for which no definite information is available for some dates.

Sources:

Line 1, 1880: Estimated on basis of cash and portfolio. *1900–35:* Annual reports of Bank of Spain. Figures exclude unused credit margins of borrowers (mainly banks). *1948–63: International Financial Statistics*, 1965–66 Supplement. (Figures include all monetary authorities.)

Line 2, 1913: Annuario Estadistico de España, 1918. *1929–35: Boletin del Consejo Superior Bancario. 1948–63: International Financial Statistics*, 1965–66 Supplement (difference between figure for "commercial and savings banks" and sum of lines 3 and 4).

Lines 3, 4, 1900: Institut International de l'Épargne, *Les Caisses d'Épargne dans le monde. 1913–63: Annuario Estadistico* and *Boletin Mensual de Estadistica* (for early years estimated on basis of deposits).

Line 5, 1900–35: Based on outstanding mortgage loans (*Memoria*, 1932; *Annuario Estadistico de España*). *1948–63:* Same as for line 6.

Lines 6–10, 1948–63: Memoria del Credito Oficial, various issues. Figures refer to "cuentas operacionales," but include undisbursed credits and are slightly below total assets.

Line 11, 1960, 1963: Annuario Estadistico de España.

Line 12, 1948–63: Annual Reports of Ministerio de Hacienda, Direccion General de Seguros.

Lines 13, 14: Information from Banco de España.

TABLE D–29

Assets of Financial Institutions in Sweden

BILLIONS OF KRONOR

	1880	1900	1913	1929	1938	1948	1960	1963
1. Riksbank	(.10)	.22	.43	.95	2.16	4.80	9.57	10.09
2. Deposit banks	(.50)	1.37	2.85	5.38	6.02	10.12	23.61	32.07
3. Postal check system[a]	—	—	—	.04	.17	1.08	2.17	2.84
4. P.O. Savings Bank[a]	—	.06	.05	.28	.62	1.92	4.73	5.93
5. Private savings banks	.15	.44	.95	2.88	3.69	6.75	16.08	19.78
6. Rural credit associations	—	—	—	.02	.12	.34	1.30	1.89
7. General Mortgage Bank[b]	.27	.29	.30	.39	.46	.65	1.30	1.56
8. Housing mortgage associations[b]	.01	.04	.10	.59	1.08	1.81	5.63	7.80
9. Building loan associations	—	.	.	.02	.13	.28	1.20	1.87
10. Ship mortgage banks[b]	—	.	.	.02	.04	.06	.06	.06
11. Cooperative Wholesale Society	—	.	.	.	.	.16	.31	.35
12. Life insurance companies[c]	.03	.15	.38	1.33	2.46	5.00	13.85	15.91
13. Friendly societies	.	.	.	.	.	.78	2.50	3.09
14. Other insurance companies[d]	.02	.05	.06	.09	.95	.98	3.57	4.00
15. State subsidiary pension fund	—	—	.04	.16	.19	.20	.22	.22
16. National Pension Fund	—	—	.04[f]	.44	.78	.78	1.34	1.34
17. National Pension Insurance Fund	—	—	—	—	—	—	.47	4.80
18. National Social Insurance Board Voluntary Insurance	—	—	—	—	.05	.13	.31	.33
19. Sickness Insurance Fund	—	—	—	—	.	.	.52	(.65)
20. Unemployment Insurance Fund	—	—	—	—	—	.	.32	.42
21. Industrial Injuries Insurance Fund	—	—	—	.07	.13	.22	.46	.52
22. Other credit institutions	—	—	.	.	.	.	1.40	3.61
Total A	1.08	2.62	5.20	12.66	19.05	36.06	90.92 (A and B)	119.13 (A and B)
Total B[e]	1.10	2.65	5.30	13.00	19.50	36.50		

( ) Estimated figures.
[a] Deposits. [b] Bonds outstanding. [c] Includes group pension plans.
[d] Local companies included only in 1960 and 1963 when they accounted for 8 per cent of total.
[e] Including rough estimate for institutions for which no specific information is available for some dates.
[f] 1914.

Sources:
1880–1948: Central Statistical Bureau, *Historisk Statistik för Sverige*, Part III (1960); information from the Bureau.
1960, 1963: Statistisk Årsbok för Sverige (1962, 1965).

Table D–30

Assets of Financial Institutions in Switzerland

BILLIONS OF FRANCS

	1860	1880	1900	1913	1929	1938	1948	1960	1963
1. National Bank	—	—	—	.43	1.29	4.08	6.40	10.27	13.91
2. Cantonal banks	.05	.50	1.26	2.87	5.82	8.15	9.68	19.86	26.07
3. Large commercial banks	.06	.26	.77	2.47	8.19	4.49	7.16	17.54	27.69
4. Local commercial banks	.13	.49	(1.60)	3.98	2.13	1.38	2.13	6.80	11.53
5. Savings banks	.15	.32			1.18	1.57	2.02	3.63	4.54
6. Credit unions	—	—	—		.24	.43	.88	1.99	2.68
7. Mortgage banks	.03	.30	(.90)		2.23	2.28	2.88	6.19	8.13
8. Confederacy Loan Office	—	—	—	.11	.15	.16	.13	—	—
9. Bank-type finance cos.[a]	—	—	·	.97	2.28	.99	.65	.87	1.60
10. Inv. cos., securities	—	—	—	—	—	—	·	2.69	3.49
11. Inv. cos., real estate[a]	—	—	—	—	—	—	·	1.38	3.60
12. Life insurance companies	·	·	.14	(.45)	(1.30)	2.68	3.91	7.77	9.80
13. Confederacy pension funds	—	—	—	—	(.20)	.62	.83	1.77	2.18
14. Railroad pension funds	—	—	—	(.10)	(.25)	.36	.42	.81	1.02
15. Canton pension funds	—	—	—	—	.10	.16	.34	1.47	1.97
16. Federal Social Insurance	—	—	—	—	—	—	.49	4.86	7.19
17. Swiss Accident Insurance	—	—	—	—	.30	.39	.54	1.63	2.10
18. Other insurance cos.	·	·	·	·	·	(1.95)	(3.30)	7.68	9.79
Total A	.42	1.87	4.67	11.38	25.66	29.69	41.76	97.21	137.29
Total B[b]	.45	2.00	5.00	11.80	27.00		43.00		

( ) Estimated figures.

[a] Market value of certificates outstanding (for line 9 until 1948).

[b] Includes rough estimates for institutions for which no specific data are available for some dates.

Sources: Statistisches Jahrbuch, various issues. Schweizerische Bundesbank, *Statistisches Handbuch des Schweizerischen Geld- und Kapitalmarktes* (1944). *Das Schweizerische Bankwesen*, various issues. For lines 2 to 7 in 1860 and 1880, unpublished estimates by Dr. F. Ritzmann, Zürich.

TABLE D–31

Assets of Financial Institutions in Thailand
BILLIONS OF BAHT

	1938	1948	1960	1963
1. Bank of Thailand[a]	.15	3.28	11.37	14.24
2. Commercial banks	.08	1.25	7.82	13.45
3. Government Savings Bank	.02[c]	.23	1.72	2.55
4. Agricultural cooperative societies	.01	.07	.38	.36
5. Bank for Cooperatives	—	.40	.31	.29
6. Industrial Finance Corp.	—	—	.04	.07
7. Insurance companies	·	·	.64	.68
Total A	.26	5.23	22.28	31.64
Total B[b]	.30	5.35		

[a] In 1938 note issues of Currency Bureau, taken over by the Bank of Thailand upon its organization in 1942; includes Exchange Fund.

[b] Including rough allowance for institutions for which no specific information is available for some dates.

[c] Government Postal Savings Office.

Sources:

Line 1: International Financial Statistics, 1965/66 Supplement.

Line 2: Bank of Thailand.

Line 3: Government Savings Bank.

Lines 4–5: Department of Credit and Marketing Cooperatives, Ministry of National Development.

Line 6: Industrial Finance Corp.

Line 7: Report on Insurance Business in Thailand of the Insurance Division, Department of Commercial Registration, Ministry of Economic Affairs.

Appendix IV

Table D–32

Assets of Financial Institutions in Trinidad

BILLIONS OF DOLLARS W.I.

	1938	1948	1960	1963
1. Currency Board[a]	1.3	18.9	33.4	30.1
2. Commercial banks	(5.0)	58.9	205.0	253.0
3. P.O. savings bank	3.1	10.5	13.9	12.3
4. Agricultural Credit Bank[b]	1.0	0.5	1.7	2.1
5. Agricultural credit cooperative	—	0.1	1.1	(.7)
6. Credit unions	.4	1.1	3.4	(4.0)
7. Building societies	3.7	5.4	6.9	8.1
8. Life insurance companies[c]	·	(5.0)	42.5	58.7
Total A	14.5	} 100.4	} 307.9	} 369.0
Total B	15.0			

( ) Estimated figures.

[a] Currency note circulation, including small amounts of notes issued by commercial banks.

[b] Loans.

[c] Assets in Trinidad.

Sources: Annual Statistical Digest, 1958, 1963, except col. 1, lines 1 and 2, which are based on data in issues of *Trinidad and Tobago Blue Book.*

TABLE D–33

Assets of Financial Institutions in the United States

BILLIONS OF DOLLARS

	1860 (1)	1880 (2)	1900 (3)	1912 (4)	1929 (5)	1939 (6)	1948 (7)	1960 (8)	1963 (9)
1. Federal Reserve Banks	—	—	—	—	5.5	19.0	50.0	53.0	58.0
2. Commercial banks	.80	2.71	10.0	21.8	66.2	66.3	155.5	257.6	312.8
3. Agencies of foreign banks	—	—	—	—	·	·	1.6	3.6	3.6
4. Mutual savings banks	.20	.92	2.4	4.0	9.9	11.9	20.7	40.6	49.7
5. Postal savings system	—	—	—	.0	.2	1.3	3.4	.8	.5
6. Savings and loan associations	·	.10	.5	1.0	7.4	5.4	13.1	71.5	107.6
7. Credit unions	—	—	—	—	.0	.2	.7	5.1	8.1
8. Sales and personal finance companies	—	·	·	·	2.5	2.9	5.7	27.5	(36.0)
9. Investment companies	—	—	—	—	3.0	2.4	3.6	(24.0)	(33.0)
10. Small business finance companies	—	—	—	—	—	—	—	.2	.6
11. Security dealers	·	·	.6	1.0	10.0	2.0	2.9	7.4	9.7
12. Land banks	—	—	—	—	1.9	2.4	1.0	2.7	3.5
13. Mortgage companies	·	(.12)	.2	.4	.8	.4	.3	2.7	4.5
14. Government lending institutions	—	—	—	.0	.4	9.8	12.5	31.1[a]	40.4[a]
15. Life insurance companies	.02	.42	1.7	4.4	17.5	29.2	56.0	119.9	141.4
16. Fraternal insurance companies	—	·	.0	.2	.8	1.2	1.9	3.2	3.6
17. Private noninsured pension funds	—	—	—	—	.5	1.0	4.6	36.9	53.8
18. Other insurance companies	(.10)	.20	.5	1.0	4.7	4.8	10.3	(29.0)	(37.0)
19. Pension, retirement, and social security funds, federal[b]	—	—	—	—	1.0	4.6	32.6	49.6	50 7

	1	2	3	4	5	6	7	8	9
20. Pension and retirement funds, state and local[c]	—	—	.0	.0	.5	1.7	4.3	20.9	28.6
Total A	1.12	4.47	15.9	33.8	132.8	166.5	}380.7	}787.3	}983.1
Total B[d]	1.20	4.60	16.0	34.0	133.5	167.0			

( ) Estimated figures.

[a] Loans outstanding (*Treasury Bulletin*, Apr. 1964, p. 128); these are slightly below total assets of lending institutions.

[b] Includes government employees and national service life funds (1948: 4.4; 1960: 10.9; 1963: 13.8).

[c] Fiscal year ending within following year.

[d] Includes rough allowance for institutions for which no specific information is available for some dates.

Sources: Cols. 1, 2:

Lines 2, 15: Historical Statistics, pp. 624, 675.

Line 4: Based on reports for three main states (New York, Massachusetts, Connecticut).

Line 6: Based on estimate of F. B. Sanborn, cited in H. M. Bodfish, ed., *History of Building and Loans in U.S.*, Chicago, 1931, p. 134.

Line 18: Based on assets of companies operating in New York and Illinois.

Cols. 3–6: Goldsmith, *Financial Intermediaries in the American Economy*, p. 73.

Col. 7: Goldsmith, Lipsey, and Mendelson, *Studies in the National Balance Sheet*, 2, 152 ff.

Cols. 8, 9: Statistical Yearbook of the U.S. (1965); Federal Reserve Bank, Flow-of-Funds Statistics; *Treasury Bulletin.*

Table D–34

Assets of Financial Institutions in Venezuela

BILLIONS OF BOLIVARS

	1913	1929	1938	1948	1960	1963
1. Banco Central	—	—	—	1.16	2.49	3.16
2. Deposit banks[a]	(.05)	(.50)	.67	(1.05)	5.94	6.83
3. Mortgage banks	—	—	—	—	.10	.31
4. Savings banks	·	·	·	·	·	.10[c]
5. Savings and loan associations	—	—	—	—	—	.07
6. Investment companies	—	—	—	—	·	.22
7. Other private credit institutions	—	—	—	—	·	.26
8. Corp. Venez. Fomento	—	—	—	.30	2.08	1.92
9. Banco Obrero	—	—	—	—	1.71	2.19
10. Banco Agricola	—	—	—	.25	1.00	1.05
11. Banco Ind. y de Fomento	—	—	—	—	.15	.23
12. Other government credit institutions	—	—	—	—	—	.06
13. Insurance companies	·	·	·	(.30)	1.01	.95
14. Social security organizations	—	—	—	—	.20	.35
Total A	} 0.05	.50	.67	3.06	14.68	} 17.70
Total B[b]		.55	.80	3.10	15.00	

( ) Estimated figures.
[a] Until 1940s also issued bank notes.
[b] Including rough allowance for institutions for which no specific information is available for some dates.
[c] 1964.

Sources:
Line 2, 1913, 1929: Annuario Estadistico (1940, 1949). *1938:* League of Nations, *Money and Banking 1942–44* (twelve banks).
Lines 1, 3–14, 1938–63: Information from Research Division, Banco Central taken from official documents.

TABLE D–35

Assets of Financial Institutions in Yugoslavia
BILLIONS OF DINARS

	1929	1938	1952	1960	1963
1. National Bank	15.21	13.58	765	1,543	2,280
2. Deposit banks	18.42	13.06	—	812[e]	2,578[e]
3. Postal savings	1.93	4.30	—	—	—
4. Credit cooperatives	(2.50)	2.44	—	—	—
5. Mortgage Bank	3.62	10.57	—	2,228[f]	4,720[f]
6. Agrarian Bank	1.00[b]	2.38	—		
7. Other government banks	2.05[c]	3.20[c]	—	—	—
8. Life insurance companies	(.80)[d]	(.80)[d]	·	92	112
9. Social insurance organizations	·	·	·		
10. Government investment loan funds	—	—	—	1,992	3,869
Total A	45.53	50.33	765	3,981[g]	7,467[g]
Total B[a]	46.50	51.50	770		

( ) Estimated figures.
[a] Including rough allowance for institutions for which no specific information is available for some dates.
[b] 1930. [c] Banks of Local Authorities and Artisans' Bank
[d] Based on face value and premium receipts.
[e] Republican and commercial banks.
[f] Business banks; specialized banks (agricultural, foreign trade, investment); economic banks.
[g] Based on consolidated balance sheet of banking system (lines 1, 2, 5 and 6).

Sources:
1929, 1938: Statistiski Godisnjak, 4, 9, and *10.*
1952–63, lines 1, 2, 6: Narodna Banka, *Statistiki Bilten. Line 8: Statistiski Godisnjak* (1964). *Line 10:* Narodna Banka, *Annual Report* (1961, 1964).

V. GROSS NATIONAL PRODUCT ESTIMATES UNDERLYING ISSUE RATIOS

NATIONAL PRODUCT IN CURRENT PRICES

For the benchmark dates 1948, 1960, and 1963 the figures in Table E–1 are with few exceptions official estimates as reproduced in *Yearbook of National Account Statistics* (United Nations) or *International Financial Statistics* (International Monetary Fund). Even in the exceptional cases, all that was required was extrapolation on the basis of adjacent years or stepping up original estimates for national income, net national product, or gross material product.

For earlier years in the case of developed countries, most of the figures were taken from standard estimates for individual countries, viz. for the United States (Kendrick; Department of Commerce); Canada (Firestone); United Kingdom (Feinstein); Germany (Hoffmann); Italy, Norway, Sweden, and South Africa (Statistical Offices); Denmark (Bjerke); Australia (Butlin); and Japan (Emi). The original data required in some cases adjustment to gross national product basis and the exact benchmark year. The figures for France, Belgium, the Netherlands, Switzerland, and New Zealand had to be pieced together from several sources (including Clark) and may be regarded as less reliable.

The situation is less satisfactory for less developed countries, except for India, where Subramonian's recent estimates were used. While some official estimates were available for 1938, the figures for earlier benchmark dates had to be derived from a variety of unofficial estimates for years generally not coinciding with the benchmark dates and usually referring to national income rather than to gross

TABLE E–1

Gross National Product, Current Prices, Benchmark Dates, 1860–1963

BILLIONS OF NATIONAL CURRENCY (1963 UNITS)

	1880[a]	1900	1913	1929	1938	1948	1960	1963
Argentina		2.0	5.6	10.0	11.3	43.8	9.54	1697
Australia		.189	.377	.816	.883	1.920	6.605	8.400
Belgium	2.6	4.5	8.0	94.0	80.0	331.8	572.3	694.8
Brazil			7.0	25.5	39.0	186	2397	9489
Canada	.581	1.032	2.700	6.166	5.165	15.450	36.281	42.968
Denmark	.840	1.480	2.500	6.010	7.574	19.556	41.145	54.996
Egypt-U.A.R.		.120	.170	.350	.193	.750	1.470	1.750
France	.255	.314	.471	3.74	3.66	70.4	296.2	395.6
Germany[b]	18.5	35.5	57.5	87.5	108.0	57.7	296.8	376.5
Great Britain	1.213	2.040	2.628	5.040	5.760	11.940	25.535	30.001
Greece			.0018	.0532	.0860	18.20	97.21	132.50
India	10.0	13.4	20.9	34.6	25.3	96.8	158.3	194.3
Israel						.459	4.301	7.323
Italy	12.6	15.0	25.7	163	164	7,483	19,937	28,186
Jamaica					.020	.060	.240	.284
Japan	.83	2.2	4.6	13.9	26.8	2,666	14,065	21,482
Mexico		1.3	1.4	4.1	7.1	30.2	154.1	192.2
Netherlands	1.40	2.01	3.14	7.27	5.87	15.05	42.73	52.16
New Zealand	.02	.04	.07	.173	.216	.480	1.311	1.595
Nigeria				.060	.045	.550	.981	1.394
Norway	.450	.808	1.364	3.196	4.308	11.589	32.340	40.252
Pakistan						20.9	33.1	40.2

Philippines			.82	1.67	1.400	6.168	12.126	17.145
Puerto Rico				.194	.209	.644	1.852	2.532
Rhodesia[c]						.059	.231	.251
Russia-U.S.S.R.		1.20	2.20	3.23	28.1	91.2	166.0	206.0
South Africa[c]			.240	.470	.640	1.470	3.830	4.760
Spain		10	13	31	31	150	615	939
Sweden	1.233	2.162	3.886	9.414	12.143	25.720	63.375	80.451
Switzerland	1.310	2.720	4.110	10.340	9.140	19.117	37.055	50.435
Thailand					1.00	18.46	53.08	68.02
Trinidad					.080	.250	.829	1.110
U.S.A.	9.3	18.7	37.3	103.1	90.5	257.4	503.8	589.2
Venezuela				2.20	2.40	7.50	23.47	26.91
Yugoslavia				84.0	65.5	1,170	3,435	5,428

[a] Figures for 1860 are .196 for France, 10.8 for Germany, .870 for Great Britain, .800 for Switzerland, and 4.5 for United States.
[b] Marks for 1860–1929, reichsmarks for 1938 and 1948; deutsche marks for 1960 and 1963.
[c] White population only.

national product, as well as from other indicators, such as indices of production and prices. These figures, therefore have little independent value as measures of national product and are used solely as denominators for the issues of financial institutions in the country.

NATIONAL PRODUCT IN CONSTANT PRICES

The figures, intended to measure the changes in the physical volume of national product on the basis of the country's prices at one date (not shown in this appendix) are usually taken from the same sources as those for national product in current prices. They are used in the form of the rate of growth of real gross national product per head as one of the independent variables in the correlation analysis of the ratios of the issues of financial institutions (and of financial instruments) to national product.

NATIONAL PRODUCT PER HEAD IN INTERNATIONAL UNITS

These figures (likewise not shown in this appendix), used as an indicator of gross national product per head in terms of the U.S. price level of 1960 of different countries at the various benchmark dates, were derived by applying to each country's figures for gross national product per head in constant prices an estimate of the 1960 purchasing power parity between the dollar and the country's currency as estimated by various authors (Rosenstein-Rodan; Kirschen). The resulting figures of gross national product per head in U.S. 1960 dollars are used only as another of the independent variables in the correlation analysis of the ratios of the assets of financial institutions and of financial instruments to aggregate gross national product in current prices.

INDEX

References to individual countries are not shown:
(1) Insofar as they appear in the 15 tables (pp. 154, 180, 186, 188, 191, 204, 209, 218, 227, 234, 238, 253, 278, 286, 345) that show information on every one of the 35 countries covered by the study, i.e., Argentina, Australia, Belgium, Brazil, Canada, Denmark, Egypt-U.A.R., France, Germany, Great Britain, Greece, India, Israel, Italy, Jamaica, Japan, Mexico, Netherlands, New Zealand, Nigeria, Norway, Pakistan, Philippines, Puerto Rico, Rhodesia, Russia-U.S.S.R., South Africa, Spain, Sweden, Switzerland, Thailand, Trinidad, U.S.A., Venezuela, and Yugoslavia.
(2) Where they are essentially limited to a restatement of figures or movements evident in tables or charts.

References to types of financial institutions do not cover the country tables of Appendix IV (pp. 502 to 551), since each of these tables contains information on virtually every type of institution.

References to authors do not include those cited in footnotes to tables.

Index